THE REAL PEOPLE OF JOYCE'S
ULYSSES

THE REAL PEOPLE OF JOYCE'S
ULYSSES

A Biographical Guide

VIVIEN IGOE

UNIVERSITY COLLEGE DUBLIN PRESS
PREAS CHOLÁISTE OLLSCOILE BHAILE ÁTHA CLIATH

2016

for Michael

First published 2016 by
UNIVERSITY COLLEGE DUBLIN PRESS
UCD Humanities Institute, Room H103
Belfield
Dublin 4
www.ucdpress.ie

© Vivien Igoe, 2016

ISBN 978-1-910820-06-3 hb

CIP data available from the British Library

Text design and layout by Lyn Davies Design
Typeset in Arnhem
Printed in England on acid-free paper by
CPI Antony Rowe, Chippenham, Wiltshire.

Supported by Dublin City Council
and Dublin UNESCO City of Literature

CONTENTS

Acknowledgements

I would like to extend my grateful appreciation first and foremost to Professor Declan Kiberd, for his unfailing kindness, help, encouragement, advice and support over many months throughout the course of my researches.

Professor Anne Fogarty, Dr Luca Crispi and Brian Donnelly from University College Dublin also provided helpful suggestions.

Thanks are due to the following people for their assistance and courtesy in answering queries: Damien Burke, Irish Jesuit Archives, Dublin; Margaret Byrne, Librarian, Law Society of Ireland, Dublin; Mary Clark, City Archivist, Dublin City Library and Archives; Noelle Dowling, Archivist, Dublin Diocesan Archives, Archbishop's House, Dublin; John Foley, Archivist, NUI, Dublin; Rebecca Hayes, Archivist, Freemason's Hall, Dublin; Andy McLaughlin, Archivist, St Paul's Retreat, Mount Argus, Dublin; Frank McGarry, Mount Jerome Cemetery; the late Shane MacThomáis, Historian to Glasnevin Cemetery Trust, Glasnevin, Dublin; Robert Mills, Librarian, Royal College of Physicians; Alan Phelan, Archivist, Erasmus High School, Dublin; Raymond Refausse, Librarian; and Susan Hood of the Representative Church Body Library, Dublin.

Sr Máire Bourke, OCD, Archivist, Carmelite Monastery, Knock, Co. Mayo; Fr Patrick Byrne, SM, Archivist, Marist Fathers, Milltown, Dublin; Fr Thomas Davitt, CM, Archivist, Vincentian Provincial Office, Dublin; Fr Ignatius Fennessy, OFM, and Fr Patrick Conlon, OFM, Archivists, Franciscan order, Killiney, Co. Dublin; Fr Hugh Fenning, OP, Archivist, St Mary's Dominican Priory, Tallaght, Co. Dublin; Fr David Kelly, OSA, Archivist, Orlagh, Rathfarnham, Co. Dublin; Brian Kirby, Archivist, Capuchin Provincial Archives, Dublin; Fr Brian Mulcahy, CP, St Paul's Retreat, Mount Argus, Dublin; Fr Vincent O'Hara, OCD, Carmelite Centre, Avila, Donnybrook, Dublin; Fr Aidan Troy, CP, Holy Cross Church, Ardoyne, Belfast.

Peter Beirne, Clare County Library; Caitlin Browne, Roscommon County Council Library; Jean Costelloe, Parnell Museum, Avondale, Co. Wicklow; Brigid Geoghegan, Westmeath County Council; Bernie Murphy, Deansgrange Cemetery; Mary O'Doherty, Royal College of Surgeons in Ireland; Nora O'Meara, North Tipperary Genealogical Services; and Tony Storan, Limerick County Council Library.

I would like to thank Hans Walter Gabler for his kind assistance. I am particularly indebted to Harald Beck, co-editor (with John Simpson) of *James Joyce Online Notes*, who provided many useful pointers and was always most generous with his time and sharing of information, as was John Simpson, former editor-in-chief of the *Oxford English Dictionary*. They both leave Sherlock Holmes in the shade. Thanks are due also to Eamonn Finn, who helped uncover material. We first met quite by chance one cold, dark November afternoon in St Patrick's graveyard, Enniskerry searching for the same gravestone of the family of Tertius Moses.

In Gibraltar, I am most grateful to Charles Durante for spending long hours over many months answering my extensive list of queries, checking details in the Garrison Library, interviewing relations of named characters, checking graveyard records, as well as locating a grave inscribed with the name of Lunita Laredo in the North Front (or Garrison) Cemetery, Gibraltar. Thanks are due also to Dominique Searle, editor of *The Gibraltar Chronicle* and to Sam Benady, Dennis Beiso and Jennifer Ballantine-Perera.

For some points of information, I would like to thank the following people, several of whom are related to characters in *Ulysses*: Patricia Boylan Ryan, Ciara Byrne, Menotti Vincent Caprani, Mary Cawley, Paul Clinch, Aidan Collins, Leo Collins, Peter Costello, Vincent Deane, Conor Dodd, Beatrice Doran, Fr Brendan Duddy, SJ, Denis Eustace, Sidney Feshbach, David Frith, Joseph C. Gallagher, Ian Gunn, Nuala Harrington Jordan, Conal Hooper, Margaret Horne, Jim Houlihan, James Hurley, Eishiro Ito, Mary Kelleher, Mary Kenny, Terence Killeen, Eithne Laracy Kavanagh, Felix Larkin, Emily Lyon O'Rourke, Charles Lysaght, Alf MacLochlainn, Kate MacLochlainn Cuffe, John McCullen, Michael McDowell, Margaret McGahon, Roland McHugh, Gerry Maginn, William Maginn, Patricia Maginn Langan, Liz Meldon, Ken Monaghan, Robert Nicholson, Andrew O'Brien, Fr Fergus O'Donoghue, SJ, Fachtna O'Donovan, Gerard O'Flaherty, Denis O'Neill, Tim O'Neill, Paola Pagnini, Homan Potterton, Justin Reynolds Piggott, Anne Ridge, John Ronayne, Stuart Rosenblatt, Aoife Ruane, Helen Rutledge, Stawell St Leger Heard, Fritz Senn, Fr Richard Eugene Sheehy, John Smurthwaite, Milo Spillane, Norma Sweny Furlong, Andrew Tierney, Mark Traynor, Roderick Trench (Lord Ashtown), Karl Troy, Claire Tunissen, Eileen Veale, Michael Veale, Tom Veale, Ged Walsh, Valerie Werner, Martin Wheeler and Gerard Whelan.

Special thanks to Patrick Shine, former Head of Survey and Mapping Dublin City Council, for his assistance in tracing streets, avenues and lanes, and pinpointing houses that had been renumbered or demolished and for his advice on maps. I would also like to thank the staff in the National Library of Ireland for their unfailing courtesy.

Aida Yared, Vanderbilt University, Nashville, Tennessee, deserves a very special thanks for her great generosity and helpful assistance with illustrations and other queries. See her remarkable website of Joycean images: joyceimages.com.

Thanks to Paddy Tutty for his help with photographs. He moved the large portrait painting of Brother Swan from the Christian Brothers' building in North Richmond Street into the daylight to get a good picture. I would also like to thank Fran Veale for his assistance with photographs. For the maps of Glasnevin, Mount Jerome and Deansgrange cemeteries, I would like to thank Tim O'Neill.

My thanks go to my husband, Michael, who greatly assisted me in various ways. Last but not least my thanks go to Fiona Dunne for her careful first edit of what was a very long manuscript and to my publisher UCD Press and editor, Noelle Moran and also to Damien Lynam for the final edit and production of the book. And finally, thanks to Brendan Kenny in Dublin City Council and Jane Alger at Dublin UNESCO City of Literature for their generous sponsorship of this publication.

List of illustrations

The majority of these photographs were taken more than a hundred years ago. Every reasonable effort has been made to trace the copyright holders of the photographs included. If there are any omissions, UCD Press will be pleased to insert the appropriate acknowledgement in any subsequent printing or editions.

List of illustrations

Appendix II: Horses in *Ulysses*

Foreword

'The ordinary is the proper domain of the artist,' said James Joyce: 'the extraordinary may safely be left to journalists.' In an age when newspapers increasingly resorted to the same sort of 'shock-horror!' stories which would animate many masterpieces of modernism from *Heart of Darkness* to *The Waste Land*, Joyce's determination to celebrate ordinary life seems quite unusual. Perhaps it was the extreme situations – from famine to land war – which characterised nineteenth-century Irish history that led Joyce to seek release in the ordinary: say, in the experience of eating a sandwich and drinking a glass of wine.

There is a sense in which *Ulysses* is presented as a text which does what traditional newspapers did before their collapse into sensationalism: offer a multi-layered account of the events of a single day: 16 June 1904. In calling himself 'a scissors and paste man', Joyce was suggesting that he had little to invent, since his main challenge was to document the real. Of course, this has always been an ambiguous challenge for Irish wordsmiths – whereas in other parts of the world, artists have to heighten their effects in order to make their material interesting, in dealing with Dublin the writer may have to scale some things down in order to make them credible. Nevertheless, Joyce was as much a stickler for the facts as any well-trained journalist of the old school – so much so that *Ulysses*, with its dense description, managed to 'paralyse Europe' in ways undreamed of by the ambitious journalist Ignatius Gallaher in *Dubliners*.

'I have put the great talkers of Dublin into my book,' said Joyce: 'they and the things they forgot.' The greatest talker of all was his father, John Stanislaus Joyce, whose phrases echo through the book: 'like a shot off a shovel', 'the weather is as uncertain as a child's bottom', and so on.

In recreating the lost Dublin of his childhood and youth, Joyce was providing the ultimate evocation of the world of his father – a place of singers, petty officials, lawyers, barflies, bailiffs, long-suffering mothers, nervous spinsters, aspiring politicians, righteous priests: in short, the seedy genteel. It was a world in which most elements were blown away by a succession of explosions: the First World War, Easter 1916, the collapse of the European ruling class, the Irish War of

Independence, all happening while Joyce wrote his memorial of a sleepy summer day in 1904. His own book was itself one of the explosions, which made most previous literature seem at once pre-modern and out-of-date; but in its actual subject-matter it was pretty old-hat. Its extreme experiments with form and style stand in marked contrast to its rather sedate, traditional content. There is through much of *Ulysses* a tremendous nostalgia for the old Edwardian world, even as the work itself makes possible a post-war modernity. *Ulysses* stands like a road-sign from the past, battered by war and revolution, pointing the way towards a wholly new future.

The characters in *Ulysses* are almost all real persons, or else they are closely based on a person or persons identifiable. Only the central figures – Leopold and Molly Bloom, Stephen Dedalus – seem to have been created out of Joyce's imagination. Everybody knows that Stephen is based to a significant degree on the young James Joyce; that Molly has elements in common with Nora Barnacle, his partner and eventual wife; and that the portrait of Leopold owes something to various characters, Irish and foreign. But in the end they are imaginative creations, whose sheer depth and complexity make the book the masterpiece it is. Moreover, that depth and complexity throw into cruel relief a certain two-dimensional shallowness in many of the other characters – as if Joyce's intent, while often celebratory or nostalgic, could also be sharply satirical. Compared with the incredible subtlety of his imagined figures, some of the real people take on the slightly ludicrous quality of caricatures, defined by a recurrent gesture or repeated trick-of-speech. It is as if cartoon drawings have been allowed to appear in a film dominated by actual persons. A paradox ensues: the real persons are made to appear less real, even as the invented ones take on an extra dimension of reality.

Vivien Igoe knows more than any living person about the real characters in *Ulysses*. She knows a lot of other things too, about graveyards, racehorses, churches, pubs, music halls. She has a cool, analytic brain along with a deep tenderness for that old Dublin world, many of whose details she learned from her mother. Vivien Igoe was one of the first curators of the Joyce Tower in Sandycove. Even as a young graduate, working for the Irish Tourist Board, she became a major source of information and illumination for such great Joycean commentators as Richard Ellmann and Fritz Senn. She was immediately recognised as a major contributor to the international community of Joyce scholars in the 1960s, helping to organise the first great symposium of their association in Dublin and providing expert and generous analysis over subsequent decades, as the body of work on Joyce grew to massive proportions. Eventually, she compiled this great catalogue of characters as part of her dissertation prepared at Joyce's own university, which it was my honour to supervise. The work was deservedly awarded a doctorate in 2011 and it is a pleasure now to see it made available in an enhanced version to the wider scholarly world.

Dr Igoe shows just how intimate a city Dublin was in 1904 and how often its networks (of lawyers, clergy, political fixers, shopkeepers, singers, housewives, librarians and academics) overlapped on one another. The Joyce family, being 'downstarts' in the social order, lived in many parts of the city and Dr Igoe reveals how their many moves facilitated the eldest son's deep knowledge not only of persons but of locales. She establishes the facts about a host of characters previously thought to be inventions. She shows just how linked were the personal histories of many of the book's characters in the years before 1904 – linkages which might have been obvious to some of Joyce's contemporary readers in Dublin but which, without this great feat of scholarship, would have been lost to us. This work is based on immense archival research in old newspapers and magazines, church records and national archives, as well as on dozens of interviews: but most of all it derives its authority from a lifetime's experience of Joyce, his world and his readers. It is not just extremely useful but also unfailingly amusing, in its deft comments and unexpected insights. It is a work in which imaginative engagement is tempered only by utter factual scruple. It is, in short, just the sort of encyclopedia that James Joyce himself would have loved.

DECLAN KIBERD
Dublin, April 2016

INTRODUCTION

They all belong to a vanished world and
most of them seem to have been very curious types.
Letter from Joyce to Mrs William Murray, 21 December 1922

The purpose of this work is to provide a reference book on the real people in James Joyce's *Ulysses* and to inform the readers of *Ulysses* today about the people of 1904 and other named figures from different periods. It gives an insight into the real personalities on which the work was based in the Dublin of 1904 and a perception of the period and its people, and social history as portrayed by Joyce in *Ulysses*.

The work focuses on the vast number of real people appearing in *Ulysses* on 16 June 1904 and others present in their memory, hallucinated or imagined. The entries include historical and contemporary people from Ireland, Gibraltar and other parts of the world.

The book contains information and biographies of many of the characters that had previously been thought to be fictional and who had been accorded little attention as a result. The intimacy of Dublin is made a reality through the personal histories of many of these individuals. Detailed information as to where they lived, worked, frequented, intermingled and found inspiration is recorded. Some people lived at different addresses in the city, which indicates in some instances the individual's rise or decline in fortune.

Many interesting facts of human interconnection become apparent, such as neighbours or street acquaintances of Joyce, or the many friends, enemies and contemporaries of his father who appear in this book. It reveals how Joyce manipulated and drew on his intimate knowledge of the city and its inhabitants in many of the neighbourhoods where he had lived, and it offers a vast mosaic of Dublin life and society in 1904.

Background information on the real people of the novel is relevant as it shows how deeply Joyce's works are embedded in the reality of Dublin. Many of the people were well known in Irish social and cultural circles and were celebrated

1

in different fields in Dublin at the turn of the century, enjoying recognition outside *Ulysses*, while others owe their immortality to Joyce. The biographical information of this eclectic mixture of people creates a vivid picture of the Dublin at the time, and throws light on many of the passages in *Ulysses*.

The Dublin of *Ulysses* had a population of only 290,638. It was a Roman Catholic city, but one in which the Protestant minority, representing about 20 per cent of the population, held most of the mercantile, professional and executive power and wealth. Virtually all the businesses were located within the boundaries of the Grand and Royal Canals. There was also dire poverty and unemployment in the city.

Many of the old, fashionable, residential districts on the north side of the Liffey had been bought by speculative landlords who let out the houses, in flats or rooms, to artisans and working-class families. Gradually, these houses fell into disrepair and degenerated into slums leading to appalling living conditions. Property on the south side of the city fared better. Many of the houses were bought by members of the legal and medical professions in areas around Merrion and Fitzwilliam Squares, and thus held both their status and their value.

There were very definite class distinctions in the Dublin of 1904 ranging from professional, lower middle class, upper working class to lower working class. It was a city of diversity, which was divided by class, wealth and religion. The literary topography and sense of place are important, as the location in which people lived, generally indicated their social status. Joyce loved the circulation of people, and as he was depicting the whole city and not just a segment of it, the characters in *Ulysses* lived in places, which encompassed the entire urban span and parts of the suburbs.

With the construction of the Dublin to Kingstown railway line in the 1830s and the introduction of the tramway system, the flight of the middle classes began and many of the wealthy professional classes moved to areas such as Rathgar, Rathmines, Terenure, Monkstown, Blackrock and Dundrum or had a house both in the country and in the city.

In the Dublin of 1904, people walked more and as a result they encountered a wide assortment of other citizens wandering through the labyrinth of streets on their way to and from work, in pubs, restaurants, churches, graveyards, hospitals, and all the various places where people intermingle. Everyone knew everyone else and if they didn't know them they knew someone who did. They were involved in and interacted with one another's lives. Therefore there was a complicated set of relationships linking politics, religion, business affairs and personal friendships.

Hundreds of names appear in *Ulysses*. Joyce was a great user of pre-existing material, which he recycled. He drew heavily from the names of his father's friends. Shortly after the death of his father, Joyce wrote to Harriet Weaver (17 January 1932), 'Hundreds of pages and scores of characters in my books came from him' (Ellmann, Richard, ed. *Selected Letters of James Joyce*. London: Faber & Faber, 1975, p. 361). Joyce himself described *Ulysses* 'as a sort of encyclopaedia' in a letter he wrote to Carlo Linati on 21 September 1920 when he sent him a schema of *Ulysses* (Ellmann, ed. *Selected Letters of James Joyce*, p. 271).

Some of the minor people have impressive lives and stories, like Gregor Grey, the artist who lived in Sherrard Street or William Gumley who fell on hard times. Other names are just mentioned or 'dropped', like Father Nicholas who was vicar in St Mary of the Angels, Church Street in 1904. He ministered there for nearly 40 years, and worked unstintingly for the rights of the people in the area. Nicholas Avenue was named after him. All these people made up the fabric of the city: 'How many! All these here once walked round Dublin. Faithful departed' (6.960–1). Many now rest in one of Dublin's three main cemeteries, Glasnevin, Mount Jerome and Deansgrange.

It is remarkable that Joyce could write about so many different Dublin characters, in some cases giving forensic attention to details about them, from portraying a city that he left for the final time in 1912. No one knew the city like he did. Dante portrayed Florence but he did not capture it in the same depth as Joyce did Dublin.

Joyce wrote *Ulysses* between 1914 and 1921. Sylvia Beach of Shakespeare & Co. first published it in Paris on 2 February 1922, on Joyce's fortieth birthday.

VIVIEN IGOE
Dublin, 2 February 2016

AUTHOR'S NOTE

I was motivated to write this book on the real people in *Ulysses* as the area I covered had not been researched before in any great detail. There were two important preceding books in the field, Shari and Bernard Benstock's *Who's He When He's at Home* (1980), which is a most useful compilation but does not provide any biographical information on the characters. The same limitation applies to *Ulysses Annotated: Notes for James Joyce's Ulysses* (1988) published by such gifted scholars as Don Gifford and Robert J. Seidman.

I wanted to provide a catalogue of people mentioned by name in *Ulysses*. It was essential that the research was undertaken to document the Dublin characters while some of their descendants were still alive who had records and pictures pertaining to the period. Being a Dubliner was an advantage as the topography in Joyce's work was familiar to me and I could relate to all the places mentioned. It also helped to be Irish to fully appreciate the Irish resonances, particularly in the areas of politics and religion.

Eileen Veale, my wonderful mother, and one of the first Dublin Joyceans, was born on 16 October 1909 in Holles Street Hospital at the time when Dr Andrew Horne was master. He was on duty there on 16 June 1904 when Mrs Purefoy was in labour with her ninth child. In selecting that surname for his fictional patient, Joyce took the name of Richard Dancer Purefoy (1847–1919), a former master of the Rotunda Hospital, the rival maternity hospital in Dublin.

As a child I mingled daily with direct descendants of named people in *Ulysses*. I attended a party at Hampstead House, Glasnevin the former home of Dr Henry Eustace (1869–1927). A descendant, Judy Eustace, was in my class at school. Miss Meldon, a granddaughter of surgeon Austin Meldon (1844–1904), was our 'drill' teacher at the same school at the Convent of the Sacred Heart, Lower Leeson Street.

'Casino', the house in Milltown where Austin Meldon was born, is close to where I live. Robert Emmet previously lived in this house. On the trail of Emmet as a child I was taken to 'The Priory' in Rathfarnham, the home of John Philpot Curran, and told that Sarah Curran had lived there. Across the road there was a tree-lined avenue named Emmet's Walk, where Emmet and Sarah used to meet. When I was researching the entries for John Philpot Curran, Sarah Curran and Robert Emmet I had already walked their territory. This applied to most of the people in *Ulysses* as every street, lane and road in Dublin has associations with some of them.

The river Dodder is 50 yards from my home. Downstream beside Lansdowne rugby ground (now Aviva) is the location where the body of Brigid Gannon was found on 23 August 1900. Constable Henry Flower from the Dublin Metropolitan Police, Londonbridge Road Station, was implicated in a case concerning the death from drowning of Gannon. So during my walks along the Dodder and through the Dublin streets, I encountered the ghosts of numerous people in *Ulysses*, in place but not in time.

As curator of the Joyce Museum in the Martello Tower in Sandycove, I encountered many writers, poets, artists, film directors, and people of all creeds and convictions. May Joyce Monaghan, Joyce's sister, was a frequent visitor and became a good friend. All the major Joycean academics and translators called, as well as students writing theses on Joyce. I assisted them with their queries and took them around Dublin on those halcyon summer evenings after work when the Tower was closed. I was in the right place at the right time and was fortunate to have met and corresponded with friends of Joyce such as Frank Budgen, Padraic Colum, Constantine Curran, Arthur Power, Paul Ruggiero, Ottocaro Weiss, and others. Those interesting days spent in Sandycove in the mid 1960s and early 1970s are recounted in my article 'Early Joyceans in Dublin' in the *Joyce Studies Annual*, xii (Summer 2001).

So having worked on Joyce and been associated with so many Joyceans like Richard Ellmann, Fritz Senn, Declan Kiberd and many others over the years, I felt it was now time to add to the Joycean scholarship and make a summitive statement with this present work on the real people in *Ulysses*. This compendium of biographies reinforces the perception of Joyce as a historian and faithful chronicler of his native city. I hope it will contribute to the advancement of knowledge in *Ulysses* and provide a comprehensive record of these people.

There are a number of people known only by context that I tried to trace and identify without success. No biographical information on them has been forthcoming so far. These include: Behan (Jarvey); Nancy Blake (Floey Dillon's friend); Lotty Clarke; Cuck Cohen; 'Bags' Comisky; John Corley; Fr Bernard Corrigan; Bob Cowley; Jack Crane; Warden Daly; Bob Doran; Miss Lydia Douce (Ormond Hotel barmaid); Mary Driscoll (servant at the Blooms home); Rev. Peter Fagan; Pat Farrel (newsboy with the *Telegraph*); James Fitzpatrick (boyhood friend of Bloom); Mrs Galbraith (friend of the Blooms); Mr Garvey (journalist with *Examiner* in Mullingar); Miss Gillespie (friend of the Dillons); Peggy Griffin; Captain Grove (Gibraltar friend of Major Tweedy); Hancock; Zoë Higgins (prostitute); Hornblower (Trinity College porter); Georgina Johnson (prostitute); R. G. Johnson; Dan Kelly; Clive Kempthorpe (Oxford student); Miss Mina Kennedy (Ormond Hotel barmaid); Mrs Kennefick; Ned Lambert (friend of Mr Dedalus); Paddy Lee; Livingstone; Florence MacCabe (fictional midwife); Paddy MacCabe (late husband of Florence); M'Conachie (friend of Corley); Daniel Magrane; Charles Albert Marsh (customer at Bella Cohen's); D. B. Murphy (seaman in cabman's shelter); Dr Murren; Lancecorporal Oliphant; 'Maggot O'Reilly' (acquaintance of Bloom); Esther Osvalt; Elsa Potter (acquaintance of Milly Bloom); Rogers (acquaintance of the Blooms); Mary Shorthall; Rev. B. R. Slattery; Miss Stack (acquaintance of Bloom); Bertha Supple (friend of Edy Boardman and Gerty MacDowell); Tighe (friend of Corley); Jesse Tilsit; and Mr and Mrs Verschoyle.

The chief fictional characters invented by Joyce, Leopold Bloom, Stephen Dedalus and Molly Bloom are composites of real people and are included. It is ironic that most of the real people in *Ulysses* are somewhat flattened or levelled in Joyce's depiction, whereas the mainly fictional Leopold and Molly Bloom are rendered with a depth unprecedented in even great literature. Joyce rarely invented anything. Most of the things he wrote were factual, which he adapted for the book. It must be emphasised that *Ulysses* is a work of fiction; the real names of people are used, but in some cases not the characters. Moses Dlugacz who appears in the 'Calypso' episode as a pork butcher was not one in fact; he was a pupil of Joyce in Trieste. He was never in Dublin and his is the only shop in Dublin mentioned in *Ulysses* that did not exist.

Almidano Artifoni appears in *Ulysses* as Stephen's voice-training teacher in Dublin. Artifoni was a real person but was neither a Dubliner nor a teacher of music. He was head of the Berlitz School of Languages in Trieste. It is possible that Artifoni's character in *Ulysses* was based on Benedetto Palmieri who was born in Naples and was employed as a singing teacher at the Royal Irish Academy of Music, in Westland Row, Dublin at the time. Palmieri lived at 14 Lansdowne Road, the location where in the 'Wandering Rocks' episode (10.128–2), 'Almidano Artifoni's sturdy trousers' were 'swallowed by a closing door' as the viceregal cavalcade passed by Northumberland Road, on its way to the Royal Dublin Society grounds. Artifoni is living at Palmieri's address at 14 Lansdowne Road. Palmieri was the singing teacher not Artifoni. When portraying the people in *Ulysses*, Joyce manipulates and abuses some of them. He treats some with contempt, some satirically, others in a disrespectful fashion, and others with affection.

He deals with various relations in a mocking fashion. Joyce did not feel in any way curtailed in including members of his own family or friends of the family for fear of offending them: he used them all. In the 'Proteus' episode Stephen recalls how his father mocks his in-laws: 'Sure he's not down in Strasburg terrace with his aunt Sally? Couldn't he fly a bit higher than that, eh?' (3.63–4). In some instances, Joyce used the names of people but not their character, as a means of revenge or to repay old scores. Sir Horace Rumbold (1869–1941) was the British minister to Switzerland in 1918. Rumbold was an enemy of Joyce following the conflict with the 'English Players' group in Zurich and Joyce's ensuing unsuccessful lawsuit in 1918–19. Joyce borrowed Rumbold's name to use for the name of the barber/hangman Harry Rumbold.

Joyce was involved in a fracas in St Stephen's Green in June 1904. Vincent Cosgrave, who was with him, abandoned him. A passer-by, Alfred Hunter, rescued Joyce. Joyce did not forget this incident and took literary revenge on Cosgrave. In the 'Circe' episode, Lynch plays the role of Judas; he abandons Stephen in his hour of need. Joyce gave him the name Lynch, as the mayor of Galway, whose name was Lynch, hanged his own son.

Sir Frederick Falkiner, the recorder of Dublin, is portrayed with both respect and affection. Joyce admired him because as the 'poor man's judge' he was reluctant to enforce the full rigours of the law on the impoverished by money-lenders. Joyce was familiar with poverty and ashamed of his family's declining fortunes caused by his improvident father. He was aware of the tricks his father used to acquire money and to avoid paying the rent.

Gogarty appears under the guise of Mulligan instead of his own name, while Russell, Koehler, Cousins and others have their own names. Joyce might have been afraid of litigation in Gogarty's case: 'That Mulligan is a contaminated bloody doubledeyed ruffian by all accounts. His name stinks all over Dublin' (6.63–4). Joyce had no love for Reuben J. Dodd, a legal accountant and money-lender. The denuding of John Joyce's pockets to pay back heavy debts to Dodd rankled deeply with Joyce, particularly since Dodd's son was his contemporary at Belvedere College. Joyce treats Dodd with utter contempt in *Ulysses*.

In this work I had to be selective, so have included only people that are named and identified in the text. Some names, not included, did not seem of major importance and several are already well known enough not to require further documentation. I have not included the names of numerous people that are alluded to through their work, or the names of the many people connected with businesses in the city.

I used the following investigative methods to research the real people in *Ulysses*. Many of the relatives of these people I interviewed provided oral family histories. Each person assisted in recording and documenting what they knew/ remembered, much of which was hitherto unrecorded or unpublished. The experience of meeting and speaking with relatives of named characters, some of whom were formerly deemed to be fictitious, proved exhilarating with the novelty of the information they provided.

Primary sources involved research in various libraries and archives both at home and abroad. *The Census of Ireland* returns for 1901 and 1911 provided information concerning personal details, such as age taken at time of the census, address, religion, marital status, and place of birth. The *Irish Civil Registration Indexes, 1845–1958* was also a useful source as were the county libraries and local heritage and genealogy centres for tracking down people living in a particular area. Other archives such as the Zurich James Joyce Foundation and the Public Record Office, Kew were consulted. I checked the burial records at Glasnevin, Mount Jerome, Deansgrange and other cemeteries.

The contemporary national and provincial newspapers circulating in Ireland in the nineteenth century provided valuable data such as death notices and obituaries. The *Irish Times* archives and the *Freeman's Journal* were particularly valuable sources for providing information. Periodicals, journals and magazines were also useful sources.

Joyce used *Thom's Directory 1904* for the events of Bloomsday. So the volumes of *Thom's Directory* were an invaluable source containing lists of government departments and offices, an ecclesiastical directory, lieutenancy and magistracy, list of institutions, trades directory of Dublin, and most importantly a street directory giving the occupiers of every building (with the exception of tenement buildings) in each street.

The Irish Law Times and Solicitors' Journal included the memoirs and obituaries of deceased members. This weekly publication (1867–1980), which started as a journal for the 'legal public', contained much useful information in tracking the many legal people in *Ulysses*.

I consulted the writings of James Joyce and his brother Stanislaus, and all of Joyce's correspondence and letters (see Bibliography for books consulted), and used many secondary sources – such as books, which contain essential biographical, background or topographical information.

Concerning the characters in Gibraltar, I had a letter published in the *Gibraltar Chronicle* and had an immediate reply from Charles Durante who was 'au fait' with Joyce and was most helpful. He spent many hours in the Garrison Library, and interviewed some descendants of the people mentioned in *Ulysses*. Exciting new information surfaced. The only person we failed to find the dates for was Father Viliplana.

For information on cricketers such as Buller and Ironmonger, I contacted Wisden who referred me to David Frith, an expert on cricket, and for information on the racehorses named in *Ulysses* I used the Archives of the British Racing Board, England and various bloodstock books.

My methodology for sourcing clergy included the Dublin Diocese Archives. I also contacted the archivist of each order mentioned in *Ulysses* and consulted the *Irish Catholic Directories* in the Jesuit Library, Milltown Park. This provided information on clergy, and dates when and where they moved, at different periods during their career. It also contained obituaries.

Guide to entries

Citations are given by episode and line number to James Joyce, *Ulysses*, edited by Hans Walter Gabler et al. (New York and London: Garland, 1984, 1986; Random House, New York: Vintage, 1986, 1993; Random House, London: The Bodley Head, 1986, 1993, 2008).

In some instances, in a character entry, a line number may be cited, but his/her name may not necessarily appear in the passage as it is merely implied.

There are numerous instances throughout *Ulysses* where people and their occupations are alluded to or thought about without the person actually being named. Some of these instances are obscure. Don Gifford, with Robert J. Seidman, *Ulysses' Annotated*, revised edition (Berkeley: University of California Press, 1988) is an essential source for my work as it gives the reader salient further information. Some citations from this book are included in character entries. Dates are given for most of the people listed in the entries. In a few cases where dates were not ascertainable, *floruit* (flourished) dates are provided. For obvious reasons line citations for Leopold and Molly Bloom, Stephen Dedalus, Malachi Mulligan and Hugh 'Blazes' Boylan are omitted as they would have been too numerous.

Entries are arranged in alphabetical sequence by the name of the subject as spelled in *Ulysses*. For example, M'Ardle, M'Cann, M'Carthy, M'Guckin, M'Manus and M'Swiney are listed as they are spelled in the text. In the case where a character is based or partly based on someone else, I cite the name of the character first, then give details on whom he/she is based. For example, Vincent Lynch is based on Vincent Cosgrave.

Abramovitz, The Rev. Leopold (1849–1905) *Rabbi*
The Rev. Leopold Abramovitch, Chazen, is identical with Abraham Lipman Abramovitz, who was reader of the Lennox Street synagogue. Born in Russia in 1849, he arrived in Dublin in 1887 and was an ordained rabbi. As well as being a Hebrew teacher he served the community as shochet (ritual slaughterman), chazen (reader) and mohel (circumciser). He lived at 3 St Kevin's Road, South Circular Road, Dublin and later at 1 Stamer Street, Dublin, with his wife Fanny, who was born in Russia in 1849. He died on 25 October 1905 and was buried in the Jewish Cemetery, Dolphin's Barn, Rialto, Dublin [03–A–24].   *Ulysses 15.3224*

Abrines, John L. (1868–1924) and Luis Richard (1870–1950) *Bakers in Gibraltar*
'... there are a few olives in the kitchen he might like I never could bear the look of them in Abrines ...' *(18.1481–2)*
The Abrines family came originally from Minorca and settled in Gibraltar. The name was originally 'Abri' but became Abrines, because the Catalan name was changed for a Castilian one. Richard and John had a bakery, R. and J. Abrines, Ltd, The Aix Bakery, 292 Main Street, Gibraltar.

Originally run by John Abrines, senior, born in 1832, the bakery was later passed on to his two sons, Luis Richard Abrines, born on 21 March 1870, died on

12 January 1950, and John L. Abrines, born on 20 February 1868, died in 1924. They later lived at 25–26 Church Street. Apart from the bakery, the Abrines had another business in Gibraltar at 27 Waterport Street, which was a groceries and provision store.

The bakery got its unusual name, 'The Aix Bakery', from the fact that the Abrines won a bread competition in Aix in France and decided to name the bakery after the French town, which was either Aix-en-Provence or Aix-la-Chapelle. In 1900, the bakery won another competition at the Colonial Bread Show Exhibition and was awarded a cup by the proprietors of Lothian Malt Preparations for 'excellence of exhibit'. The Aix Bakery, which made hovis, helium and plasmon bread, produced a large proportion of Gibraltar's bread. It closed down in the 1960s but the building may still be seen on the Main Street.

Adams, Dick (1843–1908) *Journalist and barrister*

'Dick Adams, the besthearted bloody Corkman the Lord ever put the breath of life in ...' *(7.679–80)*

Richard Adams was born on 6 January 1843 in Cork. He was the eldest son of Bryan Adams and Frances (née Donovan). He started work as a journalist with the *Cork Examiner*. After a time in London working for the *Morning Star*, he subsequently moved to the *Freeman's Journal* in Dublin.

He became a member of the Irish Bar in 1873. His first engagement in the Four Courts came in connection with the state trials of 1881, for the prosecution of Parnell and others for conspiracy. He gained notoriety for his defence of James FitzHarris, who was charged with collusion in the Phoenix Park murders. He became crown prosecutor for Cork.

On 9 March 1894, Adams became county Cork judge for Limerick and held this post until his death. Noted for his wit and humour, Adams died on 4 April 1908 in London and was buried at St Mary's Cemetery, Kensal Green.

Adderly, C. (*fl.* late 1800s–early 1900s) *Cyclist*

'... C. Adderly and W. C. Huggard, started in pursuit.' *(10.1260)*

Adderly was one of the nine quartermile flat handicappers who took part in the Trinity College bicycle races on the afternoon of 16 June 1904.

Agatha, Sister (b. 1862) *Nun*

Based on **Margaret Claffey** *Daughter of Patrick Claffey*

'Sister? Pat Claffey, the pawnbroker's daughter.' *(8.153–4)*

Leopold Bloom thinks that Pat Claffey's daughter became a nun at Tranquilla Convent, founded in 1833 by the Carmelites. It was located at 59 Upper Rathmines Road, Dublin, and was adjacent to Rathmines Castle.

Patrick Claffey the pawnbroker and his wife Margaret (née Grehan) had a number of children. Three of their daughters entered the Dominican order: Annie, Elizabeth and Margaret. Annie, whose name in religion was Sister Mary Patricia, died aged 21 in 1890 in Bavaria. Elizabeth was born in 1860 and entered the Dominicans at Mount Sion, Blackrock, Co. Dublin, and was known as Sister Mary Bonaventura. Margaret, known as Sister Mary Hyacinth was born in 1862 and entered the same convent but was later transferred to the Dominican convent at 18 Eccles Street.

Sister Agatha was modelled on one of the three daughters, possibly Margaret as she was based in Eccles Street at the same time that the Blooms lived in 7 Eccles Street. Claffey's daughter appears as Sister Agatha in the 'Circe' episode.

Ulysses 13.780; 15.3435

Aldborough, Lord (1733/4–1801) *Politician*
'Near Aldborough house Father Conmee thought of that spendthrift nobleman.' *(10.83–4)*
Edward Augustus Stratford, 2nd earl of Aldborough, was the eldest son of Martha (née O'Neale) and John Stratford, MP for Baltinglass, Co. Wicklow.

Following the death of his first wife in 1787, he married Anne Henniker, only daughter of Sir John Henniker, who brought him a large fortune that enabled him to free his estates from encumbrances.

Known for his eccentricity, Aldborough had a mania for building and had various town and country houses constructed both in England and Ireland. In 1796, Aldborough House in Portland Row, Dublin, was erected as his private residence but he never actually lived there as his wife did not like it. This was the last of the great eighteenth-century houses to be built in Dublin.

The extravagant and ostentatious Aldborough died on 2 January 1801 at his residence, Belan House, Ballitore, Co. Kildare, during a party. He left 54 wills.

Aldborough was interred in a vault at St Thomas's Church in Marlborough Street, Dublin. In 1922 during the Civil War, the church was extensively damaged and later demolished. The remains of those interred were transferred from St Thomas's in 1925–6 to a plot in Mount Jerome Cemetery, Harold's Cross, Dublin [AC–94–17333].

Aldworth, Elizabeth (née St Leger) (1695–1775) *First lady Freemason*
'There was one woman ... hid herself in a clock to find out what they do be doing ... That was one of the saint Legers of Doneraile.' *(8.971–4)*
Elizabeth Aldworth was the only daughter of the Right Honourable Arthur St

Leger, First Baron Kilmayden and Viscount Doneraile, and Elizabeth Hayes, daughter and heiress of John Hayes of Winchilsea.

Elizabeth Aldworth is credited as being the first lady Freemason. The exact date of her initiation into Masonry is not known but as the date of her marriage bond is 1713, it is believed that it took place sometime between 1710 and 1713 at Doneraile Court, Co. Cork, where she lived with her father. The story goes that Elizabeth was reading in the library and fell asleep and awoke to the sound of voices in the adjoining room. The only way out of the library was through the Lodge Room, which was used for Masonic purposes. Part of the wall dividing the two rooms was in the process of being removed to make an arch. From behind the loosely placed bricks of the dividing wall, Elizabeth observed the proceedings of the Lodge. There was only one course of action to be taken in the circumstances and she consented to 'pass through the impressive ceremonials she had already in part witnessed'.

The Honourable Mrs Aldworth died in 1775 and was buried in the Davis vault beneath the old Cathedral of St Finbarr in Cork. When the present nineteenth-century St Finbarr's Cathedral was built, her remains were moved and placed in the floor of the small chamber situated in the Great Tower. Elizabeth Aldworth is commemorated by a brass memorial in St Finbarr's Cathedral.

Alexander, Charles McCallom (1867–1928) *Revivalist*
'Torry and Alexander last year.' *(8.17)*
Charles McCallom Alexander was a minister and song leader, who, with Reuben Archer Torry, conducted revival services and a 'Mission to Great Britain', 1903–5. They came on a mission to Dublin in March–April 1904.

Alexander, Frederick *Racehorse owner*
Frederick Alexander was the owner of Throwaway, the horse that won the Gold Cup race held at Ascot at 3.00 pm on 16 June 1904.   *Ulysses 16.1278*

Alexander, Rev. Dr William (1824–1911) *Church of Ireland primate*
'... the most reverend Dr William Alexander, archbishop of Armagh, primate of all Ireland ...' *(15.1422–3)*
William Alexander was born on 13 April 1824 at Garvagh, Co. Derry, in the parish of Errigal, where his father, the Rev. Robert Alexander, was curate. He was made bishop of Derry and Raphoe in 1867 and became archbishop of Armagh and primate of All Ireland in 1896. He held that office for 15 years.

His Dublin-born wife, Cecil Frances Humphreys (1818–95), wrote almost 400 hymns, including 'All Things Bright and Beautiful', 'There Is a Green Hill Far Away', 'St Patrick's Breastplate' and 'Once in Royal David's City'.

William Alexander wrote many theological works such as *Primary Convictions* (1893). His collected poems were published in 1887 under the title *St Augustine's Holiday and Other Poems*. He retired to Torquay in England where he died on 12 September 1911, and was buried with Mrs Alexander in the cemetery of St Columb's Cathedral, Derry.

Archbishop Alexander is commemorated in St Columb's Cathedral where there is an image of his head on a corbel in the nave.   *Ulysses 15.1479*

Allingham, William (1824–89) *Irish poet and editor*
'*Laurence Bloomfield in Ireland* by William Allingham (second edition, green cloth, gilt trefoil design, previous owner's name on recto of flyleaf erased).' *(17.1388–90)*
William Allingham was born on 19 March 1824 in Ballyshannon, Co. Donegal. He was educated in Ballyshannon and in Killeshandra, Co. Cavan. His first volume of poems dedicated to Leigh Hunt was published in 1850 and included his popular poem, 'The Fairies'.

Fraser's Magazine issued Allingham's long narrative about landlords and tenants entitled *Laurence Bloomfield in Ireland* in 12 instalments during 1863. It was published in book form in 1864.

Editor of *Fraser's Magazine* from 1874–9, Allingham published *Flower Pieces and Other Poems* in 1888. He died on 18 November 1889 in Hampstead, London. His ashes were returned to Ballyshannon where they were interred in the Church of Ireland cemetery.

Laurence Bloomfield in Ireland by William Allingham is contained in Bloom's library.

Anderson, Mary (1859–1940) *Actress*
'Quite so, Martin Cunningham said. Mary Anderson is up there now.' *(6.219)*
Mary Anderson, daughter of Charles Anderson and Marie Antoinette (née Leugers), was born on 28 July 1859 in Sacramento, California. Her first public stage appearance  as Juliet was in Louisville, Kentucky, in November 1875 when she was 16. She received favourable reviews and continued with great success in various productions in Pittsburgh, Boston and New York.

Anderson first visited Europe in 1879, and thereafter toured the US and Canada. The most prominent actress of the era in the US, during the height of her acting career, she returned to London in September 1883 and played to full houses. She remained for five years, returning to the States in 1888 and a few months later became ill from exhaustion and dispersed her company. Anderson returned to Europe in 1889 to recuperate and more or less gave up the professional stage except for a few occasions where she made an occasional appearance for charity.

In 1890, Anderson married Antonio de Navarro, an American who practised at the London Bar. They settled in Broadway in Worcestershire, England, where they raised their two sons. She wrote her memoirs, *A Few Memories* (1896), and co-authored a playscript with Robert Hichens based on his book *The Garden of Allah*, which was later staged in the United States.

In the *Freeman's Journal*, on 16 June 1904, the Ulster Hall in Belfast advertised the visit of the world-renowned actress Mary Anderson (Madame de Navarro) in the balcony scene from *Romeo and Juliet*. The concert was in aid of the Holy Cross Church in Ardoyne. Other eminent artistes listed for the concert included conductor Herr Louis Werner, cellist Clyde Twelvetrees and baritone William Ludwig.

Mary Anderson died on 29 May 1940 in Broadway, Worcestershire, England, where she had strong connections with the monastery, schools and church of the Passionist Fathers.

Andrews, William Drennan (1832–1924) *Judge*

'... and master Justice Andrews, sitting without a jury in the probate court, weighed well and pondered the claim ...' *(12.1115–17)*
William Drennan Andrews, son of John Andrews and Sarah (née Drennan) was born on 24 January 1832 in Comber, Co. Down. His father was one of the most successful flax spinners in Ulster. His maternal grandfather, William Drennan, of Cabin Hill, was a well-known United Irishman and poet.

Andrews was called to the Irish Bar in 1855, and became queen's counsel in 1872. He was appointed judge in the Exchequer Division of the High Court of Justice, Ireland. This was later merged with the King's Bench Division.

In 1904, Andrews was judge of the Probate and Matrimonial Bench of the King's Bench Division. He retired in 1909 after over 27 years as a judge in the High Court. He became an honorary bencher of King's Inns, Dublin. He spent his retirement between Comber, Co. Down, and his Dublin home at 51 Lower Leeson Street. He died on 3 December 1924.

Apjohn, Percy *Bloom's boyhood friend*

'To Master Percy Apjohn at High School in 1880 he had divulged his disbelief ...' *(17.1635–6)*
It is likely that the name of the fictional Percy Apjohn was derived from that of Thomas Barnes Apjohn (1839–1911) who in 1904 lived in Rutland House, Dolphin's Barn. Percy Apjohn was one of Bloom's schoolmates who attended the Erasmus High School at 40 Harcourt Street, Dublin.

Thomas Apjohn's wife Kathleen died at Rutland House on 7 September 1905 and in 1908 he left and moved to live with his sister, Mrs Annie Barnes, at 40 Brighton Square, Rathgar.

Apjohn died on 4 August 1911 at 40 Brighton Square, Rathgar. He was buried in Mount Jerome Cemetery, Harold's Cross, Dublin [C111–12248].

Ulysses 8.404; 15.3326–8; 16.756–60; 17.51; 17.1251–2; 17.2317

Ardilaun, Lord (1840–1915) *Son of brewer Benjamin Lee Guinness*
'Still the other brother lord Ardilaun has to change his shirt four times a day, they say.' *(5.306–7)*
Arthur Edward Guinness was born on 1 November 1840 at St Anne's, Clontarf, Co. Dublin, at the Guinness family home. The eldest son of Sir Benjamin Guinness, he was named after his great-grandfather, Arthur Guinness (1725–1803), founder of Guinness's Brewery.

Educated at Eton College in England and Trinity College Dublin, he was elected MP for Dublin, 1868–9 and 1874–80. He was head of the Guinness brewing business from 1868 until 1876 when he sold his half-share to his brother, Edward Cecil. In 1880, he was created Baron Ardilaun, of Ashford in Co. Galway, and lived at times in Ashford Castle on Lough Corrib.

A philanthropist, he restored Marsh's Library in St Patrick's Close and extended the Coombe Lying-In Hospital. It was through his intervention that St Stephen's Green was transformed from a swampy waste into a public park given to the people of Dublin in 1880. The grateful citizens erected a statue of Lord Ardilaun by Thomas Farrell, RHA, on the Green's west side, at the site of the original entrance.

Lord Ardilaun died on 20 January 1915 at St Anne's, and was buried at All Saints Church, Raheny, Co. Dublin.

Artifoni, Almidano (1873–1950) *Music teacher of Stephen Dedalus*
'*Eccolo*, Almidano Artifoni said in friendly haste. *Venga a trovarmi e ci pensi. Addio, caro.*' *(10.358–9)*
Almidano Artifoni was born on 5 March 1873 in Bergamo, in Lombardy. After graduating from the Scuola Superiore di Commercio in Genoa, he taught for five

years at the Berlitz School of Languages in Hamburg, Germany where he became the director.

In 1900, Artifoni came to Trieste and was the temporary Spanish teacher when the Berlitz School opened in 1901. Two other teachers at the school, Joseph Guye and Paolo Scholz, took it over in 1907, although Artifoni continued to list himself as the director until 1911.

Artifoni taught accountancy at the evening school of the Società degli Impiegati, Via Giotto. He probably helped Joyce get a job teaching English in this school between 1910 and 1913. He remained in

Trieste after the First World War, working for the law courts as an accountancy expert.

Joyce borrowed Almidano Artifoni's name for Stephen's voice-training teacher in Dublin on account of its musicality or maybe to mark the fact that Artifoni had given him a job in Trieste. Almidano Artifoni never visited Dublin.

Artifoni died on 25 August 1950 in Trieste and was buried in the Catholic Cemetery of St Anna, Via dell'Istria 206, Trieste [Communal burial section 2936 Row 5].

Ulysses 10.338; 10.344; 10.355; 10.362–3; 10.1101; 10.1281; 15.2501

Atkinson, F. M'Curdy (1878–1973) *Dublin literary figure*
'I hardly hear the purlieu cry
Or a Tommy talk as I pass one by
Before my thoughts begin to run
On F. M'Curdy Atkinson ...' (9.1143–6)
Frederick McCurdy Atkinson was born on 31 October 1878. A contributor to *Dana* he was a tall quiet Irishman whose outward reserve hid the scholarship and sense of fun that lay beneath. While at Trinity College Dublin he became a friend of E. V. Longworth. Both were widely read and belonged to George Moore's inner circle. Moore consulted them about the critical judgements he made on English and French writing in his novel, *Hail and Farewell*.

Atkinson worked for several years as resident reader and general editor for Heinemann at 21 Bedford Street, London. He lived for some years at 12 Bryanston Street, Marble Arch, and died aged 95 on 19 March 1973 at 9 Eaton Terrace, London. His funeral took place at Golders Green Crematorium two days later.

Ulysses 9.1141; 15.2525

Balfe, Michael W. (1808–70) *Irish composer*
'Pupil of Michael Balfe's, wasn't she?' *(8.418)*
Michael Balfe, son of Michael William Balfe, a dancing schoolteacher and Catherine (née Ryan), was born at 10 Pitt Street (now Balfe Street) in Dublin on 15 May 1808. From an early age Balfe displayed great musical talent. At the age of nine he performed on his violin in the Rotunda Concert Rooms. This was followed by other

performances in the Crow Street Theatre. Balfe's first musical composition, 'The Lover's Mistake', was published in December 1822 by Isaac Willis in Westmoreland Street, Dublin.

On the death of his father in January 1823, Balfe left for London to pursue his musical career. He gave his first concert in March 1823 at Drury Lane where he performed a concerto for violin.

Balfe travelled around Europe to Italy where he was commissioned by La Scala in 1826 to write music for the ballet *La Perouse*. He moved to Paris where Rossini arranged an engagement for him to sing Figaro in *The Barber of Seville*, at the Theatre des Italiens in 1827. He wrote several operas for Drury Lane of which *The Siege of Rochelle* (1835) was the most popular. His *Falstaff* was produced in 1838 with Luigi Lablache, the Italian opera singer, in the title role.

The Bohemian Girl (1844) was produced with great success for Drury Lane. The best-known song from the opera is 'I Dreamt I Dwelt in Marble Halls'. Other Balfe operas include *The Sicilian Bride* (1852) and *The Rose of Castille* (1857).

Balfe wrote 28 operas but is best remembered for *The Bohemian Girl*. He died on 20 October 1870 at his home, 'Rowney Abbey', in Hertfordshire and was buried in Kensal Green Cemetery, London. He is commemorated by a tablet in Westminster Abbey, London and in Dublin in St Patrick's Cathedral by a stained glass window by Ballantine and a brass by Sawier (of Dublin), that bears the inscription:

In memory of M. W. Balfe the most celebrated genial and beloved of Irish musicians. Commendatore of the Order of Carlos III in Spain. Chevalier of the Legion of

Honour in France. Born in Dublin 15th May 1808. Died 20th October 1870. Erected by RP Stewart 1879.

Ulysses The Bohemian Girl, 11.659; The Rose of Castille, 7.471–2; 7.591; 11.13–14; 11.329; 11.779–82; 11.1271; 12.185; 14.1510; 15.1731; The Siege of Rochelle, 10.557; 13.313

Ball, Sir Robert Stawell (1840–1913) *Astronomer and mathematician*

'*The Story of the Heavens* by Sir Robert Ball (blue cloth).' *(17.1373)*

Robert Ball was born at 3 Granby Row, Rutland Square (now Parnell Square), Dublin, on 1 July 1840. He was the son of Robert Ball, a civil servant and Amelia (née Hellicar).

Ball's education started at Dr John Lardner Burke's school in North Great George's Street; he later attended Dr Brindley's School at Tarvin Hall near Chester, England, where he excelled in science and mathematics. When he was 17 his father died and Ball entered Trinity College Dublin as a sizar and then a scholar.

In 1865, Ball became tutor to the children of Laurence Parsons, the 3rd earl of Rosse (1840–1908), Birr Castle, Co. Offaly. He took the post on condition that he could use the giant telescope in the demesne. It was here that Ball had his first experience in practical astronomy and made many observations of nebulae.

Ball was professor of astronomy at Trinity College and astronomer-royal for Ireland from 1874 to 1892 and worked at Dunsink Observatory, Castleknock, Co.

Dublin. He was president of the Royal Zoological Society of Ireland and was knighted in 1886. He moved to Cambridge in 1892 where he was Lowndean professor of astronomy and geometry.

Popular as a lecturer, Ball was known to a wide audience through his many popular science and astronomy books, in particular *The Story of the Heavens* (1886).

Ball died in Cambridge on 25 November 1913. He was buried in St Giles's churchyard, Cambridge, England. *Ulysses 8.110; 15.1011; The Story of the Heavens, 8.110*

Bandmann-Palmer, Mrs Millicent (1865–1905) *Actress*

'*Leah* tonight. Mrs Bandmann Palmer ... Hamlet she played last night. Male impersonator.' *(5.194–6)*

Millicent Palmer, or Millie, as she was known, was an American actress. Her husband Daniel Edward Bandmann (1840–1905), was a Shakespearean actor from Germany. They settled in England in 1867.

Mrs Bandmann-Palmer made her first tour of the British Isles in 1883 and directed her own company. The 18-year-old actor, Clarence Derwent, who was in her troupe, wrote in his diary in 1902 that she 'was very short, very fat and very popular in the provinces. She weighed 200 pounds and while she may not seem

the ideal Hamlet, actually Hamlet is referred to as "fat and scant of breath" and so Mrs Bandmann-Palmer chose to play Hamlet quite frequently.'

The *Freeman's Journal* for 16 June 1904 advertised her performance for *Leah* in the Gaiety Theatre in Dublin. She played the part of Hamlet at the Gaiety on 15 June 1904. The same newspaper reported that she played the part of the prince and 'to say the least sustained it creditably'.   *Ulysses 6.185; 15.496; 17.2079; 17.2256–7*

Bannon, Alec *(fl. late 1800s–early 1900s)* *Friend of Mulligan and admirer of Milly Bloom*
'I got a card from Bannon. Says he found a sweet young thing down there. Photo girl he calls her.' *(1.684–5)*
Alec Bannon is described as a student and 'a young gentleman'.

Joyce met Mr A. E. Bannon, when John Stanislaus Joyce was working on the electoral register in Mullingar, Co. Westmeath, in 1900 and 1901. Bannon was a local man who had made a name for himself through his work as the district councillor for Mullingar.

John Stanislaus Joyce knew Bannon through his work and it is likely that on his visit to Mullingar with James that he stayed in his house at Portloman on the shores of Lough Owel. Members of the Bannon family are buried in the cemetery at Portloman.   *Ulysses 4.407; 14.497; 14.653–4; 14.1211; 15.2239*

Bapty, Walter *(1850–1915)* *Professor of singing*
'How Walter Bapty lost his voice.' *(11.927)*
Born in Leeds, England, Walter Bapty first came to Dublin as a young boy soprano to sing at two public concerts in the Rotunda where he was a great success. Aged 17, he sang as a solo tenor at the principal choral concerts in Dublin.

A Freemason, Bapty was a member of Israel Lodge, which he joined in 1871. In 1872, he made his first professional début at the old Exhibition Palace in

Earlsfort Terrace. Four years later he was appointed as vicar-choral of St Patrick's Cathedral. He sang at the early performances of the Dublin Musical Society and became a member of the Dublin Glee and Madrigal Union, succeeding Barton M'Guckin as a member of the union. When M'Guckin left Ireland to live in London, Bapty was regarded as the principal tenor in Ireland and sang several times at the Covent Garden Promenade concerts.

One of the promoters and organisers of the first Feis Ceoil (the annual Dublin music festival), Bapty acted as adjudicator at the vocal competitions. In 1884 Bapty lived at 177 Strand Road, Sandymount before moving to 22 Upper Pembroke Street, Dublin.

Bapty lost his voice in the early 1900s but after a lengthy period abroad under medical supervision it returned. He died at his home on 2 April 1915 and was buried in St Patrick's Cathedral churchyard.

Barlow, John (1822–1912) *Mace bearer and officer of commons to Dublin*
'And old Barlow the macebearer laid up with asthma, no mace on the table, nothing in order ...' *(10.1008–9)*
John Barlow, born in Dublin in 1822, worked as a corporation official in the city. He was first elected to the annual posts of mace bearer and officer of commons at a meeting of Dublin Corporation held on 24 April 1866. Barlow carried the mace as a symbol of authority before the lord mayor or his deputy. He was aged 82 in 1904 so was aptly described as 'old Barlow'.

Barlow died on 27 May 1912 at his home, 95 Ranelagh Road, Dublin, and was buried in Glasnevin Cemetery, Finglas Road, Dublin [BE 34.5 Dublin Section].

Barraclough, Arthur (1839–1905) *Professor of singing and Italian*
'While Goulding talked of Barraclough's voice production ...' *(11.796–7)*
Arthur Barraclough, originally from London, came to Dublin to teach music and singing. From 1868 his name appears in various newspapers advertising his singing classes. Barraclough made his first appearance as a vocalist in Dublin at the Orange Hall in York Street on 15 January 1868.

In 1876, Barraclough published *Observations on the Physical Education of the Vocal Organs*. A short time later he produced his book *A Guide to Italian Pronunciation* for the use of students of singing.

Barraclough died on 28 October 1905 at his home, 24 Pembroke Street Lower, Dublin, and was buried in Mount Jerome Cemetery, Harold's Cross, Dublin [A12–388–12285]. *Ulysses 16.1823*

Barrington, Jonah (1760–1834) *Judge and historian*
'Must ask Ned Lambert to lend me those reminiscences of sir Jonah Barrington.' *(10.781–2)*
Jonah Barrington was born at Knapton near Abbeyleix, Co. Laois. He spent much of his youth at his grandparents' mansion at Cullenaghmore in Laois where his ancestors had resided since the reign of James I.

Barrington studied law at Trinity College Dublin. He was called to the Bar in 1788 and served in the Irish parliament from 1790 until its dissolution in 1800. He was appointed judge of the Admiralty Court in 1798.

Barrington lost his sinecure in 1800 by opposing the Act of Union. He was knighted in 1807. He went to France some years later to escape his creditors and was stripped of his office when it was discovered that he had misappropriated court funds.

He is best remembered for his three-volume *Personal Sketches and Recollections of His Own Times* (published 1827–32). His two-volume *Historic Memoirs of Ireland* (1809, 1833) was later retitled *The Rise and Fall of the Irish Nation*. He died on 8 April 1834 in Versailles.

Barrow, Miss Eliza (1863–1911) *Murder victim*

'Phial containing arsenic retrieved from body of Miss Barron which sent Seddon to the gallows.' *(15.4541-2)*

Miss Eliza Barrow, whom Joyce refers to as Miss Barron, was poisoned by arsenic at 63 Tollington Park, London. She was a wealthy lodger with Mr and Mrs Frederick Seddon. She signed over a controlling interest of all her savings to Frederick Seddon in return for free accommodation and a small annuity for the rest of her life. She died on 14 September 1911 and was buried in a pauper's grave in Islington Cemetery, High Road, East Finchley, London.

Barry, Mrs Yelverton (1736–1805) *Accuser of Leopold Bloom*

This name is a fictional name based on a reversal of the name Barry Yelverton, politician, judge and orator. Barry Yelverton was born on 28 May 1736 in Cork. He was the son of Francis Yelverton and Elizabeth (née Barry).

Yelverton became one of the most able speakers in the House of Commons. In July 1782, he was appointed attorney general, and in December 1783 became the chief baron of the Irish Court of Exchequer. In December 1800, he was created Viscount Avonmore.

Yelverton lived in some style at Fortfield House, Terenure, which he built, sparing no expense, in 1785. Known as one of the greatest orators of the Bar of Ireland, he died in 1805 at Fortfield House and was buried in Rathfarnham churchyard. There is no tombstone to his memory but a plaque in Rathfarnham church, erected by Sir William Cusack Smith, commemorates him.

Ulysses 15.1013; 15.1036; 15.1076; 15.1092; 15.1110; 15.4550

Barton, Sir Dunbar Plunket (1853–1937) *Judge and writer*

'Judge Barton, I believe, is searching for some clues.' *(9. 520)*

Dunbar Plunket Barton, son of T. H. Barton, was born on 29 October 1853. He was educated at Harrow and Oxford.

Barton was called to the Irish Bar in 1880 and was judge of the High Court of Justice, Ireland, King's Bench Division, from 1900 to 1904, and Chancery of the Division, from 1904 to 1918. In 1904 his Dublin address was 19 Clyde Road, Ballsbridge.

Interested in Shakespeare, he was a member of the British Empire Shakespeare

Society and attended many meetings of its Dublin branch. His publications include: *Links between Ireland and Shakespeare* (1919); *Bernadotte and Napoleon* (1920); and *Timothy Healy: Memories and Anecdotes* (1933).

He died on 11 September 1937 at his London residence, 2 Gray's Inn Square and was buried at the Extra-Mural Cemetery, Brighton.

Barton, James (1848–1913) *Hackney driver*

'*A hackney car, number three hundred and twentyfour, with a gallantbuttocked mare, driven by James Barton, Harmony avenue, Donnybrook, trots past.*' *(15.3726–8)*

James Barton was born in Co. Wicklow. In 1901 he was working as an agent and living with his sister Elizabeth at 7 Floraville Road, Pembroke West, Dublin. In 1904, he was living at 'Rose Cottage', 3 Harmony Avenue, Donnybrook. Barton kept pony traps and a hackney car for private hire. He was 55 in 1904 when he chauffeured Boylan around the streets of Dublin. Barton died on 23 March 1913 and was buried in Mount Jerome Cemetery, Harold's Cross, Dublin [A45–255–14033]. *Ulysses 11.878–9*

Bass, William Arthur Hamar (1879–1952) *English racehorse owner*

'*... Mr W. Bass's bay filly* Sceptre *on a 2 ½ mile course.*' *(16.1284–5)*

William Arthur Hamar Bass, son of Hamar Alfred Bass and Louisa (née Bagot) was born on 24 December 1879. He was the nephew of the brewer Michael Arthur Bass (1837–1909), 1st Baronet Burton.

Educated at Harrow, he went to Trinity College, Cambridge, then joined the army. Following the death of his uncle, he succeeded to the baronetcy of Stafford in 1909.

Bass owned a number of racehorses, including Sceptre who finished third behind Throwaway and Zinfandel in the Gold Cup race at 3.00 pm on 16 June 1904.

A supporter of the London Film Company, Bass was also the first chairman of the Provincial Cinematograph Theatres, which were founded in 1909, the same year Joyce negotiated the opening of the Cinematograph Volta in Mary Street, Dublin.

Sir William Bass, 2nd Baronet, died on 28 February 1952 and was buried at Newchurch, Needwood, Burton-on-Trent.   *Ulysses 12.1221, 14.1161; 16.1280*

Bateman, Kate (1843–1917) *Actress*

'Poor papa! How he used to talk of Kate Bateman in that.' *(5.197–8)*

Kate Bateman was born in Baltimore in the United States in 1843. The eldest of three daughters, she was a child prodigy and made her début on the New York stage aged six. In 1863, Kate appeared at the Adelphi Theatre, London, in a role for which she was perhaps best remembered, the heroine in the drama by Augustin Daly, *Leah, the Forsaken*. She ran an acting school from 1892 and appeared only rarely on the stage later in life.

Bateman died in London on 8 April 1917 and was buried in Old Hendon churchyard, in the London borough of Barnet.   *Ulysses 12.199*

Beaufoy, Philip (1878–1947) *Short-story writer and novelist*
'Our prize titbit: *Matcham's Masterstroke*. Written by Mr Philip Beaufoy, Playgoers' Club, London.' *(4.502–3)*
Philip Beaufoy, also known as Philip Beaufoy Barry, were the pseudonyms of Philip Bergson, of the London Playgoers' Club, Clement's Inn. Bergson, the son of Michael Bergson, a professor of music, and Catherine (née Levison), was born in London in 1878 and educated at the City of London School. In 1891 he lived at 92 Percy Road, Hammersmith and worked as a 'shorthand writer'.

Under the name Philip or P. Beaufoy, he wrote numerous trashy stories for the British weekly magazine *Tit-Bits* between 1897 and 1904. *Tit-Bits* had a huge circulation; it featured 'human interest' stories many of which were rehashed and rewritten from other sources. The story attributed to Philip Beaufoy in *Ulysses* appears to be fictional. Beaufoy also wrote novels. These included *The Dosing of Cuthbert* (1927), *The Red Book of Boys' Stories* (1927) and *The Mystery of the Blue Diamond* (1928).

He died on 19 January 1947 and was cremated at Golders Green in North London. His last address was Heathfield Hotel, Guilford Street, London.   *Ulysses 15.825–7*

Bellew, Lord (1830–95) *Testified against Orton in the Tichborne Case*
'… as the evidence went to show and there was a tattoo mark too in Indian ink, lord Bellew was it …' *(16.1345–6)*
Edward Joseph Bellew was born on 3 June 1830 in Dublin. He was the son of Patrick Bellew, 1st Baron Bellew of Barmeath, and Anna de Mendoza. Educated at Stonyhurst College, he was sheriff of Co. Louth in 1854, and was a major in the Louth Militia.

Bellew attended school with Roger Charles Tichborne (1829–54), the missing heir impersonated in the nineteenth-century law case. Bellew was subsequently involved with the celebrated Tichborne Case. He testified decisively against Arthur Orton, Tichborne's impersonator. Bellew had remembered that Roger Charles Tichborne had tattoos in 1847 to which Bellew had personally added the letters 'T. C. T.' in Indian ink. Orton's body had no such tattoo.

Lord Bellew died on 28 July 1895 in Germany, and was buried in Frankfurt-am-Main, Germany.

Bellingham, Mrs *One of Bloom's three accusers of sexual misconduct*
The name is likely to be linked to that of Sir Edward Henry Charles Patrick Bellingham. He was born in 1879, 5th Baron Bellingham, and former Lt Colonel in the Royal Dublin Fusiliers. On 11 June 1904 he married Charlotte Elizabeth, daughter of Alfred Payne and widow of Frederick Gough. At the time of this fashionable wedding, Bellingham was a lieutenant in the Royal Scots Guards.

Ulysses 15.1025; 15.1044; 15.1050; 15.1074; 15.1090; 15.1102; 15.4550

Benady Brothers

Mesod Benady (1863–1946), Samuel Benady (1865–1940) *Gibraltar grocers*

'... I was a bit wild after when I blew out the old bag the biscuits were in from Benady Bros and exploded it Lord what a bang all the woodcocks and pigeons screaming ...' *(18.830–2)*

The Benady brothers were Mesod Benady and Samuel Benady. They were both educated in England, which was unusual at that time. In 1899, they took over the family business in Engineer Lane, Gibraltar which consisted of a grocers, and provision merchants store, which was founded in 1863 by their uncle Samuel Benady. Here amongst other goods they sold Twining teas, Suchard chocolates and biscuits manufactured by Huntley & Palmers and Jacobs. The Benady firm was eventually taken over by Marcos Elias.

Samuel Benady died in Madeira in 1940 and was buried there.

Bennett, Gordon (1841–1918) *American sportsman and journalist*

'Gordon Bennett cup.' *(6.419)*

Gordon Bennett was born on 10 May 1841 in New York City. His father, James Gordon Bennett, senior (1795–1872), worked his way up from proofreader to founder, editor and publisher of the *New York Herald*. In 1866 he passed on the management of the *New York Herald* to his son, who left New York for Paris in 1877 where he launched the *International Herald Tribune*.

In 1900 the Coupe Internationale de l'Automobile was established and named after Gordon Bennett. This was the precursor of the Grand Prix series of races. The Gordon Bennett Cup was held in Ireland on 2 July 1903. It was the first international motor event to be held in Ireland.

He died on 14 May 1918 in Beaulieu-sur-Mer on the Côte d'Azur, France, and was buried in Paris in the Cimetière de Passy.   *Ulysses 6.370; 15.3004; 16.1241*

Bennett, Sergeant-Major *British soldier in Portobello Barracks*

Based on **Andrew Percy Bennett (1866–1943)** *Consul-general in Zurich*

'... sergeantmajor Bennett, the Portobello bruiser, for a purse of fifty sovereigns.' *(10.1134–5)*

Andrew Percy Bennett was born on 30 July 1866 in Fulbourn, Cambridgeshire. A noted cricketer, he was educated at Laurie House, Broadstairs; Cambridge House, Margate; and New Zealand University.

He was the consul-general in Zurich during the First World War when Joyce lived there. He died on 3 November 1943 at Hove in Sussex, England.

Ulysses 12.939; 15.627; 15.4793; 15.4796

Beresford, John

'A rump and dozen, says the citizen, was what that old ruffian sir John Beresford called it but the modern God's Englishman calls it caning on the breech.' *(12.1338–40)* There were two John Beresfords: The Citizen confuses the two. Sir John Poo Beresford (*c.* 1768–1844) is not associated with any charges of flogging whereas the same cannot be said for the Rt. Hon. John Beresford (1738–1805), MP for Co. Waterford, and chief commissioner of the Revenue.

John Beresford (1738–1805) Statesman and MP

John Beresford was born on 14 March 1738 in Dublin. He was educated in Kilkenny and Trinity College Dublin. In 1760, he was called to the Bar. He was an MP for Co. Waterford for 45 years.

From 1780 to 1802 Beresford was chief commissioner of the Revenue, which gave him immense power. He was responsible for bringing James Gandon to Ireland to build the new Custom House; Beresford had the quays extended and other structural work carried out on the streets of Dublin such as the opening up of Sackville Street (now O'Connell Street).

He had a riding school to train his horses near the Custom House; this was one of the main sites where floggings and other forms of torture took place on the rebel Irish in Dublin in the aftermath of the 1798 rebellion.

Beresford died on 5 November 1805 in Walworth in Co. Derry. Beresford Place in Dublin is named after him.

Sir John Poo Beresford (c. 1768–1844) Admiral and MP

Born in Ireland, John Poo Beresford entered the navy in 1782 and served in America, the West Indies and the American War of 1812. He was MP for Coleraine, Berwick and Chatham. He was created a baronet in 1814. He died in Bedale, Yorkshire in 1844.

Bergan, Alf (1879–1947) *Assistant to the sub-sheriff*

'Little Alf Bergan popped in round the door and hid behind Barney's snug, squeezed up with the laughing.' *(12.249–50)*

Alfred Bergan, son of Edward Bergan and Isabella (née Walsh), was born in Co. Wicklow in 1879. Small in stature and known as a practical joker, he was an assistant to the sub-sheriff of Dublin and later worked as a clerk in the offices of David Charles, solicitor, of 4 Clare Street, Dublin. He was a close friend of both Joyce and his father. Occasionally he accompanied Joyce on his walks around Dublin. Bergan attended the same funerals as the Joyce family, such as that of Matthew F. Kane who was drowned on 10 July 1904.

Nichevo in the *Irish Times*'s 'An Irishman's Diary' describes him as:

a remarkable little man who knew more about the City of Dublin than anyone else of my acquaintance. There never was a more typical Dubliner. He would listen to the conversation for a time during which he invariably puffed at a rather foul-smelling pipe, then he would deliver himself of his comments. These comments were unique. Bergan had a flow of language-vituperative, caustic, penetrating but always witty which flooded the room in which he was. But his views were not so amusing as his

method of expression. I have a suspicion that Joyce owed at least something to Bergan's vocabulary, which was racy of the streets of Dublin. His accent was rich and delicious; what an actor that little man would have been!

Bergan lived at different addresses on the north side of the city. In 1904, he was living at 141 Clonliffe Road. Later he lodged at 2 Claude Road with Mrs Refausse, the widow of an official in the General Post Office. This later proved convenient for Joyce as Bergan was living in close proximity to his ageing father, John Stanislaus Joyce, who had lodgings with a Mrs Metcalfe at 25 Claude Road.

Joyce corresponded with Bergan in the 1930s especially around the time of his father's death. Bergan was the named executor of John Stanislaus Joyce's will and it was through him that James Joyce organised the gravestone for his father in Glasnevin Cemetery, Finglas Road, Dublin.

Bergan died on 27 December 1947 in Drumcondra Hospital, Whitworth Road, where John Stanislaus Joyce also died.　　*Ulysses 8.320; 11.438; 12.273; 12.278; 15.481; 15.484*

Best, Richard (1872–1959) *Librarian and Celtic scholar*

'It is clear that there were two beds, a best and secondbest, Mr Secondbest Best said finely.' *(9.714-15)*

Richard Best was born in the north of Ireland. He spent his early student years in

Paris where he studied Old Irish with d'Arbois de Jubainville and also met J. M. Synge and Stephen McKenna, the Irish linguist and scholar.

In 1904, Best became assistant director of the National Library in Dublin and was promoted director in 1924. An intimate friend of George Moore, he is credited as being one of the few people with whom Moore never quarrelled. There are numerous references to Best in Moore's *Hail and Farewell*.

Best's relationship with Joyce was less agreeable. He always maintained that in the library scene in *Ulysses*, Joyce worked off an old grudge against him. The two men corresponded over a number of years.

Best's earliest publication was a translation of de Jubainville's *Irish Mythological Cycle and Celtic Mythology* in 1903. His major work was the two-volume *Bibliography of Irish Philology and Manuscript Literature, Publications 1913–1941*. This was published in 1942 and is an indispensable work of reference. Other publications include *Bibliography of the Publications of Kuno Meyer* (1923), *The Martyrology of Tallaght* (1931), *The Book of Leinster*, formerly *Lebar na Nuachongbala* (1954) and *Lebor na Huidre: Book of the Dun Cow* which he co-edited with Osborn Bergin (1929).

He retired in 1947 and died on 25 September 1959 at his home at 57 Upper Leeson Street, Dublin and was buried in Deansgrange Cemetery, Deansgrange, Co. Dublin [66–H–South West].   *Ulysses 9.74; 9.90; 9.240; 9.263; 9.275; 9.512; 9.527; 9.618; 9.735; 9.768; 9.793*

Billington, James (1847–1901) *English hangman*
'... *Billington executed the awful murderer Toad Smith* ...' *(12.425)*
James Billington came from Farmworth near Bolton in Lancashire and had a lifelong fascination with hanging. He was originally a barber and continued for a time to shave men between hangings. He was also landlord of the Derby Arms Hotel in Bolton. Billington carried out his first execution on 26 August 1884 at Armley Jail in Leeds.

According to the *Weekly Freeman*, 14 January 1899, he had carried out work in Ireland during his vacation:

> On Saturday he hanged a man named Patrick Holmes at Kilkenny. On Tuesday he killed another murderer in Armagh Jail, while still another victim awaited his hands in the same building on Friday. Many years have passed since so many executions took place within a few days in this country. We trust that when he leaves our shores, Billington will not be summoned back again for the rest of his life.

Billington contracted a cold at the scaffold on 3 December 1901 and died from pneumonia on 20 December. He had carried out 151 executions during his career as a hangman. He was succeeded by one of his sons, who had gained ample experience as his assistant.

Blackburn/Blackburne, R. T. (1857–1922) *Secretary to Dublin County Council*
'... an orangeman Blackburn does have on the registration and he drawing his pay ...' *(12.1590–1)*
Robert Thomas Blackburne was born in Co. Dublin. His father worked as an official in the old Grand Jury Office, Rutland Square (now Parnell Square).

He was secretary to the Grand Jury and to Dublin County Council. A justice of the peace, Blackburne was a member of Lodge 25 of the Masonic order, which he joined in 1884, but he took no part in politics beyond voting for the unionist side.

Blackburne lived at 'Cameron Lodge', Raheny before moving to 15 Belgrave Square, Rathmines, where he lived in 1904. He died on 30 August 1922 in Dublin.

Blackwood, Sir John (1722–99) *Irish politician and Mr Deasy's reputed ancestor*
'But I am descended from sir John Blackwood who voted for the union.' *(2.278–9)*
The son of Sir Robert Blackwood, 1st Baronet, John Blackwood first entered the House of Commons in 1761 for Killyleagh and remained in office until 1768; he returned for Bangor in 1776. He was MP for Killyleagh again until 1790 and afterwards for Bangor until 1798. Blackwood, 2nd Baronet, died on 27 February 1799 at Balleileidy, Co. Down.   *Ulysses 2.282; 15.3994*

Blake, Phil (1869–1918) *Journalist*
'Phil Blake's weekly Pat and Bull story.' *(7.94)*
Phil Blake, son of Philip Blake, was born on 19 January 1869 at Ladyrath, Co. Meath.

He was a well-known figure in Dublin in artistic, theatrical and musical circles and was a member of the Carl Rosa and Rousby opera companies. In 1898, he joined the art staff of the *Freeman's Journal* where he worked for ten years. He left for Sydney, Australia in 1908 where he settled and established the Pictorial Advertising Company. He died in Sydney on 16 July 1918.

Blavatsky, Helena Petrovna (1831–91) *Theosophist*
'That Blavatsky woman started it. She was a nice old bag of tricks.' *(7.784–5)*
Born in Russia on 31 July 1831, Helena Petrovna Blavatsky was the daughter of Colonel Peter Von Hahn and Helena Fadeyeva, an author.

An adventurous and controversial woman, she travelled widely in connection with her work and interest in spiritualism and the occult. She went to Mexico, India, Tibet, Europe and the United States. In 1875, she founded the Theosophical Society with Colonel H. S. Olcott in New York, and the following year she published a textbook for her supporters, *Isis Unveiled: A Master Key to the Mysteries of Ancient and Modern Science and Theology*. One of her many followers was W. B. Yeats who described her as 'a great passionate nature, a sort of female Dr Johnson'.

Blavatsky died on 8 May 1891 at 19 Avenue Road, St John's Wood, London; her ashes were scattered in various places connected with her including the river Ganges in India where she had lived for a time.

Ulysses 7.784; 9.65–6; 9.71; Isis Unveiled, 3.41–2; 7.784; 9.279; 15.2268–9; The Key to Theosophy, 1.652–3; 2.159

Bleibtreu, Karl (1859–1928) *German writer, poet, critic and dramatist*
'Herr Bleibtreu, the man Piper met in Berlin, who is working up that Rutland theory ...' *(9.1073–4)*
Karl Bleibtreu was born on 13 January 1859 in Berlin, Germany. He theorised that Roger Manners (1576–1612), the 5th earl of Rutland, wrote Shakespeare's plays. Bleibtreu died on 30 January 1928 in Locarno, Switzerland.

Bloom, Leopold (b.1866) *Advertising canvasser for the* Freeman's Journal
'He's a cultured allroundman, Bloom is ...' *(10.581)*
Leopold Bloom, a fictional character, son of Rudolph Virag and Fanny (née Higgins)
was born on 6 May 1866 in Dublin.

Bloom is a composite character and an amalgam of various people, developed from individuals Joyce knew in Trieste, Zurich and Dublin. One of these was **Italo Svevo (1861–1928)** [Ettore Schmitz], the novelist, and a pupil and friend of Joyce. Born in Trieste, with a Jewish Italo-German background, he was a wealthy Jewish businessman. He is one of Joyce's chief sources for the Jewish lore in *Ulysses* as during their friendship he provided Joyce with an understanding of the large Jewish community in Trieste. Svevo was 21 years older than Joyce. The age difference between Joyce and Svevo was similar to that of Stephen and Bloom. The night-time walk of the middle-aged Bloom with young Stephen Dedalus in *Ulysses* might be inspired by the walks which Svevo and his young teacher of English used to take in Trieste

Another Triestine model for Bloom was **Teodoro Mayer (1860–1942)** a Hungarian Jew, owner and founder of *Il Piccolo della Sera*. There are many parallels between Bloom and Mayer, including an interest in stamps.

In Dublin, Joyce's friend, **J. F. Byrne (1880–1960)**, also contributed to the make up of Bloom. Bloom is the exact same weight and height as Byrne – being the 'length – five feet nine inches and a half' and the 'body's weight of eleven stone and four pounds'.

Byrne lived at 7 Eccles Street between 1908 and 1910 where Joyce visited him during his two Dublin trips in 1909. Joyce chose this address for Bloom in 1904. (In 1904, 7 Eccles Street was vacant.)

Alfred H. Hunter (1866–1926) is another model for Bloom. There are many similarities between Bloom and Hunter, which could not be coincidental. Joyce had met Hunter only once or twice. Hunter clearly made an impression on Joyce after he allegedly rescued him from an assailant on the night of 22 June 1904. [Joyce planned to write a story for *Dubliners* titled 'Ulysses' describing the day's wanderings of Hunter around the city.]

There are close resemblances between the Hunters and the Blooms. Alfred Hunter, a Presbyterian, son of William H. Hunter was born at Mount Pottinger, Ballymacarret, Co. Down near Belfast on 30 August 1866, the same year as Leopold Bloom so they would have been the same age in 1904.

Hunter married Marion Bruère Quin in London on 22 August 1899 in St Saviour's Church, Pimlico. Born in Kingstown (now Dún Laoghaire) in 1864, she was the daughter of Francis Quin, a professor of music and Menella (née Wilcox) who lived at 61 Mount Street, and later 1 Mount Street Crescent, Dublin. Her father, a Freemason, was grand organist of the Dublin Masons.

Hunter, who both lived and had an office at 1 Clare Street, worked as an advertising agent or canvasser. Bloom worked as an advertising canvasser for the *Freeman's Journal* from 1902 onwards. Hunter's wife was named Marion, as was Bloom's wife. Another similarity with the Blooms was that the Hunters lived at a number of different addresses in the city. These included 1 Clare Street, 95 Mount Street, 28 Ballybough Road, 23 Great Charles Street (off Mountjoy Square), May Street (off Clonliffe Road), then back to 23 Great Charles Street.

Hunter died on 12 September 1926 aged 60 and was buried in Mount Jerome Cemetery, Harold's Cross, Dublin [B68–359–5924]. There is a memorial stone over his grave, on which his name is inscribed amongst others.

Bloom, Marcus (b. 1861) *Dentist, LDS, RCSI, MOS, London*
'As he strode past Mr Bloom's dental windows ...' *(10.1115)*
The family of Marcus Bloom (Blum) was of German origin and first appeared in Dublin in 1840. His grandfather was Joseph Blum, a toy importer and commission agent. His father Mark Joseph Bloom (1846–94), a dentist, was one of the founders of the Dental Hospital in Dublin in 1876 where he worked.

Marcus Bloom was a dentist like his father and they are both listed in the *Dental Register*, first issued in 1879. Father and son practised at 23 Westland Row, before moving a few doors to 18 Westland Row in 1883.

Marcus Bloom moved his practice to 2 Clare Street in 1893 where Dr Sigerson was a neighbour at 3 Clare Street. Bloom served as dental surgeon to St Patrick's College Maynooth, Co. Kildare and lectured on dental surgery at St Vincent's Hospital. He was also surgeon at the Dental Hospital and St Joseph's Hospital for Children.

At his own request, Bloom had his name removed from the *Dental Register* in 1905. He gave retirement from practice as the unconvincing reason for the request. It could have been provoked by some other reason such as professional misconduct. *Thom's Directory* continued to list his name and dental qualifications until 1917.

In 1911, Marcus Bloom is listed as being single and living at 10 Tritonville Road, Sandymount, with his 80-year-old widowed mother Catherine and two sisters, Florence Pollock and Beatrice Bloom, both professors of music. His father, like the fictional Leopold Bloom, became a Catholic on marriage and his family are listed as Roman Catholics. Mrs Bloom lived at 10 Tritonville Road until 1922.   *Ulysses 15.4351*

Bloom, Marion 'Molly' (b. 1870) *Concert soprano and wife of Leopold Bloom*
The fictional Marion 'Molly' Bloom, daughter of Major Tweedy and Lunita Laredo, was born in Gibraltar on 8 September 1870. Molly, a composite character, is partly based on Joyce's wife Nora Barnacle (1884–1951) as well as other women, including one of Mat Dillon's daughters, who had Spanish features. But her black hair came

from Amalia Popper, a pupil of Joyce in Trieste. She had the same first name as Alfred Hunter's wife Marion.

Nora was a vital source of literary inspiration for Joyce. Many of the character-istics of Molly bear resemblances to those of Nora Barnacle. In 1904, Nora wrote unpunctuated letters to Joyce. Molly Bloom's interior monologue of eight long sentences in the final episode of *Ulysses* is written in the same unpunctuated style and many of the locutions undoubtedly come from Nora.

Blum, Sir Julius (1843–1911) *Under-secretary of the Egyptian Treasury*
'You have heard of von Blum Pasha.' *(15.721–2)*
Julius Blum was born in Budapest, Hungary in 1843. In 1869 he became director of the Austro-Egyptian Bank in Alexandria. An extremely able man, he was appointed state secretary in the Egyptian Ministry of Finance in 1877 and, two years later, pasha and minister of finance, positions he held until 1890. Known as 'Blum Pasha', he left Egypt to become director of the Austrian Credit-Anstalt in Vienna.

He died on 17 November 1919 in Vienna.   *Ulysses 17.1747*

Blumenfeld, Ralph David (1864–1948) *Newspaper editor*
'Now he's got in with Blumenfeld. That's press. That's talent.' *(7.688)*
Ralph Blumenfeld was born on 7 April 1864 in Watertown, Wisconsin and in 1884 started his career in journalism with the *Chicago Herald*. Three years later he paid his first visit to London where he reported on Queen Victoria's jubilee for United Press. It was shortly after this that James Gordon Bennett put him in charge of the Paris edition of the *New York Herald*.

Blumenfeld was editor of the *Daily Mail* in London from 1900 to 1902, and from 1904 until 1932 he was editor-in-chief of the London *Daily Express*.

Known as the 'Father of Fleet Street', Blumenfeld died at his country home, 'Great Eaton', Dunmow, in Essex, England on 17 July 1948.

Boardman, Baby, Edy and Jacky (*fl.* nineteenth century) *Boardman family*
'Edy straightened up baby Boardman to get ready to go ... and it was high time too because the sandman was on his way for Master Boardman junior.' *(13.605–7)*
The Joyce family lived at 13 North Richmond Street, Dublin from late 1894 or early 1895 to 1897. The Boardman family lived across the road at 1 North Richmond Street. It comprised Mr John (b. 1845) and Mrs Mary Boardman (b. 1849) and their six children Mary (b. 1870), Katherine (b. 1874), Elizabeth (b. 1881), Edward (b. 1883), Eleanor (b. 1885) and Francis (b. 1888).

Edy Boardman, one of Gerty McDowell's companions, seems to combine the name of Eily and Eddie, two family members.

Ulysses 13.13; 13.20; 13.33; 13.38; 13.66; 13.71; 13.76; 13.92; 13.146; 13.165; 13.218; 13.243; 13.253; 13.266; 13.359; 13.383; 13.521; 13.684; 13.767; 15.88; 15.90; 15.1595; 15.1597

Bobricoff, Nickolai Ivanovitch (1839–1904) *Russian general*

'Or was it you shot the lord lieutenant of Finland between you? You look as though you had done the deed. General Bobrikoff.' *(7.601–2)*

Born on 27 January 1839 in St Petersburg, Bobrikoff (Bobrikov) began his career as a soldier. Aged 19, he became an officer in the Russian army.

In 1898, he was appointed as governor-general and commander-in-chief of the military district of Finland (1898–1904) by Tzar Nicholas II.

On 16 June 1904 at 11.00 am (Central European Time), Bobrikoff was shot and fatally wounded by Eugen Schaumann, the son of Senator Schaumann, a Finnish aristocrat.

Bohee, James (1844–97) and George (1856–c. 1906) *American minstrels*

The Bohee brothers were American minstrels who moved to England in 1881. They appeared in Dublin in August 1894 performing in the Leinster Hall in Hawkins Street before a large and appreciative audience.

The Bohee brothers performed on banjos manufactured by James Bohee, which were 'remarkable for their brilliancy and volume of tone'. Those who were fortunate enough to visit the Leinster Hall were impressed with the fine entertainment presented by the Bohee brothers. They played banjos while they sang and danced.

Ulysses 15.412

Boucicault, Dion (1820/2–90) *Playwright*

'Dion Boucicault business with his harvestmoon face in a poky bonnet.' *(8.601–2)*

Dionysius Lardner Boucicault, originally Boursiquot, was born at 47 Lower Gardiner Street, Dublin.

Boucicault spent his earliest years in Dublin, before moving to London where he received his formal education. For a short time he worked as an apprentice in civil

engineering, but left to join the theatre. His first successful play, a five-act comedy of manners, entitled *London Assurance*, was staged at Covent Garden in 1841.

Boucicault returned to Ireland three times, to find source material for his works. His play, *The Colleen Bawn*, adapted from Gerald Griffin's novel, *The Collegians*, was produced in Dublin in 1861, after successful runs in New York and London. He was manager, actor and playwright and created many lavish productions. His successful plays earned up to five million dollars during his lifetime.

In 1864, Boucicault's play, *Arrah-na-Pogue*, was staged at the Theatre Royal in

Hawkins Street, Dublin. *The Shaughraun* was given its first production in Dublin in 1874 with Boucicault playing the hero, Conn.

Boucicault died in New York in September 1890. He was buried in Mount Oak Cemetery, New Jersey.

Ulysses Arrah-na-Pogue, 12.193; The Colleen Bawn, 6.186; 12.194; 16.1052; The Lily of Killarney, 6.186; 12.197; 13.314–15; 13.1212–13; 18.347–8; The Shaughraun, 8.441–2

Boyd, John (1867–1932) *Civil servant*

'Boyd? Martin Cunningham said shortly. Touch me not.' *(10.967)*

John Boyd was born in Scotland. He lived in 34 South Circular Road (Dolphin's Barn), Dublin, in 1901 with his wife Annie, two of his brothers, his sister-in-law and a servant. He worked at the State Solicitor's Office in Dublin Castle for 41 years. He was a colleague of Matthew Kane, who worked in Dublin Castle as the chief clerk in the office of Sir Patrick Coll, the crown solicitor.

John Boyd, Matthew Kane and John Stanislaus Joyce were a familiar threesome at various funerals in Dublin. Boyd was on the Kane Family Fund Committee, which was set up after Matthew Kane's death by drowning on 10 July 1904. Boyd attended all the meetings concerning the fund, which were held at intervals from 22 July to 23 August 1904. Others connected with the Kane Family Fund included Roger Greene, solicitor; John Clancy, sub-sheriff; Adam S. Findlater; J. Wyse Power; and F. F. Chance.

At the time of his death on the 23 May 1932, Boyd, now a widower, was living at the Clarence Hotel, 6 Wellington Quay, Dublin. He was buried in Glasnevin Cemetery, Finglas Road, Dublin [PH 77 Section 3].

Boylan, Hugh 'Blazes' *Impresario and advertising man*

Partly based on **Augustus Boylan** (1872–1963) *Tenor*

'Blazes Boylan, Mr Power said. There he is airing his quiff.' *(6.196)*

The fictional character Hugh 'Blazes' Boylan, Molly Bloom's lover, is a composite character. Partly, he is based on a horse dealer named James Daly who had premises at Island Bridge, Dublin and on another horse dealer named Ted Keogh. But Blazes Boylan for the most part is based on Augustus Boylan the tenor.

Augustus Boylan, son of Patrick Boylan and Mary (née Brian), was born at 10 Pim Street, Dublin, on 7 December 1872. Aged 15 he started his apprenticeship as a cooper in Guinness's Brewery. After seven years as an apprentice cooper, learning to make casks, he officially became an employee of the company and his 42 years' service in the cooperage began.

The Boylan family had been in this exclusive trade for generations and were members of the Venerable Regular Dublin Coopers Society, which received its charter from Charles II in 1666. Boylan's father and grandfather had both worked as coopers with Guinness.

Boylan also pursued his interest in singing and the theatre and for many years sang at concerts in Dublin and throughout the country. He recounted in a later interview that he was one of the first people to meet John McCormack when he came to Dublin.

Boylan won first prize at several competitions of the Oireachtas and Leinster Feis and in 1901 was awarded second place in the tenor competition in the Feis Ceoil. In 1904, he sang in the Feis Ceoil (in which Joyce participated) as one

member of a quartet, which won the prize-winning anthem. He also sang with the baritone J. C. Doyle, in various concerts. Songs associated with Boylan include 'Seaside Girls', 'The Young May Moon' and 'Love's Old Sweet Song'.

A member of St James's Gate Choir in James's Street and the Palestrina Choir in the Pro Cathedral in Marlborough Street for 37 years, Boylan sang on the same platform as John McCormack. In 1904 they sang at a concert held at the Rotunda to raise funds for McCormack's first American tour. It was so popular that another one was held at the Mansion House. On both these occasions Boylan's singing was well received and certainly contributed to the success of the tour in America, which established McCormack's reputation.

Boylan married Catherine Justice, a talented pianist from Mill Street in Co. Cork, in 1906. They had one daughter, Mona, and two sons, Patrick and Brendan. They lived at 2 Mayfield Villas, South Circular Road, Kilmainham, 1908–16. In 1926, they were living at 133 James's Street. They later moved to 41 Sandymount Road near Star of the Sea Church where they lived for the remainder of their lives. Their nephew, the Very Rev. Canon Boylan, was parish priest there for a time.

Katherine Boylan died on 3 July 1963 and Augustus died shortly afterwards on 23 July. Both were in their 90s. Boylan was buried in Glasnevin Cemetery, Finglas Road, Dublin [A1 263 St Brigid's].

Bracegirdle, Mrs Anne (*c*. 1663–1748) *English actress*

'*Amours* of actresses. Nell Gwynn, Mrs Bracegirdle, Maud Branscombe. Curtain up.' *(13.856–7)*

No precise date of birth is available for Anne Bracegirdle due to differing records of her life. Her grave in the cloisters of Westminster Abbey, London gives her age at death as 85, which would suggest she was born in 1663.

Known for her beauty and tremendous popularity with audiences, she was much admired by men, some of whom actually fought over her. William

Congreve, the dramatist with whom her name was linked, wrote plays especially for her and left her a legacy when he died in 1729.

Always discreet about her private life, she was charitable to the poor in London's Clare Market and in the area around Drury Lane.

Mrs Bracegirdle retired from the stage in 1706 at a relatively early age and died in 1748.

Brady, Dr Francis (1859–1915) *Molly Bloom's doctor*
'... *old doctor Brady with stethoscope* ...' *(15.4359)*
Dr Francis Brady, LRCSI, a justice of the peace, was born in Co. Donegal and studied medicine at the Royal College of Surgeons in Ireland in Dublin. In 1904 he lived at 58 Main Street, Carnew, Co. Wicklow, with his wife Harriette and 12-year-old son Cecil.

Dr Francis Brady, 'The Castle', Carnew, died in Dublin on 14 February 1915 and was buried at Carnew.   *Ulysses 17.2140; 18.576*

Brady, Joe (1857–83) *Member of the Invincibles*
'And it turned out to be a commemoration postcard of Joe Brady or Number One or Skin-the-Goat.' *(7.702–3)*
Joseph Brady was the youngest of a very large family, who lived at 22 North Anne

Street in Dublin. He was a good singer and member of the choir in the Franciscan Capuchin church, in nearby Church Street.

Brady worked as a stonecutter but was also a member of the Invincibles. He was 26 when he was hanged on Saturday 14 May 1883 at Kilmainham Gaol for his part in the Phoenix Park murders. The murders occurred on 6 May 1882 when Lord Frederick Cavendish, the new chief secretary for Ireland, and Thomas Henry Burke, the under-secretary, were assassinated.   *Ulysses 7.639; 12.460*

Braime, Mr (*fl.* late 1800s–early 1900s) *Horse trainer*
Herbert Braime was the trainer for Mr Fred Alexander's horse Throwaway, who won the Gold Cup race held at 3.00 pm at Ascot on 16 June 1904. Wiliam Lane rode Throwaway.   *Ulysses 16.1285*

Brandes, Georg (1842–1927) *Literary critic*
'Mr Brandes accepts it, Stephen said, as the first play of the closing period.' *(9.418)*
Georg Brandes was born on 4 February 1842 in Copenhagen, Denmark. He was educated at the University of Copenhagen.

He travelled widely in Europe from 1865 to 1871 visiting universities and studying literature. His first important work was *Aesthetic Studies* (1868). He became the leading northern European critic of the 'new breaking through' in Scandanavian and European thought. His work, *Main Currents in the Literature of the Nineteenth Century*, was published between 1872 and 1875. He spent time in Berlin from 1877 to 1883 returning to Copenhagen where he headed the group 'Det Moderne Gjennembruds Maend' ('The Men of the Modern Breakthrough').

Brandes wrote a study of William Shakespeare (1896–8) which William Archer translated into English. He died on 19 February 1927 in Copenhagen.

Brangan, Rev. Thomas (1856–1937) *Prior, Order of St Augustine, John's Lane, Dublin*
A native of Laytown, near Drogheda, Co. Louth, Thomas Brangan entered the Augustinian order at Orlagh, Rathfarnham, Co. Dublin, in 1876 and was ordained priest in Rome in 1882.

Father Brangan was a member of the community of Augustinian Friars in John's Lane, Thomas Street, in Dublin, from 1889 and was prior at John's Lane from 1903 to 1907.

He died on 5 December 1937 at Orlagh House, Rathfarnham, Co. Dublin, and was buried in the Augustinian Plot, Glasnevin Cemetery, Finglas Road, Dublin [DH South St Brigid's]. *Ulysses 12.934*

Branscombe, Maud (*fl.* 1875–1890s) *English actress*
'... 2 fading photographs of queen Alexandra of England and of Maud Branscombe, actress and professional beauty:' *(17.1778–10)*
Maud Branscombe was a minor English actress. She made her first appearance on the New York stage in 1876.

John Hollingshead in his *Gaiety Chronicles* (1898) wrote 'though a very short lady, she had a most pretty and effective face that could give any expression,

and the result was that she soon became the most photographed young person in the world'. Branscombe and beauty were synonymous. In 1877 alone, over 28,000 copies of her photograph were sold.

She performed at the Queen's Royal Theatre in Dublin in November 1883 with her London Comedy and Burlesque Company, and in December 1884, was among the principal artistes who performed in the Gaiety Theatre in the grand Christmas pantomime, *Jack and the Beanstalk*. *Ulysses 13.857*

Brayden, William Henry (1865–1933) *Barrister and editor*
'WILLIAM BRAYDEN, ESQUIRE, OF OAKLANDS, SANDYMOUNT' *(7.38–9)*

William Henry Brayden, son of William H. Brayden and Elizabeth (née Windrum), was born on 30 September 1865 in Armagh. He was educated at the Royal School in Armagh and at University College Dublin.

From 1885 to 1887, he was a parliamentary reporter for the House of Commons. He was editor of the Dublin *National Press*, 1890–2. This was absorbed by the *Freeman's Journal* where he was appointed editor in 1892, a position that he held until 1916. He left when the *Freeman's Journal* building was utterly destroyed in May of that year.

Known as a brilliant and capable journalist, Brayden was awarded an OBE in 1916 in recognition of his services during the First World War. He was the representative in Dublin of the Associated Press of America and of the *Chicago Daily News*.

He lived at 'Oaklands', 57 Serpentine Avenue, Sandymount, and later at 8 Duncairn Terrace, Bray, Co. Wicklow. He was author of *Republican Courts in Ireland* (1920); *The Irish Free State: A Survey of the Newly Constructed Institutions of the Self-Governing Irish People, Together with a Report on Ulster* (1925); and *Touring for Health and Pleasure on Great Southern Railways* (1935).

He died on 17 December 1933 at his home in Bray and was buried at St Peter's cemetery, Little Bray, Co. Wicklow.

Browne, Mervyn (1851–1924) *Professor of music, organist and pianist*
'Who was telling me? Mervyn Browne. Down in the vaults of saint Werburgh's lovely old organ ...' *(6.608–10)*
Mervyn Browne began his career as an accountant for Pigott & Co., pianoforte and musical instruments merchants, music sellers and publishers at 112 Grafton Street, Dublin.

He used this address for advertisements he placed with the *Irish Times*, such as: 'Mr Mervyn Browne having completed his engagement as *Ad Interim* organist of St Matthias's Church will be happy to renew his deputizing engagements.' Browne joined the Freemasons in June 1874 and was organist with the Lodge for 13 years. In 1877 Browne's address was 55 Mountjoy Street, Dublin.

By 1883, Browne was giving his pianoforte, singing and harmony classes at 59 Harcourt Street. The following year he had moved to 63 Harcourt Street and had taken on another position as organist at All Saints Church, Blackrock.

Browne had his own orchestral band, and performed at various functions all over the country. During the ball season, he advertised his services as a 'Dance pianist', offering to attend anywhere in Ireland with his band. By 1888, he was operating his business and advertising as, 'Professional Dance Pianist, Orchestral Band from 78 Lower Mount Street'.

In 1904, Browne lived at 48 Drumcondra Road and the following year he moved to 42 Charles Street Great. In 1911, his address was 60 Chapel Street, Lismore, Co. Waterford. He was cathedral organist at Lismore for a time.

He died aged on 13 February 1924 at his residence, 24 Russell Avenue, Drumcondra, Dublin, and was buried in Mount Jerome Cemetery, Harold's Cross, Dublin [A19–227–13994].

Buller, Captain (1846–1906) *Cricketer*

'Still Captain Buller broke a window in the Kildare street club with a slog to square leg.' *(5.560–1)*

Charles Buller, the son of Sir A. W. Buller, MP, was born on 26 May 1846 in Colombo, Sri Lanka. He was an outstanding athlete. He entered Harrow School in Middlesex in September 1860 and left in the summer of 1864. Buller played in the Harrow XI, 1861–4 and was captain in 1864. He played in a match against Eton College at Lord's in 1861.

A man of fine physique, Buller played cricket for Harrow and Middlesex and also for I Zingari (the Gypsies), a travelling club founded in 1845.

This club played regularly in Dublin and Buller is listed as having played on two occasions, including matches between Ireland and I Zingari. The first was on 11 September 1867, a two-day match when I Zingari won by seven wickets; and again on 28 August 1868, a two-day match resulting in a draw. Both matches took place at the Viceregal Grounds, in Phoenix Park, Dublin.

Buller's batting style was right-hand bat and his bowling style was round arm right-arm slow.

In the 1860s, cricket matches took place in Trinity College Park against various English teams, such as the three-day match Ireland v. All England Eleven held in June 1868, but only those teams for which a scorecard was available are included in the database of the cricket archives. It is possible that Buller played on a team here.

Captain Buller died on 22 November 1906 in Cobb, Lyme Regis, Dorset, England. According to his obituary he was 'one of the most attractive of batsmen and, perhaps, the handsomest man the cricket field has ever known'. One could choose a worse epitaph.

Burke, O'Madden *Journalist*

Based on **William O'Leary Curtis (1863–1923)** *Journalist*

'Mr O'Madden Burke, tall in copious grey of Donegal tweed, came in from the hallway.' *(7.505–6)*

O'Madden Burke was based on a journalist named William O'Leary Curtis who matriculated in 1887 at University College Dublin. A patriot and scholar, O'Leary

Curtis was the principal speaker at the Manchester Martyrs Commemoration at Bloomsbury Hall, Hart Street, Manchester in 1902. He was known to Joyce and Stanislaus in 1904 and is mentioned in Joyce's broadside, *Gas from a Burner* (1912).

He worked for a time on the *Weekly Independent* and is described as being widely read and having a pompous, full-mouthed manner of speech and no settled journalistic position. He was tall and thin and dressed 'in copious grey of

Donegal tweed' to suit his melancholy temper. In *Ulysses*, O'Madden Burke introduces Stephen to a group in the newspaper office: 'Youth led by Experience visits Notoriety'.

O'Leary Curtis was living at Alpha House, Sherrard Street Upper, Dublin in 1903, and by 1911 had moved to 34 North Great George's Street. He died on 22 February 1923 at North Great George's Street and was buried in St Maelruain's Cemetery, Tallaght.

Ulysses 7.508; 7.572; 7.589; 7.592; 7.598; 7.609; 7.623; 7.641; 7.695–6; 7.725; 7.774; 7.888; 7.896; 10.410; 11.270; 15.1694

Burke, Col Richard (1838–1922) *Fenian*

'... he prowled with colonel Richard Burke, tanist of his sept, under the walls of Clerkenwell ...' *(3.246–8)*

Richard O'Sullivan Burke was born in Dunmanway, Co. Cork. He joined the Cork Militia in 1853 and then went to sea and travelled the world, ending as a colonel in the US army. During the American Civil War (1861–5) he was involved in the organisation of Fenian circles. Thomas J. Kelly, a Fenian who also fought in the American Civil War, recommended Burke to James Stephens as an arms supplier

for the Fenians in Ireland. Under the pseudonym of Edward Winslow, Burke purchased and imported some 2,000 rifles from the United States, which were stored in Liverpool.

Burke organised the rescue of Thomas Kelly and Timothy Deasy in Manchester on 18 September 1867. Betrayed by a spy, he was arrested on 27 November and imprisoned in Clerkenwell House of Detention in London. An attempt was made to free him, resulting in the Clerkenwell explosion in which a number of people were killed and maimed. Burke was sentenced to 15 years imprisonment but feigned insanity and was transferred to Broadmoor Asylum in Berkshire. He was released in 1872 and returned to the United States where he worked in engineering whilst continuing his efforts for the Fenian cause. He died in Chicago in 1922 and was buried at Mount Olivet Catholic Cemetery, Cook County, Chicago, Illinois.

Bushe, Charles Kendal (1767–1843) *Jurist and barrister*

'Kendal Bushe or I mean Seymour Bushe.' *(7.743)*

Charles Kendal Bushe was born in Kilmurry, Co. Kilkenny, on 13 January 1767. He was the only son of the Rev. Thomas Bushe (1727–95), rector of Mitchelstown, Co. Cork, and his wife Catherine (née Doyle).

Bushe started his schooling at Mr Shackleton's Academy in Ballitore, Co. Kildare. He continued his education at the French Huguenot School in Portarlington, Co. Laois, before entering Trinity College Dublin where he obtained a BA degree in 1787. He was called to the Irish Bar in 1790.

Bushe entered the Irish parliament in 1796 as MP for Callan, Co. Kilkenny. An ally of Grattan, he was strongly opposed to the Act of Union and spoke out against it in the Union debate in 1800; he refused the post of master of the rolls to remain silent on the issue. Bushe wrote his satirical pamphlet, *Cease Your Fuming*, around this time. Sir Jonah Barrington (1760–1834), the judge and historian, described Bushe as 'incorruptible'. Bushe received the freedom of the city of Dublin for his efforts in defence legislation.

Bushe became solicitor-general in 1805 until being appointed lord chief justice in 1822. He lived at 5 Ely Place and during the last year of his life moved to 17 Upper Mount Street.

Bushe who according to Grattan 'spoke with the lips of an angel', died at his son's residence, 'Furry Park', Howth Road, Dublin, in early July 1843, and was buried on 10 July in Mount Jerome Cemetery, Harold's Cross, Dublin where he is commemorated by a monument [Vault C14–1582].

Bushe, Seymour (1853–1922) *Barrister*

'He would have been on the bench long ago ... only for ... But no matter.' *(7.744–5)*

Seymour Bushe was born on 5 April 1853. He was the fourth son of the Rev. Charles Bushe, rector of Castlehaven, Co. Cork, and Emmeline (née Cogill). His grandfather was the Rt. Hon. Chief-Justice Bushe of Kilmurry, Co. Kilkenny.

Bushe was educated in Dublin at Trinity College where he was a scholar of classics, senior moderator and Berkeley gold medallist. He was a member of the

College Historical Society and recipient of a gold medal in oratory. He was called to the Irish Bar in 1879, became queen's counsel in 1892, and bencher of King's Inns in 1896. He was called to the English Bar in 1899. In 1901, he was senior crown prosecutor for the city and county of Dublin and made a king's counsel in 1904. He was justice of the peace for Co. Cork.

J. B. Hall in his book, *Random Records*, wrote that Bushe was one of the most memorable men of the Irish Bar, 'possessed of a brilliant and fascinating eloquence, a copiousness of diction and richness of imagery, together with close and connected reasoning'. At the height of his fame, people thronged the courts to hear his eloquence and brilliant wit. Bushe eloped with the Hon. Kathleen Maude, daughter of the Rt. Hon. Viscount Hawarden, of 15 Ely Place in 1885. The following year he married her as she had been divorced by her husband for 'open and criminal adultery' with Bushe. It was an awkward situation in Victorian Dublin. Bushe continued to practise law in Dublin for the next 18 years before migrating to London where he was admitted to King's Counsel. He lived at 49 Drayton Gardens, London where he died on 27 January 1922. He was buried in Brookwood Cemetery, Brookwood, Surrey.

Ulysses 6.470; 7.741; 7.755–6; 14.959; 15.1000–1; 17.792

Butt, D., SJ *Dean of studies and professor of English at UCD*
Based on **Rev. Joseph Darlington, SJ** (1850–1939) *Dean of studies, UCD*
'... of the dean of studies, Father Butt, in the physics' theatre of university College, 16 Stephen's Green, north ...' *(17.144–5)*
Joseph Darlington was born at Wigan in Lancashire on 5 November 1850. Educated at Rossal School and Brasenose College in Oxford, he was ordained as an Anglican priest before converting to Catholicism in 1878.

He entered the Society of Jesus at Milltown Park in Dublin on 10 July 1880. He studied at the Royal University in Dublin and Louvain in Belgium where in 1889 he was ordained priest.

Darlington returned to Ireland in 1890 and taught English and philosophy at University College Dublin until 1909. He was prefect of studies and was assistant to the president of the University, Father William Delany for many years. He helped Father Delany set up a university library, purchasing books from booksellers on the quays and at auctions. Father Joseph Darlington died on 18 July 1939 in Dublin and was buried in the Jesuit Plot in Glasnevin Cemetery, Finglas Road, Dublin [AH–GH 30–40.5].   *Ulysses 9.763–4*

Butt, Isaac (1813–79) *Barrister, politician and founder of the Home Rule Movement*
'... Michael Davitt against Isaac Butt ...' *(15.4684)*
Isaac Butt, only son of the Rev. Robert Butt, a Protestant rector, and Berkeley (née Cox) was born on 6 September 1813 in Glenfin, Co. Donegal.

Butt had a brilliant academic career at Trinity College Dublin. In 1838, he was called to the Irish Bar. In opposition to Daniel O'Connell and the Repeal Association, he founded *The Protestant Guardian*, which championed the unionist cause. Butt became more liberal following the Great Famine (1845–9).

He defended William Smith O'Brien and many of the Fenians after the abortive rising of 1848 and was engaged in several major law cases.

Butt stood for election on a Home Rule ticket in 1871 and was returned as MP for Limerick. His leadership was usurped and he lost control of the Home Rule Party with the rise of Parnell and his new policy of obstruction.

Isaac Butt died on 5 May 1879 at his residence, 'The Cottage', Clonskeagh Road, Dublin. The house is marked with a plaque. He was buried in the south-east corner of the Protestant cemetery, Stranolar, Co. Donegal. He is commemorated by Butt Bridge in Dublin, which links Tara Street and Beresford Place. *Ulysses 7.707*

Byrne, Davy (1861–1938) *Publican*

'He entered Davy Byrne's. Moral pub. He doesn't chat. Stands a drink now and then.' *(8.732–3)*

Davy Byrne was the son of Andrew Byrne, a shipping and general merchant from Arklow, Co. Wicklow. Aged 12, he left home in 1873 and came to Dublin to seek em-

ployment. He was apprenticed in a public house in Baggot Street before moving to the Scotch House pub on Burgh Quay, of which he later became part-owner. (The Scotch House no longer exists.)

Byrne had worked and saved enough money to buy the then disreputable tavern at 21 Duke Street from Matthew Riley and on 11 January 1889 placed his own name over the door and there it has remained ever since. Davy was a good listener and had a way of winning friendships and retaining them. His pub became the haunt of poets, artists, writers, scholars and politicians. These included James Joyce, Michael Collins, Arthur Griffith, F. R. Higgins, Pádraic Ó Conaire, Tom Kettle, Liam O'Flaherty and William Orpen, who was one of Byrne's greatest friends. Byrne's last address in Dublin was 10 Merrion Road, Ballsbridge. Regarded as one of the outstanding characters of his time, Byrne died on 10 September 1938. He was buried in Glasnevin Cemetery, Finglas Road, Dublin [NH 46 St Brigid's].

Ulysses 8.697; 8.809; 8.815; 8.824; 8.833; 8.937; 8.942; 8.947; 8.957; 8.961; 8.969; 8.975; 8.982; 8.987; 8.991; 8.1003; 8.1013; 8.1024; 8.1026

Byrne, Louis (1859–1932) *Dublin city coroner*

'So he was before he got the job in the morgue under Louis Byrne.' *(6.885)*

Louis Byrne was born in Dublin in 1859. He worked as a clerk in the firm of Messrs

John Power and Co., whiskey distillers and then in the Accountant's Office in Dublin Corporation. He subsequently studied medicine and qualified as a doctor.

Byrne was elected Dublin city coroner on 20 January 1900 in succession to Dr J. E. Kenny. As coroner, one of his working addresses was the City Morgue, located at 3 Store Street. He had residences at 50 Merrion Square and 79 Harcourt Street. Byrne also served as surgeon at Jervis Street Hospital for 40 years.

During his 32 years as city coroner, Byrne attended over 2,000 inquests. He attended the inquest of the well-known Dublin citizen, Stephen Cunningham, owner of the Ship Hotel on Lower Abbey Street, who committed suicide at his residence in Ely Place near George Moore's home.

Byrne was still working as coroner and surgeon at Jervis Street Hospital at the time of his death on 26 November 1932 at his residence, 'Flowergrove', Rochestown Avenue, Dún Laoghaire. He was buried in Deansgrange Cemetery, Deansgrange, Co. Dublin [13–H3–North].

Byrne, Madam T. Leggett, and Talbot Haslam Leggett (1867–1948) *Dance teachers*
'The poetry of motion, art of calisthenics. No connection with Madam Legget Byrne's or Levenston's. Fancy dress balls arranged. Deportment.' *(15.4042–3)*
Talbot Haslam Leggett Byrne married on 21 July 1890 aged 23, and shortly afterwards he and his wife, known as Madam Leggett Byrne, moved to Dublin from England to teach dancing. A brilliant and popular team, they held an unchallenged sway for over 40 years teaching and promoting dance in Dublin. They operated from 68 Mountjoy Square West and 27 Adelaide Road teaching all types of dancing, including classes in ballet, ballroom and children's fancy dancing. Deportment was also included in their varied programme.

The Leggett Byrnes were the first to open a ballroom in Dublin, at the Adelaide Hall, Adelaide Road. The hall had a dancing licence, which was unusual at the time and enabled them to hold dances until after midnight on Saturdays. It became the most popular winter rendezvous in the city.

Many eminent people including young officers of the Dublin garrison as well as members of the viceregal household attended the classes and dances at Adelaide Road, which were run with Victorian decorum.

Known as the dancing master *par excellence*, Leggett Byrne died on 16 April 1948 at the Royal West Sussex Hospital, Chichester, England.

Cadogan, George Henry (1840–1915) *Lord lieutenant of Ireland*
'The cabby read out of the paper he had got hold of that the former viceroy, earl Cadogan, had presided at the cabdrivers' association dinner in London somewhere.' *(16.1662–4)*
The son of Henry Charles Cadogan and Mary (née Wellesley), George Henry Cadogan, 5th earl of Cadogan, was born at Durham on 9 May 1840. Educated at Eton College and Christ Church, Oxford, he was elected MP for Bath in 1873.

In June 1895, Cadogan became lord lieutenant of Ireland (1895–1902). He obtained better terms of purchase for Irish tenants and appointed commissions to investigate intermediate education (1899) and university education (1901). He retired in July 1902.

Cadogan died on 6 March 1915 at his residence, Chelsea House, Cadogan Place, London.

Caffrey, Cissy (*fl.* late 1800s–early 1900s) *Friend of Gerty MacDowell*
'... Cissy Caffrey and Edy Boardman with the baby in the pushcar and Tommy and Jacky Caffrey, two little curlyheaded boys, dressed in sailor suits with caps to match ...' *(13.12–15)*
The Joyce family lived at 13 North Richmond Street from late 1894 or early 1895 until 1897. Joyce used the names of many of his neighbours in this area around North Richmond Street. Characters from five of the 20 houses on the street appear in his works.

Richmond Parade was a small street running almost parallel to North Richmond Street; directly behind the Joyces' home at 13 North Richmond Street was 6 Richmond Parade where the Caffrey family lived. Members of the family lived here from 1879 to 1899. John Caffrey, a turf and coal merchant lived here with his wife and children. Cissy Caffrey and her younger brothers, the twins Tommy and Jacky, lived here; they appear in *Ulysses* with Edy Boardman who lived around the corner in 1 North Richmond Street where John Boardman was the head of the household.

Ulysses 13.16; 13.24; 13.26; 13.29–31; 13.35; 13.243; 13.249; 13.251; 13.253; 13.306; 13.352; 13.254; 13.382; 13.481; 13.492; 13.505; 13.678; 13.682; 13.711; 13.715; 13.754; 13.767; 15.41–3; 15.54; 15.68; 15.131–2; 15.237; 15.3995; 15.4001; 15.4374; 15.4380; 15.4389; 15.4404; 15.4415; 15.4592; 15.4631; 15.4647; 15.4650; 15.4654; 15.4740; 15.4777

Callan, Nurse (b. 1886) *Nurse at Holles Street Hospital*

'Must call to the hospital. Wonder is nurse Callan there still.' *(13.959–60)*

Nurse Callan, in *Ulysses*, had a house in Holles Street where Bloom lived. It over-looked Holles Street Maternity Hospital where she worked. According to the text, Nurse Callan was keen on Dr O'Hare who worked in the same hospital.

In 1901, an Ellen Callan, born in Drogheda, Co. Louth in 1886, was a servant in 45 South Richmond Street with a family named Wall. In 1911, she is recorded as working as a nurse in Cowper Road, Rathmines.

Perhaps she was the Nurse Callan who worked Holles Street Hospital in 1904.

Ulysses 14.800; 14.830; 14.1395; 15.2611; 17.1847

Callinan/Callanan, Christopher (1844–1909) *Journalist*

'Bloom was pointing out all the stars and the comets in the heavens to Chris Callinan and the jarvey: the great bear and Hercules and the dragon, and the whole jingbang lot.' *(10.567–9)*

Christopher Callanan was the eldest son of William Callanan, of Ballahow House, Nenagh, Co. Tipperary. He was born in Dublin and worked as a journalist for over 40 years in the Dublin press including the *Freeman's Journal*. Renowned for his gaffes and malapropisms, Callanan was a brother-in-law of Ignatius/Fred Gallaher.

In 1901, Callanan was living with another brother-in-law, Peter O'Sullivan, and his family at 20 Donnycarney, Clontarf West, Dublin. Other members of the Callanan family living there included his sister Mary Anne Callanan, and his brother Daniel Callanan, who worked as a commercial clerk in the wholesale paper trade. Callanan later moved to 1 Russell Street.

He died on 16 December 1909 at the Mater Misericordiae Hospital, Eccles Street, Dublin.

(Callanan not Callinan is the correct spelling. This seems another case of Joyce's misspelling, like Devan for Devin and Wetherup for Weatherup).

Ulysses 7.690–1; 10.555; 10.572; 15.1655; 15.4341; 17.2137

Cameron, Sir Charles (1830–1921) *Public analyst and medical health officer for Dublin*

'The lord mayor was there, Val Dillon it was, and sir Charles Cameron ...' *(10.537–8)*

Charles Cameron, son of Captain Ewen Cameron, a Scottish soldier and Belinda (née Smith) was born in Dublin on 16 July 1830.

Cameron studied medicine in Dublin at the Apothecaries' Hall, the Dublin School of Medicine and the Ledwich Medical School, in Peter Street, graduating in 1865. He was appointed professor of hygiene and political medicine (1867–1920) and chemistry (1875–1920) at the Royal College of Surgeons in Ireland.

Well known for his important contribution to public health and hygiene, he was appointed the first public health analyst for Dublin in 1862 and held the post until his death. In 1874, he was appointed as Dublin medical officer of health and later chief sanitary officer. He was responsible for many reforms in public health including the provision of better accommodation and public housing for the poor.

Author of *The History of the Royal College of Surgeons in Ireland and of the Irish Schools of Medicine* (1886), he died on 27 February 1921 at 27 Raglan Road, Dublin, and was buried in Mount Jerome Cemetery, Harold's Cross, Dublin [C116–3518].

Campbell, Foxy
Nickname for **Fr Richard Campbell, SJ (1854–1945)** *Master at Belvedere College*
'... Foxy Campbell, Lanternjaws.' *(3.112)*
Richard Campbell was born in Sackville Street (now O'Connell Street), Dublin, on 24 January 1854. He was the son of John Campbell, twice lord mayor of Dublin. Educated at Belvedere College in Dublin and Downside Abbey in England, he entered the Society of Jesus at Milltown Park when he was 19.

From 1893 to 1897, he was on the teaching staff of the Junior House, Belvedere College, when Joyce was a student there (Joyce attended Belvedere 1893–8). Father Campbell then spent periods at other Jesuit houses in Ireland, including Rath-

farnham Castle where he was minister under Father John Sullivan as rector. In 1926, he was transferred to the Church of St Francis Xavier, Gardiner Street and remained there until 1943, his longest period in any one place.

He spent the remaining two years of his life at Milltown Park where he died on 1 April 1945 in his ninety-second year. He was buried in the Jesuit Plot, Glasnevin Cemetery, Finglas Road, Dublin [AH–GH 30–40.5]. He was nicknamed 'Foxy Campbell' or 'Lantern Jaws'.

Campbell, Henry (1858–1924) *Dublin town clerk*
'... bore a distant resemblance to Henry Campbell, the townclerk ...' *(16.661)*
Henry Campbell was born in Kilcool near Newry, Co. Down. When he had finished his schooling he went to live with his uncle in Newcastle-on-Tyne in England and secured a job with the North-Eastern Railway Company.

While in England, Campbell became involved with the Irish literary and political societies in the area. His work on behalf of the nationalist cause so impressed Parnell that he offered him a job as his private secretary, which Campbell accepted. They remained close friends up to Parnell's death. Campbell

was amongst the minority who remained faithful to Parnell after the 'split' in the Irish Parliamentary Party when Captain William O'Shea named him as co-respondent in his divorce action against his wife Katharine.

Campbell had served as MP for South Fermanagh in 1885 and 1886–92 as a member of the Home Rule Party.

Defeating seven other candidates for the position, he was elected Dublin town clerk on 24 May 1893 by a Parnellite corporation and remained in that position until his resignation in 1920. He was conferred with a knighthood the following year.

Campbell's Dublin residence was 71 Shanaganagh, Rathmichael, Co. Dublin, and his office was in City Hall, Lord Edward Street. On his retirement he moved to Greenwood Park in Newry, Co. Down.

He died on 6 March 1924 in a London nursing home.   *Ulysses 16.908; 16.1019; 16.1355*

Cannon, Herbert Mornington 'Morny' (1873–1962) *Jockey*
'Zinfandel's the favourite, lord Howard de Walden's, won at Epsom. Morny Cannon is riding him.' *(8.830–1)*
Herbert Mornington Cannon, known as 'Morny', was born on 21 May 1873. He got the unusual name of Mornington from a winning colt of that name, which his father, the

jockey Tom Cannon (1846–1917) rode to victory the day of his birth at Bath in Avon.

Morny was just 13 when he rode his first winner. During his successful career he won a number of major races such as the 2,000 Guineas, St Leger, the Derby, the Oaks and other major races. He won the Ascot Gold Cup in 1902, riding William the Third. He rode Zinfandel, the horse favoured to win the 1904 Gold Cup.

When he retired from racing, Morny lived at Brighton in Sussex for many years. His great-nephew is the racing legend Lester Piggott.

Carey, James (1845–83) *Member of the Invincibles*
'That fellow that turned queen's evidence on the invincibles he used to receive the, Carey was his name, the communion every morning. This very church.' *(5.378–80)*
James Carey was born in James's Street in Dublin, the son of a bricklayer. He followed the same trade and eventually became a successful builder and owner of a considerable amount of slum-tenement properties. He lived in 19a Denzille Street

near the Church of St Andrew or All Hallows in Westland Row where he attended mass each day. According to the reporter, J. B. Hall, Carey had a 'reputation for ostentatious piety'.

Carey became a city councillor and joined the Fenians. He became a leader in a Fenian splinter group known as the Invincibles, whose aim was 'to remove all the tyrants of the country'. On 6 May 1882, he was implicated in the murders of the new chief secretary, Lord Frederick Cavendish, and the under-secretary, Thomas Henry Burke, near the Viceregal Lodge in the Phoenix Park.

Carey was arrested along with 16 of the Invincibles. He turned Queen's evidence during the trial in February 1883 resulting in the hanging of five of his associates. Eight others received sentences of long-term imprisonment.

The British authorities shipped Carey and his wife and six children secretly on the *Kinfauns Castle* to the Cape of Good Hope. He used the name Power and shaved off his beard as a disguise. On reaching Cape Town, Carey and his family transferred to another vessel, the *Melrose Castle*, bound for Durban and Port Elizabeth. On board was Patrick O'Donnell, a Donegal man who had lived in the United States since his part in the Fenian rising of 1867. He discovered Carey's identity and shot him dead on 29 July 1883.

Carey was buried in the prison burial ground at Port Elizabeth. O'Donnell was executed at Newgate Prison, England on 17 December 1883; a monument commemo-rating him was erected in Glasnevin Cemetery, Finglas Road, Dublin.

Ulysses 5.381; 8.442; 16.1054

Carlisle/Carlyle, James (1839–1907) *Manager of the* Irish Times
'James Carlisle made that. Six and a half per cent dividend.' *(8.337)*
James Carlyle was born in Dumfries, Scotland, on 12 April 1839. In 1869 Major Laurence Knox, founder and proprietor of the *Irish Times*, invited Carlyle to Dublin to work as the commercial manager of the paper. After Knox's death two years later, Carlyle took over management of the paper for the trustees. When Sir John Arnott acquired it in 1873, Carlyle retained his post with added responsibilities. As a result of his keen business acumen the circulation and revenue of the paper increased. In 1900 it was formed into a limited company.

Carlyle was an active Mason throughout his life and a supporter of Masonic charities. He was a governor of the Masonic Female Orphan School. He was for many years a member of the Institute of Journalists, having joined the Irish Association District at its formation.

Carlyle was associated with the *Irish Times* for nearly 40 years. He died on 28 December 1907 at his residence 'St Catherine's', Ailesbury Road, Donnybrook.

Carr, Private Harry *British soldier*

Based on **Henry Carr (1894–1962)** *British consular official in Zurich*

'PRIVATE CARR

Bennett? He's my pal. I love old Bennett.' *(15.626–7)*

Henry Carr was born in Sunderland and grew up in Co. Durham. He moved to Canada aged 17. In 1915 he volunteered for military service and served on the Western Front in the Canadian Black Watch Regiment.

Carr was badly wounded, taken prisoner and invalided from his regiment. He was 'exchanged' and sent to Zurich where he worked as an official of the British consulate. A tall, good-looking young man, he was a member of the cast of the 'English Players', a company that had been formed by Joyce and his friend Claud Sykes to produce plays in English. Carr was cast as Algernon Moncrieff in the group's production of *The Importance of Being Earnest*. He acquitted himself well in the role and bought some fancy clothes to play the part. As an amateur, Carr received only ten francs and he took umbrage at the manner in which Joyce gave him the money. A serious quarrel ensued with Joyce after the performance of the play on 29 April 1918 in the Theater zu den Kaufleuten on Pelikanstrasse. This created intense hostility between them resulting in Joyce's unsuccessful lawsuit of 1918–19.

Carr met Nora Tulloch in Zurich, married her in England and moved back to Canada where he worked as a company secretary. In 1928 he met Noelle Bach, divorced Nora and married Bach in 1933. They moved to England, where Carr joined a foundry company. Carr died in London in 1962.

Ulysses 15.48; 15.60; 15.66; 15.615; 15.619–20; 15.3995; 15.4001; 15.4373; 15.4393; 15.4409; 15.4446; 15.4462; 15.4466; 15.4492; 15.4565; 15.4572; 15.4596; 15.4625; 15.4643; 15.4719; 15.4741; 15.4745; 15.4785; 15.4795

Casement, Roger (1864–1916) *Patriot*

'Casement, says the citizen. He's an Irishman.' *(12.1545)*

Roger Casement was born on 1 September 1864 in Sandycove, Co. Dublin. He was the son of Captain Roger Casement of the 3rd Dragoon Guards and Anne (née Jephson) from Mallow, Co. Cork. Aged 20 he left for Africa and in 1892 joined the British colonial service there.

Casement exposed the atrocities committed by European employers in the Belgian Congo in a report he wrote in 1904. This resulted in some reforms. He was promoted to consular-general at Rio de Janeiro and examined conditions in the rubber plantations in Peru. He was knighted in 1911. He retired from the colonial service in 1913.

That year, Casement joined the Irish National Volunteers and raised funds for the purchase of arms. On the outbreak of the First World War he went to Germany to appeal for armed aid in the hope of getting help to win Irish independence. He returned by submarine and was arrested at Banna Strand in Co. Kerry. He was brought to London to stand trial where he was charged with high treason, found guilty and executed by hanging at Pentonville Prison, London, on 3 August 1916.

His remains were returned to Ireland, and after a state funeral were interred on 1 March 1965 near the circle at the main entrance gate of Glasnevin Cemetery, Finglas Road, Dublin [A 16 Tower Circle Section]. A stone slab, marks his grave:

Ruarí/MacCasmainn/Roger Casment/a d'fulaing bás/as son/na hEireann/
3 Lúnasa 1916/+/R.I.P.

Casey, John Keegan (1846–70) *Poet and Fenian*

'... does anybody hereabouts remember Caoc O'Leary, a favourite and most trying declamation piece by the way of poor John Casey and a bit of perfect poetry in its own small way.' *(16.426–8)*

John Keegan Casey, son of a small farmer and teacher, was born near Mullingar, Co. Westmeath, on 22 August 1846. When he was eight years old, his father got a post as headmaster in Gurteen School near Ballymahon in Co. Longford. Casey later worked as an assistant teacher in the school and wrote poetry. His best-known poem, 'The Rising of the Moon', commemorating the 1798 rebellion, was written when he was 16. It later became a popular ballad.

Casey moved to Dublin in the 1860s and contributed to the *Nation* under the pen name 'Leo' and joined the Fenians. A collection of his poems *A Wreathe of Shamrocks*, was published in 1866.

In 1867 Casey, one of the main figures in the rising of that year, was imprisoned without trial for eight months. He was released provided he went to Australia and did not return, but he remained in Dublin in disguise and continued to write poetry.

He died of consumption on 17 March 1870 and was buried in Glasnevin Cemetery, Finglas Road, Dublin [NC 7 South].

Note: Bloom confuses John Keegan the poet and author of 'Caoc the Piper' with John Keegan Casey.

Castletown, Lord (1849–1937) *Reported on the state of Irish forests*

'Larches, firs, all the trees of the conifer family are going fast. I was reading a report of lord Castletown's ...' *(12.1259–61)*

Bernard Edward FitzPatrick, only son of John FitzPatrick, 1st Baron Castletown, and Augusta (née Douglas) was born on 29 July 1849. He was MP for Portarlington, 1880–3, before succeeding his father in the barony, becoming 2nd Baron Castletown and entering the House of Lords.

Lord Castletown was appointed to examine the forestry of Ireland in 1907. The forests had suffered greatly as a result of the Land Purchase Acts (1882). His report, which listed specific recommendations for 'a national scheme of afforestation', was presented to parliament and published in Dublin on 6 April

1908. The same year, Castletown was made a knight of the Order of St Patrick and admitted to the Irish Privy Council. Between 1906 and 1910, he was chancellor of the Royal University of Ireland.

Lord Castletown died at 'Granston Manor', Co. Laois, at which point the baronetcy became extinct.

Chamberlain, Joseph (1836–1914) *English politician and statesman*
'That horsepoliceman the day Joe Chamberlain was given his degree in Trinity he got a run for his money.' *(8.423–4)*
Joseph Chamberlain, son of Joseph Chamberlain and Caroline (née Harben) was born in Camberwell, London in 1836. He was educated at Univeristy College and

was then a businessman in Birmingham. He became a member of the Liberal Party and introduced social reforms. His pioneering work in clearing slums made him a national political figure.

He was appointed by Gladstone as president of the Board of Trade in 1880 but resigned from Gladstone's cabinet due to the issue of Home Rule for Ireland and became leader of the Liberal Unionists. His name was connected with the British policy that resulted in the Boer War (1899–1902). He was doubly unpopular when he came to Dublin on 18 December 1899 to receive an honorary degree at Trinity College. To mark the occasion, an anti-Boer War meeting and demonstration was organised by John O'Leary, Maud Gonne and others, which the police interrupted.

Chamberlain gave up political life in 1906 and died in 1914. He was buried in the Unitarian Section in Birmingham General Cemetery, Key Hill, Birmingham, England.   *Ulysses 15.791*

Charles, Father (1821–93) *Priest*

'Then perform a miracle like Father Charles.' *(15.1838)*
Father Charles of Mount Argus was born John Andrew Houben on 11 December 1821 in Holland. He was the second son of Peter Houben and Johanna Elizabeth Luyten.

He served as a conscript in the army and joined the novitiate of the Passionists in Belgium aged 24 where he was given the name Charles. He was ordained in Tournai on 21 December 1850, just four months after his father's death.

He came to Ireland in July 1857 to the newly founded

monastery at Mount Argus in Harold's Cross in Dublin where he spent nine years before returning to England. He was recalled to Mount Argus in January 1874 and remained there for the rest of his life. Many cures were attributed to him and his fame spread rapidly.

Joyce's friend, J. F. Byrne (Cranly), recounts in his book, *Silent Years*, how his eye problems were treated unsuccessfully by two eye specialists before being cured by Father Charles.

Father Charles died on 5 January 1893. He was entombed in a white marble sarcophagus in the church at Mount Argus. He was beatified by Pope John Paul II in 1988 and canonised by Pope Benedict XVI in 2007.

Chatterton, Abraham (1862–1949) *School friend of Leopold Bloom*

'(*Halcyon Days, High School boys in blue and white football jerseys and shorts, Master Donald Turnbull, Master Abraham Chatterton … stand in a clearing of the trees and shout to Master Leopold Bloom.*)' *(15.3325–9)*

Abraham Chatterton was a nephew of the Judge Hedges Eyre Chatterton (1819–1910).

Chatterton was one of Bloom's school friends at the Erasmus High School, Harcourt Street in Dublin. Aged 18, he entered Trinity College Dublin and in 1895 was working as a land agent with an office at 26 Westland Row.

On 9 November 1900, Chatterton was appointed registrar and bursar of the Erasmus High School in Harcourt Street. He was living at 16 Pembroke Road, Ballsbridge, with his wife, Elizabeth Eva, and daughter. They had moved to live in Enniskerry, Co. Wicklow by 1903. He retained his office in Westland Row and continued to work in the Erasmus High School.

Chatterton later worked as estate agent for Lord Powerscourt. He was responsible for what is now named the Chatterton plantation in the Powerscourt demesne, Enniskerry, Co. Wicklow. He died on 4 August 1949 at Delgany, Co. Wicklow, and was buried in St Patrick's churchyard, Powerscourt, Enniskerry.

Chatterton, Hedges Eyre (1819–1910) *Judge*

'Old Chatterton, the vicechancellor, is his granduncle or his greatgranduncle. Close on ninety they say.' *(7.262–3)*

Hedges Eyre Chatterton was born in Cork on 5 July 1819. He was the eldest son of Abraham Chatterton and Jane (née Tisdall). Educated at Trinity College Dublin, in 1840 he entered King's Inns, Dublin, and the following year Lincoln's Inn, London. He was called to the Irish Bar in 1843.

In 1867 he was appointed attorney general and the same year became MP for Dublin University, and vice-chancellor, a post he held for 37 years.

Chatterton's wife Mary died in 1901. In 1904 he retired and the same year married Florence Henrietta, widow of Captain Edward Croker. They lived in Newtown Park House, in Newtownpark Avenue, Blackrock, Co. Dublin.

Chatterton died on 30 August 1910 and was buried in Deansgrange Cemetery, Deansgrange, Co. Dublin [18–T1–South].

Childs, Thomas (1823–99) *Murder victim*
'That is where Childs was murdered, he said. The last house.' *(6.469)*
Thomas Childs was the son of Alexander Childs of Arran Quay who had worked as a carver and gilder for the lord lieutenant amongst others. In 1899, Thomas was a wealthy unmarried man of 75 who lived alone at 5 Bengal Terrace, Finglas Road. He was described as a person of solitary habits who seldom mixed with his neighbours. His house was full of books which he had inherited from his deceased brother, the Rev. Edmond Childs, MA, a Church of Ireland clergyman formerly curate of St Nicholas Within.

Childs was murdered on Saturday 2 September 1899. Nothing was found to be missing from the house and under his copy of the *History of the Bible* was his will dated 1882. It showed that his brother Samuel was the principal beneficiary.

Samuel Childs, of 51 St Patrick's Road, Drumcondra, was charged with his brother's murder. Samuel had retired as an accountant from Brooks Thomas, a Dublin firm of builders' providers in February 1899. He had a paltry pension of £52 per annum to support a wife and family. At the time of the murder he was unemployed.

Childs was tried and acquitted in October 1899, with Seymour Bushe as the defence counsel. Timothy Healy, QC, MP appeared for Childs in the police court and in the court of trial.

Thomas Childs was buried in Mount Jerome Cemetery, Harold's Cross, Dublin [C110–1343].   *Ulysses 7.748–9; 14.958; 14.1017; 15.761*

Citron, Israel (1875–1950) *Neighbour of Bloom*
'Wonder is poor Citron still in Saint Kevin's parade.' *(4.205)*
Israel Citron was born in Russia on 4 September 1875, son of Isaac Citronremblatt and Rachel (née Waldstein). He lived at 17 St Kevin's Parade, South Circular Road, Dublin and was a neighbour of Bloom when he lived in Lombard Street West.

He worked as a travelling draper in Dublin. In 1911 he lived at 26 Longwood Avenue, South Circular Road with his wife Rose (née Seltser) and infant daughter, Clara. They later moved to 39 Emorville Terrace. Citron died in 1950 and was buried in the Jewish cemetery in Manchester.

Claffey, Patrick (1825–96) *Dublin pawnbroker*
Patrick Claffey was a pawnbroker with two shops at 65–66 Amiens Street and 28 Talbot Street, Dublin. The latter was established in 1850 and was advertised as a 'First Class Pawn Office'.

Claffey donated to many charities in Dublin such as Jervis Street Hospital and the Mansion House Relief Fund. He was a guardian of the South Dublin Union, based in the workhouse in James's Street. He first lived at 30 Nicholas Street with his wife Margaret (née Grehan) and later moved to 'St Mary's', Mount Merrion Avenue, Blackrock, in 1884. The Joyces lived at 'Leoville', 23 Carysfort Avenue, Blackrock, from early 1892 to 1893. They would have known Claffey or at least known of him because they frequented pawnshops, as did many people then.

A member of the board of the Blackrock Commissioners, Claffey was involved through his business interests, with banks such as the National and Hibernian Bank and in the Dublin Artesian Mineral Water Company.

Claffey died in 1896 at 2 Woodstock Villas, Terenure, Co. Dublin, and was buried in Glasnevin Cemetery, Finglas Road, Dublin [HD 50 Garden].   *Ulysses 8.153–4*

Claver, St Peter, SJ (1580–1654) *Jesuit missionary*
'Sermon by the very reverend John Conmee S. J. on saint Peter Claver S. J. and the African Mission.' *(5.322–3)*
St Peter Claver was born on 26 June 1580 in Catalonia, Spain. He entered the Society of Jesus in 1602, sailed to Cartagena de Indias in Colombia in 1610 and was ordained priest there on 19 March 1616.

He died in Cartagena on 8 September 1654 and his remains were interred in St Peter Claver Church, Cartagena, Colombia. He was beatified on 20 July 1850 and canonised on 15 January 1888. He was declared patron of the Negro Missions on 7 July 1896.

Clay, Robert Keating (1835–1904) *Solicitor*
'I see Keating Clay is elected vicechairman of the Richmond asylum ...' *(15.2932–3)*
Robert Keating Clay was the son of William Keating Clay, a solicitor from Meadow Bank in Terenure, Co. Dublin. He was admitted a solicitor in 1860. Six years later, he entered into partnership with Messrs Casey and Clay. In 1891, he became a member of the Council of the Incorporated Law Society of Ireland; from 1899 to 1900 he was vice-president and elected president for the year 1903–4.

Clay was elected deputy chairman of the Richmond Asylum in June 1904. This was considered the most important asylum in the country comprising a large complex of buildings designed by Francis Johnston. Located on Grangegorman Road, it consisted of the Richmond Penitentiary (1812), the Richmond Lunatic Asylum (1814), and the Grangegorman Mental Hospital (1816). A Mason, Clay was grand treasurer of the Grand Lodge of Ireland.

In 1904, Clay was practising with George Collins in the firm Casey & Collins at 21 St Andrew's Street, and his residence was 'Anglesey', 6 Killiney Road, Dalkey, Co. Dublin.

He died on 4 July 1904 in London and was buried in Mount Jerome Cemetery, Harold's Cross, Dublin [C38–12362].

Cleary, OSF Rev. P. J. (1835–1909) *Guardian of Adam and Eve's Church*
Patrick Joseph Cleary, son of William Cleary and Mary (née Corcoran), was born in Woodtown, Killucan, Co. Westmeath, on 31 July 1835.

Aged 24 he joined the Irish Franciscans, and was ordained priest in Rome on 26 March 1864. Father Cleary was a vicar to the Poor Clare sisters on Nun's Island in Galway in 1870. Three years later he was elected guardian in the Galway friary, and was a preacher and missioner. In 1879 he moved as guardian to the friary in Waterford.

In 1881 Father Cleary was appointed guardian of Adam and Eve's Church, Merchant's Quay, Dublin, where he remained for the rest of his life, residing in Presbytery House, Merchant's Quay. He died on 8 February 1909 and was buried in the Franciscan Plot, Glasnevin Cemetery, Finglas Road, Dublin [CH 10 South St Brigid's].   *Ulysses 12.929–30*

Clinch, Mrs (1865–1962) *Friend of the Blooms*
'O but the dark evening in the Appian way I nearly spoke to Mrs Clinch O thinking she was. Whew!' *(13.866–7)*
Mrs Mary Clinch (née Powell) was the youngest daughter of Major Malachy Powell. She was born on 6 February 1865 in the Curragh, Co. Kildare, when her father was stationed there. In 1891 she married James F. Clinch, a railway accountant

secretary. In 1901, they lived at 47 Leinster Road, Rathmines; by 1911, they had moved to 29 Leinster Road West where they lived with their six children. Mrs Clinch died on 9 July 1962 at her home, 'Lissarda', Granville Road, Stillorgan, and was buried at St Paul's Retreat, Mount Argus, Harold's Cross, Dublin.

Two of Malachy Powell's four daughters, Mrs Joe Gallaher (Louisa) and Mrs Clinch, appear as friends of the Blooms in their early married life.

Cochrane (1895–1986) *Pupil in Mr Deasy's school*
'You, Cochrane, what city sent for him?' *(2.1)*
Of the pupils mentioned in Mr Deasy's school, only the name of Cochrane can be traced as a resident of the Dalkey area.

John Gordon Cochrane, son of Charles Henry Cochrane and Margaret (née Gordon), was born on 2 May 1895. His father, a solicitor and commissioner for oaths, had an office at 29 South Frederick Street, Dublin. In 1904, the family lived at Cambridge House, 38 Ulverton Road, Dalkey.

He died on 13 January 1986 in Vancouver, British Columbia, Canada. John Cochrane may have attended the Clifton School, Dalkey, where Mr Deasy's original, Francis Irwin, was headmaster, and where Joyce taught for a few weeks in 1904.

Coffey, Rev. Francis J. (1843–1917) *Chaplain, Glasnevin Cemetery*
'Father Coffey. I knew his name was like a coffin. Dominenamine.' *(6.595)*
Francis Coffey was born in December 1843 in the parish of SS Mary and Peter, Dublin. He was admitted to Holy Cross College, Clonliffe, Dublin in September 1860, and completed his studies in 1867. He worked as Catholic curate at St Paul's Church, Arran Quay.

Father Coffey was also acting-chaplain at Glasnevin Cemetery for a number of years including 1904. He performed the absolution, the final phase of the funeral before burial. He lived at 65 Dalymount, Phibsborough and later at 339 North Circular Road.

Father Coffey was known as a very charitable man, giving books and papers to St Joseph's Library and the Visiting Association of Charity. Between services, Father Coffey fed the cemetery birds. The birds became so accustomed to this that when there was an unusual number of funerals, which prevented him from coming out, the birds would go into the chapel to seek him out. It was always known from the trail of birds by which gate Father Coffey had left the cemetery. He received the remains of many of the characters mentioned in *Ulysses* including Matthew Kane on 14 July 1904.

Father Coffey died on 3 December 1917 at St Vincent's Hospital, 58 St Stephen's Green, Dublin, and was buried in Glasnevin Cemetery, Finglas Road, Dublin [RA 9.5 Dublin Section].   *Ulysses 11.1036; 15.1237–8; 15.1240*

Cohen, Mrs Bella (1850/1–1905/6) *Brothel-keeper in Monto*
'*The door opens. Bella Cohen, a massive whoremistress, enters. She is dressed in a threequarter ivory gown, fringed round the hem with tasselled selvedge …*' *(15. 2742–4)*
Bella Cohen ran her brothel at 82 Tyrone Street Lower in Monto, Dublin's red light district. She was born Ellen Cohen in Gloucester, England. From 1883 she lived in Dublin. She had four previous addresses before she moved to Tyrone Street in 1888 where she remained until 1905.

In 1885, the area around what was known as 'Monto' was one of the worst slums in Europe. During its heyday between 1860 and 1900, Monto contained 1,600 prostitutes. It derived the nickname Monto from Montgomery Street, the heart of the brothel quarter, and was unique in Britain and Ireland in its lack of police interference.

Monto was also known as 'the Kips', 'the Digs' and 'the Village'. It was organised to cope with the needs of all classes; the well-off clients were catered for in what were known as 'flash houses', which were well-maintained, and lavishly furnished unlike some of the other houses in the street. Those of middle-income were accommodated in less salubrious houses, without trimmings, such as piano players or chandeliers, and the lower-income groups such as soldiers and sailors were catered for in some of the tenement houses in Purdon Street,

Elliott Place and Faithful Place. Bella Cohen had either died or retired by 1905.

Ulysses 15.1287; 15.3108; 17.2055

Cohen, Old *Former owner of the Bloom bed*

Based on **David Abraham Cohen** (1861–1932) *Gibraltarian shopkeeper*

'... the lumpy old jingly bed always reminds me of old Cohen ...' *(18.1212–13)*

David Abraham Cohen was born in Gibraltar in 1861 where he had a shop at 22 Engineer Lane. He stocked the best English, French and Spanish boots and shoes and also made shoes to order.

Cohen lived here with his wife Sara, two children Judith and Abraham, and his domestic servant, Geronima.

Cohen died on 4 November 1932 and was buried in Gibraltar in the Jewish section of the North Front (or Garrsion) Cemetery, Devil's Tower Road. The cemetery is situated at the south end of Gibraltar overlooking the Straits.

Bloom believes that Cohen was the seller of his (Bloom's) bed, which Major Tweedy, bought from Lord Napier. Napier was governor of Gibraltar (1876–83).

Ulysses 18.1498

Collins, Dr

The Dr Collins in *Ulysses* is a combination of two doctors named Collins. Joyce used the address of one, Dr John Rupert Collins, in Pembroke Road, and the manner of the other, Dr Joseph Collins, a prominent American neurologist whom he met in Paris in 1921. Molly Bloom memorialises the latter Dr Collins's manner in *Ulysses*.

Dr John Rupert Collins (c. 1878–1966) *Doctor consulted by Molly Bloom*

'... Dr Collins for womens diseases on Pembroke road ...' *(18.1153–4)*

John Rupert Collins was the son of the Rev. T. R. S. Collins, chaplain and private secretary to the Rev. Joseph Ferguson Peacocke, DD, the Church of Ireland archbishop of Dublin. In 1904, father and son are both listed as living at 65 Pembroke Road, Dublin.

John Rupert Collins graduated in medicine from Trinity College Dublin in 1901. In 1913 he took the MRCP, London and was elected FRCP in 1931. He held the appointment as honorary clinical pathologist and honorary physician to the General Hospital, Cheltenham, in England. He died in 1966.

Dr Joseph Collins (1866–1950) *American neurologist*

'... still I liked him when he sat down to write the thing out frowning so severe his nose intelligent like that you be damned ...' *(18.1172–4)*

Joseph Collins was born in Brookfield, Connecticut, USA on 22 September 1866. He studied medicine at New York University, receiving his MD in 1888. He was appointed professor of neurology in the New York Post-Graduate Medical School in 1907. A founder of the Neurological Institute of New York, he wrote a number of books. He died on 11 June 1950.

Colum, Padraic (1881–1972) *Poet, playwright and novelist*

'I liked Colum's *Drover*. Yes, I think he has that queer thing genius.' *(9.302–3)*

Padraic Colum, son of Patrick and Susan Colum, was born on 8 December 1881, in the workhouse in Longford when his father worked there as master. He lost his job and went to the United States, returning three years later to work as station-master in Glasthule, Co. Dublin.

Colum was educated locally and after finishing school worked in the Irish Railway Clearing House on Kildare Street in Dublin. He began to write and was awarded a four-year scholarship that enabled him write full-time. In 1903 *Broken Soil*, later rewritten as *The Fiddler's House*, was produced by the Irish Literary Theatre followed by *The Land* (1905) staged by the Abbey Theatre, Dublin. The best of his early poems appeared in Arthur Griffith's paper, the *United Irishman*. These included 'The Drover', 'The Plougher' and 'The Poor Scholar', which were later included in his first book of poems, *Wild Earth*, published in 1907 and dedicated to 'Æ who fostered me'.

Together with a few friends, Colum founded a literary magazine, *The Irish Review* in 1911. It was short-lived, but during its brief existence it published poems, plays, criticisms and reviews.

Colum married Mary Maguire and in 1914 they moved to the United States and both taught at Columbia University. They remained in New York for the rest of their life together, with the exception of three years, 1930–3, when they lived in France. They renewed their acquaintance with James Joyce in Paris, where Colum helped him by typing and making some suggestions with his work in progress.

Colum's *Collected Poems* was published in 1953. The next year he was awarded the Gregory Medal by the Irish Academy of Letters for outstanding literary work.

After his wife's death in New York on 22 October 1957, Colum divided his time between the United States and Ireland. When in Dublin he stayed with his sister at 11 Edenvale Road in Ranelagh.

University College Dublin and Columbia University honoured Colum with doctorates in 1958. In 1959, he published *Our Friend James Joyce*. As well as plays he published 61 books, and various poetic broadsheets illustrated by Jack B. Yeats and published by the Cuala Press. Colum died on 11 January 1972 in Enfield, Connecticut. He was buried beside his wife Mary in St Fintan's Cemetery, Sutton, near Howth in Co. Dublin. Their grave [B20] is marked by a large Celtic cross. *Ulysses 9.290–1; 9.301–5; 'The Drover', 9.303; 'A Poor Scholar of the Forties', 9.304–5; 9.510–11*

Compton, Private *British soldier in Nighttown*

Based on **Mr Compton** (*fl.* 1880s–1900s) (**Christian name unknown**) *British consular official in Zurich*

'PRIVATE COMPTON

He doesn't half want a thick ear, the blighter.' *(15.4391–2)*

Private Compton was based on a British consular official in Zurich named Compton with whom Joyce had a row in 1918. Compton was the business manager of the 'English Players', a company formed by Joyce and his friend Claud Sykes to produce plays in English.

Joyce chose the name to settle old scores. Compton appears as a British soldier in Nighttown with Private Henry Carr who knocks Stephen down. No biographical information has been forthcoming so far on Compton.

Ulysses 15.48; 15.60; 15.64; 15.617; 15.624; 15.3995; 15.4001; 15.4398; 15.4401; 15.4463; 15.4483; 15.4494; 15.4601; 15.4627; 15.4769; 15.4774; 15.4792

Concone, Giuseppe (1801–61) *Instructor of singing and pianoforte*

'... and in old Madrid Concone is the name of those exercises he bought me ...' *(18.617–18)*

Giuseppe Concone was born on 12 September 1801 in Turin, Italy. He studied music in Turin and moved to Paris in 1837 where he became famous as a teacher of singing, the pianoforte and the theory of music and composition. He published a large number of popular and effective vocal exercises for singers.

Concone returned to Turin in 1848 and was appointed organist of the Royal Chapel. He died on 1 June 1861 in Turin.

Conmee, Rev. John, SJ (1847– 1910) *Superior, St Francis Xavier's Community*

'The superior, the very reverend John Conmee S. J. reset his smooth watch in his interior pocket as he came down the presbytery steps.' *(10.1–2)*

John Conmee was born into a wealthy farming family on 25 December 1847 at Glanduff near Athlone, Co. Westmeath.

He commenced his education at Castleknock College and when he was 16 changed to the Jesuits at Clongowes Wood College, Sallins, Co. Kildare. In 1869, he joined the Society of Jesus at Milltown Park in Dublin and continued his studies at the Jesuit houses of Roehampton and Stoneyhurst in England. He returned to Ireland in 1873 and spent five years teaching at Tullabeg, Co. Offaly. He then went to Innsbruck where he studied theology and travelled widely in Europe. Archbishop Croke ordained him priest in 1881.

Father Conmee moved to Clongowes Wood College as prefect of studies. In 1885, he was appointed rector, a position he held until 1891. James Joyce was a pupil here from September 1888 to December 1892.

Father Conmee was appointed the superior at St Francis Xavier's Community in Gardiner Street in 1898. In 1905 he was elected provincial of the society and in 1909,

when his term as provincial ended, he was appointed rector of Milltown Park. The Catholic Truth Society published his book *Old Times in the Barony* in 1910.

Father Conmee died on 13 May 1910 and was buried in the Jesuit Plot in Glasnevin Cemetery, Finglas Road, Dublin [AH–GH 30–40.5].

Ulysses 5.322–3; 5.331; 9.211; 10.10; 10.12; 10.19; 10.21; 10.26; 10.30; 10.33; 10.40; 10.46; 10.49; 10.51; 10.54; 10.62–3; 10.68; 10.73; 10.77; 10.79; 10.81; 10.83; 10.85; 10.87; 10.93; 10.96; 10.98–9; 10.101; 10.104; 10.107; 10.113; 10.115; 10.120–1; 10.123–4; 10.128; 10.131; 10.136–7; 10.142–3; 10.148; 10.151; 10.153; 10.155; 10.161; 10.171; 10.174; 10.178; 10.180; 10.184; 10.189; 10.193; 10.203; 10.213; 10.264; 10.842; 10.965; 14.1154; 14.1159; 15.3673; 15.3675; 15.4141; 17.790; Old Times in the Barony, 10.161–2

Conneff, Thomas (1867–1912) *Athlete*

Thomas Conneff, son of James Conneff and Marcella (née Rourke), was born on 10 December 1867 in Kilmurry, Co. Kildare. His first established competitive appearance was in Co. Kildare where he won both the half-mile and the one mile open handicap at the Amateur Athletic Club sports competitions in Carbury in 1885. He dominated the Irish athletic scene of the time over various distances.

He emigrated to the United States in 1888 and in 1893 he broke the world amateur record for the one mile at Holmes Field, Cambridge, Massachusetts, at 4 minutes, 17 and 4.5 seconds. He later surpassed this in 1895 when he broke the world all-comers' record for the mile at 4 minutes, 15 and 3.5 seconds. His mile record remained intact for 16 years, until 1911.

His athletic career over, he joined the American army and fought in the Spanish-American War. He died of drowning near Manila in October 1912. At the time he was serving with the 7th United States Cavalry regiment. *Ulysses 12.181*

Connellan, Rev. Thomas (1854–1917) *Editor and evangelist*

'Mr Bloom turned at Gray's confectioner's window of unbought tarts and passed the reverend Thomas Connellan's bookstore. *Why I left the church of Rome.*' *(8.1069–71)*

The Rev. Thomas Connellan was born in Geevagh, Co. Sligo, in 1854. He described himself as 'editor and evangelist' and had a bookstore at 51b Dawson Street, which specialised in Protestant propaganda. Here he held a Connellan Mission with regular gospel meetings, Bible readings and classes. The Connellan Mission later moved to 108 St Stephen's Green.

Connellan regularly addressed meetings at various venues such as the Christian Union Building, Kingstown Congregational Church, the Ringsend Mission Hall and the Metropolitan Hall, Lower Abbey Street, where his 'Testimony Meetings' were 'assisted by several Converts from the Church of Rome'. He specialised in trying to convert Catholics to his own faith.

Connellan's residence in 1904 was at Elmgrove, Blackrock, Co. Dublin. He later lived at Stillorgan Park. He died in 1917 and was buried in Mount Jerome Cemetery, Harold's Cross, Dublin [B36–366–11645].

Conroy, Rev. Bernard Francis (1865–1940) *Curate, St Mary's Star of the Sea Church*
'Poor pa. That was Mr Dignam, my father. I hope he's in purgatory now because he went to confession to Father Conroy on Saturday night.' *(10.1172–4)*
Bernard Francis Conroy was born in Dublin and entered Holy Cross College, Clonliffe, Dublin, on 2 February 1878, after which he went to St Patrick's College Maynooth. He worked in Wicklow parish and in 1903 he was transferred to St Mary's Star of the Sea, on Leahy's Terrace in Sandymount where he was curate in 1904. Father Conroy lived at 5 Leahy's Terrace, Sandymount, a road alongside the church leading to Sandymount strand.

In 1917 he was curate in Dalkey, Co. Dublin, and in 1921 was promoted to parish priest at Barndarrig, Kilbride, Co. Wicklow, where he remained for the rest of his life.

He died on 18 April 1940 in Barndarrig, Kilbride, Co. Wicklow.   *Ulysses 15.1129*

Constable 57 C *Dublin Metropolitan Police*
Based on **John Broderick (b. 1870)** *Constable, Dublin Metropolitan Police*
'Constable 57 C, on his beat, stood to pass the time of day.' *(10.217)*
John Broderick was born in Monasterevin, Co. Kildare, on 20 October 1870. When he finished school he worked as a farmer. He joined the Dublin Metropolitan Police (DMP) on 22 April 1892. From 30 September 1893, he was attached to Division 'C'. His warrant number was 9737.

57 C was a white metal DMP divisional number worn by the DMP man. It was affixed to the high collar of the tunic. This indicated that he was attached to 'C' Division of the DMP, the headquarters of which was in Store Street north of the Liffey. It was called the Rotunda Division. DMP Barracks in the 'C' Division were Fitzgibbon Street, Ballybough, Clontarf and Summerhill.

In 1911, Broderick lived at 9 Hibernian Avenue, North Dock, with his 20-year-old wife Marion and his eight-month-old son Thomas Ignatius.

Broderick remained with Division 'C' until 1 January 1924 when he retired aged 54 with a pension of £165.13.4 per annum.   *Ulysses 10.218–20; 10.225–6*

Cooper Oakley, Mrs (1854–1914) *Theosophist*

'Mrs Cooper Oakley once glimpsed our very illustrious sister H. P. B.'s elemental.' *(9.70–1)*

Isabel Cooper, daughter of Henry Cooper, was born in India in 1854. Aged 23, she was immobilised by an accident for several years which allowed her time to read numerous books, including Helena Petrovna Blavatsky's *Isis Unveiled* and prompted her research into spiritualism.

In 1881 she entered Girton College, Cambridge, where she met A. J. Oakley and Dr Archibald Keightley and in 1884 they all joined the Theosophical Society. That same year Isabel Cooper and Oakley were married.

Mrs Cooper Oakley became a committed theosophist and close associate of Blavatsky. She travelled to India with her in 1884 and later took care of her when she was seriously ill.

In 1912 Mrs Cooper Oakley published some of her early articles in one volume, titled *The Comte de St Germain*. She published many books but this is perhaps the book for which she will be best remembered.

She died on 3 March 1914 in Budapest, Hungary.

Corbett, James J. (1866–1933) *American heavyweight boxer*

'But the best pucker for science was Jem Corbet before Fitzsimons knocked the stuffings out of him, dodging and all.' *(10.1147–9)*

James J. Corbett was born on 1 September 1866 in San Francisco. Known as 'Gentleman Jim Corbett', he was over six foot in height, handsome and college educated. As well as being a skilled boxer, he had an acting career and performed in various theatres.

On 7 September 1892 he knocked out John L. Sullivan in the twenty-first round and won the World Heavyweight Boxing Championship in New Orleans, Louisiana. He lost his title five years later to Bob Fitzsimmons on 17 March 1897 in Carson City, Nevada.

Corbett died on 18 February 1933 in Bayside, New York, and was buried in the Cypress Hills Cemetery in Brooklyn.

Corley, Patrick Michael *Grandfather of John Corley*

Could be based on **Michael Corley (1850–1916)** *Commercial traveller*

'His grandfather Patrick Michael Corley of New Ross had married the widow of a publican there ...' *(16.133–5)*

Joyce knew a Michael Corley who lived on the North Circular Road and met him on one of his trips to Dublin from Trieste when Corley wanted to borrow money from him. He reported that Corley was delighted to hear that he was in one of his stories ('Two Gallants' in *Dubliners*).

There is only one Michael Corley living in Dublin recorded in the *Census of*

Ireland, Dublin 1901 and *1911*. He was a commercial traveller born in Swinford, Co. Mayo, in 1850. In 1901 he was living at 15 Gardiner Place, Dublin, with his wife and six children and, by 1911, he was a widower living as a boarder at 1 Bride Road. He died at the South Dublin Union Workhouse on 1 January 1916 and was buried in Glasnevin Cemetery, Finglas Road, Dublin in the poor ground [XA 37.5. St Paul's].   *Ulysses 16.129–30; 16.132; 16.143; 16.160; 16.164; 16.174; 16.194; 16.197; 16.180*

Costello, Francis Xavier 'Punch' (1881–1948)   *Medical student*
'Hereupon Punch Costello dinged with his fist upon the board and would sing a bawdy catch *Staboo Stabella* ...' *(14.313–14)*
Francis Xavier Costello was born in Dublin, seventh son of Thomas J. Costello who lived at 25 Eccles Street. He was educated at Belvedere College, Dublin, and then studied at the Catholic University School of Medicine at Cecilia Street, Dublin where he qualified as a doctor in 1901. He was awarded the additional qualification of licentiate in midwifery of the Royal College of Surgeons in Ireland, and licentiate in midwifery of the Royal College of Physicians of Ireland, on 8 November 1904. In 1906, he lived at 27 Morehampton Road, Donnybrook, Dublin.

Costello worked as a medical officer in remote areas of the East. He moved around to different locations with the same company. In 1911, his address was c/o Messrs Jardine, Matheson & Co. Ltd, Hong Kong. By 1921, he was at the Eastern Extension Telegraph Company in Singapore and in 1931 he was with the same company in Cocos Island, located in the Pacific Ocean, 340 miles off the shore of Costa Rica, where he was based until 1941.

Costello returned to Ireland in 1942 and lived at 5 Northumberland Avenue, Dún Laoghaire, Co. Dublin. He died on 20 August 1948 and was buried in Glasnevin Cemetery, Finglas Road, Dublin [K 47 Curran Square].
Ulysses 14.193; 14.229; 14.324; 14.401; 14.416; 14.544; 14.806; 14.817; 14.841; 14.853; 14.1208; 15.1795; 15.2151; 15.2238

Courtenay, Colonel Arthur Henry (1852–1927)   *Barrister and soldier*
'There master Courtenay, sitting in his own chamber...' *(12.1115)*
Arthur Henry Courtenay, was born on 16 October 1852, the son of Thomas Lefroy Courtenay, and Jane Caroline (née Morris) of Grange, Co. Antrim, and of 14 Fitzwilliam Square, Dublin.

Educated at Trinity College Dublin, he was called to the Irish Bar and appointed master of the Common Pleas in 1883. He was master of the High Court of Justice in Ireland, King's Bench Division, in 1904.

He was colonel commanding the 3rd and 4th (Cameronians) Scottish Rifles in the South African War. He was subsequently on the headquarter's staff, York, and was attached to the Ministry of National Services.

In 1887 and 1909, Courtenay was high sheriff of Galway. He died on 19 May 1927 in Tunbridge Wells, Kent. He was buried in Lymington Cemetery.

Cousins, James H. (1873–1956) *One of Stephen's creditors*

'... Cousins, ten shillings...' *(2.257)*

Poet, playwright and teacher, James Henry Cousins was born on 22 July 1873 at

18 Cavour Street, Belfast. He was educated at the local national school and aged 12 became an office boy and then private secretary to Sir Daniel Dixon, lord mayor of Belfast.

His first collection of poetry, *Ben Madighan and Other Poems*, was published in 1894. He moved to Dublin where he began to write and associate with writers of the literary revival. He acted in minor parts for the newly formed Irish National Theatre Society. His plays included *The Sleep of the King* (1902), *The Racing Lug* (1902) and *The Sword of Dermot* (1903).

In 1903, Cousins married Margaret Gillespie who campaigned for women's rights throughout her life. They lived at 22 Dromard Terrace, Sandymount. From 1905, he was assistant headmaster at the Erasmus High School in Harcourt Street, Dublin, for eight years. Cousins and his wife moved to Liverpool in 1913 and then to India where he became literary editor for *New India*, published by theosophist Mrs Annie Besant.

Apart from visits to the United States, Europe and Japan, Cousins spent the rest of his life in India where he published numerous books on theosophy, art, education and philosophy. His *Collected Poems* was published in 1940. *We Two Together*, his autobiography written with his wife, was published in Madras in 1950.

Margaret died in March 1954 and Cousins on 20 February 1956 at the Mission Hospital, Madanapallee, a town located in the Chittoor district of Andhra Pradesh state, India.

Crampton, Sir Philip (1777–1858) *Surgeon*

'Sir Philip Crampton's memorial fountain bust. Who was he?' *(6.191)*

Philip Crampton was born on 7 June 1777 at 16 William Street, Dublin. He was the son of Dr John Crampton of 12 Gardiner Place, Dublin. He studied medicine at the Royal College of Surgeons and was appointed surgeon to the Meath Hospital.

In 1800, Crampton married Selina Cannon, the daughter of Patrick Hamilton Cannon, an officer of the 12th Dragoons. They lived at 14 Merrion Square and also had a country residence on Merrion Avenue, Blackrock, Co. Dublin.

Crampton opened one of the first private medical schools in the city behind his house in Dawson Street in 1804. He became surgeon to the Lock Hospital (which moved from Townsend Street to Donnybrook in 1792) before being appointed surgeon general to the forces in Ireland and surgeon in ordinary to King George IV and Queen Victoria. He was president of the Dublin College of Surgeons three times, and was created a baronet in 1839.

Crampton died on 10 June 1858 and was buried in Mount Jerome Cemetery, Harold's Cross, Dublin [Vault C87–2286].   *Ulysses 8.711*

Cranly *Stephen's companion and friend*

Based on **John Francis Byrne (1880–1960)** *Friend of James Joyce*

'Cranly, I his mute orderly, following battles from afar.' *(9.136)*

John Francis Byrne was born on 11 February 1880 in East Essex Street, Dublin. His father had been a farmer for most of his life in Co. Wicklow and had moved to Dublin to work in the dairy and general provisions business. He died before his son had reached his fourth birthday. Byrne was educated at the Holy Faith Convent in Clarendon Street and the Carmelite Seminary at 41 Lower Dominick Street, and on 3 September 1892 he entered Belvedere College. Four months later, his mother died and relatives subsequently took care of him.

Byrne was perhaps the closest friend that Joyce had. They first met when Joyce was 11 and had entered Belvedere College in 1893. Byrne matriculated early and went to University College in 1895. At the beginning of the academic year 1898–9 Joyce joined him. It was late in October 1898 that Joyce gave the name of 'Cranly' to Byrne. In 1903 Byrne lived at 100 Phibsborough Road while Joyce was nearby at 7 St Peter's Terrace.

Byrne's last fixed abode in Dublin was 7 Eccles Street where he lived from 1908 until April 1910 with his cousins, Mary and Cicely Fleming, and his dog, Boy. Joyce was a frequent visitor during the two trips he made to Dublin in 1909 and on occasion stayed overnight. Byrne emigrated to the US in February 1910. He lived at 70 Wilson Street, Brooklyn, New York.

Byrne's memoir, *Silent Years*, was published in 1953. He died in New York in 1960.
Ulysses 1.159; 2.307; 3.451; 9.21; 9.978

Crawford, Myles *Editor of the* Evening Telegraph

Partly based on **Patrick Meade (1858–1928)** *Subeditor and later editor of the* Evening Telegraph

'Myles Crawford began on the *Independent*. Funny the way those newspaper men veer about when they get wind of a new opening.' *(7.307–9)*

Myles Crawford, editor of the *Evening Telegraph*, is partly based on a well-known journalist Patrick Meade. Meade was born in November 1858 in Deer Park, Lismore, Co. Waterford son of John Meade and Honora (née Corbett) who had a grocery and public house on Main Street, Lismore.

Meade joined the staff of the *Cork Herald* as a young man and reported on many important events for the paper in the late 1870s and early 1880s. He covered the counties of Cork and Kerry when evictions were frequent. Meade moved to the *Freeman's Journal* around 1888 and represented the paper in the gallery of the House of Commons in the stormy days of Home Rule and land agitation. He later became editor of the Dublin *Evening Telegraph*. Described as a large, kind man with red hair, a red face and a short temper, he dressed flamboyantly and sported a flower in his buttonhole. From around 1890 to 1895, he lived at 16 Stamer Street, Dublin.

By 1901, Meade was a widower with two sons. He and his family boarded with his sister-in-law at 105 South Circular Road, Portobello. He later moved to 49 Sherrard Street Upper in Dublin where he and his sons had lodgings with the Conway family.

He died on 3 August 1928 at the residence of his sister Margaret Meade, Main Street, Lismore, Co. Waterford. He was buried in the family burial ground in Lismore Cemetery.

Ulysses; 7.380; 7.453; 7.457; 7.474; 7.480; 7.532; 7.539; 7.549; 7.585; 7.605; 7.627; 7.644; 7.649; 7.676; 7.684; 7.705; 7.773; 7.777; 7.797; 7.802; 7.956; 7.967; 7.981; 7.991; 7.1004; 7.1008; 7.1015; 7.1031; 7.1051; 7.1074; 15.806; 15.810; 15.1142

Crimmins, William C. (1863–1926) *Publican*

'How do you do, Mr Crimmins? ... I was afraid you might be up in your other establishment in Pimlico.' *(10.720–2)*

William C. Crimmins was born in Co. Limerick. He was a graduate of Trinity College Dublin. He was a tea, wine and spirit merchant at 27–28 James's Street, and had a house nearby at 61 Pimlico and later a residence, 'Sunnyside', in Dalkey, Co. Dublin.

Crimmins was a guardian of the district council of the South Dublin Union, the weekly meetings of which were held in the institution's boardroom in James's Street.

Married with a daughter, Crimmins died on 24 November 1926 at 'Sunnyside', Vico Road, Dalkey and was buried in Glasnevin Cemetery, Finglas Road, Dublin [CH 37 St Brigid's].

Crofton, J. T. A. (1838–1907) *Employee at the Collector-General's Office*

'... *Crofton out of the Collector-general's* ...' *(15.4350)*

James Thomas Ambrose Crofton was an associate of John Stanislaus Joyce in the Collector-General's Office in 1884.

Crofton lived outside Ireland between 1899 and 1907. Just two weeks after his return in August 1907, he suffered a chill that resulted in his death within a week.

Crofton, a justice for the peace, formerly of Rathgar, died on 22 August 1907 at Kingstown (now Dún Laoghaire), Co. Dublin. His son, the Rev. A. Paget Crofton, officiated at the funeral. He was buried in the family grave in Mount Jerome Cemetery, Harold's Cross, Dublin [C107–3523].

Ulysses 6.247; 12.1678; 12.1632; 12.1670; 12.1752; 12.1768; 15.1678

Crotthers, J. *Scottish medical student*
Based on **Robert Crothers (1879–1940)** *Medical Student*
'Mr J. Crotthers (Disc. Bacc.) attributes some of these demises to abdominal trauma ...' *(14.1256–7)*
J. Crotthers is modelled on a Dr Robert Crothers. The records and registers at the National Maternity Hospital, Holles Street, which listed intern and extern births, indicate that Robert J. Crothers, a medical student, worked at the hospital from 26 August to 12 September 1903. Joyce was in Dublin at the time that Crothers was working at the National Maternity Hospital. Early drafts show that Joyce knew his name was spelt Crothers and not Crotthers.

Robert Crothers was born in 1879 in Banbridge, Co. Down. He was educated at St Mungo's Academy in Glasgow and studied medicine at the University of Edinburgh, lodging at 25 South Clerk Street, Edinburgh. He returned to Banbridge and lived at Donard View House, where he had a medical practice.

Crothers went to Hastings in Sussex, where he practised for some years before moving to 139 Western Road, Brighton where he practised from 1920 to 1937. His last address was 107 King's Road, Brighton. Crothers died in 1940 at Hove, Sussex, England.   *Ulysses 14.192; 14.233; 14.887; 14.1204; 15.1792; 15.2238*

Crotty, Leslie (1853–1903) *Baritone*
'Who's that? Ned Lambert asked. Is that Crotty?' *(10.399)*
Leslie Crotty, son of the Rev. William Crotty was born in Galway. He was a well-known baritone singer with the Carl Rosa English Opera Company. The company, which first came to Dublin around 1872, produced many of the operas mentioned in *Ulysses*.

Crotty sang in Dublin during the company's Italian opera season, which had become an annual event extending over three to four weeks. In the Gaiety Theatre in December 1878, Crotty sang in *Il Trovatore*; Joseph Maas sang in *Maritana* with Georgina Burns playing the part of the heroine.

Ruy Blas by Filippo Marchetti was performed in 1886 with Crotty playing Don Sallust de Bazan. Crotty, based in Drury Lane, London, normally stayed with his brother William Haliday Crotty at 15 Sherrard Street Lower when in Dublin.

When the English opera season opened in the Gaiety on 18 August 1890, Crotty performed in *Maritana*, and *The Lily of Killarney* 'in a part in which he has had many triumphs, and his rendering of the principal baritone songs was very much appreciated'. For the 1891 Dublin season he performed in *Carmen*, *The Huguenots*, *The Talisman* and *The Bohemian Girl*.

In August 1892 Leslie Crotty and Madame Georgina Burns whom Crotty later married, left the Carl Rosa Opera Company to form their own light opera company with a number of well-known artistes.

The company toured and gave many performances throughout the United Kingdom. In Dublin they were known as the Burns-Crotty Concerts and performed at various venues such as the Rotunda and the Antient Concert Rooms.

In July 1894, a competition for the 'Leslie Crotty Prize', took place at the Royal Academy of Music in London. In the same year Crotty composed the music for a new song 'Star of Twilight' for Madame Georgina Burns.

Crotty eventually settled in Newcastle where he taught music for some years. He died on 18 April 1903 and was buried in Newcastle-on-Tyne.

Cuffe, Joseph (1841–1908) *Cattle dealer*

'... Mr Joseph Cuffe, a worthy salesmaster that drove his trade for live stock ...' *(14.570–1)*
The Cuffe family came originally from Co. Galway and were resident in Dublin since the early nineteenth century. Joseph Cuffe was born in 1841 in Mountjoy Square, Dublin and was one of eight children, son of Laurence Cuffe and Bedelia (née Byrne). His father was a cattle merchant in Smithfield, an area in Dublin used for horse fairs and where country traders brought their livestock to sell.

Joe joined as a partner in the family business with Laurence Cuffe & Sons, cattle, corn, and wool salesmen, at 5 Smithfield, near the cattle market on the North Circular Road, with offices nearby in Church Street. He married a Miss Moran and had a family of five children.

The Cuffes had farms at Ballymacarney, Co. Meath; Westbrook near Rathnew in Co. Wicklow; and land in Donabate and Swords in north Co. Dublin. Here animals from various parts of the country en route to Dublin would be rested and fattened for export. The custom at the time was to drive the cattle in herds on the hoof to Dublin. This journey was managed by drovers; the animals lost a lot of condition en route. In more recent times, cattle were transported to Dublin by rail.

Cuffe, who lived in Elgin Road, Ballsbridge, died on 12 February 1908 at 6 Lower Fitzgibbon Street. He was buried in Glasnevin Cemetery, Finglas Road, Dublin [Vault 58 O'Connell Circle].   *Ulysses 6.392; 12.105; 12.837; 15.1008; 15.4338; 17.485; 17.2139*

Cunningham, Martin *Employee at Dublin Castle*

Based on **Matthew F. Kane (1865–1904)** *Chief clerk of the Crown Solicitor's Office*
'It is not for us to judge, Martin Cunningham said.' *(6.342)*
The character of Martin Cunningham is based on Matthew F. Kane, chief clerk of the Crown Solicitor's Office in Dublin Castle who appears in *Ulysses* under his own name. Like Kane, Cunningham was also employed at Dublin Castle.

Joyce possibly derived the name from a well-known Dubliner named Stephen Cunningham (1861–1908). He wrote a weekly column about Dublin life and had friends in the newspaper business. He was onetime proprietor of the Ship Hotel in Lower Abbey Street. Cunningham was a neighbour of George Moore in Ely Place.

George Moore moved from London in 1901, to settle at 4 Upper Ely Place, Dublin. Shortly after his arrival, he fell out with his neighbours, one of whom was Stephen Cunningham who lived next door in 3.

Cunningham set up the the Gallaher Memorial Fund on 10 November 1893 to raise funds for the family of Joe Gallaher, the journalist who died on 19 October 1893. Cunningham hanged himself in his home at 3 Upper Ely Place, on 22 April 1908. He was buried in Glasnevin Cemetery, Finglas Road, Dublin [TC 56.5 Garden].

Ulysses 5.331; 6.1; 6.8; 6.34; 6.86; 6.95; 6.104; 6.109; 6.113; 6.133; 6.141; 6.146; 6.151; 6.188; 6.192; 6.219; 6.250; 6.259; 6.277; 6.282; 6.286; 6.289; 6.295; 6.305; 6.325; 6.334; 6.336; 6.339; 6.367; 6.369; 6.403; 6.415; 6.420; 6.456; 6.473; 6.491; 6.526; 6.529; 6.718; 6.735; 6.737; 6.1006; 6.1020; 6.1024; 7.165; 10.956; 10.959; 10.964; 10.967; 10.975; 10.978; 10.983; 10.987; 10.993; 10.999; 10.1014; 10.1023; 10.1029; 10.1032; 10.1038; 12.411; 12.761; 12.1587; 15.1140; 15.3854; 15.3857; 15.3859; 15.3862; 16.504; 16.1257; 17.1238; 18.1266

Cuprani/Caprani, Menotti (1866–1931) *Compositor/linotype operator*
'Double marriage of sisters celebrated. Two bridegrooms laughing heartily at each other. Cuprani too, printer. More Irish than the Irish.' *(7.98–100)*
Menotti Caprani was the eldest son of Giuseppe Fidel Caprani, who was born in Vercano, Domaso, Italy and Ann (née Bennett). Giuseppe and Ann met in London and married on 1 November 1863 in St Mary's Chapel, Moorfields, London. They lived at 13 Shoe Lane, Holborn, after their marriage.

Menotti Caprani, one of eight children, was born on 11 November 1866 at 28 Wilderness Lane, Salisbury Square, London. He was educated at the Central Model Boys' School in Marlborough Street, Dublin. As a boy he was interested in boxing and fought in matches in the Antient Concert Rooms in Great Brunswick Street (now Pearse Street).

Caprani worked as a compositor or linotype operator in the *Freeman's Journal* and was a member of the chapel (i.e. the printer's union) of the paper in the early 1900s. With the closure of the *Freeman's Journal* in 1924, he moved to the *Irish Independent* where he worked in the same capacity until his death.

Caprani lived on the north side of Dublin, in the North Strand and East Wall areas. At the time of his marriage he was living at 12 Annesley Place. Caprani and his brother married two sisters named O'Connor in a double wedding, which Bloom recalls.

Caprani married Margaret, daughter of John O'Connor, a silversmith from 1 East Road, on 8 August 1893 in St Laurence O'Toole's Church. They lived on Richmond Road, Merville Avenue, Fairview, and finally at 72 St Declan's Road, Marino.

Caprani died on 25 February 1931 at his home in St Declan's Road. He was buried in Glasnevin Cemetery, Finglas Road, Dublin [VH 128.5 St Brigid's].

Curran, Constantine P. (1883–1972) *Lawyer and author*

'Curran, ten guineas.' *(2.256)*

Constantine P. Curran was born on 30 January 1883 in Dublin to a nationalist family. His father Patrick worked as superintendent in the telegraph service in the GPO and his mother Mary (née McGahan) was a farmer's daughter from Co. Monaghan.

The family lived in Manor Street and later at 6 Cumberland Place near the Christian Brothers O'Connell School in North Richmond Street, where Curran had been educated. He was taught by Brother Swan whom he later described as 'soaked in old Dublin history and much sought after as a lecturer to Dublin clubs and literary societies'.

Curran won a gold medal in 1899 for English literature. The same year he entered University College, where he met and remained a lifelong friend of James Joyce. He graduated with a BA degree in 1902 and obtained his MA in 1906.

At this time Curran was living at 6 Cumberland Place, North Circular Road, and it was in the garden of this house in the summer of 1904 that he took the famous photograph of Joyce with his hands in his trouser pockets, sporting a yachting cap. Asked what he was thinking about when being photographed, Joyce replied, 'I was wondering would he lend me five shillings.' Curran appears as one of Stephen's debtors in *Ulysses*.

Curran was called to the Bar but never practised and worked instead in the Accountant General's Office in the Four Courts. From 1946 to 1952 he was registrar of the Supreme Court. He was a member of the Royal Dublin Society from 1927 and was elected its vice-president in 1971. He was elected as a member of the Royal Irish Academy in 1946 and was conferred with an honorary D. Litt by the National University of Ireland in 1949.

Curran's works include *The Rotunda Hospital: Its Architects and Craftsmen* (1945); *Dublin Decorative Plasterwork of the Seventeenth and Eighteenth Centuries* (1967); *Newman House and University Church* (1953); *James Joyce Remembered* (1968); and *Under the Receding Wave* (1970).

Curran died on 1 January 1972 at his home, 42 Garville Avenue, Rathgar, and was buried in Deansgrange Cemetery, Deansgrange, Co. Dublin [121–K–St Patrick].

Curran, John Philpot (1750–1817) *Lawyer, orator, politician and patriot*

'Who have you now like John Philpot Curran? Psha!' *(7.739–40)*

John Philpot Curran, son of James Curran and Sarah (née Philpot), was born in Newmarket, Co. Cork, on 24 July 1750. He was educated at Trinity College Dublin and called to the Bar in 1775. He was MP for Rathcormack, Co. Cork from 1783 to 1797, and again in 1800.

Curran appeared in all the 1798 trials for the leading United Irishmen including Napper Tandy, William Drennan and Wolfe Tone. He opposed the Act of Union and supported Catholic Emancipation.

Curran was appointed master of the rolls in 1807. He retired in 1814. His town house in Dublin was 4 Ely Place, between Merrion Row and Hume Street. He travelled frequently to London and it was on a visit here that he became ill and died, in Brompton, in October 1817. He was buried in one of the vaults in Paddington

Church. Twenty years later on a November day his remains were brought to Glasnevin Cemetery, Finglas Road, Dublin where he was buried by torchlight. He is commemorated by an eight-foot-high, classical sarcophagus, from the design of John Thomas Papworth, and modelled on the tomb of Scipio Barbatus in Rome. It bears the simple inscription: CURRAN [LMN 51–7 Curran's Square Section].

He is commemorated in St Patrick's Cathedral by a white marble bust executed by Christopher Moore in London in 1841.

Curran, Sarah (1782–1808) *Robert Emmet's fiancée*
'… the Tommy Moore touch about Sara Curran and she's far from the land.' *(12.500–1)*
Sarah Curran was born in Newmarket, Co. Cork, youngest daughter of John Philpot Curran. When she was eight, the family moved to 'The Priory' in Rathfarnham, Co. Dublin. Her parents separated when she was 12 and she was sent to be cared for by the Rev. Thomas Crawford, a friend of her father in Lismore, Co. Waterford.

Sarah met Robert Emmet when she was 18 and they became secretly engaged. When John Philpot Curran discovered Emmet's interest in his daughter, he discouraged his visits to the house.

After Emmet's execution, on 20 September 1803, Sarah sought refuge with friends named Penrose, in Cork. She married Captain Robert H. Sturgeon, a nephew of Lord Rockingham, in November 1805. They lived in Hythe, Kent in England. She never recovered from Emmet's execution and died of consumption on 5 May 1808. She was buried in the family vault in Newmarket, Co. Cork.

Cusack, Michael (1847–1906) *Co-founder of the Gaelic Athletic Association*
'Come around to Barney Kiernan's, says Joe. I want to see the citizen.' *(12.58)*
Michael Cusack, on whom the Citizen is based, was born on 20 September 1847 in Carron on the eastern edge of the Burren in north Clare, son of Matthew Cusack and Bridget (née Flannery). He attended the local national school and left Carron when he was 17.

Cusack became a teacher and taught at various schools including the District Model School in Enniscorthy, Co. Wexford; St Colman's College, Newry; Blackrock College, Dublin; St John's College, Kilkenny; and Clongowes Wood College, Sallins, Co. Kildare.

Cusack opened the successful Civil Service Academy in Gardiner Street, Dublin. Here students trained for entrance examinations to Trinity College Dublin, to law and medical schools, the constabulary, the army and the navy.

With Maurice Davin from Carrick-on-Suir, Cusack founded the Gaelic Athletic Association in Hayes' Commercial Hotel in Thurles, Co. Tipperary in November 1884. Maurice Davin was elected president. Present at the meeting was John Wyse Power, then editor of the *Leinster Leader*. Charles Stewart Parnell, Michael Davitt and Dr Thomas Croke became patrons.

Cusack also became involved in the Irish language movement, and was founder of a weekly newspaper, *The Celtic Times*, which was devoted to Irish culture, 'native games' and athletics.

Michael Cusack, also known as 'Citizen Cusack', died on 28 November 1906 and was buried in Glasnevin Cemetery, Finglas Road, Dublin, on the left-hand side on the perimeter of the old O'Connell Circle [DG 163.5 Garden].

Ulysses 12.63; 12.119; 12.130; 12.137; 12.143; 12.147; 12.218; 12.239; 12.264; 12.300; 12.377; 12.409; 12.426; 12.432; 12.479; 12.498; 12.519; 12.523; 12.679; 12.701; 12.818; 12.829; 12.831–2; 12.859; 12.883–6; 12.921; 12.949; 12.1015; 12.1052;; 12.1058; 12.1141; 12.1150; 12.1156; 12.1161–3; 12.1180; 12.1190; 12.1197; 12.1203; 12.1235; 12.1239; 12.1262; 12.1296; 12.1301; 12.1330; 12.1338; 12.1346; 12.1352; 12.1364; 12.1377; 12.1385; 12.1400; 12.1409; 12,1430; 12.1432; 12.1473; 12.1489; 12.1491; 12.1502; 12.1504; 12.1512; 12.1539; 12.1541; 12.1545; 12.1552; 12.1623; 12.1642; 12.1654; 12.1657; 12.1666; 12.1672; 12.1674; 12.1762; 12.1765; 12.1784; 12.1797; 12.1807; 12.1810; 12.1852; 12.1899; 14.22; 15.1616; 15.1932; 15.1949; 15.4339; 15.4523; 15.4620; 15.4622; 15.4840; 17.1019

D'Arcy, Bartell *Tenor*

Based on **Bartholomew M'Carthy (1840–1926)** *Tenor*

'Bartell d'Arcy was the tenor, just coming out then.' *(8.181)*

Bartholomew M'Carthy, son of Bartholomew M'Carthy of Prussia Street, was

a well-known tenor at St Mary's Pro-Cathedral, Marlborough Street, Dublin. He initially sang under the name Bartholomew M'Carthy, but after 1879 appeared as Bartle M'Carthy.

M'Carthy also worked as a hatter. He married Frances Molloy, a teacher, in 1886. They lived at 5 Thornville Avenue in Crumlin and later moved to Dolphin's Barn.

He sang in many concerts between 1871 and 1893 sharing the stage with performers such as Walter Bapty, Miss Dubedat, John Glynn the organist and

conductor, Benjamin Dollard and John Stanislaus Joyce. He joined the D'Oyly Carte Company on a trip to the United States and performed in *The Gondoliers* in New York in January 1890. He returned to Dublin and was principal tenor in the Pro-Cathedral, Marlborough Street.

M'Carthy died on 6 March 1926 at 44 Kenyon Street, Ashton-under-Lyne in Lancashire, and was buried nearby at Audenshaw Cemetery.

Ulysses 10.539; 15.4342; 18.273; 18.1295

Darling, Grace (1815–1842) *Victorian heroine*

'Wreckers. Grace Darling. People afraid of the dark.' *(13.1069–70)*

Grace Darling was born on 24 November 1815 at Bamburgh, Northumberland. She was with her father William Darling, a lighthouse keeper, in the Longstone Lighthouse on one of the Farne Islands on 7 September 1838 when the vessel *Forfarshire* foundered on rocks and split in two in stormy weather.

Grace rowed in heavy seas to the shipwreck with her father to rescue the survivors. Nine of the 63 people on board survived.

Grace Darling, who became legendary for her involvement with this sea rescue, died aged 26 on 20 October 1842. She was buried in St Aidan's churchyard, Bamburgh, on the coast of Northumbrland. Her memorial is sited in the churchyard so that it may be seen by passing ships and she is commemorated by the Grace Darling Museum, opposite St Aidan's Church.

Davis, Thomas Osborne (1814–45) *Founder of the* Nation, *poet and editor*

'... a remarkably noteworthy rendering of the immortal Thomas Osborne Davis' evergreen verses ...' *(12.915–16)*

Thomas Osborne Davis was born on 14 October 1814 in Mallow, Co. Cork, son of John Thomas Davis and Mary (née Atkins).

Davis graduated from Trinity College Dublin in 1836. He was called to the Bar in 1838 but never practised, preferring a career in literature and journalism.

With John Blake Dillon and Charles Gavan Duffy, in 1842, he founded the *Nation*, a weekly newspaper that became the organ of Young Ireland, the nationalist movement led by the three editors. The paper sowed the seeds of a revival of Irish literature, the precursor of the Irish Literary Revival that emerged in the late 1800s and early 1900s.

The *Nation* ceased publication in 1891 owing to changing political conditions. It had its offices on the site later occupied by the *Irish Independent* on Middle Abbey Street.

Davis wrote 50 ballads and songs including 'A Nation Once Again', 'The West's Awake' and 'Lament for Owen Roe O'Neill'.

Davis died on 16 September 1845 at 67 Lower Baggot Street, Dublin, and was buried in Mount Jerome Cemetery, Harold's Cross, Dublin [C5474–115].

Ulysses 'The Green above the Red', 15.4517; 'A Nation Once Again', 12.891

Davitt, Michael (1846–1906)

Founder of the Irish National Land League, politician and author

'... Michael Davitt against Isaac Butt ...' *(15.4684)*

Michael Davitt, son of Martin Davitt, and his wife Catherine, was born in Straide, Co. Mayo, on 25 March 1846. In 1851, the family was evicted due to arrears in rent and forced to emigrate to Lancashire, England.

Davitt joined the Fenians in 1865 and became organising secretary for England and Scotland. He was arrested and sentenced to 15 years in 1870 for buying arms. Released in 1878, he returned to Ireland and founded the Land League with

Parnell. In 1882 he was elected MP for Co. Meath; for North Meath in 1892, and for South Mayo in 1895–9. Like Parnell he saw the winning of the land war as a step to independence. With the revelations of the O'Shea divorce case, the fall of Parnell and the split in the Irish Parliamentary Party, the cause was set back for generations. Davitt withdrew from politics in 1899 and devoted his later life to travel and writing.

His publications include *The Prison Life of Michael Davitt* (1878); *Leaves from a Prison Diary* (2 vols, 1885); *The Defence of the Land League* (1891); *The Boer Fight for Freedom* (1902); *Within the Pale* (1903); and *The Fall of Feudalism in Ireland* (1904).

Davitt died in Dublin on 31 May 1906 and was buried in the grounds of Straide Abbey, Co. Mayo. The Michael Davitt Museum, Straide, Foxford, Co. Mayo commemorates him.

Dawson, Charles 'Dan' (1839–1917) *Baker, politician and lord mayor*

'Did you read Dan Dawson's speech? Martin Cunningham asked.' *(6.151)*

Charles 'Dan' Dawson was born in Limerick. He owned the Dublin Bread Company with business addresses in Dublin at 148 Great Britain Street and 27 Lower Stephen Street.

In 1881 he was elected to serve on the council of the Home Rule League and was an MP for Co. Carlow. He was lord mayor of Dublin in 1882 and 1883. During this period he was also the first president of the Catholic Commercial Club and secretary of the Irish Forestry Society. In 1904, he was comptroller of rates for Dublin Corporation.

Dawson lived at 19 Ardeevin Road, Dalkey, Co. Dublin, and later at 'Malabar', 52 Merrion Road, Dublin. Described as one of Dublin's merchant-politicians, Dawson died on 17 March 1917. He was buried in Glasnevin Cemetery, Finglas Road, Dublin [EA 5.5 South].   *Ulysses 7.276; 8.381–2; 10.538; 15. 435*

Deane, Sir Thomas (1792–1871) *Architect*

'Handsome building. Sir Thomas Deane designed.' *(8.1174)*

Sir Thomas Deane, son of Alexander Deane and Elizabeth (née Sharpe), was born on 4 June 1792 in Cork. He was 14 when his father, a builder and architect, died. His mother took over the family business and Thomas joined her.

Deane was mayor of Cork on three occasions (1815, 1830 and 1851) and was knighted in 1830. He designed a number of buildings in Cork including the commercial buildings, on South Mall, Queen's College, his residence at Dundanion Castle, in the Blackrock area of Cork and the Bank of Ireland.

In 1846 Benjamin Woodward joined the architectural practice and five years later this consisted of Deane, his son Thomas Newenham Deane, and Woodward. The partnership produced what is perhaps its best-known building, Oxford's University Museum (1854–60).

Deane went into semi-retirement and remained in Cork until 1860. The practice of Deane and Woodward continued until Woodward's death in May 1861, and then Deane's son, Thomas Newenham Deane, took it over.

Thomas Deane died on 2 October 1871 at his residence, 26 Longford Terrace, Monkstown, Co. Dublin, and was buried in St Michael's churchyard in Blackrock, Co. Cork.

Ulysses 8.1174; 8.1180–1

Deasy, Garrett *Headmaster of Private School*

Partly based on **Francis Irwin (b. 1859)** *Headmaster, Clifton School, Dalkey*

'I foresee, Mr Deasy said, that you will not remain here very long at this work.'
(2.401–2)

Francis Irwin, on whom the fictional Garrett Deasy is partly based, was an Ulster Scot. He attended Trinity College Dublin, though there is no record of his graduation. He was a mathematical and classical tutor and was the founder and headmaster of Clifton School, Summerfield Lodge on Dalkey Avenue, where Joyce taught for a few weeks in 1904.

A bachelor, Irwin was a member of the Church of Ireland and pro-British. He lived with an older widowed sister of private means, named Anna Jane Knox Gore, at 4 Derrynane Terrace, in Dalkey.

Ulysses 2.131; 2.135; 2.183; 2.186; 2.191; 2.206; 2.218; 2.225; 2.229; 2.236; 2.242; 2.249; 2.261; 2.265; 2.278; 2.282; 2.289; 2.305; 2.319; 2.321; 2.331; 2.338; 2.361; 2.374; 2.380; 2.385; 2.387; 2.405; 2.410; 2.415; 2.420; 2.424; 2.436; 2.442; 3.19; 7.520; 7.531; 15.2497; 15.3981; 15.3986; 16.158

Dedalus, Katey, Boody, Maggy and Dilly *Stephen's sisters*

Based on **sisters of Joyce**

James Joyce had six sisters, Margaret Alice, Eileen Isabella, Mary Kathleen, Eva Maria, Florence Elizabeth and Mabel Josephine. According to family sources, it seems likely that Boody was based on Joyce's sister Mary Kathleen, and Maggy was based on Margaret Alice (Poppie).

Margaret Alice, daughter of John Stanislaus Joyce and Mary Jane (née Murray), was born at 41 Brighton Square, Rathgar on 18 January 1884. Being the eldest daughter, she took over the running of the household at 19 when her mother died on 13 August 1903 at 7 St Peter's Terrace, Phibsborough. She left home, 44 Fontenoy Street, on 20 August 1905, to become a Sister of Mercy in New Zealand. Her name in religion was Sister Mary Gertrude. She died in New Zealand in March 1964.

Mary Kathleen Joyce, known as May, was born on 18 January 1890, at 1 Martello Terrace, Bray, Co. Wickow. She married Jack Monaghan in 1918 and lived in Oughterard, Co. Galway. She was widowed young and had a son Ken, and two daughters. She returned to live in Dublin where she died on 8 December 1966. She was buried in Mount Jerome Cemetery, Harold's Cross, Dublin [C140–36288]

Ulysses Katey: *10.233, 10.258; 10.270; 10.275; 10.279; 10.285; 16.274* Boody: *10.233; 10.258; 10.260; 10.262 10.266; 10.268; 10.273; 10.283; 10.286; 10.290; 10.293; 16.274* Maggy: *10.261; 10.272; 10.278; 10.280; 10.285; 10.289; 10.292; 10.872; 16.274* Dilly: *10.288; 10.645; 10.660; 10.666; 10.668; 10.671; 10.675; 10.680; 10.686; 10.696; 10.701; 10.705; 10.711; 10.863; 10.874; 10.1227; 15.4147; 15.4202; 16.270*

Dedalus, Mary (née Goulding) *Stephen's mother*

Based to a large extent on **Mary Jane Joyce (née Murray) (1859–1903)** *Joyce's mother*

'A statement explanatory of his absence on the occasion of the interment of Mrs Mary Dedalus (born Goulding), 26 June 1903 ...' *(17.951–2)*

Born in Dublin, Mary Jane Murray was the daughter of John Murray and Margaret Theresa (née Flynn), originally from Leitrim. One of four children, her father had a business as a tea and wine merchant at the Eagle House in Roundtown (now Terenure).

Mary Jane (known as May) studied music at the school run by her two aunts, the Misses Flynn, at 15 Usher's Island, Dublin. She met John Stanislaus Joyce when he joined the choir at the Church of the Three Patrons, Rathgar. They married on 5 May 1880 in the Church of Our Lady of Refuge, Rathmines, when she was 20 and her husband 31.

From her marriage until her death, Mary Jane lived at 17 different addresses. In the first 14 years of her marriage she had 16 or 17 pregnancies and bore six sons and six daughters. They included John Augustine (1880) who died a few days after birth, James Augustine (1882–1941), Margaret Alice (1884–1964), John Stanislaus (1884–1955), Charles Patrick (1886–1941), George Alfred (1887–1902), Eileen Isabella (1889–1963), Mary Kathleen (1890–1966), Eva Mary (1891–1957), Florence Elizabeth (1892–1973), Mabel Josephine (1893–1911) and Frederick William (1895), born dead.

She died aged 44 on 13 August 1903 and was buried in Glasnevin Cemetery, Finglas Road, Dublin. [FX 6.5–7 Dublin Section].

Ulysses 1.198; 1.204–5; 1.208; 1.218; 15.4157; 15.4172–4; 15.4181; 15.4187; 15.4195; 15.4201; 15.4211; 15.4231; 15.4237; 17.143

Dedalus, Simon *Stephen's father*

Based to a large extent on **John Stanislaus Joyce (1849–1931)** *Father of James Joyce*

'A gifted man, Mr Bloom said of Mr Dedalus senior, in more respects than one and a born *raconteur* if ever there was one.' *(16.260–1)*

John Stanislaus Joyce, only child of James Augustine Joyce and Ellen (née O'Connell), was born on 4 July 1849 in Cork. He attended St Colman's College in Fermoy. His father died on 28 October 1866 and John Stanislaus entered Queen's College Cork, where he attempted to study medicine but failed.

On his twenty-first birthday he received £1,000 and inherited properties in Cork. He moved to Dublin in 1874–5 and in 1877 invested money in the Dublin and Chapelizod Distillery, which went bankrupt in 1880. The same year, he took a position in the Office of the Collector of Rates for Dublin and met Mary Jane Murray. They married on 5 May 1880 and had ten surviving children. He was a heavy drinker who could not manage money with the result that he lost his job and his family descended rapidly into financial ruin.

John Stanislaus died on 29 December 1931 at Drumcondra Hospital, Whitworth Road, and was buried in Glasnevin Cemetery, Finglas Road, Dublin [FX 6.5–7 Dublin Section].

Ulysses 4.114; 6.6; 6.35; 6.41; 6.44; 6.48; 6.51; 6.63; 6.93; 6.101; 6.107; 6.136; 6.152; 6.156; 6.195; 6.198; 6.255; 6.268; 6.271; 6.274; 6.281; 6.291; 6.296; 6.303; 6.331; 6.341; 6.353; 6.371; 6.409; 6.412; 6.414; 6.419; 6.455; 6.457; 6.470; 6.492; 6.563; 6.567; 6.570; 6.573; 6.598; 6.641; 6.645; 6.650; 6.711; 7.47; 7.239; 7.250; 7.276; 7.288; 7.318; 7.329; 7.351; 7.354; 8.517; 10.667; 10.669; 10.672; 10.676; 10.681; 10.690; 10.694; 10.697; 10.702; 10.706; 10.713; 10.741; 10.883; 10.886; 10.889; 10.891; 10.897; 10.904; 10.907; 10.914; 10.924; 10.953; 10.1199; 10.1201; 11.192; 11.201; 11.216; 11.253; 11.255; 11.259; 11.271; 11.282; 11.440; 11.448; 11.459; 11.470; 11.476; 11.492; 11.496; 11.509; 11.536; 11.584; 11.600; 11.645; 11.657; 11.787; 11.800; 11.849; 11.992; 11.1146; 11.1160; 11.1204; 11.1219; 11.1272; 15.1141; 15.2654; 15.3538; 15.3942; 15.4925; 16.378; 16.1259; 17.138; 17.538; 17.1238; 17.2139; 17.2264; 18.1088; 18.1266; 18.1290

Dedalus, Stephen
Based to a large extent on **James Joyce (1882–1941)**

Although Stephen Dedalus is a fictional character, he is based to a considerable degree on the young James Joyce. Joyce's early life is related in *Stephen Hero* and *A Portrait of the Artist as a Young Man* at the end of which Stephen Dedalus leaves Ireland for the continent in high spirits 'to forge in the smithy of my soul the uncreated conscience of my race'. He is summoned back to Dublin by his father when his mother is dying. He appears again in the first episode of *Ulysses* defeated, disillusioned and resentful and still in mourning for his mother who died in August 1903.

Delany, Richard (1842–1912) *Timekeeper*
'The hoarse Dublin United Tramway Company's timekeeper bawled them off:
—Rathgar and Terenure!
—Come on, Sandymount Green!' *(7.4–7)*
Richard Delany, born in Queen's County, a well-known character in Dublin, was a timekeeper who worked for the Dublin United Tramway Company. Jacques M'Carthy in an article in *Sport* (1888) wrote, 'You just peep over and see if Delany, the commander-in-chief of the tram cars is gone, for he appears to me to never leave the place, and is there shouting, "Go on, Rathmines!" night, noon and morning the whole year round.'

Delany lived at 63 Connaught Street, Phibsborough. He died on 10 May 1912 and was buried in Glasnevin Cemetery, Finglas Road, Dublin [QD 63 Garden].

Delany, Fr William, SJ (1835–1924) *President, University College Dublin*
'Amongst the clergy present were the very rev. William Delany, S. J., L. L. D.;' *(12.927–8)*
William Delany, son of John Delany and Mary (née Brennan), was born on 4 June 1835 in Leighlin Bridge, Co. Carlow.

In 1856 Delany joined the Society of Jesus. He took his first vows at Clongowes Wood College, Sallins, Co. Kildare in 1858 and two years later was transferred to St Stanislaus College, Tullabeg, near Tullamore in Co. Offaly where he was made rector in 1870.

Apart from three years that he spent in Rome, Father Delany remained at Tullabeg for the next 20 years. He was rector of University College Dublin from 1883 to 1909 and subsequently president. He lived at 86 St Stephen's Green. He

was involved in the initial work leading to the foundation of the Royal University and is credited with being chiefly responsible for the emergence of the National University in 1908.

From 1909 to 1912, Father Delany was provincial of the Jesuit order in Ireland. He died on 17 February 1924 at the Jesuit house, 35 Lower Leeson Street. He was buried in Glasnevin Cemetery, Finglas Road, Dublin in the Jesuit Plot where his name is inscribed 'Gulielmus Delany obit 17/2/1924' on the Jesuit memorial at the grave [AH–GH 30–40.5].

Dennany, Thomas H. (c. 1840–1910) *Monumental sculptor*
'The stonecutter's yard on the right ... Fragments of shapes, hewn ... The best obtainable. Thos. H. Dennany, monumental builder and sculptor.' *(6.459–62)*
Thomas H. Dennany, son of James Dennany and Kate (née Hammond), was born in Drogheda c. 1840. By 1867 he was working as a stonecutter in Prospect Avenue. All funerals to Glasnevin passed up Prospect Avenue to avoid the tax on carriages as there were toll gates at the junction of the roads leading to the villages of Glasnevin and Finglas. The Stone and Marble Works continued under the Dennany name until 1910.

Dennany was responsible for a number of monuments in Glasnevin Cemetery including the O'Connell crypt.

He died on 22 June 1910 at his home, Marble Works, Prospect House, Prospect Avenue, Glasnevin. He was buried in Glasnevin Cemetery, Finglas Road, Dublin, in an unmarked grave [HC 73 Garden].

Devan, Harry *Son of Tom Devin*
Based on **Thomas (1889–1919)** or **William Devin (1892–1952)** *Sons of Tom Devin*
'[Milly is] well on for flirting too with Tom Devans two sons imitating me whistling

with those romps of Murray girls calling for her can Milly come out please shes in great demand to pick what they can out of her round in Nelson street riding Harry Devans bicycle at night ...' *(18.1023-7)*

Harry Devin is based on either of Tom Devin's two sons, Thomas Valentine or William Augustine.

Devan/Devin, Tom (1865-1937) *Dublin Corporation official*

'From its sluice in Wood quay wall under Tom Devan's office Poddle river hung out in fealty a tongue of liquid sewage.' *(10.1196-7)*

Tom Devin was born in Dublin. He worked on the clerical staff of Dublin Corporation for almost 50 years. On account of some disagreement with the town clerk he was banished from the City Hall to the City Cleansing Department at 15-16 Wood Quay. It is with this office that his name is connected in *Ulysses*, albeit spelled 'Devan'. The department was the centre of controversy on account of repeated delays in the construction of a centralised sewage system for Dublin.

Devin married Emily (née Byrne) from Kingstown (now Dún Laoghaire) in February 1888. She occasionally sang with the Moody Manners Opera Company under the name Madame de Vere. They had two sons, Thomas born in 1889 and William born in 1892. In 1901 they lived at 100 North Strand Road and in 1911 at 40 Rathgar Avenue. They later moved to 26 Upper Beechwood Avenue, Ranelagh. Emily died in 1920.

Devin was on the same ship from the North Wall that Joyce and Nora took on 8 October 1904 when they eloped to the continent.

For many years Devin was a member of the Dolphin Rowing Club. Following his retirement he was associated with the Knights of St Columbanus.

Devin died on 28 February 1937 at 26 Upper Beechwood Avenue, Ranelagh. His second wife, Mrs T. Devin, and two sons, who were well known in Dublin business, musical and sporting circles, survived him. He was buried in Glasnevin Cemetery, Finglas Road, Dublin [MC 22.5 South].

Dick, Doctor *Doctored Dublin pantomimes*

Pseudonym for journalist, based on **Denis James Downing** (1871-1909) *Journalist and amateur entertainer*

'... following the precedent of Philip Beaufoy or Doctor Dick ...' *(17.649-50)*

Denis James Downing was born in Fermoy, Co. Cork. He started his career as a journalist in Cork before moving to Dublin, where he was on the staff of the *Freeman's Journal* for many years. He then joined the *Irish Independent* as a sporting correspondent.

Under the pen name 'Doctor Dick', he contributed to the sport pages of the *Irish Independent*. He was a good musician and was responsible for the local themes included in several of the Dublin pantomimes. Downing wrote the 'local verses and references' of the pantomime *Robinson Crusoe*, performed at the

Theatre Royal in 1899, and for *Jack and the Beanstalk*, staged during the Christmas season, 1902–3.

In 1904 Downing lived at 3 Leinster Square, Rathmines. He died on 17 June 1909 and was buried in Glasnevin Cemetery, Finglas Road, Dublin [KB 275 South].

Dickinson, Mrs Emily (née Parnell) (1841–1918) *Sister of Charles Stewart Parnell*
'Mad Fanny and his other sister Mrs Dickinson driving about with scarlet harness.' *(8.513–14)*
A sister of Charles Stewart Parnell, Emily was born at Avondale, Rathdrum, Co. Wicklow. Her brother John Howard Parnell described her as a great pianist and dancer and favourite of her father. Her father objected to her proposed marriage to Captain Arthur Monroe Dickinson and disinherited her. She did marry Captain Dickinson in 1864 and some years after his death, married Captain Cuthbert S. Bengough Ricketts. She wrote a biography of Parnell, titled *A Patriot's Mistake* (1905). She died in the infirmary of the South Dublin Union Workhouse on 18 May 1918.

Dillon, Mathew (1821–1899) *Friend of the Joyce family*
'The first in the lilacgarden of Matthew Dillon's house, Medina Villa, Kimmage road, Roundtown, in 1887 ...' *(17.467–8)*
Mathew Dillon was an old friend of the Joyce family. They were neighbours for a time when the Joyces lived at 41 Brighton Square, Rathgar, 1882–4.

Mat Dillon married Sarah (née Beaumont) in the late 1850s. Their son Arthur Mathew was born in 1861 and their daughter Beatrice (Attie) in 1862. The Dillons lived at 13 Belgrave Road, Rathmines, 1865–6. Another son, William, was born on 1 October 1865 but did not survive long.

On 16 April 1866, a notice in the *Freeman's Journal* stated that Brighton House in the Barony of Rathdown was for sale. This is a large, double-fronted, red-brick house opposite the Rathgar Methodist Church. Mat Dillon bought it and moved to it with his family, which comprised his wife Sarah, son Arthur Mathew, and his bevy of daughters, Tiny, Attie, Floey, Maimie, Louy, Hetty, Sara and Nannie. He lived in it for over 28 years (1866–94) entertaining his relatives and political friends, and using his spacious well-stocked garden to play bowls.

Dillon, who worked as a representative for various firms, had an office in 10 St Andrew Street, Dublin, from 1870 to 1889. He then worked from home for a period, before moving to 61 South William Street. He was associated with the Commercial Travellers' Association in Dublin and contributed to various charities, such as the Catholic Institution for the Deaf and Dumb. The *Freeman's Journal* and *Irish Times* of 17 August 1870 noted that 'Mrs Dillon, Brighton House, Rathgar' donated parcels of linen for the wounded soldiers of the French army. She died aged 39 on 29 January 1874.

When the Joyce family lived at 1 Martello Terrace, Bray, Co. Wicklow (May

1887–91), they attended a party in Dillon's house in Roundtown (now Terenure). This is the house where the (fictitious) party in *Ulysses* took place in May 1887 and where Molly first met Leopold Bloom. Molly's father, Major Brian Cooper Tweedy, was a friend of Mat Dillon.

Dillon's house is marked by a plaque at 11 Brighton Road, Rathgar:

James Joyce's

Ulysses

'Mat Dillon'

Lived here.

Dillon spent his last years living with his daughter, Beatrice (Attie), who had a boarding house at 22 St Lawrence's Road, Clontarf. He died in 1899 and was buried in Glasnevin Cemetery, Finglas Road, Dublin, with his wife Sarah, son Arthur (d. 1912) and two of his daughters, Beatrice (d. 1916) and Florence (d. 1919) [GC 45 South].

Ulysses 6.697; 13.1091; 13.1107; 15.3162; 17.57; 17.1336; 17.2136; 18.1327

Dillon, Valentine Blake (1847–1904) *Lord mayor of Dublin and solicitor*

'Lord mayor had his eye on her too. Val Dillon. Apoplectic.' *(13.892–3)*

Lord mayor of Dublin 1894–5, Alderman Valentine Blake Dillon of the Rotunda Ward, was a solicitor with offices at 7 Rutland Square East (now Parnell Square) and 12 Andrew Street.

One-time solicitor and advisor to Parnell, Dillon had been election agent for a number of the Liberal candidates in the 1890s. He was the Parnellite nominee to succeed Peter McDonald as the representative for North Sligo in April 1891 but was unsuccessful against the McCarthyite candidate, Alderman Bernard Collery.

Dillon served on the board of the Richmond Asylum, the South City Markets, the National Telephone Company and was associated with the Catholic Commercial Club for ten years.

He died on 31 March 1904 at his home in Leeson Park and was buried in Glasnevin Cemetery, Finglas Road, Dublin [MD 67 Dublin New Chapel].

Ulysses 8.159; 10.538; 15.1008; 15.4337; 17.2136; 18.428–9

Dinneen, Fr Patrick (1860–1934) *Lexicographer and editor*

'Mr Lyster! Father Dineen wants ...

O, Father Dineen! Directly.' *(9.967–8)*

Patrick Dinneen was born at Carn, Rathmore, Co. Kerry, on 26 December 1860.

Aged 20 Dinneen entered the Society of Jesus at Milltown Park, Dublin. He attended University College Dublin in 1883 when it was run by the Jesuits and continued his Latin studies with Gerard Manley Hopkins as his lecturer. He was ordained priest in 1894 and taught in the Jesuit schools of Mungret, Co. Limerick, and Clongowes Wood College, Sallins, Co. Kildare.

With the consent of his superiors, Dinneen left the Society of Jesus in 1900 to devote his time to Irish studies and scholarship and earned his living solely by writing in Irish. He joined the Gaelic League, became a friend of Patrick Pearse and wrote fiction and drama in Irish. He edited and produced editions of the works of the Irish poets Aodhagán Ó Rathaille (1900), Eoghan Ruadh Ó Súilleabháin (1901), Seán Mac Domhnaill (1902), Séafradh Ó Donnchadha (1902), Piaras Feiritéir (1903) and Tadhg Gaelach Ó Súilleabháin (1903), and also of Geoffrey Keating's *Foras Feasa ar Éirinn* (1908–14). He is perhaps best remembered for his *Foclóir Gaedhilge agus Béarla: An Irish English Dictionary* (1904; enlarged editions, 1927, 1934). Dinneen died on 29 September 1934 in Dublin and was buried in Glasnevin Cemetery, Finglas Road, Dublin. His grave is marked with a Celtic cross [CH 83.5 St Brigid's].

Dixon, Joseph Francis (b. 1870) *Medical student*
'Still I got to know that young Dixon who dressed that sting for me in the Mater and now he's in Holles street where Mrs Purefoy.' *(8.429–431)*
Joseph Francis Dixon was born in Dublin on 13 August 1870, son of Joseph Dixon and Henrietta (née Richardson). In 1904, his address was 12 Conyngham Road, Dublin, south of Phoenix Park.

Dixon studied medicine at Trinity College Dublin and was conferred with an MD in December 1904. In 1911, Dr Dixon was a senior medical officer at the Three Counties Asylum, near Hitchen in Hertfordshire, England.

Ulysses 14.125; 14.189; 14.229; 14.259; 14.334; 14.355; 14.469; 14.505; 14.582; 14.589; 14.614; 14.623; 14.665; 14.703; 14.726; 14.801; 14.1400; 15.1797; 15.2238

Dlugacz, Moses (1884–1943) *Jewish pork butcher*
'Better a pork kidney at Dlugacz's.' *(4.45–6)*
Dlugacz was an ardent Zionist and adopted Dubliner. He is the only shopkeeper mentioned in *Ulysses* whose name is not listed in *Thom's Directory*. His name was transposed from Trieste to Dublin.

Dlugacz was a pupil of Joyce in Trieste, studying English with him from 1912 until the start of the First World War. Dlugacz gave courses in Hebrew and it is likely that Joyce learnt some Hebrew from him, such as the Zionist national anthem, part of which Bloom chants to Stephen in the 'Ithaca' episode.

Dlugacz worked as chief cashier in the office of the Cunard Line in Trieste. He organised special rates to help poor Jews travel on ships to the United States. With the onset of the war this office closed and he then worked in a small store in the Via Torrebianca, which supplied provisions to the Austrian army then fighting on the Austro-Italian front along the Isonzo river near Trieste.

Dodd, Reuben J. (1847–1931) *Legal accountant and moneylender*
'The devil on moneylenders. Gave Reuben J a great strawcalling. Now he's what they call a dirty jew.' *(8.1158–9)*

Reuben J. Dodd was born in Dublin. A moneylender, legal accountant and agent for the Patriotic Assurance Company and Mutual Assurance Company of New York, he had an office at 34 Ormond Quay Upper. He married Bridget Frances (née McEvoy) in 1876. In 1904, Dodd, a Catholic, was living at 90 South Circular Road, Portobello close to Dublin's Jewish quarter. He later moved to 65 Pembroke Road, Dublin with his wife, son Reuben J. Dodd junior, and two of his daughters.

Reuben Dodd died on 24 February 1931 and was buried in Glasnevin Cemetery, Finglas Road, Dublin [ZB 68 South].

Ulysses 6.264–5; 6.278; 6.286; 8.52; 10.892; 10.1193; 11.438–9; 11.1180; 12.1100; 15.1262; 15.1918; 15.1921; 15.2145

Dodd, Reuben J. junior (1879–1957) *Solicitor*
'Reuben J's son must have swallowed a good bellyful of that sewage.' *(8.52–3)*
Reuben J. Dodd, son of Reuben J. Dodd and Bridget Frances (née McEvoy) was born in Dublin. He was educated at Belvedere College, Dublin where he was a schoolmate of James Joyce, and later at Trinity College Dublin where he graduated with a BA degree in 1901.

Dodd served his apprenticeship with Peter J. McCann, 5 College Green, Dublin, and was admitted to the roll of solicitors in 1901. Dodd practised at various addresses in Dublin including 34 Upper Ormond Quay in 1904. His final work address was 5 Gardiner Place and his last residence was 65 Pembroke Road, Ballsbridge, Dublin. He died on 3 October 1957 and was buried in Glasnevin Cemetery, Finglas Road, Dublin [ZB 69.5 South].

Doherty, Rev. William (1872–1923) *Priest at St Mary's Pro-Cathedral*
William Doherty was born in Dublin. In 1904, the Rev. William Joseph Doherty was curate-in-charge at St Mary's Pro-Cathedral in Marlborough Street, Dublin, where he remained until 1917. He lived at 82 Marlborough Street. In 1917, he was transferred to St Paul's, Arran Quay, where he spent the rest of his life. The Rev. William J. Doherty, 38 Arran Quay, died on 4 February 1923 and was buried in Glasnevin Cemetery, Finglas Road, Dublin [WF 59.5 Section 4].　　*Ulysses 12.933*

Dolan, Father *Prefect of studies at Clongowes Wood College*
Based on **Father James Daly, SJ** (1847–1930) *Prefect of studies at Clongowes Wood College*
'*(Twice loudly a pandybat cracks, the coffin of the pianola flies open, the bald little round jack-in-the-box head of Father Dolan springs up.)*' *(15.3667–8)*
James Daly was born in Galway on 21 February 1847. He was educated at Tullabeg, Co. Offaly, and at the Jesuit College in Namur, Belgium. He entered the Society of Jesus at Milltown Park, Dublin, on 4 November 1864.

After his Jesuit training at Milltown, Roehampton, Stonyhurst and St Beuno's in Wales, he was ordained priest in 1878. He taught at Belvedere College for four years and was then prefect of studies at the Jesuit College in Limerick.

Father Daly was moved as prefect of studies to Clongowes Wood College, Sallins, Co. Kildare in 1887 aged 41 and his impact was immediate. The pupils' outings to Punchestown races were cancelled as they interfered with study time. Father Daly was prefect of studies during Joyce's time at Clongowes Wood College, from September 1888 until December 1892.

A strict disciplinarian, Father Daly was always on the move from one class to another making speeches to the pupils. If there was a slacker present in the class he was reproached for his idleness and told how it endangered the bright future that lay before him. All this was punctuated by loud-resounding strokes of the pandy-pat, not administered one after another quickly, but at regular intervals.

Father Daly's health began to fail in 1917 and he was moved to Galway to see if the bracing air would improve his health. He spent the last years of his life under the care of the Alexian Brothers at Twyford Abbey, near London.

Father Daly died on 27 January 1930 and was buried at St Mary's Catholic Cemetery, Harrow Road, Kensal Green, London [Jesuit Plot 24 NE].   *Ulysses 7.618*

Dollard, Ben *Singer and friend of Simon Dedalus*
Based on **Christopher Dollard** (1839–85) *Bass singer*
'... Ben Dollard base barreltone ...' *(18.1285)*
John Stanislaus Joyce had a friend named Christopher Dollard, a well-known amateur bass singer in the 1880s. It is likely that Ben Dollard was based on Christopher Dollard.

Christopher Dollard was the youngest son of James Dollard, of Foxhall, Raheny, Co. Dublin. John Stanislaus Joyce and Dollard occasionally shared the same platform at concerts and Dollard's rich bass voice received much praise in the press from 1863.

At the annual meeting of friends of the Irish Academy of Music held at 36 Westland Row in December 1870, Dollard was nominated among others for the Council of the Academy. He married Lilly Kennedy, a solicitor's daughter, from Kingstown (now Dún Laoghaire) on 3 June 1871.

Two 'Grand Concerts' were held in Dublin's Antient Concert Rooms on 27 and 28 April 1880, under the patronage of Edward Dwyer Gray, MP, lord mayor of Dublin and owner of the *Freeman's Journal*. The concerts raised funds for an orphanage that looked after 170 children. The conductor was Professor W. G. Goodwin, and the artistes included Mr J. S. Joyce and Mr Christopher Dollard, and other well-known amateur singers of the 1880s.

On the Feast of the Epiphany, 6 January 1884, Archbishop Patrick John Ryan of

Philadelphia celebrated high mass at St Mary's Star of the Sea Church in Sandymount. Joseph Zangl composed the music and Christopher Dollard was a second bass member of the choir. Dollard died on 14 May 1885 at 27 Upper Temple Street and was buried in Glasnevin Cemetery, Finglas Road, Dublin [D 35 O'Connell Circle].

Ulysses 8.117; 8.839; 10.539; 10.791; 10.893; 10.906; 10.911; 10.916; 10.921; 10.925; 10.932; 10.940; 10.945; 10.950; 11.435; 11.442; 11.449–51; 11.472; 11.481; 11.528; 11.538; 11.586; 11.652; 11.758; 11.772; 11.800; 11.997; 11.1074; 11.1139; 11.1151; 11.1154; 11.1157; 11.1163; 11.1168–9; 11.1173–6; 11.1178; 11.1214; 11.1272; 15.1664; 15.1668; 15.2604; 15.2608; 15.2617; 15.4342; 17.2138

Dolmetsch, Arnold (1858–1940) *Musician*

'... an instrument he was contemplating purchasing from Mr Arnold Dolmetsch ...'
(16.1764–5)

Arnold Dolmetsch was born on 24 February 1858 in Le Mans, France. He learned his skills as an instrument-maker in the family business. He studied music at the Conservatoire in Brussels and later at the Royal College of Music in London.

In 1893 Dolmetsch reproduced a particular lute and made clavichords and harpsichords for a company in Boston. He set up a workshop in Haslemere, Surrey where he made copies of every kind of musical instrument from the fifteenth to the eighteenth centuries.

On 16 June 1904, Joyce wrote to the London Academy of Music to request Dolmetsch's address to purchase a lute from him but the latter did not have one available at the time. Joyce wanted the instrument for a concert tour he had planned from Falmouth to Margate in which he would mainly sing old English songs.

Dolmetsch was created a chevalier of the Légion d'Honneur by the French government. He died on 28 February 1940 in Surrey.   *Ulysses 15.2508–9*

Dowden, Edward (1843–1913) *Professor of English*

'William Shakespeare and company, limited. The people's William.
For terms apply: E. Dowden, Highfield house ...' *(9.729–30)*

Edward Dowden was born in Cork on 3 May 1843, son of John Wheeler Dowden, a landowner and linen merchant, and his wife Alicia (née Bennett).

Dowden was educated at Queen's College Cork, and Trinity College Dublin, where he graduated in 1863. He taught at Alexandra College, Earlsfort Terrace, Dublin, resigning in 1867 when he was appointed to the newly founded chair of English literature at Trinity. He remained professor of English literature there until his death.

A noted Shakespearean scholar, Dowden made his name as a critic and his most influential work was *Shakespeare: A Critical Study of His Mind and Art* (1875). *Shakespeare*, a primer, was published two years later. His *Life of Shelley* (1886) became a standard work. He also wrote short biographies of Montaigne, Browning and Southey.

A strong opponent of Home Rule, Dowden made it clear that he had no wish to be classed as an Irish writer. His lack of understanding of Anglo-Irish literature made him unpopular with some, including W. B. Yeats.

During the 1870s he lived at 50 Wellington Road, Ballsbridge. He died on 4 April 1913 at his home, 'Rochdale', 11 Orwell Road, Rathgar, and was buried in Mount Jerome Cemetery, Harold's Cross, Dublin [C5–14017].

Ulysses 9.727; Shakespeare: A Critical Study of His Mind and Art, 9.1072–3; The Sonnets of William Shakespeare, 9.732–3; 14.359–60

Dowie, John Alexander (1847–1907) *Evangelist*
'Elijah is coming. Dr John Alexander Dowie restorer of the church in Zion is coming.' *(8.13–14)*
John Alexander Dowie, son of John Murray Dowie, was born on 25 May 1847 in Edinburgh. His family moved to Australia when he was 13. He worked in a grocery shop for eight years before studying theology in Edinburgh. Returning to Australia

as an evangelist and faith healer, he became the congregational minister in 1870 near Adelaide.

By the 1880s, Dowie had attracted many followers and in 1888 moved to the United States where in 1896 he founded the Christian Catholic and Apostolic Church in Chicago and the City of Zion in 1901. Dowie announced that he was 'Elijah the Restorer' and 'First Apostle of the Christian Catholic and Apostolic Church in Zion'. He conducted an 'Around the World' campaign, preaching in many countries and cities of the world and was in Europe 11–18 June 1904. He was not in Dublin on 16 June nor was he scheduled to be there.

In 1906 the inhabitants of Zion City accused him of misuse of funds and 'polygamous teaching, and other grave offences'. Dowie died in the City of Zion, Illinois, on 9 March 1907.   *Ulysses 14.1584; 15.1752; 15.2205; 17.791*

Doyle, Henny (*fl.* 1860s–1900s) *Friend of the Blooms*
'... not like that other fool Henny Doyle he was always breaking or tearing something in the charades ...' *(18.322–3)*
Henny Doyle was related to Luke and Caroline Doyle. Like them, he was a friend of the Blooms from their courtship days. No biographical information has been forthcoming so far on Doyle.   *Ulysses 13.1112*

Doyle, J. C. (1866–1939) *Baritone*

'*Là ci darem* with J. C. Doyle, she said, and *Love's Old Sweet Song*.' *(4.314)*

John C. Doyle was born in Dublin to a musical family. A baritone, he won the Feis Ceoil in 1899. As a young man he formed The Bohemian Quartet with his brother. He was regarded as a top vocalist and performer among the Irish musicians in the early twentieth century and sang at concerts, soirées and salons in Dublin and other parts of the country, and also performed in England and Scotland. With his fine voice and his matinée-idol good looks, Pathé described him as 'the darling of the Irish concert platform'.

Doyle shared the stage with Joyce and John McCormack for the 'Grand Concert' held in the Antient Concert Rooms in Great Brunswick Street (now Pearse Street) on 27 August in 1904, the last night of Horse Show week. He sang 'Stars above' and 'The Ould Plaid Shawl'. The *Freeman's Journal* reported that 'Mr. J. C. Doyle sang a number of songs in first-rate style'.

Doyle worked his entire life in the civil service in the Telegraphs Office, in the General Post Office in Dublin. By 1911 he was the assistant superintendent. He

was not a full-time professional singer as he had a wife, Elizabeth Mary, and eight children, and could not risk the financial insecurity of a musical career.

Doyle was a great friend and early promoter of John McCormack, who was 18 years his junior. In 1905, Doyle was living at 46 Arranmore Terrace, North Circular Road, and by November the same year he had moved to 'Glendhu', 11 Lindsay Road in Glasnevin.

He died at his home in Lindsay Road, on 14 October 1939 and was buried in Glasnevin Cemetery, Finglas Road, Dublin [HH 51.5 St Brigid's].   *Ulysses 6.222*

Doyle, Luke (1827–85) *Building surveyor*

'In Luke Doyle's long ago. Dolphin's Barn, the charades. U. p: up.' *(8.274)*

Luke Doyle lived at 4 Londonbridge Road, Irishtown from 1856 until 1867 before moving to 8 Camac Place, Dolphin's Barn, Dublin where he lived with his wife Caroline Mary. By 1883 they had moved to a larger residence Mount Brown House, 4 Mount Brown, Kilmainham, Dublin.

Doyle began his career as a carpenter and builder, and later became a loss adjuster, working with insurance companies in the business area of Dame Street. From 1850 until 1855 he had an office at 8 Anglesea Street and then moved to 9 Temple Bar in 1856 where he remained until his death.

A close friend of John Stanislaus Joyce, Doyle died on 27 August 1885 at Mount Brown House and was buried in Goldenbridge Cemetery, Dublin [GG 2² Canal Section].   *Ulysses 13.1106; 17.1261; 17.1338; 17.1347*

Drumont, Edouard Adolophe (1844–1917) *French journalist*
'M. Drumont, famous journalist, Drumont, know what he called queen Victoria? Old hag with the yellow teeth. *Vieille ogresse* with the *dents jaunes*.' *(3.230–3)*
Edouard Adolphe Drumont was born in Paris on 3 May 1844. A French editor and journalist, he was noted for his anti-Semitic ideas. His book *La France Juive*, which attacked the role of the Jews in France, was published in 1886. Six years later, he founded the newspaper *La Libre Parole* that he used to further promote his anti-Semitic views. During the Dreyfus Affair he was one of most strident of Alfred Dreyfus' accusers.   *Ulysses 3.493; 15.4501*

Dubedat, Miss (b. 1860) *Soprano and music teacher*
'May I tempt you to a little more filleted lemon sole, miss Dubedat? Yes, do bedad. And she did bedad. Huguenot name I expect that. A miss Dubedat lived in Killiney, I remember.' *(8.888–90)*
The daughter of Mrs Robert Dubedat, Marie (Martha J.) was born in Dublin on 25 January 1860 at Compton House, South Circular Road. She was a soprano and classical singer known in musical circles in Dublin in the late 1800s. Marie Dubedat seems to have been a stage name – her real name was Martha J. Dubedat. In 1894 a Miss C. and a Miss M. Dubedat lived at 18 Charleville Road, Rathmines. Martha who was a teacher of singing performed in concerts in Dublin during the 1880s and the 1890s. These included a performance of a romanza for soprano voice in an opera by Meyerbeer at one of the series of Dublin Popular Concerts, held in the Antient Concert Rooms in Great Brunswick Street (now Pearse Street). From 13 November 1893, for a few nights *The Fisherman's Daughter* was performed at the Queen's Royal Theatre, Hawkins Street, in which Miss Dubedat played the part of Kitty. In 1894 she sang in the Queen's Royal Theatre and the Leinster Hall, Hawkins Street.

On 3 February 1894, a benefit concert was held at the Queen's Royal Theatre for Mr. J. W. Whitbread, at which Mr Pat Kinsella played Rory O'More from Samuel Lover's novel and Miss Dubedat sang 'Going to Kildare'. In the same year she also performed at the Leinster Hall, Hawkins Street.

Dubedat seems to have spent a lot of time in England, as evidenced by the social columns in the *Irish Times*: 'Miss Dubedat has returned to her residence, 18 Charleville Road, Rathmines, from England.'

A Miss Dubedat of Ballsbridge was a member of the senior vocal class at the Academy in 1867. She was also awarded the Academy's certificate of proficiency as a teacher of singing in 1903. It is possible that this is the same person and that she qualified as a teacher when her singing career had ended. In 1904, the Misses Dubedat are recorded as living at Wilmount House, Killiney.   *Ulysses 15.4355–6*

Dudley, earl of/William Humble Ward (1867–1932) *Lord lieutenant of Ireland*
'William Humble, earl of Dudley, and lady Dudley, accompanied by lieutenant-

colonel Heseltine, drove out after luncheon from the viceregal lodge.' *(10.1176–8)*
William Humble Ward, 2nd earl of Dudley, was born on 25 May 1867 at Dudley

House, Park Lane in London. He was the son of William Ward, the 1st earl of Dudley and Georgiana (née Moncreiffe).

Educated at Eton College, Dudley was 17 when his father died and he inherited some 25,000 acres in Worcestershire as well as collieries and ironworks. He married Rachel Gurney in September 1891. He entered politics as a Conservative and was elected to London County Council in March 1895 to represent Finsbury, and as mayor of Dudley in 1895 and 1896.

In August 1902 he was appointed lord lieutenant of Ireland. He was extravagant, travelled widely and entertained lavishly. He hosted two successful royal visits. His term in Ireland ended in December 1905 on the defeat of the Balfour ministry.

He then got the post of governor-general of Australia, which he held from 1908 until 1911. He served in the First World War and then retired to his estates. He married Gertie Millar, the actress, in April 1924, after the death of his first wife.

Dudley died on 29 June 1932 at 17 Park Lane, London, and was buried in the gardens of his home at 'Himley Hall', Wolverhampton, England.

Dudley, Lady (1876–1920) *Vicereine*

'Lady Dudley was walking home through the park to see all the trees that were blown down by that cyclone last year and thought she'd buy a view of Dublin.' *(7.700–2)*

Rachel Gurney, younger daughter of Charles Henry Gurney, a Quaker banker from Norfolk, was born in England.

Described as being 'beautiful as a marble statue ... a carved lily', she married William Humble Ward, 2nd earl of Dudley at Chelsea in London on 14 September

1891. He was lord lieutenant of Ireland 1902–5.

When Dudley was governor-general in Australia, Lady Dudley launched Lady Dudley's Bush Nursing Scheme, a hospital for Australians, but the project failed through lack of finance. The couple had seven children and separated in 1912.

During the First World War, Lady Dudley set up a hospital for Australians in northern France and in 1918 was awarded the Royal Red Cross and appointed CBE.

The earl of Dudley and Lady Dudley often stayed in 'Screebe Lodge' in Connemara, Co. Galway, when he was lord lieutenant. She loved the area and returned to visit in June 1920. She drowned while swimming in Screebe Lake adjoining 'Screebe Lodge' in Connemara on 26 June 1920. She was buried in the grounds of Winley Chapel adjoining Lord Dudley's Worcestershire seat.   *Ulysses 10.1176; 15.2718*

Dudley, Rev. Nicholas (1852–1932) *Curate at St Agatha's Church*
'Off an inward bound tram stepped the reverend Nicholas Dudley C. C. of saint Agatha's church, north William street, on to Newcomen bridge.' *(10.110–12)*
Henry Dudley was born in Cornmarket in the parish of St Audoen's in Dublin. Father Dudley was named Henry and not Nicholas as stated in *Ulysses*. He received his ecclesiastical education in Holy Cross College, Clonliffe, Dublin and went to St Patrick's College Maynooth, Co. Kildare to continue his studies. He was ordained priest in 1882 and appointed curate in Halston Street, where he remained for 18 years. He was next appointed to St Agatha's Church, North William Street, where he was curate and administrator for 13 years.

In 1904, while he was attached to St Agatha's Church, Dudley lived at 8 Margaret Place. Margaret Place was a row of ten houses on 'Circular Road', now incorporated into North Circular Road. He then moved to 10 Richmond Place in 1907.

In 1913, Archbishop Walsh appointed Father Dudley parish priest of the newly created parish of Glasnevin, which had formerly been part of the parish of Drumcondra. He then lived at 20 and 44 Ballymun Road. In 1924, he was created a canon and a member of the Diocesan Chapter. The Rev. Henry Canon Dudley died on 9 June 1932 in the Mater Misericordiae Hospital, Dublin, and was buried in Glasnevin Cemetery, Finglas Road, Dublin [WB 81.5 Section 5].

Duggan, Mrs (b. 1860) *Acquaintance of Bloom*
'Worst of all at night Mrs Duggan told me in the City Arms. Husband rolling in drunk, stink of pub off him like a polecat.' *(13.963–4)*
Mrs Duggan was an acquaintance of Bloom at the City Arms Hotel, Prussia Street. A Joseph Duggan lived nearby at 35 Prussia Street with his sister Anna Maria. He was 54 in 1904 and his sister 44. Joyce was probably misled by *Thom's Directory* into thinking that the Duggans were married. This could possibly be the Mrs Duggan in the City Arms.

Dunlop, Daniel (1868–1935) *Theosophist*
'Dunlop, Judge, the noblest Roman of them all ...' *(9.65)*
Daniel Dunlop, son of Alexander Dunlop, and Catherine (née Nicol) was born on 28 December 1868 in Kilmarnock, Scotland.

He attended the local primary school and then worked as an apprentice in a machinery factory in Ardrossan in Ayrshire, and later took a job in Glasgow.

Dunlop moved to Dublin where he worked with a wine and tea merchant. He was a friend of W. B. Yeats and George Russell and became involved with the Irish Theosophical Society. In October 1892, he founded and was editor of the *Irish Theosophist* to which he contributed articles under the pseudonym Aretas. Dunlop was editor of *The Path*, a theosophical journal published in London, and was president of the Theosophical Society in America.

In later life he moved to the United States and became assistant manager of the American Westinghouse Electrical Company in 1896. On returning to England, he became the director of the British Electrical Manufacturers' Association in London and played an important role in developing the British electrical industry.

Dunlop died on 30 May 1935 in London. *Ulysses 3.193*

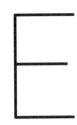

Edward VII (1841–1910) *King of England*
'Mr Deasy stared sternly for some moments over the mantelpiece at the shapely bulk of a man in tartan filibegs: Albert Edward, prince of Wales.' *(2.265–7)*
Albert Edward Prince of Wales was the eldest son of Queen Victoria and Albert of Saxe-Coburg-Gotha. He was born on 9 November 1841. He was educated at the universities of Edinburgh, Oxford and Cambridge. He was a prominent figure in public life but Victoria excluded him from any involvement in government.

As king of England he reigned for nine years from 1901 to 1910. He proved to have great skill in dealing with his ministers and with foreign rulers. Edward VII died on 6 May 1910 and was buried at St George's Chapel, Windsor Castle in Berkshire. His tomb is on the south side of the High Altar.

Ulysses 2.299; 5.74–5; 5.193; 6.551–2; 7.17; 7.28; 7.542–3; 11.1050; 12.1399–406; 12.1523–5; 15.4371; 15.4435–6; 15.4454–5; 16.515; 16.1197–201; 16.1202; 17.1779; 18.481–2; 18.500–2

Egan, Alfred William (1839–1912)
Secretary of the British and Irish Steampacket Company
'Martin Cunningham frequently said he would work a pass through Egan ...'
(16.504–5)
Alfred William Egan was born in Co. Dublin. He was the first secretary of the British and Irish Steampacket Company, 3 North Wall Quay, from 1836 to 1867. His son Alfred W. Egan succeeded him in 1870.

In 1904, Egan lived at 'Lucerne' in Dalkey, Co. Dublin. He later moved to 9 Sandycove Avenue East, Kingstown (now Dún Laoghaire).

Egan died aged on 28 March 1912 at his residence, 'Bayview', Sandycove, and was buried in Deansgrange Cemetery, Deansgrange, Co. Dublin [9–O1–South].

Egan, Kevin *Fenian exile in Paris*
Based on **Joseph Theobald Casey (1846–1911)** *Fenian exile in Paris*
'Patrice ... Son of the wild goose, Kevin Egan of Paris.' *(3.163–4)*
Joseph Theobald Casey was one of four brothers, the others being Patrick, Andrew and James, in a Kilkenny family related to James Stephens, the Fenian

95

leader. The Caseys ran a small hardware business. Joseph Casey was baptised in St Mary's Cathedral, Kilkenny, in April 1846.

Casey was a former Fenian and quite elderly when Joyce met him in the winter of 1903 on his first visit to Paris. At the time, Casey was living as a virtual exile and working as a typesetter on the European (Paris) edition of the *New York Herald*.

Casey was allegedly involved on 18 September 1867 with other armed men in the rescue of two Fenian leaders, Thomas Kelly and Timothy Deasy, from a police van in Manchester, resulting in the death of Sergeant Charles Brett.

Casey was arrested and jailed in Clerkenwell Jail in London. On 13 December 1867, a keg of gunpowder caused an explosion at the base of the wall of the prison with the intention of bringing about the escape of Casey and his leader, Colonel Richard Burke (1838–1922). There were civilian deaths and numerous horrific injuries, which caused public outrage. Casey was acquitted at his trial after lengthy proceedings. Living in Paris, he felt abandoned by his former colleagues and also by his wife. Patrice was his French-born son. Casey died on 8 June 1911 in France. *Ulysses 3.216; 3.249–50; 3.263; 12.1203; 15.4498; 15.4500; 15.4502*

Eglinton, John *Librarian*

Pseudonym for **William Kirkpatrick Magee (1868–1961)** *Writer, librarian and editor of* Dana

'John Eglinton shifted his spare body, leaning back to judge.' *(9.152)*

William Kirkpatrick Magee son of Rev. Hamilton Magee and Emily (née Kirkpatrick), was born on 16 January 1868 at 41 Eccles Street, Dublin. Magee was descended from clergymen on both sides of his family; Rev. Hamilton Magee, a native of Belfast, was sent by the synod of the Presbyterian Church in 1852 to oversee the 'Irish Mission' for the conversion of Catholics in Dublin.

Magee attended the Erasmus High School at 40 Harcourt Street in Dublin (now demolished), where he was a classmate of W. B. Yeats. He entered Trinity College Dublin in 1887, and was awarded the vice-chancellor's prize for verse in 1889 and 1890, and for prose in 1892 and 1893. He spent time in Germany and later worked as a schoolteacher in Drogheda. He took the name 'Eglinton' from a street where his parents lived in Kingstown (now Dún Laoghaire), Co. Dublin.

With the help of Edward Dowden, Magee obtained a post in the National Library as assistant librarian in 1895. He remained in the job for 26 years. His early ambition to become a poet was thwarted by Yeats's success.

Magee was a member of the theosophical movement in Dublin and included among his friends Æ, Stephen McKenna and George Moore. With Frederick Ryan, Magee co-edited *Dana* the short-lived monthly magazine from May 1904 to April 1905. Among the contributors were James Joyce, Æ, George Moore, Padraic Colum, Stephen Gwynn, Seumas O'Sullivan, Horace Plunkett, Oliver Gogarty and Alfred Webb. Joyce submitted a story titled 'A Portrait of an Artist', which was rejected but he was paid for a poem that was published, apparently the only contributor to receive a fee.

In 1911, Magee was living at a boarding house at 7 Hume Street, Dublin, which was near the National Library. He married Marie Louise O'Leary on 6 April 1920. She was an assistant in the library and had converted to Protestantism. To have more time for his writing Magee, now aged 53, took an early pension offered by the British to those civil servants not wishing to continue employment under the new Free State. He was not sympathetic towards the new Ireland and in late 1923 the couple moved to Prestatyn in Wales, where their son was born. They remained in Wales until 1929 when they left to live in Bournemouth. Their home in Bournemouth was 21 Carbery Avenue.

Magee's two most significant books were *Irish Literary Portraits* (1935) and *Memoir of Æ* (1937). His early volumes *Two Essays on the Remnant* (1894) and *Pebbles from a Brook* (1901) were also well received.

Trinity College Dublin awarded Magee an honorary degree in 1952. Magee, whom Moore described as 'a sort of lonely thorn tree', died on 9 May 1961 at 36 St Catherine's Road, Bournemouth, England. He had a private funeral.

Ulysses Eglinton: *9.18; 9.43; 9.58; 9.79; 9.100; 9.126; 9.141; 9.225; 9.232; 9.359; 9.368; 9.392; 9.408; 9.412; 9.516; 9.618; 9.660; 9.684; 9.795; 9.886; 9.949; 9.970; 9.993; 9.1017; 9.1027; 9.1061; 9.1064; 9.1098; 9.1126; 15.2248; 15.2256* Magee: *9.412; 9.451; 9.780; 9.819–20; 9.870; 9.900*

Emmet, Robert (1778–1803) *Patriot*

'Down there Emmet was hanged, drawn and quartered. Greasy black rope.' *(10.764-5)*
Robert Emmet, son of Dr Robert Emmet the state physician, was born on 4 March 1778 at St Stephen's Green. He spent his early years at 124 St Stephen's Green West (now demolished), where the family lived for almost 20 years. He was educated at Samuel Whyte's Academy at 79 Grafton Street and entered Trinity College Dublin in 1793.

Emmet, a brilliant orator at the Trinity's Historical Society's debates, became one of the leaders of the United Irishmen in the college. This involvement ended his prospects of a professional career. A warrant was issued for his arrest in 1799 but was not enforced.

He travelled on the continent in 1802 and interviewed Napoleon. On his return to Dublin he prepared plans for an insurrection, which broke out on 23 July 1803, taking the authorities by surprise. With a hundred followers, Emmet left his depot in Marshalsea Lane to attack Dublin Castle. They encountered Lord Kilwarden, the chief justice, and his nephew, passing in a coach. Emmet's undisciplined men murdered them both and the horrified Emmet first fled to the hills and then to a house in Harold's Cross to see Sarah Curran, his fiancée. He was discovered and arrested by Major Sirr, tried for treason and found guilty. He made what became a famous oration from the dock, and was executed the following day, 20 September 1803, outside St Catherine's Church, Thomas Street.

His body was removed in a cart, first to Newgate and then to Kilmainham

Gaol, until arrangements were made for interment. He was buried in Bully's Acre in the grounds of the Royal Hospital nearby. Soon after his remains were removed privately and buried elsewhere. The location remains a mystery.

A statue was placed opposite Emmet's birthplace on the west side of St Stephen's Green on 13 April 1966. The bronze statue is a replica of the statue by sculptor Jerome Connor (1876–1943) in Washington, which was commissioned by a group of Irish Americans in 1916 and unveiled by President Wilson in 1917.

Ulysses 6.977–8; 10.767–8; 10.791; 11.61–2; 11.1275; 12.180; 12.500–1; 12.525–678; 13.618–19; 15.1561–2; 15.3199; 15.3387–90; 16.1534–5

Eustace, Dr Henry Marcus (1869–1927) *Superintendent of Hampstead Hospital*
'He has recently escaped from Dr Eustace's private asylum for demented gentlemen.' *(15.1776–7)*
Dr Henry Marcus Eustace, second son of Dr John Eustace and Maria Elizabeth (née Neilson) was born in 1869. He graduated from Trinity College Dublin in 1890 and took a bachelor of medicine degree in 1892, and three years later the degree of MD. He worked for a time at the Royal Hospital, Morningside, Edinburgh, and later at the Rotunda Hospital in Dublin.

The Eustaces were a well-known Dublin medical family, originally Quakers from Cork. They were advocates of a form of treatment for mental patients known as 'The Moral Treatment'. The Eustace family actually lived with the patients.

Only the wealthy could afford to stay at the Eustace establishment at Hampstead House, in Glasnevin, Dublin. Dr John Eustace and two partners founded it in 1825. Eustace was the sole owner of Hampstead Asylum in 1830.

Dr Henry Marcus Eustace was superintendent at Hampstead Asylum in 1904. He is listed as a physician and surgeon at 41 Grafton Street, and his residences were at 'Hampstead' and 'Elmhurst' in Glasnevin where he had his private asylum. He was a member of the British Medical Association and the Royal Academy of Medicine. Dr William Nielson Eustace, his brother, was also a doctor who worked at 'Hampstead', 'Elmhurst' and 'Highfield'. He graduated from the Royal College of Surgeons in 1901.

Dr Henry Marcus Eustace died as he had lived, with his patients in December 1927 and was buried in the Friends' Burial Ground, Temple Hill, Blackrock, Co. Dublin [Grave No. 109].

Evans, Thomas Henry (1863–1942) *Attendant in the National Library, Dublin*
'Will you please ... Evans, conduct this gentleman ...' *(9.599–600)*
Thomas Henry Evans was born in Bray, Co. Wicklow. He began as a library assistant

in Dublin's National Library when he was 15 and became senior library assistant. He continued to work in the National Library until his retirement in 1927.

Evans married in 1886 and in 1901 lived at 12 Chester Road, Rathmines, with his wife Elizabeth and two children, Frances and Henry. He was living at 4 Airfield Road, Rathgar in 1904. In 1911 he had moved to 230 Merrion Road, Ballsbridge, and his final address was 62 South Circular Road, Kilmainham.

An accomplished baritone, Evans sang at many concerts. He was an enthusiastic cyclist and competed in races against Harry Reynolds, Charles Pease, Tom Goss and other well-known cyclists of the day. In his later years he was an active member of the Old Timer's Club, which included many who had ridden boneshakers and penny-farthings, the earliest models of bicycle.

Evans worked in the National Library for almost half a century from 1878 to 1927. He died on 21 March 1942 and was buried in Mount Jerome Cemetery, Harold's Cross, Dublin [B7–371–17634].

Everard, Sir Nugent Talbot (1849–1929) *Gentleman farmer and tobacco grower*
'You could grow any mortal thing in Irish soil, he stated, and there was that colonel Everard down there in Navan growing tobacco.' *(16.995–6)*
Nugent Talbot Everard was born in October 1849, son of Captain Richard Everard and his wife, Matilda Arabella, daughter of the Marquis d'Amboise. He lived at 'Randlestown', Navan, Co. Meath, an important early eighteenth-century house, demolished in the 1980s.

Everard was educated at Harrow and Trinity College Cambridge, where he graduated with an MA degree. He entered the army and was colonel commanding the 5th Battalion Prince of Wales (Leinster) Regiment. He married Sylvia Humphreys of Ballyhaise, Co. Cavan in 1873.

At 'Randlestown', Colonel Everard farmed his land and bred pedigree Shropshire sheep, Yorkshire pigs, Hereford cattle, and horses. He showed his Herefords and horses at the Royal Dublin Society shows, winning many prizes.

A member of the Council of the Royal Dublin Society for 32 years, Everard was president of Meath County Council and chairman of the Agriculture and Technical Instruction Committee for 20 years. He was a keen supporter of the Irish Agricultural Organisation, founded by Sir Horace Plunkett.

Colonel Everard is best remembered for his attempts to introduce tobacco growing into Ireland. The Department of Agriculture decided to confine experiments to those carried out under the supervision of Colonel Everard. While he demonstrated the possibility of growing the plant, the scheme failed on the manufacturing side.

Colonel Everard played a prominent part in Ireland's industrial revival and was president of the Irish Industrial Development Association for 17 years. He was also a senator and was re-elected in April 1929. He died on 11 July 1929 at his residence in Randlestown and was buried in Donaghpatrick, Co. Meath.

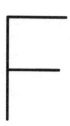

Falkiner, Sir Frederick (1831–1908) *Lawyer and recorder of Dublin*

'Sir Frederick Falkiner going into the freemasons' hall. Solemn as Troy.' *(8.1151–2)*

Frederick Falkiner, third son of Richard Miles Falkiner and Tempe (née Litton), was born at 'Mount Falcon', Borrisokane, Co. Tipperary. Aged 20, he married Adelaide Matilda Sadleir from Ballinderry Park in Co. Tipperary. He graduated from Trinity College Dublin in 1852 and the same year was called to the Irish Bar and joined the north-east circuit. He became queen's counsel in 1867.

Falkiner was appointed law adviser to Dublin Castle in 1875. The following year he was appointed recorder of Dublin on the death of Sir Frederick Shaw, and was recorder from 1876 to 1905.

Falkiner was knighted in 1896 during the viceroyalty of Earl Cadogan. As the 'poor man's judge' he had a reputation for compassion.

Falkiner was a bencher of the King's Inns in 1905 and chancellor to four bishops of the Church of Ireland. He was also governor of King's Hospital (the Blue Coat School) in Blackhall Place. He published *A History of the Bluecoat School* in 1906. His *Literary Miscellanies: Tales of the Bench and Assizes* was published posthumously in 1909. He lived at 4 Earlsfort Terrace in Dublin.

Falkiner died on 23 March 1908 in Funchal, Madeira, where he was buried. He is commemorated by a stained glass window on the north side of the Lady Chapel in St Patrick's Cathedral, Dublin.

Ulysses 7.698–9; 8.1153–9; 12.1095; 12.1121; 12.1875; 15.1162; 15.1164–5

Fanning, 'Long' John *Sub-sheriff of Dublin*

Based on **John Clancy (1845–1915)** *Dublin City Council sub-sheriff*

'The tall form of long John Fanning filled the doorway where he stood.' *(10.997–8)*

John Clancy was born in Co. Sligo. His father worked as an official with the Customs Service.

In 1859 Clancy was working at the firm of H. W. Scott, shipping agent and insurance broker, Eden Quay in Dublin. Aged 19, he was appointed outdoor manager at Palgrave Murphy, the Dublin shipping company, a post he held for 12 years.

Clancy was an ardent nationalist from his youth and held extreme views. He

was on close terms with James Stephens and in 1867 was imprisoned as a Fenian. He later became interested in Land League agitation and the Home Rule movement, resulting in a further term of imprisonment under Foster's Coercion Act.

Clancy was elected to Dublin City Council for the Inn's Quay Ward in 1883, though he was not returned at the next municipal elections because of his campaign in favour of markets near East Arran Street and Charles Street (later Ormond Markets). He was elected for the South Dock Ward, which he represented until 1913; he was then elected for the Clontarf Ward. Clancy lived in 7 North Richmond Street near the Joyce family who lived there from late 1894 or early 1895, to 1898.

During his time as sub-sheriff he frequently held sittings at Green Street Courthouse. Clancy was presented by his colleagues on Dublin City Council with an aldermanic gold chain and illuminated address in July 1914. Known as the Clancy Chain, this is now held in Dublin's Mansion House and is worn as a chain of office by the deputy lord mayor.

Clancy was proposed and elected to the office of lord mayor of Dublin at a Dublin City Council meeting on 23 January 1915 but died before assuming office. He was caught in a rainstorm on his way home to 'Ardeevin', 43 Hollybrook Road, Clontarf and developed pneumonia. He was returning from the City Council meeting that had elected him lord mayor.

Alderman Clancy, lord mayor elect, died two days later on 25 January 1915, and was buried in Glasnevin Cemetery, Finglas Road, Dublin [VF 5.5 South].

Ulysses 7.106; 10.995; 10.1001; 10.1013; 10.1017; 10.1021; 10.1027; 10.1030; 15.1174; 15.1175

Farley, Rev. Charles, SJ (1859–1938) *Priest at Church of St Francis Xavier*
'Sorry I didn't work him about getting Molly into the choir instead of that Father Farley who looked a fool but wasn't.' *(5.331–3)*

Charles Farley was born on 1 August 1859, the son of Joseph Farley, victualler of 8 South Great George's Street, Dublin. The family residence was 'Avon Cottage', Mount Merrion Avenue, Co. Dublin. Charles's mother carried on the business after his father's death.

Aged 18, Charles entered the Society of Jesus at Milltown Park, Dublin. He then served as prefect to Tullabeg, Co. Offaly for four years and in 1886 went to St Beuno's in north Wales where he was ordained priest in 1888.

On his return to Ireland, Father Farley moved around the various Jesuit houses. He spent 1911 to 1938 based at Gardiner Street, Dublin, his longest period in any one place. Here he was bursar for the province and assisted in the office of *The Messenger*, a Jesuit publication. But his main work was as director to the Commercial Sodality, which he took on from 1914 until his death.

Father Farley died in Dublin on 20 August 1938. He was buried in the Jesuit Plot in Glasnevin Cemetery, Finglas Road, Dublin [AH–GH 30–40.5]. *Ulysses 15.1711*

Farrell, Cashel Boyle O'Connor Fitzmaurice Tisdall (b. 1851)
Dublin eccentric nicknamed 'Endymion'

'Cashel Boyle O'Connor Fitzmaurice Tisdall Farrell, murmuring, glassyeyed, strode past the Kildare street club.' *(10.919-20)*

'Endymion' was the nickname of James Farrell, a Dublin eccentric. Born on 17 June 1851, he was the son of Joseph Farrell and Margaret (née Boyle). His father, a merchant and ship-owner, also owned property and lived in the quays area of Dundalk, Co. Louth.

Farrell worked for a time in Dublin as an excise officer but was injured when he tried to rescue a colleague who had fallen into a brewery vessel. He never recovered from his injury and lost his job. He became eccentric and suffered from delusions. In his youth he was an accomplished pianist and remained so for the rest of his life. He lived in rented accommodation at various addresses in Dublin, which included boarding houses in Pleasants Street, off Camden Street, 7 Charlemont Road, Clontarf and Baggot Street.

Gogarty describes the flamboyantly dressed Farrell in the opening chapter of his book, *As I Was Going down Sackville Street*:

> He wore a tailcoat over white cricket trousers, which were caught in at the ankles by a pair of cuffs. A cuff-like collar sloped upwards to keep erect a little sandy head, crowned by a black bowler some sizes too small ... Under his left arm he carried two sabres in shining scabbards of patent leather. His right hand grasped a hunting crop such as whippers-in use for hounds.

Farrell read in the National Library. When he left for home he would cross into the middle of the street and halt, then produce a large compass from his pocket and set his course for home. Many passers-by were amused by this behaviour. At the Ballast Office clock, by which all watches were set, Farrell would salute it with drawn sword, much to the delight of the crowd of bystanders who gathered to watch. He would then take a large alarm clock from his pocket, set it and carefully replace it in his pocket, from which it began to ring loudly as he left.

In 1911 Farrell was 60 and living in a boarding house at 84 Lower Baggot Street. Details of his final years are unknown.

Ulysses 8.302; 9.1115–16; 10.1102; 10.1106; 10.1261; 15.2308

Faure, François Félix (1841–99) *President of France*

'... Félix Faure, know how he died? Licentious men.' *(3.233–4)*

François Félix Faure, son of a furniture maker, was born in Paris on 30 January 1841.

He worked as a merchant and tanner in Le Havre and became very wealthy. He was elected to the National Assembly in August 1881 and took his seat as a member of the Left. He was mainly involved in matters concerning economics, railways and the navy.

By 1894 Faure had obtained cabinet rank as minister of the marine in the administration of Charles Dupuy. The following year, on the resignation of President Casimir-Perier, he was unexpectedly elected president of the republic. The Dreyfus Affair, the political scandal that divided France during the 1890s and early 1900s, marred the latter days of his presidency. He died suddenly from apoplexy at the Élysée on 16 February 1899. Other reports claimed that his death was the result of sexual excess, which sparked off numerous rumours and jokes. Faure was buried in Père Lachaise Cemetery in Paris.

Field, William, MP (1843–1935) *Cattle traders' president*

'I wrote last night to Mr Field, M. P. There is a meeting of the cattletraders' association today at the City Arms hotel.' *(2.415–17)*

William Field was born in June 1843 over the family shop at 6 Main Street, Blackrock,

Co. Dublin. He was the son of John Field, a nationalist and victualler, and Grace (née Byrne).

He was educated at St Laurence's School, a boarding school run by the Rev. Dr James Quinn located at 16–17 Harcourt Street, Dublin. It later became the Catholic University School now located in Lower Leeson Street.

On his father's death in 1867, Field inherited the family business, consisting of two shops, one in Blackrock and the other in Monkstown in Co. Dublin. He was one of the founders of the Irish Cattle Traders and Stockowners Association, the Dublin Victuallers Association and the National Meat Traders Federation of Britain. He was also president of each of these organisations.

A promoter of temperance, Field was a member of the committee that erected the statue of Father Mathew in Sackville Street (now O'Connell Street), Dublin. In the 1892 general election, Field was elected as a Parnellite MP, defeating William Martin Murphy. He became chairman of the Parnell Commemoration Committee, formed in 1892.

On 14 April 1898 his fellow townsmen presented him with a silver salver and an address, which hangs today in the hallway of the senior college in Blackrock beside the public library.

Field's publications include *Distress in the West and South of Ireland* (1898) and *Ireland and Imperial Expenditure: More Light on the Financial Relations Question. How Ireland Is Drained through Government Departments. Suggested Economies, Remedies and Reforms* (1906).

Field died at 20 Idrone Terrace, Blackrock, Co. Dublin, on 29 April 1935 and was buried in the family plot in Tully churchyard, Lehaunstown, Cabinteely, Co. Dublin.

Ulysses 12.827–8

Figatner, Aaron (1853–1922) *Jeweller*

'Bloowhose dark eye read Aaron Figatner's name. Why do I always think Figather? Gathering figs, I think.' *(11.149–50)*

Aaron Figatner was born in Kracow. He was a well-known betting man and had a second-hand jeweller's shop at 25 Wellington Quay, Dublin.

In 1904 his residence was at 1 Lower Dominick Street. He later moved to 335 North Circular Road, where he lived with his two children and wife Julia whom he married in 1901. All are listed as being Roman Catholic. Figatner died on the 8 June 1922 and was buried in Glasnevin Cemetery, Finglas Road, Dublin [DH 23 St Brigid's].

Ulysses 15.4357

Findlater, Adam (1855–1911) *Dublin businessman*

'Then, lo and behold, they blossom out as Adam Findlaters or Dan Tallons.' *(4.127–8)*

Adam Findlater was born on 25 January 1855, eldest son of John Findlater and Mary (née Johnston). He was educated at the Erasmus High School, Harcourt Street and Trinity College Dublin. He was called to the Bar in 1906 but never practised. His residence was at Primrose Hill, Kingstown (now Dún Laoghaire). The Findlater family came from Scotland to Dublin in 1823 where Alex Findlater set up a business selling whiskey, wine and ales. In the 1860s, he underwrote the cost of building the Presbyterian Church, which stands on the corner of Parnell Square. It is now a landmark and known as Findlater's Church.

Adam Findlater was the owner and managing director of a successful Dublin grocery chain, which was founded by his forefathers, in the early years of the previous century. Alex Findlater & Co., Ltd, tea, wine, and spirit and provision merchants, had their main premises at 29–32 Sackville Street Upper (now

O'Connell Street). The tea and wine was packaged as Findlater's own brand and the shops were known for their high quality food and wines. Findlater's Burgundy advertised in the *Irish Times* on 16 June 1904 appears in *Ulysses* when Bloom drinks it in Davy Byrnes.

Findlater was chairman of the board of directors of The Empire Palace Theatre in Dublin, which he took over from Dan Lowrey. He had the interior completely revamped. He was on many public boards and had a wide range of interests from politics to theatre.

Adam Findlater died on 18 January 1911 and was buried in Mount Jerome Cemetery, Harold's Cross, Dublin [C81–392].

Fingall, Lady (1866–1944) *Patroness of the Irish Industries Association*
'... it opened up new vistas in his mind such as Lady Fingall's Irish industries ...'
(16.1807–8)
Elizabeth Mary Margaret Plunkett, countess of Fingall, was born on 24 May 1866 in Mountbellew, Co. Galway, daughter of George Burke of Danesfield, Co. Galway. She married Plunkett – Lord Fingall and the 11th earl – and lived at Killeen Castle, Co. Meath. The castle was originally founded by Hugh de Lacy in 1181 and passed by marriage to Sir Christopher Plunkett in 1403.

Lady Fingall was active in the Irish Industries Association, 21 Lincoln Place, Dublin. The association encouraged cottage industry in Ireland and sponsored benefit concerts. Her memoir, *Seventy Years Young*, was published in 1937. She died on 28 October 1944 and was buried at Killeen Castle, Dunsany, Co. Meath where the medieval chantry church contains the tombs of various members of the Plunkett family.

Finucane, Dr Thomas Dawson (1823–1920) *Dignam's doctor*
'Doctor Finucane pronounced life extinct when I succumbed to the disease from natural causes.' *(15.1210–12)*
Thomas Dawson Finucane was born in Donegal. He qualified in 1855 as a licentiate of the Apothecaries' Hall, Dublin and of the Faculty of Physicians and Surgeons of Glasgow.

Dr Finucane came to Blackrock, Co. Dublin in 1855 and established a medical hall at 34 Main Street. A former resident medical officer at the Coombe Maternity Hospital, he was a member of the Dublin Obstetrical Society and attended the society's meetings in the Royal College of Physicians in Kildare Street. Among his publications was a paper entitled 'Views and observations of the asiatic cholera'.

Dr Finucane was a well-known and popular man among all classes of the Blackrock community. He was on call frequently for medical emergencies, as recounted in the press. An accident was reported in Blackrock on 30 September 1867: 'An old woman named Roche, was accidentally knocked down on Friday last, at Blackrock, by some boys who were playing in the street, and had her arm broken. Dr Finucane was in immediate attention.' John Stanislaus Joyce and his family lived at 'Leoville', 23 Carysfort Avenue, Blackrock from 1892–3, so Dr Finucane would have been known to the family. In *Ulysses*, Dr Finucane attended Paddy Dignam in his last illness.

Dr Finucane died aged 97 at 35 Main Street, Blackrock, Co. Dublin on 11 June 1920 and was buried in Deansgrange Cemetery, Deansgrange, Co. Dublin [63–Q–South West].

FitzGerald, Lord Edward (1763–98) *United Irishman*
'Somewhere here lord Edward Fitzgerald escaped from major Sirr. Stables behind Moira house.' *(10.785–6)*
Edward FitzGerald was born in Carton House, Co. Kildare, on 15 October 1763, son of the 1st duke of Leinster and Emilia Mary, daughter of Charles, duke of Richmond.

FitzGerald served in the American War of Independence where he was wounded at the Battle of Eutaw Springs in September 1781. He returned to Ireland and served as MP for Athy and Kildare. In 1792 he visited Paris, where the radical thinking of the French Revolution impressed him. Following a remark in which he agreed to the abolition of all hereditary titles, he was removed from the British army.

In 1796, Lord Edward joined the United Irishmen. He became president of the Military Committee and was committed to armed revolution with the help of a French invasion. He was regarded as the main force behind the plans for the 1798 rebellion. Due to delays by the French and the infiltration of spies into the movement, members of the United Irishmen were arrested at Oliver Bond's house in Bridge Street, Dublin.

Lord Edward went into hiding in the house of a supporter, Nicholas Murphy, at 151–152 Thomas Street. Meanwhile his wife Pamela was given sanctuary nearby in the earl of Moira's house at Usher's Quay. Occasionally they met in the stables behind the house; but as there was a reward of £1,000 for Lord Edward, an informer betrayed him. Major Henry Charles Sirr (1764–1841), the town major, notorious for his use of informers and for the viciousness of his police, arrested Lord Edward on 19 May 1798 in Murphy's house. In the ensuing struggle, FitzGerald killed one of his attackers and was himself badly wounded.

He was brought to Newgate Prison and died of his injuries there on 4 June 1798. He was buried directly under the chancel in St Werburgh's Church in Werburgh Street, Dublin. *Ulysses 10.791; 15.4686*

FitzGerald, Thomas (1513–37) *Rebel*
'We are standing in the historic council chamber of saint Mary's abbey where silken Thomas proclaimed himself a rebel in 1534. This is the most historic spot in all Dublin.' *(10.407–9)*
Thomas FitzGerald, 10th earl of Kildare, was known as Silken Thomas on account

of the silk his men wore on their helmets. When his father, Gerald FitzGerald, who was lord deputy, was summoned to England in February 1534, Thomas in his absence was appointed deputy governor of Ireland. As a result of a false rumour that his father had been executed in the Tower of London, Thomas rode through Dublin on 11 June 1534, accompanied by 140 horsemen, to the Chapter House of St Mary's Abbey where he summoned the council. He flung down his sword and publicly renounced his allegiance to King Henry VIII, lord of Ireland.

He attacked Dublin Castle the following month but his army was routed and he retreated to his stronghold in Maynooth, Co. Kildare. While Thomas FitzGerald was gathering reinforcements, an English force under Sir William Skeffington defeated the stronghold. When the garrison agreed to surrender they were promptly killed – an incident that is still remembered as the 'Pardon of Maynooth'.

FitzGerald was sent as a prisoner to the Tower of London on October 1535 and was executed with five of his uncles at Tyburn on 3 February 1537.

Ulysses 3.314; 10.415–16; 12.1861–2; 16.558

Fitzgibbon, Justice Gerald (1837–1909) *Judge and prominent Freemason*

'Mr Justice Fitzgibbon, the present lord justice of appeal, had spoken and the paper under debate was an essay (new for those days), advocating the revival of the Irish tongue.' *(7.794–96)*

Born in Dublin on 28 August 1837, Gerald was the son of Gerald Fitzgibbon, QC (1793–1882), master in Chancery in Ireland, and Ellen (née Patterson).

Educated at Trinity College Dublin, he was called to the Irish Bar in 1860 and the following year to the English Bar. In 1876 he was law adviser at Dublin Castle  and was solicitor-general, 1877–8. He was made a lord justice of appeal in 1878.

Fitzgibbon was the commissioner of national education in Ireland, 1884–96, and was regarded as one of those who were attempting to Anglicise Ireland. A Freemason and conservative, he was believed to be anti-Home Rule.

Fitzgibbon lived at 10 Merrion Square, Dublin, and at Howth, Co. Dublin. He died on 14 October 1909 and was buried in St Fintan's Cemetery, Sutton.

Ulysses 7.807; 14.493–5; 15.4343

FitzHarris, James 'Skin-the-Goat' (1833–1910) *Cab driver*

'F to P is the route Skin-the-Goat drove the car for an alibi, Inchicore, Roundtown, Windy Arbour, Palmerston Park, Ranelagh. F. A. B. P. Got that? X is Davy's publichouse in upper Leeson street.' *(7.667–9)*

James FitzHarris, known as Skin-the-Goat, was born on 4 October 1833 at Clonee, Co. Wexford. From a family of evicted farmers, he was forced to seek employment

in Dublin. He became a well-known Dublin jarvey or cab driver and was described as coarsely cheerful and robust. He got the nickname from a goat he found plucking at the straw that filled a horse's collar. He killed the goat, skinned it and used its hide to cover his knees while driving. Another story is that he sold the hide of his pet animal to pay for his drinking debts.

FitzHarris drove the Invincibles to the Phoenix Park on 6 May 1882 when Lord Frederick Cavendish, the newly appointed chief secretary for Ireland and Thomas Henry Burke, the under-secretary, were as-sassinated. It is not known whether FitzHarris was a member of the Invincibles but he was included among a number of men who were arrested and put on trial. Five were sentenced and executed at Kilmainham Gaol.

FitzHarris had been offered bribes by the British government in Ireland to inform on the men. He was offered £10,000, a substantial sum in those days, and transport to any foreign place of his choice if he divulged information. He declined, and although not guilty of murder, was sentenced to penal servitude for his part in the affair.

FitzHarris later declared: 'I came from Sliabh Buidhe where a crow never flew over the head of an informer.' He died on 6 September 1910 in the South Dublin Union Workhouse in James's Street. He was buried in Glasnevin Cemetery, Finglas Road, Dublin. A memorial plaque was erected by the National Graves Association on his grave and unveiled on 14 July 1968 [VH 159 St Brigid's].

Ulysses 7.64–41; 7.703; 16.323–4; 16.596; 16.688; 16.985; 16.1066–9; 16.1357

Fitzsimmons, Robert James 'Bob' (1863–1917) *English heavyweight boxer*
'The best pucker going for strength was Fitzsimons. One puck in the wind from that fellow would knock you into the middle of next week, man.' *(10.1145–7)*
Robert Fitzsimmons was born in Helston, Cornwall, England on 26 May 1863. When he was nine his family emigrated to New Zealand, where he later became a blacksmith. He took up boxing and some of his early fights were bare-knuckle events. In 1883 he was boxing professionally in Australia.

Fitzsimmons moved to the United States where he became world middle-weight champion on 14 January 1890 when he knocked out Jack Dempsey in New Orleans. On 17 March 1897 he became world heavyweight champion when he knocked out Jim Corbett in the fourteenth round. It is claimed that he won the title with his 'solar plexus' punch, which became legendary, although Fitzsimmons himself may never have used the phrase. Fitzsimmons lost the title to the American heavyweight champion James Jeffries (1875–1953) in 1899.

Fitsimmons's book, *Physical Culture and Self-Defence*, was published in 1901.

In November 1903 he made boxing history by defeating George Gardner, the world light-heavyweight champion and became the first boxer to win titles in three weight divisions.

Fitzsimmons, who was one of the hardest punchers in boxing, died on 22 October 1917 in Chicago and was buried in Graceland Cemetery.

Fitzsimon, H. O'Connell (1864–1950) *Superintendent of Food Market*
'... and thither come all herds and fatlings and firstfruits of that land for O'Connell Fitzsimon takes toll of them, a chieftain descended from chieftains.' *(12.89–91)*
A relation of Daniel O'Connell, Henry O'Connell Fitzsimon was born in Dublin.

He was a corporation officer and superintendent of the Food Market in St Michan's Street, Dublin. The new corporation Food Market was set up in 1899. He married a widow with five children, Elizabeth Mallins (née O'Connor) in 1907. They had two more children. In 1911 they were living at 46 Clyde Road, Ballsbridge.

He died on 6 July 1950 and was buried in Glasnevin Cemetery, Finglas Road, Dublin [JF 12 Dublin Section].

Flanagan, Rev. J. (1872–1935) *Curate, Pro-Cathedral*
John Flanagan was born on 24 February 1872 in Upper Baggot Street, Dublin. He entered Holy Cross College, Clonliffe, Dublin, in 1886, where he was ordained priest in 1896.

Father Flanagan was appointed curate in Balbriggan, Co. Dublin, and shortly afterwards was transferred to St Michael's and John's parish, Dublin. In 1901 he was appointed curate to the Pro-Cathedral and lived adjacent to it at 82 Marlborough Street. He was appointed administrator to the Pro-Cathedral in 1922. During his time there, he was chaplain to Lorcan Sherlock, lord mayor of Dublin.

Father Flanagan moved to Fairview as administrator in 1926 and in 1933 was appointed canon of the parish. During his nine years in Fairview he built a new church and the school of St Vincent de Paul in Marino.

He died on 16 December 1935 and was buried in Glasnevin Cemetery, Finglas Road, Dublin [RB 75 South].   *Ulysses 12.937–8*

Flavin, Rev. J. (1858–1920) *Curate, Pro-Cathedral*
James Flavin was born in Clashmore, Co. Waterford, and was educated at Melleray, Co. Waterford. He was admitted to Holy Cross College, Clonliffe, Dublin on 1 September 1877 and after two years went to St Patrick's College Maynooth, Co. Kildare.

Father Flavin was curate for almost ten years at St Mary's Pro-Cathedral, Marlborough Street, Dublin. During that time he organised the establishment of four new conferences of the St Vincent de Paul Society and the building of several schools. He became parish priest in Arklow, Co. Wicklow in 1915. He died on 12 September 1920 at Harrogate, North Yorkshire, England.   *Ulysses 12.934*

Fleming, Jack (*fl.* 1880s–1920s) *Collector of rates*

'Jack Fleming embezzling to gamble then smuggled off to America. Keeps a hotel now.' *(5.546-7)*

In 1883 the collector-general of rates appointed Jack J. Fleming to assist John Stanislaus Joyce with collecting the rates in the Rural Districts as the area was too large an area for just one man to cover.

No biographical information has been forthcoming so far on Fleming.

Fleming, Mrs *Cleaning woman in Bloom's household*

Based on **Mary Fleming** (1856–1909) *Cousin of J. F. Byrne*

'But I wish Mrs Fleming had darned these socks better.' *(6.106)*

Mary Fleming was born in Dublin. In 1901 she lived at 20 Essex Street East with her sister Cicely, a dressmaker, and cousin, J. F. Byrne. Mary is listed as head of the family and her occupation as vestment maker.

They moved to 7 Eccles Street where Mary and her sister lived from 1910 until 1912. James Joyce was a frequent visitor during the two trips, which he made to Dublin in 1909, when he stayed overnight in the house.

In his book, *Silent Years*, Byrne relates that one evening when Joyce was in 7 Eccles Street, a friend of his two cousins called to the house. The conversation was confined almost entirely to Mary and the visitor, with Mary doing most of the talking and trying to go one better than the visitor. The visitor mentioned a family she knew where the husband had died, leaving a widow with three children, and, what was worse, a child that would not be born for six months. Mary displayed no sympathy but responded, 'Why that's nothing. *My* father was dead years before I was born.' Mary did not like Joyce and Joyce certainly did not like Mary. Her incessant conversation obviously got on his nerves. That is why in *Ulysses* Mary Fleming is portrayed as the cleaning woman in the Bloom household.

Ulysses 6.17; 6.237; 17.315; 18.947; 18.1082

Flood, Henry (1732–91) *Politician and orator*

'Grattan and Flood wrote for this very paper, the editor cried in his face.' *(7.738)*

Henry Flood, the son of Warden Flood, chief justice of the King's Bench in Ireland, and Isabella Whiteside, was born in Co. Kilkenny. He entered Trinity College Dublin aged 15 and three years later went to Christ Church in Oxford where he graduated with an MA degree in 1752. He was admitted as a member of the Inner Temple, London, but did not seek entry to the King's Inns and never practised law in Ireland.

Flood entered the Irish parliament for Kilkenny in 1759 and later served for the borough of Callan. One of the finest orators of his day, he soon became leader of the opposition where he played a prominent part in political opposition to English dominion. He was a supporter of Henry Grattan but later quarrelled with him. He obtained a seat for Winchester in the English parliament in 1783 but proved a failure and was not returned to parliament after the 1790 general election. Flood retired to his seat at Farmley in Co. Kilkenny where he died on 2 December 1791. He was buried in Burnchurch graveyard in Co. Kilkenny.

Ulysses 7.731–2

Flower, Constable Henry, DMP 9397 (b. 1867)
Bloom used Henry Flower as his pen name
'Henry Flower Esq,
c/o P. O. Westland Row,
City' *(5.62–4)*
Henry Flower, son of James Flower, was born in Kilcormick, in the town of Kenagh, Co. Longford, in 1867. Before joining the Dublin Metropolitan Police (DMP) aged 20 in June 1887, he worked as a labourer. Flower was attached to Division 'F' in

November 1887, Division 'C' in January 1890 and Division 'A' in June 1900. His warrant number was 9397. He resigned from the DMP on 17 October 1900.

Constable Henry Flower, DMP, of Londonbridge Road police station was implicated in a case concerning the 'death from drowning' of Brigid Gannon, aged 30. She was a respectable domestic servant working at 124 Lower Baggot Street whose body was found in the river Dodder beside Lansdowne Road rugby ground (now Aviva) between Londonbridge Road and Herbert Park early on the morning of 23 August 1900.

Constable Flower had been with Gannon the night before her body was found. This he denied. Margaret Clowry, a friend of the deceased, identified the dead woman as Brigid Gannon, a serving girl, of 124 Baggot Street. Clowry claimed that she had been with Flower and Gannon for a time the night before her body was recovered.

There was a powerful case against Flower but it was thrown out by the grand jury after the judge hinted that the drowning might have been accidental. Henry Flower and some members of his family, including his father James Flower, and two brothers, George and Francis Flower also in the DMP, left Dublin in haste.

Forty years later an elderly dying woman in a tenement admitted that she had pushed Brigid Gannon into the Dodder, taken her cash and set up Henry Flower.

Ulysses 5.303; 11.296; 11.1262; 15.733; 15.2478; 15.2627; 15.3212; 17.1797; 17.1841; 17.2252

Fogarty, Patrick (1869–1907) *Grocer*
'I wonder how is our friend Fogarty getting on, Mr Power said.' *(6.454)*
Patrick Fogarty was born in Co. Tipperary. In 1897 he was a wine and spirit merchant with premises at 133 North Strand Road, Dublin. By 1902 the public house was under new ownership.

He is listed with premises at 36 Townsend Street in 1901, trading as a grocer, tea, wine and spirit merchant. By 1902 he had moved to a small shop at 35 Glengariff Parade, with his wife and three young daughters. Mr and Mrs Conlon, spirit merchants and grocer, had occupied these premises up to 1901.

Fogarty is described in the story 'Grace' in Dubliners as having 'a pale oval face, with a fair trailing moustache'.

A friend of Power, Kernan and Cunningham, he was supposedly an incompetent grocer, and was owed money by various customers. He appears in 'Grace' as 'A modest grocer' and a friend of Kernan's with 'a small shop on Glasnevin Road'. He would have been well known to the Joyce family as they lived in close proximity at 32 Glengariff Parade, 1901–2. He died on 23 June 1907 and was buried in Glasnevin Cemetery, Finglas Road, Dublin [EK 272 St Brigid's].

Fottrell, Sir George (1849–1925) *Solicitor, clerk of the crown and peace*
'An article of headgear since ascertained to belong to the much respected clerk of the crown and peace Mr George Fottrell ...' *(12.1871–2)*
George Fottrell was born in Dublin on 6 February 1849, son of George Drevar Fottrell, solicitor and member of the well-known firm of Dublin solicitors, Messrs George D. Fottrell & Sons.

Fottrell was educated at Belvedere College and the Catholic University. He served his apprenticeship with his father and was admitted to the roll of solicitors maintained by the Law Society in Easter Term, 1871.

In 1885 he was appointed by the lord lieutenant to the office of clerk of the crown for the county and city of Dublin at Green Street, and in 1895 to the joint office of clerk of crown and peace, which he held to the end of his life. Fottrell was awarded a knighthood in 1918 in recognition of his public services.

A keen cyclist, he generally cycled from his home, 'Dunmara', Ballybrack, Co. Dublin, or from his other residence at 8 North Great George's Street, to his office at 46 Fleet Street. Sir George Fottrell, died on 1 February 1925 at 8 North Great George's Street, Dublin and was buried in Glasnevin Cemetery, Finglas Road, Dublin [VA 23 South]. The firm George D. Fottrell & Sons continued in Dublin until 2003. *Ulysses 15.895*

Franks, Dr Hy (b. 1852) *Quack doctor*
'That quack doctor for the clap used to be stuck up in all the greenhouses ... Dr Hy Franks.' *(8.96–8)*
Dr Hy Franks was one of the pseudonyms of John Farlow, son of Samuel and Patti (née Farlow) of 3 Blacquiere Bridge Road, Phibsborough, Dublin. Samuel Farlow died at his residence in January 1877 aged 63, leaving property, which was sold.

From his share of the proceeds John started his own business, a chemist shop at 14 Berkeley Road. He advertised in newspapers, offering remedies for various disorders such as appeared on 27 August 1890 in the *Irish Times*: 'Nervousness, Physical and Functional Weakness, Blood and Skin Diseases cured by Dr Henry

Franks. Describe case by letter, or call. Address 14 Berkeley Road, Phibsborough, Dublin. Thousands cured annually.' He also advertised using posters pasted up on Dublin urinals, offering treatment for venereal diseases.

In November 1893 at the Southern Police Court in Dublin, he was prosecuted under the Criminal Law Amendment Act in the name of Adam J. Farlow of 14 Berkeley Road, chemist, alias Dr Henry Franks, alias J. Wilsome. The charge was of endeavouring to procure a lady for immoral purposes.

Farlow was found guilty and sentenced to one year in prison. The trial received widespread publicity and as a result he was expelled from the Pharmaceutical Society of Ireland and lost his business in Berkeley Road. The court proceedings in the case are of interest as other characters mentioned in *Ulysses* were involved, such as Mr Tobias, solicitor, Mr Carlyle, manager of the *Irish Times*, and Mr Mallon, assistant commissioner of the Dublin Metropolitan Police.

Friery, Christopher (1859–1926) *Solicitor*

'... the day we met Mrs Joe Gallaher at the trottingmatches and she pretended not to see us in her trap with Friery the solicitor ...' *(18.1068–70)*

The son of Irish parents, Miles Friery and Jane (née Burns), Christopher Friery was born in Liverpool. His father died when he was two and he was brought up in Swords, Co. Dublin, by his maternal grandmother.

Friery was admitted a solicitor in Easter Term 1888 and is listed until 1925. He was appointed coroner for north Co. Dublin in 1894. His residence was 'Fox Hall', Raheny, and he operated his solicitor's practice from 52 Rutland (now Parnell) Square where he later resided. An enthusiastic racegoer, he is reputed to have sold three of his racehorses to King Edward for £5,000. These included Jewman, Giltrim and Flying Silver.

Friery went bankrupt and was struck off the roll of solicitors but continued as coroner.

A well-known and colourful figure in the city and county of Dublin, Christopher Friery died on 3 February 1926 at his residence, 52 Rutland Square, and was buried in Glasnevin Cemetery, Finglas Road, Dublin [GC 65–66.5 South].

Froedman, Francis (1838–1925) *Pharmaceutical chemist*

'... as certified by the graduated machine for periodical selfweighing in the premises of Francis Froedman, pharmaceutical chemist of 19 Frederick street, north ...' *(17.92–4)*

Francis Froedman, born in St Petersburg in Russia, was a pharmaceutical chemist with premises at 46 Dorset Street Upper and 19 North Frederick Street. He later moved from North Frederick Street to Upper Dorset Street. Froedman died on 5 December 1925 at 19 North Frederick Street where his son Oscar lived. He was buried in Mount Jerome Cemetery, Harold's Cross, Dublin [A16–334–15093].

G

Gahan, W. H. T. (1881–1963) *Cyclist and vicar*

'Bang of the lastlap bell spurred the halfmile wheelmen to their sprint, J. A. Jackson, W. E. Wylie, A. Munro and H. T. Gahan, their stretched necks wagging, negotiated the curve by the College library.' *(10.651–3)*

Walter Henry Townsend Gahan, son of Frederick Gahan and Katherine (née Townsend) was born on 3 January 1881 in Magherabeg, Co. Donegal. By 1901 the family was living at 199 Kenilworth Square, Rathmines and Walter was studying divinity at Trinity College Dublin.

In 1902 Gahan began cycling for the college. He came fourth in the half-mile bicycle handicap race held on the afternoon of the 16 June 1904 at College Park in Trinity College Dublin. This was the first event on the day's card of a combination meeting of the Dublin University Bicycle and Harrier Club.

On completion of his studies, Gahan lived at Tyrellspass, Co. Westmeath where he married Florence Greeson. He worked as a curate in various places including Clonfadoran, Co. Westmeath, 1905–8, Castle Ennis, 1908–9 and St John's in Kilkenny, 1909–12. He was rector of Gorey, Co. Wexford, 1912–25, before moving to Natal as vicar of Tugela and later as vicar of Pinetown, Kwasulu-Natal (1944–57) in South Africa.

He died on 6 June 1963 and was buried in the St John's Anglican Cemetery.

Ulysses Trinity College Races: 5.550–4; 8.156; 10.651–3; 10.1246–60; 13.132–6

Gallagher, Michael (*fl.* late 1700s–1800s) *Carpenter*

'... Michael Gallagher, carpenter, Dufery Gate, Enniſcorthy, county Wicklow, the fineſt place in the world.' *(17.1405–7)*

This name was inscribed in ink on the flyleaf of a French book in Bloom's library titled *Short but yet Plain Elements of Geometry* by F. Ignat. It stated that the book was the property of Michael Gallagher and that if lost should be restored to him. The inscription was dated 10 May 1822.

Gallagher, William (1846–1921) *Josie Powell's father*

'Father Conmee began to walk along the North Strand road and was saluted by Mr William Gallagher who stood in the doorway of his shop.' *(10.85–6)*

William Gallagher lived at 14 Richmond Place in 1890. By 1893, he had moved to 8 North Richmond Street where for a time he was a neighbour of John Stanislaus Joyce and his family who lived in 13 North Richmond Street, 1894–7. Joyce would have been a teenager at the time. Gallagher lived here until 1908 at which time he was listed at 8, 9 and 10 North Richmond Street.

Gallagher had a shop at 4 North Strand Road from 1871 and is described as a purveyor, grocer, coal and corn merchant. This shop was still in his ownership in 1921.

He had five sons and at least two daughters, including Mary Josephine or 'Josie', who married Charles Powell, the son of Major Malachy Powell.

Gallagher died in January 1921 and was buried in Glasnevin Cemetery, Finglas Road, Dublin [ED 36.5 Dublin Section].

Gallaher, Gerald (1889–1946) *Pupil at Belvedere College*
'Yes: they were from Belvedere … And his name? Ger. Gallaher. And the other little man? His name was Brunny Lynam. O, that was a very nice name to have.' *(10.41–5)*
Gerald Gallaher was born on 4 January 1889, son of Joseph John Gallaher, a journalist, and Louisa (née Powell). His father died on 19 October 1893 at his residence, 17 Stamer Street, South Circular Road, when Gerald was four.

He attended a boarding school in Banagher, Co. Offaly, in 1901 and then moved to St Vincent's College, Castleknock, Co. Dublin. In *Ulysses* he was a Belvedere College boy. He became an electrical engineer and worked for the Electricity Supply Board at the Pigeon House in Ringsend.

In 1911 Gerald was living with his widowed mother Louisa Gallaher, his maternal grandmother, Louisa Powell (b. 1835), and brother Brendan (b. 1872) at 44 Grosvenor Road, Rathmines. In 1926 he married Eileen Short of 72 Leinster Road, Rathmines and they lived at 41 Mountain View Road, Ranelagh.

Gerald Gallaher died on 25 October 1946 at his residence, 41 Mountain View Road, Ranelagh, and was buried in Glasnevin Cemetery, Finglas Road, Dublin [QD 125.5 Garden].

Gallaher, Ignatius *Journalist*
Based on **Fred Gallaher (1854–1899)** *Journalist*
'Gallaher, that was a pressman for you. That was a pen.' *(7.629–30)*
Ignatius Gallaher was modelled on Fred Gallaher, one of the best-known journalists of his time. Born in Cork on 19 April 1854, he was the son of John Blake Gallaher and Mary (née Russell).

By 1859 the family had moved from Cork to 7 Oriel Street Upper in Dublin. They then moved to 16 Nelson Street. His father was appointed chief subeditor of the *Freeman's Journal*, a position he held for many years. His brother Joe was also a journalist.

Gallaher was educated at the College of the Immaculate Conception, Upper Mount Street, Dublin, and aged 15 joined the *Freeman's Journal*. John Blake Gallaher and his two sons, Fred and Joe, were at one time all working for this newspaper.

Gallaher was later the editor of the Irish newspaper *Sport*. He covered various sporting events and occasionally judged competitions organised by the Irish Amateur Athletic Association and other bodies. He travelled widely covering international sporting fixtures on the continent and the United States.

He married Sarah Martin in 1874 and they lived at 37 Blessington Street, and later at 151 Rathmines Road and 13 Castlewood Avenue, Rathmines.

According to Myles Crawford in *Ulysses*, Gallaher made an inspired scoop when he was first to convey by telegraph the news of the Phoenix Park murders of 1882 to the *New York World*, supplying a map of the murderers' escape route. The Ship pub was the centre of press gatherings in those days and prominent among the nightly gatherings was Fred Gallaher.

On 12 February 1890, Gallaher was formally appointed to a prominent position on the *Sportsman*, and was based permanently in London. He was also an employee of the Irish-born English publisher, Alfred C. Harmsworth, on either the *London Daily Mail* or the *London Evening News*, where T. P. O'Connor (1848–1920) got him a position.

Gallaher later worked in Paris. He died of cardiac failure on 2 May 1899 in the sub-district of St Sepulchre, London. His body was subsequently taken to St Bartholomew's Hospital in London and he was buried at St Mary's Catholic Cemetery, Kensal Green, London [Plot 676 P].   *Ulysses 6.58; 7.626; 7.651; 7.732*

Gallaher, Mrs Joe (1862–1916) *Friend of the Joyce family*

'... the day we met Mrs Joe Gallaher at the trottingmatches ... with Friery the solicitor ...' *(18.1068–70)*

Mrs Louisa Gallaher (née Powell) was born in Co. Kildare, daughter of Major Malachy Powell and Louisa (née Matthews). She married Joe Gallaher, a journalist with the *Freeman's Journal*, on 3 July 1884 at St Kevin's Church, Harrington Street, Dublin. They lived for a time at 13 Castlewood Avenue, Rathmines, and were neighbours of the Joyces who lived directly opposite at 23 Castlewood Avenue, 1884–7.

The Gallahers had five children. Louisa was widowed on 19 October 1893 when her husband died aged 38 at their residence, 17 Stamer Street, South Circular Road. He was buried in Glasnevin Cemetery, Finglas Road, Dublin [CC 52 Garden]. After his death, The Gallaher Memorial Fund was set up by the Institute of Journalists to raise funds for his family. The total amount received was £426. 16s. 6d.

Louisa Gallaher was selected for a post in Dublin Corporation on 15 December 1893. She lived at Harold's Cross Road in 1901 and had moved by 1911 to 44 Grosvenor Road, Rathmines, where she lived with her 76-year-old mother, Louisa Powell, her two sons Gerald and Brendan, aged 22 and 29 respectively, and some other relations. She died on 18 April 1916 at 148 Rathgar Road and was buried with her father in Glasnevin Cemetery, Finglas Road, Dublin [BF 202 Garden].

Ulysses 15.4349

Gamble, Major (1837–1912) *Secretary of Mount Jerome Cemetery*
'His garden Major Gamble calls Mount Jerome. Well, so it is.' *(6.768)*
George Francis Gamble was born in Middlesex, London. He was attached to the Royal Marine Light Infantry and served in that corps for 18 years, mostly at Mediterranean stations. He married in Dublin in 1866.

Major Gamble retired in 1872 to take up the position of registrar and secretary at Mount Jerome Cemetery, left vacant by the death of Charles Bolton Johnston. He lived for a time at 2 Papermill Lane, Rathmines, and then at 1 Mount Jerome, Harold's Cross. He also had a country residence 'Slivethou', in Brittas, Co. Wicklow.

Gamble undertook various reforms in the management of the cemetery and extended the grounds. He was a frequent contributor to the press and a keen gardener. He was secretary of Mount Jerome for 40 years.

He died on 22 February 1912 at his residence in Mount Jerome and was buried in Mount Jerome Cemetery, Harold's Cross, Dublin [C13–12362].

Gann, Joe (*fl.* late 1800s–mid 1900s) *Staff member, British consulate in Zurich*
'... i hanged Joe Gann in Bootle jail on the 12 of February 1900...' *(12.419–20)*
Joe Gann derives his name from a member of the British consulate in Zurich, Switzerland, who offended Joyce. Joyce used Gann's name to settle old scores due to his failure to give testimony concerning Henry Carr's offensive behaviour towards him (Joyce) in his unsuccessful lawsuit 1918–19. No biographical information has been forthcoming so far on Gann.

Garryowen (b. 1876) *Champion Irish red setter*
'... and the photograph of grandpa Giltrap's lovely dog Garryowen that almost talked it was so human ...' *(13.232–3)*

Garryowen, the Irish red setter, was born in 1876 by Champion Palmerston out of Champion Belle. He was named after a place named Garryowen in Limerick. Bred by James J. Giltrap, his successful career in the show ring spanned a number of years.

Garryowen won first prize and a silver cup in his class at the National Dog Show at Birmingham in November 1880. In November 1882 at the Birmingham Dog Show he won first prize in the champion class of Irish setters.

In early May 1883 the British Kennel Association's first dog show was held at Aston near Birmingham. In the Irish red setter class, the main prize was awarded to Mr Giltrap's 'famous prize dog Champion Garryowen'. A couple of months later in the same year Garryowen won the champion prize at Crystal Palace Dog Show in London.

In the champion class of the Irish setter, at the dog show held at the Royal Zoological Society in Dublin in August 1884, Garryowen won first prize. By now he had won an amazing 34 major prizes. At this show, Garryowen wore a collar on which were displayed the numerous medals won on former occasions. Garryowen had become a household name.

He was the subject of a painting by the famous animal portraitist, Walter Osborne, RHA (1859–1903). The famous Garryowen pipe tobacco was named after him and his portrait appeared on the tin of Garryowen Flake, another pipe tobacco, and was used in advertisements throughout the country.

Ulysses 12.118–21; 12.407; 12.715–16; 12.753; 12.1693–6; 15.663–7; 15.4339; 15.4630 (song)

Geary, James W. (1853–1930) *Sexton, Prospect Cemetery*

'On the curbstone before Jimmy Geary, the sexton's, an old tramp sat, grumbling, emptying the dirt and stones out of his huge dustbrown yawning boot.' *(6.464–6)*
James Geary, son of Thomas Barrington Geary, a solicitor, was born in Dublin. The Dublin Cemeteries Committee at Glasnevin employed Geary for more than half a century. He was sexton before succeeding John O'Connell as superintendent.

Geary was involved with various activities in his native city especially charities and sport. He was a member for the Neptune Rowing Club in his youth. In 1904 Geary was living with his wife Mary and two daughters at 18 Oak Terrace, North Circular Road.

He died on 1 February 1930 at his home, 18 Frankfort Avenue, Rathgar, and was buried in Glasnevin Cemetery, Finglas Road, Dublin [DH 9 St Brigid's].

Geraghty, Michael E. (1864–1905) *Plumber*

'An old plumber named Geraghty.' *(12.20)*
In 1904, Michael E. Geraghty lived at 29 Arbour Hill, near Stonybatter, Dublin. In *Ulysses* Geraghty is referred to as the plumber who cheated Moses Herzog. Geraghty later moved to 4 Prebend Street, Constitution Hill. Prebend Street consisted of 20 tenement houses in Constitution Hill.

He died at his home in Prebend Street on 28 August 1905 and was buried in Glasnevin Cemetery, Finglas Road, Dublin [XE 233.5 St Patrick's].

Gilligan, Philip (1843–1901) *Publican*

'... Philip Gilligan (phthisis, Jervis Street hospital) ...' *(17.1252–3)*
Philip Gilligan owned the Oval Bar at 78 Middle Abbey Street, Dublin. In many instances it was known just as Gilligan's pub. He was associated with the Licensed Grocers' and Vintners' Association for many years, becoming its chairman in

1890. On vacating this position in 1891, he was thanked for 'his energetic, dignified and impartial conduct of the affairs of the association'.

Representing the North City Ward, Gilligan was a poor law guardian of the North Dublin Union. He was also connected with and attended the meetings of the Dublin Charities Fund Committee from 1880.

When Parnell arrived in Dublin from Kilkenny on 23 December 1890, Gilligan was among those who met him at Kingsbridge Station. Others present included John Clancy, the sub-sheriff, and John Henry Menton.

Gilligan was among the invited guests to the annual municipal visit to St Kevin's Reformatory School in Glencree, Co. Wicklow. He was a regular attendee at this event, being involved in social issues of the day.

Gilligan lived at 150 Rathgar Road, Dublin. He died on 10 October 1901 in Jervis Street Hospital and was buried in Glasnevin Cemetery, Finglas Road, Dublin [1A 73 South].   *Ulysses 8.157; 17.544*

Giltrap, James J. (1832–99)   *Law agent and breeder of Garryowen*
'... because she had found out in Walker's pronouncing dictionary that belonged to grandpapa Giltrap about the halcyon days what they meant.' *(13.342–4)*
James J. Giltrap was the father of Josephine Mary Giltrap, who married William A. Murray. Giltrap had a law agency at 2 Morgan Place beside Dublin's Four Courts.

The Giltraps were friends of the Gogartys. In March 1885, at the formation of the Irish Red Setter Club, Giltrap was elected honorary secretary with Dr Henry Gogarty as honorary treasurer. Giltrap assisted with entries and the organisation of shows for the Irish Kennel Club, giving his office address as Morgan Place, Dublin. In 1889 Giltrap lived at 20 Stamer Street off the South Circular Road, Dublin, before moving in 1892 to a location named the Pembroke Kennels in Merrion, Dublin. His last move was to 3 Bengal Terrace on the Finglas Road. Their neighbour, Thomas Childs of 5 Bengal Terrace, was murdered on 2 September 1899.

Giltrap is portrayed as Gerty McDowell's maternal grandfather in *Ulysses*. He died on 1 September 1899 at Our Lady's Hospice, Harold's Cross, and was buried in Glasnevin Cemetery, Finglas Road, Dublin [2D 52 Garden].
                                       Ulysses 12.120; 12.753; 13.83; 13.232–3

Giuglini, Antonio (1827–65)   *Italian tenor*
'How Giuglini began.' *(13.1001)*
Antonio Giuglini was born in 1827 in Fano in the province of Pesaro and Urbino in the Marche region of Italy. He studied under Cellini and made his début at Fermo, Italy. His first season was in 1855 at La Scala in Milan.

Giuglini went to London in 1857, where he starred in several major roles including the first performances of Gounod's *Faust* and Verdi's *Un Ballo in Maschera*. His usual stage partner was soprano Thérèse Tietjens.

Giuglini was a great favourite in Dublin. He and Thérèse Tietjens sang in Dublin at the Theatre Royal in a series of operas in August 1859 including *Les Huguenots, Il Trovatore, Lucrezia Borgia, Norma, La Favorite, Don Giovanni, La Zingara* and *I Puritani*.

Giuglini's career ended in 1864 due to insanity, and he died in Pesaro, Italy in 1865.

Gladstone, William Ewart (1809–98) *British prime minister*

'Prayers for the conversion of Gladstone they had too when he was almost unconscious.' *(5.323–4)*

William Ewart Gladstone was born at 62 Rodney Street, Liverpool, England, on 29 December 1809, the son of John Gladstone, a wealthy merchant, and Anne (née Mackenzie Robertson).

Educated at Eton College and Oxford University, Gladstone was elected to parliament in 1832 as a Conservative and held junior offices in Peel's government of 1834–5. In 1846 when the Conservative Party split, Gladstone followed Peel in becoming a Liberal-Conservative.

Gladstone joined the Liberals in 1859 and became their leader in 1867. The following year he became prime minister for the first time, his administration lasting until 1872. He was prime minister again from 1880 to 1885, in 1886, and from 1892 to 1894. He spent 63 years in the House of Commons. He was never able to carry Home Rule for Ireland, which he strongly advocated.

Gladstone died on 19 May 1898 and was buried in the North Transept, Westminster Abbey, London.

Ulysses 2.397–8; 6.2; 8.423–4; 12.219; 12.874; 15.146; 16.590–2; 16.1366–9; 16.1395; 17.1649–50; 17.1789–90

Glynn, John M. (1834–93) *Organist*

'Mr Bloom looked back towards the choir. Not going to be any music. Pity. Who has the organ here I wonder? Old Glynn he knew how to make that instrument talk, the *vibrato*: fifty pounds a year they say he had in Gardiner street.' *(5.394–7)*

John Glynn born in Dublin, was the son of John Glynn, a clerk of works at City Hall. His early education was at Mr Nattin's school in South Richmond Street, Dublin. A gifted musician, he was taught music by James Wilkinson, an eminent organist.

Glynn's first professional appointment was at St Peter's Church, Drogheda, Co. Louth. He moved to Dublin as organist for the Dominican Church, Old Denmark Street and from there he went to the Church of St Nicholas of Myra, Francis Street, where he remained until 1866.

He was appointed to the Vincentian Church, Phibsborough, and was then organist at the Dominican Church, Dominick Street, a position he retained until

1887, when he succeeded Hamilton Croft as organist and choirmaster of the Jesuit Church in Gardiner Street. Glynn inaugurated the new organ built by John White who worked on many of the organs in Dublin in the nineteenth century.

A director of the Cecilian Society, Glynn conducted the first Cecilian Festival held in St Andrew's Church, Westland Row, in 1879.

In 1877 Glynn lived at 6 Lennox Street in Portobello, and by 1884 had moved to 10 Lennox Street.

At the Thomas Moore centenary celebrations in 1879, Glynn presided as organist, and opened the exhibition in the Rotunda in 1882, where he conducted several 'Grand Concerts' during that season. He was professor of music in many schools and convents in Dublin and was examiner for the organ and pianoforte in the Royal Irish Academy of Music, Westland Row. He was an examiner in music at the intermediate examinations.

Glynn composed church music and his best compositions include 'Tota Pulchra', 'Ecce Cor', 'Jesu Doloris', 'Inviolata', and 'O Cor Voluptus'. He also composed ballads and pianoforte pieces, notably the 'Memories of Erin', dedicated to Mrs Joseph Robinson; 'La Coronella'; and the song 'Where the Lovely Rivers Flow'. He was the first to organise Vespers in Dublin. Glynn's main residence was in Baldoyle, Co. Dublin. He also stayed at 6 Temple Street North, close to St Francis Xavier's Church. At the time of his death Glynn had been organist of St Francis Xavier's Church, Gardiner Street for six years, 1887–93.

He died on 26 August 1893 at his home in 'The Mall', Baldoyle, Co. Dublin, and was buried in Glasnevin Cemetery, Finglas Road, Dublin [BI 227 St Brigid's].

Ulysses 11.1197; 15.1953

Goldberg, Owen *Bloom's school friend*
Based on **Marcus Goldberg** (1850–1936) *Dentist*
'In 1884 with Owen Goldberg and Cecil Turnbull at night on public thoroughfares between Longwood avenue and Leonard's corner and Leonard's corner and Synge street and Synge street and Bloomfield avenue.' *(17.48–50)*
Marcus Goldberg was born in 1850 in Poland. His wife Leah (née Mitavsky) was also born there. The Goldberg family lived at 90 Longwood Avenue, South Circular Road, Dublin in 1901 and in 1904 at 31 Harcourt Street, where Marcus Goldberg practised as a dentist. He eventually moved to England with his wife. He died in Hove, Sussex in 1936.   *Ulysses 8.404*

Goldwater, Joseph (*fl.* late 1880s–early 1900s) *Neighbour of Bloom*
Joseph Goldwater lived at 77 Lombard Street West and was a neighbour of the Blooms when they lived in the same street, 1892–3. At the end of the nineteenth century, the Dublin Hebrew Young Men's Association met at Goldwater's house.

Ulysses 15.3222

Gomez, Fernando (1847–97) *Matador*

'... at the bullfight at La Linea when the matador Gomez was given the bulls ear ...'
(18.625–6)

Fernando Gomez was born in Seville in Spain on 18 August 1847. He had an interest in bullfighting from an early age. He began in the bullring as a banderillero and eventually graduated as a matador at the age of 30 on 7 October 1877.

Gomez introduced a daring pass on his knees. He was gored by a bull a number of times and was seriously injured on two occasions. He had an unrivalled skill with the large cape used at the start of a fight, but was not an expert at killing off the bull, possibly due to the shortness of his legs.

Known as one of Spain's great matadors, he died of a heart attack aged 50 on 2 August 1897 at Gelves, in the province of Seville.

Gonne, Maud (1866–1953) *Irish nationalist and suffragette*

'Maud Gonne's letter about taking them off O'Connell street at night: disgrace to our Irish capital.' *(5.70–1)*

Maud Gonne was born on 21 December 1866 in Hampshire, England. She was the daughter of Captain Thomas Gonne (1835–86) of the 17th Lancers and Edith (née Cook) (1844–71). Gonne was educated privately in France when her mother died.

In 1882 she accompanied her father when he was posted to Dublin Castle and remained with him until his death four years later.

In 1886 John O'Leary introduced her to Fenianism and on 30 January 1889 he sent her to the Yeats home at Bedford Park in London, to visit John Butler Yeats. William Butler Yeats, his 23-year-old son, fell in love with her. Although she refused his numerous proposals of marriage and caused him much pain, she had a significant role in his life. She played the leading role in his play, *Cathleen ni Houlihan* in 1902.

While recuperating from illness in France, sometime after 1887, Maud Gonne met Lucien Millevoye, the politician, and helped with the publication of his book *La Patrie*. They had two children, a son Georges, who was born in 1891 and died 18 months later, and a daughter Iseult (1895–1954), after whose birth, the couple lived apart.

Gonne led agitation over land during the famine of the 1890s in Mayo and Donegal and assisted in securing the release of Irish political prisoners from Portland Gaol. She also founded a revolutionary women's society, Inghinidhe na hÉireann (the Daughters of Ireland).

In February 1903 she married Major John MacBride in Paris. Their son Seán was born in 1904. The marriage failed and MacBride returned to Ireland. Gonne remained in France until 1917 and edited *L'Irlande Libre*. Following MacBride's execution for his part in the 1916 Easter Rising, she returned to Ireland and was involved in the anti-conscription campaign there. She was arrested in Dublin and served six months in Holloway Prison but was released on grounds of illness. During the War of Independence she worked for the White Cross for the relief of victims of violence. She opposed the Anglo-Irish Treaty of 1921 and with Hanna Sheehy-Skeffington and Charlotte Despard founded the Women's Prisoners' Defence League. She was imprisoned during the Civil War and went on hunger strike with 90 other people.

Maud Gonne lived in Roebuck House, Clonskeagh, Dublin, and in 1938 published *A Servant of the Queen*, an account of her life until her marriage.

She died on 27 April 1953 and was buried in the Republican Plot in Glasnevin Cemetery, Finglas Road, Dublin. Her son, Seán MacBride, the republican, politician, lawyer and recipient of the Nobel Peace Prize who died in 1988, was buried with her [TD 24–25.5 South New Chapel].   *Ulysses 3.233; 8.423–4*

Goodwin, Professor William (1839–92) *Professor of music*

'Poor old professor Goodwin ... Oldfashioned way he used to bow Molly off the platform.' *(4.291–3)*

From 1857 to 1864 William Goodwin, professor of music, worked as organist at St Peter's Church in Phibsborough, Dublin. During this period he lived in various locations in the vicinity, never staying in any one very long.

He conducted concerts at various venues around the city and appears as early as November 1863 conducting a concert at the Pillar Room in the Rotunda. In July 1874 he conducted a concert consisting mostly of selections from Haydn, Handel and other eminent composers in the Church of SS Augustine and John in Thomas Street. In November 1878 he conducted a concert at the Rotunda to raise funds for the education of children in Bulgaria under the care of Irish nuns.

Goodwin was a well-known teacher of music in several Dublin schools, including the Catholic University School, run by the Marist Fathers in Leeson Street, where he taught from the late 1860s to 1878. He also taught at the Royal Hibernian Military School in Phoenix Park, a school for orphans and destitute children of soldiers who had either died, were killed or were away in the service of the crown.

On 27 and 28 April 1880, two 'Grand Concerts' were held in the Antient Concert Rooms, under the patronage of Edward Dwyer Gray, MP, lord mayor of Dublin and owner of the *Freeman's Journal*. The conductor was Professor W. G. Goodwin and the artistes included among others, Mr J. S. Joyce, Mr Christopher Dollard, and other well-known amateur singers in the 1880s.

In 1881 Professor Goodwin was appointed as local secretary to the board of Trinity College Dublin. A 'Complimentary Concert to Professor W. G. Goodwin' was held on 3 September 1885 in the Antient Concert Rooms. A number of Goodwin's friends volunteered their services, including John Stanislaus Joyce.

Goodwin's compositions included 'Silent Love', 'Hail, O Mary, Queen of May' and 'Discite a Me'. The latter piece was composed and arranged with organ accompaniment, and was advertised in the *Nation* in June 1890. His publications included *Goodwin's Hand Book of Singing for the Use of Schools*.

Professor Goodwin lived at the following addresses in Dublin: 81 Phibsborough Road, 1857–8; 6 Villa Bank, Phibsborough, 1859–60; 1 Elm Villas, Glasnevin Road, Phibsborough, 1861–3; 1 Madras Place, North Circular Road 1864; 12 Magowen Terrace, Ranelagh,1867–9; 3 Bloomfield Avenue, South Circular Road, 1870–3; 2 Harrington Terrace, 1876; 26 Frankfurt Avenue, Rathmines, 1878; 57 Belgrave Square, Rathmines, 1883–4; [missing from *Thom's Directory 1885–90*]; 'Pearemount', 122 Harold's Cross, 1890–1; 74 Harold's Cross, Dublin, 1892. Goodwin died on 4 August 1892 and was buried in Glasnevin Cemetery, Finglas Road, Dublin [YC 20.5 Garden].   *Ulysses 8.185; 8.188; 8.193; 11.466; 15.4018; 15.4047; 17.2134; 18.336; 18.1333*

Gorman, Rev. Bernard, ODC (1864–1938) *Provincial, St Teresa's Church*
Bernard Gorman was born on 22 August 1864 in Dublin. Educated at Castleknock College, Dublin, he entered the Carmelite novitiate at Loughrea in Co. Galway. He continued his studies at Parma and Venice and was ordained priest on 6 October 1895.

Father Gorman was master of studies in St Mary's, Morehampton Road, Dublin and was then transferred to St Teresa's, Clarendon Street where he spent most of his religious life. He was provincial of the Discalced Carmelites Friary in Clarendon Street, at the time of his death on 26 June 1938. He was buried in Glasnevin Cemetery, Finglas Road, Dublin in the Carmelite Plot [TE 20.5 South New Chapel].

Ulysses 12.931

Gorman, Rev. Timothy (1845–1922) *Parish priest of SS Michael and John's Church*
Timothy Gorman was born in 1845 in the parish of St Andrews in Westland Row in Dublin. He entered Holy Cross College, Clonliffe, Dublin, in September 1860 before continuing his studies at St Patrick's College Maynooth, Co. Kildare. He was ordained priest in August 1869 and his first appointment was to a curacy at St Paul's Church, Arran Quay in Dublin. In succession he officiated as curate in St Kevin's, Dublin; and in Blackrock, Ballybrack and Dalkey.

Father Gorman was administrator at St Mary's Pro-Cathedral in Marlborough Street from 1890 to 1897 and was then promoted to parish priest in the parish of St Michael and John's, Lower Exchange Street, Dublin. In 1904 he was transferred to the parish of Bray, Co. Wicklow, and nominated archdeacon of Glendalough. In 1906 he was made vicar forane. In 1912 he was transferred to the new St Columba's parish in Drumcondra and lived at 'Invermore', 87 Iona Road, Glasnevin. He died on 25 November 1922 and was buried in Glasnevin Cemetery, Finglas Road, Dublin [XB 79 South].

Ulysses 12.937

Goulding, Richard *Stephen's uncle*
Based on **William Murray** (1857–1912) *Joyce's maternal uncle*
'Richie Goulding and the legal bag. Goulding, Collis and Ward he calls the firm. His jokes are getting a bit damp.' *(6.56–7)*
William Murray, son of John Murray and Margaret (née Flynn) was born in Eagle House, Roundtown (now Terenure).

William married Josephine Giltrap. As well as appearing under his own name in *Ulysses*, he also takes on the persona of Richie Goulding, Mr Dedalus's brother-in-law and accountant for Collis & Ward. Like Richie, Murray was fond of music and opera.

Murray worked as a cost accountant at the law agency of James J. Giltrap, at 2 Morgan Place, near the Four Courts. In 1899 on the death of Mr Giltrap, his father-in-law, he moved to a firm of solicitors, Collis & Ward, at 31 Dame Street.

Murray lived at various addresses in Dublin. He died on 29 November 1912 at 6 O'Connor Terrace, Ballybough Road, Dublin and was buried in Glasnevin Cemetery, Finglas Road, Dublin [AG 135.5 Garden].

Ulysses 8.320; 10.471–2; 10.1191; 11.354; 11.390; 11.521; 11.523; 11.570; 11.609; 11.643; 11.768; 11.784; 11.786; 11.797; 11.828; 11.1028; 11.1070; 11.1164; 11.1227; 13.846; 15.2788; 15.4174; 17.141; 17.539; 17.952; 18.1299

Goulding, Sara *Stephen's aunt*
Based on **Mrs William Murray** (1863–1924) *Joyce's aunt*
'His pace slackened. Here. Am I going to aunt Sara's or not?' *(3.61)*
Sara Goulding, aunt Sara, Richie Goulding's wife, was based on Joyce's aunt Josephine Murray. The daughter of James J. Giltrap, she was born in 1863 and educated at a convent school at Glossop in Derbyshire, England.

Josephine Giltrap met William A. Murray (1857–1912), 'nuncle Richie', when he worked as an accountant with her father, in his law agency office situated near the Four Courts at 2 Morgan Place. They married, had seven children and lived at different addresses around the city, including Ontario Terrace, Holles Street, and on the north side of Dublin at Northbrook Villas, 19 Foster Place, Ballybough Road, and 6 O'Connor Terrace, Ballybough.

When her father, James J. Giltrap, died on 1 September 1899, her husband William Murray lost his job and found employment as a freelance cost accountant for a firm of solicitors, Collis & Ward, at 31 Dame Street.

Josephine Murray survived her husband by 12 years. She died on 15 November 1924 at 10 Fairfield Road, Fairview, Dublin, and was buried in Glasnevin Cemetery, Finglas Road, Dublin [AG 135.5 Garden].   *Ulysses 6.051*

Grant, Ulysses S. (1822–85) *President of the United States*
'... when general Ulysses Grant whoever he was or did supposed to be some great fellow landed off the ship ...' *(18.681–3)*
Ulysses S. Grant was born on 27 April 1822 in Point Pleasant, Ohio, son of Jesse

Root Grant, a tanner, and Hannah (née Simpson). He entered the United States Military Academy at West Point aged 17.

He was elected eighteenth president of the United States in 1869. After the close of his second term of office he embarked on a two-year world tour from 1877–9 that included a visit by boat to Gibraltar on 17 November 1878.

Grant and his family were left destitute when he was swindled and lost all his financial assets. He completed his *Memoirs* just a couple of days before he died. The book proved successful and earned the family over $450,000.

Ulysses S. Grant died on 23 July 1885 at Mount Gregor, Saratoga County, New York. A large mausoleum marks his burial place in New York City's Riverside Park.

Grattan, Henry (1746–1820) *Politician, patriot and orator*

'Why not bring in Henry Grattan and Flood and Demosthenes ...' *(7.731)*

Henry Grattan was born in Dublin on 3 July 1746, son of James Grattan, MP and Mary (née Marlay). He was educated at Trinity College Dublin and graduated with a BA degree in 1767. He studied law at the Middle Temple and was called to the Irish Bar in 1772. He also wrote for the *Freeman's Journal*.

Grattan was MP for the borough of Charlemont in the Irish parliament in 1775. He replaced Henry Flood as leader. When the Irish parliament achieved independence in 1782, it became known as 'Grattan's Parliament'. Dublin responded with pealing bells, cheering crowds and bonfires. During this period, Grattan led the demand for Catholic Emancipation, introducing a bill that was defeated in 1794. The rising of the United Irishmen in 1798 distressed him and after it he returned as MP for Wicklow to fight the Act of Union but to no avail. In 1805 he sat in the English parliament for Malton, and for Dublin, 1806–20. In one of his first speeches there he said of the Irish parliament: 'I watched by its cradle; I followed its hearse.'

Grattan died at 68 Baker Street, London on 4 June 1820 and was buried in the North Transept of Westminster Abbey.

Grattan Bridge in Dublin is named after him and he is commemorated by a statue by John Henry Foley outside Trinity College Dublin, a bust by Peter Grant in Merrion Square and a marble statue by Chantry in City Hall.

Ulysses 2.270; 3.259–60; 7.87; 7.91–2; 7.348; 7.738–9; 10.352; 15.4683; 15.4883

Gray, Sir John (1815–75) *Doctor, parliamentarian and newspaper proprietor*

'He halted on sir John Gray's pavement island ...' *(7.1067)*

John Gray, son of John Gray and Elizabeth (née Wilson), was born in Claremorris, Co. Mayo, on 13 July 1815. He studied medicine at Glasgow University and graduated in 1839. He settled in Dublin and married Mary Anna, only daughter of James Dwyer of Limerick.

Gray initially practised medicine but in 1841 he became political editor and joint proprietor of the *Freeman's Journal*.

He was a supporter of the repeal movement led by Daniel O'Connell. With O'Connell, and others, he was tried and sentenced during the state trials, 1843–4.

Gray became the sole proprietor of the *Freeman's Journal* in 1850, increasing its size, reducing its price and boosting circulation. Two years later he was appointed chairman of the Dublin Corporation's Waterworks Committee and as a corporation member is best known for bringing a fresh water supply from Vartry in Co. Wicklow to the city of Dublin. The Vartry water supply scheme involved sand beds which were used to filter the water. When the system came into operation in 1867, Dublin became the first city in northern Europe with a fully filtered water supply. Bloom recalls the details of the Vartry scheme's construction in the 'Ithaca' episode.

Gray was knighted in June 1863. He declined the position of lord mayor of Dublin in 1868. He lived at Charleville House, Rathmines (now St Louis Convent), and at 'Vartry Lodge', Ballybrack, Co. Dublin.

Gray was MP for Kilkenny from 1865 until his death on 9 April 1875 at Bath in England. He was buried in Glasnevin Cemetery, Finglas Road, Dublin [Vault 8 O'Connell Tower Circle]. His grave is marked with a memorial by sculptor Thomas Farrell (1827–1900), who is also responsible for the marble statue of Gray erected by public subscription in 1879. This is sited on O'Connell Street at the junction with Abbey Street. A bust at Roundwood Reservoir, Co. Wicklow also commemorates him.   *Ulysses 6.258; 11.762–3*

Green, M. C. (*fl.* late 1800s–early 1900s) *Cyclist*
'Thither of the wall of the quartermile flat handicappers, M. C. Green ...' *(10.1258)*
M. C. Green was one of the nine quarter-mile flat handicappers who took part in the Trinity College Dublin bicycle races in the afternoon of 16 June 1904.

Greene, Roger (1846–1909) *Solicitor*
'Passing by Roger Greene's office and Dollard's big red printinghouse ...' *(10.1205–6)*
Roger Greene was born in 1846 in Rathkeale, Co. Limerick. He served his apprenticeship with Mr Thomas Lynch, in Upper Sackville Street (now O'Connell Street), Dublin. He established an extensive practice with offices at 11 Wellington Quay where he was the senior partner. A well-known and popular solicitor, Greene presided at several of the meetings for the Kane Family Fund in 1904 after the drowning of Matthew Kane.

He died at his residence, 6 Cabra Road, Dublin on 31 October 1909. He was buried in Glasnevin Cemetery, Finglas Road, Dublin [TA 6 Section 5] where John O'Connell the superintendent of Glasnevin Cemetery received his remains and the Rev. Francis J. Coffey read the prayers at the graveside.

Greene, Rev. Thomas Robert (1847–1914) *Free Church preacher*
'The reverend T. R. Greene B. A. will (D. V.) speak.' *(10.69–70)*

Thomas Robert Greene was born in Wicklow. He was the son of the Rev. Thomas Francis Greene and Elizabeth (née Heighington). As a child he lived at Donoughmore and later at Donard in Co. Wicklow where his father was vicar, 1852–61.

Greene was educated at Trinity College Dublin where he graduated with a BA degree in 1867. The following year he studied divinity also at Trinity.

During his career he was attached to Tuam, 1870; Armagh, 1871; Duagh (Ardfert), 1870–1; Roscrea (Killaloe), 1871–3; Macully (Ossory), 1873–6; Cloydagh and Bilbo (Leighlin), 1876–82; St Thomas's Church, Marlborough Street, Dublin, 1882–3; and the Sunday School Society Ireland, 1883. His last post was as incumbent of the Free Church, Great Charles Street, Dublin, where he remained, 1891–1913. In 1904 he was living at 27 Drumcondra Road Lower. He later moved to 25 Eccles Street North.

The Rev. Greene died at Ballinroan House, Baltinglass, Co. Wicklow on 27 October 1914. He was buried in Kiltegan Cemetery, Co. Wicklow.

Gregory, Lady Augusta (1852–1932) *Playwright and folklorist*

'Longworth is awfully sick, he said, after what you wrote about that old hake Gregory.' *(9.1158–9)*

Lady Gregory was born Isabella Augusta Persse on 15 March 1852 at Roxborough House, Co. Galway. She was the youngest daughter of Dudley Persse and his second wife, Frances (née Barry).

She was educated privately and during her first 27 years did not move far from the confines of the estate and spent her time visiting the tenants in the cottages, learning Irish and teaching at Sunday school.

On 4 March 1880 she married Sir William Gregory, a widower, 35 years her senior who owned an estate at Coole Park, near Gort, Co. Galway. He had a house in London where they lived when not abroad. The Gregorys' only child, William Robert, was born in May 1881. (He was later killed in the First World War.) On the death of her husband in 1892, Lady Gregory resided at Coole Park and published her husband's autobiography in 1894.

Lady Gregory was already gathering the legends and folktales of her native county in the 1890s. She published English versions of the old heroic sagas under the titles *Cuchulain of Muirthemne* (1902) and *Gods and Fighting Men* (1904). Her publications on folktales and folk history include *A Book of Saints and Wonders* (1906), *The Kiltartan History Book* (1909), *The Kiltartan Wonder Book* (1910) and the two-volume *Visions and Beliefs in the West of Ireland* (1920).

In 1896 she met W. B. Yeats who became a frequent visitor to Coole Park, spending two or three months there each year for 20 years. The Irish Literary Revival was just beginning, and many of the major literary figures availed themselves of her hospitality at Coole Park.

In 1897 Lady Gregory, W. B. Yeats and Edward Martyn met in the home of the Comte Florimond de Basterot in Duras, Co. Galway. It was at this meeting that the dramatic movement, which led to the Abbey Theatre, was initiated.

The Irish National Theatre was founded in 1904 from a merger with the Irish Literary Theatre Society and the National Dramatic Company owned by the Fay brothers, William and Frank. At William Fay's suggestion, Annie Horniman, an English heiress, bought the Mechanics Theatre in Abbey Street. This was refurbished as the Abbey Theatre and opened on 27 December 1904 with a performance of Yeats's *On Baile's Strand* and Lady Gregory's *Spreading the News*.

Between 1901 and 1928, Lady Gregory wrote over 40 plays, most of which were produced at the Abbey. She was an active director of the Abbey from its foundation until 1928 when ill health forced her to retire to Coole Park, though she continued to visit Dublin regularly until 1930 to keep an eye on the theatre.

Lady Gregory died on 22 May 1932 at Coole Park and was buried in the New Cemetery, Bohermore, Galway. *Ulysses 9.274; 9.709; 12.68–9; Cuchulain of Muirthemne, 9.1161–5*

Grey, Gregor (*c.* 1850–1920) *Artist*
'Gregor Grey made the design for it.' *(7.686)*
Gregor Grey, one of 16 children, was the son of Charles Grey (*c.* 1808–92), RHA, the eminent portrait and landscape painter who was born in Greenock, Scotland and settled in Dublin.

All of Gregor's 14 brothers were artists and six were full members of the Royal Hibernian Academy. They included: Edwin Landseer Grey; Alfred Grey, a painter of landscapes and cattle; Charles Malcolm Grey, a wood engraver; James Grey, a painter; and Edward Grey, who was regarded as the leading wood engraver of his day in London. Gregor's only sister married an artist, Walter Mills.

From 1877 to 1911 Grey, who painted mainly pastoral scenes, exhibited his works at the Royal Hibernian Academy in Abbey Street. In 1906 and 1907 he exhibited at the Oireachtas exhibition. He had a reputation for being a close and earnest student of nature.

In 1904 Alfred, Gregor and George Grey were living at 1 Sherrard Street Lower in Dublin before moving to 7 Sherrard Street.

Gregor Grey died on 17 November 1920 in the Richmond Asylum and was buried in Mount Jerome Cemetery, Harold's Cross, Dublin, in common ground [A3–227]. The Grey family vault is also in Mount Jerome.

Griffith, Arthur (1871–1922) *Journalist and politician*
'What Arthur Griffith said about the headpiece over the *Freeman* leader: a homerule sun rising up in the northwest from the laneway behind the bank of Ireland.' *(4.100–3)*
Arthur Griffith, son of Arthur Griffith, a printer, and Mary (née Phelan), was born at 61 Upper Dominick Street, in Dublin, on 31 March 1871. He was educated at Strand Street Christian Brothers School. He worked as a printer for the *Irish Independent* and the *Nation*. He joined the Gaelic League and the Irish Republican Brother-

hood and in 1889 with William Rooney, he founded the Celtic Literary Society.

Griffith joined John MacBride in South Africa in 1896 and supported the Boers. He returned to Dublin after two years to edit the *United Irishman*, a new weekly newspaper that crusaded for Irish independence. He urged passive resistance to British rule in Ireland and in a series of articles, published in 1904 as a book titled *The Resurrection of Hungary: A Parallel for Ireland*, he outlined a new policy advocating that Irish MPs withdraw from Westminster and establish a national assembly in Ireland with recognition of the crown, on the Hungarian model.

The *United Irishman* ceased publication in 1906 and Griffith launched a new paper *Sinn Féin* that continued until its suppression in 1914. Griffith joined the Irish Volunteers in 1913 and took part in the landing of arms at Howth in July 1914. He founded *Nationality* (1915–19), which he jointly edited with Seumas O'Kelly. Though he did not partake in the 1916 Rising he was arrested, as the British associated Sinn Féin with the rebellion. Eamon de Valera assumed the Sinn Féin presidency and Griffith became a vice-president. In 1918 he was elected MP for Cavan. He led the delegation that negotiated the Anglo-Irish Treaty in 1921. He replaced de Valera and was the head of the first provisional government of the Irish Free State.

Griffith died on 12 August 1922 in Dublin and was buried in Glasnevin Cemetery, Finglas Road, Dublin [ZE 22 South New Chapel].

Ulysses 3.227; 5.71; 8.462; 12.1538; 12.1574–7; 15.4685; 18.386; 18.1228; The Resurrection of Hungary, 12.1635; 15.1546–7

Gumley, William (1849–1920) *Night watchman for Dublin Corporation*
'Gumley? He said. You don't say so? A friend of my father's, is it?' *(7.648)*
William Gumley was born in Wales. In 1904 he was living at 13 Fontenoy Street with his wife Charlotte, eight children and a servant. He was a neighbour of John Stanislaus Joyce who was living at 44 Fontenoy Street in 1905. Gumley was an accountant for a land agent but in *Ulysses* is portrayed as being down on his luck and working as a night watchman for Dublin Corporation.

William Gumley and his family later moved to a large red-bricked house at 62 Lindsay Road in Glasnevin.

His last address in Dublin was 107 Railway Street. He died a widower on 17 March 1920 in the North Dublin Union Workhouse and was buried in Glasnevin Cemetery, Finglas Road, Dublin, in an unmarked grave [FD 70 St Patrick's].

Ulysses 7.645; 7.649; 12.1101; 16.109; 16.944; 16.1726

Gunn, Michael (1840–1901) *Proprietor and manager of the Gaiety Theatre*
'... when Michael Gunn was identified with the management of the *Flying Dutchman*, a stupendous success ...' *(16.860–1)*
Michael Gunn was born in Dublin. His father had a business with pianoforte and harmonium importers, publishers and sellers of sheet music, at 61 Grafton Street, Dublin. There was also a branch in Cork. His father drowned in 1861

when a horse-drawn tram in which he was travelling overturned into the Grand Canal lock at Portobello in Dublin. The business was then taken over by his sons Michael and John.

The Gunn brothers built the Gaiety Theatre in Dublin's King Street. On 1 July 1871 the foundation stone was laid when the brothers were given letters patent to build 'a well regulated theatre and therein at all times publicly to act, represent or perform any interlude, tragedy, comedy, prelude, opera, burletta play, farce or pantomime'.

The building with seating for 2,000 people was completed in six months and opened in 1871. The Gaiety became the leading playhouse staging Shakespeare and the classics. Its long operatic tradition began in 1872; Italian and English operas were performed there as well as pantomime. It attracted many famous actors over the years such as Sir Henry Irving and Sarah Bernhardt. Michael Gunn was a friend of nearly all the great artistes and composers of his time.

In 1874 the brothers acquired the old Theatre Royal at Hawkins Street and with it the royal patent of Charles II, which Michael Gunn transferred to the Gaiety. Six years later the Theatre Royal was destroyed by fire. Gunn was anxious to rebuild it but many difficulties ensued. In its place he built the Leinster Hall, a concert room, which opened in 1885.

It is perhaps as theatrical manager and proprietor of the Gaiety that Gunn is best remembered. The theatre enjoyed huge popularity with the playgoers of Dublin. He was involved in its management from 1871 until his death and had introduced the masterpieces of modern theatrical and musical composition to Irish audiences as well as a great variety of drama.

A former member of Dublin Corporation, Michael Gunn lived at 69 Merrion Square. He died on 17 October 1901 at his London residence, 'St Selskar's', Eton Avenue, Hampstead. He was buried in St Pancras Cemetery, Camden.

Ulysses 11.1050; 17.420; 17.426; Mrs Michael Gunn, 18.1111

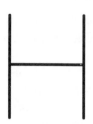

Hackett, Rev. M. A. (1850–1911) *Parish priest, St Margaret's Church, Finglas*
Martin Hackett was born in Dungarvan, Co. Waterford, in August 1850. He was admitted to Holy Cross College, Clonliffe, Dublin, in September 1869 and had completed his studies by 1874.

The Rev. Martin Hackett, CC was parish priest at St Margaret's Church, Finglas, Co. Dublin, from 1902 to 1911. Following his short pastorate in Finglas, Father Hackett died on 8 January 1911 in a private hospital in Mountjoy Square and was buried in Glasnevin Cemetery, Finglas Road, Dublin [GH 13 St Brigid's].

Ulysses 12.934–5

Haines *English friend of Mulligan*
Based on **Richard Samuel Chenevix Trench (1881–1909)** *Friend of Oliver Gogarty*
'They halted while Haines surveyed the tower and said at last:
Rather bleak in wintertime, I should say. Martello you call it?' *(1.541–2)*
Richard Samuel Chenevix Trench was born on 6 October 1881 in England, the elder son of Major-General Frederick Trench. The family consisted of two sons and

three daughters. Richard Samuel, known as Samuel, had interesting family connections: his father was the second son of the Most Rev. Richard Chenevix Trench, archbishop of Dublin, 1864–84.

Major-General Frederick Trench was military attaché at St Petersburg, 1883–6, and wrote a number of books on military topics. Samuel was 12 years old when his father was found dead aged 57 at Braemar, Scotland with a bottle of poison next to him. He was suffering from an incurable and painful disease. He was buried in the Dean Cemetery in Edinburgh.

Richard Samuel Chenevix Trench was educated at Eton College. At the time he attended Eton College, his home address in the *Eton School Register 1893–99* was listed at 28 Castle Hill Avenue, Folkestone, Kent. He then went to Balliol College in Oxford where he also joined the Oxford Gaelic Society and learned to speak Irish. Here he first met Oliver St John Gogarty at the weekly Irish classes held sometime between January and June 1904. Trench was three years younger than Gogarty.

In September 1904, Trench stayed in the Martello Tower in Sandycove,

Co. Dublin, as a guest of Oliver St John Gogarty. Joyce was also in the Tower and Trench's eccentric behaviour was responsible for Joyce's sudden departure. Trench appears in *Ulysses* as the Englishman Haines.

An enthusiastic supporter of the Gaelic Revival, Trench assumed the additional name of Dermot by deed poll on 3 March 1905. His only published work was a 1907 pamphlet entitled *What Is the Use of Reviving Irish?*

Trench died suddenly aged 27, on 1 June 1909 at Orpington House, Hivings Hill, in Chartridge, a small village near the market town of Chesham in Buckinghamshire. An inquest was held the following day, which gave the cause of death as follows: 'Shot himself in the ear and forehead while temporarily insane.' His funeral service was held in London at the Holy Trinity Church, Sloane Street, and he was interred at Brompton Cemetery, London.

Ulysses 1.49; 1.162; 1.284; 1.318; 1.328; 1.334; 1.344; 1.352; 1.359; 1.365; 1.393; 1.425–6; 1.430; 1.439; 1.449; 1.469; 1.474; 1.478; 1.487–8; 1.491; 1.520; 1.537; 1.541; 1.545; 1.553; 1.558; 1.562; 1.566; 1.572; 1.603; 1.609; 1.611; 1.615; 1.618; 1.633; 1.639; 1.642; 1.645; 1.693; 1.715; 1.718; 1.730; 9.91; 9.306; 9.513; 9.559; 9.1114; 9.1130; 10.1044; 10.1048; 10.1054; 10.1060; 10.1068; 10.1076; 10.1082; 10.1091; 10.1224; 14.1012; 14.1032; 15.4695; 15.4700, 15.4704

Hall, Jack B. (1851–1931) *Dublin Journalist and author*
'They're gone round to the Oval for a drink. Paddy Hooper is there with Jack Hall.'
(7.455–6)
Jack B. Hall was born in Dublin. He was educated at Belvedere College near his home in Eccles Street. His father worked in the *Freeman's Journal* as a member of the commercial staff.

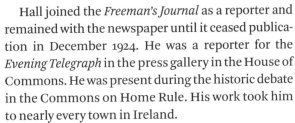

Hall joined the *Freeman's Journal* as a reporter and remained with the newspaper until it ceased publication in December 1924. He was a reporter for the *Evening Telegraph* in the press gallery in the House of Commons. He was present during the historic debate in the Commons on Home Rule. His work took him to nearly every town in Ireland.

Hall was in the Gaiety Theatre in 1882 during the Carla Rosa Opera Company's performance of *Maritana* when the proprietor Michael Gunn told him about the Phoenix Park murders. Hall got the news into the midnight edition of the *Evening Telegraph*, publishing the first report of the Phoenix Park murders which had taken place on 6 May in 1882. He also reported on the last public execution in Ireland, the hanging of an innocent man in Galway Jail. He was present at the hanging and fainted when the drop fell.

Hall was a competent critic, writing, for example, about Mary Anderson (1859–1940), the American actress who appeared in Belfast's Ulster Hall in June 1904. He was also an artist and had his works exhibited at the Hibernian Academy.

He wrote *Random Records of a Reporter* (1928), with a foreword by his friend and fellow journalist, the Rt. Hon. T. P. O'Connor, MP (Tay Pay). Hall did the accompanying sketches for the book.

In 1911 he was living at 21 Rathgar Road with his family and father, also named Jack Hall, then 86 and a retired advertising canvasser. In November 1930, when Hall had entered his eightieth year and was still working as a journalist, a special 'J. B. Hall Presentation Fund' was organised with the intention of purchasing an annuity for him.

Hall, one of the most notable journalistic figures of his time, died at his home in Rathgar on 27 July 1931 and was buried in Glasnevin Cemetery, Finglas Road, Dublin [EG 168.5 Garden].

Hand, Stephen (1873–1924) *Clerk in Dublin Corporation and bettor*

'The ruffin cly the nab of Stephen Hand as give me the jady coppaleen.' *(14.1514–15)*
Stephen Hand was born in Dublin. He was a clerk with Dublin Corporation and entered the Corporation's permanent service in 1917 becoming a well-known official. He lived in Phibsborough in 1901, and by 1911 had moved to 82 Aughrim Street, with his wife Catherine and five children.

Hand retired on a pension in March 1923 under the Local Government Act, 1919. He was responsible for the supervision of all matters dealing with the franchise and jurors' lists. He died on 24 January 1924 at his residence, 98 North Circular Road, and was buried in Glasnevin Cemetery, Finglas Road, Dublin [PH 147 St Brigid's].   *Ulysses 15.2092–3*

Harmsworth, Alfred Charles (Baron Northcliffe) (1865–1922) *Editor and publisher*

'Ignatius Gallaher we all know and his Chapelizod boss, Harmsworth of the farthing press ...' *(7.732–3)*
Alfred Charles Harmsworth was born in a house named 'Sunnybank' on the Liffey in Chapelizod near Dublin on 15 July 1865. He was the eldest son of Alfred Harmsworth, a barrister, and Geraldine (née Maffett).

The family moved to London when Alfred was two years old. He was educated at Stamford Grammar School, Lincolnshire and Henley House School, Hampstead, where due to his interest in journalism he started a school magazine. He worked occasionally for the *Hampstead and Highgate Express* as a young reporter.

In 1887 he formed a publishing business with his brother Harold and started the popular weekly journal, *Answers*. In 1894 he acquired the *London Evening News*, and in 1896 founded the *London Daily Mail*, which changed the face of English journalism. He was created baronet in 1903 and baron in 1905. In 1908 he became chief proprietor of *The Times*. He considered himself to be a champion of the 'newspapers of the future' and was created viscount in 1917.

Viscount Northcliffe died on 14 August 1922 at his home 1 Carleton Gardens,

London and was buried at Finchley Cemetery, Finchley, London. He is commemorated by a bronze bust on the south front of St Dunstan-in-the-West Church, facing Fleet Street, London.   *Ulysses 11.1023-4*

Harrington, Timothy (1851–1910) *Politician*
'Timothy Harrington, late thrice Lord Mayor of Dublin, imposing in mayoral scarlet, gold chain and white silk tie, confers with councillor Lorcan Sherlock, locum tenens.'
(15.1377-80)

Timothy Harrington was born east of Castletownbere, Co. Cork. He was the son of Ellen (née O'Sullivan) and Denis Harrington, a tenant farmer who was evicted from his holding just outside the town shortly after the Famine.

Harrington was educated at Trinity College Dublin. He joined the teaching staff in the Dominican schools in Tralee and in 1877 founded the *Kerry Sentinel* (now *The Kerryman*). His outspoken views soon attracted the attention of Parnell who offered him the position as secretary of the Land League.

Harrington became an active member of Parnell's Home Rule Party. He was MP for Kerry in 1880 and MP for Westmeath for 1883–5. He was also MP for Dublin City Harbour Division. As honorary secretary to the Irish Parliamentary Party, he devised a 'Plan of Campaign', which he published in October 1886 in *United Ireland*. This was the newspaper founded by Parnell that became the official organ of the Land League and the Irish Parliamentary Party.

Harrington was called to the Irish Bar in 1887 and acted as a counsel for Parnell during the sittings of the commission on 'Parnellism and Crime' (1888–9). He was in the United States on a fund-raising tour on behalf of the 'Plan' when the split occurred in December 1890. He sent a telegram to Parnell: 'My heart is with you, though my head is against you.' Harrington supported Parnell and continued to do so on his return, unlike Tim Healy, John Dillon and others.

On 24 August 1891 Harrington married Elizabeth O'Neill from Cavendish Row. He became a member of Dublin City Council in 1899 and represented the North Dock Ward. He served three consecutive terms of office as lord mayor of Dublin, 1901–4.

Harrington appeared for Constable Henry Flower of the Dublin Metropolitan Police who was implicated in a case concerning the 'death from drowning' of Brigid Gannon whose body was found in the river Dodder near Lansdowne rugby ground (now Aviva) on 23 August 1900. Harrington had a town house at 6 Cavendish Row and a suburban residence in Artane. He had disposed of both properties by 1905 and moved to 70 Harcourt Street in Dublin.

He died on 12 March 1910 and was buried in Glasnevin Cemetery, Finglas Road, Dublin, very close to Parnell [UG 4 Dublin Section].

He is commemorated by a bronze bust by the sculptor Audrey Rynhart in Castletownbere at the east end of the town on the site of his former home.

Harris, Frank (1856–1931) *Writer and editor*

'Nor should we forget Mr Frank Harris. His articles on Shakespeare in the *Saturday Review* were surely brilliant.' *(9.440–1)*

Frank Harris was born James Thomas in Galway on 14 February 1856. He was the son of Thomas Harris, a naval officer from Fishguard in Wales. Aged 12 he was sent as a boarder to school in Wales but ran away and went to the United States when he was 14 and then travelled to the continent before settling in London. He was editor of the *Evening News* (1882–8) and the *Fortnightly Review* (1886–94). He next edited the *Saturday Review* (1894–8), an influential periodical in which he published the work of Thomas Hardy, H. G. Wells, Arthur Symons and George Bernard Shaw.

Harris published a series of articles on Shakespeare in the *Review* that he published as *The Man Shakespeare and His Tragic Life Story* (1909).

His other publications include: short stories; a novel *The Bomb* (1909); two plays; and lives of Shakespeare, Wilde and Shaw. Perhaps he is best remembered for his autobiography, *My Life and Loves* (4 vols, 1922–7) a boastful and unreliable memoir. He was married three times.

Harris died in Nice, France on 26 August 1931 and was buried in Nice at the Cimetière Caucade.

Harris, Morris (1823–1909) *Antique dealer*

'Or will I drop into old Harris's …' *(8.552)*

Morris Harris, son of John Harris and Catherine (née Wade) was born in Spitalfield, London. He came to Dublin from Portsmouth in *c.* 1860.

Harris, lived at 44 Heytesbury Street, 152 Leinster Road, Rathmines and 22 Windsor House, Windsor Road, Rathmines. He dealt in antiques, plate, objets d'art and jewellery at 30 Nassau Street, Dublin.

His sound judgement and expertise in antiques, for half a century, brought him in to contact with many distinguished people both in Ireland and abroad.

He was very much at home amongst the curios and art treasures of his Nassau Street business. Known for his charitable disposition, he took a deep interest in the Masonic schools. Harris died on 17 June 1909 at Windsor House, and was buried in the Jewish Cemetery, Dolphin's Barn, Rialto, Dublin [A].

Hart, Michael (1859–98) *Journalist*

'… Michael Hart (phthisis, Mater Misericordiae hospital) .' *(17.1254–5)*

Michael Hart was the son of Patrick Hart of Collooney, Co. Sligo, and Mary Anne (née McDonnell). He was a friend of John Stanislaus Joyce and is described as a deceased friend of Bloom. Hart was a well-known sports journalist and was knowledgeable about horseracing. He worked as a tipster for the racing paper *Sport*, and attended the races dressed in particularly flashy clothes. He spoke French and was known as 'Monsart', that is, Monsieur Hart. He also wrote doggerel: a newspaper-type headline in the 'Aeolus' episode in *Ulysses* reads 'Lenehan's Limerick'.

In December 1889 Hart was involved with the Christmas and New Year pantomime at the Queen's Theatre in Dublin, *Dick Whittington and His Wonderful Cat*. He was employed to inject some local colour and allusions into it and was described as 'that talented young Dublin man'.

His last address was 111 Marlborough Street. He died of phthisis (pulmonary consumption) on 27 April 1898 at Jervis Street Hospital and was buried in Glasnevin Cemetery, Finglas Road, Dublin [UH 175 St Brigid's].

Harty, George Spencer (1838–1922) *Engineer for Dublin Corporation*
'… the borough surveyor and waterworks engineer, Mr Spencer Harty, C. E., on the instructions of the waterworks committee …' *(17.172-4)*
George Spencer Harty was born in Tralee, Co. Kerry. He was first engaged by Dublin Corporation in 1861 as an assistant borough surveyor and was employed on the construction of the Vartry water supply scheme. In 1887 he was appointed borough surveyor and engineer. During his term of office the streets of Dublin were paved with stone and wood in place of macadam. The construction of the Corporation Fish, Fruit and Vegetable Markets was carried out under his supervision. He was also connected with the extension of the city boundaries.

The chief work carried out by Harty was the Main Drainage Scheme, by which the river Liffey ceased to be the city's main sewer. He prepared the plans and supervised the work and was held in high esteem by the Corporation. Harty was living at 5 Trevelyan Terrace, Brighton Road, Rathgar in 1904.

Harty retired after 50 years of public service in 1910; the Corporation gave him the freedom of the city, and his colleagues presented him with an illuminated address and casket. His name will be forever linked with the numerous improvement schemes that kept pace with the natural development of the city at that time.

Harty was president of the Institute of Civil Engineers in Ireland for many years and held a foremost place in his profession. He died on 22 August 1922 at his residence, 'Ranelagh', 76 Merrion Road, Ballsbridge, Dublin.

Hastings, Lord (1842–68) *English racehorse owner*
Henry Weysford Rawdon-Hastings, 4th marquess of Hastings and the second son of George Rawdon-Hastings and Barbara (née Yelverton), was born on 22 July 1842 in Middlesex, England. He attended Eton College from 1854-5, and Christ Church Oxford from 1860-1.

Elected as a member of the Jockey Club on his twenty-first birthday, he was master of the Quorn Hunt in 1866 but had little or no interest in hunting.

His horse, Repulse, won the 1,000 Guineas in 1866. It was ridden by Tom Cannon (1846–1917), the father of 'Morny' Cannon. Hastings lost a fortune in five years due to his reckless gambling, not only on the turf, but also at Crockford's gaming club.

He died on 10 November 1868 at 34 Grosvenor Square, London, and was buried at Kensal Green Cemetery, London. *Ulysses 2.301–3*

Hauck, Minnie (1852–1929) *American soprano*

'… *and cools herself flirting a black horn fan like Minnie Hauck in* Carmen.' *(15.2744–5)*

Minnie Hauck, daughter of James Hauck, a German carpenter, was born Amalia Mignon Hauck in New York City on 16 November 1851. At the age of 15 she was the

leading soprano in the Christ Church choir in New York. In early 1868 she appeared as Amina in *La Sonnambula* by Vincenzo Bellini. The same year she sang at Covent Garden, London. When she was 17 she travelled to Europe and sang at the Grand Opera House in Vienna. Her singing career later took her to Moscow, Berlin and Brussels.

Miss Hauck sang in London with Mr Mapleson at Her Majesty's Theatre when the opera season opened on 2 April 1878. She sang in over a hundred different roles but was especially famous for the title role of *Carmen* in Georges Bizet's opera, which she performed in Brussels in 1878, and on her various tours that included the Gaiety Theatre in Dublin.

She married Baron Ernst von Hesse-Wartegg, the Austrian writer, in 1881. She died on 6 February 1929 near Lucerne in Switzerland.

Hayes, Barter (1829–1908)

Chief inspector of police, Great Southern and Western Railway

Barter Hayes was born in Cork in 1829. Being from Cork, Hayes may have been a friend of John Stanislaus Joyce. In 1904 he lived at 25 Conyngham Road, Dublin and was the chief inspector of police for the Great Southern and Western Railway Company. He was employed with the company for 22 years, from 1 April 1883. He resigned aged 76 on 31 October 1905. He died on 12 November 1908 at 74 St Lawrence's Road, Clontarf, Dublin. *Ulysses 15.4357–8*

Hayes, Michelangelo (1820–77) *Illustrator and caricaturist*

Michelangelo Hayes, RHA was born in Waterford on 25 July 1820, son of portrait painter Edward Hayes, RHA (1797–1864). He was noted for his sporting and military paintings – several depicting scenes from the Crimean War. Many of his works were engraved. He executed the Charles Bianconi (1786–1875) prints, which comprised a series of four plates, published as *Car-Travelling in Ireland* in 1836 by Ackermann.

Hayes married a sister of Peter Paul McSwiney of Sackville Street (now O'Connell Street), Dublin. When he was lord mayor, McSwiney had appointed Hayes his secretary. Hayes painted a view of Sackville Street, with the General Post Office, Nelson's Pillar, and the Mart of Messrs McSwiney and Co., which was exhibited at the RHA in 1854. He was appointed city marshall of Dublin in 1867. He was involved in a libel action for caricaturing Sir William Carroll, MD, a former lord mayor.

Hayes accidentally drowned in a tank on top of his house at 4 Salem Place, Dublin on 31 December 1877. He was buried in Glasnevin Cemetery, Finglas Road, Dublin [MC 94.5 South]. *Ulysses 12.189*

Hayes, Mrs *Acquaintance of Molly Bloom*

Based on **Mrs Letitia Hayes (née Powell) (1857–1936)** *Daughter of Major Powell*

'... and you had on that new hat of white velours with a surround of molefur that Mrs Hayes advised you to buy because it was marked down to nineteen and eleven ...' *(15.548–51)*

This name is more than likely derived from Mrs Leitita Hayes (née Powell) who was born on 10 September 1857 in Aldershot. She was a daughter of Major Malachy Powell. In 1880 she married John Joseph Hayes a medical practitioner in Hedon, Yorkshire, who died six years later. By 1901 she was living at Kenilworth Road, Rathmines and in 1911 she was living at 44 Grosvenor Road, Rathmines with her widowed mother, Louisa Powell, aged 76, her sister Louisa Gallaher and other relations. She died in June 1936 in England.

Two other daughters of Powell's, Mrs Clinch and Mrs Joe Gallaher, also appear in *Ulysses*.

Healy, Very Rev. John (1841–1918) *Archbishop of Tuam*

'... Waddler Healy ...' *(12.194)*

John Healy, son of Mark Healy and Mary (née Gallagher), was born on 14 November 1841 at Ballinafad, Co. Sligo. He was educated locally and subsequently entered the Diocesan Seminary in Summerhill near Athlone. He continued his studies at St Patrick's College Maynooth, Co. Kildare where he was ordained priest in 1867. He was appointed to the chair of theology at Maynooth, a post he held until 1883. During this time he was editor of the *Irish Ecclesiastical Record*. He was appointed titular bishop of Macra and coadjutor bishop of Clonfert in 1884.

Healy succeeded to the See of Clonfert in 1896. On 17 March 1903 he became archbishop of Tuam. He enjoyed writing verse; his best-known poem is 'Red Hugh's Address to His Soldiers before the Battle of the Curlew Mountains'. He revived the ancient pilgrimage to Croaghpatrick where St Patrick prayed and fasted for 40 days.

Healy's publications include *Ireland's Ancient Schools and Scholars* (1893), *The Centenary History of Maynooth* (1895), *St Patrick in the Far West* (1904) and *The Life and Writings of St Patrick* (1905). He contributed to the *Irish Monthly* and the *Dublin Review*. Archbishop Healy was described by a colleague as 'tall, blonde, rough, strongly built, though inclined to waddle in his gait'.

He died at the Archbishop's Palace, Tuam, Co. Galway, on 16 March 1918. He was buried in the Cathedral of Tuam between the graves of his two predecessors, Dr McHale and Dr McEvilly, in the chancel facing the high altar.

Healy, Timothy (1855–1931) *Politician, patriot and governor-general of Ireland*
'He is sitting with Tim Healy, J. J. O'Molloy said, rumour has it, on the Trinity college estates commission.' *(7.800–1)*

Timothy Healy, second son of Eliza (née Sullivan) and Maurice Healy, was born on 17 May 1855 in Bantry, Co. Cork. He was educated at the Christian Brothers School in Fermoy, Co. Cork. He left school aged 14 and came to Dublin to live with an uncle, before going to Newcastle-upon-Tyne in 1871 to work as a railway clerk with the North Eastern Railway Company. He became involved with the Home Rule policies

of the local Irish community. He moved to London in 1878 and became parliamentary correspondent for the *Nation* for which he wrote numerous articles in support of Parnell.

Parnell brought him into the Irish Parliamentary Party and supported him as a nationalist candidate for Wexford in 1880 when Healy was returned unopposed to parliament. Backed by Parnell, he was elected MP for Monaghan (1883) and South Londonderry (1885), which seat he held for just a year. He was elected in 1886 for North Longford.

Healy became a master of parliamentary procedure and achieved the 'Healy Clause' in the 1881 Land Act, which provided that no rent should be charged on tenants' future improvements.

Healy married Eliza Sullivan in 1882 and in 1884 he was called to the Irish Bar and built up a practice in land law. According to J. B. Hall in his *Random Records of a Reporter*, Healy's 'iron voice was a weapon with which he helped to overcome many an adversary'.

When the crisis arose over Parnell's involvement with the O'Shea divorce case in 1890, Healy became bitterly opposed to Parnell. Gladstone had stated that Liberal support for Home Rule would no longer be possible if Parnell remained leader of the Home Rule Party and Healy was of the opinion that Gladstone's

Liberal support was vital. Parnell refused to yield and the party split. Healy's betrayal of Parnell prompted the young James Joyce to write his poem titled 'Et Tu Healy!' which his father had printed as a broadside by the firm Alleyn and O'Reilly. Healy was involved with the murder case of Thomas Childs, but Joyce chose not to mention him or give him the credit in this context, as he disliked him.

Healy launched the *National Press* on 7 March 1891 to counteract the *Freeman's Journal*, then edited by the Parnellite Edward Byrne. Healy was expelled from the party in 1902. He held the North Louth seat from 1891 to 1910; thereafter he got a seat in North East Cork, which he resigned in 1918 in favour of a Sinn Féin prisoner. The same year he became a king's counsel and a bencher of Gray's Inn.

In 1922 Healy was appointed governor-general of the new Irish Free State, a position he held until his retirement in 1928.

He died aged on 26 March 1931 at his home in Chapelizod, Co. Dublin, and was buried in Glasnevin Cemetery, Finglas Road, Dublin [CE 4 South New Chapel].

Healy is commemorated by a bronze bust by Joseph Davidson in the King's Inns, Henrietta Street, Dublin, and by the The Tim Healy Pass from Adrigole Bridge in Co. Cork to Lauragh Bridge in Co. Kerry.

Ulysses 7.619–20; 7.802; 14.494–5; 15.4343; 16.1301; 16.1327–9; 18.1420

Heblon

Pseudonym for **Joseph K. O'Connor** (1878–1960) *Dublin solicitor*

'... Heblon's *Studies in Blue* ...' *(17.650)*

Joseph K. O'Connor was born in Co. Limerick and educated at Mount Melleray College, Co. Waterford; Crescent College, Limerick; Clongowes Wood College, Co. Kildare; and King's College, London. He worked as a civil servant attached to the Dublin police courts for some years and was the author of a collection of short stories titled *Studies in Blue* which was about Dubliners and the law (1903). He resided at 97 St Stephen's Green South.

O'Connor was called to the Irish Bar in 1906 and took silk in 1924. He was associated with many notable murder trials and was standing counsel for the Dublin United Tramways Company and a number of trade unions. In 1933 he was appointed judge of the Circuit for Cork County and City, a position he held until his retirement in 1947.

O'Connor died in June 1960 at his home, 'Shandy Lodge', Whitegates, Castleknock, Co. Dublin and was buried in Mulhuddart Cemetery, Co. Dublin.

Heenan, John C. (1833–73) *American boxer*

'In Clohissey's window a faded 1860 print of Heenan boxing Sayers held his eye.' *(10.831–2)*

Born in Troy, New York on 2 May 1833, John C. Heenan had a career spanning 1858–63. He boxed under the name of 'The Bernicia Boy' so called after his Californian residence.

Heenan's most memorable fights were against the champion Tom King and John Morrissey. He claimed the latter's title in 1859 after Morrissey had retired from boxing. Heenan was heavyweight boxing champion from 1859–62. Perhaps his most outstanding fight was against Thomas Sayers on 7 April 1860 in Farnborough, England, which was declared a draw after 37 rounds.

Heenan died at Green River Station, Wyoming on 28 October 1873 and was buried at St Agnes Cemetery, Albany, New York.   *Ulysses 12.955*

Hengler, Albert (1862–1937) *Circus proprietor*
'The irreparability of the past: once at a performance of Albert Hengler's circus in the Rotunda, Rutland square, Dublin, an intuitive particoloured clown ...' *(17.975-7)*
Hengler's Circus was established by Frederick Charles Hengler (1820–87) and continued by his son Albert Hengler. It opened in Glasgow in 1867 and was based on the site of the former Prince's Theatre in West Nile Street before moving in 1885 to Wellington Street. In 1904 it moved to the Hippodrome in Sauchiehall Street.

This had a magnificent motor-powered sinking circus arena, which could change in minutes into a lake ten foot in depth. Horses plunged dramatically from great heights and Indians shot the rapids in canoes. Dams were burst, bridges blown up and ships wrecked by tidal waves.

The Hengler management established permanent circuses in large cities like Edinburgh, Glasgow, Liverpool, Hull, London and Dublin. The Dublin location was initially sited in Great Brunswick Street (now Pearse Street) before a permanent structure was erected in the Rotunda Gardens, on the east side of Rutland Square (now Parnell Square), near Great Denmark Street. This contained a large amphitheatre, that could hold several thousand people. The circus performed to capacity audiences and took place in Dublin until 1904. Often there were long queues of people, who failed to gain admittance, due to the popularity of the show. Hengler's Circus remained at Sauchiehall Street, Glasgow until competition from cinemas and other forms of entertainment forced its closure in 1924.   *Ulysses 4.349; 16.412; 17.975-7*

Henry, James (1855–1916) *Assistant town clerk, Dublin Corporation*
'There's Jimmy Henry, Mr Power said, just heading for Kavanagh's.' *(10.982)*
James Henry was born in Ballinasloe, Co. Galway, in 1855. He was the son of William Joseph Henry who was appointed town clerk in 1864.

James Henry was elected to the office of assistant town clerk of Dublin Corporation on 23 September 1878 and remained in that post until late 1915. During any absence of the town clerk, Henry filled his post admirably and his unassuming nature and retiring disposition won him many friends.

Henry lived at 15 Haddon Road, Clontarf, with his wife Eliza, and later on the North Circular Road. He died on 11 January 1916 at his residence, 'Glenside', Charleville Terrace, North Circular Road and was buried in Glasnevin Cemetery, Finglas Road, Dublin [YC 48.5 Section 7].   *Ulysses 15.4349*

Herzog, Moses (*fl.* late 1800s–early1900s) *Peddler of groceries*
'For nonperishable goods bought of Moses Herzog, of 13 Saint Kevin's parade in the city of Dublin, Wood quay ward, merchant ...' *(12.33–4)*
Moses Herzog, who lived at 13 St Kevin's Parade, South Circular Road, Dublin between 1894 and 1906, a few doors from Citron and Maliansky, was a one-eyed Dublin Jew and peddler, trading as an itinerant grocer travelling around the city. He shared the house with relations, Isaac Herzog, a Polish Jew and widower, and his son Abraham, who were born in 1843 and 1882 respectively; both were also peddlers. Herzog was renowned for slipping out of the synagogue at St Kevin's Parade during the long services of the High Festivals to have a drink.
Herzog left Ireland for South Africa in 1908.   *Ulysses 15.3222; 15.4357–8*

Heseltine, Lt Col Christopher (1869–1944) *Aide-de-camp to the lord lieutenant*
'... accompanied by lieutenantcolonel Heseltine, drove out after luncheon from the viceregal lodge.' *(10.1176–8)*
Christopher Heseltine was born on 26 November 1869 in South Kensington, London. He joined the Imperial Yeomanry and served in South Africa in the Second Boer War. He subsequently rose to the rank of lieutenant colonel in the Royal Fusiliers in the First World War and was made an officer of the Order of the British Empire.
A noted sportsman and cricketer, he played for Hampshire Country Cricket Club between 1895 and 1904 and for the Marylebone Cricket Club between 1892 and 1914. Predominantly a bowler, he played two test matches for England against South Africa during Lord Hawke's tour of 1895–6. He was later president of the Hampshire Cricket Club.
Heseltine was an extra aide-de-camp in the lord lieutenant's household from 1902 to 1906. Being a cricketer he would have played on the viceregal cricket grounds in the Phoenix Park, where Captain Buller played on two occasions.
Lt Col Heseltine died on 13 June 1944 at Walhampton in Lymington, Hampshire, England. His funeral took place at Boldre Church, Lymington.   *Ulysses 10.1222*

Hickey, Rev. Louis J. (1840–1907) *Provincial of St Saviour's Dominican Priory*
Joseph Patrick Hickey, son of Michael Hickey and Mary (née O'Toole) was born on 8 September 1840. He entered the Dominican order at St Mary's Priory in Tallaght. He took the name Louis in religion and studied at the Angelicum, San Clemente, Rome, Viterbo in Italy, and Louvain in Belgium. In 1863 he was ordained priest at Esker, Galway by Bishop Derry of Clonfert.
Father Hickey taught theology in Cork from 1863 until October 1871 when he

was appointed prior of the Dominican house in Tallaght. In 1873 he returned to teach in Cork, then moved to Tralee where he served two successive terms as prior. From 1880 until 1887, he moved between Dublin and Cork, after which he was prior of San Clemente in Rome for ten years. During this time, he was in the Congregation of the Holy Office and travelled in the course of his work to Lyons, Avila and Lisbon.

Father Hickey was elected provincial of the Irish Province of the Order in 1896. He remained at St Saviour's Dominican Priory, Dominick Street Lower, Dublin until 1904 when his term as provincial ended.

Father Hickey died on 3 July 1907 in San Clemente, Rome.   *Ulysses 12.930*

Higgins, Francis (1746–1802) *Betrayer of Lord Edward FitzGerald*

'That ruffian, that sham squire, with his violet gloves gave him away.' *(10.788–9)*
Born in Downpatrick, Co. Down, Francis Higgins, known as the 'Sham Squire', came to Dublin with his poverty-stricken parents. He worked as an errand boy, a waiter in a porterhouse in Lord Edward Street and as an attorney's clerk. He converted to Protestantism, and by posing as one of the landed gentry, enticed a lady of means, Mary Anne Archer, into marriage. A sentence in Newgate Prison ensued for this offence.

Despite this, he became an attorney in 1780 and also made a large fortune from the operation of shady gaming houses. He lived in a fine house in a fashionable area at 72 St Stephen's Green for 17 years.

When Higgins got possession of the *Freeman's Journal*, he attacked government opponents and libelled Grattan, and especially the United Irishmen.

As a government informer in 1798, he revealed Lord Edward FitzGerald's hiding place in Thomas Street to Major Charles Sirr for £1,000. He was also implicated in the murder of Oliver Bond, the United Irishman who died suddenly in prison in September 1798.

Higgins died on 19 January 1802 at 72 St Stephen's Green, and was buried in Kilbarrack Cemetery in Sutton, Co. Dublin.   *Ulysses 7.348; 12.180*

Holohan, Hoppy (*fl.* late 1800s–early 1900s) *Pub frequenter*

'Who was telling me? Holohan. You know Hoppy?' *(5.96)*
Holohan was a real person whose name was mentioned in a letter from a suspicious Joyce to Nora dated 7 August 1909. Holohan appeared as a guest in Finn's Hotel in Leinster Street where the 19-year-old Nora worked as a chambermaid in the early months of 1904. He tried unsuccessfully to seduce her. Holohan could well have served as the model for the Holohan in Joyce's fiction. He derived the name 'Hoppy' from a bad leg, which caused him to hop or limp. No biographical information has been forthcoming so far on Holohan.   *Ulysses 7.642–3; 15.1726; 15.4346*

Hooper, Alderman John (1845–97) *Journalist and politician*

'... an embalmed owl, matrimonial gift of Alderman John Hooper.' *(17.1338–9)*

John Hooper, son of John Hooper and Mary (née Keneally) was born in Millstreet, Co. Cork. He joined the *Cork Daily Herald* in 1861 and then became a leader writer on the *Freeman's Journal* in Dublin. He spent 18 months as Westminster

correspondent. He returned to Cork as editor of the *Cork Daily Herald* (which he later owned), and developed the paper into 'one of the sturdiest of Nationalist organs'.

Hooper was elected to Cork Corporation and in 1883 became an alderman. Parnell and members of the parliamentary party noticed his abilities and in 1885 Hooper was asked by Parnell to stand as a Nationalist for South-East Cork. He was elected and took his seat in the Commons the same year.

In December 1887 along with other Nationalists, Hooper was imprisoned in Tullamore Jail for his support of the Plan of Campaign (a scheme employed by tenant-farmers against landlords, 1886–91). His particular 'crime' was the publication of reports of meetings of suppressed branches of the National League.

Hooper sided with the anti-Parnell faction at the time of the 'split'. In 1891, persuaded by Timothy Healy and others, he came to Dublin to manage the *National Press*, the anti-Parnell paper that was launched in March of that year.

The *National Press* ceased after Parnell's death and Hooper became editor of the *Evening Telegraph*, which was in the same group as the *Freeman's Journal*. He kept the issue of Home Rule and the land and university question before the Irish public.

Alderman Hooper's Dublin adddresses included 13 Upper Gardiner Street; 2 Royal Terrace, Fairview; and 22 Belvidere Place, Mountjoy Square. He died on 20 November 1897 at his residence in Mountjoy Square and was buried in Glasnevin Cemetery, Finglas Road, Dublin [ZG 178.5 Garden].   *Ulysses 6.950; 17.1334; 17.2140*

Hooper, Paddy (1873–1931) *Journalist*
'Then Paddy Hooper worked Tay Pay who took him on to the *Star*.' *(7.687)*

Paddy Hooper, son of Alderman John Hooper, was born on 1 June 1873. He joined the staff of the *Freeman's Journal* as a reporter and was transferred to the London office in the late 1890s where he served for nearly 20 years, eventually becoming the London correspondent. He studied law and was called to the English Bar.

Hooper was recalled to Dublin in 1916, to become editor of the *Freeman's Journal*, a position he held until the publication ceased in 1924. After the paper closed, he continued his association with journalism.

He was Irish correspondent of a group of American publications and contributed to a number of Irish journals. During the 'troubles' he incurred the hostility of the British authorities and was imprisoned in Mountjoy Jail for a time. In 1927 he was elected to the Irish senate and was vice-chairman of Seanad Éireann. He was known for his unselfish public service and was described as being 'a brother to many men'.

Senator Hooper died on 6 September 1931 at his residence, 102 Morehampton Road, Donnybrook, Dublin, and was buried in Glasnevin Cemetery, Finglas Road, Dublin [AH 174.5 St Brigid's]. *Ulysses 7.456*

Horne, Sir Andrew (1856–1924) *Master at the National Maternity Hospital*
'She's in the lying-in hospital in Holles street. Dr Horne got her in.' *(8.281–2)*
Andrew Horne, son of Junius Horne and Frances (née Banfield), was born at 5 Society Street in Ballinasloe, Co. Galway, on 8 August 1856. His father was a wealthy merchant and the family lived over his shop.

Horne commenced his education locally and at the age of 12 in 1868 entered Clongowes Wood College, Sallins, Co. Kildare where he remained for five years.

He started his medical studies at the Carmichael School of Medicine, North Brunswick Street (now Pearse Street) and obtained the licentiate of the Royal College of Surgeons in 1877. He spent six months as a postgraduate student in St Vincent's Hospital, Dublin and continued at the Mater Misericordiae Hospital.

Horne was assistant master at the Rotunda Hospital after which time he did postgraduate work in Vienna, returning home in December 1883. He married Margaret Norman on 28 November 1884 and they had five children, four of whom survived infancy.

The family lived for ten years at 28 Harcourt Street where Horne had a private practice. It was an irregular lifestyle with many night calls to the outer suburbs of Dublin, mostly by horse-drawn carriage. Colman Saunders, a distinguished paediatrician, gives a description of Dr Horne going to Glenageary. He was 'dressed in the uniform of the Consultant of those days – a top hat, frock coat and a long black overcoat with an astrakhan collar and carrying a massive black bag'.

In March 1894 when the National Maternity Hospital, Holles Street, Dublin, was founded, Dr Horne became joint master and subsequently master. He remained for 30 years, from 1894 to 1924. He was involved in the foundation of the Women's National Health Association, the Society for the Prevention of Cruelty to Children and many other public organisations.

He was the vice-president of the Royal College of Physicians of Ireland, 1894–6, and president, 1908–10, and received a knighthood in 1913. Other appointments included the presidency of the obstetrical section of Ireland's Royal Academy of Medicine, and the vice-presidency of the obstetrical section of the British Medical Association. Sir Andrew Horne died on 5 September 1924 at his home, 94 Merrion Square, and was buried in Glasnevin Cemetery, Finglas Road, Dublin [FD 46 South New Chapel].

Ulysses 14.74; 14.78; 14.85–6; 14.205; 14.332; 14.421; 14.501; 14.504; 14.724; 14.834; 14.1201; 14.1403

Huggard, W. C. (*fl.* **late 1800s–early 1900s**) *Cyclist*
'Thirther of the wall the quartermile flat handicappers ... and W. C. Huggard, started in pursuit.' *(10.1258–60)*
W. C. Huggard was one of the nine quartermile flat handicappers who took part in the Trinity College Dublin bicycle races on the afternoon of 16 June 1904.

Hughes, Rev. John, SJ (**1843–1912**) *Church of St Francis Xavier*
'It was the men's temperance retreat conducted by the missioner, the reverend John Hughes S. J., rosary, sermon and benediction of the Most Blessed Sacrament.' *(13.282–4)*
John Hughes was born in Ballybough Road, Dublin. He was educated with the Jesuits at Belvedere College, Dublin, and at Clongowes Wood College, Sallins, Co. Kildare.

He entered the newly founded Irish Jesuit novitiate at Milltown Park, Dublin on 4 November 1860. Father Hughes worked in several of the Jesuit houses and was rector of St Ignatius in Galway for three years. He was later attached to the Church

of St Francis Xavier and was resident in the presbytery in Gardiner Street. Here he directed a sodality and was a member of the Catholic Truth Society.

Known for his erudition in philosophy and theology, Father Hughes was an excellent preacher and missioner and gave retreats to priests and to the laity. He spent his final years in Milltown Park.

He died on 16 June 1912 and was buried in Glasnevin Cemetery, Finglas Road, Dublin, in the Jesuit Plot. His name is inscribed in Latin, 'Joannes Hughes', on the headstone [AH–GH 30–40.5]. *Ulysses 15.1128–30*

Hungerford, Margaret (**1855–97**) *Irish novelist*
'... Molly bawn she gave me by Mrs Hungerford on account of the name I dont like books with a Molly in them like that one he brought me about the one from Flanders ...' *(18.656–8)*
Margaret Hungerford (née Hamilton) was born on 27 April 1855 in Rosscarbery, Co. Cork where her father was a rector. Her first marriage in 1872 was to Edward

Argles, a solicitor with whom she had three daughters, who died six years later.

In 1882 Margaret married Thomas Henry Hungerford (1858–97) from Cahirmore House, Rosscarbery. He was from a landed family and was a descendent of Captain Thomas Hungerford, who settled in Cork in 1640 and bought large estates around Rosscarbery. Owing to the disapproval of Thomas's father to the marriage, Margaret and Thomas Hungerford settled some miles away in Bandon, Co. Cork.

Hungerford wrote her first novel, *Phyllis*, in 1877. Her second, *Molly Bawn* (1878), was the novel for which she will be best remembered. She coined the idiom 'Beauty is in the eye of the beholder', that appears in *Molly Bawn*.

Her first books were published anonymously. She later used the name 'Mrs Hungerford'; in the United States she used the pen name 'The Duchess'. Between 1877 and 1893 she produced 27 books, as well as working as a journalist. Her books were always in demand.

Margaret Hungerford died in Bandon, Co. Cork on 24 January 1897.

Hurley, Rev. Walter, CC (1854–1914) *Curate, St James's Church*
Walter Hurley was born in January 1854 in Ballyadams, Co. Kildare. He was admitted to Holy Cross College, Clonliffe, Dublin, in September 1871. He finished at Holy Cross College in October 1875 and was ordained priest in Rome.

In 1904 Father Hurley was curate in St James's Roman Catholic Church, James's Street, Dublin. In 1909 he was curate in Dalkey, Co. Dublin, and in 1911 he was parish priest in Saggart, Co. Dublin. Father Walter Hurley died on 10 February 1914. *Ulysses 12.935*

Hutchinson, Joseph (1852–1928) *Lord mayor of Dublin 1904*
'... and Hutchinson, the lord mayor, in Llandudno ...' *(10.1010)*
Joseph Hutchinson was born in Borris-in-Ossory, Co. Laois. He moved to work in Dublin aged 15. He was first elected to Dublin City Council on 15 October 1890, representing the Merchant's Quay Ward. He remained a Dublin city councillor until January 1912 during which time he served on numerous council committees.

He was a member of the Commission on City Hospitals in 1892, 1895 and 1898–9 and served on the Markets Construction Committee, which was responsible for matters connected with the new market for the sale of fish, fruit and vegetables.

Hutchinson served as high sheriff of Dublin city in 1896 and an unusual number of branches of the National Foresters came into existence as a result. He had previously established the Irish National Foresters' Benevolent Association, which spread through Ireland, Great Britain, America, South Africa and Australia.

He was elected lord mayor of Dublin in 1904, in succession to Councillor Harrington and served for two consecutive terms of office, 1904–5 and 1905–6.

Hutchinson lived with his wife and eight children at 'Ivy Cottage', 55 Hollybank Road, Drumcondra, Dublin. He died on 23 October 1928 and was buried in Glasnevin Cemetery, Finglas Road, Dublin [BH 147 Section 3].

Hyde, Douglas (1860–1949) *Writer and Gaelic revivalist*
'He's quite enthusiastic, don't you know, about Hyde's *Lovesongs of Connacht*.'
(9.93–4)
Douglas Hyde, son of Elizabeth (née Oldfield) and Arthur Hyde, rector of Tibohine, Frenchpark, Co. Roscommon, was born on 17 January 1860 in Castlerea, Co. Roscommon.

Educated at Trinity College Dublin, he studied divinity and graduated in 1885. He then studied law and took his LL.D in 1888.

Hyde's real interests were in language and literature. The names of those who formed the nucleus of the Irish Literary Revival are recorded in his diaries of this period. These include W. B. Yeats, John O'Leary, Maud Gonne, Katherine Tynan and Dr George Sigerson, to whom he dedicated his *Love Songs of Connacht* (1893), which was published under the pen name 'An Craoibhín Aoibhinn' ('The Little Sweet Branch').

Hyde's first collection of folktales, *Beside the Fire*, was published in 1890. He founded the National Literary Society in Dublin in May 1892, and was elected its president. In July 1893 he founded the Gaelic League with Eoin MacNeill and Father Eugene O'Growney, remaining its president until 1915. The league's aim was the 'de-Anglicisation of Ireland' by reviving and preserving Irish as a spoken language.

Hyde's *Literary History of Ireland* was published in 1899. His play *Casadh an tSúgáin* was staged at the Gaiety Theatre, Dublin, in 1901, the first play in Irish ever to be produced at a professional theatre. It was translated by Lady Gregory as *The Twisting of the Rope*.

In 1905 Hyde was appointed to the chair of modern Irish at the Catholic University (which became University College Dublin in 1908) where he remained until 1932. During this time he lived at 1 Earlsfort Place and 65 Adelaide Road. Following his retirement in 1932 he moved back to Ratra near Frenchpark. With the adoption of the Irish Constitution in 1938, Hyde was elected the first president of Ireland. He turned the Viceregal Lodge in the Phoenix Park into Áras an Uachtaráin, the president's house. Hyde suffered ill health from 1940 but continued in office until 1945, when he retired to a residence provided by the government in the Phoenix Park. He died on 12 July 1949 and was buried at the graveyard of the Protestant Church, Portahard, near Frenchpark in Co. Roscommon.

Ulysses An Craoibhín Aoibhinn, 12.725; Love Songs of Connacht, 9.514; 'My Grief on the Sea', 3.397–8; 7.522–5;
'The Necessity for de-Anglicising Ireland', 12.725; The Story of Early Gaelic Literature, 9.96–9

Hynes, Joseph M'Carthy 'Joe' *Newspaper reporter*

Partly based on **Matthew J. Hynes** (1866–1948) *Librarian in the Chief Secretary's Office*

'The wellknown and highly respected worker in the cause of our old tongue, Mr Joseph M'Carthy Hynes, made an eloquent appeal ...' *(12.907–9)*

It is possible that Joseph M'Carthy Hynes is partly based on a Matthew J. Hynes who was born in Galway. He attended college in Blackrock, Co. Dublin where he was an intermediate examination prize-winner. He worked as a clerk in the General Register Office in 1901. At the time he was married and living at 58 Rosemount, Dundrum, Co. Dublin. By 1911 Matthew J. Hynes was working as a librarian in the Chief Secretary's Office and was a widower living in Clontarf. He was keen on sport, especially rugby and occasionally engaged in sporting journalism. His last address in Dublin was East Wall Road. He died in early April 1948.

Ulysses 6.111; 6.504; 6.719; 6.735–6; 6.678; 6.880; 6.884; 6.891; 6.895; 6.898; 6.919; 6.925; 7.76; 7.105; 7.111; 7.115; 7.117; 8.1058; 12.5; 12.1152; 13.1046; 13.1243; 15.1191; 15.1194; 15.1659; 15.4342; 16.1248; 16.1254; 16.1260; 17.1239; 18.38

Ibsen, Henrik (1828–1906) *Norwegian dramatist*
'... Stephen thought to think of Ibsen, associated with Baird's the stonecutter's in his mind somehow in Talbot place ...' *(16.52–4)*
Henrik Ibsen, son of Knud Ibsen and Marichen Altenburg was born on 20 March 1828 in the small port town of Skien in Norway.

With the publication of *Brand* (1866) and *Peer Gynt* (1867), Ibsen became known in Scandinavia. Edmund Gosse, whose early critical work was devoted to Scandinavian literature, helped introduce Ibsen's name to England, where he became a major dramatist. London drama critic William Archer, also provided encouragement. He translated and produced Ibsen's *Pillars of Society* in London in 1880. Archer also translated and produced other works by Ibsen, such as *A Doll's House*, *Ghosts* and *Hedda Gabler*.

Shortly before the publication of Ibsen's play *When We Dead Awaken* (1899), Joyce had an article entitled 'Ibsen's new drama' accepted by the prestigious *Fortnightly Review* in 1900. Archer relayed a message to Joyce on 23 April 1900, that he wished to pass on the author's thanks.

Ibsen died on 23 May 1906 in Christiania (now Oslo) and was buried in the Graveyard of Our Saviour (Var Frelsers Gravlund) in central Oslo.

He is commemorated with the Ibsen Museum in Oslo, situated in his former home in Henrik Ibsens gt. 26 by the Royal Castle. Ibsen lived in this apartment from 1895 until his death and it was here that he wrote his last two plays, *John Gabriel Borkman* (1896) and *When We Dead Awaken* (1899).

Ingram, John Kells (1823–1907) *Irish poet and scholar*
'They rose in dark and evil days. Fine poem that is: Ingram.' *(10.790)*
John Kells Ingram was born on 7 July 1823 at the rectory in Templecarne, Co. Donegal. He was educated locally and at Trinity College Dublin.

Ingram spent 55 years at Trinity, having been professor of oratory, professor of Greek, librarian, senior lecturer and vice-provost. He was commissioner for the Publication of the Ancient Laws and Institutions of Ireland, president of both the Royal Irish Academy and the Statistical Society of Ireland, and a member of the board of the National Library of Ireland.

Ingram published widely on sociology, economics and religion and his *History of Political Economy* (1888) was translated into eight languages. He is remembered best for 'The Memory of the Dead', a martial poem, which was known as the 'Irish Marseillaise'. He published it anonymously in the *Nation* when he was 20 though he did not formally acknowledge it until he was 77, as he was reluctant to be associated with the sentiments expressed in it. Ingram had never displayed any other nationalist sympathies.

He died on 1 May 1907 and was buried in Mount Jerome Cemetery, Harold's Cross, Dublin [C3367–127].

Invincibles
Founded in December 1881, the Irish National Invincibles was a small splinter group of Fenians whose mission was to assassinate key figures of the British government in Ireland.

The Invincibles assassinated Lord Frederick Cavendish (1836–82) the new chief secretary for Ireland and Thomas Henry Burke (1829–82) the under-secretary on 6 May 1882. James Carey, one of the members turned informer, and five members of the group were hanged for murder.

Ulysses 5.378–9; 7.632–3; 7.639–40; 7.652; 7.667–9; 7.703; 8.442–3; 12.460; 12.480; 14.12446; 16.323–4; 16.590–2

Iremonger, James (1877–1956) *Cricketer and star batsman*
'... Iremonger having made a hundred and something second wicket not out for Notts ...' *(16.1683–4)*
James Iremonger was born in Yorkshire on 7 March 1877. His family came from Nottingham and he played for the county from 1897 until 1914.

Iremonger's best season was 1904 when with the aid of six centuries, he scored in 1,983 runs, 34 innings, an average of 60.09. In the summer of 1904 he hit the highest of his four scores of 200 or more: 272 against Kent at Trent Bridge, in the course of which he shared three partnerships exceeding 100.

A star batsman, Iremonger developed into a capital medium-pace bowler. He was appointed coach to Nottinghamshire at the end of the 1921 season, a post he held until his retirement in 1938. He also excelled as an Association footballer with Notts Forest for 15 years, playing as left full-back. He gained international honours for England on three occasions, against Scotland and Germany in 1901 and against Ireland in 1902.

Iremonger who lived at 70 Crosby Road, West Bridgford, Nottingham died in Nottingham on 25 March 1956.

Irwin, Thomas Caulfield (1823–92) *Irish poet and writer*
Thomas Caulfield Irwin was born at Warrenpoint, Co. Down, on 4 May 1823, son of a wealthy physician. He was educated privately and travelled extensively in Europe, North Africa and Syria, accompanied by his tutor.

Irwin had intended to study medicine but the family fortune had dwindled considerably. He joined the staff of the *Irish People*, the Fenian newspaper edited by John O'Leary whose offices were at 12 Parliament Street. As well as contributing to the *Nation*, the *Bell* and the *Dublin Magazine*, Irwin wrote a volume of prose and at least seven collections of poetry. His works include *Versicles* (1856), *Irish Poems and Legends* (1869), *Pictures and Songs* (1880), *Sonnets on the Poetry and Problem of Life* (1881) and *Poems, Sketches and Songs* (1889).

Irwin married and had one son who died in childhood. A natural eccentric, by all accounts he lived a desultory and rather unhappy life. He was observed around the Dublin streets cutting 'a weird and uncouth but venerable figure'. Irwin was a vegetarian with a special affection for cats. He lived at 1 Portland Street, North Circular Road, and later at 41 St Stephen's Green.

He died on 20 February 1892 at his home, 36 Upper Mountpleasant Avenue, Rathmines, and was buried in Mount Jerome Cemetery, Harold's Cross, Dublin [C946–93]. *Ulysses 9.283*

Isaacs, Rufus, 1st marquis of Reading (1860–1935) *British lawyer and politician*
'At the bar, English or Irish: exemplars, Seymour Bushe, K. C., Rufus Isaacs, K. C.' *(17.791–2)*
Rufus Isaacs, son of Joseph Isaacs, a Jewish fruit merchant at Spitalfields, was born on 10 October 1860 at 3 Bury Street, London. He entered the family business aged 15 and later worked on the stock exchange.

Isaacs was called to the Bar in 1887 and in 1903 his name came to the fore in the Bayliss v. Coleridge libel suit, and in the Whitaker Wright case in 1904. He led for the prosecution in the Frederick Seddon poisoning case (1912). The same year he entered the House of Commons as Liberal MP for the Reading constituency (1904–13). During this time he served as lord chief justice, attorney general and in March 1910 he succeeded Sir Samuel Evans as solicitor-general and was knighted; he was raised to the peerage as Baron Reading Erleigh in 1914.

Isaacs died on 30 December 1935 at 32 Curzon Street, London, and his ashes were interred in the Golders Green Jewish Cemetery, also known as 'Hoop Lane' Jewish Cemetery, Golders Green, London.

Iveagh, Lord (1847–1927) Guinness, Edward Cecil *Partner in Guinness brewery*
'Lord Iveagh once cashed a sevenfigure cheque for a million in the bank of Ireland. Shows you the money to be made out of porter.' *(5.304–6)*
Born at St Anne's, Clontarf, Dublin on 10 November 1847, Edward Cecil Guinness, 1st earl of Iveagh, was the third son of Sir Benjamin Guinness the brewer. He was the younger brother of Arthur Guinness, 1st Baron Ardilaun.

Educated at Trinity College Dublin, he served as sheriff of County Dublin in 1876 and nine years later as high sheriff. When the family business was formed into a public company in 1886, he became chairman and the richest man in

Ireland after floating the company on the stock market. He operated the largest brewery in the world on 64 acres. He retired a multi-millionaire at the age of 40

but continued as chairman of the company and its main shareholder.

Guinness was created Baron Iveagh in 1891. The same year he founded the 'Iveagh Trust' and was a most generous philanthropist, clearing slum areas in the city and building houses for the poor. He was created earl of Iveagh in 1919 and Viscount Elveden, of Elveden in the County of Suffolk.

Lord Iveagh died on 7 October 1927 at Grosvenor Place in London and was buried at Elveden in Suffolk.

Ulysses 11.1014–15; 12.281–2; 15.4146

Ivers, Rev. John M. (1853–1910) *Curate St Paul's Church, Arran Quay*
John Michael Ivers was born in Kingstown (now Dún Laoghaire) in 1853. He was educated for the priesthood at Holy Cross College, Clonliffe, Dublin, and was ordained priest in 1891. His first appointment was to a curacy in Roundwood, Co. Wicklow and he was later transferred to Wicklow town.

The Rev. John M. Ivers was then appointed curate-in-charge, St Paul's Church, Arran Quay, Dublin, which is where he was in 1904. He acted as chaplain to the North Dublin Union and assistant chaplain at Glasnevin Cemetery. He lived at 65 Dalymount, Phibsborough, at the same address as the Rev. Francis J. Coffey. In late 1909 he was promoted parish priest to the Church of the Immaculate Conception in Enniskerry, Co. Wicklow.

Father Ivers died on 17 February 1910 and was buried in Glasnevin Cemetery, Finglas Road, Dublin [ID 24.5 South]. *Ulysses 12.929*

J

Jackson, George A. (b. 1866) *Scenery designer and artist*
'... scenery by George A. Jackson ...' *(17.424)*
George A. Jackson was a scenery designer, who made the sets for the pantomime *Sinbad the Sailor* held in Dublin's Gaiety Theatre in January 1893.

He also designed the sets for the Christmas pantomime *Little Red Riding Hood* in the same theatre. The *Irish Times* reported that the last scene was the best: 'the Valley of Wisteria and Laburnum. It is a triumph alike for Mr George A. Jackson, the resident scenic artist, and for Mrs Gunn, who designed the costumes.' The same year, Jackson designed the scenery in the Leinster Hall for the annual ball in aid of the Children's Orthopaedic Hospital, Great Brunswick Street (now Pearse Street), 'The background was stage scenery, forming a picturesque set arranged by Mr G. A. Jackson.'

An artist named George Jackson, who was born in Bristol in 1866, lived as a boarder in 702 Northumberland Road, Dublin, and was possibly the same man.

Jackson, J. A. (1877/8–1957) *Cyclist and barrister*
'J. A. Jackson, W. E. Wylie, A. Munro and H. T. Gahan, their stretched necks wagging, negotiated the curve by the College library.' *(10.652–3)*
James Alfred Jackson, son of Thomas Stewart Jackson, was born in Co. Antrim. He was educated at Coleraine Academical Institution and Trinity College Dublin where he studied law. He was a noted athlete and won many awards as a track cyclist. He was the winner in the half-mile bicycle handicap race held on the afternoon of the 16 June 1904 at College Park in Trinity College Dublin. This was the first event on the day's card of a combination meeting of the Dublin University Bicycle and Harrier Club. W. E. Wylie, who came second in the race, had attended the same school and university as Jackson.

Jackson worked as a legal clerk with the Land Commission and lived at 7 Fitzwilliam Street, Dublin. In June 1913 he was called to the Bar and continued with the Land Commission for many years. He died in Coleraine in October 1957.

Jacquard, Joseph Marie (1752–1834) *French inventor of a loom*
'... and our Huguenot poplin that we have since Jacquard de Lyon and our woven silk and our Foxford tweeds ...' *(12.1245–6)*

Joseph Marie Charles, nicknamed 'Jacquard', was born on 7 July 1852 in Lyon, France. He was the son of Jean Charles, a master weaver, and Antoinette (née Rive).

Jacquard inherited his father's house in 1772, including looms and workshop. By 1800 he had invented a treadle loom, followed by a loom for weaving fishing nets. The 'Jacquard' loom that simplified the weaving of silk fabrics with complex patterns came into being in 1804. He displayed his programmable loom at the industrial exhibition in Paris and by 1812 there were over 11,000 Jacquard looms in France. Due to its success Jacquard was rewarded with a pension in 1806 and earned a royalty on each machine.

He died on 7 August 1834 in Oullins (Rhône). A statue in Lyon commemorates him.

Jeep, Johannes (1582–1644) *German composer*

'Even more he liked an old German song of Johannes Jeep about the clear sea and the voices of sirens ...' *(16.1812–13)*

Johannes Jeep was born in Dransfeld, near Göttingen, Germany, in 1582. He was a composer and kapellmeister to Count Hohenlohe at Weickersheim from 1613 to 1640.

Jeep composed a book of psalms and several books of secular songs, which appeared in many editions. They were popular in the seventeenth century.

Jeep died in 1644 at Hanau, Germany.

Jeffs, J. B. (*fl.* late 1800s–early 1900s) *Cyclist*

J. B. Jeffs was one of the nine quartermile flat handicappers who took part in the Trinity College bicycle races in the afternoon of 16 June 1904.   *Ulysses 10.1259*

Jenatzy, Camille (1868–1913) *Belgian racing-car driver*

'Lay you two to one Jenatzy licks him ruddy well hollow.' *(14.1559–60)*

Camille Jenatzy's red beard earned him the nickname 'Le Diable Rouge' ('The Red Devil'). He was the first driver to exceed 100 km/h in 1899, in an electric car named 'La Jamais Contente'.

Jenatzy won the 1903 Gordon Bennett Cup in Athy, Ireland, in a German Mercedes. He was scheduled to drive in the Gordon Bennett Cup race near Homburg, a village close to Frankfurt in Germany on 17 June 1904. Having won the race in 1903, he was predicted to be the winner. However, Thery, the French driver, who drove a Richard-Brasier car, defeated Jenatzy by 11 minutes and 20 seconds. Baron de Caters, a German driver, finished third.

Jenatzy died on 9 December 1913 in a shooting incident at Habay-la-Neuve, in the Belgian Ardennes. He was buried at the Laeken Cemetery in Brussels.

Joachim of Flora or Fiori (*c.* 1132–1202) *Italian abbot and mystic*

'Nor in the stagnant bay of Marsh's library where you read the fading prophecies of Joachim Abbas.' *(3.107–8)*

Father Joachim of Flora was an Italian Cistercian abbot and mystic. He was born at Celico near Cosenza *c.* 1132. The son of Maurus de Celico, a notary holding high office under the Norman kings of Sicily, he was placed in the court as a young boy.

Joachim was converted to Christianity on a pilgrimage to the Holy Land. He retired to the Cistercian Abbey of Sambucina, Italy *c.* 1159, and devoted himself to lay preaching. He was ordained priest in 1168. He devoted himself entirely to studying the Bible endeavouring to interpret the hidden meaning of the scriptures.

Joachim was elected abbot but found the duties of office difficult, so he appealed to Pope Lucius III, who relieved him of the temporal care of his abbey and suggested he repair to whatever monastery suited his work best. He spent a year and a half at the Abbey of Casamari working on his three great books, *Liber Concoridiae Novi ac Veteris Testamenti*, *Expositio in Apocalipsim*, and *Psalterium Decem Cordarum*. He retired to the hermitage of Pietralata and then founded the Abbey of Flora (or Fiore) in Calabria. He died in Calabria on 30 March 1202.

Ulysses 10.852–3

Johnson, Rev. James (*fl.* 1870–1900) *Presbyterian minister*
'The truth, the whole truth and nothing but the truth, so help you Jimmy Johnson.' *(12.1038–9)*
The Rev. James Johnson was a Scots Presbyterian who called himself 'the apostle of Truth'. He wrote a number of guides for Christian living, which include, *Learning to Float; or, Saved through Faith* (1890); *Learning to Fly; or, the Assurance of Faith* (1890); *Learning to Run in the Way of Holiness* (1890); and *Learning to Walk in the Paths of Righteousness* (1890). Johnson's name became a popular expression.

Johnston, Rev. Gilmer *Protestant minister who baptised Bloom*
May be based on **Rev. Albert Edward Johnston (*fl.* late 1800s–early 1900s)** *Incumbent St Nicholas Without*
'Bloom (three times), by the reverend Mr Gilmer Johnston M. A., alone, in the protestant church of Saint Nicholas Without, Coombe ...' *(17.542)*
The Rev. Gilmer Johnston, MA, is the Church of Ireland clergyman who administered the first of Bloom's three baptisms. No record of a Rev. Gilmer Johnston's incumbency has been discovered in the Protestant church of St Nicholas Without, the Coombe. However a Rev. Albert Edward Johnston was curate there 1887–8.

The parish of St Nicholas Without, which comprised a long strip between New Street and the river Poddle, formerly used the North Transept of St Patrick's Cathedral as its parish church. It was reunited to St Luke's (which had been formed from part of it) in 1861, and both parishes occupied the same church, which became St Luke and St Nicholas Without.

Joly, Professor Charles Jasper (1864–1906) *Astronomer*
'If I could get an introduction to professor Joly or learn up something about his family.' *(8.573–4)*
Charles Jasper Joly was born on 27 June 1864 at St Catherine's Rectory, Top Hill,

Tullamore, Co. Offaly. He was the son of Rev. John Swift Joly of Tullamore and Elizabeth (née Slater).

Joly was educated at Trinity College Dublin where he obtained an MA degree in 1889 followed by a fellowship. In 1897 he was appointed royal astronomer for Ireland at Dunsink Observatory, Co. Dublin. He published numerous papers on astronomy and mathematics and edited *Quaternions* by Rowan Hamilton (1899–1901). He was elected fellow of the Royal Astronomical Society in 1898 and fellow of the Royal Society in 1904. He was Andrews professor of astronomy in the University of Dublin; a trustee of the National Library; president of the International Association for Promoting the Study of Quaternions; and member of the Royal Irish Academy. He went on an expedition to Spain in 1900 to observe the total eclipse occurring that year. He published a *Manual of Quaternions* in 1905.

Joly died on 4 January 1906 at his residence in Dunsink, Co. Dublin, and was buried in Mount Jerome Cemetery, Harold's Cross, Dublin [C16–12330].

Jubainville, Marie Henri d'Arbois de (1827–1910) *Professor of Celtic literature*
'I was showing him Jubainville's book.' *(9.93)*
Marie Henri d'Arbois de Jubainville was born in Nancy, France on 5 December 1827. He studied at the École Nationale des Chartes, Paris, and obtained a degree of palaeographic archivist and philologist. He was then in charge of the departmental archives of Aube, a French department in the Champagne-Ardenne region in north-eastern France and remained there until 1880. He was appointed professor of Celtic literature at the Collège de France, a higher education and research establishment in Paris, in 1882.

An authority on Celtic language and literature, Jubainville wrote and edited many books on the subject including *Introduction à l'Étude de la Littérature Celtique* (1883); *Études de Droit Celtique* (1895) and *Les Principaux Auteurs de l'Antiquite à Consulter sur l'Histoires des Celtes* (1902). His book *Le Cycle Mythologique Irlandaise* (*The Irish Mythological Cycle and Celtic Mythology*), was translated by Richard Best, librarian at the National Library of Ireland (1903). A review of the book appeared in the *Freeman's Journal*, 4 March 1904. Jubainville died on 26 February 1910 in Paris.

Judge, William Quan (1851–96) *Irish-American theosophist and mystic*
'... Judge, the noblest Roman of them all ...' *(9.65)*
William Quan Judge was born in Dublin on 13 April 1851, son of Frederick H. Judge and Alice Mary (née Quan). His mother died, and in 1864 his father emigrated to New York, with his children. They settled in Brooklyn.

Judge passed the New York state Bar examination and travelled widely in the Americas in connection with his work. At 21 he became a US citizen.

It was around 1874 that Judge first met Helena Petrovna Blavatsky. He became a student and co-worker of Blavatsky and in 1875 assisted her and Colonel H. S. Olcott in founding the Theosophical Society in New York. Judge became a crucial figure in the early advancement of theosophy and was later head of the 'powerful' Aryan Theosophical Society in New York City.

He wrote a number of articles and contributed to the *Irish Theosophist* from 1893 to 1895. He also wrote books, including *The Ocean of Theosophy* (1893).

He died on 21 March 1896.

Junius (*fl.* **mid 1700s–early 1800s**) *Anonymous writer*
'Who is Junius? says J. J.' *(12.1633)*
Junius was the pseudonym of an anonymous writer of stinging, and anti-government letters, which appeared in the *Public Advertiser* in London 1769–72, satirising George III and his ministers.

The letters were often attributed to the Dublin-born Sir Philip Francis (1740–1818) who was a clerk in the War Office, and who became one of the four newly appointed councillors of the governor-general of India in 1774.

He was educated at St Paul's School with Henry Sampson Woodfall, the owner and editor of the *Public Advertiser*, an anti-government newspaper. Junius later granted full ownership and copyright of the letters to Woodfall who later published them in Pater Noster Row, London.

Kane, Matthew F. (1865–1904) *Dubliner drowned on 10 July 1904*
'Matthew F. Kane (accidental drowning, Dublin Bay) ...' *(17.1253)*
Matthew F. Kane, son of John Kane and Elizabeth (née Doyle) was born on 5 March 1865 in Dublin. At the time the family lived at 13 North Anne Street.

Kane married Mary Kavanagh in 1887 and they settled at 75 Lower Drumcondra Road. He worked in Dublin Castle as the chief clerk in the office of Sir Patrick  Coll, the crown solicitor. John Stanislaus Joyce, who was a friend and neighbour, lived nearby at 2 Millbourne Avenue in 1894. Kane remained at this address until 1899 when he moved to 73 South Circular Road, Portobello.

Kane was squat and had a long black beard and was thought to look like Shakespeare. Joyce's brother, Stanislaus Joyce, in his book, *My Brother's Keeper*, describes him as 'shrewd, and his energy and self-confidence caused him to be regarded by his friends as very reliable and level-headed'.

On 10 July 1904, Kane in the company of five others left Dublin port in the fishing boat *Annie* for a cruise in Dublin Bay. At 4.00 pm when the boat was about two miles north north-east of Kingstown harbour (now Dún Laoghaire) Kane went swimming. After about four minutes and when he was 30 yards from the boat he got into difficulties. He was retrieved from the water in a weakened state; resuscitation was carried out on him for one hour but he did not respond. The verdict of death was from heart disease.

Kane's funeral travelled from St Michael's Church, Kingstown to Glasnevin Cemetery. When the cortège reached Sandymount, it would have followed the exact same route to Glasnevin as that of the funeral of Paddy Dignam in *Ulysses*.

Similar to Paddy Dignam, Kane was aged 39, with five young children. A Kane Family Fund Committee was set up to raise funds for the support of his children.

Among the many mourners listed in the *Freeman's Journal* who attended his funeral on Thursday 14 July 1904 were: J. S. Joyce, J. A. Joyce and Charles P. Joyce;

John Wyse Power; Alf Bergan; Alfred H. Hunter; Tom Devin; John Clancy (sub-sheriff); J. H. Menton; Gregor Grey; and Sir Frederick Falkiner. The Rev. Francis J. Coffey, CC, read the prayers at the graveside. Matthew F. Kane was buried in Glasnevin Cemetery, Finglas Road, Dublin [11 238.5 St Brigid's].

On 16 June 1988, a new gravestone was unveiled for Kane. The inscription reads:

MATTHEW F. KANE/1865–1904/Chief Clerk/Chief Crown Solicitors Office/
Dublin Castle/Beloved Friend/Of Countless Dubliners/And model in JAMES JOYCE'S/
ULYSSES/For/Patrick Dignam/Martin Cunningham /William Shakespeare/
Matthew F. Kane./Accidental drowning/Dublin Bay.

Kavanagh, Charles 'Charley' (1851–94) *Former city marshal of Dublin*
'Charley Kavanagh used to come out on his high horse, cocked hat, puffed, powdered and shaved.' *(8.506)*
Charles 'Charley' Kavanagh was one of the city marshals before John Howard Parnell (1843–1923). Kavanagh died on 20 June 1894 at his residence, 21 Upper Gardiner Street, and was buried in Glasnevin Cemetery, Finglas Road, Dublin [VG 4 Garden].

Kavanagh, Michael (1860–99)
Hack-car driver for the Invincibles
'Where it took place. Tim Kelly, or Kavanagh I mean.' *(7.639)*
Michael Kavanagh, a member of the Invincibles was the hackney car driver of the getaway cab for the Invincibles after the Phoenix Park murders on 6 May 1882. He lived at 9 Townsend Street, Dublin. He died in England.

Kavanagh, Rev. P. J. (1838–1918) *Irish priest, poet, and historian*
'... the rev. P. J. Kavanagh, C. S. Sp. ...' *(12.928–9)*
Patrick J. Kavanagh, son of Laurence Kavanagh and Catherine (née Prendergast),

was born in Wexford town on 12 March 1838. He entered the Franciscan order at the friary of Fonte Colombo in Italy on 5 February 1861. He took the name Fidelis in religion and was ordained priest in Rome on 31 March 1866.

On his return to Ireland, Father Kavanagh ministered in a number of friaries. His publications include *The Wexford Rebel and Other Poems* (1917) and a book titled *Patriotism* (1914). He also wrote the very popular *The Insurrection of 1798* (1874), which was printed in six editions, including a centenary edition in 1898.

He died on 17 December 1918 and was buried in the Franciscan tomb in the old graveyard beside the Wexford Franciscan Friary. His name is inscribed on the common tombstone, which commemorates all the friars interred there. Kavanagh was an OFM, a member of the Order of Friars Minor (Franciscans) and not CSSp as mentioned in *Ulysses*.

Kelleher, Cornelius 'Corny' *Undertaker's ssistant*

Based on **Simon Kerrigan (1855–1936)** *Undertaker*

'... Kelleher bagged the job for O'Neill's. Singing with his eyes shut. Corny.' *(5.12–13)* Simon Kerrigan, an undertaker, was born in Dublin. In 1904 he was the manager of the funeral establishment of H. J. O'Neill, undertaker and job carriage proprietor, at 164 North Strand Road, Dublin.

Kerrigan died in 1936 and was buried in Glasnevin Cemetery, Finglas Road, Dublin [VC 38 Dublin Section].

Ulysses 6.112; 6.504; 6.523; 6.583; 6.632–3; 6.652; 6.683; 6.688; 6.732; 6.798; 8.441; 10.97; 10.207; 10.215; 10.218–19; 10.221; 12.364; 12.1034; 12.1081; 12.1169; 15.4319; 15.4321; 15.4811; 15.4825; 15.4831; 15.4834–5; 15.4852; 15.4859; 15.4867; 15.4880; 15.4887; 15.4889; 15. 4895; 15.4902; 15.4904; 15.4910; 15.4913; 15.4917–18; 16.70; 16.1260

Kelly, Timothy (1863–83) *Member of the Invincibles*

Timothy Kelly was described as 'a good son of aged parents'. He was a fresh-faced,

20-year-old coachbuilder from 12 Redmond's Hill in the Bishop's Square area of Dublin city. He was a member of the choir with the Franciscans in Church Street and it was here that he first encountered Joe Brady with whom he formed a close friendship.

Kelly was implicated with the Phoenix Park murders on 6 May 1882 in which Lord Frederick Cavendish, the new chief secretary for Ireland, and Thomas Henry Burke, the under-secretary, were assassinated.

Kelly was the youngest of the men arrested for alleged complicity in the murders. He was tried in Green Street Courthouse and found guilty on the third day of his third trial. He was executed by hanging on 9 June 1883 in Kilmainham Gaol prison yard. *Ulysses 7.639*

Kendal, William Hunter (1843–1917) *Actor-manager*

'... and only time we were in a box that Michael Gunn gave him to see Mrs Kendal and her husband at the Gaiety ...' *(18.1110–12)*

William Hunter Kendal, was born William Hunter Grimston, son of Edward

Hunter Grimston, and Louisa (née Rider), on 16 December 1843 in London. He launched his career at 18 on the London stage at the Soho Theatre in 1861. The following year he went to Glasgow, where he remained until 1866 before moving back for his second appearance in London at the Haymarket Theatre. He remained for six years acting in various roles in the Court Theatre and the Old Prince of Wales Theatre. He married Madge (née Robertson), an actress, on 7 August 1869 and they became a successful acting duo. Kendal always acted opposite his wife and their careers became inseparable.

From the period 1879–88 he became lessee and manager in partnership with John Hare of St James's Theatre where they produced a variety of plays.

William Hunter Kendal and Mrs Kendal toured in the United States and Canada from 1889 to 1895 with huge success. They had houses at 12 Portland Place, London, and 'The Lodge', Filey, Yorkshire. Kendal died on 6 November 1917.

Kendall, Marie (1874–1964) *English actress, singer and comedienne*

'A charming soubrette, great Marie Kendall, with dauby cheeks and lifted skirt smiled daubily from her poster ...' *(10.1220–1)*

Marie Kendall was born on 28 July 1874 at Victoria Park, Hackney, in London. Her father was a prosperous manager on the theatrical circuit in Lincolnshire until he lost all his money speculating in railways.

Kendall made her first stage appearance in London at the age of five as 'Baby Chester'. She made her initial début at Haymarket in London where she played Desdemona to Ira Aldridge's Othello. She acted a variety of roles but became famous for her pantomime performances.

Kendall was at the peak of her musical career at the end of the nineteenth and the early twentieth centuries. She is described as having a 'figure trim and flitsome as a dragonfly'. On 16 June 1904 the *Freeman's Journal* and the *Evening Telegraph* advertised the 'Great Marie Kendal' at the Empire Palace Theatre at 7.30 pm.

Famous for her vivacious personality and clear diction when singing, Marie Kendall died on 5 May 1964 in Clapham, London. Her ashes were scattered over Clapham Common close to where she lived.   *Ulysses 10.380; 10.495; 10.1141*

Kenny, Dr Robert, FRSCI (1846–1909) *Surgeon*

'Dr Bob Kenny is attending her.' *(9.826–7)*

Robert Kenny, son of Martin Kenny, a member of a Carlow family, was born in Co. Galway in 1846. He studied medicine in Dublin at the Catholic University School of Medicine at Cecilia Street. In 1873 he became a licentiate of the Royal College of

Surgeons in Ireland. The following year he became a licentiate of midwifery and a licentiate of the Apothecaries' Hall, Dublin. He was visiting surgeon to the North Dublin Poor Law Union Hospital, a charitable institution, and to Cabra Auxiliary Hospital. Kenny was called in during Mrs Joyce's terminal illness at 7 St Peter's Terrace, Phibsborough, shortly before she died, aged 44 on 13 August 1903.

Dr Kenny lived at 30 Rutland Square West (now Parnell Square). His brother, Dr Joseph E. Kenny who died in 1900, was the city coroner and MP for St Stephen's Green Division, and a close friend of Charles Stewart Parnell.

Dr Kenny was a member of the Moore Memorial Concert Committee and a director of the New Irish Peat Products Company.

He died of pneumonia aged 63 on 30 July 1909 at his residence. He had a huge funeral with 50 carriages following the cortège. Among the attendees were John Stanislaus Joyce, James Joyce, and numerous other characters that appear in *Ulysses*.

He was interred at the family burial ground at Goldenbridge Cemetery, Dublin [FF 31 Barrack Section].

Keogh, Myler (1867–1916) *Boxer*

'Myler Keogh, Dublin's pet lamb, will meet sergeantmajor Bennett, the Portobello bruiser, for a purse of fifty sovereigns.' *(10.1133–5)*

Myler Keogh, eldest son of James Keogh and Anne (née Valentine), was born in Donnybrook, Dublin, on 26 December 1867. His father, who was also a boxer, worked in a sawmill in Donnybrook.

For some of the 1890s, Myler Keogh was middle-weight champion boxer of Ireland. His first recorded fight was on 22 August 1889 and his last on 9 October 1903. Most of his fights took place in the Antient Concert Rooms, Dublin,

A tournament was held at the Antient Concert Rooms in February 1897 between Eddie Connolly and Myler Keogh. They boxed three rounds of three minutes each.

Keogh, who worked as a labourer, married Mary Byrne in 1892. After she died in 1901 he was living at 1 Treacy's Cottages, Donnybrook, with his sister also called Mary. He married Elizabeth Tobin in 1907 and they lived at 10 The Crescent, Donnybrook.

Keogh died on 9 June 1916 and was buried in Deansgrange Cemetery, Deansgrange, Co. Dublin [108–T3–North]. *Ulysses 12.939; 12.955; 12.960; 12.965; 12.971; 12.985*

Kernan, Tom *Tea salesman*

Based on **R. J. Thornton** (1851–1903) *Commercial traveller and salesman*

'... Tom Kernan that drunken little barrelly man that bit his tongue off falling down the mens W C drunk in some place or other ...' *(18.1264–6)*

Tom Kernan is a composite character, John Stanislaus Joyce providing some of his traits. Kernan was based on R. J. Thornton a neighbour and friend of Joyce who lived in North Richmond Street in the 1890s. The Joyces lived in 13 North Richmond Street in late 1894 to early 1895–7. Thornton was godfather of two of the Joyce children: Mabel, the tenth child who was born in 1893 and Freddie, the eleventh child born in the early autumn of 1894, who only survived a few weeks.

Thornton worked as a commercial traveller from 19 Eustace Street and from 1897 as a tea-taster at Pulbrook, Robertson & Co., tea importers, 5 Leinster Chambers, 43 Dame Street. In a letter to C. P. Curran dated 14 July 1937 Joyce wrote, 'My father's old friend R. J. Thornton ("Tom Kernan") used to tell me about Giuglini flying his kite on Sandymount Strand when he was a boy.' Stanislaus described Thornton as an amusing, robust, florid little elderly man and Mrs Joyce gave him the nickname 'the dicky bird'.

In 1869 Thornton married Lydia (née Crossley) who was English. They had two sons, Richard, born 1873, and John, born 1887. Their daughter, Eveline, born in 1884, lent her name to the story in *Dubliners*. Thornton lived as a lodger in Middle Gardiner Street in 1901. He died on 2 November 1903 at 10 Upper Mercer Street, a tenement building, and was buried in Glasnevin Cemetery, Finglas Road, Dublin [CJ 199 St Patrick's].

Ulysses 5.20; 6.109; 6.142; 6.455; 6.503; 6.536; 6.541; 6.654–6; 6.660; 6.664; 6.669; 6.687; 6.689–90; 8.372; 8.760; 10.673; 10.717; 10.742; 10.754; 10.773; 10.781; 10.796; 10.1183; 11.775; 11.797; 11.991; 11.1039; 11.1148; 11.1272; 15.1141; 15.1522; 16.1259; 17.1239; 17.1980; 17.2075

Keyes, Alexander (1853–1931) *Tea merchant*
'Two crossed keys here. A circle. Then here the name. Alexander Keyes, tea, wine and spirit merchant.' *(7.142–3)*
Alexander Keyes was born in Co. Dublin. In 1894 he is listed as a grocer and spirit dealer at 128 Capel Street. His residence at the time was at 128 Lower Drumcondra Road. His business in Capel Street was taken over by James Cassidy who had left his employment with Captain Tom Cunniam in Werburgh Street.

On 2 September 1899 Thomas Childs of 5 Bengal Terrace was murdered. His brother Samuel Childs was arrested and tried for fratricide. Alexander Keyes was on the jury. James Joyce sat in the gallery, taking notes which he made use of in *Ulysses*. But he does not include the fact that Keyes was on the jury.

Keyes then opened a luncheon bar at Ballsbridge and is listed as being a tea, wine and spirit merchant at 5–6 Ballsbridge. In 1911, when Keyes was living at 36 Belgrave Road, Rathmines, with his wife Mary Josephine, daughter Annie and son Alexander (a rent collector and estate agent), he gives his occupation as a commercial traveller.

Keyes died on 15 March 1931 at 6 Rugby Road, Ranelagh, Dublin, and was buried in Glasnevin Cemetery, Finglas Road, Dublin [JC 54 South].

Ulysses 6.741; 7.25; 15.1682; 15.4337; 16.1258–9; 17.587; 17.2046–7; 18.1343

Kinsella, Pat (1845–1906) *Comedian and proprietor of the Harp Music Hall*
'Where Pat Kinsella had his Harp theatre before Whitbred ran the Queen's.' *(8.600–1)*

Pat Kinsella was a popular Irish comedian who spent over 20 years on the stage. Born in Dublin in 1845, he was the son of Thomas Kinsella, a porter at H. M. Customs. Pat Kinsella moved to Liverpool when he was 23 and worked as a music hall artist. The following year he married Flora Yarnold, who was also employed in music halls.

Kinsella lived mainly in Dublin in the 1880s and 1890s but he and Flora visited Liverpool frequently. He performed in theatres around England and Ireland. He appeared in the Queen's Royal Theatre, Dublin, where in 1891 he gave a selection from his 'Popular Comicalities'.

In the 1890s, Kinsella was well known as the proprietor of the old Harp Theatre, a music hall located formerly at 1–3 Adam Court, off Grafton Street. A brief description of it appeared in 1915:

> A matter of twenty-five years or so ago, there flourished in a court off the lower end of Grafton Street, Dublin, a comic music-hall run by one Pat Kinsella, pronounced locally as Kinsh-la. Its audience was peculiar, consisting chiefly of soldiers, generally in the state specified by the Dublin Metropolitan Police as 'having dhrink taken'.

Kinsella was very popular in Ireland as a variety artist, and enjoyed great success in England and Scotland. He moved to Liverpool at the end of his career in the early 1900s. He died from 'excessive drinking' on 30 April 1906 at 9 Christian Street, Liverpool. His wife died in London five years later.

The Empire Buffet occupied the site of the Harp Theatre in 1904, adjacent to the Browne and Nolan printing works.

Kock, Charles Paul de (1793–1871) *French novelist*
'Get another of Paul de Kock's. Nice name he has.' *(4.358)*

Charles Paul de Kock was the posthumous son of Jean Conrad de Kock, a Dutch banker who was guillotined during the French Revolution. Charles Paul was born at Passy in Paris on 21 May 1793. He lived mostly on the Boulevard St Martin. He began work aged 15 as a banker's clerk, but gave up the idea of a career in banking when his first novel, *L'Enfant de Ma Femme*, was published at his own expense in 1811. Nine years later he started writing his successful series of novels dealing with low and middle-class

Parisian life in the first half of the nineteenth century. His novels were translated into several languages and were more popular abroad than they were in France. They were published in collected editions in England and the US between 1902 and 1904. His *Memoires* were published in 1873.

Charles Paul de Kock died in Romainville, Seine-Saint-Denis, France on 27 April 1871 and was buried at Cimetière des Lilas, in the eastern suburbs of Paris.

Ulysses 11.500; 11.987; 15.1023; 15.3045; 18.969

Koehler *One of Stephen's creditors*
Based on **Thomas Keohler/Keller (1873–1942)** *Theosophist and minor poet*
'... Koehler, three guineas ...' *(2.258)*
Thomas Keohler, son of Joshua William Keohler, was born in Belfast on 19 June 1873. The family moved to Cheshire, England in 1876 where his father ran a flour mill in Runcorn. They soon returned to Ireland and settled in Dublin where Thomas worked as a clerk at W. and R. Jacob and Co., Ltd which he left in January 1902 for the post of secretary at Messrs Hely, Ltd Stationers & Printers, Dame Street. He rose to the position of company secretary, and remained with Helys for over 40 years. He was a friend of Joyce, Yeats and George Russell who included Keohler's work in *New Songs: A Lyric Selection* (1904).

Keohler was a member of the Abbey Theatre Business Committee and was one of the original signatories of the National Theatre Manifesto. Closely associated with the Irish Literary Revival, he wrote about the opening performances on 27 December 1904 of the Irish National Theatre at the new theatre in Abbey Street in John Eglinton's *Dana*. He also wrote non-political pieces for Griffith's *United Irishman* and essays for *The Shanahcie*, a short-lived literary quarterly published by Maunsel & Co., Middle Abbey Street.

Keohler changed his name to Keller in 1914, probably because Keohler sounded too German. (Joyce spelt the name, Koehler, in *Ulysses*.) By 1911 he was living at 19 Gilford Avenue, Sandymount, with his wife Agnes (née Baxter) and daughter Katherine.

Keller was deeply interested in literature, though his own literary output was not large. He published a small book of poems, *Songs of a Devotee* in the Tower Press series (1906). He was keenly interested in music, played the piano and was music critic to a daily paper.

Keller died on 26 May 1942 at his home in 12 Charleville Road, Rathmines, and was buried in Mount Jerome Cemetery, Harold's Cross, Dublin [C103–24548].

L

Lablache, Luigi (1794–1858) *Italian basso*

'Lablache, said Father Cowley.' *(11.1150)*

Luigi Lablache was born on 6 December 1794 in Naples, Italy. He was the son of Nicholas Lablache, a merchant from Marseilles, and Maria Francesca Bietagh, 'of Irish descent'.

Due to his superb bass voice Lablache's fame grew rapidly throughout Europe. His first appearance in Paris and London was in 1830 after which he performed in both places frequently, often followed by tours of the 'provinces', including Dublin.

Lablache made his Dublin début in the Theatre Royal in Hawkins Street on 30 August 1841 as Giorgio in Bellini's *I Puritani*, with Giulia Grisi as Elvira and Giovanni Mario as Arturo – all of whom had created their roles in that opera in Paris in 1835. The conductor in Dublin was Julius Benedict (of *The Lily of Killarney* fame). Lablache also sang Oroveso in *Norma* with Grisi and Mario that season. He returned the following year for repeat performances of *I Puritani* and *Norma* (with the same casts) and as Henry VIII in *Anna Bolena*. On this occasion the conductor was Michael Costa.

Lablache excelled in tragedy and comedy. He was a noted actor particularly as Leporello, the conniving servant in *Don Giovanni*, perhaps one of his finest impersonations. Other roles included Geronimo in *La Gazza Ladra*; Dandini in *La Cenerentola*; Assur in *Semiramide*; and Caliban in *The Tempest*.

Lablache died in Naples on 23 January 1858 and was buried in Maisons-Laffitte Cemetery, Rue du Souvenir, Saint-Germain-en-Laye in north-western Paris.

Lalor, James Fintan (1807–49) *Land agitator*

'In 1885 he had publicly expressed his adherence to the collective and national economic programme advocated by James Fintan Lalor ...' *(17.1645-7)*

James Fintan Lalor was born on 10 March 1807 at Tinnakill House, Raheen, Co. Laois. He was the son of Patrick Lalor, the first Catholic MP for Co. Laois, and his wife Anna (née Dillon). For health reasons he was educated privately at home. At the age of 17 he attended St Patrick's College, Carlow, and then spent some time in France.

In a series of controversial and stirring letters, which he wrote for the *Nation* in

1847, he advocated 'the land of Ireland for the people of Ireland'. He also wrote for the *United Irishman* and the *Irish Felon*, advocating a policy of land nationalisation. He was deeply interested in agrarian reform for Ireland and his aim was to secure land rights for all.

Following the attempted rising in 1848 by William Smith O'Brien at Ballingarry, Co. Tipperary, Lalor was arrested in Templederry but released four months later on account of his poor health. He continued his work unabated but his health deteriorated. Lalor died on 27 December 1849 in Dublin. Twenty-five thousand people attended his funeral. He was buried in Glasnevin Cemetery, Finglas Road, Dublin [TD 24–25.5 South].

Lane, William (1883–1920) *Jockey*

'A whacking fine whip, said Lenehan, is W. Lane. Four winners yesterday and three today. What rider is like him?' *(14.1136–8)*

William Lane, also known as Willie and Wallie Lane, was the son of a Chelsea jobmaster.

Lane rode Fred Alexander's five-year-old Throwaway, winning the Gold Cup race at Ascot on 16 June 1904. The same day, Lane also won the New Stakes on Mr L. Neumann's Llangibby and the St James's Palace Stakes on Mr S. Darling's Challenger.

At the Ascot meeting the previous day, Lane rode four winners, including the Ascot Biennial Stakes on Fred Alexander's Andover; the Coronation Stakes on Major Eustace Loder's Pretty Polly; and the Fern Hill Stakes on Mr L. Neumann's Petit Bleu.

Lane was champion jockey in 1902 and had an excellent partnership with the brilliant filly, Pretty Polly, in 1904. That year he won the 1,000 Guineas, the Oaks, the Coronation Stakes, the Nassau Stakes, the St Leger and the Park Hill Stakes. He was also successful in the St James's Palace Stakes, the Ascot Gold Cup, the Norfolk Stakes, the Gordon Stakes, the Goodwood Cup, the Yorkshire Oaks, the Gimcrack Stakes and the Doncaster Cup.

Tragically, later in 1904 Lane had a fall at Lingfield, which ended his career as a jockey. He died on 27 June 1920 and was buried at St Peter and St Paul Church burial ground, Lingfield.   *Ulysses 16.1279*

Langtry, Lillie (1853–1929) *Actress and mistress of the Prince of Wales*

'... and that Mrs Langtry the jersey lily the prince of Wales was in love with ...' *(18.481–2)*
Lillie Langtry (née Emilie Charlotte le Breton), daughter of the Rev. William Corbet le Breton and Emilie Davis (née Martin) was born on 13 October 1853 in the rectory of St Saviour's Parish Church in Jersey where her father was rector and also dean of Jersey, one of the Channel Islands.

When she was 20 Lillie met and married Edward Langtry, a wealthy Irish landowner, and they moved to live in London's Belgravia. A noted beauty, she was portrayed by the painter Millais holding a lily, the emblem of Jersey. He titled it *A Jersey Lily*.

In May 1877 the Prince of Wales, Albert Edward, fell in love with her. Their ensuing liaison was widely publicised. Throughout her life Langtry had many well-known lovers including Louis of Battenberg, Robert Peel, Arthur Jones and George Baird. Encouraged by her playwright friend, Oscar Wilde, she became an unsuccessful actress but still managed to fill the theatre to capacity on account of her beauty and the patronage of the Prince of Wales. From 1892 to 1897 Lillie Langtry lived at 21 Pont Street, London. Now a hotel it is marked with a plaque erected by the Greater London Council.

Langtry divorced her husband and in 1899 got married for a second time to Hugo Gerald de Bathe, a leading racehorse owner. They retired to Monte Carlo ultimately living in separate residences. She died there in 1929 and was buried in the churchyard of St Saviour's Church in Jersey to which her father had been attached. Her grave is marked with a marble bust sculpture.

Lanner, Katty/Katti (1831–1908) *Dancer and choreographer*

'The Katty Lanner step.' *(15.4044)*

Katharina (Katti) Josefa Lanner was born in Vienna, Austria, on 14 September 1831. She was the daughter of Josef Lanner (1801–43), the Austrian composer and violinist, and Franciska (née Jahns). She studied at the ballet school of the Vienna Court Opera, and made her début aged 14 on 4 August 1845. She worked with various German ballet companies in Berlin, Munich and Dresden. In February 1864 she married the composer Johann Geraldini who was also director of the Viennese Ballet Company, and toured Europe, Russia and the United States.

Lanner was at the height of her career as a dancer in New York in 1870 and in London in 1871 when she danced the part of Giselle in Adolphe Adam's classic ballet with the Neapolitan dancer Giuseppe Venuto de Francesco.

Lanner first appeared at Drury Lane in London in 1871. Four years later she returned to London where she set up home at 40 North Side, Clapham Common. In 1876 she took over the National Training School of Dancing of which she later became owner. At this time, Lanner became romantically involved with Giuseppe Venuto de Francesco. Her marriage to Johann Geraldini, which produced three daughters, broke up and he returned to Vienna where he died in 1904.

Lanner produced many ballets and pantomimes and trained a number of students for the stage. She was ballet mistress at Her Majesty's Theatre, London, from 1877 to 1881 and her last performance was in this theatre on 16 July 1878, when she appeared as Elena in *Robert le Diable* (*Robert the Devil*). In 1887 she became ballet mistress at the Empire Theatre in Leicester Square, which at that time was a variety theatre.

Before her retirement in 1907, she had choreographed more than 36 ballets. Katti Lanner died on 15 November 1908 at 40 North Side, Clapham Common, and was buried in West Norwood Cemetery, Norwood, London.   *Ulysses 18.269*

Laracy, John (1842–1906) *Superintendent DMP*
John Laracy was born in the parish of Pitt near Gowran in Co. Kilkenny in 1842. He joined the Dublin Metropolitan Police (DMP) when he was 20, and remained with the force for 44 years, serving in four different divisions. During this time he rose from sergeant in 1875 to inspector in 1881 and was promoted superintendent in 1883. Laracy lived in Grove Park, Rathmines 1896–9 and at 81 Ranelagh Road in 1901.

On the occasion of Edward VII's visit to Dublin with Queen Alexandra in 1904,

Laracy was among the forces present, along with superintendent Flower, who organised the ceremonial escorts and policing of the enormous crowds waiting at Kingsbridge and lining the route of their journey up Parkgate Street, through the Phoenix Park to the Viceregal Lodge.

Superintendent Laracy was also responsible for police arrangements for the arrival of the lord lieutenant and Lady Aberdeen in early February 1906. It was at this period and in the discharge of his duties that he contracted a severe chill. Attached to the 'B' Division of the DMP Headquarters, he died of pneumonia on 21 February 1906 at his residence in Lower Castle Yard.

Superintendent Laracy was buried in Glasnevin Cemetery, Finglas Road, Dublin [FE 106.5 Garden].   *Ulysses 15.4350*

Laredo, Lunita (1864–97) *Molly's Spanish-Jewish mother*
'... my mother whoever she was might have given me a nicer name the Lord knows after the lovely one she had Lunita Laredo ...' *(18.846–8)*
A Luna Laredo was born in Gibraltar on 2 August 1864, daughter of Samuel Laredo and Esther Nahom. Her full name was Luna de Samuel Laredo. Luna was a common Jewish female first name, and Laredo was a Jewish family name.

Joyce revised the original name Luna Laredo before changing to Lunita Laredo in the Rosenbach Manuscript. It is possible that he got the name from the *Gibraltar Directory and Guidebook*.

Luna Laredo died aged 33 in Gibraltar on 30 December 1897. Her date of death according to the Jewish calendar was 5 Tebet 5658. This means that she died days after the feast of Hanukkah, which commemorates the rededication of the Jerusalem temple by the Maccabees after the desecration by the Seleucid Hellenists in the second century BC.

She was buried in the Jewish section, North Front Cemetery, Devil's Tower Road, Gibraltar [Grave number 14L]. The cemetery is situated at the south end of Gibraltar overlooking the Straits and on a clear day the Atlas Mountains may be seen.

Beside the cemetery there is a path called the Mediterranean Steps, which goes around the Rock and terminates on the eastern side. *Ulysses 4.60; 18.282–3*

Lavery, Rev. John (1858–1915) *Priest, St Peter's Presbytery*

John Lavery, son of Surgeon-Major Lavery, JP, was born on 14 January 1858 in Co. Armagh. His family was prominent in the legal profession for several generations both north and south. He was admitted to the Vincentians in 1882 and was ordained priest in 1887. He was appointed to St Mary's parish, Lanark, in Scotland. He was based in Castleknock College, Co. Dublin from 1890–2, and then moved to St Vincent's, Sundays Well in Cork.

Father Lavery was a member of the Vincentian community at St Peter's Church, Phibsborough, in Dublin from 1897 to 1903. He would have been known to the Joyce family as this was their parish church and close to 7 St Peter's Terrace where they lived from 24 October 1902 until late March 1904. Father Lavery went to Lanark in 1904 and returned to Cork in 1910, where he remained for the rest of his life.

He died on 21 August 1915 in Cork and was buried in the old seminary graveyard on Temple Road, Blackrock, Co. Dublin. On the sale of this property, he was exhumed with the other Vincentians and reinterred in Deansgrange Cemetery, Deansgrange, Co. Dublin [170–82–AO–North]. *Ulysses 12.932–3*

Lemaire, Madeleine (1845–1928) *French watercolourist*

'Won't you come to Sandymount,
Madeline the mare?' (3.21–2)

Madeleine Lemaire, also known as Madeleine Jeanne Lemaire, was born in 1845 in Ares, south-west of Bordeaux in France. A watercolourist, she did illustrations for *L'Abbé Constantin* by Ludovic Halévy (1834–1908), the French writer. She painted portraits but was perhaps best known for her wonderful paintings of flowers, examples of which include her *Peonies* which are in the University of Dundee Fine

Art Collection in Scotland and her *Choix d'Oeillets* in the Musée des Augustins in Toulouse in France. Lemaire won many awards including the prestigious Legion of Honour in 1906. She died in 1928 in Paris.

As well as punning on the name of Madeleine Lemaire, these lines in *Ulysses* may also be a play on the name of Philippe-Joseph Lemaire (1798–1880), the French sculptor whose work is represented in the pediment of the Église de La Madeleine and the Arc de Triomphe, Paris.

Lenehan, T. *Journalist*

'Lenehan came out of the inner office with *Sport's* tissues.' *(7.387)*
Lenehan is a composite creation. His name is borrowed from Matthew Linehan, a reporter for the *Irish Times*, and his personality from Michael Hart, a well-known sports journalist who was a friend of John Stanislaus Joyce. Hart appears under his own name in *Ulysses*. There were three Linehan brothers, Matthew, John and Vincent, all of whom were journalists. In some cases, the name was spelt Lenehan, as with John Lenehan, who worked as a journalist with *Sport*.

John Lenehan (1865–1935) *Journalist*
John Lenehan was born in Cork in 1865 and worked in Dublin as a journalist with the *Freeman's Journal* and *Sport*. He studied law and was called to the Bar in 1891. He then pursued a legal career working as county court judge in Co. Tyrone. He died in 1935.

Matthew Linehan (1868–1939) *Journalist*
A member of a distinguished Co. Cork family, Matthew Linehan was born in Cork in 1868. He came to Dublin as a youth and worked on the reporting staff of the *National Press*.

In 1904 he had a BA degree, and was working as a journalist and living with his brother Henry at 186 Clonliffe Road, Drumcondra. This seemed to have been the Linehan family home in Dublin as two of his sisters, Agnes and Emily, were also listed in the 1911 census as living here. Linehan joined the staff of the *Irish Times* where he was chief reporter for a number of years. He became a well-known sporting journalist with a particular interest in lawn tennis and rugby football.

Linehan was called to the Bar in 1907. He left the *Irish Times* to pursue a career in law and took up an official position in the Four Courts, which he held until his death. Another brother, Henry Vincent Linehan, was also a well-known sporting journalist for the *Irish Times*. All three brothers worked in journalism. Matthew Linehan died on 20 March 1939 at his residence, 39 Wellington Road, Ballsbridge, and was buried in Deansgrange Cemetery, Deansgrange, Co. Dublin [2–N2–West].

Ulysses Lenehan, T.: *7.300; 7.393; 7.401; 7.416–17; 7.420; 7.437; 7.442; 7.447; 7.465; 7.468; 7.475; 7.496; 7.504; 7.507; 7.513; 7.574; 7.587; 7.590; 7.595; 7.606; 7.611; 7.675; 7.687; 7.690; 7.695; 7.759; 7.778; 7.875; 7.891; 7.1028; 8.829; 8.844; 10.395; 10.484; 10.490; 10.494; 10.498; 10.511; 10.517; 10.522; 10.524; 10.529; 10.536; 10.541; 10.551; 10.575; 10.579; 10.1204; 11.228; 11.233; 11.240; 11.256; 11.263; 11.289; 11.338; 11.362; 11.372; 11.377; 11.387; 11.395; 11.404; 11.415; 11.428; 12.1178; 12.1208; 12.1215; 12.1218; 12.1226; 12.1265; 12.1318; 12.1389; 12.1536; 12.1548; 12.1554; 12.1622; 12.1649; 14.173; 14.191; 14.217; 14.338; 14.417; 14.506; 14.529; 14.1122; 14.1127; 14.1137; 14.1161; 15.1142; 15.1700; 15.1733; 15.2238; 15.3728; 15.3739; 15.3742; 15.3747; 15.3752; 15.4342; 16.146; 17.2137*

Lever, Captain John (1824–97) *Owner of shipping company and MP*
'... Captain John Lever of the Lever Line.' *(16.968)*

John Orrell Lever, son of James Lever from Manchester, was a manufacturer and businessman. He was a director of the South Wales Railway and the Atlantic Royal Mail Steam Navigation Company.

He owned the ships in the Galway-Halifax experiment of the mid nineteenth century and established Galway as a packet-station. The aim was to develop Galway as a transatlantic port in the second half of the nineteenth century. Lever was an MP for Galway Borough and sat in the House of Commons for two periods between 1859–85. He died on 4 August 1897. *Ulysses 16.981–2; 16.1076*

Lidwell, George (1864–1919) *Solicitor*
'George Lidwell, suave, solicited, held a lydiahand.' *(11.567)*
George Lidwell was born in Co. Fermanagh and was a solicitor at 4 Capel Street, Dublin. He was a well-known practitioner in the Dublin Police Courts with offices at 33 Upper Ormond Quay.

Lidwell was a friend of John Stanislaus Joyce. They attended funerals, and drank together at the Ormond Hotel, which was close to one of Lidwell's offices at 4 Capel Street. Due to his precarious accommodation arrangements, John Stanislaus used Lidwell's office as his postal address.

When Joyce was having problems with George Roberts in Maunsel concerning the publication of *Dubliners*, he engaged Lidwell as his solicitor.

Lidwell lived at 91 Clonskeagh Road in 1901. In 1911 he was living at 10 Sandymount Road. He had nationalist tendencies and was treasurer of the 5th (Dublin) Battalion of the Volunteers based in Sandymount.

Lidwell always conducted his cases with ability and fairness both for his clients and with consideration for those opposed to him. He died on 23 July 1919 at his home 6 Corrig Avenue, Kingstown (now Dún Laoghaire). He was buried in Glasnevin Cemetery, Finglas Road, Dublin [DA 68.5 Section 5].

Ulysses 11.227; 11.563; 11.566; 11.711; 11.718; 11.720; 11.758; 11.769; 11.815; 11.819; 11.924; 11.947; 11.950; 11.955; 11.1038; 11.1110; 11.1158; 11.1209; 11.1212; 11.1272; 15.4349

Lind, Jenny (1820–87) *Swedish soprano*
'Must be abstemious to sing. Jenny Lind soup: stock, sage, raw eggs, half pint of cream.' *(11.699–700)*
Jenny Lind, daughter of Niclas Lind and Anne-Marie Fellborg, was born on 6 October 1820 in Stockholm, Sweden. One of the most famous sopranos of her day, she performed in Sweden, Europe and America. She met the conductor and pianist

Otto Goldschmidt on her American tour. They married in February 1852 and she took the name Jenny Lind-Goldschmidt. From 1840 she was a member of the Royal Swedish Academy of Music. She spent the last years of her life in England and was a professor of singing at London's Royal College of Music.

Lind was not all that interested in food and was noted for the moderation of her diet. A nourishing but bland soup, Soup a la Cantatrice (Professional Singer's Soup) was renamed in her honour.

Known as the nightingale of Sweden, Lind died on 2 November 1887 in Malvern, Worcestershire and was buried in the Great Malvern Cemetery. She is commemorated in Poets' Corner, Westminster under the name 'Jenny Lind-Goldschmidt'.

Livermore Brothers (*fl*. 1894–1903) *Minstrel performers*

'Even the bones and cornerman at the Livermore christies.' *(15.410)*

The Livermore Brothers, a popular troupe of court minstrels, first performed in Dublin in January 1894 for a short season in the Round Room, at the Rotunda, Rutland Square (now Parnell Square). The company returned in 1889 and according to the *Irish Times*, had 'a sparkling programme of refined negro minstrelsy and comicalities, consisting of new and pathetic ballads, quartettes, operatic selections, comic songs and other attractive items specially written, composed and arranged by the proprietors'. As the years went by, the troupe increased in number.

The group returned to Dublin almost every year from 1889, and performed in the Rotunda. Their final appearance in Dublin was in April 1903.

Logue, Michael Cardinal (1840–1924) *Archbishop of Armagh*

'... *His Eminence Michael cardinal Logue, archbishop of Armagh, primate of all Ireland* ...' *(15.1420-2)*

Michael Logue, son of Michael Logue, a blacksmith, and Catherine (née Durning),

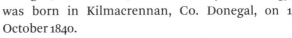

was born in Kilmacrennan, Co. Donegal, on 1 October 1840.

Logue studied at St Patrick's College Maynooth, Co. Kildare from 1856 to 1866. He was then appointed to the chairs of theology and belles lettres in the Irish College in Paris and ordained priest the same year. He remained in Paris for eight years, returning to become administrator in an Irish parish. In 1876 he was appointed to the chairs of Irish and dogmatic theology at Maynooth.

Logue became archbishop of Armagh in December 1887 and in January 1893 Pope Leo XIII created him a cardinal. Known for his guarded opposition to Parnell, he endorsed the Anglo-Irish Treaty in 1921.

He died at the archbishop's residence in Armagh on 19 November 1924 and was buried in the grounds of St Patrick's Cathedral, Armagh.

Longworth, Ernest Victor (1874–1935) *Editor and barrister*
'Longworth will give it a good puff in the *Express*.' *(9.302)*
Ernest Victor Longworth, son of Daniel Longworth of Ryde, was born in England. He was educated at the Erasmus High School and Trinity College Dublin where he was auditor of the Historical Society.

From 1901 to 1904, Longworth was editor of the *Daily Express* in Dublin, which was a conservative and pro-British paper. He published some reviews by Joyce including a critical review of *Poets and Dreamers* by Lady Gregory on 26 March 1903. The same year he was called to the Irish Bar.

Longworth lived at 4 Hume Street, and was a friend of George Moore who lived close by at 4 Upper Ely Place. He practised as a barrister and was of great assistance to Moore, who consulted him for advice concerning possible libel actions when writing *Hail and Farewell*.

Longworth settled in London in the 1920s and continued his friendship with Moore. He died in Ewell, Surrey on 15 January 1935 and was buried in Epsom Cemetery [Plot L31 B. G. S.].
Ulysses 9.1141

Love, Hugh C. (1871–1948) *Civil servant and landlord*
' The reverend Hugh C. Love, Rathcoffey. Present address: Saint Michael's, Sallins.' *(10.437–8)*
Hugh Coffey Love was born on 5 December 1871 in Belfast, son of John Love and Mary Jane (née Coffey). He was an Episcopalian (Church of Ireland) and worked as a civil servant in the grade of second-division clerk in the Education Office, Dublin.

Love married in 1899 and in 1901 lived at Farranboley in Dundrum, Co. Dublin. In 1904 he was living on the north side of the city at 3 Conquer Terrace, Clontarf. In 1911 he had moved with his wife and five children to 4 Seaview Terrace, Clontarf. He was later superintendent officer of the Ministry of Education in Northern Ireland and lived at 18 Belmont Park, Belfast. He died on 31 May 1948 and was buried in Dundonald Cemetery, Belfast.

Lovebirch, James (pseudonym) (*fl.* 1910–25) *Writer*
'Mr Bloom, alone, looked at the titles. *Fair Tyrants* by James Lovebirch.' *(10.601–2)*
James Lovebirch (pseudonym) wrote pornographic novels published between 1910 and 1925, one of which, *Fair Tyrants*, appears recurrently in *Ulysses*. This book is unknown. Some of Lovebirch's books that were published survive, such as *Les Cinq Fessées de Suzette*, published in Paris in 1910 by Roberts et Dardaillon. The Librairie Artistique published a further edition in 1924. It is listed along with his other books in the Catalogue des Livres Imprimés of the Bibliothèque Nationale [RES P-Y2–669].
Ulysses 15.1018; 18.493; 18.1396

Lowrey, Dan (1823–97) *Impresario*

'They passed Dan Lowry's musichall where Marie Kendall, charming soubrette, smiled on them from a poster a dauby smile.' *(10.495-6)*

The son of the weaver Patrick Lowrey, Dan Lowrey was born in Roscrea, Co. Tipperary. The family moved to Leeds where Dan spent his youth. He worked as a dyer in the mills and as a comic singer in the local taverns. He did well, eventually owning his own tavern. He returned to Ireland, living first in Belfast, and then in Dublin, where in December 1879 he opened Dan Lowrey's Star of Erin Music Hall in Dame Street and Crampton Court. It later became the Olympia Theatre.

Lowrey died on 16 August 1897 and was buried in Mount Jerome Cemetery, Harold's Cross, Dublin [B5–360–5772].   *Ulysses 12.747*

Loyola, St Ignatius (1491–1556) *Founder of the Society of Jesus*

'Chuck Loyola, Kinch, and come on down.' *(1.231-2)*

Ignatius Loyola was born in 1491 in the Basque province of Guipúzcoa in north-eastern Spain.

While studying in Paris, he met Francis Xavier and other scholastics who formed a community, taking vows of chastity and poverty. Pope Paul III gave formal approval in Rome on 27 September 1540 and the Society of Jesus was founded. Ignatius Loyola saw the society grow from eight members to over a thousand in his lifetime with houses and colleges all over Europe.

Ignatius Loyola died on 31 July 1556 in Rome. He was beatified by Pope Paul V on 27 July 1609 and canonised by Pope Gregory XV on 12 March 1622. His body lies under the altar designed by Pozzi in the Gesu, at Piazza del Gesu in Rome.

Ulysses 12.1687; Spiritual Exercises, 9.163

Lucas, Dr Charles (1713–71) *Irish physician, politician and patriot*

'Where are you now? Established 1763. Dr Lucas.' *(7.739)*

Charles Lucas was born on 16 September 1713, in Co. Clare. He came to Dublin and practised as an apothecary in Charles Street. In 1735 he published a pamphlet on the abuses in the sale of drugs, resulting in an act for the inspection of medicines.

Lucas campaigned against corruption in the city administration, and advocated parliamentary independence for Ireland. He was threatened with imprisonment and escaped to the continent in 1748, where aged 35 he studied medicine and qualified as a doctor in Leiden.

Lucas practised medicine in London from 1753 to 1761. He returned to Dublin and was elected MP for the city, a position he held for ten years. He became a regular contributor to the *Freeman's Journal* after its foundation in 1763. He usually wrote as 'Civis' or 'A Citizen'.

His writings included a number of political pamphlets, printed in *The Great Charter of the City of Dublin* (1749). This was a formidable piece of work focusing on long-forgotten rights.

Lucas, of whom Grattan said had 'laid the groundwork of Irish liberty', died on 4 November 1771 at his home in Henry Street and was buried in St Michan's Church, Church Street, Dublin 7. He is commemorated by a statue in City Hall, Cork Hill, Dublin.

Ulysses 12.69–70

Ludwig, William (1847–1923) *Baritone with the Carla Rosa Company*
'... who reminded him a bit of Ludwig, alias Ledwidge, when he occupied the boards of the Gaiety ...' *(16.859–60)*
William Ludwig, born William Ledwidge in Dublin on 15 July 1847, adopted the name 'Ludwig' as his surname was so consistently misprinted in concert programmes.

Ludwig was educated at the Christian Brothers School, North Richmond Street. He started his career as a singer at St Paul's Church, Arran Quay, with his lifelong friend J. J. Fagan. He played small parts in the Gaiety Theatre, at the Aldwych, the Strand, London, under John Hollingshed's management. After some engagements with small opera companies, he joined the Carl Rosa Opera Company in London in 1874. The company first came to Dublin around 1872 and produced many of the operas mentioned in *Ulysses*.

In the spring of 1875, Ludwig performed in the Gaiety Theatre, Dublin in *Martha*, *Fra Diavolo*, *Maritana* and *The Bohemian Girl*. From 6–10 December 1875 he sang in a different opera on five consecutive nights at the Theatre Royal, Dublin. These included *Il Trovatore*, *The Marriage of Figaro*, *Maritana*, *The Siege of Rochelle* and *Fra Diavolo*.

Ludwig's appearance as Vanderdecken in *The Flying Dutchman* at the Gaiety in 1877 caused a sensation in the world of opera. He was perhaps the greatest Vanderdecken of his day and Wagner is said to have given him a score of *The Flying Dutchman* inscribed 'To the incomparable Vanderdecken'. He was invited to America to sing the part and this tour proved so successful that he returned some years later.

In 1879 Ludwig and Barton M'Guckin formed a concert party for performances throughout the provinces, which proved a great success. Ludwig visited Dublin frequently to sing at the Gaiety, the Rotunda, the Leinster Hall, the Antient Concert Rooms and other Dublin venues. He also staged his own series of concerts each year around Horse Show Week.

In August 1881 Ludwig appeared with Turner, M'Guckin and Crotty in a series of operas at the Gaiety. The operas included *Mignon*, *Zampa*, *Maritana*, *Lohengrin*, *The Bohemian Girl* and *Carmen*. An enthusiastic crowd in the Abbey Theatre greeted his last performance as Vanderdecken on 1 February 1911 with Vincent

O'Brien conducting. For 34 years, Ludwig remained unrivalled as Vanderdecken.

Ludwig lost his voice shortly afterwards following an operation. T. P. O'Connor and friends organised a benefit concert for him in 1912. This ensured that he had an annuity, following his retirement from the stage.

'The great Dublin favourite of the Carl Rosa Opera Company', William Ludwig died on 25 December 1923 in West Kensington, London.

Luigi *Fisherman in Gibraltar*

'... old Luigi near a hundred they said came from Genoa ...' *(18.975–6)*

Luigi was a typical Italian/Maltese first name in Gibraltar. The links between Catalan Bay and Italy (specifically Genoa) are well known, so there is every possibility that 'Luigi' is based on a typical Catalan Bay villager.

Lynam, Brunny *Pupil at Belvedere Collge*

Based on **Bernard Lynam (1880–1945)** *Doctor*

'And the other little man? His name was Brunny Lynam. O, that was a very nice name to have.' *(10.43–5)*

Bernard Lynam is listed as a member of Joyce's year entering University College, Dublin in 1898. There were 64 students listed as entrants for that year.

The son of Matthew Lynam and Lucy (née Murphy), Bernard Malachi Lynam was born on 10 May 1880 at Bellaghy, Co. Derry. Educated locally at Magherafelt he entered University College Dublin in 1898, the same year as James Joyce. His studies were interrupted for various reasons, including his work with the army. He eventually qualified as a doctor in Edinburgh in 1917. He had a medical practice in Randalstown, Co. Antrim and died at his home, New Street, Randalstown on 28 July 1945. He was buried at St Mary's churchyard, Bellaghy, Co. Derry.   *Ulysses 10.46; 10.52*

Lynch, Vincent *Stephen's acquaintance at UCD*

Based on **Vincent Cosgrave (1877–1926)** *College acquaintance of Joyce*

'Lynch! Hey? Sign on long o' me. Denzille lane this way.' *(14.1572)*

Vincent Cosgrave was born on 22 November 1877 and lived as a boy at 5 Synott Place, which stretches from Dorset Street to Leo Street in Dublin. The family moved to 9 St Joseph's Street in the same vicinity.

Cosgrave was educated at Belvedere College, which he entered in 1892. It was here that he first met Joyce. Cosgrave left Belvedere before Joyce, matriculating in 1895, but they met again as students at University College Dublin, where Cosgrave studied medicine. There is no record in the National University of Ireland Archives that Cosgrave graduated.

Cosgrave was present when Joyce was involved in a fracas in St Stephen's Green in June 1904, but fled the scene. A man named Alfred Hunter rescued

Joyce and took him home. Joyce took literary revenge on Cosgrave and used him as the model for Lynch in *Ulysses*.

Cosgrave died on 1 September 1926 when he drowned in the Thames close to Downshams Barge Road, London. His address at the time was Brighton Hall Hotel, Cartwright Gardens, Russell Square, London.

Ulysses 14.190; 14.211; 14.410; 14.506; 14.784; 14.809; 14.1001; 14.1206; 14.1268; 15.62; 15.74; 15.101–2; 15.108; 15.113; 15.119; 15.128; 15.1762; 15.2048; 15.2054; 15.2058; 15.2067; 15.2083; 15.2122; 15.2196; 15.2239; 15.2285; 15.2290; 15.2294; 15.2508; 15.2557; 15.2589; 15.2595; 15.2644; 15.2650; 15.2710; 15.3415; 15.3535; 15.3537; 15.3550; 15.3555; 15.3567; 15.3573; 15.3589; 15.3619; 15.3624; 15.3639; 15.3659; 15.3665; 15.3819; 15.3872; 15.3879; 15.3895; 15.3905; 15.3925; 15.4009; 15.4250; 15.4260; 15.4463; 15.4724–5

Lyon, Abraham (1853–1923) *Magistrate and alderman*

'On the steps of the City hall Councillor Nannetti, descending, hailed ... Councillor Abraham Lyon ascending.' *(10.970–1)*

Abraham Lyon was born in Dublin, one of two sons of George Lyon and Alice (née Brownrigg), from Baltinglass, Co. Wicklow. When both brothers were young, their father died. Their mother took them to Cloughban near Clonroche in Co. Wexford,

where she worked as a housekeeper for her brother, Father Abraham Brownrigg, who was parish priest.

Abraham came to Dublin as a young man and worked as a salesman for Scotch whiskey, an insurance agent, and a secretary for the Family Grocers and Purveyors Association. He established a reputation for business integrity, which remained with him all his life. From 1873 to 1879 he lived at 104 North Strand, Dublin.

Lyon married Emily Anne Harvey from London in 1880. They lived at 73 Amiens Street and then moved to 1 Hollybank Terrace, Howth Road, Clontarf where they remained until 1894. Their final address was 'Altona', Howth Road, Clontarf where they lived with their five children.

Lyon served as Dublin city councillor for Clontarf from 1901 to 1905 and was appointed a justice of the peace in 1907. Always popular in commercial circles, Lyon died on 7 April 1923 at his home on Howth Road. He was buried in Glasnevin Cemetery, Finglas Road, Dublin [DG 168 Garden].

Lyons, Frederick M. 'Bantam' (1858–1908) *Punter*

'Ascot. Gold cup. Wait, Bantam Lyons muttered. Half a mo. Maximum the second'. *(5.532–3)*

Frederick M. Lyons, son of Martin Lyons and Julia (née Clare), was born in 1858.

His father was a commercial traveller who started his own stationery business. He had printing works at 6 Ormond Quay, Dublin, and much of his work was connected with the legal business. His workshop was located at 16 Usher's Court. Martin Lyons, lived at 113 Lower Gardiner Street and died on 2 February 1871. He was buried in Glasnevin Cemetery.

His sons, Frederick and James, who joined the business, had a stationer's shop at 56 Grafton Street, which dealt in high-class writing paper. Frederick lived at 5 Longford Street. He died on 28 September 1908 and was buried in Glasnevin Cemetery, Finglas Road, Dublin [SA 47 South].

Ulysses 5.108–9; 5.523; 5.527; 5.535; 5.539; 8.989; 8.997; 8.1016; 8.1023; 10.517; 12.400; 12.1554; 15.1839; 15.4346; 16.1287; 16.1290; 17.334

Lyster, Thomas William (1855–1922) *Librarian*

'QUAKERLISTER
(*a tempo*) But he that filches from me my good name ...' *(9.917–18)*
Thomas William Lyster, son of Thomas Lyster of Rathdowney and Jane (née Smith), was born on 17 December 1855 in Kilkenny. He was baptised in the Church of Ireland. His father died when Lyster was comparatively young, and he was left as the family's main support.

Lyster was educated at the Wesleyan Connexional School at 79 St Stephen's Green South, Dublin and later at Trinity College Dublin, where he graduated with an MA in German and English. He was employed as a civil servant in the Department of Agriculture and in 1878 started work in the National Library as assistant librarian. By the age of 28 he had translated, revised, enlarged and annotated Heinrich Duntzer's *Life of Goethe* (1883).

In 1880 Lyster was appointed as an examiner in English under the Intermediate Education Board and was editor of *The Intermediate School Anthology* and *Halls' History of English Literature* producing several textbooks. He also published works on Shakespeare and Milton.

Lyster was often involved in controversy. For example, the nationalist newspaper *The Leader* objected to his lecturing to a Catholic body because he was a Protestant, while the *Irish Protestant* complained that the National Library had failed to acquire some notable anti-Catholic literature.

Lyster succeeded William Archer as librarian in 1895 and remained in the post for 25 years, during which period he lectured on library topics and highlighted the importance of local newspapers and ephemera. He encouraged the application of the Dewey decimal classification system. He was elected a member of the Royal Irish Academy in 1913.

After his retirement in 1920, Lyster married Jane (née Robinson Campbell). They lived at his residence at 10 Harcourt Terrace, a ten-minute walk from the

National Library. He died suddenly on 12 December 1922 at his home and was buried in Deansgrange Cemetery, Deansgrange, Co. Dublin [45–M2–South]. A brass plaque in the National Library was unveiled by W. B. Yeats, a lifelong friend, in commemoration:

1855–1922

IN MEMORY OF THOMAS WILLIAM LYSTER

FOR TWENTY FIVE YEARS THE ABLE AND ENLIGHTENED LIBRARIAN

OF THIS LIBRARY WHOSE ENTHUSIASTIC LOVE OF BOOKS AND

WHOSE KINDLY NATURE ENDEARED HIM TO ALL WHO KNEW HIM

THE TRIBUTE OF MANY FRIENDS

MCMXXIII

Ulysses 9.1; 9.581; 9.967; 15.2244; 15.4680

Maas, Joe (1847–86) *English tenor*
'Most beautiful tenor air ever written ... *Sonnambula*. He heard Joe Maas sing that one night.' *(11.610–11)*
Joseph Maas was born in Dartford, England and started his career as a ten-year-old solo choirboy at Rochester Cathedral, Kent. In 1869 he went to Milan to continue

his musical studies. Two years later he had great success at a London concert when he took the place of John Sims Reeves (1821–1900), a leading English tenor.

Maas became the principal tenor in the Carl Rosa Opera Company and performed for them on 1 December 1878 in the Gaiety Theatre, Dublin sharing the platform with Leslie Crotty and Georgina Burns. He visited Dublin on many occasions with the company. Maas died on 16 January 1886 at his London residence. He was buried in Rochester Cathedral, Medway.

MacCabe, Edward Cardinal (1816–85) *Archbishop of Dublin*
'... the cardinal's mausoleum.' *(6.534)*
Edward MacCabe was born in Dublin and educated at Father Doyle's School on the quays and at St Patrick's College Maynooth, Co. Kildare where he was ordained priest in 1839. He was parish priest in Kingstown (now Dún Laoghaire) where he built a church and hospital. He was an assistant to Cardinal Cullen in 1877 and succeeded him as archbishop in March 1879. He was created cardinal in March 1882.

He died at his residence in Eblana Avenue, Kingstown, on 11 February 1885 and was buried in Glasnevin Cemetery, Finglas Road, Dublin [C 31 St Laurence's]. His elaborate canopied monument was erected in 1887. It was designed by the architect George Coppinger Ashlin (1837–1921), a former pupil of Edward Pugin. Sir Thomas Farrell (1827–1900) sculpted the figure of Cardinal MacCabe.

MacConsidine, Donal (*fl.* 1800s) *Gaelic poet*
' ... which is found in the satirical effusions ... of Donal MacConsidine ...' *(12.728–9)*

Domhnaill Mac Consaidín was a Gaelic scribe and poet who lived in Co. Clare, from the townland of Caherbannagh in the parish of Kilnamona. He lived for a time in Jail Street, now O'Connell Street in Ennis, Co. Clare.

MacCormack/McCormack, John (1884–1945) *Tenor*
'O yes, we'll have all topnobbers. J. C. Doyle and John MacCormack …' *(6.221–2)*
John McCormack, son of Andrew McCormack and Hannah (née Watson), was born in Athlone, Co. Westmeath, on 14 June 1884.

McCormack was educated by the Marist Brothers in Athlone and at Summerhill College in Sligo. In 1902 he obtained a position with the Palestrina Choir in the Pro-Cathedral in Dublin.

Tutored by Vincent O'Brien, McCormack entered the tenor competition in the 1903 Feis Ceoil. Professor Luigi Denza, the composer and adjudicator from the London Academy of Music, awarded McCormack the gold medal. As a result he was offered concert engagements throughout the country and his career blossomed.

McCormack and Joyce appeared in the same concert in the Antient Concert Rooms, Great Brunswick Street (now Pearse Street), on 27 August 1904.

McCormack studied in Italy under Sabatini and made his operatic début at the Royal Opera Covent Garden in *Cavalleria Rusticana* in 1907, and continued with appearances with the Chicago, Boston and Metropolitan opera companies in the United States. After several opera seasons, he proved to be the greatest concert attraction of his time. In 1928 he was made a papal count in recognition of his work for Catholic charities.

He died at his home, 'Glena', Rock Road, Booterstown, Co. Dublin, on 16 September 1945. He was buried in Deansgrange Cemetery, Deansgrange, Co. Dublin [119–20–EF–St Patrick].

He is commemorated by a statue by the sculptor Elizabeth O'Kane in Dublin's Iveagh Gardens.

MacDonnell, Sir Anthony (1844–1925) *Under-secretary to the lord lieutenant*
'Then the old specimen in the corner who appeared to have some spark of vitality left read out that sir Anthony MacDonnell had left Euston for the chief secretary's lodge or words to that effect.' *(16.1665–7)*
Anthony MacDonnell, son of Mark M. Garvey MacDonnell and Bedelia (née O'Hara), was born on 7 March 1844 at Carracastle, a small town near Swinford, Co. Mayo. He was educated at Summerhill College, Athlone, and Queen's College Galway, where he graduated with a BA degree in 1864.

He entered the Indian civil service and was posted to Bengal in 1865. He rose rapidly and in 1889 became chief commissioner of Burma. In 1893 he was lieutenant-governor of Bengal, becoming a member of the viceroy's executive council. He was awarded a knighthood that year.

In 1895, he became lieutenant governor of the Northwest Provinces, later known as the United Provinces of Agra and Oudh, and in 1901 was made president of the Indian Famine Commission but resigned the same year due to ill health and returned to London.

MacDonnell was appointed permanent under-secretary to the lord lieutenant of Ireland, a post he held from 1902 to 1908. On his retirement he was elevated to the House of Lords and given the hereditary title of 1st Baron MacDonnell of Swinford, Co. Mayo. He died at his London home on 9 June 1925 and was buried in Putney Vale Cemetery in south-west London.

He is commemorated with a statue by British sculptor Sir George Frampton (1860–1928) at Lucknow, India, which was erected in 1907.

MacDowell, Mrs (1850-1915) *Mother of Gerty*
Possibly based on **Mrs Mary MacDowell (b. 1850)** *Widow*
'It was too blooming dull sitting in the parlour with Mrs Stoer and Mrs Quigley and Mrs MacDowell and the blind down ...' *(10.1124-6)*
A Mrs Mary MacDowell lived at 10 Greenfield, Claremont Road, Sandymount, in 1904. She had then one son, Robert, aged 26, and three daughters, Ada, Florence and Alice who were aged 24, 14 and 11.

The fictional 21-year-old Gerty was a resident of Sandymount.

MacFadden, Constable *Member of the DMP*
'The baby policeman, Constable MacFadden, summoned by special courier from Booterstown, quickly restored order ...' *(12.577-9)*
Two members in the Dublin Metropolitan Police (DMP) had the surname McFadden.

Robert McFadden, DMP, Number 5474, was born in 1831, at St Mary's, Dublin. He was 5 feet 9 inches tall. He served in the 'A' Division from 1856 to 1862. He never served in Booterstown, which was the 'F' Division.

Thomas McFadden, DMP, Number 6584, was born in 1840 at Kilrea in Co. Derry. He was 5 feet, 10.75 inches tall, and served in the 'A' and 'D' Division from 1863 to 1867. He never served in the 'F' Division.   *Ulysses 12.582*

MacHugh, Professor Hugh *Scribe and editor*
Based on **Hugh MacNeill (1866-1935)** *Classical scholar and tutor*
'What about that leader this evening? professor MacHugh asked ...' *(7.378)*
Hugh MacNeill, was born at Glenarm, Co. Antrim, on 27 January 1866. He was one of five children of Archibald MacNeill, a merchant and Rosetta (née McAuley). He came from an illustrious family of scholars and administrators; he was a brother of Professor Eoin MacNeill, of James MacNeill, second governor general of the Free State and of Charles MacNeill, the antiquarian.

MacNeill was educated at Belvedere College, Dublin and was resident at 86 St

Stephen's Green when he matriculated in 1884. He lived at 9 Fitzgibbon Street when he graduated from University College Dublin with a BA degree in Latin and Greek in 1888. He then worked for a period at University College. In the Michaelmas term, 1889–90, he was tutor for matriculation Latin and in the Hilary term, 1889–90, he was tutor for matriculation Latin and French. His employment with the college continued until *c.* 1913. He supplemented his tutor's salary with examining for the Royal University and the Intermediate Examination Board.

He held an office in the Literary and Historical Society in the 1880s, and was involved along with Fr Delany and Fr Darlington with the society, which was revived after a gap of six years in 1897.

A friend wrote of MacNeill at this period: 'He did not much care for getting on in the world; indeed, his quixotic disinterestedness was the despair of his friends; it seemed as though on principle he acted in opposition to his interests. Such men are rare and are, therefore, the more attractive.'

MacNeill married Mary Abigail Murphy at the Pro-Cathedral on 3 August 1896. At the time he was living at 18 Charlemont Place. By 1900 the family had moved to a house named 'Aberdelgie' in Harbour Road, Howth. They later moved back

to the south side and from 1911 lived at various addresses in the Ranelagh area which included 6 Sandford Parade, on Sandford Road, Annaville House, Upper Annaville and 13 Charlemont Place. They had three sons and two daughters.

MacNeill frequented the offices of the *Freeman's Journal* and *Evening Telegraph* in North Princes Street. He arrived early and remained all day reading the papers, admonishing members of staff if they arrived late. He was given the exalted title of professor.

In the 1930s he was a permanent fixture in the *Irish Times* newsroom though he had never worked for the newspaper in any capacity. Known as one of the *Irish Times*'s characters, he lived on cups of tea, and ate buns, purchased by members of staff from the nearby Bewley's Oriental Cafe in Westmoreland Street. He dressed carelessly and had a dangling red beard. He slept in the *Irish Times* offices, or in a telephone kiosk on College Green. He died in the South Dublin Union Workhouse, James's Street on 13 October 1935.

Ulysses 7.237; 7.256; 7.270; 7.299; 7.325; 7.348; 7.394; 7.407; 7.461; 7.470; 7.484; 7.501; 7.547; 7.578; 7.637; 7.791; 11.268; 15.927

Mack, Mrs Annie (1831–1907) *Noted madam of Monto*
'Is this Mrs Mack's?' *(15.1285)*
Annie Mack was born Annie Alexander in Scotland in 1831. When she arrived in

Dublin sometime around 1879 she was already twice widowed. She was one of the best-known madams of Monto, reputed to have had up to a dozen 'houses of pleasure'. She was so renowned that the area was sometimes referred to as 'Mack's Town'. In 1888 she is listed as a tenant at 85 Lower Mecklenburgh Street, renamed Tyrone Street around this time (now Railway Street).

Mrs Mack had two establishments in Tyrone Street Lower in 1904, 85 and 90. In the mid nineteenth century when the Prince of Wales (later King Edward VII) was serving with the army and stationed at the Curragh in Co. Kildare, he frequented Monto and used the services provided by Annie Mack; it is rumoured that he arrived by means of 'secret tunnels' constructed underground.

Oliver St John Gogarty gives a description of Mrs Mack in *Tumbling in the Hay*:

> Her face was red-brick. Seen sideways, her straight forehead and nose were outraged by the line of her chin, which was undershot and outthrust, with an extra projection on it like the under-jaw of an old pike ... Avarice was written by Nature's hieroglyphic on the face of Mrs Mack.

Mrs Mack was also a costumier for prostitutes. In 1901, she is listed as being a lodging house keeper at 85 Tyrone Street Lower with one widowed servant from Liverpool and with five lodgers who were all single females in their early 20s. She obviously employed them as their occupations included a dressmaker from Bristol, a milliner from Co. Louth, a lace maker from Tullow, a waitress from Woolwich, and a housemaid from Limerick.

By the time Mrs Mack ceased to run her brothels she had accumulated quite a degree of wealth. She retired to her native Scotland where she died in Dunoon on 9 October 1907.

MacKenna, Stephen (1872–1934) *Linguist, scholar and nationalist*
'Mallarmé, don't you know, he said, has written those wonderful prose poems Stephen MacKenna used to read to me in Paris.' *(9.112–13)*
Stephen MacKenna was born on 15 January 1872 in Liverpool of Irish parents,

Captain MacKenna and Elizabeth Mary (née Deane).

He was educated at Ratcliffe College, a boarding school in Leicestershire; his first job was as a bank clerk in Dublin. He subsequently worked in journalism in London. He lived in Brixton and joined the Irish Literary Society and Young Ireland, a nationalist movement.

In the late 1890s MacKenna moved to Paris where he led an impoverished and bohemian life. Here he met Maud Gonne and John O'Leary, and J. M. Synge who became his best friend.

Aged 25 MacKenna fought for the Greeks against the Turks in the Greco-Turkish War in 1897. This reignited his great love for Greek literature. As European correspondent for the *New York World*, he covered the Russo-Japanese War of 1904–5, and interviewed Tolstoy. Following an argument with the owner Joseph Pulitzer, he resigned from the paper in 1907 and returned to Dublin and became a leader writer with the *Freeman's Journal*, promoting the Irish language. At this period he commenced his work on the translation of the *Enneads* by Plotinus.

MacKenna's close circle of friends included many of the most important figures of the literary revival who were invited to his 'evenings' at his home at 5 Seaview Terrace in Donnybrook. Padraic Colum remembers this as an era when intellectual contacts were easily made in Dublin. MacKenna who once said, 'I am not a man of the pen', was known as a great conversationalist.

After the death of his wife Marie in July 1923 and following his own disillusionment over the Anglo-Irish Treaty, MacKenna moved to London. He continued his work on the *Enneads* (1917–30), which is regarded as one of the best English translations of a Greek classic.

He died on 8 March 1934 at Grovelands Hospital, Southgate, London.

MacKernan/McKernan, Mrs Elizabeth (1867–1923) *Joyce's landlady*

'... Mrs MacKernan, five weeks' board.' *(2.258–9)*

Mrs Elizabeth McKernan (née Darragh) was born on 25 September 1867 in Co. Antrim. She married Daniel McKernan from Antrim in 1895.

Joyce rented a very large room spanning the top of the house where Mrs McKernan and her family lived at 60 Shelbourne Road, Ballsbridge, Dublin, from late March to 31 August 1904. Joyce spelt the name MacKernan. The spelling in the census return is McKernan. Joyce paid the rent with money he had borrowed from Oliver St John Gogarty, J. F. Byrne and George Russell.

The McKernan family comprised Elizabeth McKernan, her husband Daniel, who was an accountant's clerk, and their three children, John, Thomas and Mary Angela. Mr McKernan qualified as an accountant in July 1911, and the family moved to Cork where his employer was Michael Buckley of Carey and Buckley, 17a South Mall. By 1922 he had moved to the Cork Distillers Company, Morrison's Island, where he was chief accountant. Mrs McKernan died in early 1923.

M'Ardle/McArdle, John (1859–1928) *Surgeon at St Vincent's Hospital*

'Bolt upright like surgeon M'Ardle.' *(8.514)*

John McArdle, second son of Robert McArdle, was born in Dundalk, Co. Louth, in September 1859. He was educated at the Christian Brothers School, St Mary's College, Dundalk, and the Catholic University School of Medicine at Cecilia Street, Dublin.

He was a demonstrator of anatomy at the Catholic University School of Medicine, and in November 1879 was appointed resident at St Vincent's Hospital run by the Sisters of Charity; it was then located at 55–59 St Stephen's Green East. In July the following year he was appointed house surgeon.

In 1882, McArdle married Madeleine Forrest, daughter of Dr King Forrest, a colleague at St Vincent's Hospital. He started a practice at 7 Upper Merrion Street and in 1884 obtained a fellowship at the Royal College of Surgeons in Ireland. He was offered a very remunerative position in America as a surgeon but turned this down, preferring to work amongst the poor of Dublin.

A popular surgeon, he sat bolt upright when he travelled through the city in his doctor's brougham drawn by his fast-trotting horse. Everybody on the street waved to him because everyone knew 'the Surgeon'.

A pioneer of abdominal surgery, McArdle held the chair of surgery at University College Dublin from 1900 until 1918. He also held other positions such as surgeon to St Patrick's College Maynooth; examiner in surgery, Royal University of Ireland; and consulting surgeon for Temple Street Children's Hospital. He was consulting surgeon to the National Maternity Hospital and was one of the original governors mentioned in the Charter of the Hospital.

With his friend John Redmond, MP, he rented the Aughavannagh Barracks in Co. Wicklow. Here, he entertained Charles Stewart Parnell and other distinguished guests.

McArdle's wife and his two daughters predeceased him. He married Eileen Nugent in 1909.

He died on 14 April 1928 at his home at 72 Merrion Square, Dublin and was buried in Glasnevin Cemetery, Finglas Road, Dublin [DF 25 South New Chapel].

M'Cann/McCann, James (1840–1904) *Chairman of the Grand Canal Company*
'Developing waterways. James M'Cann's hobby to row me o'er the ferry. Cheaper transit. By easy stages.' *(6.447–8)*
James McCann was born in May 1840 in Toomes, Co. Louth, son of a farmer, James McCann, and Dorothy (née Hickey). Following his education at the Christian Brothers School in Drogheda he worked as a clerk in the Drogheda Steampacket Company. He spent ten years working in the Hibernian Bank, College Green, Dublin, before becoming a successful stockbroker.

McCann purchased an extensive property in Co. Meath in the 1890s where he founded a sawmills and a furniture factory. His businesses were hindered by the lack of an adequate transport system and he strongly advocated the commercial development of the canals, which were a cheaper mode of transport than the rail system.

McCann had a great interest in inland navigation in Ireland, and was elected in 1891 as member of the Grand Canal Company and the following year as chairman. The company had a fleet of trade boats on the Grand Canal, which operated to central and southern Ireland.

From 1900, McCann was MP for the St Stephen's Green Division of Dublin. He lived at Simmonscourt Castle, Simmonscourt Road, in Ballsbridge, which he purchased in 1878, and also had a residence at Teltown, Navan, Co. Meath. He died on 12 February 1904 and was buried in Glasnevin Cemetery, Finglas Road, Dublin [V 47 O'Connell].

McCann, Philip *Friend of Stephen at UCD*

Based on **Francis Sheehy-Skeffington** (1878–1916) *Writer*

'McCann, one guinea.' *(2.256)*

Francis Skeffington, son of Dr Joseph Bartholomew Skeffington, was born in 1878 in Bailieborough, Co. Cavan.

He was educated at University College Dublin where he revived the Literary and Historical Society and became its first auditor in 1897. A non-conformist, he

was known as a socialist and pacifist. From 1902 until 1904, Skeffington was registrar of University College but resigned after a dispute with the president, Father William Delany, SJ, concerning the rights of women to academic status. He was editor of the *Nationalist* with Tom Kettle in 1905 and later also of the *Irish Citizen* (1912), a feminist weekly. He founded the monthly journal, the *National Democrat*, with Frederick Ryan. He contributed to many newspapers including the *Manchester Guardian*, and *L'Humanité*. His works include a *Life of Michael Davitt* (1908) and a novel, *In Dark and Evil Days* (published posthumously).

He married Hanna Sheehy (1877–1946), a daughter of David Sheehy, MP. Hanna was a suffragette, feminist and nationalist, and co-founder with Margaret Cousins of the Irish Women's Franchise League. He adopted his wife's surname.

Sheehy-Skeffington supported the Home Rule Bill. He was a friend of some of the 1916 leaders but as a pacifist was against violence. His only involvement in the Rising was an attempt to prevent Dublin citizens from looting.

On 25 April 1916 he was arrested and shot without trial the following day in

Portobello Barracks in Rathmines. He was buried in Glasnevin Cemetery, Finglas Road, Dublin [ZA 16–17.5 South]. Sheehy-Skeffington is commemorated by a bust sculpted by Gary Trimble at the entrance gate to Cathal Brugha Barracks (formerly Portobello), Dublin.

M'Carthy/MacCarthy, Denis Florence (1817–82) *Irish poet, scholar and translator*
'Denis Florence M'Carthy's *Poetical Works* (copper beechleaf bookmark at p. 5).'
(17.1363–4)
Denis Florence MacCarthy was born in Dublin. He was educated locally and at St Patrick's College Maynooth, Co. Kildare, where he studied for the priesthood for a time before changing to law. He was nearly 50 when he was called to the Bar but never practised.

In 1834 he started to contribute prose and poetry to the *Nation*, the *Dublin Magazine* and other periodicals. He was appointed professor of English literature in the Catholic University in 1854. This was situated at 85 and 86 St Stephen's Green; the two houses were then combined and known as St Patrick's House (later renamed Newman House).

MacCarthy had nine children and lived for a time at Summerfield House on the corner of Dalkey Avenue and Old Quarry. In 1904 a portion of it was used by Clifton School, the founder of which was Francis Irwin, an Ulster Scot who appears in *Ulysses*.

MacCarthy's publications include *The Book of Irish Ballads* (1846), *The Poets and Dramatists of Ireland* (1846), *Ballads, Lyrics and Poems* (1850), *Underglimpses and Other Poems* (1857), *The Bell-Founder, and Other Poems* (1857), *Irish Legends and Lyrics* (1858) and *Poems* (1882).

He published translations from the Spanish of 13 plays by Pedro Calderón de la Barca (1600–81). One of these included *The Purgatory of St Patrick*. Some of the translations were assembled in a *MacCarthy Memorial Volume* (1887). MacCarthy died on 7 April 1882 at 28 Mount Merrion Avenue, Blackrock, where he had lived during his final years. He was buried in the family vault in Glasnevin Cemetery, Finglas Road, Dublin [Vault JA 44.5 Chapel Circle].

M'Carthy, Jakes
Based on **John 'Jacques' McCarthy (1857–1901)** *Journalist*
'Put us all into it, damn its soul. Father, Son and Holy Ghost and Jakes M'Carthy.'
(7.621–2)
John McCarthy, better known under his pen name 'Jacques', was a famous football reporter of his day. He wrote in a racy style for the *Freeman's Journal* on Irish rugby from about 1875 to the early 1900s.

Reporting on an international rugby match in which Ireland triumphed over England, a player named Ryan scored a brilliant try. McCarthy wrote, 'Ryan crossed the line festooned with Saxons.' This catchphrase then became associated with

him. Jacques (pronounced 'Jakes'), who lived at 8 Cumberland Place, North Circular Road, was once asked to define the three forms of football. He thought for a moment and replied, 'In rugby you kick the ball; in soccer you kick the man if you can't kick the ball; in Gaelic you kick the ball if you can't kick the man; and the use of the knife is forbidden before half time.'

Terence O'Hanlon, a journalist with the *Irish Independent* wrote in the *Capuchin Annual*, 'Jacques was a rolling stone who, despite his brilliance, sometimes found himself out of a job and on his uppers.' One of these spells of inactivity occurred during the Russo-Japanese War of 50 years ago. He was talking to a colleague on O'Connell Bridge. A newsboy ran past with an evening papers placard bearing in large type the words 'Situation in the Far East'. 'I wonder,' said Jacques to his friend, 'should I apply for it.'

McCarthy was a conspicuous figure in the world of sport, whose wit, genial temperament and kindly nature won him friends in many circles. He died in Our Lady's Hospice, Harold's Cross, Dublin, on 6 April 1901 and was buried in Glasnevin Cemetery, Finglas Road, Dublin [RD 31.5 Garden].

M'Carthy/McCarthy, Justin (1830–1912) *Journalist, novelist and politician*
'... Justin M'Carthy against Parnell ...' *(15.4684)*
Justin McCarthy, eldest son of Michael Francis McCarthy, was born in Cork on 22 November 1830.

Educated at a classical school in Cork city, he served his apprenticeship as a journalist with the *Cork Examiner*, before moving to Liverpool in 1852 to work on

the *Northern Times*. In London he represented the *Morning Star* in the House of Commons. He became foreign editor and in 1864 chief editor. From 1870 he was leader writer for the *Daily News*.

In 1879 McCarthy was elected MP for Longford, and in 1886–92 for Derry City. He led the majority anti-Parnellite wing of the Irish Parliamentary Party after 'the split' over Parnell's leadership in 1890. He resigned from the chairmanship of the party in 1896 due to ill health.

McCarthy wrote largely on history, fiction and biography. His publications included *Dear Lady Disdain* (1875), *The Story of an Irishman* (1890), *A History of Our Own Times* (5 vols, 1877–1901), *The Story of Mr Gladstone* (1898), *Reminiscences* (1899), *Mononia* (1901) and *Irish Recollections* (1912). He died in Folkestone, Kent, on 24 April 1912 and was buried in Hampstead Cemetery, London.

M'Coy, C. P.
Clerk in the Midland Railway and formerly ad man for the Freeman's Journal
Based on **Charles Chance (1863–1915)** *Commercial clerk*
'Wish I hadn't met that M'Coy fellow.' *(5.211–12)*
Charles Chance, a commercial clerk, was a friend of John Stanislaus Joyce. He was born in Dublin. In 1886 he married and by 1901 was boarding at a house owned by Patrick O'Neill at 83 Ballybough Road, Mountjoy. His wife Mary was a concert singer and performed under the name 'Marie Tallon' in a number of concerts during the 1890s.

Charles Chance and his family later moved to live with his mother, Mrs Ellen Chance, at 24 Belvidere Place, Dublin. In 1911, he is listed as an unemployed clerk. Chance, a widower, died on 19 August 1915 and was buried in Glasnevin Cemetery, Finglas Road, Dublin [EE 232 Garden].

Ulysses 4.454; 5.82; 5.85; 5.88; 5.95; 5.137; 5.153; 5.164; 5.169; 5.175–6; 5.320; 6.114; 6.889; 10.487; 10.491; 10.493; 10.498; 10.508; 10.512; 10.523; 10.525; 10.540; 10.550; 10.580; 10.1204; 11.972; 13.788; 15.1142; 15.4346; 16.523; 16.1261; 16.1263

M'Guckin, Barton (1853–1913) *Tenor*
'Ah, what M'Guckin! Yes. In his way. Choirboy style.' *(11.611–12)*
Barton M'Guckin was born in Dublin on 8 August 1853. He started his singing

career as a chorister in Armagh Cathedral School. He became the first tenor attached to St Patrick's Cathedral in Dublin.

M'Guckin was a member of the Dublin Glee and Madrigal Union, before pursuing an opera career, mainly in England. He made his début in 1875 at the Crystal Palace in London. He then travelled to Milan for further studies.

He was a leading member of the Carl Rosa Opera Company from 1880, when he performed in the first London production of Frederic Hymen Cowen's *The Corsair*. He continued with the company until 1887. He performed major roles in London and the provinces as well as in America and Australia. M'Guckin often appeared in the same operas with Leslie Crotty, starring in Goring Thomas's *Esmeralda* in 1883 and in *Nadeshda* in 1885.

M'Guckin was the first tenor to sing Verdi's *Otello* in English. He played principal roles in *Lohengrin* and in *Faust*. He also played Don José in *Carmen* and Eleazar in Halévy's *La Juive*.

In 1907 he was the conductor of the orchestral concerts held at the concert hall, seating up to 2,000 people at the Irish International Exhibition held in Dublin in what is now Herbert Park, Ballsbridge.

M'Guckin died on 17 April 1913 and was buried in Stoke Poges, England.

M'Manus/McManus, Monsignor Miles (1827–1919)
Parish Priest of St Catherine's Church

Miles McManus was born in Dublin in 1827. After a distinguished student career in St Patrick's College Maynooth, Co. Kildare, McManus commenced his ministerial career in 1851 as chaplain to the Convent of Mercy in Baggot Street, Dublin. Two years later he was moved to a curacy in the church of St Nicholas of Myra, Francis Street. He was parish priest in Celbridge, Co. Kildare, 1853–64.

In 1904 McManus was appointed vicar general and domestic prelate to the pope. He was parish priest at St Catherine's Church, Meath Street, Dublin where he remained for the rest of his life.

He died on 26 January 1919 and was buried in Glasnevin Cemetery, Finglas Road, Dublin [C 32.5 St Laurence's]. *Ulysses 12.935*

M' Swiney/McSwiney, Peter Paul (1810–84)
Businessman, politician and lord mayor

'Selling tapes in my cousin, Peter Paul M'Swiney's. Not likely.' *(6.71)*

Peter Paul McSwiney was related to Daniel O'Connell, and also a first cousin of

James Joyce's paternal grandmother, Ellen O'Connell. Originally from Cork city, he came to Dublin and opened a drapery store named The New Mart on Sackville Street (now O'Connell Street) in May 1853.

In 1863 McSwiney was elected city councillor of the North Dock Ward and the following year was elected lord mayor of Dublin. He laid the foundation stone of the memorial round tower for Daniel O'Connell in Prospect Cemetery in Glasnevin on 8 August 1864. He was elected lord mayor for a second time in 1875. He was involved with the Dublin and Chapelizod Distillery Company and invested a large sum of money in the enterprise, but it was unsuccessful and closed in 1877.

McSwiney invested money in enlarging The New Mart in 1878 but an economic depression followed and by 1882 the company was bankrupt. The following year it was sold to M. J. Clery from Limerick. McSwiney who served on Dublin City Council for 13 years, lived at 71 Lower Baggot Street. He died on 15 August 1884 and was buried in Glasnevin Cemetery, Finglas Road, Dublin [MC 79.5 South].

Madden, Dodgson Hamilton (1840–1928) *Judge and author*

'So Mr Justice Madden in his *Diary of Master William Silence* has found the hunting terms ...' *(9.582–3)*

Dodgson Hamilton Madden born on 28 March 1840, was the only son of the Rev. Hugh Hamilton Madden, chancellor of Cashel. Educated at Trinity College

Dublin, he was called to the Irish Bar in 1864. In 1888 he was solicitor-general for Ireland. From 1887 to 1892, he was MP for Dublin University and from 1892 judge of the High Court of Ireland, King's Bench Division.

Madden was president of the British Empire Shakespeare Society's Dublin branch. He took as his motto Dr Johnston's dictum: 'He that will understand Shakespeare must not be content to study him in the closet; he must look for his meaning sometimes among the sport of the field.'

His publications include *Treatise of Deeds* (1868); *Practice of Land Judges Court* (1870); *The Diary of Master William Silence; A Study of Shakespeare and of Elizabethan Sport* (1897); *Shakespeare and His Fellows: An Attempt to Decipher the Man and His Nature* (1916); *A Chapter of Medieval History: The Fathers of Literature of Sport, and Horses* (1923).

Madden lived at 'Nutley', Booterstown, Co. Dublin and also at 'The Orchard', East Sheen, Surrey where he died on 6 March 1928. He was buried in Deansgrange Cemetery, Deansgrange, Co. Dublin [9 –W–South].   *Ulysses 9.519–20; 9.687–8; 9.1073–5*

Madden, Herbert Otto (1872–1942) *Jockey*

'Sceptre with O. Madden up.' *(7.388–9)*

Herbert Otto Madden was champion jockey on four occasions between 1898

and 1904. In 1898 he won the Derby on Jeddah at 100/1. On 16 June 1904 Madden rode Sceptre in the Ascot Gold Cup. She finished third behind Throwaway and Zinfandel.

Madden who was under some suspicion of pulling Wool Winder up in the 1907 Derby retired in 1909 to take up training horses but came back to racing owing to a shortage of jockeys during the war years 1914 to 1918. He won the Oaks on Sunny Jane in 1917. He was later the owner, breeder and trainer of Chapeau who won the Ebor Handicap at York.

Madden died in 1942.   *Ulysses 5.532; 10.511; 14.1129*

Madden, William *Medical student*

Based on **Thomas Joseph Madden** (1880–1927) *Medical student at the Catholic University School of Medicine*

'... his fellows Lynch and Madden, scholars of medicine ...' *(14.190)*

Thomas Joseph Madden, son of Michael Madden and Mary Anne (née Lowry), was born on 31 January 1880 in Roscrea, Co. Tipperary. He studied medicine at the Catholic University School of Medicine at Cecilia Street, Dublin. He wrote the 'Medical Notes' in *St Stephen's*, the college magazine, and was for several years medical subeditor. He was a member of the Literary and Historical Society at college. An ardent nationalist, he was an associate of Thomas Kettle. He was among those who objected to the playing of 'God Save the King' at the conferring ceremonies held in the Royal University in 1905.

Madden was a medical student at Holles Street Maternity Hospital from about 1 July to 5 September 1903. In 1905 he was appointed dispensary doctor in Kiltimagh, Co. Mayo, with Dr Frank Ronayne as his locum. He resided at the Railway Hotel before moving to 8 George's Street in Kiltimagh. He married May McDonnell in 1913 and they had seven children.

John Redmond nominated Madden to the provisional committee of the Irish Volunteers in 1914. He was the first man in Kiltimagh to own a car. He died in 1927 and was buried in the local cemetery at Kilkinure.

Ulysses 14.203; 14.210; 14.219; 14.423; 14.1001; 14.1209; 15.1788; 15.2238

Magennis, William (1869–1946) *Professor of metaphysics, UCD*
'He is a man of the very highest morale, Magennis.' *(7.788)*
William Magennis was born on 18 May 1869 in Belfast, Co. Down. He was educated at the Christian Brothers School in Belfast, Belvedere College and University College Dublin where he graduated in 1888 with a BA degree. The following year he was awarded his MA.

Around this time he became editor of the *New Ireland Review* and assisted with *The Lyceum* (1887–94), a monthly magazine founded by two brothers, Fathers Tom and Peter Finlay. He read a paper to the Literary and Historical Society,

'Irish Democracy', an occasion at which Father Finlay was in the chair and Gerard Manley Hopkins was a member of the audience. He was auditor and gold medallist in the Literary and Historical Society from 1888 to 1889 and maintained involvement with the society over a long period as student and professor. Magennis was in the chair when Joyce read his paper 'Drama and Life' on 20 January 1900 and also presided on 15 February 1902 when Joyce gave his talk on 'James Clarence Mangan'.

Magennis was called to the Bar in 1893. From 1889 till 1909 he held the post of professor of philosophy at University College. He then became professor of metaphysics, a position he held until 1941.

From 1922 to 1927 Magennis represented the National University of Ireland in the Dáil. He was a member of the Censorship Board from 1934 and was a senator from 1938 until his death. In 1941 he was awarded a D. Litt. He lived at 3 Herbert Street, Dublin before moving to Greenpark, Stillorgan Road.

Magennis was among the first generation of professors at University College Dublin. He died on 30 March 1946 and was buried in Glasnevin Cemetery, Finglas Road, Dublin [TD 71 Section 8].   *Ulysses 7.782*

Maginni, Denis J. (1846–1915) *Professor of Dancing*
'Mr Denis J Maginni, professor of dancing & c, in silk hat, slate frockcoat with silk facings, white kerchief tie, tight lavender trousers, canary gloves and pointed patent boots, walking with grave deportment ...' *(10.56–8)*
Denis J. Maginni, whose birth name was Maginn, was born in Dublin on 27 September 1846. He was the son of Catherine (née Bulger) and Denis Maginn.

Maginni started his career as a law clerk. He was living at 37 Lower Gloucester Street, Dublin, when he married Mary (née Healy) on 1 July 1872. At the birth of their first child in 1874 they were living at 23 Cumberland Street. At this time he

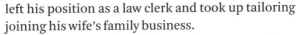

left his position as a law clerk and took up tailoring joining his wife's family business.

He moved with his family to 13 Eden Quay and then to 112 Lower Gardiner Street. It was at this address that the first advertisements for his dancing classes appeared. He changed his name to Signor Maginni as it sounded Italian and more appropriate for a teacher of dancing.

Maginni moved next to 25 Upper Gloucester Street, then to North Great George's Street, first to 28 and finally to 32 where he lived with his wife, four surviving children and a relative named Michael Healy, a tailor's foreman. In 1901, Maginni is listed at this address with the title professor of dancing. It was here that he ran his most successful dance academy.

He rented an extra room in 35 North Great George's Street for his dancing academy. Maginni was seen walking daily in the street and was described as a dark, middle-aged, dapper little man. His four children predeceased him; two died in 1902, one in 1906 and the last in 1910. His wife Mary died in 1909.

By 1911, Denis Maginni was the only remaining member of the Maginni family in 32 North Great George's Street. He moved to live for a short time with his relative Michael Healy, who rented three rooms in 35 and was caretaker there. Maginni died on 12 April 1915 and was buried in Glasnevin Cemetery, Finglas Road, Dublin, in the same grave as his wife, Mary, and daughter, Elizabeth [QI 242.5 St Brigid's].
              Ulysses 8.98; 10.600; 10.1239; 15.4032; 15.4041; 15.4059; 15.4079; 15.4089; 15.4097; 15.4102

Maher, Rev. Thomas, SJ (1859–1917) *Church of St Francis Xavier*
Thomas Maher was born on 29 September 1859 at Whitehall, Paulstown in Co. Kilkenny. He attended Carlow College for three years and continued his studies at

the Jesuit school at Tullabeg, Co. Offaly. On 9 September 1876 he entered the Society of Jesus in Milltown Park, Dublin.

In 1904, Father Thomas Maher was a member of the Jesuit Community of the Church of St Francis Xavier, Upper Gardiner Street, Dublin. He died on 27 March 1917 at Willesden, England. He was buried at St Mary's Cemetery, Harrow Road, Kensal Green [Plot No. 3991].

Ulysses 12. 931–2

Mallarmé, Stéphane (1842–98) *French symbolist poet*

'France produces the finest flower of corruption in Mallarmé ...' *(9.108–9)*

Stéphane Mallarmé was born in Paris on 18 March 1842. He was an English teacher in various lycées, mostly in Paris. He was renowned for his 'salons', which he held at his home on the Rue de Rome. Regular visitors included Paul Valery, W. B. Yeats, Paul Verlaine, Stefan George and other intellectuals of the day.

Mallarmé's works include *Herodiade (c.* 1864), *L'Après-Midi d'un Faune (c.* 1865), *Les Mots Anglais* (1878), *Poesies* (1887), *Les Dieux Antiques* (1879), *Vers et Prose* (1893) and *Un Coup de des Jamais n'Abolira le Hazard* (1897).

Mallarmé is considered one of the founders of modern European poetry. He died on the 9 September 1898 in Valvins, Vulaines-sur-Seine, and was buried in the cemetery of Samoreau (Seine-et-Marne), France in 1898.

Ulysses 9.112–13; L'Après-Midi d'un Faune, 3.441–4

Mallon, John (1839–1915) *Assistant commissioner of the DMP*

'... after a strong hint to a blind horse from John Mallon of Lower Castle Yard ...' *(16.1191–2)*

John Mallon was born on 10 May 1839 in the parish of Killevy, Flurrybridge, Co. Armagh. He joined the Dublin Metropolitan Police (DMP) on 1 December 1858.

During his career with the DMP he was attached to Divisions 'F', 'B', and 'G'.

In 1869, Mallon was promoted from sergeant to inspector and five years later was appointed superintendent. John Mallon, superintendent 'G' Division, DMP lived at 38 North Circular Road, Dublin in 1884.

He was appointed assistant commissioner in 1893, at the headquarters of the DMP in Dublin Castle, Lower Castle Yard.

From 1860 until his retirement, Mallon's work was intricately bound up with public life in Dublin. He was associated with political cases, which occurred in connection with Fenian and agrarian agitation. It was through his work that the murderers of Lord Frederick Cavendish, chief secretary of Ireland, and Thomas Henry Burke, the under-secretary, were traced, and sufficient evidence gathered to justify the convictions that followed.

Mallon retired on 1 January 1902 and moved to his ancestral home at Meigh just outside Newry.

He died on 9 October 1915 and was buried in Meigh, Newry, Co. Down.

Malone, Rev. Charles (1841–1924) *Church of the Three Patrons*
'Bloom (three times) ... and by the reverend Charles Malone C. C., in the church of the Three Patrons, Rathgar.' *(17.542–6)*
Charles Malone was one of three curates in the Church of the Three Patrons in Rathgar. This was the only parish he ever worked in.

Father Malone was associated with the parish of Rathgar from 1876 when he became a curate. At the time he was living at 25 Rathmines Road. He then moved to 50 Rathgar Road. In 1906 he became parish priest of Rathgar and inaugurated the new bell in the Church of the Three Patrons that year. Rathgar became a separate parish from Rathmines when the church was dedicated in 1882.

Father Malone baptised both Stephen and Bloom at the Church of the Three Patrons, Rathgar.

He died at his residence, 50 Rathgar Road, on 18 November 1924 and was buried in Glasnevin Cemetery, Finglas Road, Dublin [B 37 St Laurence's].

Mapas/Malpas, John (*fl.* **eighteenth century**) *Donor of obelisk for Killiney Hill*
'... the Mapas obelisk ...' *(12.1455)*
Col John Malpas owned lands in the area of Rochestown and Dalkey. His main residence was Rochestown House. In 1740 he built a house named 'Mount Malpas', which is now Killiney Castle. Malpas had the cone-shaped obelisk constructed on Killiney Hill in the grounds of his residence. It was a folly designed to provide employment for the poor. On the base of the obelisk is inscribed: 'Last year being hard with the poor, the walls around these hills and this were erected by John Malpas, esq. June, 1742.'

Joyce misspelled the name Malpas as Mapas.

Marcella, The Midget Queen *Singer at the World's Fair Waxwork Exhibition*
Based on **Elizabeth Paddock** (1878–1955) *Singer*
'Giants, though that is rather a far cry, you see once in a way, Marcella the midget queen. In those waxworks in Henry Street I myself saw some Aztecs ...' *(16.849–51)*
Elizabeth Paddock, daughter of George and Elizabeth Paddock, was born in Liverpool in 1878. Both her parents were dead by 1893 and she was adopted by an Englishman, Charles Augustus James, and his wife, Minnie. James was an auctioneer from Derbyshire who settled in Dublin in the early 1890s. He had a hardware and

fancy goods business at 30 Henry Street, which he named The World's Fair Stores.

The premises comprised four storeys. Here he had a small theatre, established his wax works and displayed the World's Fair Waxwork Exhibition where 'Marcella, the Midget Queen' first performed in 1893, singing popular lyrics of the day. She was small in stature with a beautiful light mezzo-soprano voice. Marcella also helped out in the shop.

In 1911 she was living with the James family and their two children, Ernest and Phoebe, at 36 Strand Road, Sandymount. Marcella died in Dublin in early 1955.

Marcellus II (1501–55) *Pope*
'... in the mass for pope Marcellus, the voices blended ...' *(1.653–4)*
The son of Ricardo Cervini, Marcello Cervini degli Spannochi was born on 6 May 1501 in Montefano near Loreto in Italy. He reigned as pope for only 22 days after his coronation in 1555. He was succeeded by Pope Paul IV (1555–9).

Giovanni Pierluigi da Palestrina (1525–94) composed the *Missa Papae Marcelli*, first performed on 27 April 1565. The first Dublin performance of the *Missa Papae Marcelli* was at St Teresa's Church, Clarendon Street, in 1898.

Marcellus II died on 1 May 1555 in Rome. His tomb is in St Peter's Basilica in the Vatican City.

Mario, Giovanni Matteo, Cavaliere de Candia (1810–83) *Italian tenor*
'*His spindlelegs and sparrow feet are those of the tenor Mario, prince of Candia.*'
(15.2484–5)
Mario was an Italian opera singer and one of the best-known tenors of the nineteenth century. Born Giovanni Matteo de Candia in Sardinia on 17 October 1810, he was the son of General de Candia, of the Italian royal army.

Mario made his début in 1838 as the hero of Meyerbeer's *Robert le Diable*. The following year he joined the company of the Théâtre Italien appearing as Nemorino in Donizetti's *L'Elisir d'Amore*. In 1839 he sang in London for the first time and made return visits with various concert tours throughout the United Kingdom.

During his career Mario played Ernesto in *Don Pasquale*, Gennaro in *Lucrezia Borgia* and Manrico in *Il Trovatore*. He sang Lyonel several times in Flotow's *Martha*, and performed it at Covent Garden during his final season in 1871, the year he retired from the stage. Mario died in Rome on 11 December 1883 and was buried in Cagliari, Sardinia.   *Ulysses 7.53–6*

Martin-Harvey, Sir John (1863–1944) *Actor and theatrical producer*
'... then we had Martin Harvey for breakfast dinner and supper ...' *(18.1055)*
John Martin-Harvey, son of John Harvey and Margaret Diana (née Goyder), was born on 22 June 1863 in Bath Street, Wivenhoe in Essex.

He joined Sir Henry Irving's company at the Lyceum Theatre in London in

1882 and had minor roles in Irving's productions for many years. On 16 February 1899 he played the lead role of Sydney Carton in *The Only Way*, in what was to become his most famous performing role. The play was an adaptation of Dickens's *A Tale of Two Cities*.

On 9 October 1899 Martin-Harvey came to Dublin to perform in *The Only Way* at the Theatre Royal for six nights. He paid many visits to Dublin in the late nineteenth and the early twentieth centuries and, according to his autobiography, his Dublin performances were a 'series of triumphs'.

He was knighted in 1921 and died on 14 May 1944 at his residence in East Sheen, Richmond, Surrey. He was buried at East Sheen Cemetery [Section H, No. 142].

Ulysses 13.416–17

Martyn, Edward (1859–1923) *Playwright*

'Did you hear Miss Mitchell's joke about Moore and Martyn? That Moore is Martyn's wild oats? Awfully clever, isn't it? ' *(9.306–8)*

Edward Martyn, son of John Martyn and Annie (née Smyth), was born on 30 January 1859 at Tulira Castle, Ardrahan in Co. Galway. His parents were wealthy landowners with extensive estates in two counties as well as property in Galway city.

Edward Martyn was eight when his father died, leaving him a considerable fortune. George Moore, from Moore Hall in the adjoining Co. Mayo, was his cousin, and as boys they were close friends.

Educated at Oxford, Martyn returned to his ancestral home at Tulira and became interested in the Irish language and in traditional and church music, immersing himself in every aspect of the Irish cultural revival. He founded the Palestrina Choir at St Mary's Pro-Cathedral in Marlborough Street in Dublin, and the Feis Ceoil, an annual festival of music.

In 1896, Martyn introduced W. B. Yeats to his neighbour Lady Gregory and with them he became a co-founder of the Irish Literary Theatre in 1899. Martyn's play *The Heather Field* and Yeats's *The Countess Cathleen* were the first productions.

Martyn wrote several plays including *Maeve* (1900), *The Tale of a Town* (1902), *Glencolman* (1912), *The Dream Physician* (1914) and *Romulus and Remus* (1916).

George Moore was a frequent visitor to Martyn in his rooms in Lincoln Place in Dublin. In Moore's three-volume autobiography, *Hail and Farewell* (1911–14), Martyn is a central figure.

Martyn's health deteriorated and he returned to Tulira and became a recluse. He died on 5 December 1923. He was the last of a family who had lived in Ireland since the twelfth century. He was buried in Glasnevin Cemetery, Finglas Road, Dublin [NB 86.5 St Paul's].

Ulysses 9.274; 9.1098

Mastiansky/Maliansky, Phineas (b. 1875) *Friend of the Blooms*
'And Mastiansky with the old cither.' *(4.205–6)*
Mastiansky is a misprint in *Thom's Directory* for Masliansky. Phineas Maliansky was born in Slutzk in the province of Minsk, Russia. In the family's moves between various addresses in Dublin's Jewish quarter between 1896 and 1906, the name is spelt in many different forms such as Masliansky, Maslianski and Mosliansky.

He married Russian-born Flora (née Leanse), in 1896 in Dublin and earned his living as a draper.

Phineas was musical with a fine singing voice, and was described as being handsome with a pointed beard. In 1901 he lived with his wife and family at 1 Emorville Square, South Circular Road. In 1904 he lived at 16 St Kevin's Parade, Portobello, off Clanbrassil Street Lower. Israel Citron was his next-door neighbour at 17, and Moses Herzog lived at 13.

Moses, Isaac and Phineas Masliansky left Dublin with their families for New York around 1906. Flora was buried in Seattle. It is likely that Phineas was buried there also.

Ulysses 15.4357

Mathew, Father Theobald (1790–1856) *Capuchin priest and Apostle of Temperance*
'Under the patronage of the late Father Mathew.' *(6.319–20)*
Theobald Mathew, son of James Mathew and Anne (née Whyte), was born on 10 October 1790 at Thomastown Castle, near Cashel, Co. Tipperary.

He was educated at St Canice's Academy in Kilkenny and St Patrick's College Maynooth, Co. Kildare. He joined the Capuchins in Church Street, Dublin, and was ordained priest on 17 April 1813.

Father Mathew worked for 20 years in Cork. He founded schools, organised charities and opened a Catholic cemetery on the site of the old botanic gardens of the Royal Cork Institution.

In 1838 Father Mathew signed a pledge of total abstinence and founded the Cork Total Abstinence Association with the words 'Here goes in the name of God.' He placed himself at the head of the movement and worked all over Ireland, halving the national alcohol consumption. He worked tirelessly during the famine of 1846–9, raising funds in England and America. Due to a breakdown in his health from overwork, he declined a bishopric.

Father Mathew died in Queenstown (now Cobh) in Co. Cork on 8 December 1856 and was buried in St Joseph's Cemetery, Cork.

In Dublin, he is commemorated by the Father Mathew Bridge, the Father Mathew Centenary Temperance Hall in Church Street, and a statue by sculptor Mary Redmond in O'Connell Street. A statue in his honour by John Foley stands on Patrick Street, Cork.

Ulysses 11.762–3; 12.689

Maxwell, Lady (1839–1914) *Visitor to Father Conmee*
'Nones. He should have read that before lunch. But lady Maxwell had come.'
(10.191–92)
Annie Quill, only daughter of Captain John Quill of the 82nd Regiment, was born in Co. Kerry. She married solicitor Patrick Maxwell (1817–97) on 29 September 1860 at Dunloe, Co. Kerry.

Lady Maxwell was widowed on 15 January 1897 when Sir Patrick died at their residence, 37 North Great George's Street, Dublin. He was buried in Glasnevin Cemetery, Finglas Road, Dublin [MB 5 Garden]. He had been on the council of the Incorporated Law Society, was elected president of the society and in 1887 was conferred with a knighthood by the lord lieutenant, the Marquis of Londonderry.

In 1904 Lady Maxwell was still living at 37 North Great George's Street. She died on 10 May 1914 at the Hotel Beau Sejour, Anseremme, Belgium.   *Ulysses 10.59*

Maybrick, Florence Elizabeth (1862–1941) *Murderer*
'... take that Mrs Maybrick that poisoned her husband for what I wonder in love with some other man ...' *(18.234–5)*
Florence Elizabeth Chandler, daughter of William Chandler and Caroline (née Holbrook), was born on 3 September 1862 in Alabama in the United States. Aged 18, she married 42-year-old James Maybrick, an English cotton broker. They lived in Virginia until 1885 and then moved to Liverpool, England.

Maybrick was addicted to arsenic and other poisons, which he took as aphrodisiacs. From 22 to 24 March 1889, Florence stayed with a cotton merchant named Alfred Brierley in a London hotel. In late March, Maybrick quarrelled with Florence about Brierley. The following month, Florence bought some flypaper with the intention of extracting poison for cosmetic use.

Maybrick died mysteriously in his home on 11 May 1889. Florence was tried for his murder but there was some doubt about her guilt on account of Maybrick's addiction. However, because of her flypaper purchase, the jury was convinced that she poisoned her husband and found her guilty on 7 August 1889. Her death sentence was commuted to life imprisonment on 22 August 1889.

After detention in Woking and Aylesbury prisons, Florence Maybrick was released on 25 January 1904. She returned to the United States and wrote her memoirs, *My Fifteen Lost Years*. In 1915 she was living as Mrs Chandler at South Kent, Connecticut. She died on 23 October 1941 and was buried in the grounds of South Kent School.

Mayers/Mayer, Frederick 'Freddy' (1863–1919) *General manager of an opera company*
'... when I sang Maritana with him at Freddy Mayers private opera ...' *(18.1293–4)*
Frederick Mayer, son of Henry J. Mayer and Sarah (née Slack), was born in Leek, Staffordshire in England. He was the general manager of Joseph Poole's new

Myriorama, established in 1837 and billed as 'Great Britain's most popular entertainment with a refined company of entertainers'. There were three Poole brothers each of whom had a Myriorama, as a travelling show. Mayer's boss was Joseph William Poole (1847–1906).

The Myriorama first performed in Dublin in 1887 at the Leinster Hall before moving to the Round Room at the Rotunda. It continued to perform in Dublin on a regular basis until about 1908. It provided exceptionally good entertainment 'with a variety of programmes presented which cannot fail to please the most fastidious'. Freddy Mayer was involved in the production of some of the operatic sketches and was described as 'Guide, Elocutionist, Humourist and Vocalist' and as a courteous business manager. He died on 29 January 1919 in Chichester, England. *Ulysses Poole's Myriorama, 18.39–40*

Meldon, Austin (1844–1904) *Surgeon*

'... as with the noted physician, Mr Austin Meldon ...' *(14.729)*

The son of James Dillon Meldon and Bedelia (née Ingham), Austin Meldon was born on 26 August 1844 in the family home 'Casino', close to the river Dodder in Milltown, Dublin.

Educated at the Jesuit College in Tullabeg, Co. Offaly, he studied at the Catholic University School of Medicine at Cecilia Street, previously the private medical school of the Society of Apothecaries. He had a brilliant career, winning gold medals in midwifery and the diseases of women and children.

In 1880 he became a member of the Royal College of Physicians. In 1889–90 he was president of the Royal College of Surgeons presiding over the surgical section

of the Royal Academy of Medicine in Ireland. For many years he was attached to the staff of Jervis Street Hospital, which was run by the Sisters of Mercy. In his latter years he was consulting surgeon there and also at the National Maternity Hospital, Holles Street. He was also a justice of the peace.

His publications include *A Treatise on Gout, Rheumatism and Chronic Rheumatic Arthritis* (1873); *A Treatise on Skin Diseases* (1873); *Fourteen Consecutive Cases of Successful Lithotomy* (1882); and *A Treatise on Gout* (1885).

Meldon was married twice, first to Margaret Ryan from Tipperary, by whom he had two children, and secondly to Katherine Pugin, by whom he also had two children. Meldon died on 28 April 1904 at his residence, 15 Merrion Square, Dublin and was buried in Glasnevin Cemetery, Finglas Road, Dublin [Vault 90 O'Connell Tower Circle].

Mendoza, Daniel (1764–1836) *Boxer*
'... Baruch Spinoza (philosopher), Mendoza (pugilist) ...' *(17.722–3)*
Daniel Mendoza, a Sephardic Jew, was born on 5 July 1764. Just 5 feet 7 inches tall and weighing 160 pounds, he was heavyweight boxing champion of England 1792–5.

Known as the 'father of scientific boxing', Mendoza died on 3 September 1836 and was buried at Brentwood Jewish Cemetery, Coxtie Green, Brentwood Borough, Essex, England.

Menton, John Henry (1859–1905) *Solicitor*
'In God's name, John Henry Menton said, what did she marry a coon like that for? She had plenty of game in her then.' *(6.704–5)*
John Henry Menton, son of Michael and Letitia Menton, was born in Roscrea, Co. Tipperary, on 22 July 1859. He was a twin brother of Henry Menton and one of 13 children.

Menton was admitted to the Roll of Solicitors on 13 December 1884 and became a prominent Dublin solicitor and commissioner of affidavits with offices at 27 Bachelor's Walk. He was involved with John Stanislaus Joyce in the elections of 1885 and 1886.

Menton died of consumption aged 45 on 5 March 1905. At the time of his death he was living at 3 Cumberland Place, North Circular Road, Dublin. He was buried in Glasnevin Cemetery, Finglas Road, Dublin [EA 72.5 South Section].
Ulysses 6.568; 6.690; 6.695; 6.707; 6.717; 6.1007; 6.1010; 6.1019; 6.1021; 6.1025; 10.937; 10.1229; 15.731; 15.1141; 15.1230; 15.1943; 15.4336; 16.1257; 17.1240; 17.2134; 18.38

Mercadante, Giuseppe Saverio Raffaelo (1795–1870) *Italian composer*
'Some of that old sacred music splendid. Mercadante: seven last words.' *(5.403–4)*
Mercadante was born on 16 September 1795 near Bari in Apulia, Italy. He studied music in Naples and began to compose opera with the encouragement of Rossini.

Mercadante worked for a time in Madrid, Lisbon, Vienna and Paris where he composed his opera *I Briganti* for four well-know singers of the time, Grisi, Rubini, Tamburini and Lablache. He was made the director of the Naples Conservatory in 1840.

Mercadante who composed 60 works, which were mainly opera, died on 17 December 1870.   *Ulysses 11.975; 11.1275; 12.1804; 16.1737–8*

Mercalli, Giuseppe (1850–1914) *Italian seismologist*
'The observatory of Dunsink registered in all eleven shocks, all of the fifth grade of Mercalli's scale ...' *(12.1858–60)*
Giuseppe Mercalli was born in Milan on 21 May 1850. He was professor of natural sciences at a seminary in Milan. He was subsequently appointed to Domodossola

and finally to Naples University. He was also a director of Vesuvius Observatory, a post he retained until his death.

He invented a five-grade seismic scale for measuring earthquakes known as the 'Mercalli scale' still in use today. He observed and reported on the eruptions at the Aeolian Islands of Stromboli, which are used worldwide by volcanologists.

Mercalli died on 19 March 1914 under suspicious circumstances.

Mesias, George Robert (1865–1941) *Merchant tailor*

'MESIAS

To alteration one pair trousers eleven shillings.' *(15.1910–11)*

George Robert Mesias, son of Hosias and Mary Mesias was born on 11 June 1865 in Russia. He came to Dublin in 1870. In 1904 he had a tailoring business at 5 Eden Quay, Dublin, with William J. Haddock and was living at 1 Mount Harold Terrace, Leinster Road, Rathmines, Dublin. He later moved his business to 8 Eden Quay and his residence to 7 Casimir Avenue, Rathmines where he lived with his Scottish-born wife, Elspeth (née Watson), son Harold, and daughters, Dorothy and Muriel. The family then moved to their final address of 7 Mayfield Road, Terenure. He was both Bloom's and Boylan's tailor.

Mesias who was Jewish but converted to the Church of Ireland, died at the Royal City of Dublin Hospital, Baggot Street, on 23 August 1941 and was buried in Deansgrange Cemetery, Deansgrange, Co. Dublin [106–M2–South].

Ulysses 6.831; 11.881; 15.1302; 15.1908; 17.2171

Michael, Brother *Infirmarian*

Based on **Brother John Hanly** (1832–97) *Infirmarian at Clongowes Wood College*

'... Brother Michael in the infirmary of the college of the Society of Jesus at Clongowes Wood, Sallins, in the county of Kildare ...' *(17.136–8)*

John Hanly was born on 24 June 1832 in Scariff, Co. Clare. He entered the Society of Jesus as a lay brother on 23 May 1858. He was amongst the last of the brothers who received their early spiritual training in Clongowes Wood College, Sallins, Co. Kildare. He remained there as infirmarian and sacristan until 1867 when he moved as sacristan to St Francis Xavier's Church, Gardiner Street, Dublin. He was appointed as buyer and dispenser in 1871 and the following year returned to Clongowes for a short time. Over the next few years he worked in Galway, University College Dublin and Limerick. He returned to Clongowes as infirmarian in 1881 and remained there for the rest of his life.

Brother John Hanly died on 25 January 1897. He was buried in the community graveyard, on the left-hand side off the driveway of limes just inside the main entrance to Clongowes Wood College.

Nearby is the grave of 16-year-old Peter Little, a pupil of the college who died in the infirmary on 10 December 1890, when Joyce was a pupil there and when Brother Hanly was the infirmarian.

Michelet, Jules (1798–1874) *French historian*
'About the nature of women he read in Michelet.' *(3.166–7)*

Jules Michelet was born in Paris on 21 August 1798. In the early 1820s he was appointed professor of history at the Collège Rollin, Paris. His patrons included Abel-Francois Villemain and Victor Cousin. In 1827 he was appointed maître de conférences at the École Normale Supérieure.

Author of many works including, *La Femme*, *Les Femmes de la Revolution* and *L'Amour*, Michelet is best known for his monumental work, *Histoire de France* (1833–67). He died on 9 February 1874 and was buried in Père Lachaise Cemetery, Paris.

Miller, Joe (1684–1738) *English actor*
'*I can't see the Joe Miller. Can you?*' *(7.582)*
Joseph Miller was born in 1684. A friend of William Hogarth (1697–1764), his favourite acting parts included the first gravedigger in *Hamlet*, Marplot in *The Busybody* and Trinculo in *The Tempest*.

Miller died on 16 August 1738. A year after his death, John Mottley (1692–1750) produced a book titled *Joe Miller's Jests, or the Wits Vade-Mecum*. This book of jokes was revised and reissued repeatedly and each time the number of jokes was added to. These jokes and quips came to be called 'a Joe Miller'.

Millevoye, Lucien (1850–1918) *French editor*
'Maud Gonne, beautiful woman, *la Patrie*, M. Millevoye ...' *(3.233)*
Lucien Millevoye was born in Grenoble on 1 August 1850. He was a minor French

journalist, right-wing politician and a lover of Maud Gonne. They first met when she went to the French Auvergne to recuperate from an illness. They planned to fight for Irish freedom and to regain Alsace-Lorraine from Germany. They had two children, Georges, born in 1891 who died of meningitis 18 months later, and a daughter, Iseult (1895–1954), after whose birth the couple lived apart. Their affair ended in 1908. Lucien Millevoye became editor of a political periodical, *La Patrie*, in 1894. He died in Paris on 25 March 1918.

Mitchel, John (1815–75) *Patriot, lawyer and journalist*
'In 1885 he had publicly expressed his adherence to the collective and national economic programme advocated by ... John Mitchel ... and others ...' *(17.1645–8)*

John Mitchel was born on 3 November 1815 near Dungiven, Co. Derry. He was educated at Trinity College Dublin and graduated in law in 1834. He practised in Newry and Banbridge, Co. Down. In 1842 he met Thomas Davis and co-edited the *Nation* with him.

On Davis's death in September 1845, Mitchel became manager and chief writer of the *Nation* but resigned in 1847. In February 1848 he founded the *United Irishman*. In May 1848 he was arrested, tried for treason-felony, convicted and sentenced to 20 years' transportation.

He escaped to the United States and worked as a journalist in New York. His *Jail Journal* was published in 1854 in his New York paper, *The Citizen*. He went to Tennessee to farm and during the Civil War lost two sons. He supported the Confederacy for which he was imprisoned for a term.

Mitchel returned to Ireland in 1874 and was elected MP for North Tipperary. He died on 20 March 1875 at Dromalane, Newry, and was buried in the Meeting House Green Cemetery, off Church Street, Newry, Co. Down.

Mitchell, Susan (1866–1926) *Writer and poet*
'Did you hear Miss Mitchell's joke about Moore and Martyn?' *(9.306-7)*
Susan Mitchell, daughter of Michael Mitchell and Kate (née Cullen), was born on 5 December 1866 in Bridge Street, Carrick-on-Shannon, Co. Leitrim. Following the death of her father in 1873, she moved to Dublin to live with two of her unionist aunts, at 21 Wellington Road.

She was educated at a private school for girls, Morehampton House in Donnybrook. In 1884 Susan moved with her aunts to Birr, Co. Offaly. It was at this time that she was drawn to Parnellism and reacted against the unionism with which she was brought up.

In late 1897 she went to London and stayed with the family of John B. Yeats. She got an office job and learned office skills and indexing and found herself surrounded by proponents of the Irish Literary Revival such as W. B. Yeats, George Moore, Edward Martyn and Lady Gregory.

In 1901 she was working in Dublin as assistant editor of the *Irish Homestead*. This amalgamated with the *Irish Statesman* under the editorship of George Russell in 1905. Mitchell worked as subeditor and contributed essays, reviews of fiction and drama critiques.

In 1908 she published two collections of verse, *Aids to the Immortality of Certain Persons, Charitably Administered* and *The Living Chalice and Other Poems*. In 1912 her final volume of poetry, entitled *Frankincense and Myrrh* appeared. She contributed a study of George Moore to a series entitled, *Irishmen Today* (1916).

She died on 4 March 1926 in Dublin and was buried in Mount Jerome Cemetery, Harold's Cross, Dublin [C115–4013].

Moisel, M. (Nisan) (*c*. 1829–1910) *Greengrocer and poultry dealer*
'They fetched high prices too, Moisel told me. Arbutus place: Pleasants street: pleasant old times.' *(4.209–10)*
M. Moisel is identified as Nisan Moisel 'with whose two sons and their families Bloom was acquainted'.

Nisan Moisel, was born in Russia, son of Wolf Hiam Moisel. He was a member of the Dublin Jewish community and lived at Kingsland Park Avenue and later at 20 Arbutus Place, a cul-de-sac off Lombard Street West.

Moisel was married twice; his first wife was Sarah Rivah (née Newman), a sister of Rev. Louis Newman, shochet of St Kevin's Parade synagogue who lived at 39 Lombard Street. Sarah Rivah was the mother of Elyah Wolf Moisel (1856–1904).

Moisel's second wife was Haya and the mother of Philip Moisel. Nisan Moisel died on 26 May 1910 and was buried at the Jewish Cemetery, Dolphin's Barn, Rialto, Dublin [06–A–12]. *Ulysses 15.3223*

Moisel, Mrs (1862–1940) *Wife of a son of Nisan Moisel*
'Funny sight two of them together, their bellies out. Molly and Mrs Moisel. Mothers' meeting.' *(8.391–2)*
Mrs Basseh (Bertha) Moisel (née Hodes), was born in Russia, daughter of Arca Hodes and Sarah (née Madalie). She married Elyah Wolf Moisel, son of Nisan Moisel and his first wife Sarah Rivah Moisel. They lived at 24 St Kevin's Road initially.

Mrs Moisel gave birth to a daughter Rebecca Ita in Lennox Street on 28 June 1889, just 13 days after Leopold and Molly Bloom's daughter Milly was born. The Moisels then lived at 2 Stamer Street, from late 1889. Elyah Wolf Moisel died in 1904 and Mrs Moisel moved from Stamer Street *c.* 1907 to 43 Bloomfield Avenue and then to 18 Synge Street. She died on 21 February 1940 and was buried at the Jewish Cemetery, Dolphin's Barn, Rialto, Dublin [02–B–07].

Moisel, Philip (1866 –*c*. 1903) *Acquaintance of Bloom*
'... Philip Moisel (pyemia, Heytesbury street) ...' *(17.1254)*
Philip Moisel, who was born in Russia on the 24 July 1866, was the son of Nisan and Haya Moisel. After his marriage *c.* 1892 to the daughter of a Church of Ireland minister from Kingsland Parade, they lived in Heytesbury Street. Towards the end of the nineteenth century, Mr and Mrs Philip Moisel emigrated to South Africa where Philip died in about 1903. His widow returned to Dublin shortly after his death.

Molloy, Rev. Gerald (1834–1906) *Rector, University College Dublin*
Gerald Molloy was born on 10 September at Mount Tallant House, Terenure, Co. Dublin. He was educated at Castleknock College, Co. Dublin and St Patrick's College Maynooth, Co. Kildare.

In 1857 Rev. Molloy was appointed professor of theology at Maynooth, a position he held until 1874. He was subsequently appointed professor of natural philosophy in the Catholic University, St Stephen's Green, a position he held until 1887.

Molloy was appointed vice-chancellor of the Royal University in 1903. His publications included *Geology and Revelation* (1870), *Gleanings in Science* (1888) and *A Treatise on the Correct Use of Shall and Will* (1897).

Rev. Molloy, who played a leading part in the direction of higher education in Ireland, died in Aberdeen on 1 October 1906 and was buried in Glasnevin Cemetery, Finglas Road, Dublin [A 32.5 St Laurence's].   *Ulysses 12.928*

Monks, Edward (1850–1941) *Printer compositor*

'... an old man, bowed, spectacled, aproned. Old Monks, the dayfather.' *(7.196–7)*

Edward Monks was born in Dublin in July 1850. He worked as a compositor in the *Freeman's Journal* where he was the dayfather in the paper's printing office. He was employed on the staff of several Dublin printing firms, including Messrs Dollard.

Monks was amongst those present at a special meeting of the Dublin Corporation held on 20 August 1922. A resolution was passed protesting against the prosecution and imprisonment of members of the Irish Volunteers. It was demanded that 'the same privileges be extended to Irishmen as have been given to Lord Northcliffe and the English Press presently opposed to the British Government.'

Monks was a trustee of the Dublin Typographical Provident Society for many years and paid tribute on behalf of that body at the funeral of Michael Collins on 28 August 1922 at Glasnevin Cemetery.

Monks lived at 13 Margaret Place, Mountjoy, Dublin, with his wife, son Edward and daughter Catherine. Margaret Place was a row of ten houses on 'Circular Road', now incorporated into North Circular Road; they are now located on the north side of North Circular Road at the Russell Street/Fitzgibbon Street junction. The family moved later to 108 Home Farm Road, Drumcondra. Edward Monks was a widower when he died on 31 July 1941 at Home Farm Road, Dublin. He was buried in Glasnevin Cemetery, Finglas Road, Dublin [KI 283.5 Section 3].

                        Ulysses 7.184–6; 7.190; 16.1258

Moore, George (1852–1933) *Novelist*

'Shall we see you at Moore's tonight?' *(9.273–4)*

George Moore was born in Moore Hall, Ballyglass, Co. Mayo, on 24 February 1852. He was the son of Mary (née Blake) and George Henry Moore, a wealthy landlord who was elected MP for Mayo in 1847.

Moore inherited his father's estate, which he left to his brother Maurice to manage. He studied painting in Paris from 1873 to 1880 after which he returned to Ireland to attend to family business. Finding that he had not the talent to become a painter, he moved to London to become a writer. During the next 15 years he wrote many novels in the naturalist vein, which included *A Mummer's Wife* (1885), *A Drama in Muslin* (1887) and *Esther Waters* (1913).

In 1901 Moore returned to Dublin in response to a telegram from his cousin, Edward Martyn: 'The sceptre of intelligence has passed from London to Dublin.' He owned a house at 4 Upper Ely Place, where he lived for the next ten years and where he wrote *The Untilled Field* (1903), *The Lake* (1905) and a portion of *Hail and Farewell* (1911–14), which is a three-volume fictionalised history of the Irish Revival, fused with what Moore is pleased to claim as his autobiography.

Moore's closest associates in Dublin were Æ, Edward Martyn and W. B. Yeats. He became involved with the Irish Literary Revival and the founding of the Irish National Theatre.

Inspired by Turgenev's *Sportsman's Sketchbook*, Moore gathered 13 short stories together and published them as *The Untilled Field* (1903), thereby giving impetus to the modern Irish short story.

After the appearance of his first volume of memoirs, Moore thought it best to leave Dublin so moved to London in 1911 where he remained for the rest of his life, apart from frequent visits to France. He continued to write novels, publishing more than a dozen including *The Brook Kerith* (1916) and *Heloise and Abelard* (1921).

In February 1923, Moore Hall was burned down. Moore wrote to a friend, 'Since the burning down of my house, I don't think I shall ever be able to set a foot in Ireland again.' He died at his London home in Ebury Street on 21 January 1933 and was cremated. An urn containing his ashes was placed in a hollow on an island in Lough Cara, Co. Mayo, near his former home.

Ulysses 7.479; 9.995; 9.1098; 9.1141; 14.780; Confessions of a Young Man, 14.496–7; Hail and Farewell, 9.306–9; 9.367

Moore, Thomas (1779–1852) *Poet and writer*

'He crossed under Tommy Moore's roguish finger. They did right to put him up over a urinal: meeting of the waters.' *(8.414–15)*

Thomas Moore was born at 12 Aungier Street, Dublin, son of John Moore, a grocer, and Anastasia (née Codd) from Cornmarket in Wexford

Moore was educated at Samuel Whyte's Academy at 79 Grafton Street where Robert Emmet was a pupil. They formed a lasting friendship until Emmet's death in 1803. After graduating from Trinity College Dublin, Moore went to London, and under the patronage of Lord Moira published his translation of the *Odes of Anacreon*. He was in great demand on the London social scene. In 1803 he was appointed admiralty registrar in Bermuda and later toured the United States where he met President Thomas Jefferson.

Moore published *Odes, Epistles and Other Poems* in 1806. His *Irish Melodies* was published in parts between 1807 and 1834. It earned him a good income and also gained him recognition as the national lyric poet of Ireland.

In 1811 Moore married Bessie Dyke, a 16-year-old actress, and remained devoted to her for the rest of his life. His *National Airs* was published in 1815, followed by his *Sacred Songs* in 1816. One of his most popular works, *Lalla Rookh*, followed in 1817.

In 1819 Moore met Lord Byron, who presented him with his memoirs. When Byron died in 1824, his relatives were opposed to their publication. Moore burnt them but in 1830 published *The Life of Byron*.

Moore's later life was marred by tragedy as all his five children predeceased him. He died at 'Sloperton Cottage', near Devizes, Wiltshire, in February 1852. He was buried in Bromham churchyard, in a vault on the north side of the church.

Ulysses 8.606–7; 11.634–5; 12.161–2; 12.500–1; 15.1960–2; 11.581–2; 15.435; 15.1323

Moreau, Gustave (1826–98) *French Painter*

'The painting of Gustave Moreau is the painting of ideas.' *(9.50–1)*

Gustave Moreau, son of Louis Jean Moreau and Adele des Moutiers, was born in Paris on 6 April 1826. A pupil of Theodore Chasseriau (1819–56), he was to some extent influenced by romanticism but developed his own distinctive symbolist style.

Moreau preferred to paint mystical, intense images suggesting long-dead civilizations and mythologies. *Oedipus and the Sphinx*, one of his first symbolist paintings, was exhibited at the Salon of 1864. Another of his early paintings, a pietà is now located in the Cathedral of Sainte-Pierre, Angoulême in south-west France.

In 1892 Moreau became a professor at the École Nationale Superieure des Beaux-Arts at 12 Rue Bonaparte, Paris. Among his pupils were Henri Matisse (1869–1954), and Georges Rouault (1871–1958) who became the first curator of the Musée Gustave Moreau, which Moreau bequeathed to the nation. It is located in Moreau's former workshop at 14 Rue de la Rochefoucauld, Paris.

Moreau died in Paris on 18 April 1898 and was buried in the Cimetière de Montmartre.

Morkan, Julia *Music teacher*

Based on **Julia Lyons (née Flynn) (1829–1905)** *Music teacher*

'Great song of Julia Morkan's. Kept her voice up to the very last.' *(8.417–18)*

Born in 1829, Julia Lyons (née Flynn) was the daughter of Patrick Flynn of Back Lane, Dublin. She married Matthew Lyons (1816–71) who predeceased her. She and her sister Mrs Ellen Callinan (née Flynn), Kate Morkan in *Ulysses*, ran 'The Misses Flynn School' at 15 Usher's Island where they taught music. Both were widows and appear under the guise of the Misses Morkan in Joyce's story 'The Dead'. They were Joyce's great-aunts and Mrs Callinan was his godmother.

Julia Lyons died on 25 August 1905 at St Monica's Widows Alms House, under the care of the Sisters of Charity at 35–38 Belvidere Place, Dublin. Mrs Callinan died in 1909.   *Ulysses 17.140–1*

Morley, John (1838–1923) *English politician and historian*
'... bearing 2000 torches in escort of the marquess of Ripon and (honest) John Morley.' *(17.1655–6)*
John Morley was born on 24 December 1838 in Blackburn, England. He worked as a journalist in London and from 1867 to 1883 was editor of the *Fortnightly Review*. For a short period he was editor of *Macmillan's Magazine*.

In 1883 Morley entered parliament at a by-election in Newcastle-upon-Tyne. He served in the House of Commons from 1883 to 1895, and from 1896 to 1908. He became secretary for Ireland in Gladstone's governments of 1886 and 1892. A passionate supporter of Irish Home Rule, he helped prepare the Irish Home Rule bills.

From 1905 to 1910, Morley was secretary for India. A pacifist, he resigned his office at the outbreak of the First World War.

Morley's chief work is his biography of Gladstone (1903). John Morley, 1st Viscount Morley of Blackburn, died on 23 September 1923 in Wimbledon, London.

Morphy, G. N. (*fl.* late 1800s–early 1900s) *Cyclist*
G. N. Morphy was one of the nine quartermile flat handicappers who took part in the Trinity College bicycle races in the afternoon of 16 June 1904.   *Ulysses 10.1259*

Mosenthal, Salomon Hermann (1821–77) *German dramatist and librettist*
'What is this the right name is? By Mosenthal it is. *Rachel*, is it?' *(5.199–200)*
Salomon Hermann Mosenthal, born in Kassel, Germany, on 14 January 1821 was a playwright, poet and archivist known for his successful opera librettos. The play *Leah the Forsaken* was an adaptation of Mosenthal's *Deborah*. John Augustin Daly (1838–99), the American playwright, wrote the translation and adaptation. Mrs Bandmann-Palmer's performance in *Leah* at the Gaiety Theatre, Dublin, was advertised in the *Freeman's Journal*, on 16 June 1904. This play was first produced in 1850 at the Royal Theatre in Berlin. Mosenthal spent much of of his life in Austria and died in Vienna on 17 February 1877.

Moses, Dancer (*fl.* 1880s–1920s)
'... as we passed a farmhouse and Marcus Tertius Moses, the tea merchant, drove past us in a gig with his daughter, Dancer Moses was her name ...' *(15.571–3)*
Dancer Moses was the daughter of Marcus Tertius Moses who had two daughters,

Amy Gwendolen, born in 1883, and Camilla Dagmer, born in 1886, who died in Arosa, Switzerland, on 1 March 1920, aged 34. It is unknown which of the daughters was known as Dancer.

Moses, Marcus Tertius (1843–1917) *Tea merchant and political figure*
'M'Coy peered into Marcus Tertius Moses' sombre office, then at O'Neill's clock.'
(10.508–9)
Marcus Tertius Moses, was a wholesale tea merchant at 14 Eustace Street and 30 Essex Street, Dublin and one of the managers of the Dublin Savings Bank in Abbey Street. He lived at 'Kilbride Tower', Herbert Road, Bray, Co. Wicklow, and also had a residence at 3 Herbert Street in Dublin.

Moses was a member of the Church of Ireland. His great-grandfather became a convert to Christianity in 1785 in Dublin. The crest for the Moses family bore a cock reguardant proper and its motto, in Hebrew, was 'I crow till I die'. This was stamped on the flap of their envelopes and is alluded to in the text.

A member of the Chamber of Commerce in Dublin, Moses was also a justice of the peace and had associations in various capacities with many different hospitals and charitable institutions in the city. These included the Royal City of Dublin Hospital, the Old Men's Asylum in Northbrook Road, the Rotunda and Adelaide Hospital, the Drumcondra Hospital, in Whitworth Road, the Royal Hospital for Incurables, King Edward's Coronation Fund for Nurses, and Dublin's Deaf and Dumb Association. He retired as chairman of the City of Dublin Nursing Institution, Ltd, in June 1914 but remained a member of the board.

A fellow of the Royal Geographical Society, Moses wrote about the island of Majorca for the *Irish Times* in 1877.

He died in Zurich, on 23 June 1917 and was buried in the Enzenbühl Cemetery. His wife and other members of his family were buried in St Patrick's Graveyard in Enniskerry, Co. Wicklow, which is the nearest one to Kilbride Church.

Moses is commemorated by a tablet in Kilbride Church, near his home in Bray, Co. Wicklow.   *Ulysses 15.571*

Most, Johann (1846–1906) *German anarchist and orator*
'Brood of mockers: Photius, pseudo Malachi, Johann Most.' *(9.492)*
Johann Most was born in Augsburg, Germany, on 5 February 1846. He worked as a bookbinder in Germany, Italy and Switzerland.

In 1867 he moved to Vienna where he became a socialist and editor of *Chemnitzer Freie Presse*. He was jailed a number of times for his political activities. He returned to Germany and worked as a journalist and was elected to the German Reichstag but was forced to leave the country on account of his activities.

Most went to London in 1878 and continued to publish his radical paper *Die Freiheit*. His paper was suppressed by the British government for its endorsement of the Phoenix Park murders. On his release in 1882 he moved to Cincinnati in the United States where he continued to publish *Die Freiheit* and books and pamphlets on anarchism, including a pamphlet titled *Down with the Anarchists!* (1901). Most died on 17 March 1906 in Cincinnati, Ohio.   *Ulysses 1.656*

Mulligan, John (1838–1912) *Bank manager*
'John Mulligan, the manager of the Hibernian bank, gave me a very sharp eye yesterday on Carlisle bridge as if he remembered me.' *(10.746–7)*
John Mulligan was born in Dublin. He was well known in business and commercial circles in the city and in 1882 was appointed a director of the Hibernian Bank at 27 College Green. The following year he became managing director, resigning in 1907 but remaining a member of the board.

When the Hibernian Insurances Company was formed, Mulligan was one of its directors. He was also a director of the Irish Catholic Church Property Insurance Company and a member of the Municipal Council of Dublin. He was associated with the male orphanage of the St Vincent de Paul Society, and gave generously to the funds of the City Labour Yard. He was an honorary trustee of the Sick and Indigent Roomkeepers' Society.

He lived at 12 Silchester Road, Glasthule, Co. Dublin and later at 'Greinan', Albert Road, Kingstown (now Dún Laoghaire). He died on 4 March 1912 and was buried in Deansgrange Cemetery, Deansgrange, Co. Dublin [79–B–North].

Mulligan, Malachi Roland St John 'Buck' *Medical student*
Based on **Oliver St John Gogarty** (1878–1957) *Poet, surgeon and senator*
'Stately, plump Buck Mulligan came from the stairhead, bearing a bowl of lather on which a mirror and razor lay crossed.' *(1.1–2)*
Oliver St John Gogarty was born at 5 Rutland Square (now Parnell Square), Dublin.

He was the son of Dr Henry Gogarty and Margaret (née Oliver) and was the eldest in a family of three sons and a daughter.

He was educated at the Christian Brothers School, North Richmond Street, and a series of Jesuit boarding schools, including Mungret in Co. Limerick, Stonyhurst College in England and Clongowes Wood College, Sallins, Co. Kildare. He attended the Catholic University School of Medicine at Cecilia Street for two years, before transferring to Trinity College Dublin. He played cricket and became the Irish cycling champion. He was academically brilliant with an incisive wit and was awarded the Vice-Chancellor's Prize for English on three occasions.

From January to June 1904 he interrupted his studies at Trinity College and went to Worcester College, Oxford, hoping to win the Newdigate Prize for Poetry. He came second to G. K. C. Bell, who later became bishop of Chichester. He was involved with the Oxford Gaelic Society and it was here that he met the Anglo-Irish Richard Samuel Chenevix Trench, who later changed his name to Dermot Chenevix Trench.

In July 1904 Gogarty acquired the lease for the Martello Tower in Sandycove, Co. Dublin. Gogarty declared that it was Joyce who leased it from the secretary of state for war but, according to the records, it was Gogarty who paid the annual rent of eight pounds. He probably took up occupation around 17 August 1904 which is the date of the covenant. Gogarty was an exceptionally strong swimmer and the Tower was close to the Forty Foot bathing place, where he swam three or four times a day. Joyce and Dermot Chenevix Trench joined Gogarty in the Tower in September 1904.

In 1906 Gogarty married Martha Duane of Moyard, Connemara, Co. Galway. The following year he graduated from Trinity and went to Vienna for postgraduate study in ear, nose and throat surgery. He purchased a house at 15 Ely Place (now demolished) as his family residence and consulting rooms. Here he held literary evenings that were attended by Moore, Yeats, Stephens, Æ, Tom Kettle, Lennox Robinson and other literati of the day.

In 1923 Gogarty became a senator of the new Irish Free State. His best-known book, *As I Was Going down Sackville Street*, was published in 1937, following which Harry Sinclair, an antique dealer, took out a libel suit against him. The case, which Gogarty lost, received widespread publicity and the costs and damages to him were substantial.

In 1939, the year *Tumbling in the Hay* was published, Gogarty left for America and, apart from a few return visits, spent the remainder of his life there. He derived his income from writing; he contributed to *Atlantic Monthly*, *Harper's Bazaar* and *Vogue*. He also wrote the novels *Going Native* (1940), *Mr Petunia* (1945), *Mourning Became Mrs Spendlove* (1948) and *Intimations* (1950). His *Collected Poems* was published in 1950 and his autobiography, *It Isn't That Time of Year at All*, in 1954.

Gogarty planned to return to Ireland in 1957, but he died that year in Beth David Hospital, New York, on 22 September. His remains were brought back to Ireland and interred in Ballynakill Cemetery near Cleggan in Connemara, Co. Galway. This was near his country house at Renvyle.

Ulysses 1.17; 1.41; 1.47; 1.50; 1.59; 1.64; 1.71; 1.85; 1.92; 1.111; 1.115; 1.121; 1.127; 1.138; 1.147; 1.179; 1.184; 1.191; 1.197; 1.219; 1.221; 1.228–9; 1.287; 1.293; 1.296; 1.318; 1.323; 1.330; 1.338; 1.342; 1.346; 1.353; 1.355; 1.360; 1.373; 1.388; 1.391–3; 1.408; 1.416; 1.427; 1.431; 1.435; 1.440; 1.446; 1.451; 1.471; 1.485; 1.494; 1.499; 1.502; 1.510; 1.523; 1.531; 1.534; 1.539; 1.543; 1.546; 1.554; 1.559; 1.564; 1.569; 1.579; 1.657; 1.660; 1.678; 1.687; 1.692; 1.697; 1.703; 1.717; 1.720–2; 1.726; 1.733; 2.255; 2.430; 3.112; 6.49; 6.63; 7.583; 9.41; 9.305; 9.369; 9.485; 9.504; 9.507; 9.515; 9.554; 9.568; 9.573; 9.605; 9.645; 9.655; 9.773; 9.792; 9.794; 9.951; 9.978; 9.1025; 9.1053; 9.1086; 9.1099–100; 9.119;

9.1125; 9.1142; 9.1155; 9.1170; 9.1176; 9.1204; 9.1209; 10.1043; 10.1049; 10.1055; 10.1071; 10.1087; 10.1224; 11.154; 14.495; 14.651; 14.655; 14.660; 14.666; 14.697; 14.704; 14.719; 14.727; 14.730; 14.964; 14.998; 14.1213; 14.1242; 14.1452; 15.1772; 15.1774; 15.2239; 15.4166; 15.4169; 15.4177; 16.264; 16.281; 16.287

Mullins, Jem/Mullin, James (1846–1920) *Physician and patriot*

'The Irish catholic peasant. He's the backbone of our empire. You know Jem Mullins?' *(16.1021–2)*

James Mullin was born in Cookstown, Co. Tyrone. Due to poor family circumstances he was obliged to work as a farm labourer from the age of 11. He then took up the trade of carpenter for nine years. He was an early member of the Fenian organisation, joining in 1865. Whilst working as a carpenter he attended the Cookstown Academy and graduated from Queen's College Galway with a BA degree.

To fund his medical studies Mullin tutored students and graduated as a doctor in 1881. He practised in London and in Cardiff where he was chairman of the local branch of the United Irish League.

Mullin's autobiography *The Story of a Toiler's Life* was published posthumously in 1921. He died in 1920.

Mulvey, Lieutenant Harry *British naval officer in Gibraltar*

Based on **William Mulvagh (1881–1952)** *Admirer of the young Nora Barnacle*

'Molly, lieutenant Mulvey that kissed her under the Moorish wall beside the gardens.' *(13.889–90)*

William Mulvagh was the eldest of nine children and son of Robert Mulvagh, a sergeant in the RIC (Royal Irish Constabulary), and Mary (née Thompson). As an RIC sergeant, Robert Mulvagh served in different police stations in Galway, including Barnaderg, Oranmore and Galway city. William was born in Co. Galway in 1881 and educated in the national schools in the towns where his father was

stationed. In Galway city, the Mulvagh family lived at 3 Mary Street, Newtownsmith (now demolished).

Mulvagh attended the Grammar School on College Road, Galway. He qualified as an auditor and accountant and was the first accountant employed in the firm of Joe Young, which manufactured mineral water in Eglinton Street. He subsequently had his own accountancy practice and lived at 5 Kirwan's Lane. He married a 19-year-old Galway girl, Margaret, in 1907 and moved to 3 Montpelier Terrace. They had a daughter Evelyn, and at the time of Evelyn's marriage in 1927 Mrs Mulvagh was deceased. William Mulvagh married Mary Frances Madden in 1932 and remained at the Montpelier Terrace address until his retirement. He moved to London with his wife to join his son Desmond and lived at 32 Charlwood Street. Mulvagh died there on 24 January 1952 and was buried in Streatham Park Cemetery, Rowan Road, London.

Ulysses 13.1282; 17.870; 17.2133; 18.818; 18.845; 18.1582

Munro, A. (1879–1958) *Cyclist and clergyman*
'... A. Munro and H. T. Gahan, their stretched necks wagging, negotiated the curve by the College library.' *(10.652–3)*
Alexander Munro was born on 30 October 1879 in Ballisodare, Co. Sligo. He was educated at Primrose Grange School, Sligo, Dundalk Academy, Co. Louth and Trinity College Dublin where he graduated with a BA degree in 1907. He joined the University Cycling Club in 1903 and came third in the half-mile bicycle handicap race held in the afternoon, 16 June 1904, at College Park in Trinity College Dublin. This was the first event on the day's card of a combination meeting of the Dublin University Bicycle and Harrier Club.

Munro continued cycling throughout his university career. Following his graduation in 1907, he married Edith Kildahl and was appointed to the church of Layde in Co. Antrim. In 1909 he moved to Conwal, Co. Donegal (1909–12) and from there to Glencolumbkille, Co. Donegal (1913–18). His final posting was to Inver, also Donegal. He died on 26 November 1958 at Cornageeha, Sligo and his funeral took place at Ballysodare Church, Sligo.

Murphy, Rev. James, SJ (1852–1908) *Provincial, Irish Jesuit Province*
James Murphy was born in Clonmel, Co. Tipperary, on 18 September 1852. He was

educated at the Catholic University School. He then attended the Catholic University for one year. Aged 17, he entered the Society of Jesus at Milltown Park, Dublin on 27 November 1869. He was ordained priest in 1887. He became provincial of the Irish Province (which included the Australian Mission) and lived in the Jesuit residence in Gardiner Street.

Father Murphy died in Tullabeg, Co. Offaly, on 22 February 1908 and was buried in the community graveyard, St Stanislaus College, Tullabeg, Co. Offaly.

Ulysses 12.932

Murphy, William Martin (1844–1919)
Entrepreneur, politician and proprietor of Independent newspapers
'How's that for Martin Murphy, the Bantry jobber?' *(12.237)*
William Martin Murphy, son of Denis Murphy, a building contractor was born on 21 November 1844, in Bantry, West Cork. He was educated at Belvedere College, Dublin.

Following the death of his father in 1863, Murphy took over the family business in Cork and transferred it to Dublin. He constructed bridges, schools and churches throughout Ireland. In 1877 he set up the Dublin Tramway Company, and bought the other two tramway companies in the city to form the Dublin United Tramways Company.

Murphy branched into railway construction and set up contracts for several important and extensive electrical railway and tramway networks in the United Kingdom and Africa. He purchased Clerys, Dublin's biggest department store, and several hotels including the Imperial, one of the city's landmarks.

An MP from 1885 to 1892, he was closely associated with T. M. Healy. He was anti-Parnell and funded the establishment of the *National Press* newspaper, the prime aim of which was to destroy Parnell.

In 1904 Murphy bought three daily newspapers and replaced them the following year with the *Irish Independent*. With control of the *Irish Independent*, he was one of the most powerful Catholics in Ireland. He was instrumental in setting up the Irish International Exhibition in 1907, following which he declined a knighthood from Edward VII.

Murphy was a member of the Dublin Chamber of Commerce and its president in 1912. In 1913 he led Dublin employers against the trade unions, an opposition that concluded in the lockout of 1913 organised by Jim Larkin.

He lived in 'Dartry Hall', Dartry. The Mill Hill Missionaries now occupy the house and the surrounding gardens and lands have been used for a housing development. Murphy died at his home in Dartry on 25 June 1919 and was buried in Glasnevin Cemetery, Finglas Road, Dublin [VT 30 Section 11 O'Connell Circle].

Ulysses 7.308; 12.220–1; 12.237

Murray, John Fisher (1811–65) *Political writer and satirist*
John Fisher Murray was born in Belfast, son of Sir James Murray, a well-known physician who invented fluid magnesia. He was educated in Belfast and at Trinity College Dublin where he graduated in 1830 with a BA degree.

Fisher contributed to *Blackwood's Magazine* and various Dublin periodicals. His publications include *The Viceroy* (3 vols, 1841), a satirical account of Dublin society, *The Environs of London* (1842), and *The World of London* (1843–5). *The Irish Oyster Eater* (1840) was considered one of his best works.

Fisher joined the Young Ireland nationalist movement in the 1840s. He died in Dublin in 1865 and was buried in Glasnevin Cemetery, Finglas Road, Dublin [NC 44 South].

Ulysses 17.1647–8

Murray, John Valentine 'Red' (1856–1910) *Joyce's maternal uncle*
'Red Murray's long shears sliced out the advertisement from the newspaper in four clean strokes.' *(7.31–2)*
John Valentine Murray, whose nickname was 'Red' Murray because of the colour

of his hair, was born in 1856 in Eagle House, Roundtown (now Terenure), Dublin. He was the son of John Murray and Margaret (née Flynn) originally from Leitrim.

John Murray senior had a business as a tea and wine merchant at the Eagle House in Roundtown. (Eagle House is now Vaughan's Eagle House at 107 Terenure Road North.) 'Red' Murray had two brothers, William and Joseph, and one sister, Mary Jane, James Joyce's mother.

He worked in the accounts department of the *Freeman's Journal*. In 1891 he married Elizabeth Harris (1874–1931), daughter of a commercial traveller. In 1897 they lived on Raymond Street off the South Circular Road; in 1894 they lived at 37 Dargle Road, Drumcondra, where his father 'old John Murray' died. In 1901 they were living at 39 Drumcondra Road by which time they had three children, Elizabeth aged nine, Isabella aged seven and Valentine John aged one year. By 1904 they had moved to 55 St Brigid's Road Lower nearby. Red Murray's daughters may have been the models for 'those Murray girls' who were friends of Milly.

Murray was still employed as an accountant at the *Freeman's Journal* when he died at his residence at St Brigid's Road Lower, Drumcondra on 30 May 1910. He was buried in Glasnevin Cemetery, Finglas Road, Dublin [IH 159.5 Section 3].

Ulysses 7.25; 7.34; 7.40; 7.49; 7.55; 7.62; 15.4342

Murray, Lindley (1745–1826) *Grammarian and author of school textbooks*
'... in it which must have fell down sufficiently appropriately ... with apologies to Lindley Murray.' *(16.1473–5)*
Lindley Murray, son of Robert Murray and Mary (née Lindley), was born on 7 June 1745 in Pennsylvania in the United States.

Murray practised as a lawyer for a time before moving to England and settling in a Quaker community in York. In 1795 he began writing school textbooks and became a best-selling author. He was renowned for his books on English grammar. His *English Grammar Adapted to the Different Classes of Learners. With an Appendix, Containing Rules and Observations, for Assisting the More Advanced Students to Write with Perspicuity and Accuracy* (1795) became a standard nineteenth-century school text. His most popular work was his *English Reader* (1799). Four million copies of his books were sold in Britain and another 16 million in America. Murray died on 16 January 1826.

Murray, William (1857–1912) *Joyce's maternal uncle*
'What? ... And Willy Murray with him, the two of them there near whatdoyoucall-him's ...' *(12.327–8)*
See also under **Goulding, Richard**   *Ulysses 12.313*

Myers, Lt John (1863–1927) *Chief fire officer, Dublin City Fire Brigade*
'(*Lieutenant Myers of the Dublin Fire Brigade by general request sets fire to Bloom.
Lamentations.*)' *(15.1930–1)*

John Myers was born in Co. Down, son of William Myers, an inspector for the
Dublin Fire Brigade. The family, comprising William Myers, a widower, and his
two sons John and Joseph, and a daughter Maggie, lived at 12 Winetavern Street,
Wood Quay, Dublin.

For over 40 years John Myers worked for Dublin Corporation, serving 32 years
with the Fire Brigade. He worked as an inspector before being appointed chief
officer of the Dublin Fire Brigade in 1918.

Myers was in charge of the Dublin Fire Brigade when the Four Courts and
parts of Sackville Street (now O'Connell Street) were
destroyed. He also dealt with the fire in the buildings
attached to the Magazine Fort in the Phoenix Park
on Easter Monday 1916.

Chief Officer Myers and his crew of seven Dublin
firemen were involved in assisting the Cork Brigade
during the burning of the centre of Cork city in 1920.

Myers, who had overseen the major change in
the Dublin Fire Brigade from horse-drawn vehicles
to motorisation, died on 19 March 1927 and was
buried in Glasnevin Cemetery, Finglas Road,
Dublin [AA 5 South].

N

Nagle, Susanna 'Susy' (1871–1951) *Acquaintance of Miss Dunne*

'If I could get that dressmaker to make a concertina skirt like Susy Nagle's. They kick out grand. Shannon and all the boatclub swells never took his eyes of her.' *(10.384–6)*
Susanna Nagle was born on 5 January 1871, the daughter of Denis Nagle, a member of the Dublin Metropolitan Police (DMP), and Mary (née Fitzsimons) of 84 Upper Dorset Street, Dublin. Her father rented houses on the north side of the city to tenants. The Nagles subsequently moved to 134 Upper Dorset Street where Mr Nagle died on 26 October 1880.

By 1894 the family had moved to 10 Jones's Road, Drumcondra where Susy Nagle set up her dressmaking business, which she later located at 90 Talbot Street. The Nagles then moved to 24 Jones's Road.

Susy married Felix O'Hanlon, from Co. Down in September 1899. He was a tailor and member of the DMP. In 1901, they lived at 24 Jones's Road with their baby, Mary Agatha. By 1911 they were living at Dorset Street Lower with two children.

Susy Nagle died at her home 20 Nelson Street, Dublin on 15 December 1951 and was buried with two of her children John and Eileen in Glasnevin Cemetery, Finglas Road, Dublin [YM 82 St Patrick's].

Nannetti, Joseph Patrick (1851–1915) *Foreman printer and politician*

'Through a lane of clanking drums he made his way towards Nannetti's reading closet.' *(7.74–5)*
Joseph Patrick Nannetti was born in Great Brunswick Street (now Pearse Street), Dublin. His father, Joseph Nannetti, was a sculptor and modeller initially with a business at Church Street before moving in 1843 to 6 Great Brunswick Street. The Nannetti family, originally from Naples, is recorded as resident in Dublin from the 1830s.

Nannetti was educated at Baggot Street Convent School and at the O'Connell Christian Brothers School in North Richmond Street. He was apprenticed to the printing trade and employed for a time in Liverpool, where he was a founder member of the Home

Rule organisation in that city. On his return to Dublin, he became a foreman printer on the *Freeman's Journal*.

In 1898 Nannetti was elected to Dublin City Council as councillor for the Rotunda Ward. In 1900 he was elected as MP for the College Green Division of Dublin, representing the Irish Parliamentary Party. He continued to serve as MP and city councillor until his death in 1915.

He was an active trade unionist and became secretary and later president of the Dublin Trades Council. He served as lord mayor of Dublin for two terms of office, 1906–7 and 1907–8. He was created justice of the peace in 1908 and was coopted as a member of the Glasnevin Cemeteries Committee.

Nannetti and his wife Mary (née Egan) lived at 24 Middle Gardiner Street, 1886–93; 18–19 Hardwicke Street, 1894–1904; 1 Juverna Terrace, Finglas, 1905–8; and 2 St Anne's Villas, Dollymount, 1909–13. Their final address was 47 Whitworth Road, Drumcondra where he died on 26 April 1915. He was buried in Glasnevin Cemetery, Finglas Road, Dublin [HF 25 South Section].

Ulysses 7.121; 7.123; 7.188; 7.975; 8.1057; 10.970; 12.850; 15.3385; 15.4337; 17.601

Napier, Lord Robert (1810–90) *Field marshal*

'... the lumpy old jingly bed ... and he thinks father bought it from Lord Napier that I used to admire when I was a little girl ...' *(18.1212–15)*

Robert Napier, son of Major Charles Frederick Napier and Catherine (née Carrington), was born on 6 December 1810 in Colombo, Ceylon.

Educated privately, Napier entered the Military Academy at Addiscombe in February 1825. He joined the Bengal Engineers, arriving in Calcutta, India in 1828. He served in the Anglo-Sikh Wars in India, the Indian Mutiny and later in China and Abyssinia. He was raised to the peerage as Lord Napier of Magdala in July 1868. He was commander-in-chief in India, 1870–5, and served as governor of Gibraltar, 1876–83. After he left Gibraltar he was promoted to field marshal.

Napier died at his residence, 63 Eaton Square, London, on 14 January 1890. He was buried in the crypt in St Paul's Cathedral.

Nelson, Horatio (Viscount Nelson) (1758–1805)

English naval hero and paramour of Lady Emma Hamilton

'Onehandled adulterer! the professor cried. I like that. I see the idea. I see what you mean.' *(7.1019–20)*

The son of the Rev. Edmund Nelson, rector of Burnham and Catherine (née Suckling), Horatio Nelson was born at Burnham, Thorpe, in Norfolk on 29 September 1758.

He went to sea aged 12 and rose rapidly through the ranks in the Royal Navy, having his own command when he was 20 in 1778. He was blinded in his right eye during the siege of Calvi on 10 July 1794. He distinguished himself in the Battle of

Cape Vincent in 1797 commanding the HMS *Captain*. Shortly afterwards he lost his right arm in the Battle of Santa Cruz de Tenerife.

In 1799 Nelson began a liaison with Emma Hamilton, wife of Sir William Hamilton, the British minister at Naples. It became one of the 'great scandals' of the period. She was the mother of his only child, Horatia.

In Britain's greatest naval victory, Nelson defeated the combined French and Spanish fleets at the Battle of Trafalgar on 21 October 1805. He was killed by a French sniper shot. He was buried at St Paul's Cathedral in the crypt directly below the dome on 9 January 1806 and is commemorated by Nelson's Column in Trafalgar Square, London.

Ulysses 6.293; 7.566; 7.1068; 7.1072; 11.762–3; 12.1193–4; 15.145; 15.1752; 15.1842; 15.4144; 16.563

Nicholas, Rev. Fr (1849–1923)
Vicar, Franciscan Capuchin Monastery, St Mary of the Angels
'... the very rev. Fr. Nicholas ...' *(12.930–1)*
Maurice Murphy was born on 22 October 1849 at Kinnagh, Co. Wicklow, son of

Patrick Murphy and Anne (née Stafford). In 1874 he joined the Order of St Francis Capuchin, entering the novitiate in Le Mans, France. He was ordained priest five years later. On his return to Ireland he was assigned to Holy Trinity, Cork, where he was guardian/superior, 1883–5.

At the refounding of the Irish Capuchin Province in 1885, he was moved to Dublin, took the name of Friar Nicholas in religion and became vicar of the Franciscan Capuchin friary, St Mary of the Angels, in Church Street. He immediately acquired adjoining property, extended the friary and added a garden. When the guardian resigned in 1886, Nicholas replaced him and ministered at Church Street for nearly 40 years until 1893.

He was president of the nearby Father Mathew Hall, 1895–1904. He was also chaplain to the lord mayor of Dublin.

Fr Nicholas died at the Capuchin friary, Church Street, on 1 November 1923 and was buried in Glasnevin Cemetery, Finglas Road, Dublin [NH 6 Section 3].

Nicholas Avenue, which links Church Street to Bow Street, is named after him. Rev. Fr Nicholas is listed as being vicar in St Mary of the Angels, Church Street, in 1904.

Noir, Jessie (b. 1857) *Dancer and choreographer*
'... ballets by Jessie Noir ...' *(17.426)*
Jessie Noir was of Scottish descent and was born in Ontario in 1857. A dancer with

her own ballet troupe she was choreographer of the Christmas pantomime *Sinbad the Sailor* at the Gaiety Theatre in Dublin, which opened on 26 December 1892. It was staged again on 30 January 1893. Forty dressmakers worked on the elaborate costumes under the supervison of Mrs and Miss Whelan.

Miss Jessie Noir who was the 'premiere danseuse' danced in what was described as the latest London novelty, the serpentine dance, introduced for the first time to Dublin. There were four ballets in the pantomime all arranged by Jessie Noir.   *Ulysses Sinbad the Sailor, 16.858; 17.423; 17.2322; 17.2328*

Nolan, John Wyse   *Friend of Martin Cunningham*
Based on **John Wyse Power** (1859–1926) *Journalist*
'John Wyse Nolan, lagging behind, reading the list, came after them quickly down Cork hill.' *(10.968–9)*
John Wyse Power was born in Waterford city in 1859. He was educated in Waterford and Blackrock College, in Co. Dublin. He worked in the civil service at Dublin Castle but felt obliged to leave on account of his political sympathies.

A fluent Irish speaker, he worked for the *Leinster Leader*, before moving to the *Freeman's Journal*. At the time of the Parnell split in 1891, he left the *Freeman's Journal* for the *Daily Independent*, which had been founded by Parnell. Wyse Power was subsequently editor of the *Evening Herald* for a few years after which he devoted his time to writing for other journals and magazines. He was the secretary of the Gaelic Athletic Association from 1884 to 1887 and was the first chairman of the Dublin County Committee in 1886. Athletics were among his main interests in life.

Wyse Power died at his home in Henry Street, Dublin, on 29 May 1926 and was buried in Glasnevin Cemetery, Finglas Road, Dublin [IC 36 South].
Ulysses 10.973; 10.979; 10.986; 10.990; 10.995; 10.1015; 10.1025; 10.1033; 10.1041; 10.1212; 12.1178; 15.1533;
15.3305; 15.4353

Nolan, Mrs John Wyse   *Proprietress of a dairy*
Based on **Mrs Jennie Wyse Power** (1858–1941) *Manager of the Irish Farm Produce Company*
'... and he coming out of that Irish farm dairy John Wyse Nolan's wife has in Henry street with a jar of cream in his hand ...' *(8.950–1)*
Jennie Wyse Power (née O'Toole) was born in May 1858 in Baltinglass, Co. Wicklow, the youngest of seven children and daughter of Edward O'Toole and Mary (née Norton). Both her parents were from farming stock and from strongly nationalistic backgrounds.

The family moved to Dublin in 1860 after her father sold his business in Baltinglass. He established a shop at 15 Redmond's Hill, then 3 Cuffe Street, and a few years later at 6 Johnson Place. He died in 1876 and his wife died the following year, after moving with the children to 45 Gloucester Place.

Jennie was educated locally and in 1881, when living at 8 St Catherine's Terrace, Clonliffe Road, she joined the Ladies Land League, which had been founded by Anna and Fanny Parnell, sisters of Charles Stewart Parnell.

On 5 July 1883 she married John Wyse Power. They lived in Naas, Co. Kildare, where he was editor of the *Leinster Leader*. In 1885 they moved to 7 Royal Terrace, Fairview, Dublin.

Mrs Wyse Power established and was manager of the Irish Farm Produce Company, 21 Henry Street, Dublin. This was a dairy and restaurant serving home-produced food. Another restaurant opened at 21 Lower Camden Street in 1908. Her home in Henry Street was a regular meeting place of Irish nationalists and it was here that the 1916 Proclamation was signed. Mrs Wyse Power was an active figure in local government, Cumann na mBan and the Irish senate.

She died on 5 January 1941 and was buried in Glasnevin Cemetery, Finglas Road, Dublin [IC 36 South].

Norman, Connolly (1853–1908)

Physician and superintendent of the Richmond Lunatic Asylum

'He's up in Dottyville with Connolly Norman. General paralysis of the insane!'
(1.128–9)

Connolly Norman was born on 12 March 1853 at All Saints Glebe, Newtown Cunningham, Co. Donegal, son of the Rev. Hugh Norman, the rector of All Saints, and Anne (née Ball). Because of his delicate health, Connolly Norman was educated at home. He studied medicine at Trinity College Dublin and the

Carmichael School of Medicine, formerly the Richmond Medical School, founded in 1826.

Norman was assistant medical officer in Monaghan Asylum from 1874 to 1881. In 1878 he became a fellow of the Royal College of Surgeons in Ireland. From 1881 to 1882 he studied at the Bethlem Hospital in London, after which he was appointed superintendent of Castlebar Asylum in Mayo, 1882–5. He married Mary Emily Kenny in 1882.

From 1886 to 1908 he was superintendent of Dublin's Richmond Asylum, which was considered to be the most important asylum in the country, comprising a large complex of buildings located on Grangegorman Road and consisting of the Richmond Penitentiary, the Richmond Lunatic Asylum and the Grangegorman Mental Hospital.

He was joint editor of the *Journal of Medical Science* and in 1890 became a fellow of the College of Physicians. He was president of the Medico-Psychological Association, 1894–5, and later vice-president of the Royal College of Physicians of Ireland. In 1907 the University of Dublin conferred him MD *honoris causa*.

He died on 23 February 1908 near his home at St Dympna's on the North Circular Road, and was buried in Mount Jerome Cemetery, Harold's Cross, Dublin [C79–80–12823].

He is commemorated by a bronze plaque on the north aisle of St Patrick's Cathedral in Dublin and in the Royal College of Physicians of Ireland in Kildare Street where a portrait of him by Sarah Cecilia Harris hangs in the Stokes Room.

Norman, Harry Felix (1868–1947) *Editor of the* Irish Homestead
'Thank you very much, Mr Russell, Stephen said, rising. If you will be so kind as to give the letter to Mr Norman ...' *(9.316–17)*
Harry Felix Norman was born in Dublin. From 1898 to 1905 he was editor of the *Irish Homestead*, a weekly journal founded by Horace Plunkett as the organ for his Irish Agricultural Organisation Society (IAOS). George Russell (Æ) took over as editor in 1905.

Norman became assistant secretary of the IAOS. He lived with his mother, Adelaide Norman, at 99 Upper Rathmines in 1911 and later moved to 14 Greenmount Road, Terenure. In 1929 he was Irish correspondent of the Horace Plunkett Foundation, 84 Merrion Square; he was then living at 5 Harcourt Terrace.

He died on 31 December 1947 and was buried in Deansgrange Cemetery, Deansgrange, Co. Dublin [29–B–St Nessan].

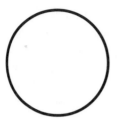

O'Brien, James Francis Xavier (1828–1905) *Politician and Fenian*
'In 1885 he had publicly expressed his adherence to the collective and national economic programme advocated by ... J. F. X. O'Brien and others ...' *(17.1645–8)*
James Francis Xavier O'Brien, son of Timothy and Catherine (née O'Brien), was born in Dungarvan, Co. Waterford, on 16 October 1828.

In 1855 he went to Paris to study medicine at the École de Médecine but due to ill health did not graduate. The following year he fought in the Nicaragua War (1856–7). He met James Stephens in New Orleans in 1858 and joined the Fenians and became a member of the supreme council. He was an assistant surgeon in the early stages of the American Civil War (1861–5).

In 1867 O'Brien participated in the Fenian rising in Cork, leading an attack on the Ballyknockane Barracks. He was arrested and sentenced to death but his sentence was commuted to penal servitude and he was released in 1869.

He became treasurer of the National League and supported Charles Stewart Parnell until 1891 when he seceded following the split in the Irish Parliamentary Party. He was MP for South Mayo from 1885 to 1895 and for Cork from 1895 to 1905.

He died on 28 May 1905 at his residence 39 Garden Road, Clapham, London and was buried in Glasnevin Cemetery, Finglas Road, Dublin [YA 34 South]. *Ulysses 4.491*

O'Brien, John Patrick (1846–1925)
Superintendent, Municipal baths and washhouses, Tara Street
'Tara street. Chap in the paybox there got away James Stephens, they say. O' Brien.' *(4.490–1)*
John Patrick O'Brien was born in 1846 in Shoreditch, Middlesex, eldest son of Patrick O'Brien, from Kilmore, near Nenagh, Co. Tipperary, and his wife Catherine.

He joined the British army as a private based at Fulwood Barracks, Lancashire with the aim of recruiting for the Fenian movement. He was discovered and in 1867 was sentenced to penal servitude for life in an English convict prison at Chatham, Kent. He was released in January 1878 with other political prisoners including Michael Davitt, Sergeant Charles M'Carthy and Corporal Thomas Chambers. O'Brien married Annie Josephine Pierce of Dublin at St Paul's Church, Arran Quay, on 5 June 1878.

He was manager of the Municipal baths and washhouses in Tara Street, for over 30 years. His wife was matron. The baths were on the south side of the Liffey and had been built in the 1880s as part of a Victorian health programme attempting to improve cleanliness and sanitation amongst the poor. They were officially opened on 12 July 1886 and closed *c.* 1960.

O'Brien and his family lived close by in tenements at 17 Tara Street later moving to 5 Wolseley Street, South Circular Road.

He died on 15 May 1925 and was buried in Glasnevin Cemetery, Finglas Road, Dublin [B1 221 St Brigid's].

O'Brien, Sir Timothy (1787–1862) *Lord mayor of Dublin*
'Timothy of the battered naggin.' *(14.1441)*
Timothy O'Brien was born at Tanakely near Birr, Co. Offaly.
O'Brien became a successful merchant and eventually governor of the Hibernian Bank. He purchased a house at 1 Patrick Street, Dublin, formerly owned by Dr John Whalley (1653–1724), the astrologer, quack and maker of almanacs, which he converted into an inn.

As an innkeeper, O'Brien was known for his short measures. He used a battered naggin for this and was nicknamed as 'The Knight of the Battered Naggin', recalling Cervantes's Knight of the Golden Basin in *Don Quixote*. The river Poddle coursed through the cellar of his house, proving most useful for the disposal of waste from his business.

As a member of the Repeal Movement, O'Brien was one of Daniel O'Connell's foremost lieutenants. He was elected an alderman to Dublin City Council and served as lord mayor of Dublin in 1844 and again in 1849. In 1846 he was elected as Liberal MP for the Royal City of Cashel and held this position until his retirement in 1859. He supported tenants' rights and the repeal of the union in parliament

As lord mayor O'Brien received Queen Victoria on her first visit to Ireland in August 1849 and in return was created 1st baronet of Borris-in-Ossory. He had a town house at 14 Merrion Square East and two country residences: 'Tudor Lodge' in Co. Dublin and another in Borris-in-Ossory, in Co. Laois.

He died on 3 December 1862 and was buried in Glasnevin Cemetery, Finglas Road, Dublin [Vault 56 Garden].

O'Brien, Vincent (1871–1948) *Composer and musician*
'(*A choir of six hundred voices, conducted by Vincent O'Brien, sings the chorus of Handel's Messiah Allelulia ... accompanied on the organ by Joseph Glynn.' (15.1953-5)*
Born in Dublin into a musical family, Vincent O'Brien's father was the organist at St James's Church. Educated at the Christian Brothers School and Belvedere College, he studied music at the Royal Irish Academy of Music in Dublin.

He was the first conductor of the Palestrina Choir founded by Edward Martyn in 1899 at St Mary's Pro-Cathedral in Marlborough Street, Dublin. He held this position from 1898 to 1902 and was also the organist from 1902 to 1946. In 1904 Vincent O'Brien was living at 109 Amiens Street. He was John McCormack's accompanist in 1913 on his first world tour.

O'Brien was the musical director of Radio Éireann, from 1926 to 1941. He wrote the opera *Hester* (1893) and his best-known compositions include 'An Easter Hymn' for solo, chorus and orchestra and 'St Patrick's Pageant Music'.

He died at his home, 37 Parnell Square, on 21 June 1948 and was buried in Glasnevin Cemetery, Finglas Road, Dublin [DD 57 South New Chapel].

O'Brien, William (1852–1928) *Nationalist, politician, land agitator and author*

'*When We Were Boys* by William O'Brien M. P. (green cloth, slightly faded, envelope bookmark at p. 217).' *(17.1370–1)*

William O'Brien, son of James O'Brien and Kate (née Nagle), was born on 2 October 1852 at 'Bank Place' in Mallow, Co. Cork. He was educated at Cloyne Diocesan College.

O'Brien worked as a reporter with the *Cork Daily Herald* from 1868 to 1876 before moving to the *Freeman's Journal* where he was employed until 1881. Subsequently he edited the *United Ireland*, a paper established by Charles Stewart Parnell as the official organ of the Land League and of the Irish Parliamentary Party. On account of its militancy, O'Brien was arrested and imprisoned in Kilmainham Gaol with Parnell in 1881. On his release in 1883 he was elected MP for Mallow and continued editing *United Ireland*.

O'Brien established the 'Plan of Campaign' with T. M. Healy, Tim Harrington and John Dillon in 1886. This was a scheme employed by small farmers against landlords to secure a reduction in exorbitant rents. He was imprisoned for six months. At the time of 'the split' in 1891, O'Brien sided against Parnell and founded the United Irish League on 23 January 1898 in Westport, Co. Mayo, with Michael Davitt as president. The League called for the division of large estates among small farmers. O'Brien seceded from the party and in 1910 founded the All for Ireland League. He favoured devolution and after 1909 retired from active politics.

O'Brien's publications include *When We Were Boys* (1890), *The Downfall of Parliamentarianism* (1918), *The Irish Revolution* (1921) and *The Parnell of Real Life* (1926). O'Brien died in Victoria's Belgravia Hotel, London, on 25 February 1928. He was buried in the graveyard of the old parish church in Mallow in Co. Cork.

Ulysses 16.1503

O'Brien, William Smith (1803–64) *Irish nationalist*

'Smith O'Brien. Someone has laid a bunch of flowers there.' *(6.226)*

William Smith O'Brien was born in Dromoland, Co. Clare, on 17 October 1803, son of Sir Lucius O'Brien. He was educated in England at Harrow and the University of Cambridge.

O'Brien was MP for Ennis, 1821–31, and for Limerick, 1835–49. He joined the Repeal Association in 1843. He seceded from this and in 1847 founded the Irish

Confederation and urged that a national guard be recruited. Following the arrests of the majority of its leaders in 1848 and the suspension of *habeas corpus*, the confederates decided on an armed rising.

O'Brien and a small party clashed with policemen in the Widow McCormack's house at Boulah Common, Ballingarry, Co. Tipperary bringing the rising of 1848 to an end. O'Brien was arrested, tried and sentenced to death. His death sentence was commuted to penal servitude and he served five years in Tasmania. He was released in 1854 and unconditionally pardoned in 1856. He returned to Ireland but took no part in politics.

He died in Bangor in Wales on 16 June 1864. He is commemorated by a marble statue by the sculptor James Farrell that was erected in 1870 at the southern end of Carlisle Bridge (now O'Connell), at the junction of D'Olier and Westmoreland Streets. In 1929 it was moved to O'Connell Street. He was buried in Rathronan Cemetery, Co. Limerick.

O'Connell, Daniel (1775–1847)

Lawyer and agitator for Catholic Emancipation in Ireland
'They passed under the hugecloaked Liberator's form.' *(6.249)*
Daniel O'Connell, 'the Liberator', was born near Cahirciveen, Co. Kerry, on 6 August 1775. He was educated at St Omer and Douai, in France. Here he witnessed the French revolutionary army in action, which left him with an abhorrence of violence.

In 1794 he studied at Lincoln's Inn in London and was called to the Irish Bar in 1798. Shortly afterwards the rebellion of 1798 broke out, which he did not support as he believed that the Irish should assert themselves politically rather than by means of force. He practised law in the south of Ireland for a decade and in 1802 married his cousin Mary O'Connell. Of their 11 children, seven survived: four sons and three daughters.

O'Connell set up the Catholic Association, to raise money for Catholic Emancipation. In 1828 he won a seat in Clare against Vesey FitzGerald. At Westminster he refused to take the Oath of Allegiance, which declared the Catholic religion to be false. Wellington agreed to grant Catholic Emancipation and in 1829 George IV assented.

O'Connell's great achievement, Catholic Emancipation, was clouded some-what by his failure to win Repeal.

He spoke in the House of Commons for the last time on 8 February 1847. He died on 15 May 1847 in Genoa. His heart was buried in Rome and his body was returned to Ireland where it was interred in the cemetery he had founded in Glasnevin. He is commemorated by a tower that dominates the entrance area of the cemetery. *Ulysses 2.271–2; 4.491; 6.79; 6.641; 6.750–2; 7.619–20; 7.707; 7.880–2; 15.4683*

O'Connell, John (1845–1925) *Superintendent of Prospect Cemetery, Glasnevin*

'Decent fellow, John O'Connell, real good sort.' *(6.740)*

John O'Connell was born in Banagher, Co. Offaly, where his family were millers. They moved to Dublin where John attended the Christian Brothers School in North Richmond Street and the Rev. Dr Doyle's Academy on Usher's Quay.

After working for a brief period in journalism, O'Connell secured a position as a clerk with the Dublin Catholic Cemeteries Committee and was soon promoted to superintendent of Glasnevin Cemetery. With this job came 'Clareville', an imposing house opposite the main gate of the cemetery, which

afforded him space to rear his 14 children with his wife Mary Ann (née Hickey). He was later promoted to secretary of the Dublin Catholic Cemeteries Committee, a position he held until his retirement.

At work, O'Connell was smartly attired with polished shoes, frockcoat and silk top hat, which he lifted in acknowledgement as the funeral barrow passed by. He was a renowned storyteller and his tales of the graveyard were legion. He received Parnell's funeral at Glasnevin and that of many of the other citizens mentioned in *Ulysses*.

He died at his residence, 4 Rutland (now Parnell) Square, on 7 January 1925 and was buried in Glasnevin Cemetery, Finglas Road, Dublin [HE 37 Dublin Section]. *Ulysses 6.710; 6.720; 6.727; 6.799; 15.1236; 15.1243; 15.1248*

O'Connor, James (1836–1910) *Journalist*

'Poor man O'Connor wife and five children poisoned by mussels here. The sewage.' *(13.1232–3)*

James O'Connor was a journalist with *United Ireland*, a paper established by Parnell as a successor to the *Flag of Ireland*, the first issue appearing on 13 August 1881. O'Connor was also MP for County Wicklow.

O'Connor's 35-year-old wife Mary and five children were poisoned by mussels collected in a pond behind their house at 1 Seapoint Terrace, Seapoint, Co. Dublin, in July 1890. Only his youngest daughter Moya survived.

A coroner's inquest held two weeks later in Blackrock concluded that a number of sewage outlets flowed into the pond leading to stagnant water that poisoned the mussels.

The funeral of his wife and four children took place on 3 July from Seapoint, travelling into the city and on to Glasnevin Cemetery. Two weeks later the O'Connor Memorial Fund was established to raise funds for a monument to erect over their grave.

The O'Connor family memorial is in the O'Connell Circle. It comprises the face of a woman and on each side, enfolded in her wings are the faces of two winged cherubs representing her four children, Annie, Aileen, Kathleen and Norah.

James O'Connor died at 18 Mellifont Avenue, Kingstown (now Dún Laoghire), on 12 March 1910. He was buried in Glasnevin Cemetery, Finglas Road, Dublin [XE 1924 Garden]. *Ulysses 17.543–4*

O'Connor, Thomas Power, 'Tay Pay' (1848–1929) *Journalist and politician*
'Then Paddy Hooper worked Tay Pay who took him on to the *Star*.' *(7.687)*
The eldest son of Thomas O'Connor and Teresa (née Power), Thomas Power O'Connor (better known as T. P. or Tay Pay) was born in Athlone, Co. Westmeath, on 5 October 1848.

He was educated at the College of the Immaculate Conception, Athlone, and Queen's College Galway, graduating in history and modern languages. He began his career in journalism at the Dublin daily, *Saunder's Newsletter*. In 1870 he

joined the *London Daily Telegraph* as a subeditor and later became London correspondent for the *New York Herald*. He founded and edited several London newspapers and weeklies including the *Star* (1887), the *Weekly Sun* (1891), the *Sun* (1893), *M. A. P.* and the literary paper, *T. P.'s Weekly* (1902).

In 1880 O'Connor was elected MP for Galway as a representative of Parnell's Home Rule League. In 1885 he married American writer, Elizabeth Paschal. The same year he was returned for Galway and also won the Scotland division of Liverpool and held that seat until his death. He successfully combined a career in politics and journalism and wrote a daily sketch of proceedings for the *Pall Mall Gazette*.

O'Connor was known as 'father of the House of Commons' and enjoyed almost 50 years of unbroken service. He became the first president of the Board of Film Censors in 1917. His books include: *Lord Beaconsfield: A Biography* (1879); *The Parnell Movement* (1886) and *Gladstone's House of Commons* (1886).

He died in London on 18 November 1929 and was buried in Kensal Green Cemetery, London.

O'Donnell, Leopold (1809–67) *Duke of Tetuan and prime minister of Spain*
'We gave our best blood to France and Spain, the wild geese … And Sarsfield and O'Donnell, duke of Tetuan in Spain …' *(12.1381–3)*
Leopold O'Donnell, son of Carlos O'Donnell y Anethan and his wife Josefa Jorris y Casaviella, was born in Santa Cruz de Tenerife on 12 January 1809.

A descendant of the O'Donnells who fled to Spain in 1690, he had a chequered military career. He was prime minister of Spain 1854–6, 1858–63 and 1864–6, and minister for foreign affairs in 1858 and 1860–3. He was duke of Tetuan, 1860–7.

O'Donnell died in Biarritz, France, on 5 November 1867. His mausoleum, sculpted by Jeronimo Suñol in Carrara marble, is in St Barbara's Church in Madrid.

O'Donovan Rossa, Jeremiah (1831–1915) *Fenian leader*
Jeremiah O'Donovan Rossa was born in Rosscarbery, Co. Cork. Educated locally, he worked as a relieving officer, distributing support during the Great Famine (1845–9).

He founded the Phoenix National and Literary Society in 1856. When James Stephens (1825–1901) came to Ireland in 1858, O'Donovan Rossa and his Phoenix Society were among the first to join the Irish Republican Brotherhood. He was tried for complicity in 'the Phoenix conspiracy' but was released. He became business manager of the *Irish People* between 1863 and 1865.

O'Donovan Rossa was arrested with John O'Leary, Charles Kickham and other Fenians and sentenced to penal servitude for life but was freed in 1871 and went to America where he edited the *United Irishman*. In 1877, he became head of the Fenians and organised a fund for a dynamiting campaign in England.

His publications include *O'Donovan Rossa's Prison Life* (1874) and *Rossa's Recollections, 1838–98* (1898).

O'Donovan Rossa died in New York on 30 June 1915 and on 1 August he was buried in the Republican Plot in Glasnevin Cemetery, Finglas Road, Dublin [TD 37 South New Chapel]. *Ulysses 12.199*

O'Dowd, Elizabeth (1839–1910) *Proprietor, City Arms Hotel*
'… in the City Arms Hotel owned by Elizabeth O'Dowd of 54 Prussia street where, during parts of the years 1893 and 1894, she had been a constant informant of Bloom who resided also in the same hotel …' *(17.481–4)*
Elizabeth O'Dowd was born in Co. Wexford. She lived at 54 Prussia Street, Dublin in 1901 and is portrayed as a hotel keeper. Joyce refers to her as Mrs Elizabeth O'Dowd. She was in fact Miss O'Dowd. Miss O'Dowd is described as a 'stout lady' and was proprietor of the City Arms Hotel, 55 Prussia Street, north of the Liffey

near the site of the former Cattle Market. She had a public house licence giving her permission to sell, spirits, sweets, mead, beer and cider. Miss O'Dowd sold the hotel on 7 November 1908 to John Conroy.

She died on 12 October 1910 at the City Arms Hotel and was buried in Glasnevin Cemetery, Finglas Road, Dublin [RF 127.5 Garden].

The Blooms lived in the City Arms Hotel from 1893 to1894. *Ulysses 12.513; 12.840; 15.4338*

O'Growney, Soggarth Eoghan/Fr Eugene (1863–99)
Professor of Irish and founder member of the Gaelic League
'... Soggarth Eoghan O'Growney ...' *(12.179-80)*
Eugene O'Growney was born on 25 August 1863 in Athboy, Co. Meath. He was educated at St Finian's Diocesan Seminary, Navan, and at St Patrick's College Maynooth, Co. Kildare. He was ordained priest in 1889 and was appointed curate at Ballynacargy, Co. Westmeath.

In 1891 he was appointed professor of Irish in Maynooth. He was editor of the *Gaelic Journal* and helped found the Gaelic League. He contributed lessons in Irish to the *Gaelic Journal* and *Weekly Freeman*, which were published in a book titled *Simple Lessons in Irish* (1894). Due to ill health, he resigned from the chair of Irish at Maynooth on 23 June 1896 and went to California. He continued his writings and contributed to American papers and to the *Weekly Freeman*.

Father O'Growney died in Los Angeles on 18 October 1899 aged 36. He was buried in the cemetery in the grounds of St Patrick's College Maynooth.

O'Hagan, Thomas (1812–85) *Barrister and jurist*
'Where have you a man now at the bar like those fellows, Whiteside, like Isaac Butt, like silvertongued O'Hagan. Eh?' *(7.706-7)*
Thomas O'Hagan was born in Belfast on 29 May 1812. He was educated at the Belfast Academical Institution and was called to the Irish Bar in 1836.

He was editor of the *Newry Examiner* from 1838 to 1841. He moved to Dublin and in 1842 he defended Gavan Duffy in a libel action. In 1849 he was made a bencher of King's Inns.

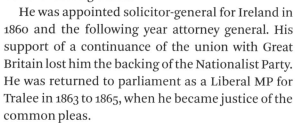

He was appointed solicitor-general for Ireland in 1860 and the following year attorney general. His support of a continuance of the union with Great Britain lost him the backing of the Nationalist Party. He was returned to parliament as a Liberal MP for Tralee in 1863 to 1865, when he became justice of the common pleas.

In 1868 O'Hagan became lord chancellor of Ireland. He was raised to the peerage and created Baron O'Hagan, of Tullahogue, in Co. Tyrone.

O'Hagan's chancellorship ended with the Gladstone ministry in 1874 but he returned as lord chancellor in 1880 and became known for his eloquent, pro-Irish appeal for the Irish Land Bill in 1881. He resigned the same year. On his retirement he was appointed vice-chancellor of the Royal University of Ireland and a knight of St Patrick.

He died on 12 January 1885 at Hereford House, London, and was buried in Glasnevin Cemetery, Finglas Road, Dublin [Vault 42 O'Connell Tower Circle].

O'Hanlon, Canon John (1821–1905)
Parish priest, St Mary's Star of the Sea Church, Sandymount
'Canon O'Hanlon put the Blessed Sacrament back into the tabernacle and genuflected and the choir sang *Laudate Dominum omnes gentes ...*' *(13.674–5)*
John O'Hanlon, son of Edward O'Hanlon and Honor (née Downey), was born in Stradbally in Co. Laois on 30 April 1821.

Aged 19 he entered St Patrick's College, Carlow, as a seminarian. Two years later he left for America and in 1843 joined the Ecclesiastical Seminary in St Louis where he was ordained priest in 1847.

O'Hanlon was editor of the *St Louis Newsletter* and two of his books, *An Abridgement of the History of Ireland* (1849) and *The Irish Emigrant's Guide to the United States* (1851) were published there.

He returned to Ireland in 1853 and was appointed curate of St Michael's and John's Church, 75 Exchange Street Lower. In June 1880, he was appointed parish priest of Sandymount, at St Mary's Star of the Sea Church. His presbytery address was 3 Leahy's Terrace, which runs alongside the church in the direction of the strand. At the time, the strand was at the end of Leahy's Terrace, as Beach Road did not exist until land was later reclaimed.

Canon O'Hanlon is best remembered for his monumental work, *The Lives of the Irish Saints* (9 vols, 1875), which took 30 years to complete, and includes the lives of 3,500 saints covering 8,500 pages.

He died on 15 May 1905 at 3 Leahy's Terrace, and was buried in Glasnevin Cemetery, Finglas Road, Dublin [EH 18.5 St Brigid's]. He is commemorated in St Mary's Star of the Sea Church by a mural tablet by sculptor G. Smyth.

Ulysses 13.448; 13.491; 13.496; 13.553; 13.572; 13.621; 13.1293; 15.1128

O'Hare, Dr John Joseph (1877–1907) *Holles Street National Maternity Hospital*
'Her he asked if O'Hare Doctor tidings sent from far coast and she with grameful sigh him answered that O'Hare Doctor in heaven was.' *(14.94–6)*

John Joseph O'Hare, son of John O'Hare, a merchant, was born on 14 October 1877 at Mayobridge, Newry, Co. Down. He attended Clongowes Wood College, Sallins, Co. Kildare and registered at University College Dublin in 1895. He lived at 41 Belvidere Place, Mountjoy Square, at the time and played soccer for Bohemians Football Club in Phibsborough.

O'Hare studied medicine at University College for seven years. Whilst there he was a member of the Scientific and Medical Society. In 1901, he was a resident pupil at the Mater Hospital, Eccles Street, and also worked in the Richmond Lunatic Asylum, Grangegorman Road. He graduated in 1902 and was awarded the degrees of MB, BCh, and BAO specialising in obstetrics which he studied at the National Maternity Hospital. In 1903 he was awarded a diploma in public health at the Royal College of Surgeons in Ireland.

Dr O'Hare was one of the assistant masters with Dr Walsh at Holles Street National Maternity Hospital in 1904. Later when working as dispensary medical officer in Newry, he contracted typhoid fever and died at 30 Hill Street, Newry on 3 May 1907 aged 30, and was buried in the family burial ground at Mayobridge, Newry.

Ulysses 13.961

O'Leary, John (1830–1907) *Fenian, journalist and editor*
'... *John O'Leary against Lear O'Johnny ...*' *(15.4685–6)*
John O'Leary was born in Tipperary on 23 July 1830. He was educated locally at the Erasmus Smith School and Carlow College.

In 1847 he entered Trinity College Dublin to study law but changed to medicine at the Queen's College in Cork and Galway, and later at medical schools in London and Paris, but never graduated.

He took part in the rising of 1848 and joined the Fenian movement. In 1863 he was appointed editor of the *Irish People*, a new Fenian weekly journal, with Thomas Clarke Luby and Charles Kickham as co-editors. He joined the Young Ireland movement and was arrested in 1865 after the Fenian uprising. He was imprisoned for five years and exiled from Ireland for a further 15, during which time he lived in Paris.

On his return to Ireland in 1885, he lived with his sister, the poet Ellen O'Leary, at 40 Leinster Road, Rathmines, which became a meeting place for young Irish nationalists and writers. Among the visitors were Douglas Hyde, T. W. Rolleston, Katherine Tynan and the young W. B. Yeats.

O'Leary's publications include *Recollections of Fenians and Fenianism* (2 vols, 1896), *Young Ireland, the Old and the New* (1885) and *What Irishmen Should Know, How Irishmen Should Feel* (1886).

O'Leary died on 16 March 1907 and was buried in Glasnevin Cemetery, Finglas Road, Dublin [RD 39 South New Chapel].

Ulysses 12.480

O'Malley, Grace 'Granuaile' (*c*. 1530–1600) *Sea captain and pirate*
'And they will come again and with a vengeance, no cravens, the sons of Granuaile
...' *(12.1373–5)*
Grace O'Malley was most likely born in Co. Mayo. She was called Granuaile, in Irish 'Grainne Mhaol' meaning 'Grace of the cropped hair'. She is associated with the west of Ireland and the coastline around Clew Bay.

Grace was married twice, first to Donal O'Flaherty and then in 1582 to Richard Burke. After the death of her second husband in 1586, Grace was taken captive by Sir Richard Bingham, a naval commander and governor of Connaught, who accused her of plundering the Aran Islands, and prepared a gallows for her execution. According to Bingham she was 'nurse of all the rebellions in the province for forty years'. She was released and fled to Ulster where she stayed with O'Neill unable to return on account of having lost all her ships. She was pardoned by Elizabeth I and returned to Connaught where she died in poverty in 1600.

According to tradition, Grace O'Malley was buried in Clare Island Abbey, Clare Island, Clew Bay, Co. Mayo. A mural stone plaque bearing her coat of arms is at the Abbey just beside the O'Malley tomb.   *Ulysses 16.558*

O'Molloy, J. J. *Solicitor*
'He spoke on the law of evidence, J. J. O'Molloy said, of Roman justice as contrasted with the earlier Mosaic code, the *lex talionis*.' *(7.755–6)*
J. J. Molloy is a composite character based on two people.

George Aloysius Moonan (1872–1945) Barrister and judge
George Aloysius Moonan, son of Richard Moonan and Mary Anne (née Tiernan) was born on 3 November 1872 in Drogheda, Co. Louth.

He put himself through college while working in the civil service. He entered University College Dublin in 1905 and obtained a BA degree. He was called to the Bar in 1911, took silk in 1930 and was appointed judge that same year. He later became a king's counsel and a circuit court judge for Counties Donegal and Sligo.

He married Mary Eveleen MacCarthy, a contralto singer, in 1901. They lived at 29 Garville Avenue, Rathgar. From 1893 he was a member of the Gaelic League and in 1899 became honorary secretary. He founded the Leinster College of Irish in 1906 to revive the Irish language and became its honorary secretary in 1913, and then honorary manager and chairman. It was based at 25 Rutland (now Parnell) Square. From 1907 to 1910 he was a council member of the National Literary Society along with O'Leary Curtis, Horace Plunkett and the O'Donoghue of the Glens.

Moonan was author (with Mary Hayden) of *A Short History of the Irish People* (1921). He died on 17 December 1945 at his residence 'Aille Méara', Foxrock, Co. Dublin. He was buried in Deansgrange Cemetery, Deansgrange, Co. Dublin [123–E–St Patrick].

John O'Mahony (1870–1904) Barrister

John O'Mahony, son of John Francis O'Mahony, was born in Cork on 27 January 1870. He worked as a journalist on the *Cork Daily Herald* and was joint editor of the *Cork Archaeological and Historical Journal*. He then moved to Dublin where he continued to work as a journalist and at the same time studied law. He was recipient of the O'Hagan Gold Medal from the Student's Debating Society of Ireland for a speech titled 'The Liberty of the Press', published in 1899. He was called to the Bar and was on the Munster Circuit. He lived in Cookstown, Tallaght, Co. Dublin, then a quiet rural area.

He married Nora Tynan on 29 April 1895 and they had three children. She was a sister of poet Katherine Tynan, and their family home was a farm named 'Whitehall', near Clondalkin.

O'Mahony was at the height of a brilliant career when he died aged 34 on 28 November 1904. He was buried in St Maelruain's Cemetery, Tallaght.

Ulysses O'Molloy, J. J.: 7.282; 7.290; 7.297; 7.301; 7.365; 7.382; 7.409; 7.424; 7.437; 7.451; 7.462; 7.467; 7.478; 7.499; 7.502; 7.545; 7.600; 7.652; 7.700; 7.727; 7.741; 7.746; 7.755; 7.760; 7.767; 7.775; 7.777; 7.782; 7.800; 7.813; 7.872; 7.906; 7.958; 7.1000; 7.1062; 7.1064; 10.433; 10.442; 10.453; 10.458; 15.938; 15.966; 15.992; 15.997; 15.1644

Opisso, Mrs Catherine Stark (1845–1923) *Dressmaker in Gibraltar*
'... and Mrs Opisso in Governor street O what a name Id go and drown myself in the first river if I had a name like her ...' *(18.1466–7)*
Catherine (or Catalina) Stark Opisso was born in Gibraltar. She worked as a milliner, dressmaker and lodging housekeeper. She lived with her son Avelino, born in 1869, who worked as a commercial clerk, and her granddaughter Catherine, born in 1890. They lived in House 9 Governor's Street. The 'house' in this context was a courtyard-style building, that contained several dwellings, now known as small flats. Mrs Opisso was a widow by 1901. Avelino died on 20 October 1905.

Mrs Opisso died on 18 April 1923.

O'Reilly, Robert (1834–1915) *Alderman, politician and merchant tailor*
'The Glencree dinner, Alderman Robert O'Reilly emptying the port into his soup before the flag fell. Bobbob lapping it for the inner alderman.' *(8.160–2)*
Robert O'Reilly was born in Co. Dublin and was a merchant tailor at 8 Parliament Street. He was a councillor for the Ward of Merchant's Quay from 1886 until 1890. During this period he served on various committees, such as the Finance and Leases, Artisans' and Labourers' Dwellings, Paving and Lighting, and Markets Construction Committees.

O'Reilly later served on the City of Dublin Distress Committee, of which he was chairman, and on the Waterworks Committee, of which he was vice-chairman. In 1891 he became an alderman and was high sheriff in 1897. In 1907 he was chairman of the Public Health Committee. A nationalist, he was alderman for the South City Ward until he was defeated in the election in January 1911 by a unionist, Ernest Bewley.

In 1911 O'Reilly was a widower living with his two daughters at 8 Parliament Street. He died in 1915 and was buried in Glasnevin Cemetery, Finglas Road, Dublin [LC 45.5 South].

O'Rourke, Larry (1840–1913) *Publican*

'He approached Larry O'Rourke's.' *(4.105)*

Larry O'Rourke was born in Carlow and was involved in the tea, wine and spirits business for many years in Dublin. He is first listed in 1884 as a tea, wine and spirit

merchant at 2 Fishamble Street. He later ran similar businesses at 9 Lord Edward Street and in 1894 opened a business at 72 and 73 Dorset Street Upper, where he remained until 1911. This building was sited at the corner of Eccles Street and Dorset Street.

O'Rourke was married with three daughters and one son. On his retirement in 1912, he moved to 11 Maxwell Road, Rathmines. He died on 29 November 1913 and was buried in Glasnevin Cemetery, Finglas Road, Dublin [WB 21.5 South].   *Ulysses 4.116; 4.119; 4.122*

O'Rourke, Tiernan (ruled *c.* 1124–72) *Prince of Breffni*

'A faithless wife first brought the stangers to our shore here, MacMurrough's wife and her leman, O Rourke, prince of Breffni.' *(2.392-4)*

Tiernan O'Rourke slew the king of Meath in 1130 and the following year devastated the country as far as Cooley and Omeath following which he battled with the men of Connaught. His wife, Devorgilla, deserted him in 1152 for Dermot MacMurrough, king of Leinster. Apparently on account of this, Roderick O'Conor, high king of Ireland, joined with O'Rourke to overthrow MacMurrough who appealed for assistance to Henry II, thus triggering the Anglo-Norman invasion of Ireland in 1169. At the time of the invasion, the O'Rourkes controlled the eastern frontier of the Meath kingdom. O'Rourke was slain by Hugo de Lacy in Meath in 1172.

Ulysses 7.536–7; 16.1470–1

O'Shea, Katharine (1845–1921) *Mistress and later wife of C. S. Parnell*

'A woman too brought Parnell low.' *(2.394)*

Katharine O'Shea, the daughter of Sir John Page Wood, 2nd baronet, of Hatherley House, and Emma Caroline (née Michell), was born on 30 January 1845 in Braintree, Essex.

On 24 January 1867 Katharine married Captain William Henry O'Shea in Brighton. O'Shea supported Parnell for the leadership of the Irish Parliamentary

 Party. He regularly held dinner parties for his business friends in London. Katharine acted as hostess, although she and O'Shea were already separated. Parnell was invited to one of these parties but failed to turn up. So Katharine went to the House of Commons in July 1880 and requested that Parnell come out and speak with her, which he did.

Two months later, Katharine became Parnell's mistress; she bore him three children between 1882 and 1884. O'Shea knew about the affair and in 1889 he petitioned for divorce, naming Parnell as co-respondent. A decree *nisi* was granted in November 1890. Parnell married Katharine on 25 June 1891 at Steyning near Brighton but died 6 October aged 45, in their home in Brighton.

Under the name of Katharine O'Shea, Mrs Charles Stewart Parnell wrote *Charles Stewart Parnell: His Love Story and Political Life* (2 vols), published in 1914.

She lived in relative obscurity and died on 5 February 1921 at 39 East Ham Road, Littlehampton, Sussex. She was buried in Littlehampton Cemetery, Sussex.

Ulysses 8.183; 15.1762

O'Sullivan, Seumas *Poet and editor*
Pseudonym of **James Sullivan Starkey** (1879–1958)
'I hope you will come round tonight. Bring Starkey.' *(9.323–4)*
Seumas O'Sullivan was born James Sullivan Starkey on 17 July 1879 in Dublin. Son of William Starkey, his father had a pharmacy in the Rathmines Medical Hall at 80 Rathmines Road. The family lived at 8 Newington Terrace.

O'Sullivan was educated at Wesley College, St Stephen's Green. He attended the Catholic University School of Medicine at Cecilia Street for a short time before becoming an apprentice in his father's pharmacy.

His literary career began in 1902 with the publication of some poems in the *Irish Homestead*, the *United Irishman* and *Celtic Christmas*. His other publications included *Verses Sacred and Profane* (1908); *The Earth-Lover and Other Verses* (1909); *Mud and Purple* (1917); *Requiem and Other Poems* (1917); *Common Adventures* (1926); and *The Rose and Bottle* (1946).

O'Sullivan founded the *Dublin Magazine* in 1923 and edited it until 1958. He lived at Grange House in Whitechurch near Rathfarnham. In 1926 he married Estella Solomons (1882–1968), the landscape and portrait painter. They lived at 2 Morehampton Road, Donnybrook.

O'Sullivan was president of Dublin PEN for many years. In 1939 he was conferred with an honorary degree by Dublin University. The Irish Academy of Letters presented him with its Lady Gregory Medal in 1957.

He died in Dublin on 24 March 1958.   *Ulysses 9.301*

Otto, Thomas (*fl*. 1880s–90s) *Comedian*

'... the grand annual Christmas pantomime *Sinbad the Sailor* ... harlequinade by Thomas Otto ...' *(17.422–7)*

Thomas Otto was responsible for the harlequinade in the pantomime, *Sinbad the Sailor*, held in Dublin's Gaiety Theatre on 26 December 1892.

In 1897 Thomas was one of three comedians named Fred, Thomas and William Otto, who also acted as clown, pantaloon and harlequin in the Dublin Gaiety pantomime, *Cinderella and the Little Glass Slipper*. They are widely recorded from 1888 to 1897, often in minstrel companies as 'The Three Ottos' all over Britain. In some advertisements they are called 'peculiar American comedians'.

Palles, Christopher (1831–1920) *Lord chief baron of the Exchequer*

'Do you know that story about chief baron Palles? J. J. O'Molloy asked. It was at the royal university dinner.' *(7.502-3)*

Christopher Palles was born on 25 December 1831 at 5 Lower Gardiner Street, Dublin, the second son of Andrew Palles and his wife Eleanor (née Plunkett). Christopher's

father had a large landed property, 'Mount Pallas', near Mount Nugent, Co. Cavan, in the family's possession since the end of the seventeenth century.

From 1837 to 1847 Palles attended Clongowes Wood College, Sallins, Co. Kildare. During this time the family moved to 25 Mountjoy Square and then to 26 Temple Street.

In 1847 Palles entered Trinity College Dublin and was called to the Irish Bar in 1853. He married Ellen Doyle from 17 Mountjoy Square on 5 August 1862. In 1872 he unsuccessfully contested Derry City for parliament. From 1872 to 1874 he was solicitor-general and attorney general. In February 1874 he was appointed lord chief baron of the Court of the Exchequer.

In 1879 Pallas moved to 28 Fitzwilliam Place and acquired a country residence near Dundrum named Mountanville House (it was subsequently named 'Knockrabo' and is now demolished). Palles took the train from the station in Dundrum, and then a tram to his workplace at the Four Courts. In the winter, he resided at his town house at 28 Fitzwilliam Place.

In 1892 he was sworn in as a member of the Privy Council of England, an almost unprecedented honour for an Irish judge who had never attained the House of Lords. On 5 July 1916 he resigned from the office of lord chief baron. Aged 79, he largely drafted the constitution for the National University of Ireland.

He died on 14 February 1920 at Mountanville House and was buried in Glasnevin Cemetery, Finglas Road, Dublin [Inner Vault D 93 Old O'Connell Circle].

Parnell, Charles Stewart (1846–91) *Politician, agitator for Home Rule*

'Parnell will never come again, he said. He's there, all that was mortal of him. Peace to his ashes.' *(6.926-7)*

Charles Stewart Parnell, politician and leader of the Irish Parliamentary Party (1880–90) was born at Avondale, Rathdrum, Co. Wicklow, on 27 June 1846. He was the son of John Henry Parnell and Delia (née Stewart).

He was educated at schools in England and at Magdalene College, Cambridge. He inherited Avondale on the death of his father and in the early 1870s concentrated on managing the estate.

He was elected MP for Meath in 1875 and joined the obstructionist wing of the Irish Parliamentary Party. In August 1877 he succeeded Isaac Butt as leader of the

Home Rule Confederation of Great Britain. He became first president of the National Land League, which was now represented in parliament. The British government passed a new Coercion Act, which Parnell opposed. He was imprisoned in 1881 and released in 1882 when Gladstone came to terms with Parnell through the 'Kilmainham Treaty'. The agitation was discontinued and the policy of land reform that began with the Land Act of 1881 was implemented.

On Parnell's release the new chief secretary, Lord Frederick Cavendish, was sent to set up a fresh era of peaceful progress. On 6 May 1882, the day of his arrival, he was murdered in the Phoenix Park with Thomas Burke, the under-secretary. The Invincibles carried out the assassination. The government introduced a new coercion bill, which Parnell opposed in parliament. However, it did honour its commitment and the Arrears Act virtually ended the land war of 1879–82.

In October 1882 Parnell founded the Irish National Land League, to replace the Land League. Following the general election in 1885, he held the balance of power and converted Gladstone to Home Rule. In April 1886 Gladstone introduced his Home Rule Bill, which Parnell regarded as inadequate but supported as a basis for further progress. It caused a split in the Liberal Party and the bill was defeated. In 1887 *The Times* published a series of articles, 'Parnellism and crime', accusing him of complicity in murder during the land war. One included a facsimile of a letter, supposedly written by Parnell after the Phoenix Park murders to Patrick Egan, a Fenian and former secretary of the Land League. It was found to be a forgery and Parnell was exonerated.

In December 1889 Parnell was named as co-respondent by Captain William O'Shea in his divorce action against his wife, Katharine. The divorce was granted and the non-conformist element in Gladstone's party was outraged, demanding that Parnell be removed as leader of the Irish Parliamentary Party. The Irish hierarchy adopted the non-conformist view. Parnell refused to yield and the party split. It marked the end of his political career.

Parnell died on 6 October 1891 in Brighton and was buried in Glasnevin

Cemetery, Finglas Road, Dublin, in what is now known as the Parnell Circle [EG 17 and FG 17 South Section].

He is commemorated by a monument in Dublin's O'Connell Street by Augustus Saint-Gaudens.

Ulysses 2.394; 6.320; 6.855; 6.919; 6.923–4; 8.183; 8.462; 8.517; 12.220–1; 15.1762; 15.4684; 16.1008–9; 16.1298; 16.1729–30; 17.507–8; 17.1649

Parnell, Frances Isabel 'Fanny' (1849–82)   *Poet and sister of C. S. Parnell*
'Mad Fanny and his other sister Mrs Dickinson driving about with scarlet harness.'
(8.513–14)
Fanny Parnell, daughter of John Henry Parnell and Delia (née Stewart), was born in Avondale, Rathdrum, Co. Wicklow in 1849. She was a sister of Charles Stewart Parnell. She published patriotic poems while in her teens in the *Irish People*, a paper founded by James Stephens in 1863.

In 1874 she visited the United States with her American mother, Delia Stewart Parnell. She wrote for the *Boston Pilot* and the *Nation* and founded the Ladies' Land League in America. Fanny also encouraged support of the Land League through her poems published in *United Ireland*, a paper established by Charles Stewart Parnell as the official organ of the Land League and of the Irish Parliamentary Party. Her publications include *The Hovels of Ireland* (1879) and *Land League Songs* (1882).

She died in Bordenstown, New Jersey, on 20 July 1882 and was buried at the Tudor family plot at Mount Auburn Cemetery, Cambridge, Massachusetts.

Parnell, John Howard (1843–1923)   *Politician and Dublin city marshal*
'John Howard Parnell translated a white bishop quietly and his grey claw went up again to his forehead whereat it rested.' *(10.1050–1)*
John Howard Parnell, son of John Henry Parnell and Delia (née Stewart), was the elder brother of Charles Stewart Parnell. He was born in Avondale, Rathdrum, Co. Wicklow. He served for a time in the Armagh Militia.

John Howard emigrated to the United States and lived in Alabama for several years where he was occupied in fruit growing. He returned to Ireland in 1872 and farmed in Co. Armagh. He inherited Avondale after the death of his brother in 1891. His election to parliament was due to his representations that unless he obtained such a remunerative post he would lose Avondale. Unable to make Avondale financially viable, he sold it in 1899.

From 1895 to 1900 he was MP for South Meath. In 1897 he was elected as Dublin city marshal and held that post until his death. His office was in The Castle Chambers at 3 Dame Street. In 1907 when he was living in Upper Mount Street, he married Olivia Isabella Smythe, 29 years his junior and widow of Archibald Mateer of Carlingford, Co. Louth. They lived at 1 Clarinda Park East, Kingstown (now Dún Laoghaire), and later moved to Sion House in Glenageary. He published *C. S. Parnell: A Memoir* in 1916.

He died on 2 May 1923 at Sion House, Glenageary, Co. Dublin, and was buried in Deansgrange Cemetery, Deansgrange, Co. Dublin [O–South West].

Ulysses 8.500; 8.706; 10.1007; 10.1045; 10.1226; 15.1412; 15.1512; 15.1516; 15.4344

Patey, T. M. (*fl.* late 1800s–early 1900s) *Cyclist*

T. M. Patey was one of the nine quartermile flat handicappers who took part in the Trinity College bicycle races in the afternoon of 16 June 1904. *Ulysses 10.1258*

Pepper, John Henry (1821–1900) *Engineer, illusionist and educationist*

'Pepper's ghost idea.' *(8.20)*

John Henry Pepper, son of John Bailey Pepper, was born at Great Queen Street in London on 17 June 1821. In 1848 he was appointed analytical chemist and lecturer at the Royal Polytechnic in Regent Street. He later became honorary director and remained in that post for 20 years.

In September 1858, Henry Dircks produced details of a device for producing 'spectral optical illusions'. Pepper recognised its possibilities and with some changes in the apparatus he showed the 'ghost' in illustration of Charles Dickens's *The Haunted Man* in December 1862. The device was patented in both the names of Pepper and Dircks but later the two fell out with each other. The exhibition became popularly known as 'Pepper's Ghost'.

Pepper's Ghost and Spectral Opera Company made regular appearances in Dublin between 1883 and 1897. The show, performed in the large concert room in the Rotunda in Cavendish Row, comprised a scientific arrangement, which enabled the reflection of the performers to be presented to the audience. It proved very popular and played to full houses for a number of years. There were many and varied productions, including a dramatised version of Dickens's *A Christmas Carol*, Wagner's *The Flying Dutchman* and Boucicault's *The Colleen Bawn*.

Pepper died at his home, 55 Colworth Road, Leytonstone, Essex, on 25 March 1900 and was buried in West Norwood Cemetery in the London borough of Lambeth. *Ulysses 8.20*

Pile, Sir Thomas (1856–1931) *Lord mayor and high sheriff of Dublin*

'... the new high sheriff, Thomas Pile ...' *(17.444–5)*

Thomas Pile was born in Dublin on 27 February 1856. He was the son of William Pile, of Tritonville Road, Sandymount. He was educated at Wesley College, Dublin.

In 1887 he was elected to Dublin City Council. He was chairman of its Electricity Committee. He started the Dublin Electricity Scheme and was responsible for the erection of the new power station at the Pigeon House.

Pile married Caroline Maude (née Nicholson) on 3 May 1892. They lived in Terenure and later moved to 'Kenilworth Lodge', Kenilworth Square in Rathgar, Dublin.

In 1898 he was high sheriff of Dublin and lord mayor 1900–1. When Queen Victoria visited Dublin in April 1900, she was welcomed by Pile, who was granted a baronetcy to mark the event. A prominent Freemason, he was also a deputy lieutenant and a justice of the peace of the City and County of Dublin.

Pile retired in 1901 and moved to London in 1905. He lived at Henley House near Regent's Park, then Kenilworth House at Willesden Lane, London.

He died on 17 January 1931 at his home, 90 Corringham Road, Hampstead, London, and was cremated at Golder's Green Crematorium.

Pinker, J. B. (1863–1922) *Literary agent*
'My literary agent Mr J.B. Pinker is in attendance.' *(15.834–5)*
James Brand Pinker, son of William Pinker and Matilda (née Humphrey) was born in East London. He worked as a clerk at Tilbury Docks then took a job on the *Levant Herald* in Constantinople. In 1888 he married Mary Seabrooke, who inherited wealth giving him freedom to pursue his career in journalism. On his return to England, he became assistant editor for the weekly illustrated magazine, *Black and White*. He got to know writers such as Bram Stoker, H. G. Wells and Henry James who contributed short stories to the magazine. This motivated him to found a literary agency in 1896 with an office at 9 Arundel Street, London.

Pinker was Joyce's literary agent in London. Philip Beaufoy claims him as his literary agent in the text.

Pinker died on 8 February 1922 at the Biltmore Hotel, New York.

Pisimbo *Gibraltar name remembered by Molly*
There are variations of the surname Pisimbo such as Pesimbo and Pisimo in Gibraltar. There is only one record of a Pesimbo/Pisimbo in the *Census of Gibraltar, 1901*. The family lived in a house at 8 Parody's Passage, Gibraltar.   *Ulysses 18.1466*

Pisimbo, Manuel Eulogio (1858–1932) *Boatman*
Manuel Eulogio Pisimbo/Pesimbo was born in Gibraltar and worked as a boatman. He married Catalina Fernandez who was born in Algatocin, Spain, in 1861. Catalina worked privately as a seamstress in Gibraltar. Their children were Manuel, a blacksmith born in 1883, Carlota, born in 1885, Francisco, born in 1886, Fanny, born in 1888, and Andras, born in 1889. Manuel Pisimbo died in 1932.   *Ulysses 18.1466*

Pitt, William (1759–1806) *British prime minister*

'Billy Pitt had them built, Buck Mulligan said, when the French were on the sea. But ours is the *omphalos.*' *(1.543–4)*

The son of William Pitt the elder, earl of Chatham, William Pitt was born on 28 May 1759 in Hayes, Kent. He was educated at Cambridge and was called to the Bar in 1780 before becoming chancellor of the Exchequer in 1782 and leader of the house.

Pitt's first administration lasted 17 years. He resigned on 14 March 1801 after King George III refused to accept Pitt's Emancipation of Catholics Bill. He remained in opposition for three years until May 1804, when he again became prime minister, a post he held until his death.

Pitt died on 23 January 1806 and was buried in Westminster Abbey, London, in the North Transept central aisle. His monument is at the west end of the nave.

Pitt was responsible for the building of the Martello Towers around the coast of Ireland as a defence against possible Napoleonic invasion. Fifteen towers, authorised by the National Defence Act of 1804, were erected between Dublin and Bray. Number 11 at Sandycove is the tower in which the opening chapter of *Ulysses* takes place.

Pokorny, Professsor Julius P. (1887–1970)
Professor of Celtic philology, linguist and scholar

'It's rather interesting because professor Pokorny of Vienna makes an interesting point out of that.' *(10.1077–9)*

Julius Pokorny was born on 12 June 1887 in Prague, son of Samuel Pokorny and Margarethe (née Riegner). He came from an Austrian Catholic-Jewish background. In 1897 the family moved to Vienna.

Pokorny was educated at the Benedictine School at Kremsmunster in Austria from 1898 to 1905. He studied law at the University of Vienna and became interested

in Welsh and Celtic studies. He visited Ireland for the first time in 1908 to learn Irish in Co. Mayo, where he met Eoin MacNeill and Richard Best, who was to remain a lifelong friend.

Pokorny qualified in 1910 with a doctorate of law from Vienna and worked as a librarian. He was appointed a lecturer in Celtic philology and Irish at the University of Vienna where he remained from 1913 to 1920. He was awarded an honorary doctorate by the National University of Ireland in 1925.

Pokorny succeeded Kuno Meyer (1858–1919) as professor of Celtic philology in Berlin University. He also took over as editor of the *Zeitschrift für Celtische Philologie*, which Meyer had founded in Germany in 1896 and which became a major influence on Celtic learning.

Due to his Jewish ancestry, Pokorny had to relinquish his post in Berlin in 1935 but somehow managed to survive in Nazi Germany until 1943. He was admitted to neutral Switzerland with refugee status as he held an Irish visa. At the request of his friend Douglas Hyde and on the instructions of Eamon de Valera Pokorny secured the visa.

He spent the remainder of his life in Switzerland and taught at Bern and Zurich universities. He retired in 1959. His publications include *History of Ireland* (1916) and *Indo-European Etymological Dictionary* (1959).

He died in Zurich on 8 April 1970. His funeral service was held in Zurich. Pokorny was cremated and his ashes were returned to Vienna.

Ponchielli, Amilcare (1834–86) *Italian composer*

'Morning after the bazaar dance when May's band played Ponchielli's dance of the hours.' *(4.525–6)*

Amilcare Ponchielli was born near Cremona, Italy, on 31 August 1834. He studied music at the Milan Conservatory and composed several operas; his best known is *La Gioconda* from which comes 'The Dance of the Hours'.

Ponchielli was appointed maestro di cappella of Bergamo Cathedral in 1881. He was also professor of composition at the Milan Conservatory. He died on 16 January 1886 in Milan and was buried in the Cimitero Monumentale, one of the largest cemeteries in Milan.

Potterton, Robert (1823–1901) *Defendant in legal case*

'An elderly female, no more young, left the building of the courts of chancery, king's bench, exchequer and common pleas, having heard in the lord chancellor's court the case in lunacy of Potterton ...' *(10.625–7)*

Robert Potterton, son of Thomas Potterton and Eleanor (née Hinds) of 'Balatalion', Kildalkey, Co. Meath, was born on 10 July 1823. He was educated at Bannow Grammar School, Wexford, and Trinity College Dublin where he graduated with a BA degree in 1853. He obtained a doctorate in 1864. He worked as a school inspector in Trim, Co. Meath and later became a district inspector working in Cork, Loughrea, Sligo, Tipperary, Limerick and Armagh.

In 1855 Potterton married Mary Kelly Waldron whose dowry was a large farm in Co. Leitrim. Sometime after 1880 they moved to Dublin to 'Alpine Lodge', at 38 Finglas Road, Glasnevin, which was incorporated into Bengal Terrace. Potterton was declared a lunatic in April 1890 and throughout the 1890s was a patient at Hampstead Asylum in Glasnevin, the hospital run by the Eustace family.

He died on 13 March 1901 at Hampstead Asylum and was buried in St James's churchyard, Athboy, Co. Meath.

Powell, Josie (1878–1967) *Girlhood friend of Molly Bloom*
'... Josie Powell that was, prettiest deb in Dublin.' *(15.441–2)*
Josie Powell was Mrs Josephine Breen's maiden name in *Ulysses*. She was a girlhood friend of Molly and was later the wife of Denis Breen.

The fictional Josie Breen (née Powell) was based on a real person named Mary Josephine Gallagher, born in 1878, the daughter of William Gallagher, a grocer and purveyor from 4 North Strand. On 20 November 1901 she married Charles Powell who was born in Aldershot on 27 April 1867, and was the second son of Major Malachy Powell. She became Mary Josephine Powell, or 'Josie Powell'. She worked for a number of years as the housekeeper at City Hall and lived nearby at 7 Cork Hill.

She died on 26 December 1967 and was buried in Deansgrange Cemetery, Deansgrange, Co. Dublin [14–B1–St Kevin]   *Ulysses 8.273; 13.814; 17.1846; 18.169*

Power, Jack *Employed by Royal Irish Constabulary, Dublin Castle*
'Mr Power gazed at the passing houses with rueful apprehension.' *(6.310)*
Jack Power is a composite character based on two people.

John Power (d. 1919) *DMP Pensioner*
Jack Power may be identified with Mr John Power who could have been an inspiration for his name. John Power was a Dublin Metropolitan Police pensioner who lived at 34 Rutland Square (now Parnell Square) until his death at the age of 54 on 14 September 1919. His late father Pierce Power, from Fermor, Tramore, Co. Waterford, was in the Royal Irish Constabulary.

Tom Devin *Dublin Corporation Official*
Joyce wrote in a letter to Alf Bergan dated 25 May 1937 that Devin 'comes into *Ulysses* under the name of Mr Power'. Joyce misspells his name as Devan in *Ulysses*. Devin was a friend of the Joyce family. He worked as an official in the Dublin Corporation Cleansing Department in Wood Quay.

The story 'Grace' in *Dubliners* states that Mr Power worked in Dublin Castle for the Royal Irish Constabulary. He has not only a wife, but also a mistress who works as a barmaid.

Ulysses Power, Jack: *6.2; 6.33; 6.73; 6.85; 6.92; 6.98; 6.112; 6.134; 6.144; 6.149; 6.194; 6.196; 6.224; 6.242; 6.250; 6.254; 6.257; 6.266; 6.275; 6.288; 6.292; 6.299; 6.335; 6.338; 6.368; 6.389; 6.411; 6.417; 6.427; 6.454; 6.468; 6.472; 6.492; 6.528; 6.532; 6.642; 6.648; 6.710; 6.920; 10.699; 10.966; 10.977; 10.982; 10.986; 10.990; 10.1025–6*

Poyntz, Samuel Robert (1842–1918) *Clothing outfitter*
'... Monsieur Poyntz, from whom I can have for a *livre* as snug a cloak of the French fashion ...' *(14.776–7)*
Samuel Robert Poyntz was born in Dublin, son of Rachel and John Poyntz (1801–77), a tailor and draper of Eustace Street who later moved to 33 Peter Street.

There were two shops in Dublin belonging to the Poyntzes. In 1884 both had their shops in Grafton Street. Poyntz, B. & Co., hosiers, glovers, and colonial outfitters at 105 and 106 Grafton Street, and Samuel Robert Poyntz, India rubber warehouse, lawn tennis and cricket outfitter at 52 Grafton Street. *The Medical Press* in 1879 carried an advertisement, for Poyntz, Peppard, Co.: 'India-Rubber, Gutta-Percha and portmanteau manufacturers, 52 Grafton Street, Dublin invite an inspection and comparison of the prices and quality of their ...'

He married Dorcas Cecilia Peppard and they had two sons, John and William. They later separated and Dorcas moved with the children to Meadowside, Hockley, Essex in England. Poyntz lived at 'Norfolk Lodge', 21 Park Avenue in Sandymount and moved to 20 Clare Street where he later had his business. Poyntz died in Clare Street on the 15 August 1918 and was buried in Mount Jerome Cemetery, Harold's Cross, Dublin [A99–218].

Price, Henry Blackwood (1849–1923) *Cousin of Garrett Deasy*
'My cousin, Blackwood Price, writes to me it is regularly treated and cured in Austria by cattledoctors there.' *(2.340–1)*
Henry Blackwood Price was a descendant of Sir John Blackwood. He was born on 28 March 1849 in Newtownard, Saintfield, Co. Down.

He was an engineer and assistant manager of the Eastern Telegraph Company in Trieste, where he became friends with Joyce. Stanislaus Joyce refers to several evenings spent at his house, singing around the piano.

Price was interested in foot-and-mouth disease and learned that there was a cure in Austria for it. He corresponded with Joyce in 1912 about an outbreak in Ireland and asked him for the address of William Field, MP, the victualler in Blackrock who was the president of the Irish Cattle Traders' Society.

When Joyce visited Ireland in 1912, Price asked him to promote a cure for the foot-and-mouth disease. An unsigned editorial appeared in the *Freeman's Journal* on 10 September 1912 titled 'Politics and cattle disease'. William Brayden, the editor, most likely wrote it. This incident finds its way into *Ulysses* with Stephen being asked to perform the same task for Mr Garret Deasy, who is modelled, at least in part, on Blackwood Price.

Henry Blackwood Price died in 1923.   *Ulysses 2.279; 2.334; 12.1277*

Purcell, Rev. Thomas (1842–1923) *St Saviour's Dominican Priory*
Thomas Purcell was born on 29 July 1842 in St Munchin's parish, Limerick, son of Richard Purcell and Catherine (née Mulqueen).

In 1867 he entered the Dominican order at Tallaght and took the name Francis in religion. He was ordained priest in Newry and worked in various places around the country. From 1897 to 1911 Father Purcell was based in Dublin as a member of the Community of St Saviour's Dominican Priory in Dominick Street Lower. He published *Mary's Guide of Honour: Manual of the Perpetual Rosary* in 1907.

From 1915 to 1917, Father Purcell moved between Athy, Cork and Kilkenny before transferring back to Cork in 1922 where he remained for the last 18 months of his life. He died on 23 September 1923 and was buried in the Dominican Plot in St Joseph's Cemetery, Cork.

Ulysses 12.936–7

Purefoy, Mina *Patient in Holles Street Maternity Hospital*
Surname is based on **Richard Dancer Purefoy (1847–1919)** *Master at the Rotunda Hospital*
'Mina Purefoy swollen belly on a bed groaning to have a child tugged out of her.'
(8.479–80)
Mina Purefoy, who is giving birth to her ninth child in Holles Street Maternity Hospital, and her husband Theodore, an accountant in the Ulster Bank, are fictitious characters. Their surname is taken from Richard Dancer Purefoy, master at the Rotunda Maternity Hospital, Dublin.

Richard Dancer Purefoy, son of Dr Thomas Purefoy and Alice Maria (née Dancer) was born in August 1847 in Cloughjordan, Co. Tipperary.

Purefoy was educated at Raphoe Royal School, Co. Donegal and Trinity College Dublin and was a gynaecologist at the Adelaide Hospital and later master of the Rotunda Hospital. He established the first pathological laboratory in the Rotunda Hospital with funds he raised from organising the 'Lucina' Bazaar.

Purefoy never married and lived with his sister Anna Catherine and three servants at his residence, 62 Merrion Square South. He was president of the Royal College of Surgeons in Ireland and of the Royal Irish Academy.

He died at his home on 27 June 1919.

Ulysses 8.277; 8.358; 8.431; 10.590; 11.903; 11.1103; 13.959; 14.510; 14.1333; 14.1335; 14.1410; 14.1434; 15.641; 15.1740; 15.4345; 15.4692; 17.2054

Pyat, Félix (1810–89) *Journalist, socialist and politician*
'That's press. That's talent. Pyatt! He was all their daddies!' *(7.688–8)*
The son of a lawyer, Félix Pyat was born in Vierzon, France. He studied law and in 1831 was called to the Bar in Paris, but quit to become a radical journalist. He was involved in the Paris Commune in 1871 before escaping to London. He was implicated with the European Revolutionary Committee in Belgium and England.

Pyat wrote a number of plays and contributed articles to several newspapers and revolutionary journals. His own paper, *Le Combat*, was suppressed and was followed on by another equally virulent paper *Vengeur*. Pyat died on 3 August 1889 at Saint-Gratien, north of Paris.

Pyper, William Stanton (1868–1942) *Journalist, translator, globe trotter*
'Piper is coming.
Piper! Mr Best piped. Is Piper back?
Peter Piper pecked a peck of pick of peck of pickled pepper.' *(9.274–6)*

William Stanton Pyper was born in Cornwall son of James Pyper a staff commander with the Royal Navy.

He was educated at the Erasmus High School, Dublin, and later became a mining engineer. A vegetarian with an interest in theosophy and journalism, he was an enthusiast of the Irish language. He was on the fringe of the Irish literary scene in the 1890s and wrote under the pseudonym 'Lugh' for the *United Irishman* between 1899–1906. Pyper and Yeats reviewed John Eglinton's *Pebbles from a Brook* for the *United Irishman*.

In 1901 Pyper lived with his parents in Killester, Co. Dublin. He travelled widely and worked at various jobs, which included translating. He subsequently emigrated but returned to Ireland after the First World War. His translation of V. I. Nemirovitch-Danchenko's *With a Diploma and the Whirlwind* was published in 1915.

Pyper died in Hendon, Middlesex in England in 1942.   *Ulysses 9.1073; 9.1076*

Quigley, Mary (b. 1878) *Nurse*
'... when here nurse Quigley from the door angerly bid them hist ye ...' *(14.318)*
A nurse named Mary Quigley was born in Galway in 1878 and spoke both Irish and English. In 1901 she lived with other hospital staff, which included two other nurses in accommodation at the Dublin City Hosptial at 16 and 18 Upper Baggot Street. It is possible that she was Nurse Quigley who worked in the National Maternity Hospital, Holles Street in 1904.

Ulysses 15.2611

Quill, Albert William (1843–1908) *Barrister and part time poet*
'(Albert Quill wrote a fine piece of original verse of distinctive merit on the topic for the *Irish Times*) ...' *(16.910–11)*
Albert William Quill, a native of Co. Kerry, was born on 13 September 1843, the son of Thomas Quill and Ellen (née O'Sullivan) of Carriganas Castle, Co. Cork. The family name Quill, an English corruption of the Irish Ó Cúil, was borne by the chief poet of Munster (Ó Cúil) in the twelfth century, while on his mother's side he traced descent from O'Sullivan Beare.

Quill was educated at Old Hall Green, Hertfordshire, and Trinity College Dublin where he graduated in 1869. He was called to the Bar in 1870 and was joint author of a number of legal textbooks.

A classical scholar, he translated the *History of Tacitus* (1892). McGee in Dublin published his *Poems* (1895). When the Russian ship, *The Palme*, went aground off the coastline in Booterstown, Co. Dublin, on 24 December 1895 in a severe storm, Quill published a poem to commemorate the event in the *Irish Times* on 16 January 1896.

In 1904 Quill lived at 1 Trevelyan Terrace, Brighton Road, Rathgar. He died on 1 February 1908 and was buried in Deansgrange Cemetery, Deansgrange, Co. Dublin [50–B–North].

Quirke, Thomas George (1865–1949) *Solicitor*
Thomas Quirke was born in England. He served his apprenticeship with William Frewin a solicitor in Tipperary and was admitted as a solicitor in Hilary term 1891.

He practised as a solicitor at 15 Frederick Street South and was professor of real property and equity for the Law Society from 1907 to 1912. He was a member of the council of the Law Society from 1913 to 1942 and was president from 1925 to 1926.

In 1904 he lived in 'Abbey View', Dalkey. He later moved to 12 Ailesbury Road and his final residence was 'Grosvenor' in Monkstown. In later years he was senior partner in the firm T. G. Quirke and Co. He died at his Monkstown residence on 9 September 1949 and was buried in Deansgrange Cemetery, Deansgrange, Co. Dublin [106–C–North].   *Ulysses 12.938*

Rabaiotti, Antonio (b. 1879) *Italian ice cream vendor*
'A onelegged sailor crutched himself round MacConnell's corner, skirting Rabaiotti's icecream car, and jerked himself up Eccles street.' *(10.228–9)*
Antonio Rabaiotti, born in Italy, was an ice cream dealer and vendor with a number of push cars or 'gondolas', selling ice cream around the Dublin streets. In 1901 he lived in Amiens Street and by 1904 he had an address at Elm View, 62a Madras Place, North Circular Road. He also had a restaurant at 65 Talbot Street, close to Monto.

By 1911 Antonio Rabaiotti was living at 4 Wexford Street with his wife Rosina and two daughters, Vittorina and Valentina. He also worked here as a fish merchant and had five Italian-born assistants in his fish shop.   *Ulysses 15.150*

Raftery, Anthony (1784–1835) *Poet*
'... of the harsher and more personal note which is found in the satirical effusions of the famous Raftery and of Donal MacConsidine ...' *(12.727–9)*
Anthony Raftery was born in Killaiden near Kiltimagh, Co. Mayo. Blinded as a child by smallpox, he attended a hedge school in nearby Bohola. He was a talented musician and violinist and became a wandering bard, known as the Kiltimagh Fiddler and the Blind Poet. He spent most of his life in the Gort and Loughrea area of Co. Galway where he encountered a variety of unfortunate people: such as evicted tenants, beggars, old soldiers, Ribbonmen, Whiteboys and vagabonds on the run.

Raftery never wrote his poems down, as they were composed in the folk idiom. The tradition was essentially oral in this period and the poems were handed down from generation to generation. One of his finest poems is 'Contae Muigheo'.

Douglas Hyde collected Raftery's poetry in *Abhráin atá Leagtha ar an Reachtuire* (1903). Irish University Press reissued Hyde's *Songs Ascribed to Raftery, Love Songs of Connacht* and *The Religious Songs of Connacht* in the 1970s.

Raftery died on Christmas Eve 1835 and was buried at Killeeneen, near Kilcolgan in the townland of Craughwell, Co. Galway. He is commemorated in the square in Kiltimagh by a plaque on a stone memorial.

Redmond, John (1856–1918) *Politician and leader of the Home Rule Party*
'... Arthur Griffith against John Redmond ...' *(15.4685)*

John Redmond, son of William Redmond, MP for Wexford, and Mary (née Hoey), was born in Kilrane, Co. Wexford, on 1 September 1856. Educated at Clongowes Wood College, Sallins, Co. Kildare and Trinity College Dublin, he became a clerk in the House of Commons.

Elected MP for New Ross in 1881, Redmond was one of Parnell's most loyal supporters. He remained faithful to Parnell after 'the split' following the O'Shea divorce case in 1890 and led the minority in support of Parnell. In 1891 he was elected Parnellite MP for Waterford and retained the seat until his death. In 1900 he became leader of the reunited Home Rule Party.

Redmond supported England in the First World War, and suffered the consequence by having his party destroyed. His publications include several volumes of Home Rule speeches and addresses.

He died in London on 6 March 1918 and was interred in the family vault in the ruins of the Knight's Templar Church of St John in Wexford.   *Ulysses 7.619–20; 16.1327–9*

Reynolds, Robert 'Bob' (1878–1959) *Cyclist*
'... Bob Reynolds, half a guinea ...' *(2.257–8)*
Robert Reynolds, known as 'Bob' was born in Hampton Street, Balbriggan, Co. Dublin. One of six children, he was son of Julia (née Carvin) and Robert Reynolds. His parents operated the first business in Balbriggan, which sold newspapers in the 1860s. Both parents died when the children were young, and relatives raised them.

Reynolds joined the local Wanderers Cycling Club as a teenager. He was a cycling companion and friend of Oliver St John Gogarty. In the 1890s Reynolds and his brother Harry, an extraordinarily talented cyclist, made cycling history partaking in many overseas events. Bob came third in the World Mile Championship at Copenhagen and competed in the grand cycling and athletic tournament held in Ballsbridge on 16 April 1900. Known for his famous pop-gun sprints, he won the Half Mile Championship of Ireland in Waterford on 2 July 1901.

Reynolds later worked as a motor and cycling agent and lived at 'Sea Breeze', 1 Convent Road, Dalkey. He had a cycle and motor depot at Wolfe Tone Place, Dalkey for a number of years and worked there as manager until the mid 1950s. He died on 25 July 1959 and was buried in Deansgrange Cemetery, Deansgrange, Co. Dublin [42 –N–St Nessan].

He is commemorated by a plaque at his birthplace in Hampton Street.

Rice, Edmund Ignatius (1762–1844) *Founder of the Irish Christian Brothers*
'... and the confraternity of the christian brothers led by the reverend brother Edmund Ignatius Rice.' *(12.1687–8)*
Edmund Rice, son of Robert Rice and Margaret (née Tierney), was born on 1 June 1762 at Westcourt, near Callan in Co. Kilkenny.

Rice was educated in Kilkenny. Aged 17, he worked as an apprentice in his uncle's victualling and ship chandelling business in Waterford. On his uncle's death in 1790 he inherited the business. He married Mary Elliott in 1785. In 1789 she had an accident and on her deathbed gave birth to a disabled daughter. Rice retired from business and devoted his life to the service of God and to helping the less fortunate.

In 1802 he established his first school for poor boys in New Street, Waterford, followed by one in nearby Stephen Street, which was relocated close by and named 'Mount Sion'. He took religious vows and in 1808 obtained papal recognition from Pope Pius VII for the Institute of the Religious Brothers of Christian Schools in Ireland. In 1820 he was elected the first superior general.

Daniel O'Connell laid the foundation stone for the North Richmond Street house and school in Dublin in 1828. The present residence includes the original house built by Rice who lived there from 1831 until 1839, when he returned to Mount Sion.

Rice retired in 1838 aged 76 having set up 22 Christian Brothers houses in Ireland and England.

He died in Waterford on 29 August 1844. In 1993 Pope John Paul II declared him venerable, and he was beatified on 6 October 1996. His remains were laid to rest at what is now the International Heritage Centre, Mount Sion, Barrack Street, Waterford.

Blessed Edmund Rice is commemorated by a statue in Green Street (also known as Edmund Ignatius Rice Street) in Callan, Co. Kilkenny, and the Edmund Rice Bridge, which spans the river Suir in Waterford city.

Rice, Ignatius J. (1870–1955) *Solicitor and law agent for Dublin Corporation*
'... had been convicted of a wastage of 20,000 gallons per night by a reading of their meter on the affirmation of the law agent of the corporation, Mr Ignatius Rice, solicitor ...' *(17.179–81)*
Ignatius J. Rice was born in Dublin and served his apprenticeship with Michael Coyle, 12 Parliament Street. He practised as a solicitor at Rutland Place until 1896. He subsequently moved to City Hall, Cork Hill, Dublin, and was employed as law agent to Dublin Corporation, where he worked for the Waterworks Committee until his retirement in 1947. In 1904 Rice was living at 1 Waltham Terrace, Blackrock.

He died at his residence 'Rose Lawn', Ballybrack, Co. Dublin, on 4 December 1955 and was buried in Deansgrange Cemetery, Deansgrange, Co. Dublin [15–N2–North].

Ricketts, Kitty *Employed at Bella Cohen's establishment*
Possibly based on **Becky Cooper** (*fl.* **early 1900s**) *Dublin prostitute*
'*Kitty Ricketts bends her head. Her boa uncoils, slides, glides over her shoulder, back, arm, chair to the ground.*' *(15. 2082–3)*
The description of Kitty Ricketts, who worked in Bella Cohen's brothel at 82 Tyrone Street Lower in Monto, suggests that she may be based on Becky Cooper.

Cooper was probably the best-known Dublin prostitute from the beginning of the century until the 1920s.

An attractive, well-dressed woman of strong character, Cooper was one of the last madams in Monto. She ran a kip house in Tyrone Street, which faced the Leinster Arms in Railway Street (formerly Tyrone Street). When the tenements in Railway Street were demolished and replaced with flats, Cooper moved to live in Liberty House Flats.

Cooper gave money to various charities and was kind and generous to the poor. When she took a fancy to a young man, she would sometimes embarrass him by buying him new clothes or giving him gifts of money.

Ulysses 15.2050; 15.2219; 15.2302; 15.2709

Riordan, Mrs 'Dante' *Widow living with the Dedaluses*
Based on **Mrs Elizabeth Conway (1827–1896)** *Governess to Joyce children*
'Mrs Riordan (Dante), a widow of independent means, had resided in the house of Stephen's parents ...' *(17.479–80)*
The daughter of Edmund Hearn, Elizabeth was born in Cork. She was supposedly a distant relation of John Stanislaus Joyce on his mother's side.

She entered a convent with the intention of becoming a nun and taught in the Convent of Mercy in Western Pennsylvania in the United States. Before taking her final vows she quit the convent when her brother died in 1862, leaving her the large sum of £30,000, which he had made trading in West Africa. She returned to Ireland and settled in Dublin where she married Patrick Henry Conway, the son of a Dublin solicitor, in 1875. He was a clerk in the Bank of Ireland. After a couple years of marriage, he absconded to Buenos Aires with most of his wife's fortune. She became an abandoned wife and was embittered as a result.

Mrs Conway joined the Joyce family as a governess to the children in the autumn of 1888 while they were living at 1 Martello Terrace in Bray. She remained with the family when they moved to their next home, 'Leoville', 23 Carysfort Avenue in Blackrock, and left between 1892 and 1893 after a disagreement about Parnell with John Stanislaus Joyce.

She moved around living with various friends for short periods of time. Stanislaus Joyce recounts in *My Brother's Keeper* that she was the most bigoted person that he ever had the misfortune to encounter.

Mrs Conway, who lived at 4 Pembroke Terrace, Merrion, in Dublin died on 16 November 1896 in Our Lady's Hospice in Harold's Cross, Dublin and was buried in Glasnevin Cemetery, Finglas Road, Dublin [GC 4.5 South].

Ulysses 6.378; 15.1714; 15.4339; 18.4

Ristori, Adelaide (1822–1906) *Italian tragedienne*
'And Ristori in Vienna.' *(5.199)*
Italian actress, Adelaide Ristori, was born on 29 January 1822 in Cividale del Friuli town in Friuli-Venezia Giulia, northern Italy. She joined the Sardinian Company

and the Ducal Company at Parma and in 1846 became the Marquesa Capranica del Grillo. She chose the part of *Francesca* for her début in Paris in 1855. Famous for her tragic roles, a version of *Leah* was adapted especially for her.

Ristori appeared in London, Madrid, and the United States. Although there is no available record that she performed in Vienna, she undoubtedly did so.

Ristori died on 9 October 1906 and was buried in Cimitero Comunale Monumentale Campo Verano, Rome.

Roberts, Frederick Sleigh (1832–1914) *1st Earl Roberts, Kandahar and Waterford*
'... darling little Bobsy (called after our famous hero of the South African war, lord Bobs of Waterford and Candahar) ...' *(14.1331–2)*
Frederick Sleigh Roberts was born in Cawnpore, India, on 30 September 1832. He was the son of General Sir Abraham Roberts (1784–1873) and his second wife, Isabella (née Bunbury) of Kilfeacle, Co. Tipperary.

Roberts was educated at Eton College, Sandhurst and Addiscombe. He entered the Bengal Artillery in 1851 and served through the Indian Mutiny and was awarded the Victoria Cross. In the summer of 1880 Roberts led the march mounted on his legendary Arab horse Vonolel from Kabul to Kandahar, to relieve the British garrison at Kandahar.

During the second Boer War in 1900, Roberts commanded the British forces in South Africa, relieving Kimberley (Cape Colony) and advancing on Pretoria. He was commander-in-chief in India from 1885 to 1893, and in 1895 was appointed commander-in-chief in Ireland and moved to Dublin where he was master of the Royal Hospital Kilmainham until 1900. In 1901 he was created earl and knight of the garter. He spent the latter years of his life living at Englemere, Ascot.

He contracted a chill when visiting troops on the front in the First World War and died three days later on 14 November 1914 in St Omer, France. He was buried in the crypt in St Paul's Cathedral, London. A statue of Lord Roberts mounted on Vonolel stands in Whitehall. He is also commemorated by a statue in Waterford.

Ulysses 18.378

Roberts, George (1872–1953) *Managing editor, Maunsel and Company*
'George Roberts is doing the commercial part.' *(9.301–2)*

George Roberts, son of Oliver Roberts and Margaret (née Gray), was born on 8 January 1872 in Castlewellan, Co. Down.

Roberts was a minor poet and actor with the Abbey Theatre. He was a founder member of the publishing house, Maunsel and Company (1905–23), with Stephen Gwynn and Joseph Maunsel Hone, from whom it derived its name. Roberts eventually became the managing editor.

Maunsel became infamous for its failure to publish *Dubliners* and its prolonged wrangle with Joyce.

Maunsel published over 500 titles which included works by W. B. Yeats, Hyde, Russell, Lady Gregory, Stephens, Colum, Shaw and Synge. It opened a branch in London but ran into financial difficulties. On its closure, Roberts worked for the Talbot Press before moving moving permanently to England in 1926, where he was employed for the publisher Victor Gollancz. His final job before he retired in 1950 was with the printing firm, Western Typesetting. Extracts from Robert's unpublished *Memoirs* were published in the *Irish Times* in July and August 1955.

Roberts died on 9 November 1953 at 44 Denning Road, London and was cremated at Golders Green.

Robinson, George Frederick Samuel (1827–1909)
English politician, statesman and marquess of Ripon
'... bearing 2000 torches in escort of the marquess of Ripon ...' *(17.1655–6)*
George Frederick Samuel Robinson Ripon, son of Lord Goderich and Lady Sarah (née Hobart), was born on 24 October 1827 at 10 Downing Street, London.

In 1853 Robinson entered the House of Commons as a Liberal for Hull. In 1859 he succeeded his father as earl of Ripon and Viscount Goderich and moved to the House of Lords. From 1863 to 1866 he served as secretary for war and was created marquess of Ripon in 1871.

Gladstone appointed Ripon as viceroy to India, a position he held from 1880 to 1884. In 1886 he was first lord of the admiralty and was secretary of state for the colonies 1892–5. In 1905 with the return of the Liberals to power, he took office as lord privy seal and leader of the House of Lords. He resigned in 1908 aged 81.

He was popular in Ireland as a supporter of Gladstone's Irish policies, including Home Rule. He died on 14 July 1909 at his home at Studley Royal, North Yorkshire, and was buried in St Mary's Church, Studley Royal Park.

Rochford, Thomas (1857–1934) *Mechanical engineer*
'Down went Tom Rochford anyhow, booky's vest and all, with the rope round him. And be damned but he got the rope round the poor devil and the two were hauled up.' *(10.500–2)*
Thomas Rochford was born in Dublin in 1857 and later lived at 2 Howth View, Sandymount. Howth View comprised of three houses, off Sandymount Road.

He later became known as 'Rochford of the Quay' as he was associated with the horrific Burgh Quay sewer disaster, which occurred on Saturday 6 May 1905 at the corner of Hawkins Street and Burgh Quay near the Scotch House (now demolished).

Constable Patrick Sheahan was on duty when his attention was drawn to a manhole on Burgh Quay. He suspected something was amiss below and descended the iron ladder to discover a sanitation worker overcome by sewer gas. The gas had also overcome a fellow worker, who went to rescue him. Before Sheahan could take action the gas overpowered him too.

Tom Rochford lowered himself with a rope and tied another around the other bodies before he too began to lose consciousness. He was hauled to safety and then the victims were brought up. Two of the men died, including Constable Sheahan.

Rochford had a number of addresses around Dublin, including 19 Wellington Quay and 22 East Essex Street, which he used to patent various inventions such as his 'programme indicators' for music halls and theatres. His last address was 24 Parliament Street.

When Rochford died on 21 February 1934 he had been retired for some years from the position of assistant main drainage engineer in Dublin Corporation. He was buried in Glasnevin Cemetery, Finglas Road, Dublin [HJ 166.5 St Patrick's].

Ulysses 8.989; 8.1001; 8.1010; 8.1014; 8.1035; 10.464; 10.481; 10.486; 10.1217–18; 11.429; 12.268; 15.1259; 15.1261; 15.4673

Rochfort, Mary (née Molesworth) (1720–c. 1790) *First countess of Belvedere*

'A listless lady, no more young, walked alone the shore of lough Ennel, Mary, first countess of Belvedere, listlessly walking in the evening, not startled when an otter plunged.' *(10.164–6)*

Mary Molesworth was born in Swords, Co. Dublin, the daughter of Richard Molesworth (1656–1758), 3rd Viscount Molesworth of Swords.

In 1736 Mary Molesworth married Colonel Robert Rochfort (1708–74), then Lord Bellfield. He was created 1st earl of Belvedere in 1753. They lived in the birthplace of her husband, Gaulstown House (also known as Gaulstown Park), the Rochfort estate near Lough Ennel in Co. Westmeath. They had five children, Jane, George, Richard, Robert and Arthur.

Mary was not destined to have a happy life. In 1743, she was maliciously accused of adultery with Arthur Rochfort, her brother-in-law, though apparently innocent. Her husband promised her a divorce if she admitted guilt. However, when she complied, he imprisoned her in Gaulstown House, where she remained a recluse in captivity for 31 years.

Robert Rochfort died in 1774. Mary instructed her son George, now the 2nd earl of Belvedere, to destroy all that belonged to him, including Gaulstown House. Robert Rochfort was interred in the family crypt at Christ Church, Gaulstown, on 19 November 1774. Mary was released and lived with her daughter Jane, now countess of Lanesbourough.

A second Gaulstown House was built on the original site. Mary eventually went to live with relations in France where she died *c.* 1790.

Gaulstown House was burned in 1922 and the Office of Public Works demolished what remained of it in 1970.

Rock, Patrick (1848–1933) *Head sheriff's bailiff*
'Rock, the head bailiff, standing at the bar blew the foamy crown from his tankard.' *(8.687–8)*
Patrick Rock, was born in Dublin and worked in the Head Sheriff's Office as bailiff. In 1907 he moved to 67 Connaught Street and remained there until 1909. In 1911 he lived at 45 Mountjoy Street, later moving to 48 Mountjoy Square where his wife Catherine died in 1921.

In January 1914 Rock gave evidence of decrees and executions against a Dublin man named McElroy charged with fraud. Mr Seymour Bushe, KC and Mr Dudley White were among those who appeared for the prisoner. Rock was probably known to Joyce through the family circumstances of frequent house moving.

Rock died on 21 January 1933 and was buried in Glasnevin Cemetery, Finglas Road, Dublin [SK 270 St Patrick's].   *Ulysses 10.935*

Rosales y O'Reilly
Composite Spanish/Irish name remembered by Molly from Gibraltar
'... Rosales y O Reilly in the Calle las Siete Revueltas ...' *(18.1465–6)*
Rosales and O'Reilly are two separate family names of people in Gibraltar. Calle las Siete Revueltas is known as City Mill Lane in English-speaking Gibraltar. This is the street, which Molly mentions, and both the name of Rosales and O'Reilly appear as people who were resident in this street.

James O'Reilly (d. 1933) *Gibraltar resident*
In the 1890s a James O'Reilly lived in House 29 Mill City Lane. A 'house' in this context means a courtyard-style building, the courtyard itself known locally as a patio. The building would contain several dwellings that would nowadays be called small flats, with communal/shared toilet facilities.

O'Reilly died on 28 March 1933 aged 59.

John Rosales (1874–1933) Tailor, Gibraltar

John Rosales was a tailor born in Gibraltar in 1874 who lived in House 29 City Mill Lane with his wife Victoria, born in 1877, daughter Araceli, born in 1901, and brother-in-law John Villa, a stoker born in 1883.

Rosenberg, Harris (b. 1844) *Neighbour of the Blooms*

Harris Rosenberg was born in Poland on 14 May 1844. He arrived in Dublin on 21 September 1895 and became a member of the Dublin Jewish community and worked as a dealer. He lived at 63 Lombard Street West, where he was a neighbour of the Blooms before later moving to 24 Lombard Street West. His wife Sarah was also born in Poland.

Ulysses 15.3222–3

Rothschild, Leopold de (1845–1917) *Banker and racehorse owner*

'... with financial resources (by supposition) surpassing those Rothschild or the silver king.' *(17.2022–3)*

Born on 22 November 1845, Leopold was the son of Lionel de Rothschild (1808–79) and his wife Charlotte. Educated at King's College School and Trinity College Cambridge, he joined the family banking business, N. M. Rothschild & Sons.

On the death of his uncle in 1874, Baron Mayer de Rothschild, he inherited Ascott House in Ascott, Buckinghamshire. Baron Leopold de Rothschild set up the Southcourt Stud in Bedfordshire and had some of the finest thoroughbred horses in Europe. His horses won a number of prestigious races including the Epsom Derby, St Leger Stakes and the 2,000 Guineas. He was the owner of the racehorses St Frusquin and St Amant, the 1904 Derby winner.

He died on 29 May 1917 and was buried in the family plot in Willesden Jewish Cemetery in North London.

Ulysses 8.831–2; 15.1848; 17.1748

Royce, Edward William (1841–1926) *English actor and stage manager*

'She heard old Royce sing in the pantomime of *Turko the Terrible* ...' *(1.257–8)*

Edward William Royce, was born in Eversholt, Bedfordshire in England on 11 August 1841. His real surname was Reddal. In 1860 he made his début at Covent Garden as a dancer in *Un Ballo in Maschera*.

In 1873 he appeared at the Gaiety Theatre in Dublin during Christmas week in *Turko the Terrible*, a pantomime by the Irish author Edwin Hamilton (1849–1919), adapted from William Brough's (1826–70) London pantomime, *Turko the Terrible; or, the Fairy Roses*. Jack B. Hall of the *Freeman's Journal* wrote that this was the best pantomime ever produced at the theatre.

Royce was under the D'Oyly Carte management for a short period in 1876 when he appeared as Ulric in *The Duke's Daughter* and Job Wort in *A Blighted Being* at the Royalty, Globe and Charing Cross theatres.

In 1882 Royce left the stage for a time due to ill health. In 1886 he travelled to Australia where he appeared in comedy, burlesque and drama. On his return to England he worked as an actor, choreographer and director. He died in London on 24 January 1926.

Rubio, Mrs *Housekeeper of the Tweedy family in Gibraltar*
'... pity I never tried to read that novel cantankerous Mrs Rubio lent me by Valera ...' *(18.1474–5)*
Rubio is a very common Spanish name in Gibraltar. There are several women named 'Maria Rubio' in the *Census of Gibraltar, 1901*, all of whom were housekeepers or servants.   *Ulysses 18.748; 18.785*

Rublin/Ruhlin, Mrs Gus (b. 1878) *Campaigner for women's suffrage*
'Unsolicited testimonials ... My bust developed four inches in three weeks, reports Mrs Gus Rublin with photo.' *(15.3257–9)*
Sarah Mulrooney, daughter of James Mulrooney and Eliza (née Rooney), was born in Sligo. She moved to New York in 1898 and stayed in Brooklyn with a relative. By 1900 she was working at the Manhattan State Hospital.

Sarah married Gus Ruhlin (not Rublin), aka 'the Akron Giant' who was a well-known boxer. Ruhlin appeared at an exhibition fight in Dublin in August 1902. On his return to the States, he set up a saloon at Myrtle Avenue, Brooklyn at the corner of Irving Avenue, where they lived.

Sarah Mulrooney now Mrs Gus Ruhlin was involved with the New York Woman Suffrage Party but after a disagreement left to set up her own party, the Progressive Political Party.

She received a lot of publicity over the years due to her initiatives in various roles. Her husband died in February 1912. In 1922 she was involved in a demonstration outside the British embassy in Washington with Terence Mac Swiney's widow following his death while on hunger strike in Brixton Prison.

Rumbold, Harry *Barber/hangman*
Based on **Sir Horace Rumbold (1869–1941)** *British diplomat*
'Quietly, unassumingly Rumbold stepped on to the scaffold in faultless morning dress and wearing his favourite flower, the *Gladiolus Cruentus*.' *(12.592–3)*
Sir Horace Rumbold, son of Horace Rumbold, 8th baronet, was born on 5 February 1869 and was educated at Eton College. He was the British minister to Switzerland in 1918. Joyce borrowed Rumbold's name to use for the barber/hangman Harry Rumbold.

Rumbold was an enemy of Joyce due to the conflict with the 'English Players' group in Zurich and his following unsuccessful lawsuit. Joyce used Rumbold's name to repay old scores.   *Ulysses 12.430; 15.1177; 15.1182–3; 15.4536; 15.4555*

Russell, George (Æ) (1867–1935) *Mystic, poet, painter and editor*

'With the approval of the eminent poet, Mr Geo. Russell'. *(8.526–7)*

The son of Thomas and Marianne Russell, George Russell, or Æ as he was commonly known, was born in Lurgan, Co. Armagh. A prominent figure in the Irish Literary Revival, he was poet, painter, mystic, organiser of the cooperative movement, economist and editor. He was educated at Power's School in Harrington Street, Dr C. W. Benson's School in Rathmines, and the Metropolitan School of Art in Kil-

dare Street, Dublin. He worked for a time as a clerk with Messrs Pim Bros, a drapers in South Great George's Street.

In 1890 he became a member of the Theosophical Society and five years later joined the Irish Literary Society, the aim of which was to advance and promote a new school of literature, which would be singularly Irish although written in the English language. In 1897 he joined the Irish Agricultural Organisation Society founded by Sir Horace Plunkett to integrate the work of the Irish cooperatives. He became the editor of its magazine, the *Irish Homestead*, and later editor of the *Irish Statesman*, which replaced the former publication.

He was vice-chairman of the Irish National Theatre, which was founded in 1902 with W. B. Yeats as president. Æ is associated mostly with his house at 17 Rathgar Avenue where he lived for 25 years and held lively literary gatherings on Sunday evenings.

His wife Violet died in 1931 and the following year Æ moved to London. He spent the remainder of his life travelling abroad and giving lectures. He died in Bournemouth on 17 July 1935. He was buried in Mount Jerome Cemetery, Harold's Cross, Dublin [A76–401–11217].

Ulysses 2.257; 8.332; 9.46; 9.104; 9.181; 9.290; 9.311; 9.316; 9.813; 10.812; 14.524

Russell, Thomas O'Neill (1828–1908) *Author and Celtic revivalist*

'O'Neill Russell? O, yes, he must speak the grand old tongue.' *(9.311)*

Thomas O'Neill Russell was born in Moate, Co. Westmeath. He was educated locally and then worked for Jacobs, the biscuit manufacturers, as a commercial traveller.

Russell was a founder member of the Gaelic League. One of his main aims was the revival of the Irish language. He attended all the meetings of the National Literary Society and was the author of many papers read at its meetings. A great admirer of Thomas Moore, he brought out a new edition, with notes of his own, of Archbishop MacHale's Gaelic version of Moore's *Melodies*. He also wrote a popular novel, *Dick Massey* (1860).

Fearing arrest on account of his association with the *Irishman*, a nationalist paper, Russell went to America in 1867, where he remained for almost 30 years. He wrote and lectured on the Irish language and was also connected with the *Chicago Citizen*. In 1882 he contributed an article, on 'Gaelic letters', to *Irisleabhar na Gaedhilge*. On his return to Dublin in 1895, he continued his work for the revival of Irish, and contributed articles to the *Freeman's Journal* on historic Irish places.

He died on 15 June 1908 in Synge Street, Dublin and was buried in Mount Jerome Cemetery, Harold's Cross, Dublin [C43–2859].

Rutland, Roger Manners (1576–1612) *5th earl of Rutland*
'Herr Bleibtreu, the man Piper met in Berlin, who is working up that Rutland theory, believes that the secret is hidden in the Stratford monument.' *(9.1073–5)*
Roger Manners, 5th earl of Rutland, was born on 6 October 1576. Educated at Oxford, Cambridge, Gray's Inn and the University of Padua, he travelled across Europe and took part in Essex's campaigns against Elizabeth I.

On 5 March 1599 Manners married Elizabeth, daughter of Sir Philip Sidney. Favoured by James I, Manners was a friend of many of the leading artists and writers of the Elizabethan-Jacobean age.

The German writer and critic Karl Bleibtreu theorised that Roger Manners wrote Shakespeare's plays.

Roger Manners died on 26 June 1612 aged 35 and his tomb is in St Mary the Virgin's Church at Bottesford, Leicestershire.

Ruttledge, Wilson Ormsby (1853–1918)
Business manager of the Freeman's Journal
'The door of Ruttledge's office creaked again.' *(7.28)*
Wilson Ormsby Ruttledge was born on 30 June 1853 in Co. Mayo. He was the eldest son of William Ruttledge of Ballyhowly, Claremorris, and Elizabeth (née Gray), a sister of Sir John Gray, founder of the *Freeman's Journal*. Both the Grays and Ruttledges were prominent landowning families.

Ruttledge, a convert to Catholicism, married Annie M. J. Martin, eldest daughter of John Martin, of 'Humevile', Rathmines and formerly of Enniscorthy, Co. Wexford. The marriage was performed on 8 August 1885 in the Church Our Lady of Refuge, Rathmines, by the Rev. M. A. Canon Fricker. The Ruttledges were married for nine years and had three sons and six daughters.

They lived at a number of addresses in the Rathgar and Rathmines area, which included 29 Leinster Road West (1889–9), 18 Stamer Street (1890–1) and 25 Garville Avenue (1893–5). This is the house where Annie Ruttledge died in September 1894. In 1893 the Ruttledges had an additional address at 1 Martello Terrace, Bray, where the Joyce family lived (1887–91). The Ruttledges subsequently moved to 65 Moyne Road, in Ranelagh and then to 120 Rathmines, which is now

Rathmines Road Upper.

Ruttledge is described as 'cashier of the newspaper' and 'advertising manager' and held a senior position with the *Freeman's Journal* on account of his connection with the Gray family.

Wilson Ruttledge died on 23 March 1918. At the date of his death his address was given as 'Highfield', Bassalegh, Newport, Co. Mayo. He was buried in Glasnevin Cemetery, Finglas Road, Dublin [ZG 111.5 Section 4].   *Ulysses 7.50; 11.965*

Ryan, Frederick (1876–1913) *Socialist, playwright and journalist*
'Fred Ryan wants space for an article on economics.' *(9.1082–3)*
Frederick Ryan was born in Dublin. In 1904 with William Kirkpatrick Magee, the pseudonym of John Eglinton, he launched and edited the short-lived *Dana*, an important magazine of the literary movement. He and Frank Fay founded the Irish National Theatre of which he was secretary for some years. His only play, *The Laying of the Foundations*, was performed here in December 1902.

Ryan contributed work to *Dana*, *New Age* and other periodicals, under his own name or under the pseudonyms of 'Irial' and 'Finian'. He was unable to make a living from journalism, so he worked in an accountant's office and devoted his free time to journalism.

He lived at 152 Leinster Road, Rathmines. From 1905 to 1907 he worked in Alexandria as editor of the *Egyptian Standard*. During this time he published a book *Criticism and Courage and Other Essays* (1906). Early in 1907, assisted by Francis Sheehy-Skeffington, he founded the *National Democrat*, a penny monthly, but it lasted only seven months. He then went to London where he edited *Egypt* for Wilfrid Blunt.

Ryan spent his final two years in Dublin. He lived with his two sisters and brother at 152 Leinster Road, Rathmines, and wrote frequently for the *Irish Nation*. He was the leading light in the reorganisation of the Dublin Socialist Party. After his return to London, he spent his holidays in Ireland, lecturing to the Dublin societies in which he was interested.

He died while visiting Wilfrid Blunt in Horsham, England on 7 April 1913 and was buried in Crawley Down Monastery, Crawley, West Sussex.

Ulysses 2.256; 9.322; 9.1084

Salmon, Dr George (1819–1904) *Provost of Trinity College Dublin*

'Provost's house. The reverend Dr Salmon: tinned salmon. Well tinned in there.'
(8.496–7)

George Salmon was born in Cork on 25 September 1819. He was educated at Mr Porter's School, Cork, and Trinity College Dublin.

Salmon was awarded a doctor of divinity in 1859 and was professor of divinity 1866–88. He became provost of Trinity College in 1888 and remained so until his death. During the 1870s he played an important part in the reconstruction of the Church of Ireland after Disestablishment and his strong Protestant views are expressed in his publication, *The Infallibility of the Church* (1889). He wrote four advanced mathematical textbooks.

Salmon died on 22 January 1904 in the Provost's House and was buried in the family vault in Mount Jerome Cemetery, Harold's Cross, Dublin [Vault C92–999].

He is commemorated by a marble statue by John Hughes in the quadrangle near the campanile in Trinity.

Sandow, Eugen (1867–1925) *Performing strongman and author*

'Must begin again those Sandow's exercises.' *(4.234)*

Eugen Sandow, often referred to as the 'Father of Modern Bodybuilding', was born Friederich Wilhelm Müller in Königsberg, Germany, on 2 April 1867. He was one of the earliest athletes to develop his musculature to predetermined dimensions. At the age of 19 he was performing strongman feats in sideshows. He was hired by the legendary Florenz Ziegfeld for his carnival show and became a star.

Sandow performed in America and all over Europe. He performed in Dublin at the Empire Theatre in

Dame Street from 2 to 14 May 1898. He was billed as the: 'Strongest man on earth! Perfect Embodiment of the Human Form; Greatest Living Authority on Physical Culture whose Colossal Feats of Strength have astounded Civilisation in Both Hemispheres.'

Sandow wrote five books, one of which, *Physical Strength and How to Obtain It* (1897), was included in Bloom's library.

Sandow died on 14 October 1925. He was buried in Putney Vale Cemetery, south-west London.   *Ulysses 17.1397; 17.1817*

Sankey, Ira D. (1840–1908) *Hymnist, gospel singer and composer*

'He infinitely preferred the sacred music of the catholic church to anything the opposite shop could offer in that line such as those Moody and Sankey hymns ...' *(16.1740–2)*

Ira D. Sankey was born on 28 August 1840 in Edinburgh, Pennsylvania. He became a celebrated gospel singer and came to the attention of the evangelist Dwight Moody (1837–99).

Sankey met Moody in 1871 and they travelled around the United States and Sweden, preaching and singing. Moody preached and Sankey sang. In 1873 they made the first of several joint trips to the United Kingdom.

Sankey died in Brooklyn on 13 August 1908.

Sayers, Tom (1826–1865) *English boxing champion*

'Myler dusted the floor with him ... Heenan and Sayers was only a bloody fool to it.' *(12.955–6)*

Tom Sayers was born in Brighton. His career took off as a prizefighter when he was 23. By the age of 31 he had won the heavyweight title of England, defeating William Perry.

On 7 April 1860 Sayers fought the American John Heenan in Farnborough, England. The match lasted for two hours and 20 minutes. There were 37 rounds, each round ending when one of the boxers was knocked down. Sayers's right arm was injured and when the American party invaded the ring, the bout was declared a draw.

This remarkable fight put an end to bare-fist prizefighting in England. After this, boxing was permitted only under the Marquess of Queensberry Rules, which were formulated six years later.

Sayers's career spanned from 1849 to 1860 and he was the first boxer to be declared the world heavyweight champion. On his retirement he lived in Camden Town in London.

He died aged 39 and was buried at Highgate Cemetery, London. His grave is marked with a memorial, which includes a statue of his faithful hound, Lion.

Scaife, C. (*fl.* late 1800s–early1900s) *Cyclist*
C. Scaife was one of the nine quartermile flat handicappers who took part in the Trinity College bicycle races in the afternoon of 16 June 1904.   *Ulysses 10.1259*

Scally, Rev. Michael D. (1843–1923) *Parish priest, Church of St Nicholas of Myra*
Michael D. Scally was born in September 1843 in Ballyshannon in south Donegal. He entered Holy Cross College, Clonliffe, Dublin, in September 1862 and was ordained priest in 1869. He worked initially in St Andrews's Catholic Church in Westland Row, Dublin and was transferred to the Church of St Nicholas of Myra, Francis Street, where he worked as administrator from 1892 until 1895. He was then promoted parish priest and remained in this parish for the remainder of his life.
    He died on 6 September 1923 and was buried in Glasnevin Cemetery, Finglas Road, Dublin [E 34 Section 13].   *Ulysses 12.936*

Sebastian, Father (1832–91) *Passionist father*
'... Father Sebastian of Mount Argus ...' *(17.2140)*
Sebastian Keens, son of Henry and Mary Keens, was born in London. He came to Dublin in 1858 and was member of the Passionist Community at Mount Argus for almost 33 years. For many years he was director of the Confraternity of the Passion, which he had introduced into Ireland.
    A well-known preacher, Father Sebastian gave retreats and missions all over Ireland and wrote a number of popular prayer manuals. He raised funds to pay off the monastery debts.
    He died on 28 September 1891 and was buried in the community graveyard, at St Paul's Retreat, Mount Argus, Harold's Cross, Dublin.

Seddon, Frederick Henry (1870–1912) *Murderer*
'Phial containing arsenic retrieved from body of Miss Barron which sent Seddon to the gallows.' *(15.4541–2)*
In 1909 Frederick Seddon purchased a house at 63 Tollington Park, London, and advertised the second floor of his house to let.
    Eliza Barrow, a neighbour, moved in with the Seddons on 26 July 1910 with her ten-year-old ward, Ernest Grant, the nephew of a friend. Barrow was moderately wealthy, having £1,500 of India Stock plus other savings. Frederick Seddon enticed her to sign over to him a controlling interest in all her assets. In return he would look after her for life, provide free accommodation and give her a small annuity.
    Miss Barrow (not Barron as spelled in *Ulysses*) became ill with stomach pains and died on 14 September 1911. She was buried hurriedly in a common grave. Initially it was thought that she died of epidemic diarrhoea but, when her cousin

Frank Vonderahe became suspicious, her body was exhumed on 15 November 1911. It was found to contain arsenic.

Frederick Seddon was found guilty of her murder and was hanged on 18 April 1912.

Seymour, Robert Francis (1882–1939) *Student and friend of Buck Mulligan*
'Seymour's back in town … Chucked medicine and going in for the army.' *(1.695–6)*
Robert Francis Seymour, son of the Rev. Robert Seymour, was born on 23 October 1882 in Armagh. He was educated at the Royal School, Armagh; St Columba's College, Dublin; and Campbell College, Belfast. In 1900 he entered Trinity College Dublin where he obtained a BA degree in 1904 and an MD in 1907.

Seymour worked in London at St Mary's and King's College Hospitals and in 1912 was appointed a medical inspector of the local government board. During the First World War he was responsible for the health of troops, rising to be a major in the Royal Army Medical Corps and receiving the Médaille du Roi Albert. After the war, his work at the Ministry of Health was concerned with tuberculosis, and later with water supplies and the administration of the Food and Drugs Acts.

Early in 1939 Seymour was promoted to principal regional medical officer for the south-west region of England. He was renowned for his great zest and energy and for his varied literary and scholarly interests. He died in Harley Street, London on 7 June 1939 and was cremated at Golders Green Crematorium.

Ulysses 1.163; 1.702–3

Sharon, Larby/Larie (b. 1863) *Merchant and grocer*
'… and the fowl market all clucking outside Larby Sharons …' *(18.1589–90)*
Larby or Larie Sharon, the correct name, was born in Tangier, Morocco, in 1863. He lived at 36 Engineer Lane, Gibraltar, with his cousin Mohamet, who was born in Tangier in 1872. They were dealers in eggs and later in poultry and had a business in Gibraltar. This is the shop that Molly remembers.

Their business was first advertised in the *Gibraltar Directory* in 1912. Located in the Moorish Market, it provided fowls, eggs and game, wholesale and retail, and boasted of devoting the 'best attention to orders'.

Shaw, George Bernard (1856–1950) *Playwright*
'And we ought to mention another Irish commentator, Mr George Bernard Shaw.' *(9.439–40)*
George Bernard Shaw, son of George Shaw and Elizabeth (née Gurly), was born on 26 July 1856 in 3 Upper Synge Street (now 33 Synge Street), Dublin. His parents eventually separated. He was educated at the Wesleyan Connexional School at St Stephen's Green South, the Central Model Boys' School in Marlborough Street and the Dublin Scientific and Commercial Day School in Aungier Street.

In October 1871 he worked in the offices of Messrs Charles Uniake and Thomas Courtney Townshend, land agents, 15 Molesworth Street, and was made chief cashier.

In 1872 George Vandeleur Lee, Mrs Shaw's music teacher, left for London, followed by Mrs Shaw. Shaw remained with his father at 61 Harcourt Street for two years, during which time he frequented the theatre, concert halls and the National Gallery of Ireland. In 1876 he went to London and earned virtually nothing between his twenty-first and thirtieth year, relying solely on his mother's support.

In 1885 he reviewed books for the *Pall Mall Gazette* and was art critic for *The World*. He was music editor for the *Star* using the pen name Corno di Bassetto and was drama critic for the *Saturday Review*.

He wrote over 50 plays and in 1926 was awarded the Nobel Prize in Literature. He was made an honorary freeman of Dublin in 1946.

Shaw's home for 40 years was at Ayot St Lawrence, Hertfordshire, where he died on 2 November 1950 aged 94. He was cremated on 23 November and his ashes, mixed with those of his wife, were scattered on the gardens of his home.

Shaw is commemorated by a statue in Dublin's National Gallery of Ireland, to which he left a third of his royalties.

Ulysses 12.1330–2; The Dark Lady of the Sonnets, 9.430–40; John Bull's Other Island, 16.1003

Sheares, Henry (1753–98) *Barrister and United Irishman*
'And the citizen and Bloom having an argument about the point, the brother Sheares and Wolfe Tone beyond on Arbour Hill ...' *(12.498–9)*
Henry Sheares was born in Cork, son of a banker and MP. Educated at Trinity College Dublin, he was called to the Bar in 1790. He served in the British army for three years but resigned and joined the United Irishmen at the instigation of his brother John. They were both executed in front of Newgate Prison in Green Street on the morning of 14 July 1798 and interred in the vaults of St Michan's Church, Church Street, Dublin.   *Ulysses 12.69–70; 12.538–9*

Sheares, John (1766–98) *Barrister and United Irishman*
John Sheares was born in Cork. He was educated at Trinity College Dublin and graduated in 1787. He was called to the Bar the same year. He visited France in 1792 and became inspired with the political ideology of the revolution. On his return to Dublin, he joined the United Irishmen and wrote for *The Press*, a nationalist newspaper. He revealed his plans to a Captain Armstrong of the militia, who informed on him. He was arrested on 21 May 1798 and found guilty of high treason. He was executed in public with his brother Henry on 14 July 1798 in front of Newgate Prison in Green Street.

He was interred in the vaults of St Michan's Church, Church Street, Dublin.

Ulysses 12.69–70; 12.498–9; 12.538–9

Sheehy, David (1844–1932) *Irish Nationalist MP*

'Still David Sheehy beat him for south Meath.' *(8.514–15)*

David Sheehy, son of Richard Sheehy, was born in Broadford, Co. Limerick. He was educated at the Jesuit school in Limerick and the Irish College in Paris.

He founded a milling business at Loughmore, near Templemore, Co. Tipperary, where he raised a family. His brother, the Rev. Eugene Sheehy, was known as 'the Land League Priest'.

Sheehy, a supporter of the Irish Republican Brotherhood and the Land League, was elected Nationalist MP for South Galway (1885–1900), and stood against and defeated John Howard Parnell for the seat of South Meath, 1903–8. During the Plan of Campaign, he served 18 months in prison. In the crisis over Parnell's leadership in December 1890, he opposed Parnell's continuing in office, thinking it would endanger the tenant farmers' fight for fair rent. He lived at 2 Belvidere Place, Dublin, adjacent to Fitzgibbon Street.

He died on 17 December 1932 and was buried in Glasnevin Cemetery, Finglas Road, Dublin [AA 25.5 South].   *Ulysses 10.17*

Sheehy, Mrs (1847–1918) *Wife of David Sheehy, MP*

'Good afternoon, Mrs Sheehy.' *(10.29)*

Bessie Sheehy (née McCoy) was born in Co. Limerick. She was the wife of David Sheehy, MP and lived at 2 Belvidere Place, Dublin. Their family consisted of two boys, Richard and Eugene, and four girls, Margaret, Hanna, Kathleen and Mary. All six children later figured prominently in the public life of the country. Hanna Sheehy married Francis Skeffington, who appears as McCann in *Ulysses*. She died on 1 January 1918 at Windsor House, Windsor Road, Rathmines and was buried in Glasnevin Cemetery, Finglas Road, Dublin [AA 25.5 South].   *Ulysses 10.17; 10.26*

Sherlock, Lorcan (1874–1945) *Secretary to Dublin Corporation and later lord mayor*

'... and Hutchinson, the lord mayor, in Llandudno and little Lorcan Sherlock doing *locum tenens* for him.' *(10.1010–11)*

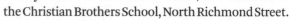

Lorcan Sherlock, son of Dublin city councillor Thomas Sherlock, was educated at

the Christian Brothers School, North Richmond Street.

In 1904 Sherlock was secretary to John Clancy, high sheriff of Dublin, and later secretary of the Dublin Cattle Traders' Association. In 1905 he had a tobacconist business in Summerhill, Dublin. He was elected a Dublin city councillor for the Mountjoy Ward, 1905–6. Three years later he became chairman of the City Council's Improvements Committee. At the time he lived in St Lawrence's Road, Clontarf.

In 1912 Sherlock was elected lord mayor. The same year, he was conferred with an honorary doctorate from Dublin University. He was re-elected lord mayor in 1913, 1914 and 1915. Apart from the Mansion House, he had his own residence at 18 Rathdown Terrace, North Circular Road, and had a business address at 24 Upper Ormond Quay.

In 1920 he was elected alderman for Mountjoy Ward. He resigned in 1921, but remained sheriff until 1944. Following his retirement from political life, Sherlock became involved in various commercial interests. He was chairman of Messrs Todd Burns and Co. and was a director of Cable and Wireless and associated companies for over 20 years.

He died on 24 December 1945 at his residence, 81 Park Avenue, Sandymount, and was buried in Deansgrange Cemetery, Deansgrange, Co. Dublin [125–E–St Patrick].   *Ulysses 15.1379–80*

Shrift, H. (*fl.* late 1800s–early 1900s) *Cyclist*
H. Shrift was one of the nine quartermile flat handicappers who took part in the Trinity College bicycle races in the afternoon of 16 June 1904.   *Ulysses 10.1259*

Shulomowitz, M. (1877–1940) *Librarian at the Jewish Library in Dublin*
'Darkshawled figures of the circumcised, in sackcloth and ashes, stand by the wailing wall, M. Shulomowitz ...' (15.3220–2)
Isaac Myer Shulomowitz (or M. Shmulovitch), son of Israel Shmulovitch was born in Lithuania, and was librarian of the Jewish Library at 57 Lombard Street West. He was a neighbour of the Blooms when they were living in the same street in the old Jewish neighbourhood of Dublin in 1892. He also lived at 4 Spencer Street and 7 Vincent Street in the same area.

Shmulowitz was a drapery traveller and the Dublin correspondent of the London Hebrew weekly, *Haychudi*. He left for South Africa in 1904 but returned some years later settling in Cork. He married Anna Elyan, daughter of the Rev. Meyer Elyan, who was minister of the Cork congregation. He died on 17 June 1940 and was buried in the Cork Jewish Cemetery.

Sigerson, Dr George (1836–1925) *Physician, poet and translator*
'Our national epic has yet to be written, Dr Sigerson says.' (9.309)
George Sigerson, son of William Sigerson and Nancy (née Neilson), was born on 11 January 1836 at Holy Hill, Strabane, Co. Tyrone. He was educated at Letterkenny Academy, Queen's College Galway and Queen's College Cork, where he graduated in medicine in 1859. He did further study in Paris under Charcot and Duchenne, and on his return to Dublin started his medical pratice.

In 1865 Sigerson married novelist Hester Varian, and they lived at 17 Richmond Hill, Rathmines, where their three children, George, Dora (the poet) and Hester were born. They later moved to 3 Clare Street.

Sigerson was Dublin's first neurologist and was professor of botany and zoology at the Catholic University. He wrote political and literary articles for the *Freeman's*

Journal, *The Irishman*, *The North British Review* and other periodicals. His books include *The Poets and Poetry of Munster* (1860), *Bards of the Gael and Gall* (1897), *The Last Independent Parliament of Ireland* (1919), *The Easter-Song of Sedulius* (1922) and *Songs and Poems* (1927).

Fellow of the Royal University, Sigerson was a founder member of the Feis Ceoil and was president of the National Literary Society from 1893 until 1925. He was a member of the Dublin Lodge of the Theosophical Society and was included among the first members of the Irish Free State senate.

He died on 17 February 1925 at 3 Clare Street, Dublin and was buried in Glasnevin Cemetery, Finglas Road, Dublin [E 28 O'Connell Circle].

Simnel, Lambert (*c.* 1475–*c.* 1534) *Yorkist pretender to the throne of England*
'... and Lambert Simnel, with a tail of nans and sutlers, a scullion crowned.'
(3.315–16)
With Perkin Warbeck, Simnel was one of the two impostors who threatened the rule of King Henry VII.

Simnel was crowned 'King Edward VI' in Christ Church Cathedral in Dublin on 24 May 1487. He invaded England that same year and was captured by Henry VII at the Battle of Stoke in June. King Henry was lenient and pardoned him with a job in the royal kitchen. Simnel later became a royal falconer and died *c.* 1534.

Simpson, Georgina (1876–1955) *Friend of the Blooms*
'... the night of Georgina Simpsons housewarming ...' *(18.172–3)*
Georgina Simpson was born in Dublin on 29 May 1876. She was the daughter of Henry Irwin Simpson and Mary (née Fox).

She worked as a telegraphist and was a friend of the Blooms in their courtship days. In 1904 she lived at 127 Tritonville Road, Sandymount, with her widowed mother and brother Robert. They later moved to 16 Serpentine Terrace, Ballsbridge. She died in 1955. *Ulysses 15.443*

Sinclair, William (1882–1937) *Grandson of Morris Harris*
'Or will I drop into old Harris's and have a chat with young Sinclair? Well-mannered fellow.' *(8.552–3)*
William Sinclair, was the son of John Sinclair and Elizabeth (née Harris) and grandson of Morris Harris (1823–1909), dealer in works of art, plate and jewellery, at 30 Nassau Street, Dublin. He was raised a Jew at his grandfather's insistence and lived with his wife Frances (née Beckett) at 'Belgrove', Stillorgan Road, Booterstown, Co. Dublin. He died on 4 May 1937 and was buried in the Jewish Cemetery, Dolphin's Barn, Rialto, Dublin [21-A-45].

Smith, Philip Henry Law (1863–1920) *Barrister*
'... shunned the lamp before Mr Law Smith's house and, crossing, walked along Merrion square.' *(10.1103–4)*
Philip Henry Law Smith was the son of Philip Smith, JP, and Delia Mary (née Banahan), of Kevitt Castle, Co. Cavan. He was educated at St Patrick's College, Cavan, and Trinity College Dublin. He was called to the Bar in 1887 and took silk in 1906. He was senior crown prosecutor of the north-west circuit and was appointed county court judge of Limerick in May 1908. He co-authored with Judge Michael P. Drummond, *The Practice of the Supreme Court of Judicature in Ireland* (1889).

In 1904 Philip Law Smith's office was located at 14 Clare Street, Dublin. He lived at 22 Ailesbury Road, Dublin. He died in Bath, England, on 5 January 1920 and was buried in the Perrymead Catholic Cemetery, Bath.

Solomons, Maurice E. (1832–1922) *Optician*
'... stared through a fierce eyeglass across the carriages at the head of Mr M. E. Solomons in the window of the Austro-Hungarian viceconsulate.' *(10.1261–3)*
Maurice E. Solomons was born on 15 September 1832, son of Elias Solomons and Sophia (née Neuberg). His father was an an optician at 27 Old Bond Street in London and came on regular trips to Dublin in the 1830s before setting up a business there.

Maurice E. Solomons was an optician at 19 Nassau Street where he manufactured spectacles, mathematical and hearing instruments. He acted as the Austro-Hungarian vice-consulate from the same address. He was also a Freemason and a director of Messrs Bolands Ltd. He was president of the Dublin Hebrew Congregation at St Mary's Abbey. He married Rosa (née Jacobs) in 1876 and their daughter Estella Solomons, the landscape and portrait painter, married James Sullivan Starkey.

He died on 18 June 1922 at his home at 26 Waterloo Road, Dublin, and was buried at the Jewish Cemetery, Dolphin's Barn, Rialto, Dublin [11–A–03].

Sprague, Horatio Jones (1823–1901) *US consul, Gibraltar*
'... and old Sprague the consul that was there from before the flood ...' *(18.683–4)*
Horatio Jones Sprague was born in Gibraltar on 12 August 1823, son of Horatio Sprague and Victorine (née Flechelle).

He was educated privately in Gibraltar and in 1846 became his father's partner. Shortly after his father's death on 20 March 1848, he succeeded him as consul. He represented the US in Gibraltar for 53 years until 1901.

One of the oldest consuls in the service of the United States at the time, Sprague died on 18 July 1901 at his residence, 34 Prince Edward's Road, Gibraltar and was buried in the North Front Cemetery.

Stanhope, Hester *Molly's friend in Gibraltar*

Based on **Emily Lyons** (*c.* 1881) *Friend of Nora Barnacle*

'... faded all that lovely frock fathers friend Mrs Stanhope sent me from the B Marche paris ...' *(18.612–13)*

Emily Lyons, from Abbeygate Street, Galway was a childhood friend of Nora Barnacle. Described as a domestic (servant) who could read and write, she left Galway aged 14 on board a sailing ship for Boston to join her mother in August 1895.

Steevens, Grissel (*c.* 1654–1747) *Founder of Dr Steevens's Hospital*

'... swineheaded (the case of Madame Grissel Steevens was not forgotten) ...' *(14.986–7)*

Grissel Steevens, daughter of John and Constance Steevens, was a twin of Richard

Steevens, the noted Dublin physician. On his death on 15 December 1710, Grissel inherited a large estate for her lifetime. His wish was that on her death any residue would be used to found a hospital in Dublin for the sick and poor. Grissel decided to build the hospital in her lifetime and to keep £100 a year for herself. This was the first public hospital founded in Dublin.

The hospital, which included a colonnaded walk and a clock tower, was designed by Thomas Burgh, who died just before it was finished. Edward Lovett Pearse supervised the completion of the hospital, which opened in 1733.

Madame Grissel as she was known, was a large lady and always went veiled in public. It was whispered she did this to hide her face, which (it was rumoured) resembled that of a pig. There was no foundation for this myth.

Grissel died on 18 March 1747 and left her estate to the governors of the hospital. She was interred in the hospital chapel. The hospital closed in 1987.

Ulysses 15.3867

Stephens, Davy (1845–1925) *News vendor*

'Davy Stephens, minute in a large capecoat, a small felt hat crowning his ringlets, passed out with a roll of papers under his cape, a king's courier.' *(7.28–30)*

Davy Stephens, or Sir Davy, as he was known, was one of the Dublin characters of the time. Known 'as prince of the news vendors', he started work aged six, selling copies of *Saunder's Newsletter* to support his widowed mother.

For 60 Years he operated from the steps of the railway station at Kingstown (now Dún Laoghaire), attending to the arrival and departure of the mail boats selling newspapers to passengers that included monarchs, viceroys and prime ministers.

In 1911 Davy Stephens was living at 33 Upper George's Street, Kingstown where he then ran a stationery business. He died on 10 September 1925 at 5 Anglesea Buildings, Dún Laoghaire and was buried in Deansgrange Cemetery, Deansgrange, Co. Dublin [2–T–North].   *Ulysses 15.1122*

Stephens, James (1825–1901) *Chief organiser of the Fenian Society*
'James Stephen's idea was the best. He knew them. Circles of ten so that a fellow couldn't round on more than his own ring.' *(8.457–8)*

James Stephens was born in Kilkenny in 1825 and trained as a civil engineer. He joined the Young Ireland movement and took part in the 1848 rising at Ballingarry, where he was wounded.

He escaped to France and on his return to Ireland founded the Irish Republican Brotherhood, or the Fenian movement. He was the chief organiser of the Fenian Society.

In 1858 he went to America to raise funds and in 1863 founded the *Irish People* to promote the Fenian cause. Stephens assured his American associates that he would lead a rising in 1865 but he postponed the action due to a disagreement that delayed the delivery of arms. He was arrested and imprisoned in the Richmond Bridewell in Dublin. He escaped shortly afterwards and went into hiding before making his way to Paris and then New York.

Denounced by the American Fenians as 'a rogue, imposter and traitor', Stephens returned to Paris, where he earned a living by teaching and through journalism. In 1886 he returned to Dublin where friends raised a public subscription for him.

He died in Blackrock, Co. Dublin, on 29 April 1901 and was buried in Glasnevin Cemetery, Finglas Road, Dublin [RD 40 South New Chapel].

Ulysses 2.272; 3.241; 4.491; 8.457–61; 12.881; 15.1534; 16.1052

Stephens, James (1880–1950) *Poet, novelist and short-story writer*
'James Stephens is doing some clever sketches.' *(9.312)*
James Stephens, son of Francis Stephens and Charlotte (née Collins), was born on 9 February 1880 at 5 Thomas Court, off Thomas Street in Dublin. Shortly after his birth, the family moved to 5 Artisan's Dwellings, off Buckingham Street, where his father died when James was two years old.

Aged six he was committed to the Meath Industrial School in Carysfort

Avenue, Blackrock, and remained for ten years. He was small and agile and one of his early ambitions was to become an acrobat 'like one of Dan Lowry's acrobats on the Olympia stage'.

When he finished his schooling, Stephens lived in York Street, Dublin, and learned shorthand and typing. He began to contribute articles and poems to the *United Irishman* in 1905.

His collection of poems, *Insurrections* was published in 1909. This was followed in 1912 by two novels, *The Charwoman's Daughter*, a portrait of Dublin slum life and poverty, and *The Crock of Gold*, considered to be his finest work.

In 1912 he went to Paris and on his return in 1915 was appointed registrar of the National Gallery of Ireland. In 1916, he published *The Insurrection of Dublin*, an account of the Easter Rising. In 1924 he resigned his post in the National Gallery and following a lecture tour in the United States, established himself as a broadcaster with the BBC in London.

His final book, *Kings and the Moon*, was published in 1938. In 1942 Stephens was put on the British Civil Pension List. He was awarded a D. Litt by the University of Dublin (Trinity College) in October 1947.

He died on the 26 December 1950 and was interred in Kingsbury Old Graveyard in north London.

Sterling, Antoinette (1850–1904) *Contralto*

'... its musicrest supporting the music in the key of G natural for voice and piano of *Love's Old Sweet Song* (words by G. Clifton Bingham, composed by J. L. Molloy, sung by Madam Antoinette Sterling) ...' *(17.1306–9)*

Antoinette Sterling was born in Sterlingville in Jefferson County, New York, on 23 January 1850. She studied singing for two years in America and in 1873 travelled to

England where she appeared at Covent Garden. Sterling was popular in Britain and Ireland and was especially known for her ballad singing. She also sang German and classical songs. On one occasion Gounod asked her to sing for him. After she had sang the final chord of 'The Better Land' he approached her, kissed her on both hands and remarked, 'I have heard every voice of any repute throughout the whole world, but this one was unique.'

Madam Antoinette Sterling's image appeared on the sheet music of 'Love's Old Sweet Song'. She died at her home in Hampstead, London on 10 January 1904 and was cremated at Golder's Green.

Stevenson, F. (*fl.* late 1800s–early 1900s) *Cyclist*

F. Stevenson was one of the nine quartermile flat handicappers who took part in the Trinity College bicycle races in the afternoon of 16 June 1904.   *Ulysses 10.1259*

Stoer, John Martin (1824–1907) *Businessman*
'One of them mots that do be in the packets of fags Stoer smokes that his old fellow welted hell out of him for one time he found out.' *(10.1142–4)*
John Martin Stoer was the husband of Mrs Stoer, a neighbour of the Dignams, and lived at Newgrove House, 15 Newgrove Avenue, Sandymount. A German Lutheran, he was born in Bavaria in 1824. He was a chemical manufacturer and businessman and was manager of Dublin Tar Company Ltd, with offices at Hanover Quay. In 1891 he started a lager brewery at Dartry on the river Dodder, which he sold two years later.

Stoer died on 20 May 1907 and was buried in Mount Jerome Cemetery, Harold's Cross, Dublin [B20–206–4467].

Stoer, Mrs (1850–1944) *Neighbour of the Dignams*
'The night of the party long ago in Stoer's ...' *(13.200–1)*
Mrs Emile Stoer, also known as Emily, lived at Newgrove House, 15 Newgrove Avenue, Sandymount, with her husband John Martin and their five children, George Louis, Annie, Emily Pauline, Edmund Maxwell and Moira.

The Stoers were generous benefactors to Catholic causes and charities. Following her husband's death in 1907, Mrs Stoer and her daughters continued this work. They are mentioned regularly in newspapers in connection with local fund-raising events. These included the sale of work in St Matthew's Parish Church, Irishtown, on 1 December 1904, which was held to raise money for the erection of a new Roman Catholic church in Ringsend.

Mrs Stoer, who was 26 years younger than her husband, died in 1944.

Ulysses 10.1125–6; 10.1143

Stoker, Sir William Thornley (1845–1912) *Surgeon*
'Because he closed my carriage door outside sir Thornley Stoker's one sleety day ...' *(15.1029–30)*
William Thornley Stoker, son of Abraham Stoker and Charlotte (née Thornley) was born on 6 March 1845 in Marine Crescent, Clontarf. Educated at Wymondham Grammar School in Norfolk, the Royal College of Surgeons in Ireland and Queen's College Galway, he graduated in medicine in 1866. He was appointed surgeon to the Royal City of Dublin Hospital and in 1873 transferred to the Richmond Hospital. Three years later he became visiting surgeon to Swift's Hospital for the Insane, a position he held for life.

Stoker was professor of anatomy at the Royal College of Surgeons in Ireland 1876–89, and was president of the college, 1894–6. During his period in office he was conferred with a knighthood.

In 1904 Stoker lived at Ely House, 8 Ely Place, where his neighbours were George Moore and Oliver St John Gogarty. Due to ill health, he resigned from the Richmond Hospital in 1910. His wife Emily died that year. The following year he was created a baronet. He sold Ely House and moved to 21 Lower Hatch Street, Dublin.

He died on 1 June 1912 at Hatch Street and was buried in Mount Jerome Cemetery, Harold's Cross, Dublin [C79–11088].

Stratton, Eugene (1861–1918) *Music-hall dancer and singer*

'... under the railway bridge, past the Queen's theatre: in silence. Hoardings: Eugene Stratton, Mrs Bandmann Palmer.' *(6.183–5)* Eugene Stratton was the stage name of Eugene Augustus Ruhlmann, who was born on 8 May 1861 in Buffalo, New York. He started his career aged ten in an acrobatic act called the Two Welsleys. In 1881 he came to Britain with the Haverley's Minstrels. He joined the Moore & Burgess Minstrels and became the chief singer and dancer. He left in 1887 to join the Bristish music-hall circuit, first as part of a double act, and then solo.

Stratton became a music-hall star as a 'Negro impersonator' and specialised in 'coon songs'. On stage a single spotlight highlighted his face as he whistled refrains and danced in his soft shoes. He was described as 'a noiseless moving shadow'. In the *Freeman's Journal* for 16 June 1904, the Theatre Royal advertised a performance that evening for Eugene Stratton, 'the world renowned comedian, in a series of Recitals from his Celebrated Repertoire'.

Stratton died on 15 September 1918 in Christchurch, Hampshire, England and was buried in Bandon Hill Cemetery, Wallington, Surrey. *Ulysses 10.141; 10.1273; 15.410*

Stubbs, George Henry (1840–1908) *Overseer of public works, the Phoenix Park*
'Saw her in the viceregal party when Stubbs the park ranger got me in with Whelan of the *Express*.' *(8.352–3)*
George Henry Stubbs, eldest son of Thomas Stubbs, was born in England. He was the overseer of public works in Dublin's Phoenix Park until 1901 and lived with his wife, Elizabeth, in a house known as 'The Cottage', within the lands of the Viceregal Lodge (it was demolished some years ago). Stubbs was involved with the upkeep of various parks in Dublin, including the Rotunda Gardens.

On his retirement in 1901, he moved to 1 Cabra Lane, Castleknock, with his family. He died on 12 November 1908 at his residence, 'Villa Park', Cabra and was buried in Mount Jerome Cemetery, Harold's Cross, Dublin [A46–407–12971].

Sullivan, John L. (1858–1918) *World heavyweight boxing champion*
John L. Sullivan, the last of the bare-knuckle heavyweight champions, was born near Boston on 15 October 1858. He was the son of emigrant parents, Michael

Sullivan from Abbeydorney, Co. Kerry, and Katherine (née Kelly) from Athlone, Co. Westmeath.

On 7 February 1882, Sullivan became heavyweight champion of America when he beat Paddy Ryan, the reigning champion, in nine rounds in ten minutes in Mississippi city. He went on his first tour abroad in November 1887, arriving in Dublin on 11 December.

The high point of Sullivan's career was his victory over John Kilrain in a fight on 8 July 1889 held in Richburg, Mississippi, which ended after 75 rounds. On 7 September 1892, Sullivan lost the title of heavyweight champion of America to James J. Corbett, when he was knocked out in the twenty-first round in New Orleans.

Sullivan had a record of 35 wins, one loss and two draws, with 30 wins by knockout. He died on 2 February 1918 and was buried in the Old Calvary Cemetery in Mattapan, near Boston.   *Ulysses 12.187*

Swan, Brother William (1834–1911) *Director of the O'Brien Institute*
'Brother Swan was the person to see.' *(10.4–5)*

William Swan was born in Dublin and was educated at the Christian Brothers O'Connell School, North Richmond Street. At the age of 16, he entered the Christian Brothers novitiate, then at Mount Sion in Waterford. He became well known for his work educating the youth of Dublin.

Brother Swan was superior of the O'Connell School from 1880 to 1894. He spent most of his life in Dublin with the exception of a few years spent in Waterford, Liverpool, Bath and Kingstown. He was transferred to the O'Brien Institute, Fairview, on 7 September 1904. At the time there was a community of five brothers and a hundred boys. He remained at the Institute until his death on 5 March 1911. He was buried in Glasnevin Cemetery, Finglas Road, Dublin [PC 54 South].

Ulysses 6.537

Sweny, Frederick William (1856–1924) *Pharmacist*
'Sweny's in Lincoln place. Chemists rarely move.'
(5.463–4)

Frederick William Sweny, one of nine children, was born at 1 Lincoln Place, Dublin. He was the son of Mark Sweny (1816–69), a medical doctor and pharmacist, the proprietor of Sweny's chemist shop at 1 Lincoln Place.

Sweny was 13 when his father died. When he had finished school, he studied pharmacy and took over the chemist shop. In 1884 he married Sarah Jane (née Owens) and they had seven children, three of whom survived. Sweny died on 11 March 1924 in Dublin and was buried in Mount Jerome Cemetery, Harold's Cross, Dublin [A10–414–16688].

Ulysses 15.340; 15.342; 17.333–4

Swift, Jonathan (1667–1745)

'Doctor Swift says one man in armour will beat ten men in their shirts.' *(15.4402)*
Jonathan Swift, son of Jonathan Swift and Abigail (née Erick), was born at 7 Hoey's Court in the parish of St Werburgh's in Dublin on 30 November 1667.

He was educated at Kilkenny College and Trinity College Dublin. In 1689 he became secretary to Sir William Temple, at Moor Park near Farnham in Surrey. Swift lived there for several years and it was where he first met Esther Johnson, known as Stella.

Following his ordination in 1694, he worked as a clergyman in Kilroot, near Carrickfergus in Co. Antrim. Sir William Temple died in January 1699 and, at 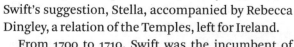 Swift's suggestion, Stella, accompanied by Rebecca Dingley, a relation of the Temples, left for Ireland.

From 1700 to 1710, Swift was the incumbent of Laracor, a village near Trim, Co. Meath. Stella lived nearby with Mrs Dingley. Here he wrote much of his longest and most ironic masterpiece, *Gulliver's Travels* (1726).

His *Journal to Stella* was written during his London stay between 1710 and 1713. He published *The Tale of a Tub* (1704) and *The Battle of the Books* (1704) anonymously, and wrote political pieces on behalf of the Tory party. Owing to the party's downfall in 1713, he decided to accept the position of dean of St Patrick's Cathedral in Dublin, where he remained until his death.

During his last years, Swift continued to work with the poor of Dublin, spending a third of his income on charities. St Patrick's Hospital in Bow Lane, off James's Street, was founded in 1745 for the treatment of mental illness with funds bequeathed by Swift.

Swift died in the autumn of 1745 and was buried beside Stella in the West End of the Nave of St Patrick's Cathedral, beneath the Latin epitaph that he composed himself, which means, 'He has gone where savage indignation can lacerate his heart no more.'

Ulysses 3.109–11; 3.113; 3.128; 7.87; Complete Collection of Genteel and Ingenious Conversation, 8.755; 8.761–2; 12.332–3; 13.1224–5; 14.666; 15.1183; Gulliver's Travels, 3.111; 12.1353; 17.1702–3; A Letter to the Whole People of Ireland, 15.4402

Swinburne, Algernon (1837–1909) *English poet*
'Like me, like Algy, coming down to our mighty mother.' *(3.31–2)*
Algernon Swinburne, son of an admiral and Lady Jane Swinburne, was born on 5 April 1837 in Grosvenor Place, London. He was educated at Eton College and at Balliol College in Oxford, where he met Rossetti and others who influenced his later life. After Mrs Rossetti's (Elizabeth Siddall's) death in 1862, Swinburne moved with Rossetti to live at 16 Cheyne Walk in Chelsea.

In 1865 his poem in classical Greek form 'Atlanta in Calydon' was published. This work revealed his great metrical skills and brought him fame. Tennyson praised his 'wonderful rhythmic invention'.

Just over five foot tall, Swinburne was highly excitable and suffered from occasional frail health and alcoholism. He stayed with his friend and fellow critic, Theodore Watts-Dunton, in his home at 11 Putney Hill, London. Watts-Dunton devotedly cared for him, curbing his heavy drinking for 30 years from 1879 until his death.

Swinburne died at Putney Hill and was buried in St Boniface's Church, Bonchurch, on the Isle of Wight.

Ulysses 1.77–8; 10.1073; 15.2527; 'Ask Nothing More of Me, Sweet', 1.463–4; Atalanta in Calydon, 9.616–17; 'Genesis', 10.1073–4; 14.1484–5; 'Hymn to Prosperpine', 9.615; 10.1073; 'The Oblation', 1.455–6; 'On the Death of Colonel Benson', 9.137–78; 'The Triumph of Time', 1.77–8; 3.31–2; 15.4180

Synge, John Millington (1871–1909) *Irish dramatist*
'Synge has promised me an article for *Dana* too.' *(9.322)*
John Millington Synge, son of John Hatch Synge and Kathleen (née Traill), was born on 16 April 1871 at Newtown Villas, in Rathfarnham, Co. Dublin.

Synge was one when his father died and his mother moved the family to 4 Orwell Park in Rathgar. He attended various schools and studied the violin at the Royal Irish Academy of Music at 36 Westland Row.

Around 1888 the family moved to 31 Crosthwaite Park West, Kingstown (now Dún Laoghaire), and Synge entered Trinity College Dublin. After obtaining his degree in 1892 he went to Germany for a year to pursue his musical studies. He dropped music as a possible career and took up literature instead, going to Paris to teach English and study at the Sorbonne. While there, he met W. B. Yeats, who told him with uncanny insight to give up an alien culture and return to the Aran Islands to live as one of the people and 'express a life that has never found expression'.

Synge spent five summers in succession on Aran. In 1901 he completed his book *The Aran Islands*. *In the Shadow of the Glen*, which he wrote in 1902, was his first play to be produced, opening on 8 October 1903. *Riders to the Sea* followed in 1904, and then *The Well of the Saints* on 4 February 1905. The same year he became a director of the Irish National Theatre Society.

Synge moved to 15 Maxwell Road, Rathmines, and then to 57 Rathgar Road to be nearer the city and the Abbey Theatre. In 1906 he fell in love with Molly Allgood, an actress who had joined the Abbey Theatre Company the previous year as Maire O'Neill.

The Playboy of the Western World caused riots when it opened at the Abbey in Dublin on 26 January 1907.

Synge's health deteriorated and he was admitted to the Elphis Nursing Home at 19 Lower Mount Street. In 1908, he moved to 47 York Road, Rathmines, where he planned to live after his marriage to Molly, but he was here for only a brief period before returning to the nursing home. His mother died and Synge returned to her residence at Glendalough House, in Glenageary, to finish his play *Deirdre*. On 2 February 1909 he entered the Elphis Nursing Home for the last time.

He died aged 38 on 24 March 1909 and was buried in Mount Jerome Cemetery, Harold's Cross, Dublin [C9468–38].

Ulysses 7.87; 9.510–11; 9.558–66; 9.570; 9.576–7; 9.1155–6; 14.1010–37; 17.49–50; In The Shadow of the Glen, 9.38–40; 9.322; The Playboy of the Western World, 10.936; Riders to the Sea, 9.322; 9.775–6; The Tinker's Wedding, 9.569

T

Talbot, Florry *Prostitute at Bella Cohen's*
Possibly based on **Florrie Power (b. 1875)** or **Fleury Crawford** (*fl.* **early 1900s**)
'Florry Talbot, a blond feeble goosefat whore in a tatterdemalion gown of mildewed strawberry, lolls spreadeagle in the sofacorner ...' (15.2073-5)
Florry Talbot worked as a prostitute at Bella Cohen's brothel at 82 Tyrone Street Lower in Monto. The madams who ran the brothels were always on the lookout for pretty young girls who came to the city seeking work. The girls generally lived in houses owned by the madams and became trapped when they fell into debt on payments for their lodgings, food and clothes. Some of them, when they had lost their looks after harrowing lives, ended up alcoholics and eventually in the Westmoreland Lock Hospital, Townsend Street, which catered for women with sexually transmitted diseases.

A Florrie Power is mentioned in the 'Circe' notes in the *Ulysses Notesheets*. Florrie Power lived at 36 Faithful Place, off Tyrone Street Lower, in Monto. She was born in 1875, so would have been 29 in 1904.

Another model for Florry Talbot could have been Fleury Crawford, whose father held a political job as a scrivener on the education board.

Ulysses 15.2127-8; 15.2134; 15.2165; 15.2195; 15.2221; 15.2232; 15.2505; 15.2510; 15.2528; 15.2532; 15.2591; 15.2648; 15.2876; 15.2919; 15.2950; 15.2953; 15.3412; 15.3542; 15.3552; 15.3571; 15.3583; 15.3635; 15.3689; 15.3722; 15.3724; 15.3737; 15.3754; 15.3795-6; 15.3817; 15.3927; 15.4028; 15.4095; 15.4101; 15.4110; 15.4118; 15.4123; 15.4207; 15.4229; 15.4292; 15.4314

Talbot de Malahide, Lord Richard (d. 1329) *Lord admiral of Malahide*
'Lord Talbot de Malahide, immediate hereditary lord admiral of Malahide and the seas adjoining.' *(10.156-7)*
The title Baron Talbot de Malahide was created in 1831 for Margaret Talbot, widow of Richard Talbot, heir of the ancient lords of Malahide. The Malahide estate dates from 1185, when Richard Talbot, a knight who had accompanied Henry II to Ireland, was granted the 'lands and harbour of Malahide'.

Lord Talbot de Malahide also holds the title 'Hereditary Lord Admiral of Malahide and Adjacent Seas' (created by Edward IV). The 7th Baron Talbot eventually inherited Malahide Castle and demesne. On his death in 1973, it passed to his sister Rose who sold it to the Irish state to pay inheritance taxes. The castle and demesne, comprising over 260 acres of parkland, is open to the public and is close to the village of Malahide, nine miles north of Dublin.

Ulysses 14.682–4; 16.133–3

Tallon, Daniel (1836–1908) *Lord mayor of Dublin*

'... the rhymes, homophonous and cacophonous, associated with the names of the new lord mayor, Daniel Tallon ...' *(17.443–4)*

Daniel Tallon was born in Rathdrum, Co. Wicklow. In 1861, he started a business in

the tailoring and outfitting line. Subsequently he was a wine merchant and grocer with premises at 46 George's Street South and 57 Stephen Street, Dublin.

In 1890 he entered Dublin Corporation as a representative of the Mansion House Ward and was elected high sheriff of Dublin in 1895. He was a member of Dublin City Council between 1891 and 1903. He was elected lord mayor of Dublin on three occasions, 1897, 1898 and 1899.

Tallon created a Mansion House Committee in 1898 to raise funds for the relief of distress due to the failure of the potato crop in the west and south of Ireland. Grants were made available for relief works, such as draining and fencing of land, the construction of cow-houses and the building of roads and piers.

In 1899, Tallon paid an official visit as lord mayor to the United States where President McKinley received him. He also helped John Redmond, MP raise funds for the proposed statue of Charles Stewart Parnell in Upper Sackville Street (now O'Connell Street).

Tallon lived at 136 Leinster Road in Rathmines before moving nearby to 5 Cambridge Road, where he died on 13 July 1908. He was buried in Glasnevin Cemetery, Finglas Road, Dublin [MC 99.5 South].

Ulysses 4.128

Taxil, Léo (1854–1907) *Anti-clerical French author*

'But he must send me *La Vie de Jésus* by M. Léo Taxil.' *(3.167)*

Gabriel Jogand-Pagès, whose pseudonym was Léo Taxil, was born on 21 March 1854 in Marseilles and first became known for anti-Catholic and anti-clerical books. A brilliant prankster, in 1885 he professed conversion to Catholicism and as a result gained an audience with Leo XIII. This was one of his many hoaxes.

Taxil's books include *Les Pornographes Sacrés: La Confession et les Confesseurs* (1882), *La Bible Amusante* (1882), *La Vie de Jésus* (1884) and *Les Debauches d'un Confesseur* (1884). Taxil died in Sceaux, south Paris on 31 March 1907.

Ulysses La Vie de Jésus, 3.161–2; 14.306–8; 15.2583–5

Taylor, John F. (1853–1902) *Barrister, journalist and orator*
'The finest display of oratory I ever heard was a speech made by John F Taylor at the college historical society.' *(7.792–3)*
John F. Taylor, son of John Taylor of Riverstown, Co. Sligo, and Maria (née Feeney) was born on 13 February 1853.

In 1882 Taylor was called to the Irish Bar and to the English Bar in 1890. For many years he contributed articles on Irish affairs, especially during the Parnell crisis to various leading publications, including the *Manchester Guardian*. He had a considerable legal practice in Dublin and was a leading member of the Connaught circuit.

Politically, Taylor was a Liberal Home Ruler and one of the finest orators of his time. He died at 4 Ely Place, Dublin, on 7 November 1902 and was buried in Glasnevin Cemetery, Finglas Road, Dublin [RB 60.5 South].   *Ulysses 9.353–4; 15.995*

Tearle, George Osmond (1852–1901) *English actor-manager*
'... Osmond Tearle (+ 1901), exponent of Shakespeare.' *(17.794)*
George Osmond Tearle was born on 26 March 1852 in Plymouth, England. He formed a succession of Shakespearean companies in London, New York and Stratford-on-Avon. He appeared regularly with his 'powerful' company at the Gaiety Theatre, Dublin during the 1890s with *Othello*, *Romeo and Juliet*, *Hamlet*, *King Lear*, *Richard III*, *Coriolanus* and *Richelieu*. His productions were always well attended.

Tearle died on 6 October 1901 while his company was playing at Newcastle-on-Tyne. He was buried at St Paul's Church, Whitley Bay, Northumberland.

Tell, William (*fl.* 1307–54) *Legendary hero in the fight for Swiss independence*
'(... William Tell and the Lazarillo-Don Cesar de Bazan incident depicted in *Maritana* on which occasion the former's ball passed through the latter's hat) ...'
(16.492–4)
William Tell, an expert shot with the crossbow, is a folk hero of Switzerland. His legend is recorded in a late fifteenth-century Swiss chronicle. He was forced by a tyrant named Gessler to prove his marksmanship by shooting an apple off his son's head; otherwise, both would be executed. Tell was promised his freedom if he was successful with his shot. Tell split the apple with a bolt from his crossbow on 18 November 1307. He went on to assist the Swiss forest cantons win independence from Austria.

Tell died by drowning in 1354 while trying to rescue a child from the Schachenbach river in Uri. The scene is depicted in a fresco in a chapel in Burglen, which, according to legend, was his home. Burglen is a municipality in the canton of Uri in Switzerland. Tell is commemorated by a statue and a monument in Altdorf, Switzerland.   *Ulysses 12.189; 13.1093*

Temple *Stephen's acquaintance at UCD and later his creditor*
Based on **John R. Elwood** (1881–1934) *College friend of Joyce*
'Temple, two lunches.' *(2.257)*

John R. Elwood was born at Carrowbehy, Castlerea, Co. Roscommon, on 17 July 1881. He was the son of Francis William Elwood, a shopkeeper and farmer, and Sarah (née Taylor). The Elwoods were a prominent family in that area.

Educated at Summerhill College in Sligo, Elwood commenced his medical studies at the Catholic University School of Medicine at Cecilia Street, Dublin in 1900.

He qualified as a medical practitioner in 1915, becoming a licentiate of the Apothecaries' Hall in 40 Mary Street, Dublin. He moved back to Carrowbehy to practise medicine. He was also involved in agricultural matters and land reclamation and devised a scheme to alleviate flooding in the area.

Elwood was known for his kindness. One stormy night he went out on a call to a poor and needy person. Travelling on foot over wet fields and bogland to reach the cottage of his patient, he contracted a chill resulting in pneumonia.

He died of at his home on 27 March 1934 and was buried in the nearby Kilruddane graveyard. His grave is marked with a Celtic cross, sited at the highest point in the graveyard.

Tennyson, Lord Alfred (1809–92) *Poet*
'Lawn Tennyson, gentleman poet.' *(3.492)*

Alfred Tennyson, son of George Clayton Tennyson was born on 5 August 1809 in Somersby, Lincolnshire. He was educated at Trinity College Cambridge. In 1830 he published *Poems, Chiefly Lyrical*. In 1833 he commenced *In Memoriam*, an elegy mourning the death of his friend Arthur Hallam, which took 17 years to complete.

Tennyson was appointed poet laureate in succession to William Wordsworth in 1850. The same year he married Emily Sellwood and settled in Farringdon on the Isle of Wight, before moving in 1869 to Aldworth, Surrey. It was during this time that he produced some of his best poems such as 'Ode on the Death of the Duke Wellington' (1852) and 'The Charge of the Light Brigade' (1854).

Tennyson died at Aldwort on 6 October 1892, and was buried in the Poets' Corner in Westminster Abbey, London. *Ulysses 9.648; 15.4395–7*

Thornton, Mrs *Midwife at the births of the Bloom children*
Based on **Mary Thornton** (*fl.* 1880s) *Midwife*
'Remember the summer morning she was born, running to knock up Mrs Thornton in Denzille street.' *(4.416–17)*

Mary Thornton was a professional midwife who lived near the Holles Street lying-in hospital at 19a Denzille Street, Dublin. This ran from Holles Street to Hamilton Row.

Mrs Thornton delivered some of the Joyce children. These included Margaret born on 18 January 1884, Stanislaus born on 17 December 1884 and Charles Patrick born on 24 July 1886, all born at 23 Castlewood Avenue, Rathmines. She also delivered Eileen, who was born in 1 Martello Terrace, Bray, Co. Wicklow, on 22 January 1889. Mrs Thornton was popular with all the Joyce family.

Ulysses 8.394; 15.1818

Tichborne, Roger Charles (1829–54) *Missing heir impersonated in legal case*
'... like the claimant in the Tichborne case, Roger Charles Tichborne, *Bella* was the boat's name ...' *(16.1343–4)*
Roger Charles Tichborne was the son of dowager Lady Tichborne. He was lost at sea when the ship *Bella* sank in 1854; his identity was assumed by Arthur Orton (1834–98), an Australian who claimed to be the missing heir, Sir Roger Tichborne.

A famous legal case ensued in the United Kingdom. Lord Bellew, a school friend of Roger Charles, testified decisively against Orton in the Tichborne case, claiming that Roger Charles had tattoos to which he had personally added the letters 'R. C. T.' in Indian ink. Following two lengthy trials, Orton was finally sentenced for perjury.

Tivy, Richard 'Dick' (1848–1928) *Cork acquaintance of Mr Dedalus and Ned Lambert*
'And how is Dick, the solid man?' *(6.561)*
Richard Tivy, was born in Cork city. He lived at 20 Summerhill in 1911 with his wife Maria and two servants. The family was well known in Cork for their interest in antiques. Tivy was secretary of a public company in Cork.   *Ulysses 6.560–3*

Tobias, Matthew (1840–1921) *Solicitor*
'... the bridewell and an appearance in the court next day before Mr Tobias ...'
(16.72–3)
Matthew Tobias, son of the Rev. James Tobias, was born in Tandragee, Co. Armagh, in November 1840. He was educated in the Wesleyan Connexional School, Stephen's Green South, Dublin. He became an apprentice to solicitor Theodore Cronhelm, and entered partnership with him on qualifying in 1871. In 1872 he married Elizabeth Cronhelm, his partner's daughter.

In 1904 Tobias had offices at 4 and 7 Eustace Street and was living at 31 Mount-pleasant Square West, Ranelagh. He later moved to a house named 'Arundel' in Sutton, Co. Dublin.

Tobias was prosecuting solicitor to the Dublin Metropolitan Police for over 25 years, and also to the Society for the Prevention of Cruelty to Children. Following an accident in 1916, he retired from his professional duties.

He died on 17 September 1921 at the residence of a relative, T. C. Tobias, barrister, 2 Connaught Place, Clonskeagh, Dublin. He was buried at Mount Jerome Cemetery, Harold's Cross, Dublin [C177–3277].

Tobin, Patrick (1863–1928) *Dublin Corporation official*
'... Gumley ... given the temporary job by Pat Tobin ...' *(16.944–5)*
Patrick Tobin, born in Co. Tipperary, was prominently connected with the Gaelic Athletic Association. On 6 April 1903 he was elected as secretary to the Paving and Improvements Committee, which was one of the standing committees of the municipal council of Dublin Corporation. By 1905 he had charge of the main drainage system and was later appointed as joint secretary to the Housing Committee.

In 1903 Tobin was living at 2 St Vincent Street North, which links Berkeley Road with Goldsmith Street in Dublin. By 1911 he had moved to a fashionable area on the east coast at 4 Sorrento Terrace, Dalkey, Co. Dublin, where he lived with his wife Anne and four children.

Tobin died on 28 September 1928. He was buried in Glasnevin Cemetery, Finglas Road, Dublin [PJ 101 St Patrick's].

Tomkins, Thomas (1572–1656) *Welsh composer*
'... and one Tomkins who made toys or airs and John Bull.' *(16.1768–9)*
Thomas Tomkins was born in St David's in Pembrokeshire. His father, also Thomas, was organist and vicar choral of St David's Cathedral.

In 1596 Tomkins was organist and master of the choristers in Worcester Cathedral. He studied under William Byrd, the composer and organist at the Chapel Royal. It is probable that Byrd found a place for him as a chorister there. Tomkins was also affiliated to Magdalen College, Oxford, in 1607. A skilled composer of keyboard and consort music, he composed many songs, anthems, liturgical music and madrigals.

He died in Martin Hussingtree, four miles from Worcester, and was buried in the churchyard of Martin Hussingtree on 1 June 1656.

Torry/Torrey, Reuben Archer (1856–1928) *American revivalist*
'Torry and Alexander last year.' *(8.17)*
Reuben Archer Torrey was a graduate of Yale University in 1875 and Yale Divinity School in 1878. He was a revivalist and, with Charles McCallom Alexander (1867–1928), a minister and song leader. They conducted revival services and a 'Mission to Great Britain', 1903–5. This included a mission to Dublin in March–April 1904.

Tree, Beerbohm (1853–1917) *English actor and stage manager*
'... that fellow in the pit at the Gaiety for Beerbohm Tree in Trilby ...' *(18.1041–2)*
Herbert Draper Beerbohm, son of Julius Beerbohm and Constantia (née Draper), was born in Kensington, London, on 17 December 1853. He was educated in Germany and went on the English stage in 1878. It was at this time that he took on the professional name Beerbohm Tree. He was involved with the Haymarket

Theatre in London, where an assortment of dramas were produced.

In 1895 Beerbohm Tree's Haymarket Company came to Dublin's Gaiety Theatre, where Tree played Svengali in a production of *Trilby*, dramatised from George du Maurier's celebrated novel, for six nights from 7 October 1895. The Gaiety's private boxes were the most expensive seats in the theatre and were from 30 to 50 shillings. The pit was just one shilling.

In 1904 Tree established the Royal Academy of Dramatic Art, and Edward VII knighted him in 1909 for his contribution to the theatre.

He died at 15 Henrietta Street, Marylebone, on 2 July 1917. He was cremated and his ashes were placed in Hampstead Cemetery, London.

Troy, Denis (1853–1943) *DMP Constable*

'I was just passing the time of day with old Troy of the D. M. P. at the corner of Arbour hill ...' *(12.1–2)*

Denis Troy, son of John Troy and Mary (née Hennessy), was born on 10 August 1853 in Roscomroe, in the Slieve Bloom Mountains between Roscrea and Kinnity in Co. Offaly.

Troy joined the Dublin Metropolitan Police (DMP) on 17 December 1880 and was attached to 'D' Division. He was stationed at Manor Street, which extends from Stoneybatter to Prussia Street. On 21 April 1884 Troy married Bridget Murphy from Co. Westmeath at St Catherine's Church in Meath Street. At the time of his marriage he was living at 42 Newmarket (off the Coombe) and Bridget was living at 48 Bellview near Ushers Quay. They moved to Arbour Hill after their marriage. Here they raised their family of five children. In 1904 they lived at 14 Arbour Hill and by 1917 had moved to 8 Arbour Hill.

Troy was employed for 40 years in the service of the 'D' Division of the DMP. On 10 August 1920 he was pensioned from the DMP, aged 67.

He died on 24 January 1943 at 8 Arbour Hill and was buried in Mount Jerome Cemetery, Harold's Cross, Dublin [A–49a–88].   *Ulysses 15.4358*

Tupper, Norman W. (*fl.* 1890s) *Chicago contractor*

'Norman W. Tupper, wealthy Chicago contractor, finds pretty but faithless wife in lap of officer Taylor.' *(12.1170–1)*

Norman W. Tupper lived at 1137 Jackson Boulevard, Chicago, with his wife Belle and two daughters. Belle was infatuated with a policeman named Sergeant Taylor, a married man with a wife and child, who lived at 1418 Warren Avenue, Chicago. One day, Tupper returned home unexpectedly and found his wife and Taylor in an embrace. After a scuffle with Tupper, Taylor escaped.

Turnbull, Donald (1859–1908) *School friend of Bloom.*

'(*Halcyon Days, High School boys in blue and white football jerseys and shorts, Master Donald Turnbull...*' (15.3325-6)

Donald Turnbull, who was born in Scotland, lived at 53 Harcourt Street in 1904. He was a fancy goods merchant and later manager of the Paris House, Grafton Street. He is named in Bloom's list of school friends at the Erasmus High School at 40 Harcourt Street, Dublin. He died on 9 January 1908 as the result of an accident and was buried in Mount Jerome Cemetery, Harold's Cross, Dublin [B26-359-7887].

Ulysses 17.48

Tweedy, Major Brian Cooper *Molly Bloom's father*

Partly based on **Major Malachy Powell (1821-1917)** *Soldier and military correspondent*

'Hard as nails at a bargain, old Tweedy. Yes, sir. At Plevna that was.' (4.63)

Major Malachy Powell supplied a number of characteristics for Molly Bloom's father, Major Brian Cooper Tweedy.

Malachy Powell was born in Thomastown, Co. Kilkenny. He joined the 1st Life Guards as a young man. On the outbreak of the Crimean War, he volunteered for service and was commissioned to the Army Transport Corps, which was known at the time as the Military Train. He distinguished himself in the Crimea and was awarded a number of medals including the Turkish Medal with Clasp.

In 1857 he married Louisa Matthews from Maidstone in Kent. They had a family of four daughters and one son. He served at the Curragh, Co. Kildare, from 1858 to 1866, and was subsequently transferred to Aldershot, Hampshire, in England. He retired from the army in 1869 and commuted his pension to buy a farm in Kilkenny. He lost the farm and his wife because of his intemperance. From 1877 to 1885 he was employed as a riding master to the Mounted Rifles of South Australia. He returned to Dublin and lived at Kenilworth Square and worked as 'Military Correspondent' for the *Freeman's Journal*.

Powell lived at 12 Stamer Street from 1888 to 1896 and was a neighbour of James J. Giltrap, William Ormsby Ruttledge, and Patrick Meade, the model for Myles Crawford. Major Powell was one of the last of the Crimean veterans when he died on 21 September 1917 at 30 Frankfort Avenue, Rathgar, aged 96. He received a public military funeral and was buried in Glasnevin Cemetery, Finglas Road, Dublin [BF 202 Garden].

Ulysses 12.1003; 15.779; 15.4612; 15.4617; 15.4622; 15.4751; 16.1442; 17.55-6; 17.1420; 17.2082; 17.2100

Tweedy, Henry R. (1855–1939) *Crown solicitor for Co. Waterford*

'Same house as Molly's namesake, Tweedy, crown solicitor for Waterford.' (6.233-4)

Henry R. Tweedy, son of John Tweedy, was born in Dublin. He qualified as a solicitor when he was 21 and developed an extensive practice at Newtownards, Co. Down.

In 1886 Tweedy married Julia McMahon and joined the Dublin firm of his brother-in-law, Aguila McMahon. On the latter's death, Tweedy became head of the firm of McMahon and Tweedy, then at 31 College Green. The office was later sited at 13 Hume Street. Tweedy was crown solicitor for Co. Waterford from 1897 to 1922. He retired in 1931.

He and his wife lived at 4 Charlemont Terrace, Dún Laoghaire (formerly Kingstown). After his wife's death in March 1937, Tweedy moved nearby to 2 Crofton Mansions, Dún Laoghaire.

He died on 2 August 1939 and was buried in Deansgrange Cemetery, Deansgrange, Co. Dublin [82–A–South West].

Twelvetrees, Mrs Clyde (1885–1970) *Participant in forest wedding*

'... wedding of ... Jean Wyse de Neaulan ... with Miss Fir Conifer of Pine Valley ... Mrs Clyde Twelvetrees, Mrs Rowan Greene ... graced the ceremony by their presence.' *(12.1267–79)*

Ethel Mary Eyre was the eldest daughter of Edmund W. Eyre, of Monkstown, Co. Dublin, city treasurer of Dublin.

On 9 May 1909 she married musician Clyde Twelvetrees youngest son of R. H. Twelvetrees of London. He was a major force in the Dublin musical scene playing in concerts at the Ancient Concert Rooms, Dublin Castle, the Rotunda, the Royal Dublin Society, the Mansion House, the Tivoli, and the Gaiety and Abbey theatres. He shared the platform with the baritone J. C. Doyle and was a member of the renowned Esposito Quartet. He died in January 1956 at 16 Nutley Park, Donnybrook.

Mrs Twelvetrees died aged 85 at her home, 33 Trimleston Gardens, Booterstown, Co. Dublin, on 27 November 1970. She was buried in St Peter's Cemetery, Little Bray, Bray, Co. Wicklow.

Twigg, Elizabeth 'Lizzie' Ann (1882–1933) *Poet*

'No time to do her hair drinking sloppy tea with a book of poetry.' *(8.332–3)*

Elizabeth Ann Twigg, better known as Lizzie Twigg, was born in Jabbalpore, a garrison town, now Jabalpur, India, daughter of William Twigg, a sergeant major in the 2nd Battalion of the Scottish Rifles (the Cameronians) and Eliza Mary (née Hayes). Lizzie's mother died in 1890 in Nainital, India, on 2 April 1890. William Twigg returned to Limerick with Lizzie, where he worked as a clerk for Great Southern and Western Railway. He married

Frances (née McCarthy) from Cork in 1892.

Lizzie was educated at the Presentation Convent in Sexton Street. In 1901 she lived with her parents at 9 Rathbane South in Limerick. She worked in London for a short time then moved to Dublin, where she did a course at St Kevin's House for Business Girls, located at 40 to 42 Rutland Square West (now Parnell Square). A number of her poems were published in the *United Irishman*. They appeared on 7 February 1903 and 6 June 1903 under the name Lizzie Twigg. She also contributed to the *Irish Rosary* almost every week, producing up to 50 poems a year. A protégé of Æ (George Russell), she also published under her Gaelic name, Éilís Ní Chraoibhín.

In 1904 Twigg published *Songs and Poems*. By 1911 she was living at 9 Rathbane South in Limerick again, but by 1923 was residing with her father at 27 O'Curry Street (formerly Frederick Street), Limerick. He died in 1927 and in 1931 she was listed as living at the same address. She spent her final years in Limerick engaged in social work and in efforts to improve housing conditions. She died at Barrington's Hospital, George's Quay, Limerick, on 3 January 1933 and was buried in Mount St Lawrence Cemetery on 5 January [No. 111 Cb].

Ulysses 8.330–1; 8.527

V

Valenti, Giulio (1860–1933) *Italian embryologist and physician*
Giulio Valenti was an Italian embryologist and physician who was professor of anatomy at Perugia, Italy, in 1893.

He was author of *Lezioni Elementari di Embriologia Applicata alle Scienze Mediche* (1893). This book provided much information on the subject of embryology for Joyce and he used it as a source for the 'Oxen of the Sun' episode. Valenti died in 1933.
Ulysses 14.1236

Valera, Juan y Alcalā-Galiano (1824–1905) *Author, diplomat and political figure*
'... I never tried to read that novel ... by Valera with the questions in it all upside down ...' *(18.1474–5)*
Juan y Alcalā-Galiano Valera was born on 18 October 1824 in Cabra in the province of Cordoba, Andalusia, Spain. He studied law at the University of Granada and Madrid before entering the diplomatic service. In 1859, he was one of the editors of *El Contemporaneo*, a liberal journal.

A major figure in the late nineteenth-century literary renaissance in Spain, his novels include *Las Ilusions del Doctor Faustino* (1875), *El Comendador Mendoza* (1877) and *Juanita la Larga* (1895). His best-known work *Pepita Jimenez* appeared as a serial in 1874.

Juan Valera died on 18 April 1905 in Madrid. A marble sculpture in Paseo de Recoletos in Madrid commemorates him.

Vance, Roygbiv *Teacher in the Erasmus High School*
Based on **James Vance (b. 1842)** *Bray chemist and friend of the Joyce family*

'Roygbiv Vance taught us: red, orange, yellow, green, blue, indigo, violet.' *(13.1075–6)*
The name of Joyce's fictional science teacher at the Erasmus High School, 40 Harcourt Street, Dublin is based on James Vance who lived at 4 Martello Terrace, Bray, Co. Wicklow. He was the father of Joyce's childhood friend, Eileen Vance. The Joyces were neighbours at 1 Martello Terrace.

Vance was born in Cork and began in medicine

but gave up and qualified as a pharmacist. He married 20-year-old Eleanor Augusta (née Atkinson) in 1879 and they had three daughters, Eileen, Norah and Violet. In 1894 Vance's wife died, aged 35, when they lived in their new home at 5 Loreto Villas, Bray. Vance then moved to live over his chemist shop at 92 Main Street, Bray. The shop still trades under the name Vance & Wilson. *Ulysses 5.42*

Vaughan, Father Bernard John, SJ (1847–1922) *English Jesuit*

'Yes, it was very probable that Father Bernard Vaughan would come again to preach ... A wonderful man really.' *(10.23-5)*

Bernard John Vaughan, was born on 20 September 1847 at Courtfield in Herefordshire, England. The son of Colonel John and Eliza Vaughan, he was from a large family. Four of his sisters entered the religious life and one of his brothers became Cardinal Herbert Vaughan, the founder of the Mill Hill Missionaries in 1866.

Vaughan entered Stonyhurst when he was 12. His great-grandfather Thomas Weld had given Stonyhurst to the Jesuits in 1794. Vaughan entered the Jesuit novitiate in December 1866, and was ordained priest on 20 September 1880.

Vaughan had already decided to make his name as a preacher. He worked tirelessly in the East End among London's poorest citizens. He visited the slums of Dublin frequently. He spoke at the Rotunda several times and at St Patrick's Training College in Drumcondra.

In his latter years he toured the world for 18 months, travelling 30,000 miles and delivering 400 speeches to half a million people. He died on 30 October 1922 and was buried in Kensal Green Cemetery, London. *Ulysses 5.398*

Veuillot, Louis (1813–83) *French journalist*

'*Un coche ensablé* Louis Veuillot called Gautier's prose.' *(3.287-8)*

Louis Veuillot was born on 11 October 1813 at Boynes in Loiret, France. At 17 he was working in a newspaper at Rouen and then at Périgueux. In 1837 he was in Paris and a year later visited Rome, where he was converted to Catholicism.

Veuillot joined the staff of the newspaper *Univers Religieux* in 1843 and became editor in 1848. It was suppressed in 1860 and revived in 1867. Due to his continued ultramontane propaganda, *Univers* was again suppressed in 1874.

His work as a journalist covering religious and political history was published in 12 volumes entitled *Mélanges Religieux, Historiques, Politiques et Littéraires* (1857–75). Veuillot died in 1883 and was buried in the Cimetière du Montparnasse, Boulevard Edouard Quinet, Paris.

Victory, Louis H. (1870–1947) *Journalist and minor Irish Revival literary figure*
Louis H. Victory was born in Dublin. A friend of George Russell (Æ), to whom he dedicated his book *The Higher Teaching of Shakespeare* (1896), he was a member of Dublin literary and artistic circles of the 1890s. He contributed regularly to the columns of the *Irish Times*.

In 1897 Victory married Laura Jean Douglas, also a journalist, in Dublin. In 1901 they lived at 2 Cabra Parade, Clontarf. Victory was managing editor of the *Leinster Leader* in Naas, Co. Kildare. He left for Australia in 1907 where he worked as a journalist. He also spent some years in the United States, where the Four Seas Company in Boston published his volume of poems, *The Loom of Orchid* (1924).

With the exception of four years, from 1917–1920, when he was on the editorial staff of the *Cork Examiner*, Victory worked abroad. Towards the end of his career, he was on the editorial staff of the *Yorkshire Herald* and returned to Dublin shortly after his wife's death in York in 1940.

Victory's works include *Poems* (1895); *Imaginations in the Dust* (1903); and *The Inwardness of Shakespeare* (1905).

Victory died on 16 November 1947 at the home of his sister, Mrs Rathborne, at 27 Upper Sherrard Street, Dublin and was buried in Deansgrange Cemetery, Deansgrange, Co. Dublin [69–L–St Mary].   *Ulysses 9.283*

Vilaplana, Fr Ildefonso (*fl.* 1910–26)
Priest at Cathedral of St Mary the Crowned, Gibraltar
'... father Vilaplana of Santa Maria that gave me the rosary ...' *(18.1464–5)*
Father Ildefonso Vilaplana was born in Lerida (Lleida) in Catalonia, Spain. He studied at Montserrat and entered the Order of St Benedict.

He worked as a priest in the Cathedral of St Mary the Crowned, on Calle Real, Gibraltar's main street. He was vicar general of the Benedictines there between 1910 and 1926. While he was working there, the bishop was Bishop Thompson. Secular clergy, mostly local priests, now run the cathedral.

Villiers de l'Isle-Adam, Philippe (1838–89)
French symbolist writer and playwright
'As for living our servants can do that for us, Villiers de l'Isle has said.' *(9.186)*
Born into poverty, Philippe Villiers de l'Isle-Adam wrote several collections of short stories and some poetry but is best known as a playwright and author of *Elen* (1865), *Morgane* (1866) and *La Revolte* (1870). His most famous work *Axel* (1890), which first appeared in symbolist reviews, provided the title for Edmund Wilson's *Axel's Castle* (1931), a study of symbolist literature. This movement included writers such as Yeats, Valéry, and Stein.

Voisin, Louis (1876–1918) *Murderer*

'Knife with which Voisin dismembered the wife of a compatriot and hid remains in a sheet in the cellar ...' *(15.4539-40)*

In October 1917 Louis Voisin was a French butcher living at 101 Charlotte Street in London. His mistress, Mrs Emilienne Gerard, was a 32-year-old French woman who lived at 50 Munster Square, east of Regent Square. Her husband was away fighting in the French army at the time.

On 31 October 1917, on the night of an air raid, Emilienne went to Voisin to shelter in his basement in Charlotte Street. When she arrived, she discovered him with his other mistress, Bertha Roche. A heated argument ensued and Roche struck Emilienne with a poker. Voisin then smothered her with a towel. They dismembered her body and took some of her remains back to her rooms at 50 Munster Square.

He kept her head and her hands in a sheet as they were still recognisable and hid them in his cellar at Charlotte Street. The sack containing the rest of her remains were left in Regent Square, where a road sweeper later discovered them.

Voisin was found guilty of the murder of Emilienne Gerard and sentenced to death on 2 March 1918. He was executed at Pentonville Prison, London. Bertha Roche, his accomplice, was sentenced to seven years' imprisonment but went insane in prison and was committed to a hospital where she died on 22 March 1919.

Wall, Thomas J. (1837–1910) *Chief divisional magistrate, Dublin*
'Got her hand crushed by old Tom Wall's son.' *(8.395-6)*
Thomas J. Wall was the son of a well-known physician in Cork city. Wall was called to the Bar in 1861 and joined the Munster circuit. He had a large practice, which included that of counsel to the Commissioners of Woods and Forests in Ireland.

In 1895 he was appointed chief divisional magistrate of the City of Dublin. He was subsequently appointed a member of the Inner Bar. As chief magistrate, he presided at a number of Board of Trade inquiries in Dublin. Perhaps the most notable was that concerning the loss of the lightship *Puffin* off the coast of Cork in 1895. In 1904 he lived at 26 Longford Terrace, Monkstown, Co. Dublin.

He died on 9 July 1910 at his residence in Monkstown and was buried in Deansgrange Cemetery, Deansgrange, Co. Dublin [92–M1–North].

Walsh, Louis J. (1880–1942) *Judge and author*
'*Art thou real, my ideal?* it was called by Louis J Walsh, Magherafelt, and after there was something about *twilight, wilt thou ever?*' *(13.645-7)*
The son of Louis Walsh and Elizabeth (née Donnelly), Louis J. Walsh was born in Maghera, Co. Derry, where his family kept a hotel. He was educated in Derry and then studied law at University College, Dublin. Joyce was involved with the Literary and Historical Society and was nominated to be treasurer of its executive on 21 March 1899, but was defeated by Louis J. Walsh, known as 'the boy orator'. On 15 February 1902 Joyce read a paper on James Clarence Mangan to the society. Walsh took exception to Joyce's omission of the fact that Mangan was one of the men of '48.

Walsh was taught Irish by Patrick Pearse. He qualified as a solicitor and returned home to practise, first to Maghera, and then to Ballycastle, Co. Antrim. In addition to his involvement with the Gaelic Leage, he devoted much of his time to the Irish language movement and to Sinn Féin. In 1919, he was a Sinn Féin candidate for North Antrim but was defeated. On the establishment of the Free State, he was appointed as a district justice for Co. Donegal.

Walsh wrote a number of books and plays, which include one of Ulster's most popular comedies, *The Pope in Killybuck*. Other works include: *The Guileless Saxon: An Ulster Comedy in Three Acts* (1917); *The Yarns of a Country Attorney: Being Stories and Sketches of Life in Rural Ulster* (1918); *John Mitchel* (1934); and *Old Friends Being*

Memories of Men and Places (1934). Walsh died on 26 December 1942 at his home in Letterkenny, Co. Donegal.

Walsh, Dr William J. (1841–1921) *Archbishop of Dublin*
'Convert Dr William J. Walsh D. D. to the true religion.' *(5.325–6)*

William J. Walsh was born on 30 January 1841 at 11 Essex Quay in Dublin. He was the son of Mary (née Pierce) and Ralph Walsh, a watch and clockmaker.

In 1853 the family moved to 19 Parliament Street. Walsh was educated at Mr Fitzpatrick's private school for Catholic children in Peter Street, St Laurence O'Toole's Seminary in Harcourt Street, and the Catholic University. In the autumn of 1858 he entered St Patrick's College Maynooth, Co. Kildare and was ordained priest on 22 May 1866. The following year he became professor of dogmatic and moral theology, a post he held until 1878, when he became vice-president of St Patrick's College Maynooth. He was president 1880–5, when he was appointed archbishop of Dublin.

Archbishop Walsh had a keen interest in public affairs and was a member of several educational and charitable bodies. He was a prolific writer and in 1908 was the first chancellor of the National University of Ireland.

The Most Rev. William Walsh, DD, archbishop of Dublin and primate of Ireland, died on 9 April 1921 at 32 Eccles Street and was buried in Glasnevin Cemetery, Finglas Road, Dublin [Vault C 45.5 St Laurence's Section].

Ward, Gerald (1877–1914) *Aide-de-camp to the lord lieutenant of Ireland*
'In the following carriage were the honourable Mrs Paget, Miss de Courcy and the honourable Gerald Ward A. D. C. in attendance.' *(10.1178–9)*
The Honorary Gerald Ernest Francis Ward, MVO, who was a lieutenant, 1st Life Guards, was born in 1877. He was a brother of William Humble Ward, earl of Dudley. In 1899 he married Lady Evelyn, a daughter of the earl of Erne.

He was killed in action aged 36 on 30 October 1914 at Zandvoorde, south-east of Ypres, where he was buried [Grave/Memorial reference – Panel 3. Cemetery memorial name Ypres [Menin Gate] Memorial].

Watchman, Minnie (1866–1921) *Member of the Jewish community*
'*Darkshawled figures of the circumcised, in sackcloth and ashes, stand by the wailing wall ... Minnie Watchman ...*' *(15.3220–3)*
Minnie Watchman (née Mark), daughter of Hillel Mark and Frea (née Sakinovski) was born in Russia. In 1901 she lived at 57 Mary Street, Dublin with her husband Jacob, and their four daughters and one son. Jacob was born in Russia, as were two of their daughters, Rachal and Hettie. She was a great-aunt of Morris Watchman,

who lived at 77 Lombard Street West in 1904 and was one time a neighbour of Bloom.

Minnie Watchman's husband Jacob, a furniture dealer, was setting up a business at 19 St Mary's Road, Dundalk, Co. Louth in 1904. Minnie is mistakenly listed in *Thom's Directory 1904* as 'Mr. Minnie Watchman' as the tenant of 20 St Kevin's Parade, South Circular Road, Dublin. She died on 17 July 1921 and was buried at the Jewish Cemetery, Dolphin's Barn, Rialto, Dublin [10–A–17].

Waters, Rev. Thomas (1863–1948) *Curate, church of St John the Baptist*
Thomas Waters was born on 5 June 1863 in Dalkey, Co. Dublin. He was educated at Ratcliffe College in Leicestershire, England. He was admitted to Holy Cross College, Clonliffe, Dublin on 1 September 1881. He then joined the Redemptorist order.

In 1904 the Rev. Thomas Waters was curate in the church of St John the Baptist, 35 Newtown Avenue, Blackrock. He died in 1948.   *Ulysses 12.929*

Weatherup, William (1832–95) *Rate collector*
'Wetherup always said that. Get a grip of them by the stomach.' *(7.342–3)*
William Weatherup, son of James Weatherup, was born in Ballycarry, Co. Antrim in 1832. He held a few positions, which included working as a 'servant' at 34 Merrion Square and later at 30 Upper Merrion Square. He then became a grocer in Blackrock before joining the Collector-General of Rates Office in January 1868, where he worked with John Stanislaus Joyce. In 1875 he lived at 37 Gloucester Street Upper.

Weatherup had 12 children. His wife, Anne, who died on 3 August 1885, was buried in Carrickbrennan churchyard, Monkstown, Co. Dublin.

Weatherup was in receipt of a pension from the Collector-General of Rates Office when he died on 2 December 1895 at his residence, 3 St Patrick's Terrace, Russell Street, Dublin. He was buried in Carrickbrennan churchyard, Monkstown, Co. Dublin.   *Ulysses 7.337; 15.4357; 16.1701*

Werner, Lewis/Louis Joseph (1860–1936) *Ophthalmic Surgeon*
'... walked as far as Mr Lewis Werner's cheerful windows ...' *(10.1106–7)*
Louis Joseph Werner was the eldest son of Louis Werner, the portrait painter who was born in Bernwiller, Alsace and who came to Dublin having received commissions to paint some portraits. He married a French girl, Augustine Fieffe (1827–1902) and remained in the city. They had three sons.

Louis Joseph, the eldest, was born in Dublin on 27 October 1860. He studied ophthalmology at Trinity College Dublin and qualified in 1884. He became a specialist in diseases of the eye and was appointed assistant surgeon in the National Eye and Ear Infirmary, 1886–97. In 1898 he was admitted as a fellow of the Royal College of Surgeons in Ireland.

Werner was appointed surgeon to the Mater Misericordiae Hospital in Eccles Street and the Royal Victoria Eye and Ear Hospital 1897–1936.

Werner was the co-author with Sir Henry Swanzy of *Diseases of the Eye* (1899).

He married Louise Giradin and they had two children, a daughter Elsa and a son Louis Emil, who became an eye surgeon. Between them, the father and son were associated with the Royal Victoria Eye and Ear Hospital and its predecessor, St Mark's, for over a hundred years.

In 1904 Werner's residence was at 31 Merrion Square North on the corner of Holles Street. He later moved to Glengyle House, Zion Road, Rathgar (now Stratford College). He died on 25 November 1936 and was buried in Deansgrange Cemetery, Deansgrange, Co. Dublin [84–C–South West].

Werner, Louis (1856–1941) *Professor of music, organist and conductor*
'Louis Werner is touring her, Mr Bloom said. O yes, we'll have all topnobbers. J. C. Doyle and John MacCormack ... The best in fact.' *(6.221–3)*
Louis Werner was born in Aldershot, England. In 1875 he took the position of organist and choirmaster with the Holy Cross Church, Ardoyne, in Belfast and remained there for 66 years. The Passionist Fathers, who had a monastery in Mount Argus in Dublin, had been in Ardoyne for just six years.

In 1889 Werner married, and lived with his wife Harriette, who was from Cloyne, Co. Cork, at 58 Antrim Road. In 1904 they lived at Duncairn Street, Clifton, Co. Antrim.

Keen to carry out the wishes of Pope Pius X for the reform of church music, Werner disbanded the mixed choir in 1905 and turned his talent to the training of an all-male voice choir in pure liturgical style. In 1906 a writer in *Nomad's Weekly and Belfast Critic* wrote of Werner that 'he must be a veritable wizard to conjure the beautiful music with which he fills the church from such an inadequate instrument.'

Werner celebrated his golden jubilee as organist and choirmaster of Holy Cross Church, Ardoyne, Belfast in 1925 and on 2 January 1936 Pope Benedict XV conferred on him the Cross of Honour for his services to church music.

Werner was prominent for some 66 years in the musical life of Northern Ireland. He was billed as the 'Conductor and Accompanist' with Miss Anderson and Company at a concert in the Ulster Hall, Belfast on 16 June 1904.

He died on 4 April 1941 at his home 150 Antrim Road and was buried in Milltown Cemetery, Belfast.

Westminster, duke of/Hugh Lupus Grosvenor (1825–99)
English racehorse owner and politician
'... the duke of Westminster's Shotover ...' *(2.301–3)*
Hugh Lupus Grosvenor, the 1st duke of Westminster, was born on 13 October 1825

at Eaton Hall in Cheshire. He was the son of Richard Grosvenor, 2nd marquess of Westminster, and Elizabeth (née Leveson-Gower). He was educated at Eton College and Balliol College, Oxford. He then served as MP for Chester.

Bend Or, one of his horses, won the Derby in 1880. He had further Derby winners in 1882, 1886 and 1899 and during his 25-year career as a breeder and owner, his horses won hundreds of races. He was the only man to have been owner/breeder of two winners of the Triple Crown. He never gambled and never even placed a bet on one of his own horses. He bred the great mare Sceptre who came up for sale as a yearling after his death.

Westminster's filly Shotover won the 2,000 Guineas in 1882 and also the Derby at Epsom Downs the same year. A large proportion of his income, that financed his lifestyle and philanthropy, was derived from the ground rents of his properties in Mayfair and Belgravia in London.

The duke of Westminster died on 22 December 1899 at St Giles House in Cranborne, Dorset. He was cremated and his ashes interred in Eccleston churchyard, Cheshire.

Whitbread, James (1848–1916) *Manager of the Queen's Royal Theatre*
James Whitbread was the lessee and manager of the Queen's Royal Theatre in Great Brunswick (now Pearse) Street for many years. Before that he was associated with the Harp Music Hall until it closed. He produced a number of his own plays for the Queen's Theatre, and these proved very popular.

Whitbread usually wrote at least one historical drama each year for the Queen's Theatre, based on an Irish theme and produced by Mr Kennedy-Miller's Company. Such plays included, *The Sham Squire* (January 1904); *Wolfe Tone* (January 1904); and *The Victoria Cross* (April 1904). This was a five-act play based on the Indian Mutiny and was 'crammed with incidents of the most exciting description'. It was considered one of the most successful of Whitbread's plays.

Whitbread left for England when the lease of the old Queen's Theatre expired. He died on 9 June 1916 in his home at 38 Londesborough Road, Scarborough and was buried at All Saints' Church, Scarborough.   *Ulysses 8.600*

White, Dudley (1873–1930) *Barrister*
'Between Queen's and Whitworth bridges lord Dudley's viceregal carriages passed and were unsaluted by Mr Dudley White, B. L., M. A., who stood on Arran quay ...' *(10.1184–6)*
Dudley White was born on 2 March 1873 in Dublin. He was the son of Dr William Dudley White, a noted physician and surgeon of Rutland Square (now Parnell Square), and Emily (née Noble).

White was educated at Belvedere College and Trinity College Dublin. In 1897 he was called to the Irish Bar and soon built up an extensive practice with a number of prominent cases. He was called to the English Bar in 1909 and the same year was appointed crown counsel for the County of Wicklow. Three years later he became crown counsel for the County and City of Dublin, a position he held until 1921. After the Anglo-Irish Treaty, he was junior state prosecutor at criminal trials in Green Street Courthouse. He had addresses at 29 Kildare Street and 20 Earlsfort Terrace. He died on 3 July 1930 and was buried in Glasnevin Cemetery, Finglas Road, Dublin [VB 9.5 Section 5].

Whiteside, James (1804–76) *Lord Chief Justice and MP*

'Why bring in a master of forensic eloquence like Whiteside?' *(7.735–6)*

James Whiteside, son of the Rev. William Whiteside, a Church of Ireland clergyman, was born on 12 August 1804 in Delgany, Co. Wicklow.

He was educated at Trinity College Dublin, and at Gray's Inn and the Inner Temple in London. He was called to the Irish Bar in 1830. In 1833 he married Rosetta, the daughter of William Napier. Known for his brilliant oratory and forensic eloquence, Whiteside soon had a large practice. He became a queen's counsel in 1842.

In 1844 Whiteside defended Daniel O'Connell at the state trials and his speech placed him at the forefront of the Bar. Shortly afterwards he travelled to Italy for health reasons. This resulted in his publication, *Italy in the Nineteenth Century* (1848).

In 1848 he was back in Ireland defending William Smith O'Brien and others at state trials in Clonmel, Co. Tipperary. Three years later he was elected Conservative MP for Enniskillen in Co. Fermanagh.

In 1852 Whiteside was appointed solicitor-general for Ireland and in 1858 attorney general. In 1859 he became MP for Dublin University and in 1866 he was appointed lord chief justice of Ireland. Perhaps one of Whiteside's greatest triumphs was in the Yelverton case in 1861 when he became known as the leading forensic orator of the period; after his celebrated speech he was cheered on entering the House of Commons.

Whiteside died in Brighton, England, on 25 November 1876. He was buried in Mount Jerome Cemetery, Harold's Cross, Dublin [C86–4872].   *Ulysses 7.707*

Wilde, Lady Jane Francesca (Speranza) (1821–96) *Poet*

'... the matchless melody endeared to us from the cradle by Speranza's plaintive muse.' *(12.538–9)*

Jane Francesca Elgee was born in Dublin in 1821, daughter of Charles Elgee and Sarah (née Kingsbury). Jane was a granddaughter of Archdeacon John Elgee of Wexford, and a grandniece of novelist Charles Maturin.

Under the pseudonym 'Speranza' she contributed poetry and prose to the *Nation*. When one of its founders, Charles Duffy, was imprisoned, Speranza replaced him as the leader writer.

In 1851 she married Dr William Wilde and had three children: William, Oscar and Isola. They lived at 21 Westland Row before moving to 1 Merrion Square, where Lady Wilde held her celebrated salons.

Following Sir William Wilde's death in 1876, she moved to London and contributed to London periodicals such as the *Pall Mall Gazette*, the *Queen*, *Tinsely's* and the *Burlington Magazine*. Her works include *Ancient Legends of Ireland* (1887), *Ancient Cures* (1890) and *Men, Women, and Books* (1891).

She died during her son Oscar's imprisonment, on 3 February 1896 at 147 Oakley Street, Chelsea. She was buried in an unmarked grave in Kensal Green Cemetery, London. She is commemorated by a plaque on the Wilde family tomb in Mount Jerome Cemetery, Harold's Cross, Dublin [C678–108].

Wilde, Oscar (1854–1900) *Poet and dramatist*
'Staunch friend, a brother soul: Wilde's love that dare not speak its name.' *(3.450–1)*
Oscar Wilde was born on 16 October 1854 at 21 Westland Row, Dublin. He was the second son of Sir William Wilde and Jane Francesca (née Elgee).

He was educated at Portora Royal School in Enniskillen, Co. Fermanagh, Trinity College Dublin and Magdalen College, Oxford, where he won the Newdigate Prize for Poetry in 1878 and graduated with first class honours in classics and the humanities.

On 29 May 1884, Wilde married Constance Lloyd, daughter of Horace Lloyd, QC. His first great theatrical success, *Lady Windermere's Fan* (1892), resulted in him becoming the most fashionable and talked-about playwright in London. This play was followed by *A Woman of No Importance* (1893), *An Ideal Husband* (1895) and *The Importance of Being Earnest* (1895).

Wilde was also beginning to achieve notoriety through his relationship with Lord Alfred Douglas, whom he had met in 1891. He was arrested and imprisoned for homosexual offences in 1895. He was released in 1897 and went to France.

He died in Paris on 30 November 1900 at the Hotel d'Alsace in the Rue des Beaux Arts. He was buried first in Bagneux Cemetery and later removed to Père Lachaise Cemetery in Paris. His unusual tomb is sculpted by Sir Jacob Epstein.

Ulysses 1.554; 9.532; 'The Critic as Artist', 9.1069; 'De Profundis', 9.454; The Picture of Dorian Gray, 1.143;
9.442–3; 9.523–5; 9.735; 9.1069; 16.1193–4; 'Requiescat', 3.83

Wilkins, William (1853–1912) *Headmaster of the Erasmus High School*
'Women never meet one like that Wilkins in the high school drawing a picture of Venus with all his belongings on show.' *(13.909–10)*
William Wilkins was born in Greece. He was educated at Trinity College Dublin, where he obtained an MA. He was appointed headmaster at the Erasmus High School, in Harcourt Street in 1879 and held that position until the summer of 1908, when he resigned. In 1904 he lived at 40 Harcourt Street with his wife and family and later moved to 8 Rostrevor Terrace, Rathgar. He published a volume of poetry entitled *Songs of Study* (1881).

He died at Harrogate in England on 31 July 1912.

Woffington, Margaret 'Peg' (1720–60) *Actress*

Margaret Woffington, known as 'Peg', was born in Dublin on 18 October 1720. She first appeared in a children's company in St George's Lane, when an Italian ropedancer named Violante recruited her. She performed at Smock Alley and various Dublin theatres until 1740 when she went to Covent Garden in London. She had a successful career as an actress until retiring in 1757.

She died in London on 28 March 1760 and was buried in a vault in St Mary's Parish Church, Teddington. *Ulysses 12.181*

Wolseley, Sir Garnet Joseph (1833–1913) *British general*
'... and father talking about Rorkes drift and Plevna and sir Garnet Wolseley and Gordon at Khartoum ...' *(18.690–1)*
Garnet Joseph Wolseley, eldest son of Major Garnet Wolseley and Frances Anne (née Smith), was born on 4 June 1833 in Golden Bridge House, Golden Bridge, Co. Dublin. In the parish of Kilmainham, the former Golden Bridge House was

situated near to Richmond Barracks, which was demolished in 1969.

Wolseley spent the first 16 years of his life in Dublin. He was educated at Hollybrook School, Upper Rathmines, and then studied surveying under Mr Callaghan, assistant of Sir William Hamilton.

In 1852 he entered the army and served in Burma, the Crimean War, the Indian Mutiny and China. He commanded in Ashanti, Soudan, Egypt and South Africa. Wolseley, who was actively employed for 50 years, was created a field marshal in 1894. He was commander-in-chief and master at the Royal Hospital in Kilmainham, Dublin, from 1890 to 1895.

Wolseley was in command of the expedition that attempted unsuccessfully to relieve General Gordon at Khartoum in 1885. The phrase 'All Sir Garnet', meaning that everything is in good order, is derived in recognition of Wolseley's military successes. Garnet Joseph Wolseley, first Viscount Wolseley, died at Menton on the French Riviera on 26 March 1913. He was buried in the Crypt of St Paul's Cathedral, London.

Woods, Patrick and Rose (*fl.* late 1800s–early 1900s)
Next-door neighbours to the Blooms
'Woods his name is. Wonder what he does. Wife is oldish.' *(4.148-9)*
Patrick and Rose Woods lived in 8 Eccles Street and were next-door neighbours of the Blooms who lived in 7. Patrick Woods, who was born in 1859 in King's County (now Offaly), worked as a carrier. His wife Rose was born in Co. Meath in 1861.

Their daughter Katie, who was unmarried, was born in Dublin in 1880 and was aged 24 in 1904. Bloom encountered her in Dlugacz's, the pork butcher shop, buying a pound and a half of Denny's sausages and 'his eyes rested on her vigorous hips'. He thought that he might catch up on her if she walked slowly, but by the time he left the shop, she was gone.

Worthington, Robert (1842–1922) *Railway contractor*
'What he wanted to ascertain was why that ship ran bang against the only rock in Galway bay when the Galway harbour scheme was mooted by a Mr Worthington ...'
(16.964-6)
Robert Worthington was born in Co. Dublin, son of R. S. Worthington, a barrister, and the grandson of Sir William Worthington, lord mayor of Dublin, 1795-6. He lived at 'Salmon Pool Lodge', Islandbridge, Dublin, and had an office at 40 Dame Street.

He constructed numerous railway lines in the south and west of Ireland including the Tralee and Dingle railway, work on which commenced in 1888. He was responsible for the construction of hundreds of miles of railways throughout the country.

In 1890 he played a prominent role in connection with the railway relief works under Arthur Balfour, then chief secretary. He was involved with the construction of the tramway between Blackrock and Kingstown (now Dún Laoghaire), and also undertook work in England and Wales, such as the renewing of the Menai Bridge, which connects Carnarvon with Anglesey.

During the last 14 years of his life he put a lot of work into planning the Galway–Barna Transatlantic Port Scheme, known as the 'Galway Harbour Scheme'. Due to strong opposition this project never materialised. Worthington died on 28 July 1922.

Wylie, William E. (1881–1964) *Barrister and cyclist*

'... like his brother W. E. Wylie who was racing in the bicycle races in Trinity college university.' *(13.134–6)*

William E. Wylie was born in Dublin. He was the son of the Rev. R. B. Wylie, a Presbyterian minister in Coleraine. He was educated at Coleraine Academical Institution, Co. Down, and studied law at Trinity College Dublin, where he gradu-

ated in 1904. He was a distinguished racing cyclist at Trinity. He built up an extensive legal practice and was one of the most successful advocates of his day.

In 1916 Wylie was captain of the Trinity College Militia and was prosecuting counsel in the trial of the 1916 leaders. In 1918 he became a bencher of the King's Inns and the following year he was appointed law adviser to the British Administration in Ireland. When the Irish Free State was established in 1922, he was appointed a judge of the High Court. He retired from the Bench in 1936.

After his retirement he devoted himself to the service of the Royal Dublin Society and was president from 1939 to 1941.

A portrait of Wylie by Leo Whelan, hangs in the Royal Dublin Society building, and the wrought-iron gates, or 'Wylie Gate', at the entrance to the Simmonscourt extension to the Royal Dublin Society grounds were named after him.

He died on 12 October 1964 in Dublin and was buried in the graveyard of St Mary's Church of Ireland, Clonsilla, Co. Dublin.   *Ulysses 10.651; 13.196*

Yeats, Elizabeth and Susan (1868–1940 and 1866–1949) *The weird sisters*

'Printed by the weird sisters in the year of the big wind.' *(1.367)*

The daughters of John Butler Yeats and Susan Mary (née Pollexfen), Susan Yeats, known as 'Lily' (b. 26 August 1866) and her sister, Elizabeth Corbet Yeats, known as 'Lollie', (b. 11 March 1868) were both born at 23 Fitzroy Road, Regent's Park, London. The sisters had associations with the Dundrum area from 1902 when they returned from London to help Evelyn Gleeson found the Dun Emer Guild at a house named 'Runnymede' on the Sandyford Road. The purpose of the industry was 'to find work for Irish hands in the making of beautiful things'.

Susan organised the embroidery workshop and Elizabeth founded the Dun Emer Press as part of the scheme in the spring of 1903 with her brother W. B. Yeats as editor. Inspired by the Arts and Crafts Movement of William Morris, and with the support of Emery Walker, Sydney Cockerell and W. B. Yeats, the sisters printed small, hand-press editions on an Albion press.

In 1908, they moved the business to their house, 'Gurteen Dhas', a four-roomed cottage in Churchtown. Here they worked under the name of the Cuala Press until 1923 when they transferred to 82 Merrion Square, before finally moving again to 133 Lower Baggot Street in 1925.

Elizabeth died on 16 January 1940 and Susan on 5 January 1949. They were buried in the same grave in St Nahi's churchyard in Dundrum, Co. Dublin.

Yeats, William Butler (1865–1939) *Poet and dramatist*

'Couldn't you do the Yeats touch?' *(9.1160–1)*

William Butler Yeats, son John Butler Yeats and Susan (née Pollexfen) was born on 13 June 1865 at 5 Sandymount Avenue, Dublin.

Shortly after his birth the family moved to London until 1880. He was educated at the Godolphin School, Hammersmith, and on his return to Dublin in 1880 attended the Erasmus High School in Harcourt Street. He subsequently studied painting at the Metropolitan School of Art in Kildare Street.

Yeats published his first poems in the *Dublin University Review*, which was founded in 1885. He became artistically and politically aware of Irish history and literature and these were soon the inspiration for and theme of his writings.

In 1887 the family moved back to London and Yeats lived between both cities.

In London he met other poets and publishers and joined the Blavatsky Lodge of the Theosophical Society. In 1889 he met and fell in love with Maud Gonne, and shortly afterwards wrote, 'From this time the troubling of my life began.' *The Wanderings of Oisin*, a series of ballads and poems, was published the same year.

In 1891 Yeats founded the Irish Literary Society in London and the following year the Irish National Literary Society. In 1893 he published *The Countess Cathleen*. His first volume of folk-stories, *The Celtic Twilight*, appeared the same year. In 1896 his friendship with Lady Gregory began and from then on he spent many summers at her home in Coole Park, Gort in Co. Galway. With the help of Edward Martyn, they began a movement for an Irish Literary Theatre, which was founded in 1898, and whose aim was for Irish playwrights to write plays about Irish themes for an Irish audience. The first productions, in the Antient Concert Rooms in 1899, were Yeats's *Countess Cathleen* and Martyn's *The Heather Field*. Yeats's *Cathleen ni Houlihan* was staged in 1902 with Maud Gonne in the lead role. The Irish Literary Theatre gained permanent premises in the Abbey Theatre in 1904, opening with *On Baile's Strand* by Yeats and *Spreading the News* by Lady Gregory.

In 1917 Yeats married Georgie Hyde-Lees. He bought 'Thoor Ballylee', near Gort, which he restored as his summer residence. In 1919 *The Wild Swans at Coole* was published, followed by *Michael Robartes and the Dancer* in 1921. In 1922 he became a senator of the Irish Free State and in 1923 was awarded the Nobel Prize in Literature. *The Tower* was published in 1928 followed by *The Winding Stair* in 1933.

Yeats died on 28 January 1939 at Cap Martin on the French Riviera, and was buried at Roquebrune. After the Second World War, his remains were brought back to Ireland and buried in Drumcliffe churchyard, Co. Sligo.

Ulysses 9.304; 15.2254; *The Wanderings of Oisin*, 9.578; *Cathleen ni Houlihan*, 1.239–41; 1.403; 9.36–40; 12.725; 12.1151; 15.4586; *The Celtic Twilight*, 10.813–14; *The Countess Cathleen*, 1.239–41; 9.822; 14.1088–9

APPENDIX I

Note on biographical entries

The biographical entries include an eclectic mixture of people from the world of entertainment, the clergy, the legal and medical professions, members of the press and sporting figures.

ENTERTAINMENT

Cultural life in Joyce's Dublin was rather limited. In 1900 Dublin had five theatres, two of which were music halls. The most popular theatrical events of the year were the pantomimes. The Gaiety and the Royal theatres played a large part in the social life of the city and relied heavily on London companies, such as D'Oyly Carte and the Carl Rosa Opera, for drama, musical comedies and light operas. The Queen's Theatre provided a staple diet of melodrama and sentimental patriotic plays, such as *The Face in the Window* or *Arrah-na-Pogue*, but by far the most popular venues for ordinary Dubliners were the Empire Palace and Tivoli. These music halls offered variety shows, which were often cheap and vulgar but always entertaining. The Abbey Theatre, which was founded in 1904 as a literary theatre, appealed only to a minority and, because of this, it often played to very poor houses.

The musical life of the city was even more limited and elitist. On the occasions when there were celebrity concerts, they were given on weekday afternoons, which ensured that the vast majority of the population could not attend. The opera seasons always included such old reliables as *The Bohemian Girl, The Lily of Killarney, Martha* and *Carmen*. Lovers of grand opera were poorly catered for. Ordinary Dubliners appreciated the concerts given by Irish artists in the Rotunda and the Antient Concert Rooms, where in 1904 James Joyce shared the platform with John McCormack. There are 48 people named in *Ulysses* connected with various forms of entertainment.

THE CLERGY

Many of the clergy named in *Ulysses* are from the Jesuit order. Joyce had 14 years' education with the Jesuits, which included Clongowes Wood College, Sallins, Co. Kildare, and Belvedere and University College in Dublin. Father John Conmee, SJ was in Clongowes Wood when Joyce was a pupil there from September 1888 to December 1892. Father James Daly, SJ, who appears as Father Dolan, was prefect of studies while Brother John Hanly, who appears under the name of Brother Michael, was the infirmarian.

Father Conmee later played a pivotal role in Joyce becoming a pupil at Belvedere College, when the Joyce family were in financial difficulties. Father Richard Campbell, SJ, nicknamed 'Foxy Campbell' or 'Lantern Jaws', was a teacher at Belvedere College when Joyce was there. Father Darlington, SJ and Father Delany, SJ were connected with his time at University College Dublin.

Other priests, both secular and from orders such as the Franciscans, Carmelites, Passionist, Vincentians and Augustinians were attached to churches around the city. The churches to which they were attached give an insight into the city at the time, and also to the people connected with them, other than the clergy, such as the organists, like John Glynn who 'knew how to make that instrument talk'.

Father Timothy Gorman was administrator from 1890 to 1897 at the Pro Cathedral in Marlborough Street and was then promoted parish priest in the parish of St Michael and John's, Lower Exchange Street, Dublin. Nearby, at the church of St Nicholas of Myra, Francis Street, Father Michael Scally worked as administrator from 1892 until 1895, when he was appointed parish priest and remained there for the rest of his life. Father Francis Coffey, who was curate at St Paul's Church, Arran Quay, was also acting-chaplain at Glasnevin Cemetery, Finglas Road, where he received the remains of so many of the characters from *Ulysses*.

The Very Rev. Canon O'Hanlon, parish priest of St Mary's Star of the Sea, Sandymount was a distinguished churchman, historian, poet and author of many works including *Lives of Irish Saints* (9 vols, 1875). There are 43 named clergy in *Ulysses.*

THE LEGAL PROFESSION

Ulysses contains a number of judges, barristers and solicitors and innumerable legal references. Some of those called to the Bar may not have been practising as barristers, but worked in other areas such as journalism, politics, business or administration. The list of characters associated with the law ranges from prominent and successful judges and lawyers, with good addresses in fashionable areas of the city, to those who were less fortunate and ended up in poor conditions.

Joyce always had an interest in law and his father encouraged him to become a barrister. He even attended some lectures. In 1899, as a 17-year-old undergraduate at University College, he attended the murder trial of Samuel Childs at Green Street Courthouse and took notes on Bushe's speech. Childs was tried and acquitted, with Seymour Bushe as the defence counsel. The case figures prominently in *Ulysses* with Joyce repeating several times that the case had been won by the eloquence of Seymour Bushe.

Tim Healy appeared for Childs both in the police court and the court of trial, but Joyce chose not to give him any credit, as he disliked him on account of the role he played in the downfall of Parnell. There are numerous cases woven throughout the text mostly relating to legal issues of the time, such as that of Florence Maybrick who poisoned her husband in 1889; and Constable Henry Flower of the Dublin Metropolitan Police who was implicated in a case concerning 'death from drowning' of Brigid Gannon whose body was found in the river Dodder on 23 August 1900. There are 48 characters named in *Ulysses* who had some connection with the law.

THE MEDICAL PROFESSION

Joyce attended lectures for a time at the Catholic University School of Medicine at Cecilia Street, Dublin and then later at the university in Paris. However, due to financial constraints, he gave up the idea of studying medicine. About *Ulysses* he remarked, 'Among other things my book is the epic of the human body.' References to embryology, anatomy and clinical medicine appear throughout the text.

Excellent clinical care for the population was provided resting on the skills, practices and traditions developed during the first half of the nineteenth century, generally considered to be the golden age of Dublin medicine.

Most of the doctors mentioned in *Ulysses* were connected with various medical institutions in the city. Connolly Norman, a distinguished psychiatrist, was superintendent to the Richmond Asylum, considered to be the most important asylum in the country. Dr Eustace, known for his progressive methods, was superintendent at Hampstead Asylum in Glasnevin. The popular surgeon McArdle, attached to St Vincent's Hospital, was renowned as a teacher of surgery and refused a remunerative position in the United States, preferring to work amongst the poor of Dublin.

The most frequently mentioned medical institutions in *Ulysses* are the National Maternity Hospital, known as 'Holles Street' and the Mater Misericordiae, and Mercer's hospitals. Many of the doctors in *Ulysses* were eminent figures in Dublin at the time. They included Louis A. Byrne, the Dublin City coroner, Sir

Thornley Stoker (brother of Abraham Stoker, author of *Dracula*), Austin Meldon, surgeon to Jervis Street Hospital, and Dr Andrew Horne who was master of Holles Street. Horne is prominent in the 'Oxen of the Sun' episode, which takes place at Holles Street. It was due to Dr Horne and the founders of this hospital that it achieved such a prominent position at the time. Many doctors, medical students and two nurses appear in this chapter. There are 32 people connected with medicine in *Ulysses*. This includes a dentist and three nurses.

THE PRESS

Several members of the press mentioned in *Ulysses* worked with the *Freeman's Journal*, which was founded in Dublin in 1763 and had a distinguished history. It supported Catholic Emancipation, the Repeal Association, the Land League and Home Rule. It backed Parnell against the anti-Parnellites. It was a supporter of non-violent nationalism as espoused by John Redmond, leader of the Irish Party. Stephen J. M. Brown, in his book *The Press in Ireland* (1937), wrote 'the *Freeman* was always moderate and cautious to a fault. Extremists looked upon it with contempt, and the more ardent spirits of the party, which it supported, were often exasperated by its hesitancy and moderation. It maintained that reputation, not always deserved, to the end.'

In 1904, the world of the press in Dublin was about to change. William Martin Murphy was planning the launch of his halfpenny *Irish Independent* in January 1905, which sealed the fate of the *Freeman's Journal*. The *Freeman* ceased publication in 1923 when it was incorporated into the *Irish Independent*.

The journalists mentioned in the 'Aeolus' episode were mainly attached to the *Evening Telegraph* and *Freeman's Journal*. William Brayden, a brilliant and capable journalist, was editor of the Dublin *National Press*, 1890–2, which was absorbed by the *Freeman's Journal*. In 1892 he was appointed as editor of the paper, a position that he held until 1916.

Patrick Meade, on whom Myles Crawford is partly based, was subeditor of the *Evening Telegraph* in 1904. He came from the *Cork Herald*, where he covered the counties of Cork and Kerry during the days when evictions were frequent. Ignatius Gallaher, also with the *Freeman's Journal*, was modelled on Fred Gallaher, who was one of the best-known journalists of the time. According to Myles Crawford in *Ulysses*, Gallaher made an inspired scoop when he was the first to convey by telegraph the news of the Phoenix Park murders of 1882 to the *New York World*. Dick Adams worked for the *Southern Reporter*, before moving to the *Freeman's Journal*. He became a barrister, and gained notoriety for his defence of James FitzHarris, who was charged with collusion in the Phoenix Park murders.

John Hooper, who began his career with the *Cork Daily Herald*, became a leader writer on the *Freeman's Journal*. Parnell used his influence to have him made a parliamentary correspondent for the paper. Hooper returned to Cork as editor of the *Cork Daily Herald*. He sided with the anti-Parnell faction at the time of 'the split'. In 1891, he returned to Dublin to manage the *Nationalist Press*, the anti-Parnell paper. On the death of Parnell, Hooper became editor of the *Evening Telegraph*, which was in the same group as the *Freeman's Journal*. Paddy Hooper, his son, was a journalist with the *Freeman's Journal* and became its editor in 1916. John 'Jacques' McCarthy, a famous football reporter, noted for his sparkling wit also wrote for the *Freeman's Journal*, from 1875 until his death in 1901.

Others like Lenehan worked for different papers, such as the *Irish Times* and *Sport*. Some of the journalists held other jobs, as perhaps they did not feel financially secure. It was part of Dublin life at the time. Journalism was perhaps more democratic than other professions as it did not require rigid qualifications. Newspapers employed a variety of people from the editor and business manager to journalists, linotype operators, compositors, printing foremen, printers, and distributors. There are 35 people named in *Ulysses* connected with the press.

SPORT

The foundation of the Gaelic Athletic Association and Gaelic League in the late nineteenth century reawakened a realisation of Irish traditions and culture across the sectarian divide in Ireland.

There are numerous sportsmen mentioned in *Ulysses*. The bicycle races at College Park include the enthusiastic cyclists of the day such as the H. T. Gahan, J. A. Jackson, A. Munro, Robert 'Bob' Reynolds and W. E. Wylie who partook in the half-mile bicycle handicap and C. M. Green, W. C. Huggard, J. B. Jeffs, G. N. Morphy, T. M. Patey, C. Scaife, H. Shrift and F. Stevenson who partook in the quarter-mile race. Boxing is featured with a match between Dubliner Myler Keogh and Sergent-Major Percy Bennett from Portobello Barracks. Other boxers mentioned include Jem Corbett, Robert Fitzsimmons, John Heenan, Daniel Mendoza, Tom Sayers and John L. Sullivan. Cricketers named include the handsome Captain C. F. Buller who played for Harrow, Middlesex and I Zingari. Camille Jenatzy and Gordon Bennett are included in connection with motor racing, then in its infancy. Jockeys are named, such as Morny Cannon, Otto Madden, and William Lane. It is good to remember too the name of a now forgotten Irish athlete, Thomas Conneff from Kilmurray, Co. Kildare who broke the world amateur record for the mile in 1893 in Cambridge, Massachusetts. His mile record remained unsurpassed for 16 years, until 1911.

APPENDIX II

Horses in *Ulysses*

Horse racing is the sport mentioned most frequently in *Ulysses*. The names of 14 horses are referred to in ten of the episodes. Four of the horses named in *Ulysses* ran in the Gold Cup, the third event which was held at Ascot at 3.00 pm on 16 June 1904.

Horses named in the text include Ceylon, Fair Rebel, John O'Gaunt, Maximum II, Nevertell, Prophesy, Repulse, Saint Amant, Saint Frusquin, Sceptre, Shotover, Sir Hugo, Throwaway and Zinfandel.

Ceylon

'*... the duke of Beaufort's Ceylon, prix de Paris. Dwarfs ride them, rustyarmoured, leaping, leaping in their, in their saddles.*' *(15.3978–9)*
Ceylon owned by Henry Charles Fitzroy Somerset, the 8th duke of Beaufort (1824–99) won the Grand Prix de Paris in 1866, a famous race for three-year-olds that is held each year at the Hippodrome de Longchamp in the Bois de Boulogne. Tom Cannon rode Ceylon in the race.

Ulysses 2.302–3

Fair Rebel

'*Fair Rebel! Fair Rebel!* Even money the favourite: ten to one the field. Dicers and thimbleriggers we hurried by after the hoofs, the vying caps and jackets and past the meatfaced woman, a butcher's dame, nuzzling thirstily her clove of orange.' *(2.309–12)*
Fair Rebel, foaled in 1899 was by Circasslan out of Liberty. She was owned and trained by W. P. Cullen, 'Rathbride Cottage', the Curragh, Co. Kildare. On 4 June 1902, at the Tipperary meeting, Fair Rebel won the Curragh Plate.

John O' Gaunt

'Bad luck to big Ben Dollard and his John O'Gaunt. He put me off it.' *(8.839)*
John O'Gaunt was bred by Sir Tatton Sykes. He was named after John of Gaunt, the son of King Edward III. A bay horse by Isinglass out of La Flèche, he was foaled in 1901. Both his dam and sire were classic winners.

Sir John Thursby bought him for 3,000 guineas. He ran in the Derby on 2 June 1904, which was won by Saint Amant. Many people including Thursby were convinced that John O'Gaunt would have won the race had it not been for the awful thunderstorm.

This was his last race. When he was preparing for the St Leger he injured himself and then went to stud. He was considered to be among the more prominent stallions. He was destroyed prematurely at the Meddler Stud at Newmarket on 7 January 1924, aged 23 and in perfect health.

Maximum II

'Ascot. Gold cup. Wait, Bantam Lyons muttered. Half a mo. Maximum the second.' *(5.532–3)*

Maximum II, a French horse by Chalet out of Urgence was foaled in 1899. Jacques de Bremond owned him. He won the Gold Cup in 1903. Ridden by G. Stern he came fourth in the Gold Cup in 1904. He never really posed a threat in this race as he was beaten in his two previous races in France before the Gold Cup.

Ulysses 15.3976; 16.1289

Nevertell

'I mean, Leopardstown. And Molly won seven shillings on a three year old named Nevertell ...' *(15.546–7)*

The only horse on record named Nevertell was foaled in 1910 by St Primus or Oppressor out of Secret. Nevertell went to stud in 1912. There is no record of Nevertell running at Leopardstown. Ironically, a horse named Never Again won at Leopardstown on 26 December 1912 at 5/2. If Molly had placed a bet of two shillings on Never Again she would have got back seven shillings!

Prophesy/Prophecy

'Prophesy who will win the Saint Leger.' *(15.1840)*

Prophecy a bay filly by Knight of St Patrick out of Endor was foaled in 1870. She ran in 93 races between 1872 and 1880 winning 29 of them.

Repulse

Repulse by Stockwell was owned by Lord Hastings (1842–68). Repulse won the 1,000 Guineas in 1866. She was a certainty for the race but only won by a short head at 2/1 on. She was ridden by Tom Cannon the father of 'Morny' Cannon, and was trained by John Day junior.

Ulysses 2.301

Saint Amant

'I could have got seven to one against Saint Amant a fortnight before.' *(8.831–2)*

Saint Amant was a colt by St Frusquin out of Lady Loverule. Owned by Mr Leopold

de Rothschild whose racing colours were blue and gold, he won the Derby in a time of 2:45.4 on 2 June 1904 leading the race from start to finish during a ferocious thunderstorm. Trained by Alfred Hayhoe he was ridden by Kempton Cannon. He also won the 2,000 Guineas in 1904 ridden by the same jockey. Apart from winning the Jockey Club Stakes as a four-year-old, the rest of his career was disappointing. He made little mark as a sire.

Saint Frusquin

'That was a rare bit of horseflesh. Saint Frusquin was her sire.' *(8.836–7)*

Saint Frusquin was foaled in 1893. His sire was St Simon and his dam Isabel by

Plebeian. He was owned and bred by Leopold de Rothschild and trained by Alfred Hayhoe. He won nine out of his 11 starts and was runner-up to Persimmon in the Derby. He beat Persimmon in the Princess of Wales's stakes at Newmarket. Ridden by Thomas Loates, in 1896, he won the 2,000 Guineas, worth over £33,000. Shortly after the Eclipse Stakes at Sandown, which he won in 1896, he broke down and never raced again.

Sceptre

'Lenehan came out of the inner office with *Sport*'s tissues.

Who wants a dead cert for the Gold cup? He asked. Sceptre with O. Madden up.' *(7.387–9)*.

Sceptre, one of the greatest fillies in history, was foaled in 1899. Her sire was the famous Persimmon (1893–1908) who was bred by Edward VII. Her dam was Ornament by Ben Or (1877–1903).

The 1st duke of Westminster bred Sceptre at his Easton Stud. Following the duke's death Robert Sievier bought her for 10,000 guineas. She won 13 of her 21 starts, including four Classic races. Sievier was a gambler and pushed Sceptre to a gruelling number of races. She won the St Leger and two days later was entered for the Park Hill Stakes in a state of exhaustion. She was sold in very poor condition to William Bass but her health improved with the careful attention of Alex Taylor, her new trainer.

Sceptre entered the Ascot Gold Cup over two and a half miles as a five-year-old. In the *Freeman's Journal* on 16 June 1904 in tips from 'Celt', Sceptre is named.

By the time she was a five-year-old, Sceptre was past her peak. In 1911 she was sold and for the remainder of her life, she had three more owners. She only bred four winners and after 1917 she had no more foals.

Known as one of the toughest and gamest fillies of her time, Sceptre died aged 27 in 1926 and is commemorated by the Sceptre Stakes, which is run each September on the second day of Doncaster's four-day St Leger Festival. It is open to thoroughbred fillies and mares aged three years or older.

Ulysses 5.532; 8.829–31; 10.507; 12.1221; 12.1228; 14.1127–33; 14.1161–2; 14.1514–17; 15.3976–7; 16.1276–89; 17.320

Shotover

The duke of Westminster owned Shotover a filly by Hermit out of Stray Shot. Trained by John Porter, she won the 2,000 Guineas in 1882 and also the Derby the same year in a time of 2:45. She is among the few fillies that have won the Derby. Tom Cannon, on both occasions, rode the horse.   *Ulysses 2.302*

Sir Hugo

'... dark horse *Sir Hugo* captured the blue ribband at long odds.' *(16.1243–4)*

Sir Hugo, foaled in 1889 was by Wisdom out of Manoeuvre. Owned by the 3rd earl of Bradford and trained T. Wadlow he won the Derby in 1892 in a time of 2:44. Frederick Allsopp rode him. Like Throwaway, Sir Hugo was a dark horse and 'captured the blue ribband at long odds'. The Derby is sometimes referred to as 'the Blue Riband' of the turf.

As a yearling, Bradford put £100 on Sir Hugo to win £10,000 as a three-year-old. He also put more bets on Sir Hugo for the same race to the tune of £8,000. The stake of the race was £6,000. So by winning the Derby in 1892, Bradford won £24,000.

Throwaway

'And that Goddamned outsider *Throwaway* at twenty to one.' *(15.2935–6)*

Throwaway was born in 1899 and was by Rightaway out of Theale. Fred Alexander at Everleigh in England bred him. Between the years of 1901 and 1905, Throwaway ran in races at Chester, Bath, Liverpool, Newcastle, Gosforth Park, Newmarket, Bibury (Salisbury), Manchester, Ascot and Doncaster.

An outsider, Throwaway won the Gold Cup

race held at 3.00 pm at Ascot on 16 June 1904. He was trained by Herbert Braime and ridden by William Lane.

Ulysses 12.1219; 12.1226; 12.1551; 12.1563; 14.1132; 15.4814; 16.1242; 16.1278; 16.1280–2

Zinfandel

'Zinfandel's the favourite, lord Howard de Walden's, won at Epsom.' *(8.830–1)*

The chestnut Zinfandel foaled in 1900 was out of Medora and by Persimmon who

won the Ascot Gold Cup in 1897. On the death of his first owner Col H. McCalmont he passed into the ownership of Lord Howard de Walden and was trained by Major Charles Beatty.

Among Zinfandel's successes were the Coronation Cup, in which he beat Sceptre and Rock Sand; the Gold Vase at Ascot (first run in 1838); the Ascot Gold Cup; the Alexandra Plate; the Manchester Cup; the Gordon Stakes at Goodwood; and the Jockey Club Cup. As a three-year-old, Zinfandel's only defeat was in the Cesarewitch at Newmarket.

Zinfandel (5/4) ridden by Morny Cannon came second in the 1904 Gold Cup. He was winner of the 1905 Gold Cup and it is rumoured that when he won the race, his owner was seated under a tree in the paddock, perusing the score of an opera.

REFERENCES

Biographical Encylopaedia of British Flat Racing, edited by Roger Mortimer, Richard Onslow, and Peter Willett. London: MacDonald and Jane's, 1978; *Encyclopaedia of Flat Racing*, edited by Roger Mortimer. London: Robert Hale, 1971; *The Racing Calendar* and *The Irish Racing Calendar* 1872–80; Igoe, Vivien. '"Spot the Winner": some of the horses in *Ulysses*', *Dublin James Joyce Journal*, 2011: 4; Igoe, Vivien. '"Spot the Winner" again: another horse in *Ulysses*', *Dublin James Joyce Journal*, 2012: 5.

APPENDIX III

Cemeteries

How many! All these here once walked round Dublin.
Faithful departed. As you are now so once were we.
(6.960-1)

Several of the Dublin characters in *Ulysses* are buried in three of Dublin's main cemeteries. These include Glasnevin, Mount Jerome and Deansgrange. Daniel O'Connell founded Glasnevin, formerly named Prospect Cemetery. The largest cemetery in Ireland, it is in use since 1832 and is the burial place for over 150 characters in *Ulysses*.

Glasnevin Cemetery is laid out in a system which involves grids. Letters denote the rows of graves running from east to west, whiles those running north to south are numbered, giving each grave a unique reference of letters and numbers. The boundary walls are marked with the letters and these can be used as a reference for locating a particular grave.

Mount Jerome situated in Harold's Cross is in operation since 1836 and is the resting place of 44 characters whilst Deansgrange, which opened in 1865 and is the largest cemetery in south Co. Dublin contains 28 named characters in the novel. Goldenbridge Cemetery, in use since 1829, is the burial place of Dr Robert Kenny, the surgeon. Walter Bapty, the professor of singing lies in the shadow of St Patrick's Cathedral in the little churchyard in Patrick Street. Seven of the Jewish characters from *Ulysses* are buried in the Jewish Cemetery in Dolphin's Barn, Rialto, Dublin 8.

Glasnevin Cemetery, Finglas Road, Glasnevin, Dublin 9
Barlow, John (1822–1912) [BE 34.5 Dublin Section]
Boyd, John Dean (1867–1932) [PH 77 Section 3]
Boylan, Augustus (1872–1963) [A1 263 St Brigid's]
Brangan, Fr Thomas B. (1856–1937) [DH South St Brigid's]
Burke, Thomas Henry (1829–82) [ZB 74 South Section E]
Byrne, Davy (1861–1938) [NH 46 St Brigid's]
Campbell, Fr Richard (1854–1945) Jesuit Plot [AH–GH 30–40.5]
Caprani, Menotti (1866–1931) [VH 128.5 St Brigid's]

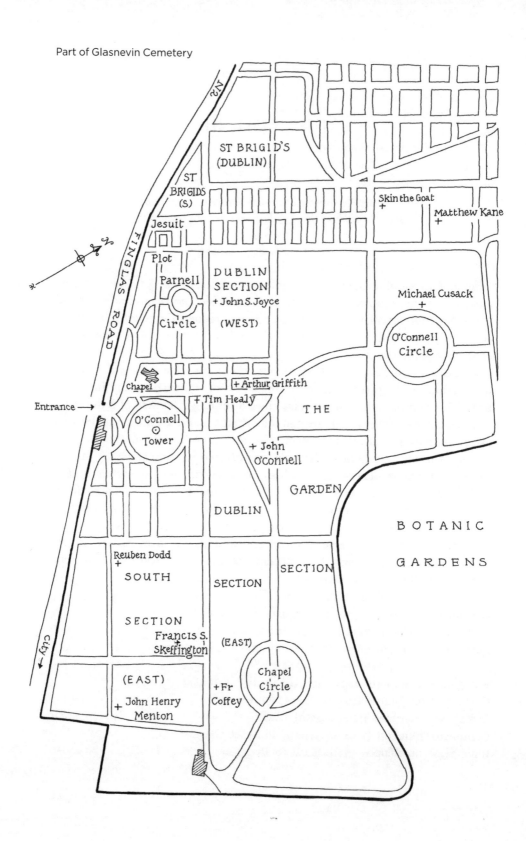

Part of Glasnevin Cemetery

Casement, Roger (1864–1916) [A 16 Tower Circle Section]

Casey, John Keegan (1846–70) [NC 7 South]

Chance, Charles (1863–1915) [EE 232 Garden]

Claffey, Patrick (1825–96) [HD 50 Garden]

Clancy, Alderman John (1845–1915) [VF 5.5 South]

Cleary, Rev. Fr Patrick Joseph (1835–1909) Franciscan Plot [CH 10 South St Brigid's]

Coffey, Rev. Fr Francis J. (1843 –1917) [RA 9.5 Dublin Section]

Conmee, Rev. Fr John (1847–1910) Jesuit Plot [AH–GH 30–40.5]

Conway, Elizabeth 'Dante' (1827–96) [GC 4.5 South]

Corley, Michael (1850–1916) [XA 37.5 Saint Paul's]

Costello, Francis (1881–1948) [K 47 Curran Square]

Crimmins, William Condon (1863–1926) [CH 37 St Brigid's]

Cuffe, Joseph (1843–1908) [Vault 58 O'Connell Circle]

Cunningham, Stephen (1861–1908) [TC 56.5 Garden]

Curran, John Philpot (1750–1817) [LMN 51–7 Curran's Square Section]

Cusack, Michael (1847–1906) [DG 163.5 Garden]

Darlington, Fr Joseph, SJ (1850–1939) Jesuit Plot [AH–GH 30–40.5]

Dawson, Charles 'Dan' (1839–1917) [EA 5.5 South]

Delany, Richard (1842–1912) [QD 63 Garden]

Delany, Fr William, SJ (1835–1924) Jesuit Plot [AH–GH 30–40.5]

Dennany, Thomas H. (c. 1840–1910) [HC 73 Garden]

Devin, Thomas (1865–1937) [MC 22.5 South]

Dillon, Mathew (1821–1899) [GC 45 South]

Dillon, Valentine Blake (1847–1904) [MD 67 Dublin New Chapel]

Dinneen, Fr Patrick (1860–1934) [CH 83.5 St Brigid's]

Dodd, Reuben (1847–1931) [ZB 68 South]

Dodd, Reuben junior (1879–1957) [ZB 69.5 South]

Doherty, Fr William (1872–1923) [WF 59.5 Section 4]

Dollard, Christopher (1839–85) [D 35 O'Connell Circle]

Downing, Denis J. (1871–1909) [KB 275 South]

Doyle, John Christopher (1866–1939) [HH 51.5 St Brigid's]

Dudley, Fr Henry (1852–1932) [WB 81.5 Section 5]

Farley, Rev. Charles, SJ (1859–1938) Jesuit Plot [AH–GH 30–40.5]

Figatner, Aaron (1853–1922) [DH 23 St Brigid's]

FitzHarris, James 'Skin-the-Goat' (1833–1910) [VH 159 St Brigid's]

Fitzsimon, H. O'Connell (1864–1950) [JF 12 Dublin Section]

Flanagan, Fr John (1872–1935) [RB 75 South]

Fogarty, Patrick (1869–1907) [EK 272 St Brigid's]

Fottrell, Sir George (1849–1925) [VA 23 South]

Friery, Christopher (1859–1926) [GC 65–66.5 South]

Gallagher, William (1846–1921) [ED 36.5 Dublin Section]

Gallaher, Gerald (1889–1946) [QD 125.5 Garden]

Gallaher, Joe (1855–93) [CC 52 Garden]

Gallaher, Mrs Joe (née Louisa Powell) (1862–1916) [BF 202 Garden]

Gannon, Brigid (1870–1900) [S 38 Poor Ground Section] (Exhumed and reinterred at Clonsilla Cemetery.)

Geary, James W. (1853–1930) [DH 9 St Brigid's]

Geraghty, Michael (1864–1905) [XE 233.5 St Patrick's]

Gilligan, Philip (1843–1901) [1A 73 South]

Giltrap, James J. (1832–99) [2D 52 Garden]

Glynn, John M. (1834–93) [BI 227 St Brigid's]

Gonne, Maud (1866–1953) [TD 24–25.5 South New Chapel]

Goodwin, William (1839–92) [YC 20.5 Garden]

Gorman, Fr Bernard, ODC (1864–1938) [TE 20.5 South New Chapel]

Gorman, Fr Timothy (1845–1922) [XB 79 South]

Gray, Sir John (1815–75) [Vault 8 O'Connell Tower Circle]

Greene, Roger (1846–1909) [TA 6 Section 5]

Griffith, Arthur (1871–1922) [ZE 22 South New Chapel]

Gumley, William (1849–1920) [FD 70 St Patrick's]

Hackett, Rev. Martin (1850–1911) [GH 13 St Brigid's]

Hall, Jack B. (1851–1931) [EG 168.5 Garden]

Hand, Stephen (1873–1924) [PH 147 St Brigid's]

Harrington, Timothy (1851–1910) [UG 4 Dublin Section]

Hart, Michael (1859–98) [UH 175 St Brigid's]

Hayes, Michelangelo (1820–77) [MC 94.5 South]

Healy, Timothy (1855–1931) [CE 4 South New Chapel]

Henry, James (1855–1916) [YC 48.5 Section 7]

Hooper, Alderman John (1845–97) [ZG 178.5 Garden]

Hooper, Patrick (1873–1931) [AH 174.5 St Brigid's]

Horne, Sir Andrew (1856–1924) [FD 46 South New Chapel]

Hughes, Fr John, SJ (1843–1912) Jesuit Plot [AH–GH 30–40.5]

Hutchinson, Joseph (1852–1928) [BH 147 Section 3]

Ivers, Michael (1853–1910) [ID 24.5 South]

Joyce, John Stanislaus (1849–1931) and Mary Jane (1859–1903) [XF 6.5–7 Dublin Section]

Kane, Matthew F. (1865–1904) [11 238.5 St Brigid's]

Kavanagh, Charles (1851–94) [VG 4 Garden]

Kerrigan, Simon (1855–1936) [VC 38 Dublin Section]

Keyes, Alexander (1853–1931) [JC 54 South]

Lalor, James Fintan (1807–49) [TD 24–25.5 South]

Laracy, John (1842–1906) [FE 106.5 Garden]

Lidwell, J. G. (1864–1919) [DA 68.5 Section 5]

Lyon, Abraham (1853–1923) [DG 168 Garden]

Lyons, Frederick M. 'Bantam' [SA 47 South]

MacCabe, Edward Cardinal (1816–85) [C 31 St Laurence's]

MacCarthy, Denis Florence (1817–82) [Vault JA 44.5 Chapel Circle]

McArdle, John (1859–1928) [DF 25 South New Chapel]

McCann, James (1841–1904) [V 47 O'Connell]

McCarthy, John 'Jacques' (1857–1901) [RD 31.5 Garden]

McManus, Rev. Miles (1827–1919) [C 32.5 St Laurence's]

McSwiney, Peter Paul (1810–84) [MC 79.5 South]

Magennis, William (1869–1946) [TD 71 Section 8]

Maginni, Denis J. (1846–1915) [QI 242.5 St Brigid's]

Malone, Rev. Charles (1841–1924) [B 37 St Laurence's]

Martyn, Edward (1859–1923) [NB 86.5 St Paul's]

Maxwell, Sir Patrick (1817–97) [MB 5 Garden]

Meldon, Austin (1844–1904) [Vault 90 O'Connell Tower Circle]

Menton, John Henry (1859–1905) [EA 72.5 South Section]

Molloy, Rev. Gerald (1834–1906) [A 32.5 St Laurence's]

Monks, Edward (1850–1941) [KI 283.5 Section 3]

Murphy, William Martin (1844–1919) [VT 30 Section 11 O'Connell Circle]

Murray, John (1856–1910) [IH 159.5 Section 3]

Murray, John Fisher (1811–65) [NC 44 South]

Murray, Josephine (1863–1924) [AG 135.5 Garden]

Murray, William (1857–1912) [AG 135.5 Garden]

Myers, John (1863–1927) [AA 5 South]

Nagle, Susanna 'Susy' (1871–1951) [YM 82 St Patrick's]

Nannetti, Joseph Patrick (1851–1915) [HF 25 South New Chapel]

Nicholas, Fr, OSFC (1849–1923) [NH 6 Section 3]

O'Brien, James Francis Xavier (1828–1905) [YA 34 South]

O'Brien, John Patrick (1848–1925) [B1 221 St Brigid's]

O'Brien, Sir Timothy (1787–1862) [Vault 56 Garden]

O'Brien, Vincent (1871–1948) [DD 57 South New Chapel]

O'Connell, Daniel (1775–1847) [Crypt beneath the Tower]

O'Connor, James (1836–1910) [XE 1924 Garden]

O'Connell, John D. (1845–1925) [HE 37 Dublin Section]

O'Donovan Rossa, Jeremiah (1831–1915) Republican Plot [TD 37 South New Chapel]

O'Dowd, Elizabeth (1839–1910) [RF 127.5 Garden]

O'Hagan, Thomas (1812–85) [Vault 42 O'Connell Tower Circle]

O'Hanlon, Canon John (1821–1905) [EH 18.5 St Brigid's]

O'Leary, John (1830–1907) [RD 39 South New Chapel]

O'Reilly, Robert (1834–1915) [LC 45.5 South]

O'Rourke, Larry (1840–1913) [WB 21.5 South]

Palles, Christopher (1831–1920) [Inner Vault D 93 Old O'Connell Circle]

Parnell, Charles Stewart (1846–91) Parnell Circle [EG 17 and FG 17 South Section]

Powell, Major Malachy (1821–1917) [BF 202 Garden]

Power, Jennie Wyse (1858–1941) [IC 36 South]

Power, John Wyse (1859–1926) [IC 36 South]

Rochford, Thomas Henry (1857–1934) [HJ 166.5 St Patrick's]

Rock, Patrick (1848–1933) [SK 270 St Patrick's]

Ruttledge, Wilson Ormsby (1853–1918) [ZG 111.5 Section 4]

Scally, Rev. Michael (1843–1923) [E 34 Section 13]

Sheehy, Bessie (1867–1918) [AA 25.5 South]

Sheehy, David (1844–1932) [AA 25.5 South]

Sheehy-Skeffington, Francis (1878–1916) [ZA 16–17.5 South]

Sigerson, Dr George (1836–1925) [E 28 O'Connell Circle]

Stephens, James (1825–1901) [RD 40 South New Chapel]

Swan, Brother William (1834–1911) [PC 54 South]

Tallon, Daniel (1836–1908) [MC 99.5 South]

Taylor, John F. (1853–1902) [RB 60.5 South]

Tobin, Patrick (1863–1928) [PJ 101 St Patrick's]

Thornton, R. J. (1853–1903) [CJ 199 St Patrick's]

Walsh, Rev. William (1841–1921) [Vault C 45.5 St Laurence's]

White, Dudley (1873–1930) [VB 9.5 Section 5]

Mount Jerome Cemetery, Harold's Cross, Dublin 6

Aldborough, Lord (1733/4–1801) St Thomas Churchyard Communal Plot [AC-94–17333]

Apjohn, Thomas Barnes (1839–1911) [C111–12248]

Barraclough, Arthur (1839–1905) [A12–388–12285]

Barton, James (1848–1913) [A45–255–14033]

Browne, Mervyn (1851–1924) [A19–227–13994]

Bushe, Kendal D. (1767–1843) [Vault C14 –1582]

Cameron, Sir Charles (1830–1921) [C116–3518]

Carlyle, James (1839–1907) [C51–11713]

Childs, Thomas (1823–99) [C110–1343]

Clay, Robert Keating (1835–1904) [C38–12362]

Connellan, Rev. Thomas (1854–1917) [B36–366–11645]

Crampton, Sir Philip (1777–1858) [Vault C87–2286]

Crofton, James Thomas Ambrose (1838–1907) [C107–3523]

Davis, Thomas Osborne (1814–45) [C5474–115]

Dowden, Edward (1843–1913) [C5–14017]

Evans, Thomas Henry (1863–1942) [B7–371–17634]

Findlater, Adam (1855–1911) [C81–392]

Mount Jerome Cemetery

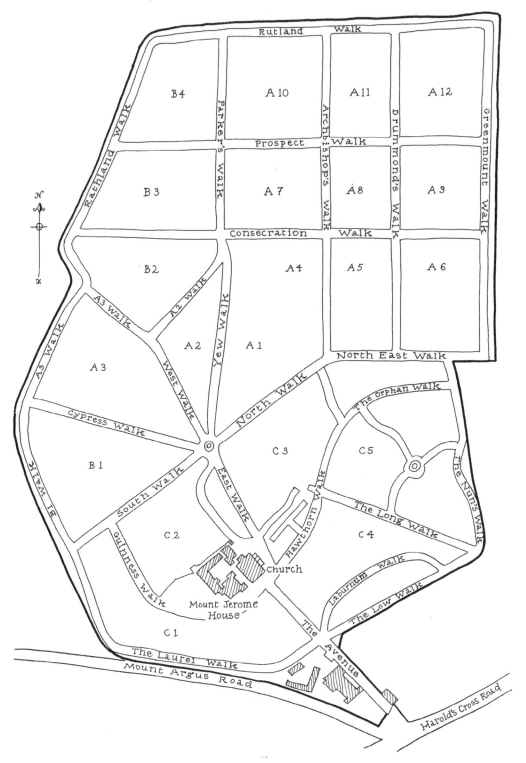

Froedman, Francis (1838–1925) [A16–334–15093]

Gamble, Major George Francis (1837–1912) [C13–12362]

Grey, Gregor (*c.* 1850–1920) [A3–227]

Hunter, Alfred (1866–1926) [B68–359–5924]

Ingram, John Kells (1823–1907) [C3367–127]

Irwin, Thomas Caulfield (1823–92) [C946–93]

Joly, Jasper (1864–1906) [C16–12330]

Joyce Monoghan, Mary Kathleen (1890–1966) [C140–36288]

Keller, T. G. (1873–1942) [C103–24548]

Lowrey, Dan (1823–97) [B5–360–5772]

Norman, Connolly (1853–1905) [C79–80–12823]

Poyntz, Samuel Robert (1842–1918) [A99–218]

Russell, George (Æ) (1867–1935) [A76–401–11217]

Russell, Thomas O'Neill (1828–1908) [C43–2859]

Salmon, George (1819–1904) [Vault C92–999]

Stoer, John Martin (1824–1907) [B20–206–4467]

Stoker, Sir William Thornley (1845–1912) [C79–11088]

Stubbs, George Henry (1840–1908) [A46–407–12971]

Sweny, Frederick William (1856–1924) [A10–414–16688]

Synge, John Millington (1871–1909) [C9468–38]

Tobias, Matthew (1840–1921) [C177–3277]

Thom, Alexander (1801–1879) [C115–5372]

Troy, Denis (1856–1943) [A–49a–88]

Turnbull, Donald Munro (1859–1908) [B26–359–7887]

Whiteside, James (1804–76) [C86–4872]

Wilde, Sir William (1815–76) [C678–108]

Wilde, Lady Jane Francesca (Speranza) (1821–96). Plaque on Wilde family tomb [C678–108]

Deansgrange Cemetery, Deansgrange, Co. Dublin

Best, Richard Irvine (1872–1959) [66–H–South West]

Byrne, Louis A. (1859–1932) [13–H3–North]

Chatterton, Hedges Eyre (1819–1910) [18–T1–South]

Curran, C. P. (1883–1972) [121–K–St Patrick]

Egan, Alfred William (1839–1912) [9–O1–South]

Finucane, Dr Thomas Dawson (1823–1920) [63–Q–South West]

Keogh, Myler (1867–1916) [108–T3–North]

Lavery, John (1858–1915) Vincentian Plot [170–182–AO–North]

Linehan, Matthew (1868–1939) [2 –N2–West]

Lyster, Thomas William (1855–1922) [45–M2–South]

McCormack, John (1884–1945) [119–20–EF–St Patrick]

Deansgrange Cemetery

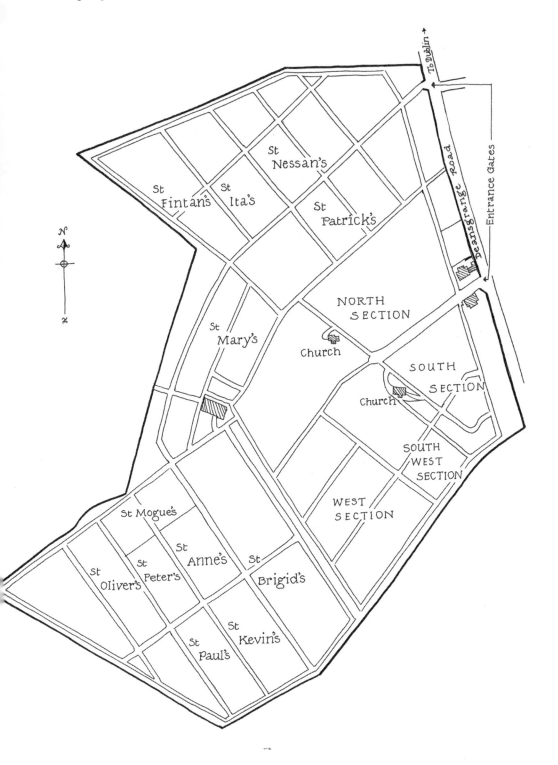

Madden, Dodgson Hamilton (1840–1928) [9–W–South]
Mesias, George Robert (1865–1941) [106–M2–South]
Moonan, G. A. (1872–1945) [123–E–St Patrick]
Mulligan, John (1838–1912) [79–B–North]
Norman, Harry Felix (1868–1947) [29–B–St Nessan]
Parnell, John Howard (1843–1923) [O–South West]
Powell, Josie (1878–1967) [14–B1–St Kevin]
Quill, Albert William (1843–1908) [50–B–North]
Quirke, Thomas (1865–1949) [106–C–North]
Reynolds, Robert 'Bob' (1878–1959) [42–N–St Nessan]
Rice, Ignatius J. (1870–1955) [15–N2–North]
Sherlock, Lorcan (1874–1945) [125–E–St Patrick]
Stephens, Davy (1845–1925) [2–T–North]
Tweedy, Henry Robert (1855–1939) [82–A–South West]
Victory, Louis Henry (1870–1947) [69–L–St Mary]
Wall, Thomas J. (1837–1910) [92–M1–North]
Werner, Louis (1860–1936) [84–C–South West]

Goldenbridge Cemetery, St Vincent Street West, Inchicore, Dublin 8
Doyle, Luke (1827–85) [GG 2² Canal Section]
Kenny, Dr Robert (1846–1909) [FF 31 Barrack Section]

St Maelruain's Cemetery, Tallaght
O'Leary Curtis, William (1863–1923)
O'Mahony, John (1870–1904)

St Patrick's churchyard, Patrick Street, Dublin 8
Bapty, Walter (1850–1915)

Friends' Burial Ground, Temple Hill, Blackrock, Co. Dublin
Eustace, Dr Henry Marcus (1869–1927) [Grave No. 109]

Jewish Cemetery, Dolphin's Barn, Rialto, Dublin 8
Abramovitz, Rev. Leopold (1849–1905) [03–A–24]
Harris, Morris (1823–1909) [A]
Moisel, Basseh (Bertha) (1862–1940) [02–B–07]
Moisel, Nisan (c. 1829–1910) [06–A–12]
Sinclair, William (1882–1937) [21–A–45]
Solomons, Maurice F. (1832–1922) [11–A–03]
Watchman, Minnie (1866–1921) [10–A–17]

Endnotes

Annotations have been limited as the full bibliography contained in this work will provide the reader with what he/she needs to know by way of reference for character entries.

ABRAMOVITZ, THE REV. LEOPOLD
Census of Ireland, Dublin 1901; *Thom's Directory 1904–7*; Hyman, Louis. *The Jews of Ireland*; Rosenblatt, Stuart. Jewish Ireland Series. *Vol. XV: Lackman-Zwirn*. *'Heritage' The A–Z DNA of Irish Jewry*.

ABRINES, JOHN L. AND LUIS RICHARD
Census of Gibraltar, 1901, Division 1, 2 and 4; *The Gibraltar Directory and Guidebook 1896*.

ADAMS, DICK
Irish Law Times and Solicitors' Journal, lxvii (1933); *Cork Examiner*, 8 Apr. 1908.

ALDBOROUGH, LORD
Carlyle, E. I. 'Stratford, Edward Augustus, second earl of Aldborough (1733/4–1801)', rev. E. M. Johnston-Liik. *Oxford Dictionary of National Biography*; Bence-Jones, Mark. *A Guide to Irish Country Houses*; Lewis, Samuel. *A Topographical Dictionary of Ireland*, vol. 1; Caufield, Catherine. *Emperor of the United States of America and Other British Eccentrics*.

ALDWORTH, ELIZABETH (NÉE ST LEGER)
Day, Brother John. *Memoir of the Honble. Elizabeth Aldworth of Newmarket Court, Co. Cork*.

ALLINGHAM, WILLIAM
Warner, Alan. *William Allingham*; Welch, Robert. *Irish Poetry from Moore to Yeats*.

ANDERSON, MARY
Roy, Donald. 'Anderson, Mary (1859–1940)'. *Oxford Dictionary of National Biography*.

ANDREWS, WILLIAM DRENNAN
Census of Ireland, Dublin 1911; *Irish Times*, 4 Dec. 1924.

APJOHN, PERCY
Thom's Directory 1904; *Census of Ireland, Dublin 1901, 1911*; *Irish Times*, 9 Sep. 1905, 12 Aug. 1911.

ATKINSON, F. M'CURDY
Stow, Randolph. 'Remembering Mr Atkinson'. Planet 71: *The Welsh Internationalist*, lxxi (October-November 1988); Moore, George. *Hail and Farewell*, edited by R. Cave; Trinity College Dublin Calendar, 1901; *The Times*, 19 Mar. 1973.

BALFE, MICHAEL W.
Barrett, William Alexander. *Balfe: His Life and Works*; Kenney, C. L. *A Memoir of Michael William Balfe*.

Endnotes

BALL, SIR ROBERT STAWELL

Ball, W. Valentine. *Reminiscences and Letters of Sir Robert Ball*; Wayman, P. A. *Dunsink Observatory 1785–1985: A Bicentennial History*.

BANDMANN-PALMER, MRS MILLICENT

New York Times, 27 Feb. 1887, 25 Jun. 1899; *Freeman's Journal*, 16 Jun. 1904.

BAPTY, WALTER

Census of Ireland, Dublin 1911; *Irish Times*, 5 Feb. 1876, 1 Nov. 1876, 2 Feb. 1877, 20 Mar. 1878, 21 Mar. 1882, 26 Jan. 1901, 3 Apr. 1915, 6 Apr. 1915; *The Musical Times*, 1 May 1915; *Thom's Directory 1884, 1904*.

BARLOW, JOHN

Census of Ireland, Dublin 1911; *Irish Times*, 28 Apr. 1866, 29 May 1912.

BARRACLOUGH, ARTHUR

Freeman's Journal, 21 Feb. 1878; *Irish Times*, 13 Dec. 1870, 28 Oct. 1905, 2 Nov. 1905, 4 Nov. 1905, 29 Nov. 1905; *The Musical Times*, 1 Feb. 1868, 1 Jan. 1878; 1 Dec. 1905; *Census of Ireland, Dublin 1911*.

BARRINGTON, JONAH

Barrington, Sir Jonah. *Personal Sketches and Recollections of His Own Times*; Barrington, Sir Jonah. *Historic Memoirs of Ireland*.

BARTON, SIR DUNBAR PLUNKET

Irish Times, 12 Sep. 1937; *Thom's Directory 1904*; *The Times*, 16 Sep. 1937.

BARTON, JAMES

Thom's Directory 1904; *Census of Ireland, Dublin 1901, 1911*; *Irish Times*, 5 Jul. 1958; *Irish Civil Registration Indexes, 1845–1958*.

BATEMAN, KATE

The Weekly Dispatch, 15 Apr. 1917.

BEAUFOY, PHILIP

The Times (legal notices), 25 Apr. 1947; Simpson, John. 'Philip Beaufoy and the philospher's tone'. *James Joyce Online Notes*. Issue 3 (April 2012).

BELLEW, LORD

Debrett's Peerage and Baronetage, edited by Charles Kidd and David Williamson.

BELLINGHAM, MRS

Adams, Robert M. *Surface and Symbol: The Consistency of James Joyce's Ulysses*.

BENADY BROTHERS

Census of Gibraltar, 1901; *Register of Births and Deaths, Gibraltar*.

BERGAN, ALF

Census of Ireland, Dublin 1901; *Irish Times*, 27 Dec. 1947, 3 Jan. 1948 (An Irishman's Diary); *Thom's Directory 1904*.

BEST, RICHARD

Irish Times, 28 Sep. 1959.

BILLINGTON, JAMES

Irish Times, 12 Jan. 1901, 21 Dec. 1901; *Weekly Freeman*, 14 Jan. 1899.

BLACKBURN/BLACKBURNE, R. T.

Census of Ireland, Dublin 1911; *Irish Times*, 2 Sep. 1922; *Thom's Directory 1884, 1904*.

BLACKWOOD, SIR JOHN

St James's Chronicle, 12 Mar. 1799.

BLAKE, PHIL

Weekly Irish Times, 19 Oct. 1918.

BLOOM, LEOPOLD

Nina Rocco-Bergera. *Itinerary of Joyce and Svevo through Artistic Trieste*, published on the occasion of the Third International James Joyce Symposium; Staley, Thomas. 'James Joyce e Italo Svevo'.

Lecture, Trieste, 24 Feb. 1965; Byrne, J. F. *Silent Years*; Hyman, Louis. *The Jews in Ireland*; McCourt, John. *The Years of Bloom, James Joyce in Trieste 1904–1920*; Gilbert, Stuart, ed. *Letters of James Joyce*, vol. 1; Raleigh, John Henry. *The Chronicle of Leopold and Molly Bloom*; Killeen, Terence. 'The original Bloom unmasked'. *Irish Times*, 16 Jun. 2008; Killeen, Terence. 'Marion Hunter revisited: further light on a Dublin enigma'. *Dublin James Joyce Journal*, iii (2010).

BLOOM, MARCUS JOSEPH
Census of Ireland, Dublin 1901, 1911; Cohen, R. A. 'A general history of dentistry from the 18th century with special reference to Irish practitioners.' *Irish Journal of Medical Science*, 1952; Lyons, J. B. *Thrust Syphilis down to Hell and Other Rejoyceana*; *Thom's Directory 1904–22*; Hyman, Louis. *The Jews of Ireland*; *Medical Directory 1898*.

BLOOM, MARION 'MOLLY'
Igoe, Vivien. *James Joyce's Dublin Houses and Nora Barnacle's Galway*; Igoe, Vivien. 'Centenary of Nora Barnacle's birth'. *Irish Times*, 21 Mar. 1984; Maddox, Brenda. *Nora: A Biography of Nora Joyce*.

BOARDMAN, BABY, EDY AND JACKY
Census of Ireland, Dublin 1901.

BOHEE, JAMES AND GEORGE
Komara, Edward M. *Encyclopaedia of the Blues*; Lotz, Rainer E. *Black People: Entertainers of African Descent in Europe, and Germany*; *Irish Independent*, 28 Aug. 1894; *Irish Times*, 1 Sep. 1894.

BOUCICAULT, DION
Hogan, Robert. *Dion Boucicault*.

BOYD, JOHN
Census of Ireland, Dublin 1901; *Irish Independent*, 24 May 1932; *Irish Times*, 22 Jul. 1904, 13 Aug. 1904, 23 Aug. 1904.

BOYLAN, HUGH 'BLAZES'
Evening Herald, 18 Jun. 1962; *Sunday Independent*, 21 May 2006; *Thom's Directory 1904, 1926, 1929*; Killeen, Terence. *Ulysses Unbound: A Reader's Companion to James Joyce's Ulysses*.

BRACEGIRDLE, MRS ANNE
Howe, Elizabeth. *The First English Actresses: Woman and Drama 1660–1700*.

BRADY, DR FRANCIS
Census of Ireland, Wicklow 1901, 1911; *Irish Civil Registration Indexes, 1845–1958*; *Thom's Directory 1904*; *Irish Times*, 16 Feb. 1915; 18 Feb. 1915.

BRANGAN, REV. THOMAS
'A beloved novice master, Fr. Thomas Brangan, OSA'. *Good Counsel*, Oct.–Dec. 1938; *The Irish Catholic Directory and Almanac*; *Irish Times*, 7 Dec. 1937, 8 Dec. 1937.

BRANSCOMBE, MAUD
Irish Times, 7 Nov. 1883, 8 Nov. 1883, 27 Dec. 1884; *News of the World*, 16 May 1886; *New York Times*, 9 Sep. 1880, 9 Nov. 1884.

BRAYDEN, WILLIAM HENRY
Census of Ireland, Dublin 1901, 1911; *Irish Independent*, 20 Dec. 1933; *Thom's Directory 1904*.

BRODERICK, JOHN
Census of Ireland, Dublin 1911.

BROWNE, MERVYN
Census of Ireland, Dublin, 1901, 1911; *Census of Ireland, Waterford 1911*; *Irish Civil Registration Indexes, 1845–1958*; *Irish Times*, 28 Feb. 1874, 29 Sep. 1877, 6 Dec. 1882, 8 Aug. 1883, 3 Nov. 1883, 22 Feb. 1888, 26 Apr. 1888, 10 May 1888, 15 Feb. 1890, 10 Jan. 1891, 30 Apr. 1904, 1 Aug. 1905; *Irish Independent*, 15 Feb. 1924; *Thom's Directory 1884–1905*.

BULLER, CAPTAIN
Hone, W. P. *Cricket in Ireland*; *Wisden Almanak*, 1907; Harrow School Register; Desborough, Lord.

Fifty Years of Sport at Oxford, Cambridge and the Great Public Schools, Eton, Harrow and Winchester, edited by R. H. Lyttelton, Arthur Page and Evan Noel.

BUSHE, SEYMOUR

Hardiman, Adrian. '"A gruesome case": James Joyce's Dublin murder case'; Hardiman, Adrian. 'How Joyce took on the law'. *Irish Times*, 10 Jun. 2006.

BUTT, ISAAC

Thornley, David. *Isaac Butt and Home Rule*; White, Terence de Vere. *The Road to Excess*.

BYRNE, LOUIS

Census of Ireland, Dublin 1901; *Irish Times*, 30 Nov. 1907, 2 May 1908, 29 Nov. 1932.

BYRNE, MADAM T. LEGGETT AND TALBOT HASLAM LEGGETT

Irish Times, 23 Jun. 1933, 20 Jul. 1940, 22 Apr. 1948, 24 Apr. 1948, 1 May 1948.

CAFFREY, CISSY

Thom's Directory 1879–99.

CALLAN, NURSE

Census of Ireland, Dublin 1901, 1911.

CALLANAN, CHRISTOPHER

Census of Ireland, Dublin 1901; *Irish Times*, 25 Dec. 1909, 30 Dec. 1909.

CAMERON, SIR CHARLES

Fleetwood, John. *History of Medicine in Ireland*.

CAMPBELL, HENRY

Clark, Mary and Hugh Fitzpatrick. *Serving the City: The Dublin City Manager and Town Clerks 1230–2005*; *Irish Times*, 7 Mar. 1924.

CAMPBELL, RICHARD, SJ

Bradley, Bruce, SJ. *James Joyce's Schooldays*; *Irish Province News*, v:2 (April 1945).

CAREY, JAMES

Corfe, Tom. *The Phoenix Park Murders: Conflict, Compromise and Tragedy in Ireland, 1879–1882*.

CARLISLE/CARLYLE, JAMES

Irish Times, 5 Jan. 1907.

CASEY, JOSEPH THEOBALD

The Anglo Celt, 10 Jun. 1911; Ryan, Desmond. *The Fenian Chief: A Biography of James Stephens*.

CHANCE, CHARLES

Census of Ireland, Dublin 1901, 1911; *Irish Times*, 11 Feb. 1895, 16 Apr. 1895, 20 Mar. 1897; *Thom's Directory 1904*.

CHARLES, FATHER

Spencer, Paul Francis. *To Heal the Broken Hearted: The Life of Blessed Charles of Mount Argus*.

CHATTERTON, ABRAHAM

Census of Ireland, Dublin 1901; *Thom's Directory 1895, 1903*.

CHILDS, THOMAS

Evening Herald, 12 Nov. 1957; Hardiman, Adrian. '"A gruesome case": James Joyce's Dublin murder case'; *Irish Times*, 4 Sep. 1899, 5 Sep. 1899, 6 Sep. 1899, 7 Sep. 1899, 8 Sep. 1899, 9 Sep. 1899, 23 Oct. 1899; *Thom's Directory 1888, 1889*.

CITRON, ISRAEL

Census of Ireland, Dublin 1901, 1911; Hyman, Louis. *The Jews of Ireland*; *Thom's Directory 1904*.

CLAFFEY, MARGARET

Census of Ireland, Dublin 1901, 1911; Simpson, John. 'Pat Claffey and the Dublin convents'. *James Joyce Online Notes*. Issue 5 (September 2013).

CLAFFEY, PATRICK

Thom's Directory 1884, 1904; *Irish Times*, 27 May 1882, 26 Dec. 1882, 19 May 1883, 20 Jul. 1883, 4 Sep. 1884, 17 Jun. 1889, 24 Jul. 1891, 2 Sep. 1891, 22 Aug. 1892, 25 Jan. 1894, 15 Feb. 1895.

CLANCY, JOHN

Irish Times, 17 Jul. 1914, 30 Jan. 1915, 2 Feb. 1915.

CLAY, ROBERT KEATING

Irish Law Times and Solicitor's Journal, xxxviii (1904); *Irish Times*, 9 Jul. 1904; *Thom's Directory 1904*.

CLEARY, OSF. REV. P. J.

Census of Ireland, Dublin 1901; *Freeman's Journal*, 10 Feb. 1909; *Thom's Directory 1904*.

COCHRANE

Census of Ireland, Dublin 1901; *Thom's Directory 1904*.

COFFEY, REV. FRANCIS J.

Census of Ireland, Dublin 1911; *Dublin Catholic Directory 1904–18*; *Irish Times*, 6 May 1913, 21 Feb. 1914.

COHEN, MRS BELLA

Fagan, Terry. *Monto, Madams, Murder and Black Coddle*; Simpson, John. 'Bella Cohen at No 82 (not 81)'. *James Joyce Online Notes*. Issue 4 (March 2013); *Thom's Directory 1883–1905*.

COHEN, OLD

The Gibraltar Directory and Guidebook 1889; *Register of Births and Deaths, Gibraltar*; *Gibraltar Census 1901, Division 2*.

COLLINS, DR JOSEPH

Lyons, J. B. *James Joyce and Medicine*; *New International Encyclopedia*; *Thom's Directory 1904*.

COLUM, PADRAIC

Bowen, Zack. *Padraic Colum*; Denson, Alan. 'Padraic Colum: an appreciation with a check-list of his publications'. *The Dublin University Magazine*, vi (Spring 1967); Igoe, Vivien. 'Padraic Colum 1881–1972'. *Ireland Today*, the bulletin of the Department of Foreign Affairs, 1981.

CONMEE, REV. JOHN, SJ

Clongownian, 1910; *Irish Ecclesiastical Record*, Feb. 1968; Conmee, Very Rev. John S. *Old Times in the Barony*.

CONNEFF, THOMAS

Simpson, John. 'Wondrous little Tommy Conneff from the short-grass county of Kildare'. *James Joyce Online Notes*. Issue 5 (September 2013).

CONNELLAN, REV. THOMAS

Census of Ireland, Dublin 1911; Gibbons, Luke. '"Famished Ghosts": Bloom, Bible wars, and "U.P. up" in Joyce's Dublin'. *Dublin James Joyce Journal*, ii (2009); *Irish Times*, 2 Jan. 1904, 10 Jun. 1905, 7 Jul. 1905, 10 Jul. 1905, 4 Jan. 1907, 28 Sep. 1908, 5 Jun. 1909; *Thom's Directory 1904*.

CONROY, REV. BERNARD FRANCIS

Census of Ireland, Dublin 1911; Donnelly, Rev. N. *Short Histories of Dublin Parishes*, part 6, section 3; *The Irish Catholic Directory and Almanac 1904–41*.

COOPER, BECKY

Fagan, Terry. *Monto, Madams, Murder and Black Coddle*; Ellmann, Richard. *James Joyce*, revised edition; Finnegan, John. *The Story of Monto*.

CORLEY, PATRICK MICHAEL

Census of Ireland, Dublin 1901, 1911; Ellmann, Richard. *James Joyce*; *Thom's Directory 1884*; Jackson, John Wyse and Bernard McGinley. *James Joyce's Dubliners: An Illustrated Edition with Annotations*.

COSTELLO, FRANCIS XAVIER 'PUNCH'

Farmar, Tony. *Holles Street, 1894–1994: The National Maternity Hospital: A Centenary History*; *Irish Times*, 21 Aug. 1948; Medical Register, General Medical Council, London.

COUSINS, JAMES H.

Cousins, James Henry and Margaret E. *We Two Together*; Dumbleton, William. *James Cousins*; Denson, Alan. *James Cousins and Margaret E. Cousins: A Bibliography*; Stephenson, Paul and Margie Waters. 'We two and the lost angel: the Cousins of Sandymount and James Joyce'. *James Joyce Quarterly*, xxxvii:1 and 2 (Fall 1999 and Winter 2000).

CRAMPTON, SIR PHILIP

O'Malley, Kevin and Eoin O'Brien, eds. *Bicentenary Account of the Royal College of Surgeons in Ireland 1784–1984*, vol. 2; *Freeman's Journal*, 12 Apr. 1834; Lyons, J. B. *James Joyce and Medicine*; O'Cleirigh, Nellie. *Hardship and High Living: Irish Women's Lives 1808–1923*; *Oxford Dictionary of National Biography*.

CRAWFORD, MYLES

Census of Ireland, Dublin 1901, 1911; *Irish Times*, 6 Aug. 1928; *Irish Independent*, 6 Aug. 1928; *Thom's Directory 1891–5*.

CRIMMINS, WILLIAM C.

Census of Ireland, Dublin 1911; *Irish Times*, 25 Nov. 1926; *Thom's Directory 1904, 1926*.

CROFTON, J. T. A.

Irish Times, 12 Aug. 1927, 31 Aug. 1927; *Thom's Directory 1884, 1888*.

CROTTHERS, J.

Census of Scotland, 1901; *England and Wales Deaths Register*, 1940; Farmar, Tony. *Holles Street, 1894–1994: The National Maternity Hospital: A Centenary History*; UK Medical Register, 1915, 1935; National Probate Register.

CROTTY, LESLIE

Hodgart, Matthew J. C. and Ruth Bauerle. *Joyce's Grand Operoar: Opera in Finnegans Wake*; *Irish Times*, 16 Aug. 1890, 19 Aug. 1890, 8 Nov. 1893, 2 Jul. 1894, 22 Sep. 1894, 19 Dec. 1894, 20 Apr. 1903, 28 Nov. 1915, 24 Oct. 1917.

CUFFE, JOSEPH

Census of Ireland, Dublin 1901; *Thom's Directory 1904*.

CUPRANI/CAPRANI, MENOTTI

Caprani, Vincent. 'James Joyce and the Grandfather'. *Ireland of the Welcomes*, Jan./Feb. 1982.

CURRAN, CONSTANTINE P.

Curran, C. P. *James Joyce Remembered*; Curran, C. P. *Under the Receding Wave*; *Irish Times*, 3 Jan. 1972.

CURTIS, WILLIAM O'LEARY

Society of Jesus, Fathers of the. *A Page of Irish History: Story of University College, Dublin 1883–1909*; *Census of Ireland, Dublin 1911*; Joyce, Stanislaus. *The Dublin Diary of Stanislaus Joyce*, edited by George Harris Healey; *Thom's Directory 1903*.

CUSACK, MICHAEL

De Burca, Marcus. *Michael Cusack and the GAA*.

DALY, FATHER JAMES, SJ

Irish Province News, Jun. 1930; Bradley, Bruce, SJ. *James Joyce's Schooldays*.

DAWSON, CHARLES 'DAN'

Census of Ireland, Dublin 1911; *Irish Times*, 14 Feb. 1881.

DEANE, SIR THOMAS

O'Dwyer, Frederick. *The Architecture of Deane and Woodward*.

DELANY, RICHARD

Census of Ireland, Dublin 1911; *Sport*, 28 Jan. 1888.

DENNANY, THOMAS H.

Census of Ireland, Dublin 1901; Simpson, John. 'Thos. H. Dennany on a spit of land'. *James Joyce Online Notes*. Issue 5 (September 2013); *Thom's Directory 1904*.

DEVAN/DEVIN, TOM

Census of Ireland, Dublin 1901, 1911; *Irish Independent*, 2 Mar. 1937, 4 Mar. 1937; *Irish Times*, 4 Mar. 1937; Ellmann, Richard, ed. *Selected Letters of James Joyce*.

DILLON, MATHEW

Freeman's Journal, 16 Apr. 1866, 15 May 1866, 23 Apr. 1867, 3 Dec. 1867, 3 Apr. 1869, 7 Jul. 1870, 13 Jul. 1870; *Irish Civil Registration Indexes, 1845–1958*; *Irish Times*, 18 Sep. 1866, 9 Nov. 1869, 30 May 1872, 29 Dec. 1873; *Nation*, 5 Nov. 1871; *Thom's Directory 1865–96*.

DILLON, VALENTINE BLAKE
  Freeman's Journal, 1 Jan. 1904; *Irish Times*, 9 Nov. 1869; *Thom's Directory 1904*.

DIXON, JOSEPH FRANCIS
  Thom's Directory 1904; UK Medical Register; *Weekly Irish Times*, 24 Dec. 1904.

DLUGACZ, MOSES
  Hyman, Louis. *The Jews of Ireland*; McCourt, John. *The Years of Bloom, James Joyce in Trieste 1904-1920*.

DODD, REUBEN J.
  Census of Ireland, Dublin 1911; *Irish Independent*, 17 Jun. 1904; *Irish Times*, 24 Feb. 1947; *Thom's Directory 1904*.

DODD, REUBEN J. JUNIOR
  Irish Times, 8 Oct. 1954, 9 Oct. 1954, 16 Oct. 1954, 27 May 1955; 23 Jun. 1955, 24 Jun. 1955, 7 Oct. 1957; *Law Directory 1904*.

DOHERTY, REV. WILLIAM
  Census of Ireland, Dublin 1911; *Irish Times*, 5 Feb. 1923.

DOLLARD, CHRISTOPHER
  Freeman's Journal, 23 Feb. 1864, 3 Jun. 1871, 2 Jun. 1875, 13 Nov. 1875, 27 Mar. 1877, 21 Apr. 1880, 2 Oct. 1882, 13 Apr. 1896; *Irish Times*, 19 May 1863, 11 Feb. 1864, 18 Dec. 1866, 28 Mar. 1867, 2 Mar. 1869, 22 Dec. 1870, 5 May 1875, 6 Oct. 1882, 1 Dec. 1882.

DOLMETSCH, ARNOLD
  Campbell, M. *Dolmetsch: The Man and His Work*; Donington, R. *The Work and Ideas of Arnold Dolmetsch*; Matthew, H. C. G. 'Dolmetsch, (Eugène) Arnold (1858-1940)'. *Oxford Dictionary of National Biography*.

DOWDEN, EDWARD
  Dowden, E. D. *Letters of Edward Dowden and His Correspondence 1843-1913*, edited by H. M. Dowden; Gwynn, E. J. 'Dowden, Edward (1843-1913)', rev. Arthur Sherbo. *Oxford Dictionary of National Biography*.

DOWNING, DENIS JAMES
  Freeman's Journal, 2 Dec. 1899; *Irish Times*, 18 Jun. 1909; *Thom's Directory 1904*; *Tuam Herald*, 26 Jun. 1909.

DOYLE, J. C.
  Dwan, Peter. *John McCormack: Icon of an Age: The Anthology*; *Irish Times*, 1 Oct. 1939, 17 Oct. 1939.

DOYLE, LUKE
  Thom's Directory 1850, 1856, 1867, 1885.

DUBEDAT, MISS
  Freeman's Journal, 3 Feb. 1894; Nolan, Anne. 'An Irishwoman's diary'. *Irish Times*, 8 Nov. 1893, 19 Jul. 1999; *Thom's Directory 1904*; Wootten, Maria. *The DuBedat Story: Killiney to Kommetjie*.

DUDLEY, LADY
  Irish Times, 26 Jun. 1920, 29 Jun. 1920, 30 Jun. 1920, 3 Jul. 1920.

DUDLEY, REV. NICHOLAS
  Census of Ireland, Dublin 1911; *The Irish Catholic Directory and Almanac 1904-32*; *Irish Times*, 10 Jun. 1932; *Thom's Directory 1904*.

DUNLOP, DANIEL
  Meyer, Thomas. *D. N. Dunlop: A Man of Our Time*.

EGAN, ALFRED WILLIAM
  Census of Ireland, Dublin 1911; *Irish Times*, 4 Feb. 1911, 13 Sep. 1911, 6 Apr. 1912; Smyth, Hazel. *The B & I Line: A History of the British and Irish Steam Packet Company*; *Thom's Directory 1904*.

EGLINTON, JOHN
  The Times, 11 May 1961.

ELWOOD, JOHN R.
  Connacht Tribune, 7 Apr. 1934; Joyce, Stanislaus. *The Dublin Diary of Stanislaus Joyce*, edited by

George Harris Healey; Gogarty, Oliver St John. *Tumbling in the Hay*; *Irish Times*, 12 Nov. 1904, 1 Jan. 1905, 13 Apr. 1912, 1 Oct. 1914; *Irish Independent*, 3 Apr. 1934; Lyons, J. B. *James Joyce and Medicine*.

EMMET, ROBERT
Reynolds, J. J. *Footprints of Emmet*; Madden, Richard R. *The United Irishmen: Their Lives and Times*.

EUSTACE, DR HENRY MARCUS
Census of Ireland, Dublin 1911; *Irish Times*, 2 Dec. 1927; Lyons, J. B. *James Joyce and Medicine*; *Thom's Directory 1904*.

EVANS, THOMAS HENRY
Census of Ireland, Dublin 1901, 1911; *Irish Times*, 23 Mar. 1942, 25 Mar. 1942; *Thom's Directory 1904–29*.

EVERARD, SIR NUGENT TALBOT
Irish Times, 30 Apr. 1904; 11 Jun. 1904; 20 Aug. 1904; 14 Oct. 1904; 22 Apr. 1905; 21 Oct. 1922; 20 Apr. 1929; 11 Jul. 1929; 20 Jul. 1929.

FALKINER, SIR FREDERICK
Irish Law Times and Solicitors' Journal, xlii.

FARLEY, REV. CHARLES, SJ
Irish Province News, iii:1 (January 1939); Robinson, Lennox. *Palette and Plough*; *Thom's Directory 1868, 1904*.

FARRELL, CASHEL BOYLE O'CONNOR FITZMAURICE TISDALL
Gogarty, Oliver St John. *As I Was Going down Sackville Street*; Simpson, John. 'Cashel Boyle O'Connor Fitzmaurice Tisdall Farrell (Endymion): the back-story'. *Dublin James Joyce Journal*, iv (2011); *Irish Times*, 21 Feb. 1934 (An Irishman's Diary).

FIELD, WILLIAM, MP
Reid, J. F. *William Field, MP: A Biography and Character Study*; *Irish Independent*, 15 Apr. 1898; 2 May 1935; *Irish Times*, 30 Apr. 1935; McGahon, Donal. '"The Light of the Village": William Field M.P.'. *Proceedings of the Blackrock Society*, ix (2001).

FIGATNER, AARON
Census of Ireland, Dublin 1901, 1911; *Irish Civil Registration Indexes, 1845–1958*; *Irish Times*, 18 Jul. 1914; *Thom's Directory 1904*.

FINDLATER, ADAM
Findlater, Alex. *Findlaters: The Story of a Dublin Merchant Family 1774–2001*; *Irish Times*, 23 Jan. 1911; *Thom's Directory 1904*.

FINGALL, LADY
Irish Independent, 30 Oct. 1944.

FINUCANE, DR THOMAS DAWSON
Census of Ireland, Dublin 1911; Lyons, J. B. 'Finucane lives! Or does he?'. *A Wake Newslitter*, x:3 (June 1973); *Irish Times*, 15 Aug. 1862, 30 Sep. 1867, 28 Nov. 1870, 28 Sep. 1906, 5 Jun. 1911, 14 Jun. 1920, 19 Jun. 1920; *Thom's Directory 1904*.

FITZGERALD, LORD EDWARD
Moore, Thomas. *The Memoirs of Lord Edward FitzGerald*, edited by Martin MacDermott.

FITZGIBBON, JUSTICE GERALD
Irish Times, 19 Oct. 1909.

FITZHARRIS, JAMES 'SKIN-THE-GOAT'
Corfe, Tom. *The Phoenix Park Murders: Conflict, Compromise and Tragedy in Ireland, 1879–1882*; *Irish Times*, 16 Aug. 2004 (An Irishman's Diary).

FITZSIMON, H. O'CONNELL
Thom's Directory 1904; *Census of Ireland, Dublin 1911*.

FLANAGAN, REV. J.
Census of Ireland, Dublin 1911; *Irish Catholic Record 1904-36*; *Irish Times*, 17 Dec. 1935; *Thom's Directory 1904*.

FLAVIN, REV. J.
Census of Ireland, Dublin 1911; *The Irish Catholic Directory and Almanac 1904-21*; *Irish Times*, 13 Sep. 1920.

FLOOD, HENRY
Kelly, James. *Henry Flood: Patriots and Policies in Eighteenth-Century Ireland*.

FLOWER, CONSTABLE HENRY DMP
Garvin, John. *James Joyce's Disunited Kingdom and the Irish Dimension*; *Irish Times*, 23 Aug. 1900, 3 Sep. 1900.

FOGARTY, PATRICK
Census of Ireland, Dublin 1901; *Thom's Directory 1897-1908*; Jackson, John Wyse and Bernard McGinley. *James Joyce's Dubliners: An Annotated Edition*.

FOTTRELL, SIR GEORGE
County Officers and Courts (Ireland) Act 40 & 41 Vict. c56, 1877; *Gazette of the Incorporated Law Society*, Mar. 1925; *Irish Times*, 2 Feb. 1925; *Thom's Directory 1904*.

FRANKS, DR HY
Irish Times, 27 Aug. 1890, 10 Nov. 1893, 24 Nov. 1893, 7 Dec. 1893, 8 Dec. 1893; Simpson, John. 'Will the real Dr Hy Franks please stand up?'. *Dublin James Joyce Journal*, iii (2010).

FRIERY, CHRISTOPHER
Irish Times, 13 Feb. 1926, 26 Mar. 1926, 27 Mar. 1926; *Law Gazette*, Feb. 1925; *Thom's Directory 1904*.

FROEDMAN, FRANCIS
Census of Ireland, Dublin 1901, 1911; *Thom's Directory 1904*.

GAHAN, W. H. T.
Evening Telegraph, 16 Jun. 1904 (last pink edition); Simpson, John. 'Wheelmen don't eat quiche'. *James Joyce Online Notes*. Issue 6 (December 2013).

GALLAGHER, WILLIAM
Census of Ireland, Dublin 1901, 1911; *Thom's Directory 1871-1921*.

GALLAHER, FRED
Freeman's Journal, 4 May 1899; *Irish Times*, 16 Apr. 1875, 19 Jul. 1886, 13 Feb. 1890, 28 Oct. 1893; Simpson, John. 'Ignatius per ignotius: the short lie and extraordinary times of Frederick Gallaher'. *James Joyce Online Notes*. Issue 5 (June 2013).

GALLAHER, GERALD
Census of Ireland, Dublin 1901, 1911; *Irish Times*, 28 Oct. 1893.

GALLAHER, MRS JOE
Census of Ireland, Dublin 1901, 1911; *Irish Times*, 28 Oct. 1893, 10 Nov. 1893, 17 Nov. 1893, 1 Dec. 1893, 8 Dec. 1893, 4 Jan. 1894, 19 Jan. 1894, 2 Feb. 1894; *Nation*, 12 Jul. 1884.

GAMBLE, MAJOR
Census of Ireland, Dublin 1901, 1911; *Irish Times*, 23 Feb. 1912; *Thom's Directory 1904*.

GARRYOWEN
Igoe, Vivien. 'Garryowen and the Giltraps'. *Dublin James Joyce Journal*, ii (2009); *Irish Times*, 22 Apr. 1880, 28 Aug. 1880, 7 Apr. 1881, 11 May 1882; Millner, Colonel J. K. *The Irish Setter: Its History and Training*, with an introduction by S. W. Carlton; *Times Literary Supplement*, 9 Jan. 1964.

GEARY, JAMES W.
Census of Ireland, Dublin 1901; *Irish Times*, 4 Feb. 1930; *Thom's Directory 1904*.

GERAGHTY, MICHAEL E.
Thom's Directory 1904-5.

GILLIGAN, PHILIP

Irish Times, 9 Sep. 1881, 24 Oct. 1881, 25 Nov. 1882, 3 Dec. 1889, 24 Dec. 1890; *Thom's Directory 1884*.

GILTRAP, JAMES J.

Freeman's Journal, 4 Sep. 1899; *Irish Times*, 22 Apr. 1880, 28 Aug. 1880, 7 Apr. 1881, 11 May 1882; *Thom's Directory 1889–99*; *Times Literary Supplement*, 9 Jan. 1964.

GIUGLINI, ANTONIO

Irish Times, 3 Aug. 1859, 5 Aug. 1859, 8 Aug. 1859.

GLYNN, JOHN M.

Igoe, Vivien. 'John M. Glynn, (1834–93): organist and professor of music'. *Dublin James Joyce Journal*, ii (2009); *Irish Catholic*, 2 Sep. 1893, 9 Sep. 1893; *Irish Daily Independent*, 28 Aug. 1893, 31 Aug. 1893; *Thom's Directory 1884*.

GOGARTY, OLIVER ST JOHN

Gogarty, Oliver St John. *It Isn't This Time of Year at All*; O'Connor, Ulick. *Oliver St John Gogarty: A Poet and His Times*.

GOLDBERG, OWEN

Thom's Directory 1901, 1904, 1910; *Census of Ireland, Dublin 1901, 1911*; *Irish Times*, 14 Jul. 1936.

GOLDWATER, JOSEPH

Hyman, Louis. *The Jews of Ireland*; *Thom's Directory 1904*.

GOMEZ, FERNANDO

Sullivan, Philip B. 'Los Toros in *Ulysses*'. *A Wake Newslitter*, xi (March 1963).

GONNE, MAUD

Gonne, Maud. *A Servant of the Queen: Reminiscences*; Yeats, W. B. *Memoirs*, edited by Denis Donoghue.

GOODWIN, PROFESSOR WILLIAM

The Musical Standard, 1881; *Irish Times*, 25 Nov. 1863, 5 Apr. 1866, 8 Jul. 1869, 13 Jul. 1876, 18 Dec. 1877, 27 Apr. 1880, 1 Dec. 1880, 31 Aug. 1885, 8 Mar. 1919; *Nation*, 14 Jun. 1890; *Thom's Directory 1858–91*.

GORMAN, REV. BERNARD, ODC

Carmel Magazine, Aug. 1938.

GORMAN, REV. TIMOTHY

Donnelly, Rev. N. *Short Histories of Dublin Parishes*; *The Irish Catholic Directory and Almanac 1904–23*; *Thom's Directory 1904*.

GRAY, SIR JOHN

Thom's Directory 1868; Ruttledge, Thomas Ormsby. 'The Gray Family of Claremorris, Co. Mayo'. *Irish Genealogist*, 1989.

GREENE, ROGER

Census of Ireland, Dublin 1901; *Irish Times*, 1 Nov. 1909, 3 Nov. 1909.

GREENE, REV. THOMAS ROBERT

Clergy of Dublin and Glendalough, biographical succession lists, complied by Canon J. B. Leslie and revised, edited and updated by W. J. R. Wallace; *Thom's Directory 1904*; *Irish Times*, 28 Oct. 1914.

GREGORY, LADY AUGUSTA

Coxhead, Elizabeth. *Lady Gregory: A Literary Portrait*; Robinson, Lennox, ed. *Lady Gregory's Journals 1916–1930*.

GREY, GREGOR

Thom's Directory 1904; *Irish Times*, 7 Jul. 1887, 15 Apr. 1887, 8 Feb. 1890, 21 Oct. 1892, 22 Oct. 1892, 7 Mar. 1894, 10 Mar. 1902, 24 May 1902.

GUMLEY, WILLIAM

Census of Ireland, Dublin 1901, 1911; *Thom's Directory 1904*.

GUNN, MICHAEL

Irish Times, 26 Oct. 1901; Watters, Eugene and Matthew Murtagh. *Infinite Variety: Dan Lowrey's Music Hall 1879–97*.

HACKETT, REV. M. A.
Irish Times, 9 Jan. 1911, 11 Jan. 1911; The Irish Catholic Directory and Almanac 1911.

HALL, JACK B.
Census of Ireland, Dublin 1911; Hall, J. B. Random Records of a Reporter, with a foreword by T. P. O'Connor; Irish Times, 8 Nov. 1930, 28 Jul. 1931; O'Hanlon, Terence. 'Further wisps of memory'. Capuchin Annual, 1953.

HAND, STEPHEN
Census of Ireland, Dublin 1901, 1911; Irish Times, 25 Jan. 1924.

HANLY, BROTHER JOHN
Bradley, Bruce, SJ. James Joyce's Schooldays; Clongownian, Jun. 1897; Memorials of the Irish Province, i:1 (June 1898); The Rhetorician, 28 Apr. 1888; Young, Peter. The Data Book of Joe Miller Jokes.

HARRIS, MORRIS
Irish Times, 26 Jun. 1909; Ellmann, Richard, ed. Selected Letters of James Joyce; Thom's Directory 1904; Rosenblatt, Stuart. Jewish Ireland Series. Vol. XV: Lackman-Zwirn. 'Heritage' The A–Z DNA of Irish Jewry.

HART, MICHAEL
Irish Times, 28 Apr. 1898; Weekly Irish Times, 28 Dec. 1889.

HARTY, GEORGE SPENCER
Census of Ireland, Dublin 1911; Irish Times, 24 Aug. 1922; Thom's Directory 1904.

HASTINGS, LORD
Davenport-Hines, Richard. 'Hastings, Henry Weysford Charles Plantagenet Rawdon, fourth marquis of Hastings (1842–1868)'. Oxford Dictionary of National Biography; Igoe, Vivien. '"Spot the Winner": some of the horses in Ulysses'. Dublin James Joyce Journal, iv (2011).

HAUCK, MINNIE
Irish Times, 6 Oct. 1877, 19 Mar. 1878.

HAYES, BARTER
Census of Ireland, Dublin 1901; Irish Times, 21 Nov. 1908; Thom's Directory 1904.

HAYES, LETITIA (NÉE POWELL)
Census of Ireland, Dublin 1901, 1911; Thom's Directory 1904.

HAYES, MICHELANGELO
Strickland, Walter G. A Dictionary of Irish Artists.

HEALY, VERY REV. JOHN
The Irish Catholic Directory and Almanac 1919; Irish Times, 18 Mar. 1918; Joyce, Rev. P. J. John Healy Archbishop of Tuam.

HENGLER, ALBERT
Turner, John Martin. Historical Hengler's Circus; Irish Times, 1871–1904.

HENRY, JAMES
Census of Ireland, Dublin 1911; Irish Times, 24 Sep. 1878, 14 Jan. 1892, 12 Jan. 1916.

HERZOG, MOSES
Census of Ireland, Dublin 1901; Hyman, Louis. The Jews of Ireland; Thom's Directory 1904.

HESELTINE, LT COL CHRISTOPHER
Thom's Directory 1904; The Times, 14 Jun. 1944.

HICKEY, REV. LOUIS J.
The Lamp, lii:267 (1897); Irish Times, 15 Jul. 1907.

HOLOHAN, HOPPY
Ellmann, Richard, ed. Selected Letters of James Joyce; Lyons, J. B. James Joyce and Medicine.

HOOPER, ALDERMAN JOHN
Francis Guy's Almanac 1879/80; Freeman's Journal, 22 Oct. 1897; Irish Times, 22 Nov. 1897, 24 Nov. 1897; Midland Tribune, 9 Jan. 1888; 22 Feb. 1888.

HOOPER, PADDY
  Irish Times, 7 Sep. 1931, 8 Sep. 1931, 9 Sep. 1931.
HORNE, SIR ANDREW
  Farmar, Tony. *Holles Street, 1894–1994: The National Maternity Hospital: A Centenary History*; *Irish Times*, 6 Sep. 1924, 10 Sep. 1924, 12 Sep. 1924, 13 Sep. 1924, 25 Jun. 1979; Stronge, John M. *Andrew Horne: Thirty Years a Master*.
HUGHES, REV. JOHN, SJ
  Irish Times, 19 Jun. 1912; *Thom's Directory 1904*.
HURLEY, REV. WALTER, CC
  The Irish Catholic Directory and Almanac 1904–15; *Thom's Directory 1904*.
HUTCHINSON, JOSEPH
  Irish Times, 27 Oct. 1928.
HYNES, MATTHEW J.
  Census of Ireland, Dublin, 1901, 1911; *Irish Civil Registration Indexes, 1845–1958*; *Freeman's Journal*, 29 Dec.1892, 1 Oct. 1906; *Irish Times*, 4 Oct. 1881, 13 Sep. 1882.
IRWIN, FRANCIS
  Census of Ireland, Dublin 1901, 1911; *Thom's Directory 1904*.
IVERS, REV. JOHN M.
  The Irish Catholic Directory and Almanac 1904–11.
JACKSON, GEORGE A.
  Census of Ireland, Dublin 1901; *Freeman's Journal*, 27 Dec. 1893; *Irish Times*, 27 Dec. 1890, 5 Jan. 1893, 11 Feb. 1893, 27 Dec. 1893, 5 Jan. 1901, 20 Nov. 1901.
JACKSON, J. A.
  Evening Telegraph, 16 Jun. 1904 (last pink edition); Simpson, John. 'Wheelmen don't eat quiche'. *James Joyce Online Notes*. Issue 6 (December 2013).
JEFFS, J. B.
  Evening Telegraph, 16 Jun. 1904 (last pink edition).
JENATZY, CAMILLE
  Irish Times, 16 Jun. 1904, 18 Jun. 1904, 20 Jun. 1904.
JOACHIM OF FLORA OR FIORI
  Catholic Encyclopaedia.
JOLY, PROFESSOR CHARLES JASPER
  Irish Times, 5 Jan. 1906, 9 Jan. 1906, 10 Jan. 1906.
JOYCE, JOHN STANISLAUS
  Jackson, John Wyse with Peter Costello. *John Stanislaus Joyce: The Voluminous Life and Genius of James Joyce's Father*.
KANE, MATTHEW F.
  Census of Ireland, Dublin 1901; *Freeman's Journal*, 14 Jul. 1904; Joyce, Stanislaus. *The Dublin Diary of Stanislaus Joyce*, edited by George Harris Healey; *Irish Times*, 14 Jul. 1904, 22 Jul. 1904, 9 Aug. 1904, 13 Aug. 1904, 23 Aug. 1904; Joyce, Stanislaus. *My Brother's Keeper*; Kane, Chris. 'James Joyce and Matthew Kane'. *James Joyce Online Notes*. Issue 5 (September 2013); *Thom's Directory 1887–1904*.
KAVANAGH, CHARLES 'CHARLEY'
  Irish Times, 25 Jun. 1894.
KAVANAGH, MICHAEL
  Corfe, Tom. *The Phoenix Park Murders: Conflict, Compromise and Tragedy in Ireland, 1879–1882*.
KAVANAGH, REV. P. J.
  The Irish Sword, xxiii (Winter 2003).

KELLY, TIMOTHY

Corfe, Tom. *The Phoenix Park Murders: Conflict, Compromise and Tragedy in Ireland, 1879–1882*; *Irish Times*, 20 Apr. 1883, 12 May 1883.

KENDALL, MARIE

Watters, Eugene and Matthew Murtagh. *Infinite Variety: Dan Lowrey's Music Hall 1879–97*.

KENNY, DR ROBERT, FRSCI

Census of Ireland, Dublin 1901; *Freeman's Journal*, 4 Aug. 1909; *Irish Independent*, 31 Jul. 1909; *Irish Times*, 17 Oct. 1900, 8 Aug. 1908; Lyons, J. B. *James Joyce and Medicine*.

KEOGH, MYLER

Census of Ireland, Dublin 1901; *Freeman's Journal*, 28 Apr. 1904, 29 Apr. 1904; *Irish Times*, 27 Feb. 1897, 29 Apr. 1904, 30 Apr. 1904; *Irish Independent*, 12 Jun. 1916; Simpson, John. 'Myler Keogh: the story of a boxing family'. *Dublin Historical Record*, lxiv:1 (Spring 2011).

KEOHLER/KELLER, THOMAS

Census of Ireland, Dublin 1911; *Dana*, i:10 (1905); *Irish Times*, 27 May 1942, 28 May 1942; Finn, Eamonn and John Simpson. 'Some notes on the triple life of Thomas Goodwin Keohler'. *James Joyce Online Notes*. Issue 1 (September 2011).

KERRIGAN, SIMON

Census of Ireland, Dublin 1901, 1911; Garvin, John. *James Joyce's Disunited Kingdom and the Irish Dimension*; *Thom's Directory 1904*.

KEYES, ALEXANDER

Census of Ireland, Dublin 1911; *Irish Independent*, 23 Oct. 1899; *Thom's Directory 1904*.

KINSELLA, PAT

Daily Telegraph, 4 May 1906; *Irish Times*, 10 Oct. 1891, 15 Oct. 1891, 17 Oct. 1891, 28 Nov. 1891, 5 Dec. 1891, 12 Dec. 1891, 19 Dec. 1891, 5 May 1906; *Liverpool Daily Post and Mercury*, 1 May 1906; *The Aeroplane*, ix (1915).

LANE, WILLIAM

Freeman's Journal, 16 Apr. 1904; *Irish Times*, 29 Jun. 1920; Igoe, Vivien. '"Spot the Winner": some of the horses in *Ulysses*'. *Dublin James Joyce Journal*, iv (2011).

LANGTRY, LILLIE

Langtry, Lillie. *The Days I Knew*.

LARACY, JOHN

Census of Ireland, Dublin 1901; *Irish Times*, 31 Jan. 1903, 27 Apr. 1904, 5 Feb. 1906, 24 Feb. 1906, 26 Feb. 1906.

LAREDO, LUNITA

Abecassis, Jose Maria. 'secs XV11 a XX, 1991, Luna Laredo, N-2.8.1864 em Gibraltar. F-30.12.1897 em Gibraltar'. *Genealogia Hebraica Portugal e Gibraltar*; Registry of Deaths of the Jewish Community No. 3; *The Gibraltar Directory and Guidebook, 1902*; Herring, Phillip F. *Joyce's Uncertainty Principle*.

LIDWELL, GEORGE

Census of Ireland, Dublin 1901, 1911; *Irish Times*, 24 Jul. 1905; *Thom's Directory 1904*.

LINEHAN, MATTHEW

Census of Ireland, Dublin, 1911; *Irish Times*, 31 Jan. 1935, 1 Feb. 1935, 21 Mar. 1939; *Thom's Directory 1904*.

LIVERMORE BROTHERS

Irish Times, 1884–1903.

LOVE, HUGH C.

Census of Ireland, Dublin 1901, 1911; Proceedings of the Belfast Natural History and Philosophical Society 1935; *School and Society: Volume 22, 1925*; *Thom's Directory 1904*.

LUDWIG, WILLIAM

Irish Times, 24 Mar. 1875, 1 Apr. 1875, 16 Apr. 1875, 30 Nov. 1875, 21 Dec. 1875, 19 Jun. 1876, 2 Aug. 1876,

9 Aug. 1876, 1 May 1878, 19 Nov. 1878, 2 Jan. 1880, 7 Jan. 1880, 4 Aug. 1880, 4 Aug. 1881, 15 May 1882, 13 Feb. 1886, 2 Oct. 1886, 9 Oct. 1886, 26 Jun. 1889, 15 Nov. 1890, 13 Feb. 1893, 1 Dec. 1894, 17 Aug. 1896, 11 Jan. 1898, 13 Jan. 1899, 18 Apr. 1901, 27 May 1902, 22 Aug. 1904, 22 Aug. 1905, 28 Aug. 1906, 6 Jun. 1907, 27 Dec. 1910, 9 Jan. 1911, 2 Feb. 1911, 24 Apr. 1912, 3 Aug. 1912.

LYNAM, BERNARD

Society of Jesus, Fathers of the. *A Page of Irish History: Story of University College, Dublin 1883–1909*; Simpson, John. 'Brunny the Medical Student'. *James Joyce Online Notes*. Issue 5 (September 2013).

LYON, ABRAHAM

Census of Ireland, Dublin 1911; *Irish Times*, 9 Apr. 1923.

LYONS, EMILY

Simpson, John. 'Emily Lyons sets sail for Boston'. *James Joyce Online Notes*. Issue 5 (December 2012).

LYONS, FREDERICK M. 'BANTAM'

Irish Times, 3 Feb. 1871; Jackson, John Wyse and Bernard McGinley. *James Joyce's Dubliners: An Annotated Edition*.

LYSTER, THOMAS WILLIAM

Irish Times, 27 Dec. 1922; MacLochlainn, A. *The National Library of Ireland, 1877–1977*.

MAAS, JOE

Irish Times, 23 Dec. 1878; 23 Jan. 1886.

MACCONSIDINE, DONAL

Ní Dheá, Éilis. 'Na Consaidínigh: grafnóirí na hInse sa 19ú haois'. *The Other Clare*, xxvi (2002).

MACCORMACK/MCCORMACK, JOHN

Ledbetter, Gordon T. *The Great Irish Tenor*.

MACDONNELL, SIR ANTHONY

New York Times, 20 Oct. 1902; *The Times*, 10 Jun. 1925.

MACDOWELL, MRS

Thom's Directory 1904; *Census of Ireland, Dublin 1911*.

MACK, MRS ANNIE

Census of Ireland, Dublin 1901; Ellmann, Richard, *James Joyce*, revised edition; Fagan, Terry. *Monto, Madams, Murder and Black Coddle*; Finnegan, John. *The Story of Monto*; Gogarty, Oliver St John. *Tumbling in the Hay*; Simpson, John. 'Summing up the madams'. *James Joyce Online Notes*. Issue 4 (October 2012); *Thom's Directory 1888–1904*.

MACKENNA, STEPHEN

Dodds, E. R., ed. *Journal and Letters of Stephen MacKenna*, with a memoir by Dodds and a preface by Padraic Colum; *The Times*, 24 Mar. 1934.

MACKERNAN/MCKERNAN, MRS ELIZABETH

Census of Ireland, Dublin 1901, 1911; *Thom's Directory 1904*.

MACNEILL, HUGH

Society of Jesus, Fathers of the. *A Page of Irish History: Story of University College, Dublin 1883–1909*; Byrne, J. F. *Silent Years*; *Census of Ireland, Dublin 1911*; Curran, C. P. *James Joyce Remembered*; Gray, Tony. *Mr Smyllie, Sir*; *Irish Times*, 26 Oct. 1935; Simpson, John. 'The reluctant professor MacHugh'. *James Joyce Online Notes*. Issue 10 (March 2016).

M'ARDLE/MCARDLE, JOHN

A History of St Vincent's Hospital: A Century of Service: The Record of One Hundred Years, published for the Centenary of St Vincent's Hospital, 23 January 1934; *Irish Times*, 18 Apr. 1928; *Thom's Directory 1904*.

M'CANN/MCCANN, JAMES

Freeman's Journal, 17 Feb. 1904; *Irish Times*, 20 Feb. 1904, 25 Nov. 1904; *Thom's Directory 1903*.

M'CARTHY, BARTHOLOMEW

Beck, Harald. 'The man behind Mr Bartell d'Arcy'. *James Joyce Online Notes*. Issue 1 (September 2011).

M'CARTHY, JOHN 'JACQUES'
Irish Times, 26 Mar. 1873, 8 Apr. 1901, 9 Apr. 1901, 13 Apr. 1901, 6 Aug. 1903, 7 Dec. 1937, 8 Mar. 1952, 2 Aug. 1971; O'Hanlon, Terence. 'Further wisps of memory'. *Capuchin Annual*, 1953.

M'CARTHY/MCCARTHY, JUSTIN
Irish Times, 4 May 1912.

M'GUCKIN, BARTON
Irish Times, 1880–1913; Shaw, G. B. *Music in London 1890–1894*.

M'MANUS/MCMANUS, MONSIGNOR MILES
Census of Ireland, Dublin 1911; Donnelly, Rev. Nicholas. *Short Histories of Dublin Parishes*; *Dublin Catholic Directory 1904–20*; *Thom's Directory 1904*.

M'SWINEY/MCSWINEY, PETER PAUL
Costello, Peter and Tony Farmar. *The Very Heart of the City: The Story of Denis Guiney and Clerys*; Clark, Mary and Hugh Fitzpatrick. *Serving the City: The Dublin City Manager and Town Clerks 1230–2005*.

MADDEN, DODGSON HAMILTON
Thom's Directory 1904; *Irish Times*, 8 Mar. 1928; *Irish Independent*, 10 Mar. 1928.

MADDEN, HERBERT OTTO
Igoe, Vivien. '"Spot the Winner": some of the horses in *Ulysses*'. *Dublin James Joyce Journal*, iv (2011).

MADDEN, THOMAS JOSEPH
Society of Jesus, Fathers of the. *A Page of Irish History: Story of University College, Dublin 1883–1909*; *Census of Ireland, Mayo 1911*; Farmar, Tony. *Holles Street, 1894–1994: The National Maternity Hospital: A Centenary History*; Lyons, J. B. *The Enigma of Tom Kettle 1880–1916*.

MAGENNIS, WILLIAM
Society of Jesus, Fathers of the. *A Page of Irish History: Story of University College, Dublin 1883–1909*; *Irish Times*, 10 Apr. 1946; *Census of Ireland, Dublin 1911*.

MAGINNI, DENIS J.
Census of Ireland, Dublin 1901, 1911; *Evening Herald*, 10 Nov. 1909, 12 Apr. 1915, 13 Apr. 1915; Graham, Godfrey. *Forty Years behind the Lens at RTÉ*; *Thom's Directory 1876–1904*.

MAHER, REV. THOMAS, SJ
Irish Province News, iv:2 (April 1942); *Thom's Directory 1904*.

MALONE, REV. CHARLES
Donnelly, Rev. N. *Short Histories of Dublin Parishes*; *Thom's Directory 1904*.

MAPAS/MALPAS, JOHN
Pearson, Peter. *Between the Mountains and the Sea: Dún Laoghaire-Rathdown County*; *Thom's Directory 1904*.

MARTIN-HARVEY, SIR JOHN
Disher, Maurice Willson. *The Last Romantic*; *Irish Times*, 6 Oct. 1899, 7 Oct. 1899, 9 Oct. 1899; Martin-Harvey, John. *The Autobiography of Sir John Martin-Harvey*.

MARTYN, EDWARD
Gwynn, Denis. *Edward Martyn and the Irish Revival*; Moore, George. *Hail and Farewell*, edited by R. Cave.

MASTIANSKY/MALIANSKY, PHINEAS
Census of Ireland, Dublin 1901; Hyman, Louis. *The Jews of Ireland*; *Thom's Directory 1904*; Rosenblatt, Stuart. Jewish Ireland Series. *Vol. XV: Lackman-Zwirn. 'Heritage' The A–Z DNA of Irish Jewry*.

MATHEW, FATHER THEOBALD
Maguire, John Francis. *Father Mathew: A Biography*; Rogers, Rev. Patrick. *Father Theobald Mathew: Apostle of Temperance*.

MAXWELL, LADY

Burke, Sir Bernard. *Burke's Landed Gentry of Ireland*; *Irish Times*, 16 Jan. 1897; *Thom's Directory 1904*; *The Solicitors' Journal and Reporter*, 6 Oct. 1860.

MAYER, FREDERICK 'FREDDY'

Irish Times, 11 Jul. 1887–1908.

MEADE, PATRICK

Irish Examiner, 7 Aug. 1928.

MELDON, AUSTIN

Medical Directory 1904; *Dublin Journal of Medical Science*, cxvii (1904).

MENTON, JOHN HENRY

Irish Law Times and Solicitors' Journal, 20 Dec. 1884; *Irish Times*, 11 Mar. 1905.

MERCADANTE, GIUSEPPE SAVERIO RAFFAELO

Kaufman, Thomas G. 'Mercadante'. *International Dictionary of Opera*, vol. 2; Rose, Michael. 'Mercadante: essay'. *New Grove Dictionary of Opera*, vol. 3.

MESIAS, GEORGE ROBERT

Census of Ireland, Dublin 1911; *Irish Times*, 30 Aug. 1941; *Thom's Directory 1904, 1929*.

MILLER, JOE

Young, Peter. *The Data Book of Joe Miller Jokes*.

MITCHELL, SUSAN

Kain, Richard M. *Susan L. Mitchell*; Pyle, Hilary. *Red-Headed Rebel: Susan L. Mitchell, Poet and Mystic of the Irish Cultural Renaissance*; *Irish Times*, 6 Mar. 1926.

MOISEL, M. (NISAN)

Thom's Directory 1904; Hyman, Louis. *The Jews of Ireland*.

MOISEL, MRS

Census of Ireland, Dublin 1901; *Thom's Directory 1900–7*; Hyman, Louis. *The Jews of Ireland*; Rosenblatt, Stuart. Jewish Ireland Series. *Vol. XV: Lackman-Zwirn. 'Heritage' The A–Z DNA of Irish Jewry*.

MONKS, EDWARD

Census of Ireland, Dublin 1911; *Irish Times*, 21 Aug. 1915, 30 Aug. 1922, 8 Dec. 1923, 1 Aug. 1941; *Thom's Directory 1904*.

MOONAN, GEORGE ALOYSIUS

Society of Jesus, Fathers of the. *A Page of Irish History: Story of University College, Dublin 1883–1909*; *Census of Ireland, Dublin 1911*; *Irish Law Times and Solicitors' Journal*, lxxix (1945); *Irish Times*, 10 May 1902, 1 Aug. 1907, 21 Aug. 1909, 2 Jun. 1910, 11 Mar. 1913, 19 Dec. 1945; Joyce, Stanislaus. *My Brother's Keeper*.

MOORE, GEORGE

Hone, Joseph. *The Moores of Moore Hall*; Moore, George. *Confessions of a Young Man*; Moore, George. *Esther Waters*; Moore, George. *Hail and Farewell*, edited by R. Cave; Moore, George. *A Drama in Muslin*.

MOORE, THOMAS

Strong, L. A. G. *The Minstrel Boy: A Portrait of Tom Moore*; White, Terence de Vere. *Tom Moore: The Irish Poet*.

MOSES, MARCUS TERTIUS

Hyman, Louis. *The Jews of Ireland*; *Irish Times*, 1877–1917; *Irish Independent*, 24 Aug. 1917; *Thom's Directory 1884, 1904*; *Tagblatt der Stadt Zürich*, 26 Jun. 1917.

MULLIGAN, JOHN

Census of Ireland, Dublin 1901, 1911; *Irish Times*, 30 Jan. 1912, 5 Mar. 1912, 6 Mar. 1912, 13 Mar. 1912; *Thom's Directory 1904*.

MULLINS, JEM/MULLIN, JAMES

Mullin, James. *The Story of a Toiler's Life*.

MULVAGH, WILLIAM
  Census of Ireland, Galway 1901, 1911; Ellmann, Richard, ed. *Letters of James Joyce*; Ó Laoi, Pádraic. *Nora Barnacle Joyce: A Portrait*; *Connacht Tribune*, 13 Jul. 1912; 4 Apr. 1922; 16 Jul. 1932; 11 Aug. 1932; *Irish Independent*, 12 Mar. 1927; 23 Jan. 1952.

MUNRO, A.
  Evening Telegraph, 16 Jun. 1904; Simpson, John. 'Wheelmen don't eat quiche.' *James Joyce Online Notes*. Issue 6 (November 2013).

MURPHY, WILLIAM MARTIN
  Morrissey, Thomas J. *William Martin Murphy*.

MURRAY, JOHN VALENTINE 'RED'
  Thom's Directory 1891, 1904.

MYERS, LT JOHN
  Census of Ireland, Dublin 1901, 1911; Geraghty, Tom and Trevor Whitehead. *The Dublin Fire Brigade: A History of the Brigade, the Fires and the Emergencies*; *Irish Times*, 21 Mar. 1927; *Thom's Directory 1904*.

NAGLE, SUSANNA 'SUSY'
  Simpson, John. 'Susie Nagle and her concertina skirt'. *James Joyce Online Notes*. Issue 3 (September 2012).

NICHOLAS, REV. FR
  Census of Ireland, Dublin 1911; *Irish Catholic Record 1924*; *Irish Times*, 5 Nov. 1923; Shaw, Fr Nessan, OFM Cap., ed. *The Irish Capuchins: Record of a Century 1885–1985*; *Capuchin Annual*, 1972; *Thom's Directory 1904*.

NOIR, JESSIE
  Irish Times, 21 Dec. 1892, 5 Jan. 1893.

NORMAN, CONNOLLY
  Irish Times, 24 Feb. 1908; *Journal of Mental Science*, Apr. 1908; Lyons, J. B. *James Joyce and Medicine*; *Medical Press and Circular*, 4 Mar. 1908; *Thom's Directory 1904*.

NORMAN, HARRY FELIX
  Census of Ireland, Dublin 1911; *Thom's Directory 1926, 1929*.

O'BRIEN, JOHN PATRICK
  Census of Ireland, Dublin 1901, 1911; *Freeman's Journal*, 5 Jun. 1878; *Irish Independent*, 15 May 1925; *Irish Times*, 13 Jul. 1886; *Nenagh Guardian*, 7 Jan. 1978; *Nation*, 21 Jul. 1877, 19 Jan. 1878; *Thom's Directory 1904*; UK Births Register 3Q 1846; *UK Census, 1861, 1871*.

O'BRIEN, SIR TIMOTHY
  James Joyce Quarterly, xix:2 (1982); *In the Shadow of St Patrick's*, facsimile edition with an introduction by Thomas Wall; *Sunday Independent*, 16 Oct. 1927.

O'BRIEN, VINCENT
  Census of Ireland, Dublin 1911; *Irish Independent*, 9 Jan. 1917; *Irish Times*, 22 Jun. 1948, 24 Jun. 1948, 14 Jun. 1984; *Thom's Directory 1904*.

O'BRIEN, WILLIAM
  O'Brien, Joseph. *William O'Brien and the Course of Irish Politics*.

O'CONNELL, JOHN
  Studies Irish Review, xciv:374 (Summer 2005).

O'CONNOR, JAMES
  Irish Times, 4 Jul. 1890, 19 Jul. 1890.

O'CONNOR, JOSEPH K.
  Census of Ireland, Dublin 1911; *Irish Times*, 9 Jun. 1960.

O'DOWD, ELIZABETH
  Census of Ireland, Dublin 1901; Raleigh, John Henry. 'Afoot in Dublin in search of the habitations of some shades'. *James Joyce Quarterly*, viii:1 (1970); *Thom's Directory 1904*; *Irish Independent*, 14 Oct. 1910.

O'HARE, DR JOHN JOSEPH
  Census of Ireland, Dublin 1901; *Irish Independent*, 4 May 1907.

O'MAHONY, JOHN
  Beck, Harald. 'The short but remarkable life of John O'Mahony'. *James Joyce Online Notes*. Issue 8 (February 2015).

OPISSO, MRS CATHERINE STARK
  The Gibraltar Directory and Guidebook 1883; *Census of Gibraltar, 1901*; *Register of Births and Deaths, Gibraltar*.

O'REILLY, LORENZO
  The Gibraltar Directory and Guidebook 1890, 1896; *Census of Gibraltar, 1901, Division 2*; *Gibraltar Register of Births and Deaths*.

O'REILLY, ROBERT
  Census of Ireland, Dublin 1911; *Irish Times*, 9 Aug. 1906, 19 Aug. 1909, 23 Nov. 1909, 17 Jan. 1911, 6 Jul. 1915; *Thom's Directory 1904*.

O'ROURKE, LARRY
  Census of Ireland, Dublin 1901; *Thom's Directory 1894–1914*.

O'SHEA, KATHARINE
  Lyons, F. S. L. *Charles Stewart Parnell*; O'Shea, Katharine. *Charles Stewart Parnell: His Love Story and Political Life*, 2 vols.

O'SULLIVAN, SEUMAS
  Miller, Liam, ed. *Retrospect: The Work of Seumas O'Sullivan and Estella F. Solomons*.

PADDOCK, ELIZABETH
  Census of Ireland, Dublin 1911; Simpson, John. 'Marcella, the Midget Queen'. *James Joyce Notes Online*. Issue 1 (September 2011).

PALLES, CHRISTOPHER
  Delany, V. T. H. *Christopher Palles: Lord Chief Baron of Her Majesty's Court of Exchequer in Ireland 1874–1916: His Life and Times*.

PARNELL, CHARLES STEWART
  Lyons, F. S. L. *Charles Stewart Parnell*; O'Shea, Katherine. *Charles Stewart Parnell: His Love Story and Political Life*, 2 vols; Parnell, John Howard. *Charles Stewart Parnell: A Memoir*.

PARNELL, JOHN HOWARD
  Census of Ireland, Dublin 1911; *Irish Times*, 4 May 1923; *New York Times*, 8 Mar. 1898.

PEPPER, JOHN HENRY
  Irish Times, 30 Apr. 1883, 31 Oct. 1892, 10 Dec. 1895; Seccombe, Thomas. 'Pepper, John (1821–1900)', rev. M. C. Curthoys. *Oxford Dictionary of National Biography*.

PILE, SIR THOMAS
  Irish Times, 19 Jan. 1931, 24 Jan. 1931.

PINKER, J. B.
  The Times, 10 Feb. 1922.

PISIMBO, MANUEL EULOGIO
  Census of Gibraltar, 1901, Division 2; *The Gibraltar Register of Births and Deaths*.

POKORNY, PROFESSSOR JULIUS P.
  Ó Dochartaigh, Pól. *Julius Pokorny, 1887–1970: Germans, Celts and Nationalism*; Senn, Fritz. 'No trace of hell'. *James Joyce Quarterly*, vii (1969–70).

POTTERTON, ROBERT
  Potterton, Homan. 'In lunacy of Potterton'. *James Joyce Online Notes*. Issue 5 (September 2013).

POWELL, JOSIE

Census of Ireland, Dublin 1901, 1911; *Irish Times*, 22 Nov. 1901.

POWELL, MAJOR MALACHY

Irish Times, 21 Sep. 1917, 22 Sep. 1917, 24 Sep. 1917, 29 Sep. 1917, 3 Jul. 2010; Tierney, Andrew. 'One of Britain's fighting men: Major Malachy Powell and *Ulysses'*. *James Joyce Online Notes*. Issue 6 (December 2013).

POWER, FLORRIE

Census of Ireland, Dublin 1911; Ellmann, Richard. *James Joyce*, revised edition; Fagan, Terry. *Monto, Madams, Murder and Black Coddle*; Herring, Phillip F., ed. *Joyce's Ulysses Notesheets in the British Museum*.

POWER, JACK

Adams, Robert M. *Surface and Symbol: The Consistency of James Joyce's Ulysses*; Joyce, Stanislaus. *The Dublin Diary of Stanislaus Joyce*, edited by George Harris Healey; Ellmann, Richard, ed. *Letters of James Joyce*.

POWER, MRS JENNIE WYSE

Neill, Marie. *From Parnell to de Valera: A Biography of Jennie Wyse Power 1858–1941*.

POWER, JOHN WYSE

Irish Times, 5 Jun. 1926.

POYNTZ, SAMUEL ROBERT

Census of Ireland, Dublin 1911; *Irish Times*, 16 Jan. 1918; *Medical Press*, 1879; *Thom's Directory 1884, 1904*.

PRICE, HENRY BLACKWOOD

Matthews, Terence. 'An emendation to the Joycean canon: the last hurrah for politics and cattle disease'. *James Joyce Quarterly*, iv:3 (2008).

PYPER, WILLIAM STANTON

McLochlainn, Alf. 'Piper and the peas' (unpublished article); *Dublin Magazine*, Jan. 1924.

QUIGLEY, MARY

Census of Ireland, Dublin 1901.

QUILL, ALBERT WILLIAM

Irish Law Times and Solicitors' Journal, xlii (1908); *Irish Times*, 3 Feb. 1908, 8 Feb. 1908; *Thom's Directory 1904*.

QUIRKE, THOMAS GEORGE

Census of Ireland, Dublin 1911; *Irish Law Times and Solicitors' Journal*, 24 Sep. 1949; *Thom's Directory 1904*.

RABAIOTTI, ANTONIO

Thom's Directory 1904; *Census of Ireland, Dublin 1901, 1911*.

REDMOND, JOHN

Gwynn, Denis. *The Life of John Redmond*; *Irish Times*, 13 Mar. 1918.

REYNOLDS, ROBERT 'BOB'

Census of Ireland, Dublin 1911; *Irish Times*, 16 Apr. 1900, 1 Sep. 1900, 3 Jul. 1901, 20 Jul. 1901, 6 Apr. 1935, 13 May 1955; *Irish Independent*, 12 Feb. 1937, 12 Jul. 1945; *Thom's Directory 1904*.

RICE, IGNATIUS J.

Census of Ireland, Dublin 1911; *Law Directory 1904*; *Law Gazette*, Dec. 1955; *Thom's Directory 1904*.

ROBERTS, FREDERICK SLEIGH

Roberts, F. S. *Forty-One Years in India*, 2 vols; Lanning, E. C. 'Vonolel: charger of Lord Roberts of Kandahar'. *Soldiers of the Queen*, the journal of the Victorian Military Society, lxxxviii (March 1997).

ROBERTS, GEORGE

The Times, 10 Nov. 1953; *Irish Times*, 12 Jul. 1955.

ROCHFORD, THOMAS

Census of Ireland, Dublin 1911; Finn, Eamonn. '"My turn now on": Rochford's invention turns up'.

James Joyce Broadsheet, lxxx (June 2008); *The Freeman's Journal*, 2 Mar. 1911; *Irish Times*, 26 Aug. 1905, 8 Jul. 1911, 3 Mar. 1934; *Irish Independent*, 8 May 1905.

ROCHFORT, MARY (NÉE MOLESWORTH)

O'Neill, Denis. *The Background of the Rochfort Family* (unpublished).

ROCK, PATRICK

Census of Ireland, Dublin 1911; *Irish Times*, 14 Jan. 1913; *Thom's Directory 1907–32*.

ROSALES, JOHN

Census of Gibraltar, 1901, Division 2.

ROSENBERG, HARRIS

Census of Ireland, Dublin 1901, 1911; *Thom's Directory 1904*.

ROYCE, EDWARD WILLIAM

Hollingshead, John. *Gaiety Chronicles*.

RUBLIN/RUHLIN, MRS GUS

Simpson, John. 'Mrs Gus Ruhlin: boxing and women's suffrage'. *James Joyce Online Notes*. Issue 3 (September 2012).

RUSSELL, GEORGE (Æ)

Eglinton, John (W. K. Magee). *A Memoir of Æ*; Moore, George. *Hail and Farewell*, edited by R. Cave.

RUSSELL, THOMAS O'NEILL

Irish Times, 16 Jun. 1908.

RUTTLEDGE, WILSON ORMSBY

Census of Ireland, Dublin 1911; *Irish Times*, 15 Aug. 1885; Ruttledge, Thomas Ormsby. 'The Ruttledge families in Co. Mayo'. *Irish Genealogist*, 1988; *Thom's Directory 1889–1904*; Adams, Robert M. *Surface and Symbol: The Consistency of James Joyce's Ulysses*; Ellmann, Richard. *James Joyce*, revised edition.

RYAN, FREDERICK

Kelly, John. '"A Lost Abbey Play": Frederick Ryan's *The Laying of the Foundations*'. *Ariel*, Jul. 1970; Sheehy-Skeffington, Francis. 'Frederick Ryan, an appreciation'. *The Irish Review*, 3 May 1913.

SANDOW, EUGEN

Chapman, David L. *Sandow the Magnificent: Eugen Sandow and the Beginnings of Bodybuilding*; Sandow, Eugen. *Strength and How to Obtain It*; *Freeman's Journal*, 7 May 1898; *Irish Times*, 7 May 1898.

SCALLY, REV. MICHAEL D.

Donnelly, Rev. N. *Short Histories of Dublin Parishes*, part 4, section 11; *The Irish Catholic Directory and Almanac 1904–24*.

SEBASTIAN, FATHER

Irish Catholic Directory 1904; *National Press*, 26 Sep. 1891, 29 Sep. 1891; Spencer, Paul Francis. *To Heal the Broken Hearted: The Life of Blessed Charles of Mount Argus*.

SEYMOUR, ROBERT FRANCIS

Census of Ireland, Dublin 1911; *The British Medical Journal*, 24 Jun. 1930; *The Times*, 8 Jun. 1939.

SHARON, LARBY/LARIE

Census of Gibraltar, 1901, Division 2; *The Gibraltar Directory and Guidebook 1912*.

SHAW, GEORGE BERNARD

Holroyd, Michael. *Bernard Shaw: The One-Volume Definitive Edition*; Holroyd, Michael. *Bernard Shaw: The Search for Love, Vol. 1, 1956–1898*; Shaw, G. B. *Music in London 1890–1894*.

SHEEHY, DAVID

Gibson, Andrew. *Joyce's Revenge: History, Politics and Aesthetics in Ulysses*; *Irish Times*, 19 Dec. 1932.

SHEEHY, MRS

Census of Ireland, Dublin 1911; *Thom's Directory 1904*.

SHERLOCK, LORCAN
   Irish Independent, 25 Dec. 1945, 26 Dec. 1945, 27 Dec. 1945; *Irish Times*, 25 Dec. 1945, 26 Dec. 1945, 27 Dec. 1945, 28 Dec. 1945.

SHULOMOWITZ, M.
   Hyman, Louis. *The Jews of Ireland*; *Thom's Directory 1904*; Rosenblatt, Stuart. Jewish Ireland Series. *Vol. XV: Lackman-Zwirn. 'Heritage' The A–Z DNA of Irish Jewry*.

SIGERSON, DR GEORGE
   Journal of the Irish Colleges of Physicians and Surgeons, iii:1 (1973).

SIMPSON, GEORGINA
   Census of Ireland, Dublin 1901, 1911; *Civil Registration Indexes, 1845–1958*; *Thom's Directory 1904*.

SINCLAIR, WILLIAM
   Colum, Mary and Padraic. *Our Friend James Joyce*; Hyman, Louis. *The Jews of Ireland*; Richard Ellmann, ed. *Selected Letters of James Joyce*; *Thom's Directory 1904*; Rosenblatt, Stuart. Jewish Ireland Series. *Vol. XV: Lackman-Zwirn. 'Heritage' The A–Z DNA of Irish Jewry*.

SMITH, PHILIP HENRY LAW
   Irish Law Times and Solicitors' Journal (1920); *Freeman's Journal*, 9 Jan. 1920.

SOLOMONS, MAURICE E.
   Census of Ireland, Dublin 1901, 1911; *Irish Times*, 19 Jun. 1922; *Thom's Directory 1904*.

SPRAGUE, HORATIO JONES
   Census of Gibraltar, Division 4, 1901; *Gibraltar Chronicle*, 19 Jul. 1901, 16 Oct. 1934; *New York Times*, 19 Jul. 1901.

STEPHENS, DAVY
   Irish Times, 11 Sep. 1925.

STEPHENS, JAMES
   Ryan, Desmond. *The Fenian Chief: A Biography of James Stephens*; Pyle, Hilary. *James Stephens: His Work and an Account of His Life*.

STOER, MRS
   Census of Ireland, Dublin 1901, 1911; *Irish Times*, 2 Dec. 1904, 20 May 1907, 11 Jun. 1910, 17 Mar. 1917; *Irish Independent*, 25 Apr. 1944; *New York Times*, 9 Nov. 1948; *Thom's Directory 1904*.

STOKER, SIR WILLIAM THORNLEY
   Irish Times, 3 Jun. 1912; *Thom's Directory 1904*.

STRATTON, EUGENE
   Freeman's Journal, 16 Jun. 1904; *Oxford Companion to Popular Music*, edited by Peter Grammond.

STUBBS, GEORGE HENRY
   Census of Ireland, Dublin 1911; *Irish Times*, 14 Nov. 1908, 21 Nov. 1908.

SULLIVAN, JOHN L.
   Irish Times, 8 Nov. 1887, 24 Nov. 1887, 13 Dec. 1887, 14 Dec. 1887, 16 Dec. 1887; Mallon, Kevin. 'Profile of a pugilist'. *Irish Times*, 29 Oct. 2008.

SWAN, BROTHER WILLIAM
   The Christian Brothers' Educational Record 1912; *O'Connell School Centenary Record*, Jun. 1928.

SWENY, FREDERICK WILLIAM
   Irish Times, 17 Oct. 1866, 12 Mar. 1924, 19 Jun. 2009 (An Irishman's Diary).

SYNGE, JOHN MILLINGTON
   Synge, J. M. *Autobiography*, edited by Alan Price; Stephen, Edward. *My Uncle John: Life of J. M. Synge*, edited by Andrew Carpenter.

TALLON, DANIEL
   Irish Times, 14 Jul. 1908; *Thom's Directory 1904*.

TAYLOR, JOHN F.
  Irish Law Times and Solicitors' Journal, xxxvi (1902); Meenan, James, ed. *Centenary History of the Literary and Historical Society of University College Dublin, 1855–1955.*

TEARLE, GEORGE OSMOND
  Irish Times, 22 Feb. 1892, 23 May 1893, 24 May 1893, 5 Nov. 1894, 4 Dec. 1896; *New York Times*, 8 Sep. 1901.

THORNTON, R. J.
  Census of Ireland, Dublin 1901; Joyce, Stanislaus. *The Dublin Diary of Stanislaus Joyce*, edited by George Harris Healey; Ellmann, Richard, ed. *Selected Letters of James Joyce*; Costello, Peter. *James Joyce: The Years of Growth, 1882–1915*; *Thom's Directory 1893–1903.*

TIVY, RICHARD 'DICK'
  Census of Ireland, Cork 1911.

TOBIAS, MATTHEW
  Census of Ireland, Dublin 1911; *Irish Times*, 19 Sep. 1921; *Irish Law Times and Solicitors' Journal*, 24 Sep. 1921; *Thom's Directory 1904.*

TOBIN, PATRICK
  Census of Ireland, Dublin 1911; *Irish Times*, 1903–28; *Thom's Directory 1903, 1911.*

TREE, BEERBOHM
  Irish Times, 19 Jan. 1895, 26 Jan. 1895.

TRENCH, RICHARD SAMUEL CHENEVIX
  Trench, C. E. F. 'Dermot Chenevix Trench and Haines of *Ulysses*'. *James Joyce Quarterly*, xiii:1 (Fall 1975); *Irish Times*, 1 Jun. 1909.

TROY, DENIS
  Census of Ireland, Dublin 1901, 1911; *Thom's Directory 1904, 1917.*

TUPPER, NORMAN W.
  National Police Gazette, 16 Sep. 1893; Simpson, John. 'Norman W. Tupper and the policeman's lap'. *James Joyce Online Notes*. Issue 2 (March 2012).

TURNBULL, DONALD
  Census of Ireland, Dublin 1901; *Irish Independent*, 22 Sep. 1917; *Irish Times*, 13 Jan. 1908, 18 Jan. 1908; *Thom's Directory 1904.*

TWEEDY, HENRY R.
  Census of Ireland, Dublin 1911; *Thom's Directory 1904.*

TWELVETREES, MRS CLYDE
  Census of Ireland, Dublin 1911; *Irish Times*, 28 Nov. 1970.

TWIGG, ELIZABETH 'LIZZIE' ANN
  Bowen, Zack. 'Lizzie Twigg: gone but not forgotten'. *James Joyce Quarterly*, vi:4 (Spring 1969); *Census of Ireland, Limerick 1911*; Register of electors 1923; *Limerick Leader*, 14 Jan. 1933.

VANCE, JAMES
  Census of Ireland, Dublin 1901, 1911.

VAUGHAN, FATHER BERNARD JOHN, SJ
  Martindale, C. C. *Father Bernard Vaughan: A Memoir.*

VEUILLOT, LOUIS
  Catholic Encyclopaedia; *Encyclopaedia Britannica*, eleventh edition.

VICTORY, LOUIS H.
  Census of Ireland, Dublin 1901; *Irish Times*, 31 May 1943, 29 Nov. 1947.

VILAPLANA, FR ILDEFONSO
  The Gibraltar Directory and Guidebook 1912, 1913.

WALL, THOMAS J.
  Census of Ireland, Dublin 1901; *Irish Times*, 11 Jul. 1910; *Thom's Directory 1904.*

WALSH, LOUIS J.
  Ellmann, Richard. *James Joyce*, revised edition; *Irish Times*, 28 Dec. 1942.

WALSH, DR WILLIAM J.
  Freeman's Journal, 21 Apr. 1921; Morrissey, Thomas J. *William J. Walsh: Archbishop of Dublin, 1841–1921*; *Thom's Directory 1841, 1853*.

WARD, GERALD
  Thom's Directory 1904; *Visitation of England and Wales*, xix (College of Arms, 1917).

WATCHMAN, MINNIE
  Census of Ireland, Dublin 1901; *Civil Registration Indexes, 1845–1958*; Hyman, Louis. *The Jews of Ireland*; *Thom's Directory 1904*.

WATERS, REV. THOMAS
  Irish Civil Registration Indexes, 1845–1958; *Thom's Directory 1904*.

WEATHERUP, WILLIAM
  Evening Telegraph, 4 Dec. 1895; *Irish Times*, 20 Mar. 1875, 7 Dec. 1895; *Thom's Directory 1878, 1883*; Simpson, John. 'William Weatherup: what the newspapers said'. *James Joyce Online Notes*. Issue 2 (February 2012).

WERNER, LEWIS/LOUIS JOSEPH
  Lyons, J. B. *An Assembly of Irish Surgeons*; Strickland, Walter G. *A Dictionary of Irish Artists*; *Irish Times*, 27 Nov. 1936; *Thom's Directory 1904*.

WERNER, LOUIS
  Ardoyne's Golden Jubilee 1952: Souvenir Brochure; *Census of Ireland 1901, 1911*; *Chronicles of Old Ardoyne, 1852–1952*; *Irish Press*, 7 Apr. 1941; *Irish Times*, 2 Jan. 1936.

WHITBREAD, JAMES
  Irish Times, 2 Jan. 1904, 4 Jan. 1904, 3 Mar. 1904, 11 Apr. 1904, 28 May 1904, 25 Jun. 1904, 10 Sep. 1904, 26 May 1911, 12 Jun. 1916; *Thom's Directory 1904*.

WHITE, DUDLEY
  Census of Ireland, Dublin 1901, 1911; *Irish Law Times and Solicitors' Journal*, xiv (1930); *Irish Times*, 5 Jul. 1930.

WILDE, LADY JANE FRANCESCA
  Ellmann, Richard. *Oscar Wilde*; Melville, J. *Mother of Oscar: The Life of Jane Francesca Wilde*; Montgomery Hyde, H. *Oscar Wilde: A Biography*; White, Terence de Vere. *The Parents of Oscar Wilde: Sir William and Lady Wilde*; Wyndham, H. *Speranza: A Biography of Lady Wilde*.

WILDE, OSCAR
  Ellmann, Richard. *Oscar Wilde*; Montgomery Hyde, H. *Oscar Wilde: A Biography*; White, Terence de Vere, *The Parents of Oscar Wilde: Sir William and Lady Wilde*.

WILKINS, WILLIAM
  Census of Ireland, Dublin 1901, 1911; *Thom's Directory 1904*.

WOLSELEY, SIR GARNET JOSEPH
  Irish Times, 26 Mar. 1913, 27 Mar. 1913; Lehmann, Joseph. *All Sir Garnet: A life of Field-Marshall Lord Wolseley*.

WOODS, PATRICK AND ROSE
  Census of Ireland, Dublin 1901; *Thom's Directory 1904*.

WORTHINGTON, ROBERT
  Irish Times, 26 Jan. 1880, 13 Jul. 1880, 21 Apr. 1881, 10 Feb. 1883, 1 Sep. 1888; *Thom's Directory 1904*.

WYLIE, WILLIAM E.
  O'Broin, Leon. *W. E. Wylie and the Irish Revolution, 1916–1921*.

Bibliography

Newspapers

The Anglo Celt
Connacht Tribune
Cork Examiner
Daily News
Daily Telegraph
Dublin Evening Mail
Dublin Evening Post
Evening Herald
Freeman's Journal
Gibraltar Chronicle
Illustrated London News
Irish Catholic
Irish Independent
Irish Press
Irish Times
Limerick Leader
Nation

National Press
Nenagh Guardian
New York Times
News of the World
Roscommon Herald
Sunday Independent
The Telegraph
The Times
Tuam Herald

Periodicals

A Wake Newslitter
Clongownian
Dana
Dublin Historical Record
Dublin James Joyce Journal
Dublin Magazine
Dublin Review

The Dublin University Magazine
Irish Catholic Directory
Irish Ecclesiastical Record
Irish Ecclesiastical Review
Irish Genealogist
Irish Homestead
Irish Law Times and Solicitors'
   Journal
The Irish Review
Irish Statesman
James Joyce Broadsheet
James Joyce Online (JJON)
James Joyce Quarterly
Joyce Studies Annual
The Musical Times
Studies Irish Review
Times Literary Supplement
The Welsh Internationalist

Contemporary Works of Reference

Burke, Sir Bernard. *A Genealogical and Heraldic History of the Landed Gentry in Ireland*. London: Harrison, Pall Mall, 1871.

—. *Burke's Landed Gentry of Ireland*. London: Burke's Peerage, 1899.

Census of Gibraltar, 1901.

Census of Ireland, 1901, 1911.

Census of Scotland, 1901.

Debrett, John. *Debrett's Peerage of England, Scotland and Ireland*. London: G. Woodfall, 1817.

Debrett's Peerage and Baronetage, edited by Charles Kidd and David Williamson. London: St Martin's Press, 1990.

Francis Guy's Almanac 1879/80.

The Gibraltar Directory and Guidebook. Gibraltar: Garrison Library Printing Establishment, 1879.

The Irish Catholic Directory and Almanac, published since 1837.

Irish Civil Registration Indexes, 1845–1958.

Thom's Official Directory of the United Kingdom of Great Britain and Ireland. Dublin: Alexander Thom & Co. Ltd, published annually.

Modern Works of Reference

Biographical Encylopaedia of British Flat Racing, edited by Roger Mortimer, Richard Onslow and Peter Willett. London: MacDonald and Jane's, 1978.

Boylan, Henry. *A Dictionary of Irish Biography*. Dublin: Gill & Macmillan, 1978.

Catholic Encyclopaedia. New York: Robert Appleton Company, 1914.

Concise Edition of Baker's Biographical Dictionary of Musicians, eight edition, revised by Nicolas Slonimsky. New York: Schirmer Books, 1993.

Crone, John S. *A Concise Dictionary of Irish Biography*. London: Longmans Green and Co. Ltd, 1928.

Dante Encyclopedia. Routledge: London, 2010.

Dictionary of American Biography. New York: Scribner, 1959.

Dictionary of Irish Biography, edited by James Maguire and James Quinn. Cambridge: Cambridge University Press published in collaboration with the Royal Irish Academy, 2009.

Dictionary of Modern Music and Musicians, edited by A. Eaglefield-Hull. London: J. M. Dent, 1924.

Dictionary of Ulster Biography, edited by Kate Newman. Belfast: Institute of Irish Studies, 1993.

Encyclopaedia Britannica, eleventh edition. Cambridge: Cambridge University Press, 1910–11.

Encyclopaedia of Flat Racing, edited by Roger Mortimer. London: Robert Hale, 1971.

Farmar, David Hugh. *The Oxford Dictionary of Saints*. Oxford: Clarendon Press, 1978.

International Dictionary of Ballet, edited by M.Bremser. Michigan: St James Press, 1993.

International Dictionary of Opera, edited by Steven LaRue. Michigan: St James Press, 1993.

Komara, Edward M. *Encyclopaedia of the Blues*. Abingdon: Routledge, 2006.

Lewis, Samuel. *A Topographical Dictionary of Ireland*. London: S. Lewis & Co., 1837.

New Grove Dictionary of Music and Musicians, 20 vols, edited by Stanley Sadie. London: Macmillan Publishers Ltd, 1980.

New Grove Dictionary of Opera. London: Macmillan Reference, 1992.

New International Encyclopedia. New York: Dodd, Mead & Company, 1902.

Oxford Companion to Popular Music, edited by Peter Grammond. Oxford: Oxford University Press, 1991.

Oxford Dictionary of National Biography. Oxford: Oxford University Press, 2004.

Strickland, Walter G. *A Dictionary of Irish Artists*. Dublin: Maunsel & Company, 1913.

Webb, Alfred. *A Compendium of Irish Biography*. Dublin: M. H. Gill & Son, 1878.

Who Was Who. Vol. 1(1897–1915). London: Adam & Charles Black, 1935.

Who's Who of British Members of Parliament: Vol. 1 1832–1885, edited by Michael Stenton. Atlantic Highlands, NJ: Humanities Press, 1976.

Books and Articles

A History of St Vincent's Hospital: A Century of Service: The Record of One Hundred Years, published for the Centenary of St Vincent's Hospital, 23 January 1934. Dublin: Browne & Nolan, 1934.

Adams, Robert M. *Surface and Symbol: The Consistency of James Joyce's Ulysses*. Oxford: Oxford University Press, 1962.

Ball, F. E. *The Judges in Ireland, 1221–1921*, 2 vols. London: John Murray, 1926.

—. *A History of County Dublin*. Dublin: Alex Thom, 1903.

Ball, Robert. *The Story of the Heavens*. London: Cassell, 1900.

Ball, W. Valentine. *Reminiscences and Letters of Sir Robert Ball*. London: Cassell, 1915.

Barrett, William Alexander. *Balfe: His Life and Works*. London: Remington and Co., 1883.

Barrington, Sir Jonah. *Historic Memoirs of Ireland*, 2 vols. London: H. Colburn & R. Bentley, 1935.

—. *Personal Sketches and Recollections of His Own Times*, 3 vols. Glasgow: Cameron, Ferguson & Co., 1876.

Bence-Jones, Mark. *A Guide to Irish Country Houses*. London: Constable, 1996.

Bennett, Douglas. *Encyclopaedia of Dublin*. Dublin: Gill & Macmillan, 1991.

Bibliography

Benstock, Shari and Bernard. *Who's He When He's at Home: A James Joyce Directory*. Urbana: University of Illinois Press, 1980.

Benzenhofer, Udo. 'Joyce and embryology: Giulio Valenti's "Lezioni Elementari Di embriologia" as a source for "Oxen in the Sun"'. *James Joyce Quarterly*, xxvi:4 (1989).

Bidwell, Bruce and Linda Heffer. *The Joycean Way*. Dublin: Wolfhound Press, 1981.

Bowen, Zack. *Padraic Colum*. Carbondale: Southern Illinois Press, 1970.

Bradley, Bruce, SJ. *James Joyce's Schooldays*. Dublin: Gill & Macmillan, 1982.

Brown, Stephen. *The Press in Ireland: A Survey and a Guide*. Dublin: Browne & Nolan, 1937.

Budgen, Frank. *James Joyce and the Making of Ulysses*. London: Grayson & Grayson, 1934.

Bulfin, William. *Rambles in Eirinn*. Dublin: Gill & Son, 1907.

Butler, Alban. *Butler's Lives of the Saints*, 4 vols, edited by Herbert Thurston, SJ, and Donald Attwater. New York: Farrar, Straus and Young, 1953.

Byrne, J. F. *Silent Years*. New York: Farrar, Straus and Young, 1953.

Campbell, M. *Dolmetsch: The Man and His Work*. London: Hamilton, 1975.

Caufield, Catherine. *Emperor of the United States of America and Other British Eccentrics*. London: Routledge & Kegan Paul, 1981.

Chambers, Anne. *Granuaile: The Life and Times of Grace O'Malley c. 1530–1603*. Dublin: Wolfhound Press, 1979.

Chapman, David L. *Sandow the Magnificent: Eugen Sandow and the Beginnings of Bodybuilding*. Urbana: University of Illinois Press, 1994.

Chart, D. A. *The Story of Dublin*. London: J. M. Dent, 1907.

Clark, Mary. *Eminent Images: The Dublin Civic Portrait Collection*. Dublin: Dublin City Council, 2009.

Clark, Mary and Hugh Fitzpatrick. *Serving the City: The Dublin City Manager and Town Clerks 1230–2005*. Dublin: Dublin City Council, 2006.

Clergy of Dublin and Glendalough, biographical succession lists, complied by Canon J. B. Leslie and revised, edited and updated by W. J. R. Wallace. Dublin: The Ulster Historical Foundation, the Diocesan Councils of Dublin and Glendalough, 2001.

Colum, Mary and Padraic. *Our Friend James Joyce*. London: Gollancz, Ltd, 1959.

Conmee, Very Rev. John S. *Old Times in the Barony*. Blackrock: Carraig Books, 1976.

Cooper Oakley, Isabel. *The Comte de St Germain*. Milan: Liberia Editrice del Dr G. Sulli-Rao, 1912.

Corfe, Tom. *The Phoenix Park Murders: Conflict, Compromise and Tragedy in Ireland, 1879–1882*. London: Hodder & Stoughton, 1968.

Costello, Peter. *James Joyce: The Years of Growth, 1882–1915*. London: Kyle Cathie Ltd, 1992.

—. *Dublin Churches*. Dublin: Gill & Macmillan, 1989.

—. *Leopold Bloom: A Biography*. Dublin, Gill & Macmillan, 1981.

Costello, Peter and Tony Farmar. *The Very Heart of the City: The Story of Denis Guiney and Clerys*. Dublin: A. & A. Farmar, 1992.

Cousins, James Henry and Margaret E. *We Two Together*. Madras: Ganesh, 1950.

Coxhead, Elizabeth. *Lady Gregory: A Literary Portrait*. London: Macmillan, 1961.

Craig, Maurice. *Dublin 1660–1860*. Dublin: Hodges Figgis, 1952.

Crispi, Luca. *Joyce's Creative Process and the Construction of Characters in Ulysses: Becoming the Blooms*. Oxford: Oxford University Press, 2015.

Curran, C. P. *Under the Receding Wave*. Dublin: Gill & Macmillan, 1970.

—. *James Joyce Remembered*. Oxford: Oxford University Press, 1968.

D'Alton, John. *The History of County Dublin*. Dublin: Hodges and Smith, 1838.

Day, Brother John. *Memoir of the Honble. Elizabeth Aldworth of Newmarket Court, Co. Cork*. Cork: Guy and Co. Ltd, 1914.

De Burca, Marcus. *Michael Cusack and the GAA*. Dublin: Anvil Books, 1989.

Delany, V. T. H. *Christopher Palles: Lord Chief Baron of Her Majesty's Court of Exchequer in Ireland 1874-1916: His Life and Times*. Dublin: Allen Figgis & Co., Ltd, 1960.

Deming, Robert H., ed. *James Joyce: The Critical Heritage*, 2 vols. London: Routledge & Kegan Paul, 1970.

Denson, Alan. *James Cousins and Margaret E. Cousins: A Bibliography*. Kendall: Alan Denson, 1967.

Desborough, Lord. *Fifty Years of Sport at Oxford, Cambridge and the Great Public Schools, Eton, Harrow and Winchester*, edited by R. H. Lyttelton, Arthur Page and Evan Noel. London: Walter Southwood and Co., Ltd. 1922.

Devoy, John. *Recollections of an Irish Rebel*. New York: Chas Young Co., 1929.

Disher, Maurice Willson. *The Last Romantic*. London: Hutchinson & Co, 1948.

Dodds, E. R., ed. *Journal and Letters of Stephen MacKenna*, with a memoir by Dodds and a preface by Padraic Colum. New York: William Morrow, 1936.

Donington, R. *The Work and Ideas of Arnold Dolmetsch*. Haslemore: The Dolmetsch Foundation, 1932.

Donnelly, Rev. N. *Short Histories of Dublin Parishes*. Blackrock: Carraig Books, 1905.

Dowden, E. D. *Letters of Edward Dowden and His Correspondence 1843-1913*, edited by H. M. Dowden. London: J. M. Dent; New York: E. P. Dutton, 1914.

—. *Shakespeare: A Critical Study of His Mind and Art*. London: Henry S. King & Co., 1875.

Dumbleton, William. *James Cousins*. London: Twayne, 1980.

Dwan, Peter. *John McCormack: Icon of an Age: The Anthology*. Zampano Productions, 2006. [4 cds plus video and booklet: John McCormack. *The letters of John McCormack to J. C. Doyle, 1884-1945*.]

Eglinton, John (W. K. Magee). *A Memoir of Æ*. London: Macmillan, 1937.

Ellmann, Richard. *Oscar Wilde*. London: Hamish Hamilton, 1987.

—. *James Joyce*, revised edition. Oxford: Oxford University Press, 1982.

—, ed. *Selected Letters of James Joyce*. London: Faber & Faber, 1975.

—, ed. *Letters of James Joyce*. London: Faber & Faber, 1966.

Fagan, Terry. *Monto, Madams, Murder and Black Coddle*. Dublin: North Inner City Folklore Group, 2000.

Farmar, Tony. *Holles Street, 1894-1994: The National Maternity Hospital: A Centenary History*. Dublin: A. & A. Farmar, 1994. [Appendix 3: Peter Costello. 'James Joyce, *Ulysses* and the National Maternity Hospital'.]

—. *Ordinary Lives*. Dublin: Gill & Macmillan, 1991.

Ferguson, Kenneth, ed. *King's Inns Barristers 1868-2004*. Dublin: Honorable Society of King's Inns in association with the Irish legal History Society, 2005.

Findlater, Alex. *Findlaters: The Story of a Dublin Merchant Family 1774-2001*. Dublin: A. & A. Farmar, 2001.

Finnegan, John. *The Story of Monto*. Cork: Mercier Press, 1978.

Fleetwood, John. *History of Medicine in Ireland*. Dublin: Richview Press, 1951.

Frazier, Adrian. *George Moore 1852-1933*. New Haven: Yale University Press, 2000.

Garvin, John. *James Joyce's Disunited Kingdom and the Irish Dimension*. Dublin: Gill & Macmillan, 1976.

Geraghty, Tom and Trevor Whitehead. *The Dublin Fire Brigade: A History of the Brigade, the Fires and the Emergencies*. Dublin: Dublin City Council, 2004.

Gibbons, Luke. *Joyce's Ghosts: Ireland, Modernism, and Memory*. Chicago: University of Chicago Press, 2015.

Gibson, Andrew. *Joyce's Revenge: History, Politics and Aesthetics in Ulysses*. Oxford: Oxford University Press, 2002.

Gifford, Don with Robert J. Seidman. *Ulysses' Annotated*, revised edition. Berkeley: University of California Press,1988.

Gilbert, John T. *A History of the City of Dublin*, 3 vols (1854-59). Dublin: Irish University Press, 1972.

Gilbert, Stuart. *James Joyce's Ulysses: A Study*. London: Faber & Faber, 1930.

—, ed. *Letters of James Joyce*, vol. 1. London: Faber & Faber, 1957.

Gogarty, Oliver St John. *It Isn't This Time of Year at All*. London: Macgibbon & Kee, 1954.

—. *Tumbling in the Hay*. London: Constable & Company Ltd, 1939.

—. *As I Was Going down Sackville Street*. London: Rich & Cowan, 1937.

—. 'They think they know Joyce'. *Saturday Review of Literature*, 18 March 1950.

Gonne, Maud. *A Servant of the Queen: Reminiscences*. London: V. Gollancz, 1974.

Gorman, Herbert. *James Joyce: A Definitive Biography*. London: John Lane. The Bodley Head, 1949.

Gosse, Edmund. *The Life of Algernon Charles Swinburne*. London: Macmillan and Co., Ltd, 1917.

Graham, Godfrey. *Forty Years behind the Lens at RTÉ*. Dublin: Ashfield Press, 2005.

Gray, Tony. *Mr Smyllie, Sir*. Dublin: Gill & Macmillan, 1991.

Greenwood, Douglas. *Who's Buried Where in England*. London: Constable, 2006.

Guest, I. 'An early "national" school: the achievements of Katti Lanner'. *Dancing Times*, November 1958.

Gwynn, Denis. *The Life of John Redmond*. London: G. G. Harrap, 1932.

—. *Edward Martyn and the Irish Revival*. London: Jonathan Cape, 1930.

Hall, J. B. *Random Records of a Reporter*, with a foreword by T. P. O'Connor. London: Simpkin Marshall; Dublin: Fodhla Printing Co., 1928.

Hamer, D. A. *John Morley: Liberal Intellectual in Politics*. Oxford: Oxford University Press, 1968.

Harbison, Peter. *Guide to the National Monuments of Ireland*. Dublin: Gill & Macmillan, 1970.

Hardiman, Adrian. '"A gruesome case": James Joyce's Dublin murder case'. *Librarians, Poets and Scholars: A Festschrift for Donal O Luanaigh*, edited by Felix M. Larkin. Dublin: Four Courts Press in association with the National Library of Ireland Society, 2007.

Hart, Clive and David Hayman, eds. *James Joyce's Ulysses: Critical Essays*. Berkeley: University of California Press, 1974.

Hart, Clive and Ian Gunn with Harald Beck. *James Joyce's Dublin: A Topographical Guide to the Dublin of Ulysses*. London: Thames & Hudson, 2004.

Herlihy, James. *The Dublin Metropolitan Police: A Short History and Genealogical Guide*. Dublin: Four Courts Press, 2001.

Herring, Phillip F. *Joyce's Uncertainty Principle*. Princeton: Princeton University Press, 1987.

—, ed. *Joyce's Ulysses Notesheets in the British Museum*. Charlottesville: University Press of Virginia, 1972.

Hodgart, Matthew J. C. and Ruth Bauerle. *Joyce's Grand Operoar: Opera in Finnegans Wake*. Urbana: University of Illinois Press, 1997.

Hogan, Robert. *Dion Boucicault*. New York: Twayne, 1969.

Hollingshead, John. *Gaiety Chronicles*. Westminster: Archibald Constable & Co., 1898.

Holroyd, Michael. *Bernard Shaw: The One-Volume Definitive Edition*. London: Chatto & Windus, 1997.

—. *Bernard Shaw: The Search for Love, Vol. 1, 1956–1898*. London: Chatto & Windus, 1988.

Hone, Joseph. *The Moores of Moore Hall*. London: Jonathan Cape, 1939.

Hone, W. P. *Cricket in Ireland*. Tralee: The Kerryman, 1955.

Howe, Elizabeth. *The First English Actresses: Woman and Drama 1660–1700*. Cambridge: Cambridge University Press, 1992.

Hutchins, Patricia. *James Joyce's World*. London: Methuen, 1957.

Hyman, Louis. *The Jews of Ireland*. Shannon: Irish University Press, 1972.

Igoe, Vivien. *James Joyce's Dublin Houses and Nora Barnacle's Galway*. Dublin: Lilliput Press, 2007.

—. *Dublin Burial Grounds and Graveyards*. Dublin: Wolfhound Press, 2001.

—. *A Literary Guide to Dublin*. London: Methuen, 1999.

—. *City of Dublin*. Hampshire: Pitkin, 1991.

In the Shadow of St Patrick's, facsimile edition with an introduction by Thomas Wall. Blackrock: Carrig Books, 1976.

Jackson, John Wyse and Peter Costello. *John Stanislaus Joyce: The Voluminous Life and Genius of James Joyce's Father*. London: Fourth Estate, 1997.

Jackson, John Wyse and Bernard McGinley. *James Joyce's Dubliners: An Illustrated Edition with Annotations*. London: St Martin's Press, 1993.

Joyce, James. *The Critical Writings of James Joyce*, edited by Ellsworth Mason and Richard Ellmann. London: Faber & Faber, 1959.

Joyce, Rev. P. J. *John Healy Archbishop of Tuam*. Dublin: Gill & Son, 1931.

Joyce, Stanislaus. *My Brother's Keeper*. London: Faber & Faber, 1958.

—. *The Dublin Diary of Stanislaus Joyce*, edited by George Harris Healey. London: Faber & Faber, 1962

Joyce, Weston St John. *The Neighbourhood of Dublin*. Dublin: Gill & Son, 1939.

Kain, Richard M. *Susan L. Mitchell*. Lewisburg: Bucknell University Press, 1972.

Kelly, James. *Henry Flood: Patriots and Policies in Eighteenth-Century Ireland*. Dublin: Four Courts Press, 1998.

Kelly, John. '"A Lost Abbey Play": Frederick Ryan's *The Laying of the Foundations'*. *Ariel*, July 1970.

Kenner, Hugh. *Dublin's Joyce*. New York: Columbia University Press, 1956, reissued 1987.

Kenney, C. L. *A Memoir of Michael William Balfe*. London: Tinsley Brothers, 1875.

Kiberd, Declan. *Ulysses and Us: The Art of Everyday Living*. London: Faber & Faber, 2009.

—. *Inventing Ireland*. London: Jonathan Cape, 1995.

—, ed. *The Students Annotated Ulysses*. London: Penguin 20th Century Classics, 1992.

Killeen, Terence. *Ulysses Unbound: A Reader's Companion to James Joyce's Ulysses*. Dublin: Wordwell in association with the National Library of Ireland, 2004.

Langtry, Lillie. *The Days I Knew*. London: Hutchinson & Co., 1925.

Ledbetter, Gordon T. *The Great Irish Tenor*. New York: Scribner's, 1977.

Lehmann, Joseph. *All Sir Garnet: A Life of Field-Marshall Lord Wolselely*. London: Jonathan Cape, 1964.

Lotz, Rainer E. *Black People: Entertainers of African Descent in Europe, and Germany*. Bonn: Birgit Lotz Verlag, 1997.

Lyons, F. S. L. *Charles Stewart Parnell*. London: Collins, 1977.

Lyons, J. B. *Thrust Syphilis down to Hell and Other Rejoyceana*. Dublin: Glendale Press, 1988.

—. *An Assembly of Irish Surgeons*. Dublin: Glendale Press, 1984.

—. *The Enigma of Tom Kettle 1880–1916*. Dublin: Glendale Press, 1983.

—. *Oliver St John Gogarty: The Man of Many Talents*. Dublin: Blackwater, 1980.

—. *James Joyce and Medicine*. Dublin: Dolmen Press, 1973.

MacLochlainn, A. *The National Library of Ireland, 1877–1977*. Dublin: Stationery Office, 1979.

McCartney, Donal. *UCD: A National Idea: The History of University College, Dublin*. Dublin: Gill & Macmillan, 1999.

McCourt, John. *The Years of Bloom, James Joyce in Trieste 1904–1920*. Dublin: Lilliput Press, 2000.

McCready, Rev. T. C. *Dublin Street Names*. Dublin: Hodges Figgis, 1892.

Madden, Richard R. *Ireland in '98: Sketches of the Principal Men of the Time*. London: Swan Sonnenschein Lowrey, 1888.

—. *The United Irishmen: Their Lives and Times*. Dublin: Mullany, 1860.

Maddox, Brenda. *Nora: A Biography of Nora Joyce*. London: Hamish Hamilton, 1988.

Maguire, John Francis. *Father Mathew: A Biography*. Dublin: Eason & Son, Ltd, 1862.

Martin-Harvey, John. *The Autobiography of Sir John Martin-Harvey*. London: Sampson Low, 1933.

Martindale, C. C. *Father Bernard Vaughan: A Memoir*. London: Longman, Green and Co., 1923.

Meenan, James, ed. *Centenary History of the Literary and Historical Society of University College Dublin, 1855–1955*. Tralee: The Kerryman, 1955.

Melville, J. *Mother of Oscar: The Life of Jane Francesca Wilde*. London: John Murray, 1994.

Meyer, Thomas. *D. N. Dunlop: A Man of Our Time*. London: Temple Lodge, 1992.

Miller, Liam, ed. *Retrospect: The Work of Seumas O'Sullivan and Estella F. Solomons*. Dublin: Dolmen Press, 1973.

Millner, Colonel J. K. *The Irish Setter: Its History and Training*, with an introduction by S. W. Carlton. London: H. F. G. Willerby, 1924.

Montgomery Hyde, H. *Oscar Wilde: A Biography*. Methuen: London, 1976.

Moore, George. *A Drama in Muslin*. Gerrards Cross: Colin Smythe, 1981.

—. *Hail and Farewell*, edited by R. Cave. Gerrards Cross: Colin Smythe, 1976.

—. *Esther Waters*. J. M. Dent: London, 1962.

—. *Confessions of a Young Man*. London: Heinemann, 1937.

Moore, Thomas. *The Memoirs of Lord Edward FitzGerald*, edited by Martin MacDermott. London: Downey & Co., 1897.

Morrissey, Thomas J. *William J. Walsh: Archbishop of Dublin, 1841–1921*. Dublin: Four Courts Press, 2000.

—. *William Martin Murphy*. Dundalk: Dundalgan Press, 1997.

—. *Towards a National University: William Delany SJ (1835–1924): An Era of Initiative in Irish Education*. Dublin: Wolfhound Press, 1983.

Mullin, James. *The Story of a Toiler's Life*. Dublin and London: Maunsel & Roberts Ltd, 1921.

Nicholson, Robert. *The Ulysses Guide: Tours through Joyce's Dublin*. Dublin: New Island, 2002.

Nina Rocco-Bergera. *Itinerary of Joyce and Svevo through Artistic Trieste*, published on the occasion of the Third International James Joyce Symposium. Trieste: Azienda Autonoma Soggiorno e Turismo, 1971.

O'Brien, Joseph. *William O'Brien and the Course of Irish Politics*. Berkeley: University of California Press, 1976.

O'Broin, Leon. *W. E. Wylie and the Irish Revolution, 1916–1921*. Dublin: Gill & Mcmillan, 1989.

O'Caithnia, Liam P. *Michael Ciosog*. Baile Átha Cliath: An Clóchomhar, 1982.

O'Cleirigh, Nellie. *Hardship and High Living: Irish Women's Lives 1808–1923*. Dublin: Portobello, Press, 2003.

O'Connor, Ulick. *Oliver St John Gogarty: A Poet and His Times*. London: Jonathan Cape, 1965.

Ó Dochartaigh, Pól. *Julius Pokorny, 1887–1970: Germans, Celts and Nationalism*. Dublin: Four Courts Press, 2004.

O'Dwyer, Frederick. *The Architecture of Deane and Woodward*. Cork: Cork University Press, 1997.

—. *Lost Dublin*. Dublin: Gill & Macmillan, 1981.

O'Hanlon, Canon John. *Lives of the Irish Saints*, 10 vols. Dublin: James Duffy, 1875–1903.

Ó Laoi, Pádraic. *Nora Barnacle Joyce: A Portrait*. Galway: Kenny's Bookshops and Art Galleries Ltd, 1982.

O'Leary, John. *Recollections of Fenians and Fenianism*. London: Downey, 1896.

O Machain, Padraig and Tony Delaney. *Like Sun Gone down: Selections from the Writings of John Canon O'Hanlon*. Kilkenny: Galmoy Press, 2005.

O'Malley, John W. *The First Jesuits*. Massachusetts: Harvard University Press, 1993.

O'Malley, Kevin and Eoin O'Brien, eds. *Bicentenary Account of the Royal College of Surgeons in Ireland 1784–1984*, vol. 2. Dublin: Glendale Press, 1987.

O'Neill, Marie. *From Parnell to de Valera: A Biography of Jennie Wyse Power 1858–1941*. Dublin: Blackwater Press, 1991.

O'Shea, Katharine. *Charles Stewart Parnell: His Love Story and Political Life*, 2 vols. London: Cassell, 1914.

Parnell, John Howard. *Charles Stewart Parnell: A Memoir*. New York: Henry Holt & Co., 1914.

Pearson, Peter. *Between the Mountains and the Sea: Dún Laoghaire–Rathdown County*. Dublin: O'Brien Press, 1999.

Power, Arthur. *Conversations with James Joyce*. Dublin: Lilliput Press, 1999.

Pyle, Hilary. *Red-Headed Rebel: Susan L. Mitchell, Poet and Mystic of the Irish Cultural Renaissance*. Dublin: Woodfield Press, 1998.

—. *James Stephens: His Work and an Account of His Life*. London: Routledge & Kegan Paul, 1962.

Raleigh, John Henry. *The Chronicle of Leopold and Molly Bloom*. Berkeley: University of California Press, 1977.

Reid, J. F. *William Field, MP: A Biography and Character Study*. London: The Meat Trades' Journal, 1918.

Reynolds, J. J. *Footprints of Emmet*. Dublin: Gill & Son, 1903.

Robinson, Lennox. *Palette and Plough*. Dublin: Browne & Nolan, 1948.

—, ed. *Lady Gregory's Journals 1916–1930*. London: Putnam, 1946.

Roberts, F. S. *Forty-One Years in India*, 2 vols. New York: Longmans, Green, 1897.

Rogers, Rev. Patrick. *Father Theobald Mathew: Apostle of Temperance*. Dublin: Richview Press, 1943.

Rosenblatt, Stuart. Jewish Ireland Series. *Vol. XII: Irish Jewish Gardens of the Dead: 1748–2006, Dublin, Belfast, Cork, Limerick and Other Burials*. Dublin: 2006.

—. Jewish Ireland Series. *Vol. XV: Lackman-Zwirn. 'Heritage' The A–Z DNA of Irish Jewry*. Dublin: 2008.

Ryan, Desmond. *The Fenian Chief: A Biography of James Stephens*. Dublin: Gill & Son, 1967.

Sandow, Eugen. *Strength and How to Obtain It*. London: Gale and Polden, 1897.

Senn, Fritz. *Inductive Scrutinies: Focus on Joyce*, edited by Christine O'Neill. Dublin: Lilliput Press, 1995.

—. *Joyce's Dislocutions: Essays on Reading as Translation*. Baltimore: John Hopkins University Press, 1984.

—. 'No trace of Hell'. *James Joyce Quarterly* (Spring 1970).

Shaw, G. B. *Music in London 1890–1894*. London: Constable, 1932.

Shaw, Fr Nessan, OFM Cap., ed. *The Irish Capuchins: Record of a Century 1885–1985*. Dublin: Capuchin Publications, 1985.

Sheehy, Eugene. *May it Please the Court*. Dublin: C. J. Fallon Ltd, 1951.

Sheehy-Skeffington, Francis. 'Frederick Ryan, an appreciation'. *The Irish Review*, 3 May 1913.

Slote, Sam, 'Notes'. James Joyce. *Ulysses: Based on the 1939 Edition*. Richmond, Surrey: Alma Classics, 2012.

Smyth, Daragh. *A Guide to Irish Mythology*. Sallins: Irish Academic Press, 1988.

Smyth, Hazel. *The B & I Line: A History of the British and Irish Steam Packet Company*. Dublin: Gill & Macmillan, 1984.

Society of Jesus, Fathers of the. *A Page of Irish History: Story of University College, Dublin 1883–1909*. Dublin and Cork: Talbot, 1930.

Somerville, E. A. O. and M. Ross (V. F. Martin). *An Incorruptible Irishman: Being an Account of Chief Justice Charles Kendal Bushe, and His Wife Nancy Crampton, and Their Times, 1767–1843*. London: Nicholson and Watson, 1932.

Spencer, Paul Francis. *To Heal the Broken Hearted: The Life of Blessed Charles of Mount Argus*. Dublin: Gill & Macmillan, 1988.

Stephen, Edward. *My Uncle John: Life of J. M. Synge*, edited by Andrew Carpenter. Oxford: Oxford University Press, 1974.

Strong, L. A. G. *The Minstrel Boy: A Portrait of Tom Moore*. London: Hodder & Stoughton, 1937.

Stronge, John M. *Andrew Horne: Thirty Years a Master*. Dublin: A. & A. Farmar, 1999.

Sullivan, Kevin. *Joyce among the Jesuits*. New York: Columbia University Press, 1958.

Synge, J. M. *Autobiography*, edited by Alan Price. Dublin: Dolmen Press, 1965.

Thornley, David. *Isaac Butt and Home Rule*. London: MacGibbon & Kee, 1964.

Thornton, Weldon. *Allusions in Ulysses: An Annotated List*. New York: Touchstone-Simon & Schuster, 1968.

Turner, John Martin. *Historical Hengler's Circus*. Liverpool: Lingdales Press, 1989.

Watters, Eugene and Matthew Murtagh. *Infinite Variety: Dan Lowrey's Music Hall 1879–97*. Dublin: Gill & Macmillan, 1975.

Wayman, P. A. *Dunsink Observatory 1785–1958: A Bicentennial History*. Dublin: Dublin Institute for Advanced Studies and the Royal Dublin Society, 1987.

Welch, Robert. *Irish Poetry from Moore to Yeats*. Buckinghamshire: Colin Smythe, 1980.

Warner, Alan. *William Allingham*. Lewisberg: Bucknell University Press, 1975.

Wheen, Francis. *Karl Marx: A Life*. London: Fourth Estate, 1999.

White, Terence de Vere. *Tom Moore: The Irish Poet*. London: Hamish & Hamilton, 1977.

—. *The Parents of Oscar Wilde: Sir William and Lady Wilde*. London: Hodder & Stoughton, 1967.

—. *The Road to Excess*. Dublin: Brown & Noland, *c*. 1946.

Wilson, T. G. *Victorian Doctor: Being the Life of Sir William Wilde*. New York: Fischer, 1946.

Woodward, Marcus, ed. *Gerard's Herbal: The History of Plants*. London: Senate, 1994.

Wootten, Maria. *The DuBedat Story: Killiney to Kommetjie*. Dublin: Tram Cottage Production, 1999.

Wright, G. N. *An Historical Guide to the City of Dublin*. London: Baldwin, Cradock and Joy, 1925.

Wroe, Ann. *Perkin: A Story of Deception*. London: Jonathan Cape, 2004.

Wyndham, H. *Speranza: A Biography of Lady Wilde*. London: T. V. Boardman, 1951.

Yeats, W. B. *Memoirs*, edited by Denis Donoghue. London: Macmillan, 1972.

Young, Peter. *The Data Book of Joe Miller Jokes*. Huddersfield: Scholfield and Sims, 1990.

Website

Beck, Harald and John Simpson, eds. *James Joyce Online Notes*. Available at: jjon.org.

Index